YOUR Health

Consulting Authors

Charlie Gibbons, Ed.D.
Associate Professor
Alabama State University
Health, Physical Education
  and Dance Department
Montgomery, Alabama; and
School Age Coordinator
Maxwell Air Force Base, Alabama

Jan Marie Ozias, Ph.D., R.N.
Director, Texas Diabetes Council; and
Consultant, School Health Programs
Austin, Texas

Carl Anthony Stockton, Ph.D.
Professor of Health Education and
  Department Chair
Department of Health, Physical
  Education and Recreation
The University of North Carolina
  at Wilmington
Wilmington, North Carolina

Orlando • Austin • Chicago • New York • Toronto • London • San Diego

Visit *The Learning Site!*
www.harcourtschool.com

For permission to reprint copyrighted material, grateful acknowledgment is made to the following sources:

Annick Press Ltd.: From *Where There's Smoke* by Janet Munsil. Text copyright © 1993 by Janet Munsil.

Bridgewater Books, an imprint of Troll Communications, L.L.C.: "How Medicine Came" from *The Circle of Thanks* by Joseph Bruchac. Text copyright © 1996 by Joseph Bruchac.

HarperCollins Publishers: From *No Measles, No Mumps for Me* by Paul Showers. Text copyright © 1980 by Paul Showers.

Highlights for Children, Inc., Columbus, Ohio: "I Need My Knees, but No More, Please" by Stan Lee Werlin. Text copyright © 1997 by Highlights for Children, Inc.

Random House Children's Books, a division of Random House, Inc.: "Greedy Mable" from *A Year Full of Stories* by Georgie Adams. Text copyright © 1997 by Georgie Adams.

Marian Reiner, on behalf of Aileen Fisher: "My Puppy" from *Up the Windy Hill* by Aileen Fisher. Text copyright © 1953 by Abelard Press; text copyright renewed 1981 by Aileen Fisher.

Marian Reiner, on behalf of Mary O'Neill: "Mark's Fingers" from *Fingers Are Always Bringing Me News* by Mary O'Neill. Text copyright © 1969 by Mary O'Neill; text copyright renewed 1997 by Abigail Hagler and Erin Baroni.

RLR Associates, New York: "Clean Water" from *Keeping Clean* by Vicki Cobb. Text copyright © 1989 by Vicki Cobb.

Adam Yarmolinsky: "A Pig Is Never Blamed" by Babette Deutsch.

ISBN 0-15-334309-5

3 4 5 6 7 8 9 10 059 10 09 08 07 06 05 04 03

Teacher Edition Contents

About This Program

The Chapters

Read-Aloud Anthology

Teacher Reference Section

Author Articles

CONSULTING AUTHORS

Charlie Gibbons

Charlie Gibbons, Ed.D., has over 25 years of university teaching experience and is presently teaching at Alabama State University in the Department of Health, Physical Education and Dance in Montgomery, Alabama. He is also Coordinator of the Maxwell Air Force Base School Age Program. Dr. Gibbons is a past president of the Alabama State Association of Health, Physical Education, Recreation and Dance and a past vice president of the Southern District American Alliance of Health, Physical Education, Recreation and Dance (AAHPERD). He is presently serving on both state and district committees. He has served on numerous public service committees providing inservice workshops and presentations on various areas of school health curricula including such topics as HIV/AIDS prevention and physical fitness for children.

Dr. Gibbons has been the recipient of both the Alabama State Association and Southern District AAHPERD Honor (1990 & 1998) and Ethnic Minority Awards (1999 & 2001).

Jan Marie Ozias

Jan Ozias, Ph.D., R.N., has extensive experience in school health services and health education from a nursing perspective. She worked as Nursing Supervisor and Administrator of Health Services in the Austin Independent School District, Austin, Texas. Dr. Ozias holds adjunct faculty appointments in both the School of Nursing and the College of Education at the University of Texas at Austin from which she also earned an M.A. in Special Education and a Ph.D. in Health Education.

Dr. Ozias has worked as Director of Medical Underwriting, Texas Healthy Kids Corporation and presently serves as Director, Texas Diabetes Council/Program at the Texas Department of Health. She is co-chief editor of School Health Alert. She writes and presents on child health for school nurses and educators. Her other activities include leadership positions in the American School Health Association, such as the Task Force on Injury Prevention and the U.S. Pharmacopoeia's ad hoc Panel on Children and Medicine (education).

Carl Anthony Stockton

Carl Anthony Stockton, Ph.D., is department Chair and Professor of Health Education in the Department of Health, Physical Education and Recreation at the University of North Carolina in Wilmington. Throughout his professional career, Dr. Stockton has taught health education classes focusing on a wide variety of health topics. His curricula have included such diverse health topics as health programs in the elementary schools, nutrition, national and international health, accident and safety education, public health administration, and the use of technology in health promotion.

Dr. Stockton is a recipient of the College Health Professional of the Year Award by the Virginia Alliance of AAHPERD. In addition, Dr. Stockton has received the 1997 Outstanding Teaching Award and the 1999 Outstanding Service Award from Radford University. In 2001 Dr. Stockton was inducted into the American Association for Health Education's (AAHE) Fellows Honorary organization. The Fellows award is given for long-term dedication to the profession of health education. Dr. Stockton is currently a director for the national board of the American Association for Health Education.

Dear Educator,

Your Health is a comprehensive program designed to provide your students with the knowledge, life skills, consumer skills, and thinking skills they need in order to achieve good health.

Knowledge includes current information, facts, and concepts in the following content areas:

- human body systems
- emotional, intellectual, and social health
- family life, growth, and development
- personal health and physical fitness
- nutrition
- disease prevention and control
- drug use prevention
- injury prevention
- community and environmental health

Life Skills are health-enhancing behaviors that help children reduce risks to their health. **Your Health** provides opportunities for children to learn and practice life skills through lessons that use real-life situations. These important skills are:

- make decisions
- manage stress
- set goals
- resolve conflicts
- communicate
- refuse risky behaviors

Thinking Skills connect to all subject areas in the school curriculum. They are essential for enabling children to use knowledge and life skills appropriately. Thinking skills include:

- critical thinking
- using facts
- problem solving

Consumer Skills are important for helping children evaluate the enormous amount of information that is transmitted to them via the media. These skills include:

- analyze advertisements and media messages
- make buying decisions
- access valid health information

We are confident that **Your Health** provides you with the tools you need to motivate your students to take an active role in maintaining and improving their health.

Sincerely,
The Authors

CONSULTING HEALTH SPECIALISTS

Harriet Hylton Barr, B.A., M.P.H., CHES
Clinical Associate Professor Emeritus
Department of Health Behavior and
Health Education
School of Public Health
University of North Carolina at
Chapel Hill
Durham, North Carolina

David A. Birch, Ph.D., CHES
Associate Professor
Department of Applied Health Science
Indiana University
Bloomington, Indiana

Glen Ceresa, D.D.S.
Clinical Instructor
Las Vegas Institute for Advanced
Dental Studies
Las Vegas, Nevada

Michael J. Cleary, Ed.D., CHES
Professor
Department of Allied Health
Slippery Rock University
Slippery Rock, Pennsylvania

Lisa C. Cohn, M.M.Sc., M.Ed., R.D.
Nutrition Educator and
Research Consultant
New York, New York

Mary Steckiewicz Garzino, M.Ed.
Director, Nutrition Education
National Dairy Council
Chicago, Illinois

Mark L. Giese, Ed.D., FACSM
Professor
Northeastern Oklahoma
State University
Tahlequah, Oklahoma

Michael J. Hammes, Ph.D.
Associate Professor
University of New Mexico
Albuquerque, New Mexico

Betty M. Hubbard, Ed.D., CHES
Professor of Health Education
Department of Health Sciences
University of Central Arkansas
Conway, Arkansas

Rama K. Khalsa, Ph.D.
Director of Mental Health
Santa Cruz County
Soquel, California

Darrel Lang, Ed.D.
Health and Physical Education
Consultant
Kansas State Department of Education
Emporia, Kansas

Gerald J. Maburn
National Vice President for Planning
and Evaluation
American Cancer Society
Atlanta, Georgia

Cheryl Miller-Haymowicz, B.S., CHES
Health Educator
Salem-Keizer Public Schools
Salem, Oregon

John A. Morris, M.S.W.
Professor of Neuropsychiatry and
Behavioral Science
University of South Carolina School
of Medicine
Director of Interdisciplinary Affairs
South Carolina Department
of Mental Health
Columbia, South Carolina

Patricia Poindexter, M.P.H., CHES
Health Education Specialist
Tucker, Georgia

Janine Robinette
Health Program Administrator
Monterey, California

Spencer Sartorius, M.S.
Administrator
Health Enhancement and
Safety Division
Montana Office of Public Instruction
Helena, Montana

Jeanne Marie Scott, M.D.
Staff Physician
San Jose State University
San Jose, California

David A. Sleet, Ph.D.
Centers for Disease Control
and Prevention
Atlanta, Georgia

Becky J. Smith, Ph.D., CHES
Reston, Virginia

Howard Taras, M.D.
Associate Professor
(Specialist in Medical Consultation
to Schools)
University of California at San Diego
San Diego, California

Pamela M. Tollefsen, R.N., M.Ed.
Program Supervisor, Health Education
Office of Superintendent of Public
Instruction
State of Washington
Olympia, Washington

Mae Waters, Ph.D., CHES
Executive Director of Comprehensive
Health Training
Florida State University
Tallahassee, Florida

Your Health and The National Health Education Standards

The National Health Education Standards were developed by representatives of various health organizations, including the American School Health Association, the Association for the Advancement of Health Education, and the American Cancer Society. The standards describe what students should know and be able to do in order to be health literate. A health-literate person obtains, interprets, and understands basic health information and services and uses that information and those services in ways that are health-enhancing.

Your Health promotes health literacy in the following ways:

- provides students with the **knowledge** they need to make informed decisions about their health.

- provides students with opportunities to learn and practice **life skills** and **consumer skills** for positive health behaviors.

- encourages the use of **thinking skills** in order to solve problems and think critically.

Every lesson in *Your Health* was developed to help students meet the Standards. A correlation to the Standards is provided on each Chapter Organizer in this Teacher's Edition.

National Health Education Standards

1. Students will comprehend concepts related to health promotion and disease prevention.

2. Students will demonstrate the ability to access valid health information and health-promoting products and services.

3. Students will demonstrate the ability to practice health-enhancing behaviors and reduce health risks.

4. Students will analyze the influence of culture, media, technology, and other factors on health.

5. Students will demonstrate the ability to use interpersonal communication skills to enhance health.

6. Students will demonstrate the ability to use goal-setting and decision-making skills to enhance health.

7. Students will demonstrate the ability to advocate for personal, family, and community health.

Curriculum Integration

Your Health is designed to allow you to integrate health into your daily planning through the use of connections to all curriculum areas. Look for Curriculum Integration in the teacher planning section at the beginning of each chapter.

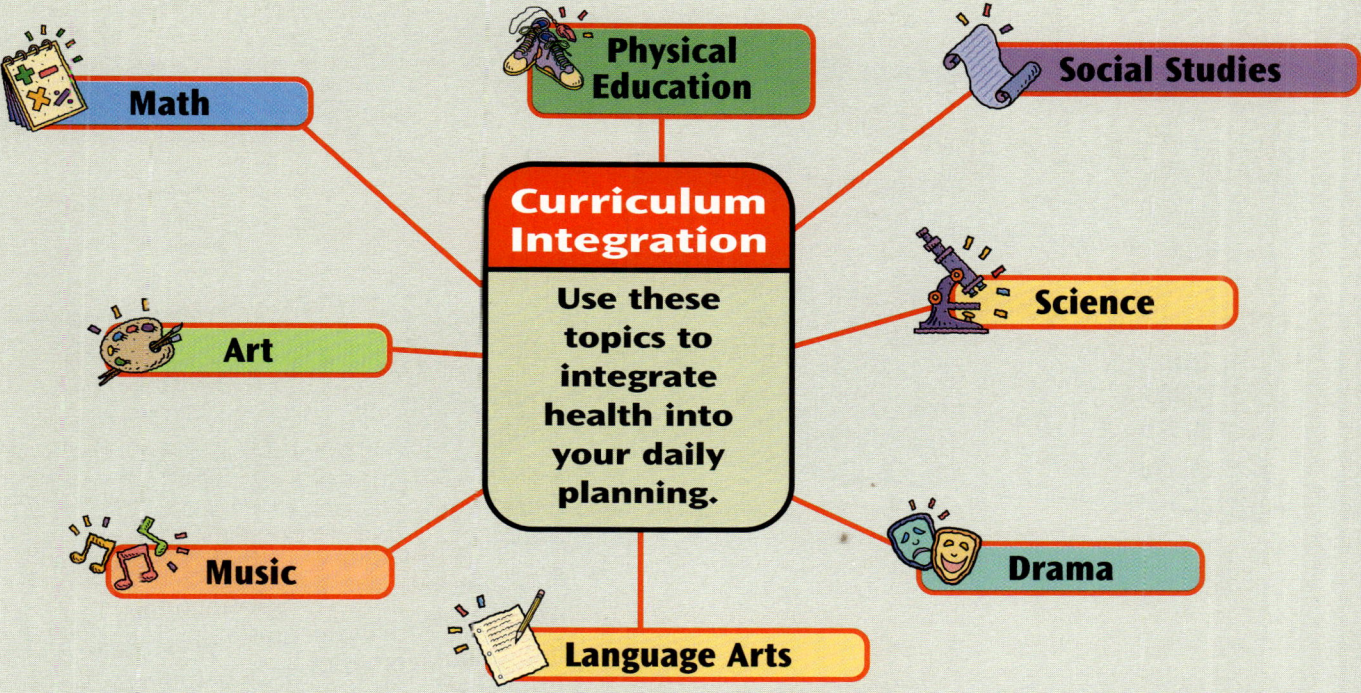

Program Assessment

Your Health provides a variety of assessment strategies and tools for assessing student health literacy. The assessment is based on the following model:

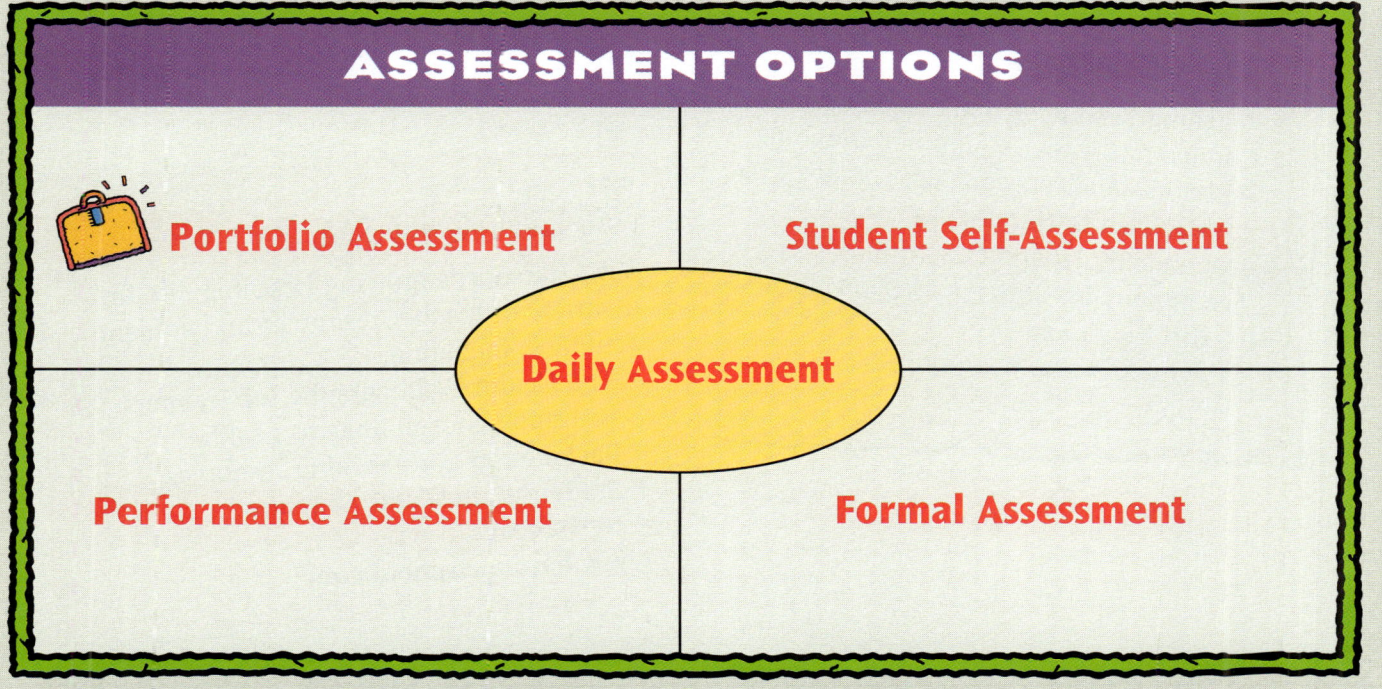

For more information, please refer to pages 2–3 in the *Assessment Guide*.

Program Components

Your Health provides components that meet a variety of instructional needs.

For Kindergarten

- colorful Teaching Charts in poster format
- comprehensive Teacher's Edition
- Activity Book
- Teaching Resources book (includes School-Home Connection letters, Take-Home Booklets, Assessment Options, and Patterns)
- Teaching Transparencies with Accompanying Copying Masters

For Grades 1 and 2

- Pupil's Editions
- comprehensive Teacher's Edition
- colorful Big Book
- Activity Book
- Assessment Guide
- Teaching Resources book (includes School-Home Connection letters, Take-Home Booklets and reproducible copies of the student Health Handbook)
- Teaching Transparencies with Accompanying Copying Masters

For Grades 3 through 6

- Pupil's Editions
- comprehensive Teacher's Edition
- Activity Book
- Assessment Guide
- Teaching Resources book (includes School-Home Connection letters, Computer Graphing Activities, and reproducible copies of the student Health Handbook)
- Teaching Transparencies with Accompanying Copying Masters
- Health Video Series
- Growth, Development, and Reproduction (an optional resource)

Technology

Visit Harcourt's growing Learning Site for a variety of teacher resources and student activities, including:

- The Health Webliography for Teachers (carefully chosen links to health background and teaching resources)
- Student Games and Activities
- Newsbreaks

www.harcourtschool.com

Contents

Chapter 5 — Preventing Disease 120

Disease Prevention and Control

Chapter 6 — Medicines and Other Drugs . 146

Drug Use Prevention

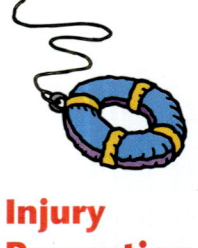

YOUR HEALTH SKILLS

The practical, important life skills and consumer skills introduced here are taught, reinforced, and assessed throughout *Your Health*. Encourage students to revisit these pages if they need help as they complete Life Skills lessons, Life Skills and Consumer Focus features, Lesson Checkups, and Chapter Reviews.

Understanding Life Skills

Set Goals

Introduce the Skill

Ask students to read the first paragraph. Then as a class, brainstorm examples of goals that people might set for themselves. What are some ways to group the goals? Possible answers: area—health, schoolwork, sports, money; time—short-, medium-, and long-term; and priority

Discuss

Why do you think setting goals is important? It helps you improve; you can achieve what you want; you feel good because you're working toward something.

Critical Thinking How is achieving a goal in life like scoring a soccer goal? It takes time and work. You may have to learn new skills. There are obstacles to overcome, such as other players and the goal keeper. It is rewarding.

Practice the Skill

Tell students they will set a short-term goal. Then, ask students to think of one task they can easily do today that would help them improve. If students have difficulty, refer back to the goals that they listed under **Introduce the Skill**, above.

Understanding Life Skills

Having good health isn't just knowing the facts. It's also thinking critically about those facts and knowing how to use them every day. The Life Skills in *Your Health* can help you do just that.

Setting Goals for Self Improvement

In soccer or ice hockey, scoring a goal is something that a team wants to do to win the game. In life, you set goals for things you want to do to improve yourself. Planning and checking your progress makes it easy. You feel better about yourself because you know you are getting closer to your goals.

▶ Roosevelt knows that it is important to his health to exercise. How can he set a goal to exercise more during the week?

Steps for Setting Goals

1. Set a goal.

2. List and plan steps to meet that goal.

3. Check your progress toward the goal.

4. Evaluate the goal.

PHYSICAL EDUCATION

Training Goals Amateur and professional athletes set goals to improve their performances. Have students select a physical activity they wish to improve. Have them set a goal to increase their speed or endurance in the activity. You may wish to refer students to the President's Fitness Challenge in the Health Handbook on pages 260–261.

Making Decisions

Decisions that affect your health are important. For important decisions, you should think carefully about all the choices and the possible results, then decide. Following the steps shown below will help you make wise decisions. Making wise decisions will help to keep you healthy.

Think about your choices!

◀ Trisha is at her friend's house after school and becomes thirsty. Her friend offers Trisha a sip of her drink. How can Trisha make the best decision?

Steps for Making Decisions

1. Find out about the choices you could make.
2. Imagine the possible result of each choice.
3. Make what seems to be the best choice.
4. Think about the result of your choice.

ix

 **LANGUAGE ARTS**

Adventure Decisions Challenge students to make a health adventure book. Each page will have a scenario with a list of possible decisions. The reader will choose from the list the most appropriate decision after reading each set of circumstances.

Make Decisions

Introduce the Skill

How did you choose what to wear to school today? Accept all reasonable answers. Students looked for clean clothes or clothes they hadn't worn recently. Some may have dressed for the weather, a sport, or a school activity. Some may just have picked a favorite color. List responses. Point out that students followed steps and used reasons to make a decision, or choice, about what to wear.

Discuss

Have students suggest decisions related to their health. Accept all reasonable answers. Possible answers: when to get checkups, whether to get vaccinated, what to eat, how much to eat, how much to exercise, personal hygiene Have students classify the decisions as those they can make and those their parents or guardians must make.

Critical Thinking **How will those decisions change as you get older?** Answers will vary. Students should realize that they will gradually assume more responsibility for their personal health.

Practice the Skill

Ask students to look at the photo and read the caption. Display the Steps for Making Decisions. Work through the steps. Have students give reasons and possible results for each of the four steps.

Introducing Health Bird

Health Bird appears periodically throughout the Pupil Edition. In most cases, Health Bird reminds students of important health tips. Other times, Health Bird adds a fun element to the pupil page. Have students watch for Health Bird as they work through each chapter of *Your Health*.

 # Life Skills
Manage Stress

Introduce the Skill

What are some examples of ways that athletes get stronger? Possible answers: running, bicycling, lifting weights; exercise in general Point out that these exercises are examples of *stress* on the body. Athletes stress, or train, their bodies and they get stronger.

Critical Thinking **What do you think would happen if an athlete's body were under training stress all day, every day?** Some students may say that the athlete will become tired or sick; others may incorrectly say he or she will get very strong. Accept all reasonable answers.

Discuss

Explain that stress can also be mental. Feeling nervous, worried, or sad can make the body tense.

Critical Thinking Direct students' attention to step 3 in the box. **Why do you think it is important to take one step at a time?** Answers will vary. It is hard to do many things at the same time. If you do just one thing at a time, it is easier and less stressful.

Practice the Skill

Ask student volunteers to provide examples of events that would be stressful. Suggest that they use the list in the first paragraph of the Pupil Edition page as a starting point. Then for each example, have students suggest ways to make the event less stressful.

Managing Stress

"I'm so stressed!" Maybe you or a parent said that today. Stress is tension in your body or your mind. Maybe you feel stress because of a class report, a quiz, or a doctor's appointment. Some stress is a normal part of life. You even need a little stress to stay healthy. But, it's important not to let stress harm your health.

▶ Tomorrow is the first day Camille is going to a new school. She is nervous about making new friends. How can she manage her stress and relax?

Steps for Managing Stress

1. Know what stress feels like and what causes it.
2. When you feel stress, think about ways to handle it.
3. Focus on one step at a time.
4. Learn ways to reduce and release tension.

x

 ## CAREER

Massage Therapist Have students use library resources to investigate the career of massage therapist and how massage helps in stress reduction. Have students share what they learn by making a small display that a massage therapy school might use at a job fair.

🍎 Refusing

...metimes people can try to make you do things you really ...n't want to do. Knowing how to refuse, or say *no*, to ...ings that are unsafe or risky can keep you healthy. This is ...so an important reason for learning more about your ...alth. Knowing how a bad choice—such as using alcohol, ...bacco, or other drugs—will affect you ...akes it easier to say *no* firmly.

Todd is at a sleep-over with his friends. Some of them want to watch a movie that he knows his family wouldn't want him to see. How can Todd refuse watching the movie?

How to Refuse

1. Say **no** and say why not.

2. State your reasons for saying **no**.

3. Suggest something else to do.

4. Repeat **no**; walk away.

xi

Refuse

Introduce the Skill

Ask a volunteer to tell about a toddler-age sibling first learning to say *no*. The toddler says *no* to almost every question, even if *no* is the wrong answer. Eventually the toddler learns how to use *no* appropriately. Explain that as students get older, it is again important for them to learn how to say *no*—this time to dangerous behaviors.

Discuss

Point out that no one enjoys being injured or ill. Refusing is a skill that can help students stay healthy.

Direct students' attention to the photo and caption. **Why should Todd refuse to watch the movie?** Answers will vary. It is important to follow family rules. The movie may have content, such as violence or bad language, that Todd's family does not want him to be exposed to.

Critical Thinking **Why is it important to be able to give reasons why not?** Answers will vary. Your refusal is stronger because you are more confident. Explaining why you don't want to do something makes you more convincing.

Practice the Skill

As a class, brainstorm a list of behaviors or substances students might need to say "no" to, such as unsafe activities, or use of alcohol, tobacco or other drugs. Pretend to be someone offering children something that is unsafe. Use the directions under How to Refuse to write a play for refusing the offer.

SCIENCE
. . . .

Myths vs. Facts Have students use library science resources to identify myths and learn the truth about the effects of drugs on the body. Have students prepare Myth and Fact posters for the classroom to help all students refuse effectively.

 # Life Skills
Communicate

Introduce the Skill

Make a web diagram to illustrate communication. Label the center *Me*. Ask students for examples of people with whom they communicate. Put those people around the center. Ask students for examples of how they communicate. Then, connect the people to the center by adding ways of communicating (words, writing, actions, e-mail, telephone, and so on).

Discuss

Explain that *communicating* is something that everyone does nearly all the time. Why do you think it is a good idea to practice this skill? Possible answers: it's an important part of daily life; getting better at it might avoid confusion and improve relations with others.

What needs might you want to communicate to your family? Possible answers: food, sleep, warm clothes, school supplies, recognition, affection, privacy; accept all reasonable responses.

Critical Thinking Why is it important to gather feedback after you have communicated your message? You need to know if your audience understood the message. You need to know about any misunderstandings so that you can do better next time.

Practice the Skill

Have students work in groups to plan a communication scenario. Ask each group to choose something they might need to communicate. Then, have them briefly explain how they would accomplish each of the four steps under How to Communicate. You may wish to have groups role play their scenario for the class.

Communicating

Communicating is another word for "sharing information." You have ideas, needs, and feelings. To meet your needs, you often need to communicate with other people. You also need to listen to people and understand their needs and feelings.

◄ Ever since Bradley's little sister was born, he feels he is getting less attention from his parents. Yet, he loves his new sister. How can he communicate his feelings to his parents?

How to Communicate

1. Understand your audience.
2. Give a clear message.
3. Listen.
4. Gather feedback.

xii

LANGUAGE ARTS

Healthful Ads Have students write and design an advertisement that advocates a healthful lifestyle choice. Have students follow the steps for communicating, including gathering feedback to be sure that their ads are effective.

Resolving Conflicts

...flict, or disagreement, is a normal part of life. ...agreeing with a classmate about how to finish a ...ject is a conflict. Bigger conflicts may lead to hurt ...ings or even violence. A fight or an argument is a ...or way to deal with a conflict. If you communicate ...ll, you often can find a peaceful way to resolve, or ...d, a conflict. You may even find ...t communicating well leads to a ...ution that is better for everyone.

...Yuriko's older brother
...took a CD from her
...room. He says that the
...CD is his, and that
...Yuriko took it from him.
...How can they resolve
...this conflict?

Steps for Resolving Conflicts

1. Use I-messages to tell how you feel.

2. Listen to each other.

3. Think of the other person's point of view.

4. Decide what to do and do it.

xiii

CAREER

Mediator Tell students to use library resources to investigate the career of mediator. Have students make a newspaper, radio, or video advertisement for the business practice of a well-qualified mediator to share what they learned.

For more information about health-related careers, visit the **Webliography** on the Teacher Resources page at:
www.harcourtschool.com/health
Keyword health careers

Resolve Conflicts

Introduce the Skill

Initiate a brief tug-o-war by offering a book or an unsharpened pencil to a student, then refusing to let go. **What are some words or pictures that describe what happened?** Accept all reasonable answers.

Discuss

Students may be familiar with *conflict* only from news stories about violence. Have students read the text and photo caption. Then ask the class to give other examples of everyday, nonviolent conflicts. **In your own words, what is a definition of a *conflict* that fits all these examples?** Possible answer: Conflict is people arguing or disagreeing, or people wanting to use the same thing at the same time.

Critical Thinking **Why might it be good to ask someone outside the conflict for help?** It's easier for that person to see both sides. If the person isn't involved, he or she will make a fairer decision.

Practice the Skill

Have students work in groups to make comic strips that show how an everyday conflict can be resolved. Suggest that students write scripts before they begin to draw. If students need help with their scripts, suggest that they start by using the Steps for Resolving Conflicts at the bottom of page xiii as the main heads for a script outline.

Being a Wise Health Consumer

Make Buying Decisions

Introduce the Skill

Have students write down the last three food items that they or a family member purchased recently. Then, ask students to write brief reasons each item was chosen. Ask volunteers to share their reasons and make a class list. (Be sensitive to socio-economic status. Avoid requiring students to disclose purchases or amounts.) **What are some ways of prioritizing items on the list?** Possible answer: 1. price, 2. freshness, 3. taste, 4. need, 5. availability, 6. nutritional value

Discuss

What are some examples of bad buying decisions? Possible answers: Product doesn't work, costs much more than similar product, is dangerous, doesn't fit right, tastes bad, isn't really needed, and so on.

Critical Thinking **How can following the Steps for Making Buying Decisions help you avoid bad buys?** You have to think carefully about all your choices before you buy. Thinking about the result of your choice helps you learn from mistakes.

Practice the Skill

Direct students' attention to the product pictures. Ask students to suppose they are shopping. Have them make a chart to compare the products. If students are having difficulty, guide them by asking: **What do these products do? What else would you want to know about these products?**

YOUR HEALTH Skills

Being a Wise Health Consumer

Being a wise consumer means making good buying decisions. As you get older, you will have more responsibility for buying health products and services. You need to learn how advertisements can mislead you. You also need to learn how to get valid, or correct, health information.

Making Buying Decisions

Advertising can help you make buying decisions. However, advertisements shouldn't be the only information you use. Using product information wisely helps you to get the most value for your money.

▲ Which of these backpacks would you choose to buy? Why?

Steps for Making Buying Decisions

1. Decide whether the item is something you need, want, or don't really need at all.

2. Compare several brands of the same item.

3. Choose the least expensive item that meets your needs.

4. Think about the result of your purchase decision.

SCIENCE

Product Testing Explain to students that there are science laboratories that test the safety and effectiveness of products. Have students design and carry out an experiment to test the effectiveness of a product. For example, students might investigate laundry detergent, stain remover, or plant food.

CAUTION: Make sure that students carry out any investigations under adult supervision and that proper safety equipment, such as goggles and an apron, are used.

xiv

 # Analyzing Advertising and Media Messages

Advertising is everywhere, even places you may not notice. Ads can give you good information about a product. They also can mislead you. Be aware of these tricks to get you to buy:

PUT DOWN

TRICK The ad says another product is bad.

TIP Maybe the other brand isn't that bad. Compare the products for yourself.

IDEAL PEOPLE

TRICK Everyone in the ad looks pretty and happy.

TIP The product doesn't make people pretty or happy. Find out what it really does.

BE COOL

TRICK People who use the product become more popular.

TIP A product can't make someone more popular.

JOIN THE CROWD

TRICK It seems like everyone is using this product and you're left out.

TIP Most people probably aren't using the product. It's wise to buy only things that you need.

STAR POWER

TRICK Your favorite sports or music star tells you to buy a product.

TIP The star can't know that the product is right for you. Find out if it really meets your needs.

How to Analyze Advertising and Media Messages

1. Find out who made the message and why.
2. Watch for tricks to make you notice or agree with the message.
3. Notice the values and points of view shown.
4. Learn whether anything is left out.

xv

Analyze Advertising and Media Messages

Introduce the Skill

Display a variety of advertisements clipped from children's magazines or printed from children's websites. Ask students to describe the first thing they notice when viewing each ad. **Would the first thing you noticed help you make a good buying decision?** Accept all reasonable answers.

Discuss

Review the ads one-by-one. For each, ask students to identify the product, what the ad claims it does, price (if listed), and any other important information. You may wish to have students make a chart to organize their information. Then, review the Tricks and Tips in the Pupil Edition. Point out the tricks used by the ads.

Critical Thinking Why is it important to be aware of advertising tricks? Possible answer: You can choose products that meet your needs rather than choosing products that only seem good.

Practice the Skill

Have students choose a category of products, such as food, games, or clothing, and collect four ads for products in the category. Have students use the steps shown in the Pupil Edition and the Tricks and Tips to analyze each of the ads. As an extension, you may wish to videotape television ads for students to view and analyze during class.

SOCIAL STUDIES

Quack Cures The Food and Drug Administration (FDA) exists, in part, because of bad medicine. Have students investigate the history of patent medicine ads, quack cures, and the FDA. Ask students to make an illustrated timeline to share what they learn.

 # Consumer Skills

Access Valid Health Information

Introduce the Skill

Share the following scenario with students: Suppose someone you don't know tells you that your bicycle is dangerous and needs an expensive repair. **What would you do? Why?** Students may suggest talking to a parent or guardian, visiting a bike shop, asking an expert, and so on. A trusted adult will know more about what to do. Accept all reasonable answers.

Discuss

Point out that students put more trust in a bike expert or someone they know well. Such people are more likely to give valid, or trustworthy, information.

Have students read the Pupil Edition page. If someone you don't know told you something about your health, who would you trust to help you decide if the information was valid? A parent, guardian, health professional; accept other reasonable responses.

Critical Thinking **Why is it important to check an answer in more than one place?** If several people agree on the answer, it is probably more trustworthy.

Practice the Skill

Challenge students to use library and other resources to find three examples of dietary guidelines: one very reliable, one reliable, and one not reliable. Ask students to provide a brief explanation of their rating for each example.

xvi

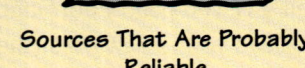 ## Accessing Valid Health Information

It's important to know the facts about your health. However, not everything you read or see is the truth. You should make sure health information is reliable, or trustworthy. The best source of health information is health professionals, such as nurses, doctors, and pharmacists. For other sources, especially the Internet, you should think about the source of the information. Also, check to see if other sources agree.

Sources That Are Probably Reliable

- College and university websites
- Science and health journals
- Major national newspapers
- National health magazines
- National health organizations, such as the American Heart Association
- Government organizations, such as the Centers for Disease Control and Prevention

Access Valid Health Information

1. Find out who is responsible for the information. Notice whether they are selling something.
2. Decide if the information is reasonable.
3. Check the information against other reliable sources. Keep a questioning attitude.
4. Discuss the information with a trusted adult or a health professional such as a nurse, doctor, or pharmacist.

You will learn and practice these important life skills as you use *Your Health*.

xvi

 ## SOCIAL STUDIES

Community Resources
Organizations such as the Consumers' Union and Better Business Bureau exist to help consumers get reliable information about products. Have students research and make a contact list for similar groups in their community. Each entry should include a telephone number, street address, web address (if available), and information the organization provides.

The Amazing Human Body

Getting enough rest, staying active, and eating right are important steps to a healthful life.

1

Using The Amazing Human Body

This section of the pupil book provides interesting and detailed information about the systems of the human body. The structure and function of each system is identified. Student activities and tips for caring for each system are also included.

Using *The Amazing Human Body* for Body-System-Specific Lessons

You may wish to use these pages to teach lessons about the structure, function, and care of the body systems. Lesson strategies are offered on the following pages.

Using *The Amazing Human Body* as a Reference Section

Some teachers prefer to integrate instruction about body systems as they teach other health content. For example, learning about the digestive system can be included with instruction on nutrition. For this reason, *The Amazing Human Body* has been designed to be used as a reference section. Cross-references to the appropriate body systems appear throughout *Your Health*. You will find these cross-references in the "Human Body Connection" feature.

ASSESSMENT GUIDE, p. 8

Name _____ Date _____

Chapter Title _____

Healthy Habits Checklist

Healthy Habits Checklist

This quiz will tell you how healthy your daily habits are. Put a check-mark in the proper column. When finished, add up your score. Take the quiz several times this year and see how your health habits improve!

	ALWAYS	SOMETIMES	NEVER
Using Life Skills			
1. I weigh options and make healthful decisions.			
2. I say *no* if I need to.			
3. I resolve conflicts peacefully.			
4. I use stress-management strategies.			
5. I communicate with others clearly.			
6. I set goals for myself and work toward attaining them.			
Making Healthy Choices			
1. I eat healthful meals and snacks.			
2. I get enough sleep.			
3. I make time for physical activities.			
4. I avoid alcohol, tobacco, and drugs.			
5. I take medicines safely.			
6. I use safety equipment when playing sports and use a safety belt in a car.			
Getting Along with Others			
1. I have some close friends.			
2. I am a responsible family member.			
3. I work well with others.			
4. I apologize when I am wrong.			
5. I feel good about myself.			
6. I get along with other students.			

Give yourself 2 points for each ALWAYS, 1 point for each SOMETIMES, and 0 points for each NEVER. Add up your score for each category.

8-12 points	4-7 points	0-6 points
You Have Healthy Habits!	You Need Improvement	Work to Do Better

Using the *Healthy Habits Checklist*

You may wish to give each student a copy of the Healthy Habits Checklist (Assessment Guide, p. 8). Explain that the checklist can be used for self-evaluation. The results need not be shared with others. Suggest that students keep their completed checklists in their portfolios. At the end of the semester or school year, provide students with another copy of the checklist. Ask them to compare their results with their attempts at the beginning of the school year.

TEACHING TRANSPARENCIES

The anatomy diagrams in *The Amazing Human Body* are included in the Teaching Transparencies package. Opportunities for using the transparencies are noted at point of use throughout this Teacher's Edition. Also, copying masters are provided for each transparency. Art labels are not included on the copying masters so that they can be used for instruction, review, or assessment.

Sense Organs

OBJECTIVE

• Identify the parts and functions of the body's sense organs.

PROGRAM RESOURCES

Teaching Transparencies 10–14

• Activity Book, p. 1

VOCABULARY

• lens
• pupil
• iris
• optic nerve
• retina
• ear canal

• eardrum
• nostril
• olfactory bulb
• olfactory tract
• nasal cavity
• taste buds

1 Motivate

Optional Materials 2 pencils, ruler, tape

Explain that some parts of the skin are more sensitive than other parts. Demonstrate this by taping two pencils about a half-inch apart on a ruler. Have volunteers close their eyes as you touch them on their fingertips, arms, necks, and so on. Ask the volunteers whether they feel one point or two points when being touched. In sensitive areas, such as the fingertips and lips, two points should be felt.

Why do you think some areas of the skin are more sensitive than other areas of the skin? Some areas have more sensors.

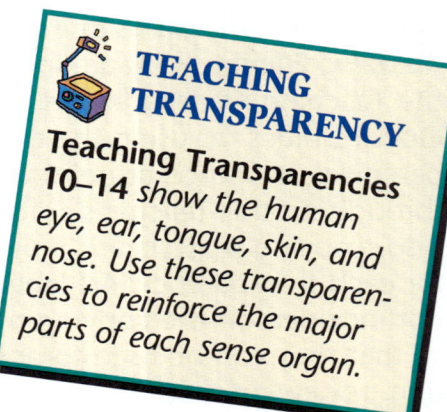

TEACHING TRANSPARENCY

Teaching Transparencies 10–14 show the human eye, ear, tongue, skin, and nose. Use these transparencies to reinforce the major parts of each sense organ.

Eye

Your eyes are protected by the bones in your skull, nose, and cheeks. Your eyelids protect your eyes automatically from dust, tiny flying objects, and sudden bright lights.

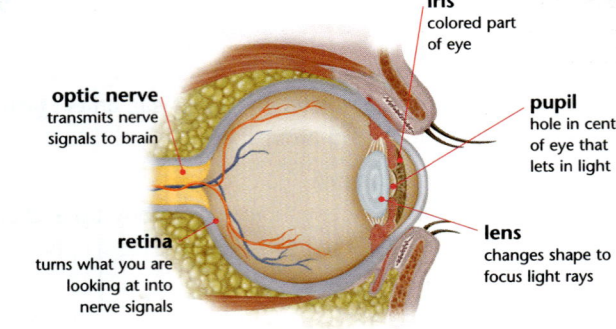

iris colored part of eye

optic nerve transmits nerve signals to brain

pupil hole in center of eye that lets in light

retina turns what you are looking at into nerve signals

lens changes shape to focus light rays

Ear

Earwax is made inside your ears to help keep them clean. Dust, dirt, and germs stick to the earwax instead of going farther into your ear. When you move your mouth by chewing and talking, old wax works its way to your outer ear.

Outer ear | Middle ear | Inner ear

eardrum moves back and forth when hit by sound waves

ear canal connects outer ear to middle ear

Caring for Your Eyes and Ears

• Have your eyesight (vision) checked every year.

• Wear safety glasses when participating in activities that can be dangerous to the eyes, such as sports and mowing grass.

• Wash in, around, and behind your outer ear. Do not try to clean your ear canal with cotton-tip sticks or other objects.

2

LANGUAGE ARTS

Story Writing Students should write short stories describing a day without one or more of their senses. Ask them to show how pleasure and safety could be affected. Encourage students to illustrate their stories. Then collect the stories to form a book titled "A Senseless Day."

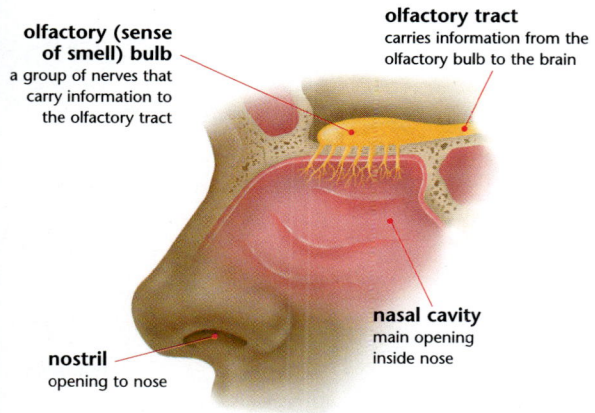

olfactory (sense of smell) bulb
a group of nerves that carry information to the olfactory tract

olfactory tract
carries information from the olfactory bulb to the brain

nostril
opening to nose

nasal cavity
main opening inside nose

Nose

The inside of your nose is lined with tiny blood vessels. When something hits you in the nose, these blood vessels can break and you can have a nosebleed.

Tongue

Germs live on your tongue and in other parts of your mouth. Germs can harm your teeth and give you bad breath.

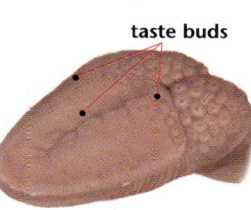

taste buds

Skin

Your skin protects your insides from the outside world. It keeps fluids you need inside your body and fluids you don't need, such as swimming pool water, outside your body.

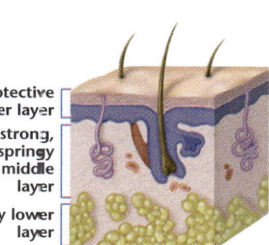

protective outer layer

strong, springy middle layer

fatty lower layer

Caring for Your Nose, Tongue, and Skin

- If you get a nosebleed, sit, lean forward slightly, and pinch just below the bridge of your nose for ten minutes. Breathe through your mouth.
- When you brush your teeth, brush your tongue too.
- Always wear sunscreen when you are in the sun.

3

MULTICULTURAL LINK

Skin Color Explain that over thousands of years groups of people who lived in very hot areas of the world developed dark skin for protection from the sun's harmful rays. People who lived in cooler parts of the world developed light skin color because the sun's rays were not as strong. People today have the skin color of their ancestors.

2 Teach

Discuss

Explain how the pupil controls the amount of light that reaches the retina to protect it from being damaged by too much light. Draw an analogy using the amount of light that could enter through a large window and a small window.

Critical Thinking How can you further protect your eyes when in bright sunlight? wear sunglasses

Learn from Diagrams

Use Transparency 11 to trace how sound waves become nerve signals the brain interprets as sound.

Which part of the ear acts like a funnel to collect the sound waves? outer ear

Discuss

Explain that different cells in the nasal cavity detect different odors.

Learn from Diagrams

Use Transparency 12 to show where the tongue senses various flavors (sweet and salty on the tip; sour on the sides; bitter in the back). Help students list foods or drinks that are examples of each flavor.

Caring for the Sense Organs

Discuss the importance of caring for the sense organs because they tell us what's going on around us. They help us enjoy and stay safe in our environment.

3 Wrap Up

Use the blackline master included in the transparency package to assess students' understanding of the parts and functions of the sense organs.

OBJECTIVE

- Identify the parts and functions of the skeletal system.

PROGRAM RESOURCES

Teaching Transparency 15

- Activity Book, p. 2

VOCABULARY

- skull
- clavicle
- rib cage
- humerus
- spine
- ulna
- pelvis
- radius
- femur
- tibia
- fibula

1 Motivate

Tell students that bones meet and link at joints. Explain that bones can't bend; however, the joints allow the bones to move. Have students form their hands into fists. Ask them to identify where joints are in a finger.

Based on the location of joints in a finger, how many bones do you think make up each finger? three

2 Teach

Discuss

Explain to students that the skull has an opening at the base to allow a bundle of nerves (spinal cord) from the rest of the body to pass through. Other openings allow signals to reach the brain from the sense organs.

What sense organs are located in the skull? eyes, ears, nose, tongue

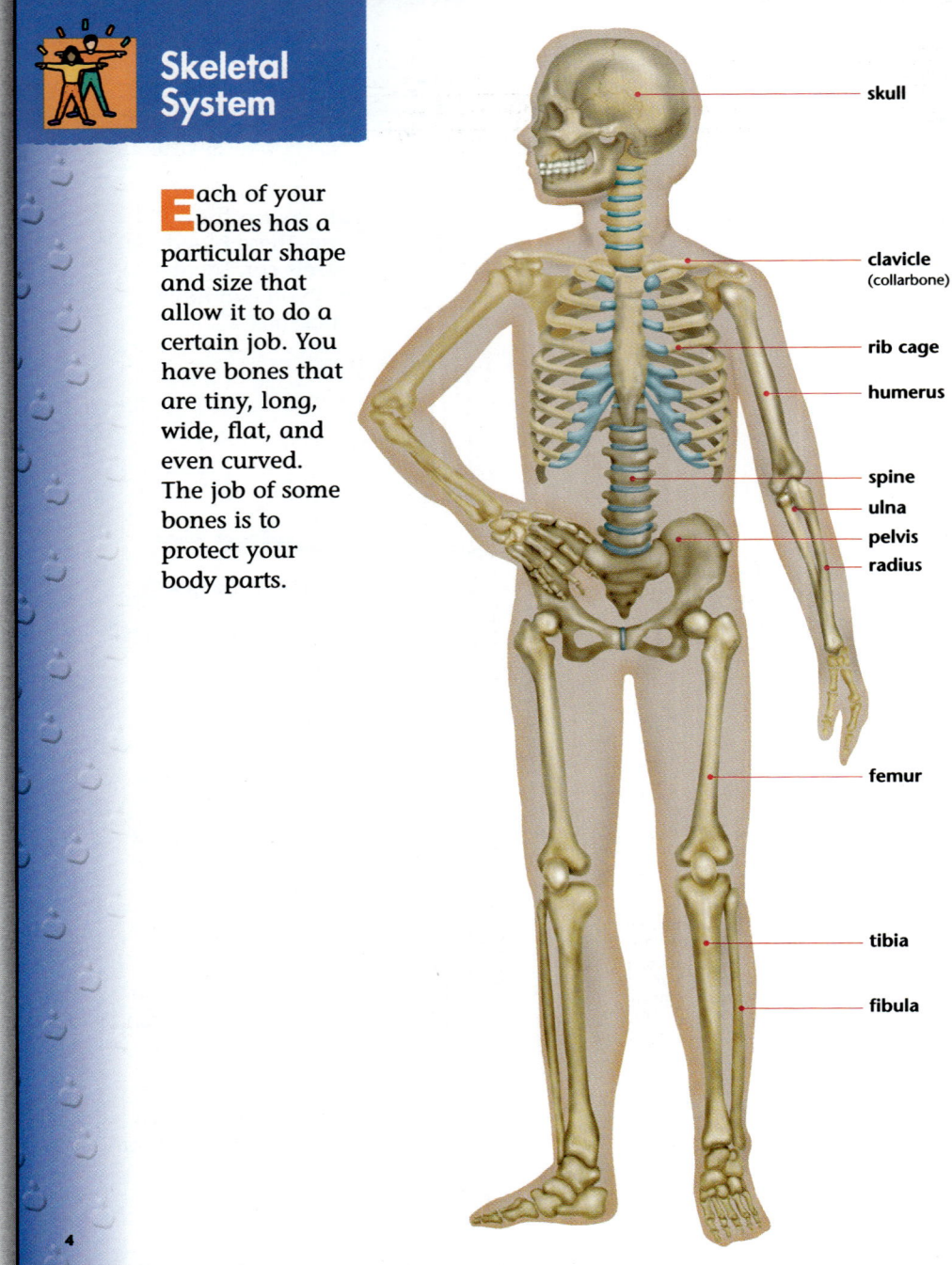

Skeletal System

Each of your bones has a particular shape and size that allow it to do a certain job. You have bones that are tiny, long, wide, flat, and even curved. The job of some bones is to protect your body parts.

- skull
- clavicle (collarbone)
- rib cage
- humerus
- spine
- ulna
- pelvis
- radius
- femur
- tibia
- fibula

4

TEACHING TRANSPARENCY

Teaching Transparency 15: The Skeletal System shows the major parts of the system.

TEACHER TIP

Learning Vocabulary Suggest that students categorize and learn the different bones by body parts, such as bones of the legs, the arms, the torso, the head. Invite students to create games based on their categories involving matching, sorting, or recall to review the parts of the skeletal system.

Bones that Protect

Rib Cage Your rib bones form a cage that protects your heart and lungs from all sides. Your ribs are springy. When something strikes you in the chest, your ribs push the object away instead of letting it hit your heart and lungs. Your ribs are connected to your breastbone (sternum) by springy material called cartilage. The springy connection lets your ribs move up and down. This happens when your rib cage gets bigger and smaller as you breathe in and out.

Skull The bones in your head are called your skull. Some of the bones in your skull protect your brain. The bones in your face are part of your skull too.

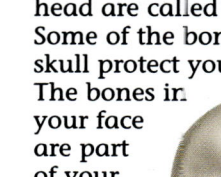

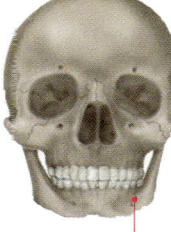

cartilage

rib

sternum

jaw

Caring for Your Skeletal System

- Calcium helps bones grow and makes them strong. Dairy products like milk, cheese, and yogurt contain calcium. Have 2–3 servings of dairy products every day.
- Exercise also makes your bones strong. When bones aren't used, they can become brittle and may break.

Activities

1. Look at the picture of the skeleton. Name a long bone. Name a short bone. Name a curved bone.

2. Put a tomato inside a wire cage. Gently throw a wad of paper at the cage. What happens? The cage protects the tomato in the same way your ribs protect your heart.

3. Measure around your rib cage with a string. How big is it when you breathe in? How big is it when you breathe out? Which measurement is greater?

5

Caring for the Skeletal System

Explain how bones store calcium from foods so they can grow, harden, and repair themselves. Other parts of the body also need calcium. If the body does not get enough calcium from foods, it will take calcium from bones.

Critical Thinking What do you think will happen to bones if calcium is taken from them? They will become weak and brittle.

Activities

Activity 1 Examples of long bones (bones of arms and legs); short bones (bones of hands and feet); curved bones (ribs).

Critical Thinking Which type of bones would allow for fine (small) movements? short bones Which type of bones would best protect the body? curved bones

Activity 2 Explain that heavier objects or ones that hit harder could break the cage or knock it off the table and ultimately damage the tomato.

Critical Thinking What are examples of situations in which a person could injure the ribs and, therefore, need special protection? Possible answers: while playing sports, while riding in a car.

Activity 3 Have students hold their measured lengths of string along a yard- or meterstick to determine distance. Explain that the ribs move up and out, causing the rib cage to become larger, when the air breathed in expands the lungs. They move down and in, causing the rib cage to become smaller, when you breathe out.

3 Wrap Up

Use the blackline master included in the transparency package to assess students' understanding of the parts of the skeletal system.

ACTIVITY BOOK, p. 2

The Skeletal System

In the space provided, write the letter of the term in Column B that best fits the description in Column A.

Column A		Column B
b	1. the collarbone	a. skull
j	2. the larger lower leg bone	b. clavicle
d	3. the bone of the upper arm	c. rib cage
e	4. supports the back	d. humerus
c	5. protects the heart and lungs	e. spine
f	6. the larger bone of lower arm	f. radius
h	7. the bone that forms the hips	g. ulna
a	8. the bones that protect the brain	h. pelvis
k	9. the smaller bone of the lower leg	i. femur
i	10. the upper leg bone	j. tibia
g	11. the smaller bone of the lower arm	k. fibula

On the lines below, write a short song to remember which bones are connected to form the skeleton.

Song ideas will vary. Check to be sure students have followed a logical order.

SCIENCE

Determining Mineral in Bones
Illustrate how minerals strengthen bones by having students feel the stiffness of a clean leg bone of a chicken. Then, place the leg bone in a jar of vinegar. Each day for a week, have students check the stiffness of the bone. (It should become flexible within a week as minerals in the bone dissolve in the vinegar.)

OBJECTIVE

• Identify the parts and functions of the muscular system.

PROGRAM RESOURCES

Teaching Transparency 16

• Activity Book, p. 3

VOCABULARY

• deltoid
• biceps
• triceps
• flexors
• abdominal muscles
• quadriceps

1 Motivate

Explain to students that you need muscles to move and that most movements take many muscles working together. For example, more than 200 muscles are used every time you take a step. About 30 muscles are used to make facial expressions. A smile alone requires 15 muscles to work.

2 Teach

Discuss

Point out to students that opposing muscles are located on the opposite sides of bones at joints. Each muscle is attached to bone by tendons.

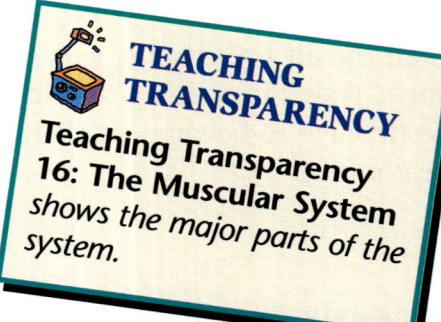

TEACHING TRANSPARENCY

Teaching Transparency 16: The Muscular System shows the major parts of the system.

Muscular System

Like your bones, each muscle in your body does a certain job. Muscles in your thumb help you hold things. Muscles in your neck help you turn your head. Muscles in your arms help you pull or lift objects.

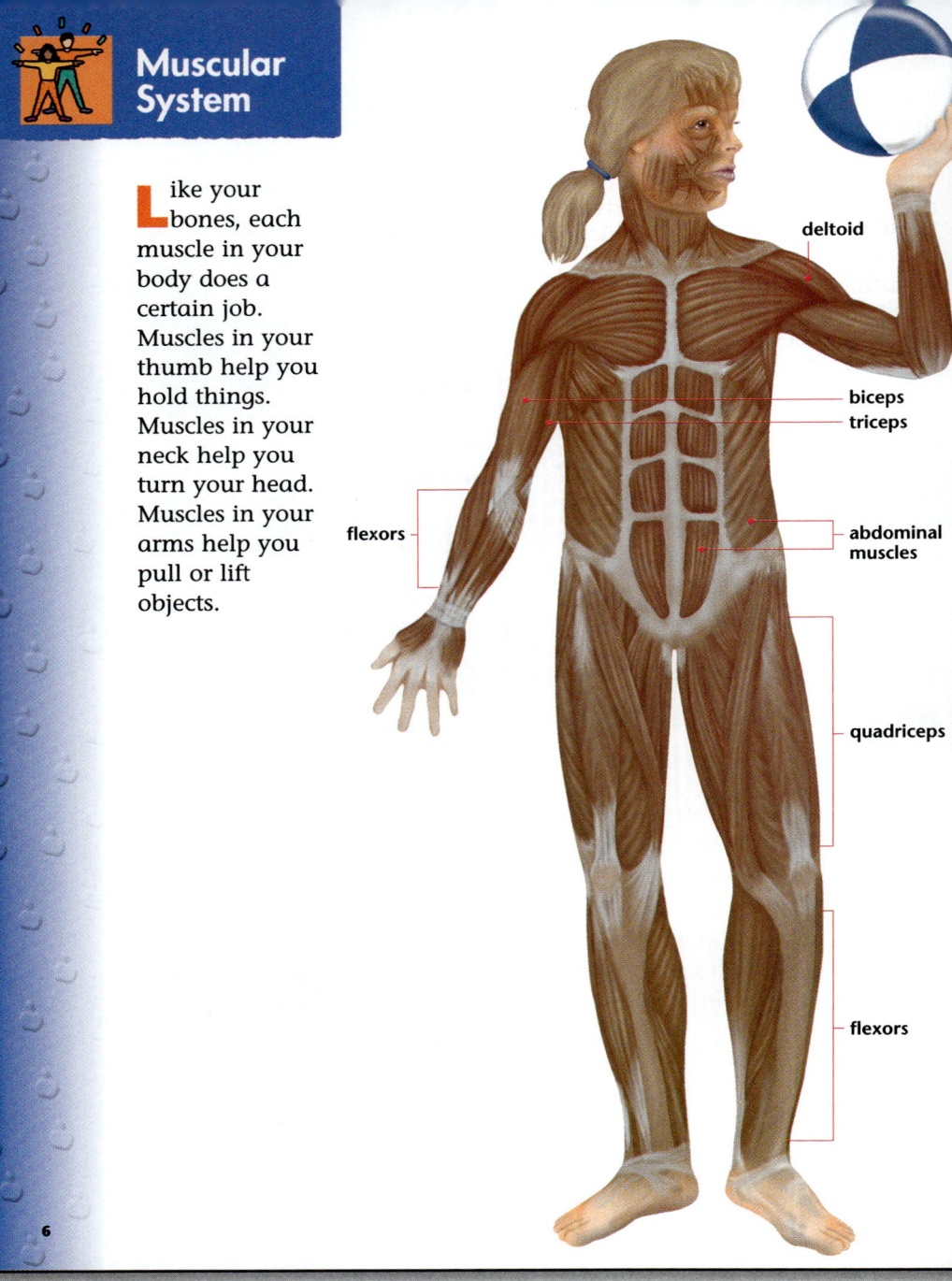

- deltoid
- biceps
- triceps
- flexors
- abdominal muscles
- quadriceps
- flexors

6

MEET INDIVIDUAL NEEDS

Kinesthetic Learners To allow students hands-on and visual experiences with the contracting and relaxing muscles, build a simple model of the arm. Use two narrow 1-foot boards, a hinge, two eye-screws, string, and a long balloon. Attach the boards using the hinge as a joint. Insert one eye-screw near the end of one board and the other midway along the other board. Partially blow up the balloon and attach it to the eye-screws with string. The balloon will become shorter and fatter as the boards are moved toward one another and will become longer and thinner as the boards are moved apart.

How Muscles Move Your Body

Muscle Pairs Your arm can reach forward and pull back. Your hand can open and close. Muscles can only pull. Moving part of your body in more than one direction takes more than one muscle. It takes a pair of muscles for your arm to bend and straighten.

 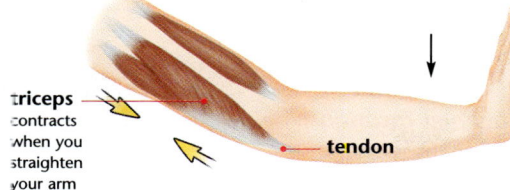

triceps contracts when you straighten your arm

tendon

biceps contracts when you bend your arm

tendon

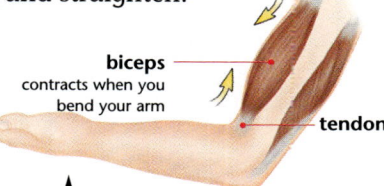

Tendons Tendons are strong strips of tough cord-like material. They connect your muscles to your bones. Your Achilles tendon is just above your heel. It connects your calf muscle to your heel bone. Your calf muscles and Achilles tendon allow you to stand on tiptoe.

Caring for Your Muscular System

- Exercise makes your muscles stronger.
- Stretching before you exercise makes muscles and tendons more flexible and less likely to get hurt.

Activities

1. Tie your shoe without using your thumb. What happens?

2. Pull up on a desk with one hand. With your other hand, feel which arm muscle is working. Now push on the desk. Which arm muscle is working?

3. Ask a friend to push down on your arms for one minute while you push up as hard as you can. When your friend lets go, what happens?

7

Care of Your Muscular System

Explain that exercise makes muscles work hard. In response, the muscles get larger and stronger to do work more easily.

Activities

Activity 1 Without the use of their thumbs, students will be unable to grasp and manipulate the strings effectively to tie their shoes.

Critical Thinking What other actions do you do every day that require the use of your thumbs? Possible answer: pick up things.

Activity 2 Pulling will primarily use the biceps muscle. Pushing will primarily use the triceps muscle. Students should be able to feel these muscles tightening and getting shorter and fatter. Reinforce that both muscles are actually involved in both movements.

What is a muscle doing when it gets shorter and fatter? contracting

Activity 3 When released, the students' arms will rise as resistance is removed.

3 Wrap Up

Use the blackline master included in the transparency package to assess students' understanding of the parts of the muscular system.

Health Background

Opposing Muscles Muscles work in pairs. Each skeletal muscle has another skeletal muscle that works gently against it. When one muscle contracts, the other muscle relaxes. The contracting muscle causes movement. The relaxed muscle stays somewhat tight to help control the movement. To return the body part to its original position, the relaxed muscle contracts and the other muscle relaxes.

For more background, visit the **Webliography** on the Teacher Resources page at:
www.harcourtschool.com/health
Keyword human body

ACTIVITY BOOK, p. 3

The Muscular System

Read the phrase. Find the term in the box that matches each phrase. Put one letter on each line. Each letter in the puzzle has a number. Use the numbers to fill in the secret message.

| biceps | deltoid | flexors | quadriceps | tendons |

1. strong strips of cord-like material

t e n d o n s
1 3 5 7 9 5 2

2. muscle that contracts when you bend your arm

b i c e p s
4 6 8 3 10 2

3. muscle of front upper leg

q u a d r i c e p s
11 15 12 7 13 6 8 3 10 2

4. shoulder muscle

d e l t o i d
7 3 14 1 0 6 7

5. muscles of lower arms and legs

f l e x o r s
16 14 3 18 9 13 2

Secret Message: What makes muscles strong?

e x e r c i s e
3 18 3 13 8 6 2 3

♪ MUSIC

Playing the Piano Muscles on the underside of the forearm have long tendons that run through the wrist, attaching to the fingers. These muscles contract to bend the fingertips toward the palm, as when playing the piano.

7

OBJECTIVE

- Identify the parts and functions of the digestive system.

PROGRAM RESOURCES

Teaching Transparency 17

- Activity Book, p. 4

VOCABULARY

- mouth
- esophagus
- liver
- stomach
- small intestine
- large intestine

1 Motivate

This is a paragraph from the book *The Magic School Bus—Inside the Body*, where students travel throughout the body in a microscopic bus. Read the following excerpt aloud: "It wasn't exactly quiet in there. The walls . . . moved in and out, churning and mashing the food into a thick liquid. The bus was turning round and round, and digestive juice splashed the windows. Now we knew how it felt to be a hamburger!"

What part of the body are the children traveling through? the stomach

Health Background

The Process of Digestion Digestion begins in the mouth as you chew and mix food with saliva. It continues in the stomach, where another chemical begins to break down the food and prepares it to enter the small intestine. As food progresses to the small intestine, many other chemicals finish digestion. Digested food passes through the walls of the small intestine and enters the blood, where it travels to all parts of the body.

For more background, visit the **Webliography** on the Teacher Resources page at:
www.harcourtschool.com/health
Keyword human body

Digestive System

Food is broken down and pushed through your body by your digestive system. Your digestive system is a series of connected parts that starts with your mouth and ends with your large intestine.

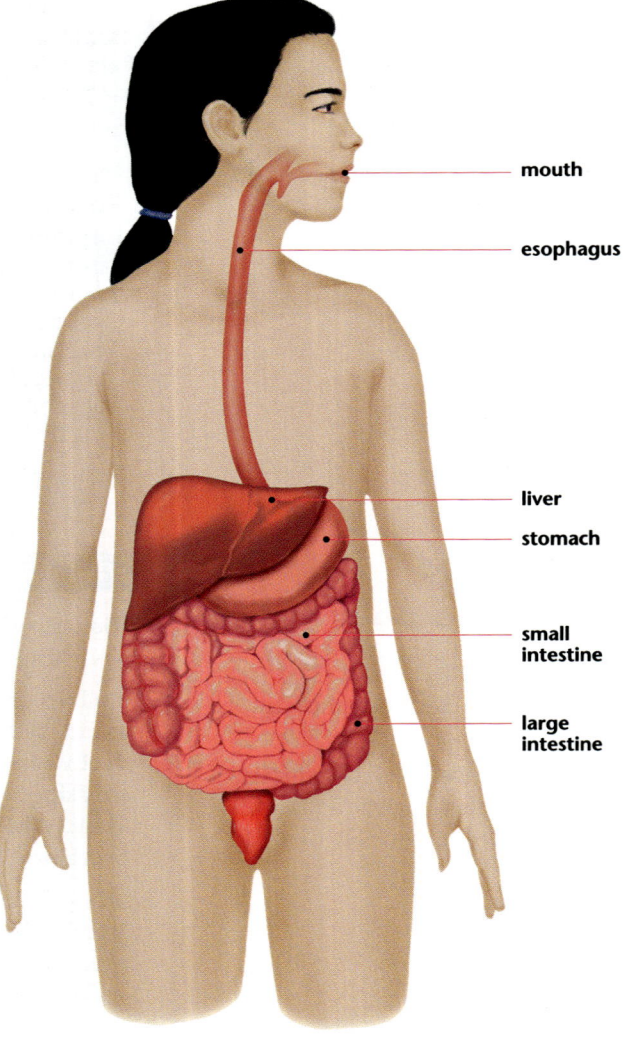

mouth

esophagus

liver

stomach

small intestine

large intestine

8

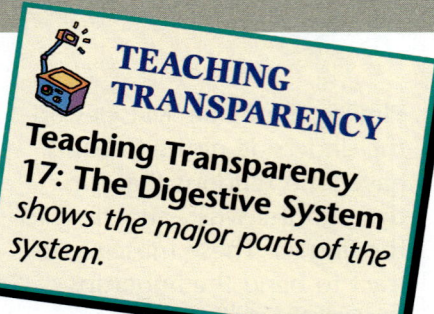

TEACHING TRANSPARENCY

Teaching Transparency 17: The Digestive System shows the major parts of the system.

MEET INDIVIDUAL NEEDS

Kinesthetic Learners Ask students to design and build mobiles with at least six facts about the digestive system, or to draw the digestive system and provide tag lines to name and identify the functions of each part.

From Mouth to Stomach

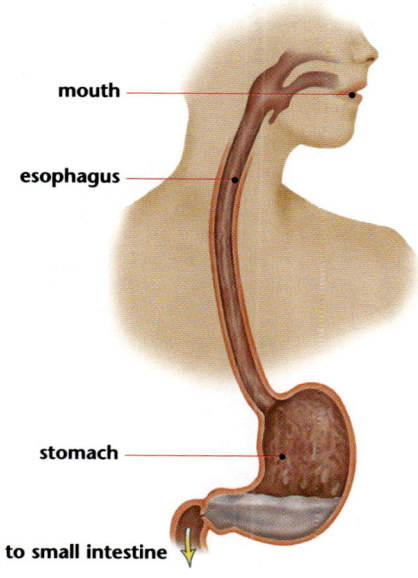

mouth

esophagus

stomach

to small intestine

Esophagus Your esophagus, or food tube, is a tube that connects your mouth to your stomach. After you swallow a bite of food, muscles in your esophagus push the food into your stomach.

Stomach Your stomach is filled with acid that helps dissolve food. The stomach walls are strong muscles that mix food with the acid. The stomach walls are protected from the acid by a thick layer of mucus. From your stomach, food moves to the small intestine and then to the large intestine.

Caring for Your Digestive System

- Chew everything you eat carefully. Well-chewed food is easier to digest.
- Do not overeat. Overeating can cause a stomachache.

Activities

1. Measure 25 feet (about 8 m) on the floor. This is how long your digestive system is.

2. Cut a narrow balloon so that it is open on both ends. Put a wad of paper in one end. Squeeze the outside of the balloon to push the paper through and out the other end. This is similar to how your esophagus pushes food to your stomach.

9

ACTIVITY BOOK. p. 4

The Digestive System

Imagine you could shrink and travel through the body in a protective bubble. What might you experience as you pass through the digestive system and travel to the body's cells? Write a short story of your experience in the space below. Be sure to tell where you are during each stage of digestion. Draw a picture to go along with your story.

Stories will vary.

_____

_____

_____

_____

_____

_____

_____

_____

_____

_____

_____

_____

_____

_____

_____

_____

 MATH

Measuring Surface Area Show how chewing food into smaller pieces increases surface area exposed to digestive juices allowing food to be broken down more easily. Have several students measure the surface of a loaf of bread while still wrapped. Open the loaf and provide slices for students to measure. Add their figures to determine the surface area of all the slices.

---

2 Teach

Discuss

Explain to students that muscles in the walls of the stomach squeeze and churn food every few minutes to make it into an almost liquid form. Only a few substances are absorbed through the stomach walls.

Caring for Your Digestive System

Thoroughly chewing food helps digestion because it does a lot of the work chemicals would have to do otherwise—breaking food into smaller parts. Also, food broken into smaller parts has more surface area to be exposed to digestive juices.

Activities

Activity 1 Tell students that the digestive system is mostly made of the intestines, which are coiled in the abdomen. Explain that digestion takes a long time. It takes three to six hours for a meal to be broken down in the stomach. The first food reaches the intestines an hour later. The trip through the intestines can take between eight and twenty-four hours, or even longer.

Activity 2 Muscles in the esophagus push food to the stomach.

3 Wrap Up

Use the blackline master included in the transparency package to assess students' understanding of the parts of the digestive system.

OBJECTIVE

• Identify the parts and functions of the circulatory system.

PROGRAM RESOURCES

 Teaching Transparencies 18 and 19

 Computer Graphing Activity, Teaching Resources p. 52

VOCABULARY

• blood vessels
• arteries
• veins
• heart

1 Motivate

Have students find the pulses on their wrists by cradling the back of one wrist in the palm of the other hand and wrapping their fingers gently around the wrist. Encourage them to press gently on their wrists with the tips of their fingers until they feel a thumping sensation. Explain that each thump is the contraction of the heart muscle pushing blood through the body's blood vessels.

In which type of blood vessel, arteries or veins, do you think you can feel the heart beating? Why? arteries, because there is more forceful movement in them as the heart pumps the blood away from the heart

Health Background

Pulse When the body is active, the muscles need more oxygen, so the heart beats faster and harder. With each beat, waves of pressure move along the arteries. This is known as pulse. Resting pulse is about 70–75 beats per minute. After exercise, pulse rate may vary.

For more background, visit the **Webliography** on the Teacher Resources page at:
www.harcourtschool.com/health
Keyword human body

Circulatory System

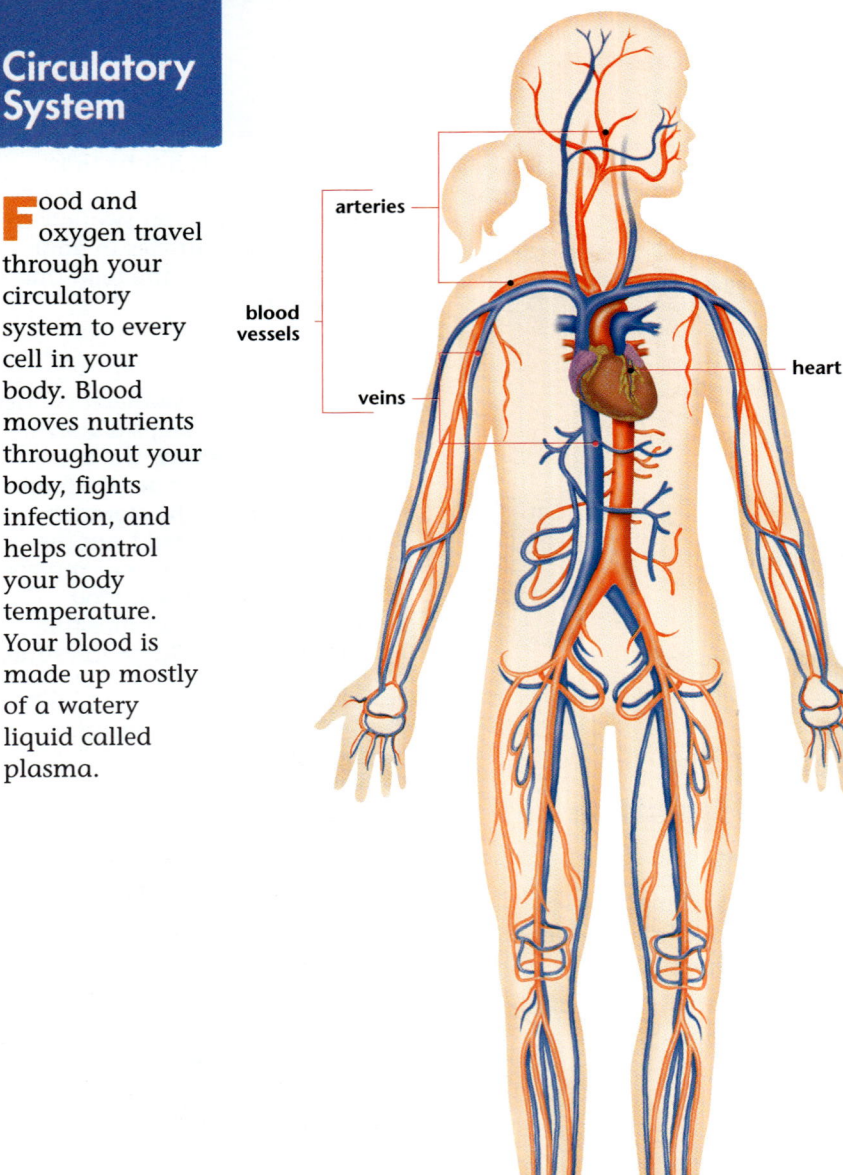

Food and oxygen travel through your circulatory system to every cell in your body. Blood moves nutrients throughout your body, fights infection, and helps control your body temperature. Your blood is made up mostly of a watery liquid called plasma.

arteries

blood vessels

veins

heart

10

Blood Vessels

Arteries Arteries carry blood away from the heart. Blood in arteries is brighter red because it has come from the lungs and has lots of oxygen. Arteries bring oxygen and nutrients to all parts of the body.

Veins Veins carry blood to the heart. Veins have one-way valves that allow blood to move only toward the heart.

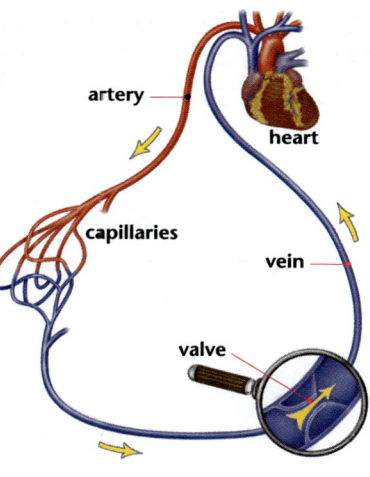

artery
heart
capillaries
vein
valve

Capillaries Capillaries are very small pathways for blood. When blood flows through capillaries, it gives oxygen and nutrients to the cells in your body. Blood also picks up carbon dioxide and other waste.

Caring for Your Circulatory System

- Never touch another person's blood.
- Eat a healthy, balanced diet throughout your life to keep excess fat from blocking the blood flowing through your arteries.
- Get regular exercise to keep your heart strong.

Activities

1. **Take the bottom out of a paper cup. Bend the top together like a clamshell. Hold the cup and drop a marble through from the bottom. Now try to drop one into the top. The clamshell-shaped cup is like the one-way valve in a vein.**

2. **Find the blue lines under the skin on your wrist. These are veins. Press gently and stroke along the lines toward your elbow. Now stroke toward your hand. What do you see?**

11

SCIENCE

Valves in the Veins Illustrate how valves in veins help blood reach the heart. Form an inclined plane by shaping a folder into an "M" and placing one end on a book. Gently thump a marble part way up the trough of the folder and allow the marble to roll back down. Explain that gravity acted against the marble. Thump the marble gently again, but this time follow it up with your finger, stopping it as it begins to roll back. Continue this until the marble reaches the top. Tell students that blood in veins, especially in the legs and feet, also work against gravity, and that valves hold blood in place (as your finger did the marble) until the next force arrives to force the blood farther toward the heart.

2 Teach

Caring for the Circulatory System

Explain to students that touching blood that has germs in it (from an infected person) could allow the germs to enter their blood through a cut or scratch. This could cause them to become ill as well.

Discuss how exercise improves the heart because it responds to hard work just like other muscles do. It gets stronger to make its work easier.

Activities

Activity 1 Tell students that blood moves through the veins with much less force than it does through the arteries. As a result, blood tends to trickle backward when no force is pushing it forward.

What are the one-way parts of the veins that prevent blood from trickling backward? valves

Activity 2 Stroking toward the elbow will result in the veins disappearing, but gradually reappearing. (Blood continues to flow from the hand.) Stroking toward the hand will result in the lines disappearing and not reappearing until pressure is released. Tell students that the blue in the veins is the blood with little oxygen. Explain that stroking toward the hand forces blood back toward the hand, blocking any more blood from entering the veins.

Critical Thinking What prevents the veins from reappearing when stroking toward the hand? Valves block the flow of blood.

3 Wrap Up

Use the blackline master included in the transparency package to assess students' understanding of the parts of the circulatory system.

Respiratory System

OBJECTIVE
• Identify the parts and functions of the respiratory system.

PROGRAM RESOURCES
 Teaching Transparency 20

 Computer Graphing Activity, Teaching Resources p. 53

VOCABULARY
- nose
- mouth
- trachea
- lungs
- diaphragm

1 Motivate

Optional Materials balloons

Provide students with identically sized balloons. Ask each student to take a deep breath and exhale as much air into the balloon as he or she can, and then pinch the end of the balloon. You do the same. Compare the different sizes of the balloons, discussing why the balloons could be different sizes (lung size, ability to fully inhale or exhale, allowing air to escape). Have students count the number of full breaths it takes to fill their balloons. You do the same. Discuss how breathing deeply allows the lungs to work more efficiently.

Health Background

Diaphragm The diaphragm forms the base of the chest and the top of the abdomen. It is the main breathing muscle. Muscles around the ribs are also involved in breathing.

Breathing To breathe in, the diaphragm contracts, pulling down the base of the lungs. Muscles around the ribs pull the front of the chest up and out. These movements expand the lungs, sucking in air. To breathe out, the diaphragm relaxes, allowing the lungs to spring back to their smaller size, pushing out air.

Your body uses its respiratory system to get oxygen from the air and get rid of excess carbon dioxide. Your respiratory system is made up of your nose and mouth, your trachea (windpipe), your two lungs, and your diaphragm—a dome-shaped muscle under your lungs.

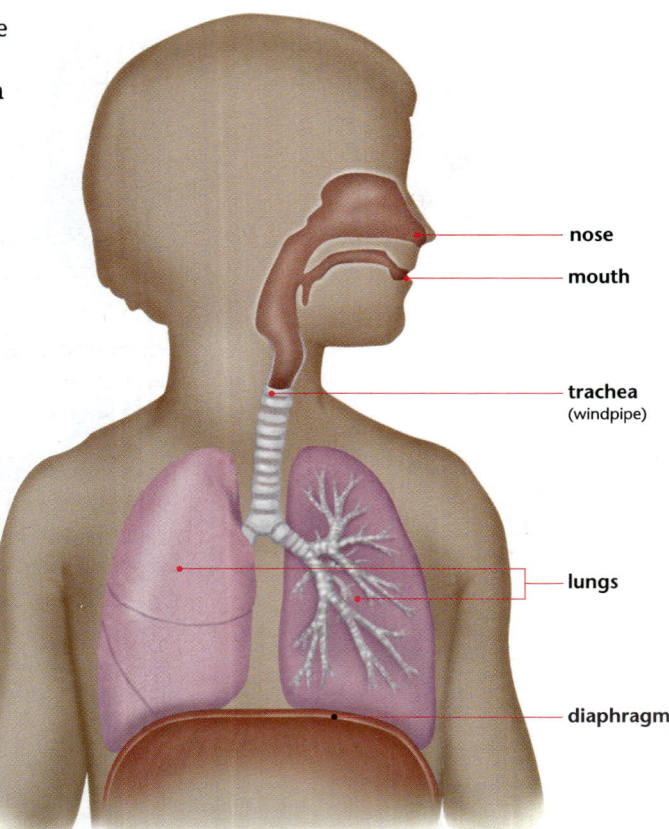

nose
mouth
trachea (windpipe)
lungs
diaphragm

12

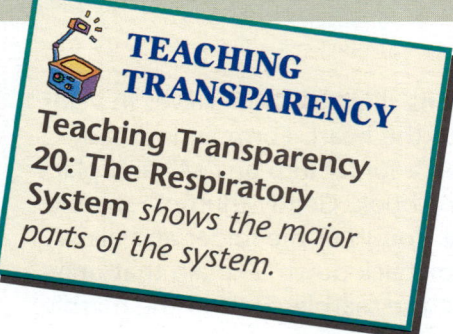

TEACHING TRANSPARENCY

Teaching Transparency 20: The Respiratory System shows the major parts of the system.

TEACHER TIP

Understanding the Body's Need for Oxygen A cell in the body may be compared with a flame. Light a candle and allow it to burn briefly while you discuss how the flame needs oxygen to burn. Then, place a glass over the candle and allow the flame to go out. Explain that the flame continued to burn until all of the oxygen trapped in the glass was used. Describe how the body's cells have similar needs and how without oxygen they would die.

Breathing

When you inhale, or breathe in, air enters your mouth and nose and goes into your trachea. Your trachea connects your nose and mouth to your lungs. Your trachea divides into two smaller tubes that go to your lungs. Your lungs fill with air. When you exhale, or breathe out, your diaphragm pushes upward. Air is forced up your trachea and out your mouth and nose.

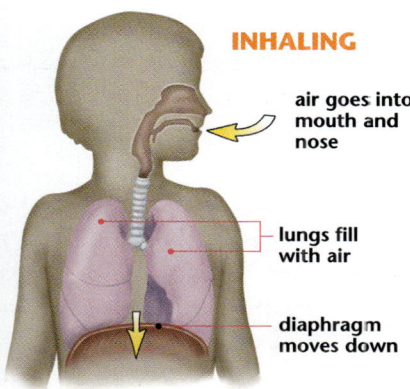

INHALING

air goes into mouth and nose

lungs fill with air

diaphragm moves down

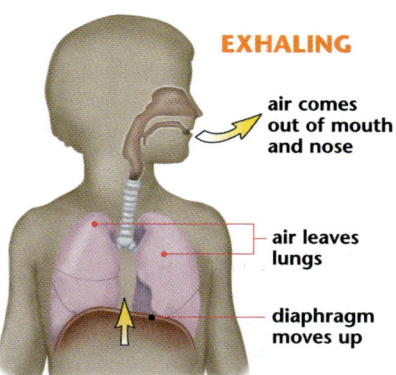

EXHALING

air comes out of mouth and nose

air leaves lungs

diaphragm moves up

Caring for Your Respiratory System

- Exercise. When you exercise your body, you exercise your respiratory system too. Your muscles use more oxygen, so you breathe faster and deeper.

- Get enough sleep to help your resistance to colds.

Activities

1. Sit in a chair and count how many breaths you take in 30 seconds. Then exercise for two minutes. When you stop, count how many breaths you take in 30 seconds. Do you breathe more while sitting or after exercise?

2. Put your hand on your bellybutton and take a deep breath in and out. How does your hand move?

13

SCIENCE

Model of Diaphragm Glue a piece of wood to the inside bottom edge of the top half of a plastic pop bottle. Secure a balloon around the base of the bottle using a rubber band. Cut a hole in the bottle's cap and insert a straw, sealing the hole with modeling clay. Attach a second balloon to the bottom of the straw using another rubber band. Screw the cap on the bottle. Demonstrate the function of the diaphragm by pulling on the bottom balloon to increase the size of the balloon inside the bottle (the lungs). Release it to decrease the size of the internal balloon.

2 Teach

Discuss

Discuss how air that is breathed in flows through the nose where small hairs filter out bits of dust and other floating particles.

Caring for Your Respiratory System

Coughing clears blockages in the throat, lungs, and breathing tubes. When you cough your vocal cords close and muscles in your chest squeeze, increasing pressure in your lungs. When the pressure becomes great, the vocal cords open and air rushes out of your mouth. The air carries dust and mucus that sometimes form the blockage.

Activities

Activity 1 Breathing rate will increase following exercise. Explain that during exercise, your brain tells you to breathe more quickly to send more oxygen to your muscles.

Activity 2 The hand moves out when deep breaths are taken in, and moves in when air is exhaled.

3 Wrap Up

Use the blackline master included in the transparency package to assess students' understanding of the parts of the respiratory system.

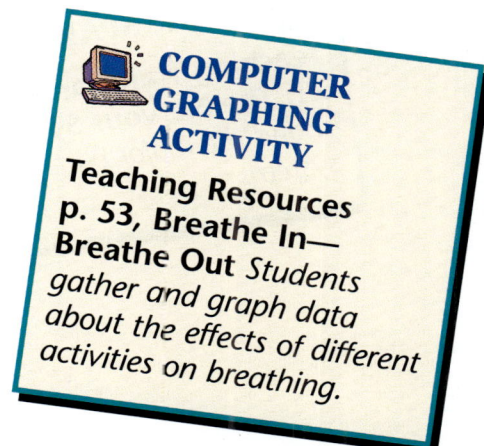

COMPUTER GRAPHING ACTIVITY

Teaching Resources p. 53, Breathe In—Breathe Out *Students gather and graph data about the effects of different activities on breathing.*

OBJECTIVE

• Identify the parts and functions of the nervous system.

PROGRAM RESOURCES

Teaching Transparency 21

• Activity Book, p. 5

VOCABULARY

• brain
• spinal cord
• nerves

1 Motivate

Ask students if they are as smart as a mouse. Yes; because a human brain is much larger than a mouse's brain. Ask if they are as smart as an elephant. Yes; even though the elephant's brain is much larger than the human brain. Explain that intelligence is not based only on brain size. It also depends on the sizes of particular parts of the brain and how the brain parts are connected. The part of the brain that involves thinking is a very large part of the human brain.

Why is the brain important to all animals? The brain is the control center, receiving and sending messages throughout the body.

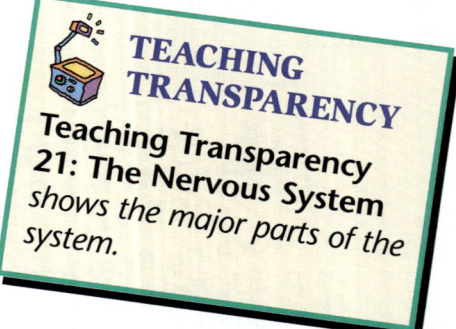

TEACHING TRANSPARENCY

Teaching Transparency 21: The Nervous System shows the major parts of the system.

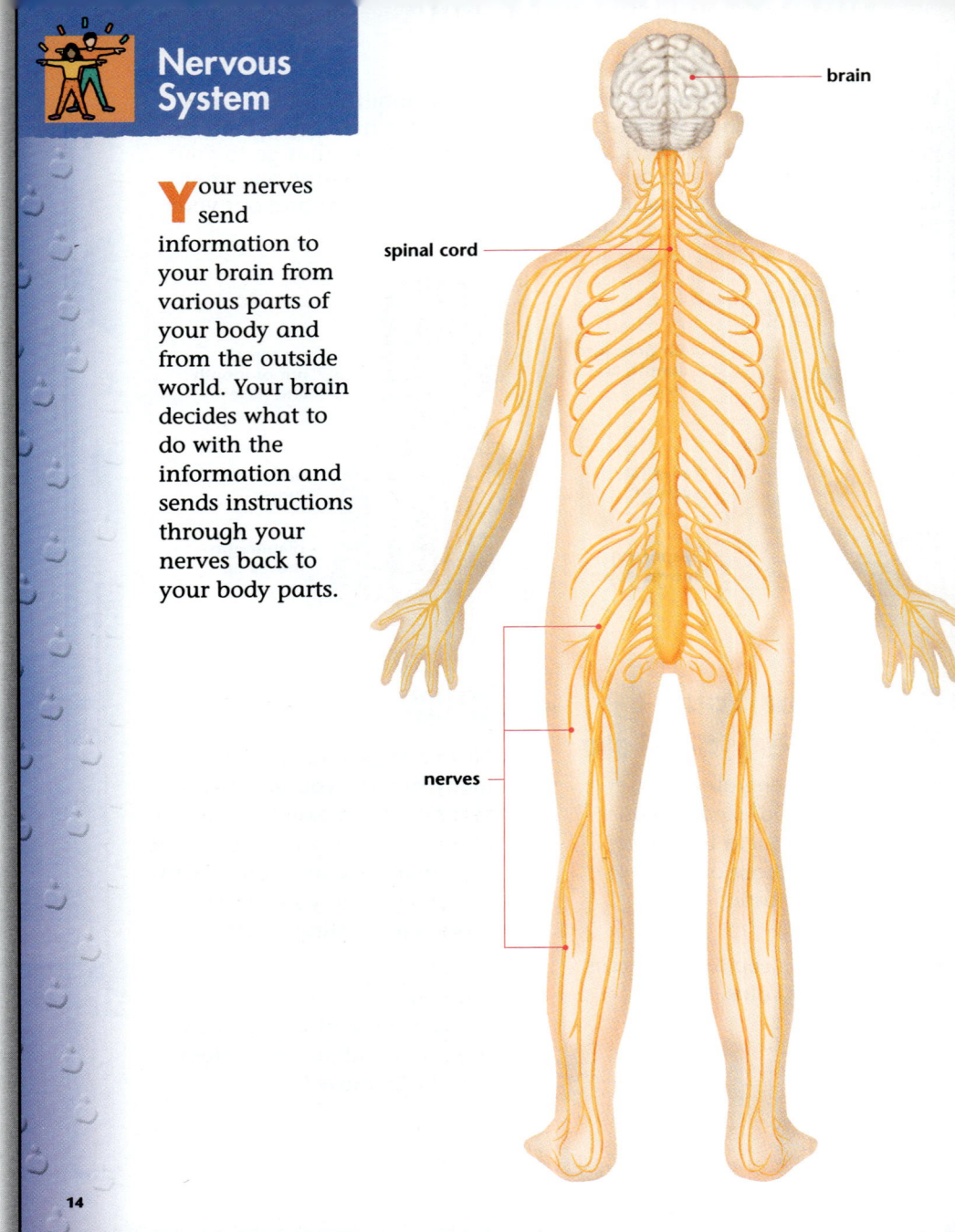

Nervous System

Your nerves send information to your brain from various parts of your body and from the outside world. Your brain decides what to do with the information and sends instructions through your nerves back to your body parts.

brain

spinal cord

nerves

14

SCIENCE

Connecting the Body Systems Have students identify all of the body systems they have studied. For each body system, ask them to brainstorm ways the brain or nerves are involved. For an example, consider the skeletal system (which may be the most difficult): nerves run through holes in the skull for messages to pass to and from the body, bones contain nerves, bones protect nerves, and so on. Other body systems will reflect a stronger role by the nervous system in their ability to do their jobs.

Your Brain

Your brain is about two pounds of wrinkled, pinkish-gray material. It's protected by your skull and cushioned by a thin layer of liquid. The brain's main connection to the body is the spinal cord.

Different parts of the brain send signals to different parts of your body. For example, the part right behind your forehead tells your body how to move. The area near the base of your neck controls your breathing and heartbeat. If you are left-handed, the right half of your brain controls your handwriting.

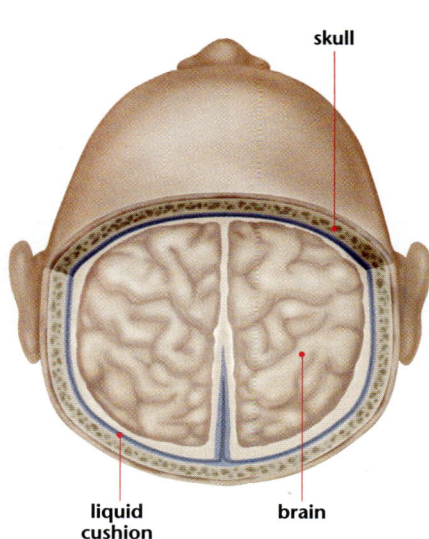

skull

liquid cushion

brain

Caring for Your Nervous System

- Many injuries to the brain are caused by car crashes. Wear your safety belt and sit in the backseat when you are in the car.
- Always wear a helmet when you ride your bike or scooter, skate, or use a skateboard.

Activities

1. Make a list of signals your nerves are sending to your brain right now. Also list instructions your brain is sending to your nerves.
2. Read a paragraph out of a book while the television is on. Do you know what the paragraph was about? Do you know what happened on television?
3. Write your name with your opposite hand ten times. Does your writing improve?

15

TEACHER TIP

Awareness Explain to students that although the brain processes thousands of messages about touch and the other senses, it often takes little notice unless some action is required. For example, once your brain has gotten used to your feet having shoes on, it takes little notice of it. However, if the shoes are uncomfortable, the brain will remind you often, until you adjust or take off the shoes.

2 Teach

Caring for Your Nervous System

Most injuries to the brain or spinal cord result from falls or crashes. Wearing a safety belt in the car prevents you from being thrown around the car if a crash were to occur. Wearing a helmet during sports provides extra protection for the head, padding it in case you fall.

Activities

Activity 1 Examples of signals from nerves might include information about the lighting, sounds, and temperature. Signals from the brain might include stimulating muscles to close the eyelids, straighten the back, or hold a pencil and write.

Critical Thinking What are some actions your brain controls even though you don't have to think about doing them? Possible answers: breathing, getting the heart to pump, digesting.

Activity 2 It would be more difficult to read and comprehend with the TV on.

Critical Thinking Why is it difficult to read and watch TV at the same time? Reading requires visual attention, reading skills, and the ability to think about what is being read. TV tends to stimulate the brain and distract you because of its sights and sounds.

Activity 3 Students probably would improve their writing as they practice. Explain that when you first learn something, it takes a while for your brain to understand what needs to be done. After performing an action repeatedly, however, your brain is able to instruct your muscles in less than a second.

3 Wrap Up

Use the blackline master included in the transparency package to assess students' understanding of the parts of the nervous system.

 CHAPTER 1

About Myself and Others

Chapter Organizer

Lesson	Objectives	Vocabulary	Program Resources
Introduce the Chapter pp. 16–17	• Preview the chapter. • Begin chapter project.		• School-Home Connection, TR p. 33 • Assessment Guide, p. 21 • Read-Aloud Anthology, p. RA-2 ✎ Teaching Transparency 1—Graphic Organizer
✔ 3•5•6 **Lesson 1 Feeling Good About Myself** pp. 18–19 *Pacing: 1 class period*	• Recognize the importance of respecting and taking care of oneself. • Describe ways to exhibit responsible behavior.	feelings respect responsible honest	• Growth, Development, and Reproduction pp. 20–25
✔ 1•3•5 **Lesson 2 Understanding My Feelings** pp. 20–23 *Pacing: 2 class periods*	• Recognize that feelings are expressed by words, actions, and body language. • Identify effective ways to change or cope with unpleasant feelings.	body language emotions self-control	• Activity Book, pp. 6–7
✔ 1•3 **Lesson 3 Dealing with Fear, Stress, Anger, and Grief** pp. 24–27 *Pacing: 2 class periods*	• List situations involving fear that require immediate help from a trusted adult. • Identify effective strategies for dealing with fear, stress, anger, and grief.	fear stress anger grief	
✔ 1•3 **Life Skills Manage Stress** pp. 28–29 *Pacing: 1 class period*	• Identify ways to manage stress. • Apply stress-management skills to situations at school.		• Activity Book, p. 8
✔ 1•3•7 **Lesson 4 Relationships with Family and Friends** pp. 30–33 *Pacing: 2 class periods*	• Describe practical methods for establishing and building healthful relationships. • Recognize the importance of standing up for personal values when faced with negative peer pressure.	relationship peers peer pressure	• Activity Book, p. 9 💵 HEALTH VIDEO: The Cleanup Kids
✔ 1•3•5 **Lesson 5 Communicating Well with Others** pp. 34–35 *Pacing: 1 class period*	• Recognize that effective communication skills include both speaking and listening skills. • Realize the importance of compassion, kindness, apology, and forgiveness.	communicate compassion apologize	• Activity Book, p. 10
✔ 1•3•5 **Life Skills Resolve Conflicts** pp. 36–37 *Pacing: 1 class period*	• Identify strategies for resolving conflicts. • Use negotiation to resolve conflicts with friends and peers.		• Activity Book, p. 11
✔ 3•5•7 **Chapter Review and Test** pp. 38–41	• Assess chapter objectives and project. • Provide extension activities.		• Chapter Test and Project Evaluation Sheet, Assessment Guide, pp. 18–21

 National Health Education Standards
A complete list of the Standards is provided on the next page.

Key: TR = Teaching Resources

National Health Education Standards

1. Comprehend concepts related to health promotion and disease prevention.
2. Access valid health information and health-promoting products and services.
3. Practice health-enhancing behaviors and reduce health risks.
4. Analyze the influence of culture, media, technology, and other factors on health.
5. Use interpersonal communication skills to enhance health.
6. Use goal-setting and decision-making skills to enhance health.
7. Advocate for personal, family, and community health.

Science
- Pets Have Feelings Too, p. 23
- Do Animals Communicate?, p. 35

Art
- Stress Drawings, p. 28

Math
- Time-Management Calendars, p. 16C
- Make Bar Graphs, p. 27

Curriculum Integration

Use these topics to integrate health into your daily planning.

Social Studies
- Role Models, p. 16C
- Pioneer Stress, p. 29
- Family Traditions, p. 31

Drama
- Role-Play, p. 26

Language Arts
- Studying and Creating Fables, p. 16C
- More Than Crying, p. 22
- Gaining Attention, p. 31

ASSESSMENT OPTIONS

Portfolio Assessment
Have students select their best work from the following suggestions:
- **Studying and Creating Fables,** p. 16C
- **Communicating Your Feelings,** p. 40
- **Managing Your Time,** p. 40

Student Self-Assessment
- **Journal Notes,** p. 21
- **Set Health Goals,** pp. 19, 23, 33, 35
- **Use Life Skills,** p. 27

Daily Assessment
- **Check Your Facts,** pp. 19, 23, 27, 33, 35

Performance Assessment
- **Chapter Project: Make a Feelings Booklet,** pp. 17, 21, 25, 31, 39
- **Project Evaluation Sheet,** Assessment Guide, p. 21

Formal Assessment
- **Chapter Review,** pp. 38–39
- **In-Book Test,** p. 41
- **Chapter Test,** Assessment Guide, pp. 18–20

Cross-Curricular Activities

Language Arts

Studying and Creating Fables

Read and discuss examples of Aesop's fables, such as "The Boy Who Cried Wolf," "The Fox and the Grapes," and "The Hare and the Tortoise." Point out that most fables contain animal characters, and that each fable leads to a moral, or lesson. Then, based on specific content of each lesson, have students write original fables with morals that you provide, such as "be your own best friend" (Lesson 1) or "good friends respect your family's rules" (Lesson 4).

Math

Time-Management Calendars

Time management takes lots of practice. Create forms for students to use to plan and monitor the progress of a specific project. You might have them use the forms to chart the Chapter Project, or you might select another long-term project assigned to them in another curricular area. Work with students to break down the project into specific small steps they can easily schedule and accomplish. Use the activity to help them learn and practice effective strategies for accomplishing long-term goals by completing a series of short-term goals. Emphasize that this procedure is often helpful in reducing stress and avoiding last-minute deadline pressure.

Social Studies

Role Models

From their study of history and current events, work with students to identify constructive role models, based on such values as honesty, responsibility, goal setting, respect for others, and communication skills—all of which are discussed in this chapter. Have students write profiles of their selected role models, pointing out the reasons that led to their choices. Then, at the conclusion of Lesson 4, tie this role-model activity into the "big kids" discussion related to page 33. Ask students to write a final paragraph for their role model profiles, explaining how they, like their role models, can make a positive difference in the lives of others.

Bulletin Board

Give each student a flat oval construction-paper link with two diagonal cut lines.

- Have students trace their handprints in the middle of their links and print their names below their handprints.

- On their links, have students write four to six interests, talents, or self-describing phrases. Caution students not to write in the area immediately above or below the two "cut lines."

- Title the bulletin board "Each of us is different and special." Post the links as independent circles around the perimeter of the bulletin board. In the center of the display, create a chart with two columns titled: *To be happy and proud, each of us should:* and *To get along with others, each of us should:* As you work through the chapter, have students fill out the chart.

- See the Teacher Tip on the bottom of page 33 for suggestions regarding changes to make to assemble the chain and revise the banner.

Resources

Books for Students

Leghorn, Lindsay. **Proud of Our Feelings.** Magination Press, 1995. Priscilla introduces her friends, each of whom is feeling and expressing a different emotion. **EASY**

Wild, Margaret. **The Very Best of Friends.** Harcourt, 1994. After the death of his owner, a cat wins the heart of his grieving mistress. **AVERAGE**

Parsons, Alexandra. **I Am Special.** Franklin Watts, 1996. Discusses what makes us unique—our feelings, our friends, and our talents. **ADVANCED**

Books for Teachers and Families

Kalish, Susan. **Your Child's Fitness: Practical Advice for Parents.** Human Kinetics Publishers, 1995. In support of children's attitudes and behaviors about fitness, this book offers solid advice to adults as they work to make family fitness a priority.

Virgilio, Stephen J. **Fitness Education for Children: A Team Approach.** Human Kinetics Publishers, 1997. This is a comprehensive resource including more than 100 practical activities and instructional materials for adults who work with children on good health and fitness.

Videos

My Body, My Buddy: Teasing & Bullying, Rainbow Educational Media, 1995. (18 minutes) Explores why some children tease and bully, how it makes others feel, and how to deal with those feelings.

Who I Am Is Fine with Me, Rainbow Educational Media, 1997. (16 minutes) Talks to students about self-respect and respect for others. Explains self-esteem and shows real-life situations.

Yes, I Can!, Rainbow Educational Media, 1997. (17 minutes) Showcases three students facing personal challenges with ways to overcome their anxieties and self doubts to succeed.

Health Video Series by Harcourt **The Cleanup Kids**
This video is referenced at point-of-use in this Teacher's Edition.

GO ONLINE Your Health Webliography

The **Webliography** provides links to the Health Background and teaching resources that will support you as you teach the topics in *Your Health*. Simply choose a keyword and you will be taken to a page of links with descriptions of the content you can obtain at each site. The **Webliography** is located on the Teacher Resources page at **www.harcourtschool.com/health** Please review websites before referring your students to them.

Organizations and Agencies

National PTA
330 N. Wabash Ave.
Suite 2100
Chicago, IL 60611
800-307-4782
The PTA provides programs and information on conflict resolution in schools, as well as on helping children build good self-concepts.

Rainbows
2100 Golf Rd. #370
Rolling Meadows, IL 60008-4231
800-266-3206
Peer support group for children who have suffered a significant loss in their lives. Assists teachers in helping students through periods of grief.

Will Rogers Institute
1640 Marengo St.
Suite 406
Los Angeles, CA 90033
877-957-7575, ext 208
Distributes free pamphlets on a variety of health-related issues such as stress, exercise, and safety.

For more information about health organizations and agencies, please see the **Teaching Resources** book.

Community Health

Health and the Arts Invite a local artist, art historian, or museum curator to talk about how artists use color and form to express specific feelings. Prior to the visit, explain to the speaker the Lesson 3 "Career" context. Encourage the speaker to bring examples of art to share and discuss with students. If possible, have the speaker engage students in an art activity based on his or her discussion. Help students see the health benefits of finding ways to express their feelings in different ways.

Note that information, while correct at time of publication, is subject to change.

Visit **The Harcourt Learning Site** for related links, activities, resources, and the health **Webliography**.

www.harcourtschool.com

"...focuses on the importance of positive interpersonal relationships as an element in individual health and well being."

—Page 52, *California Health Framework*

CHAPTER SUMMARY

In this chapter students

- learn positive strategies pertaining to self-respect, self-control, and effective communication skills.
- examine and practice methods for dealing with fear, anger, stress, and grief.
- recognize the importance of building and maintaining positive relationships with family members and peers.

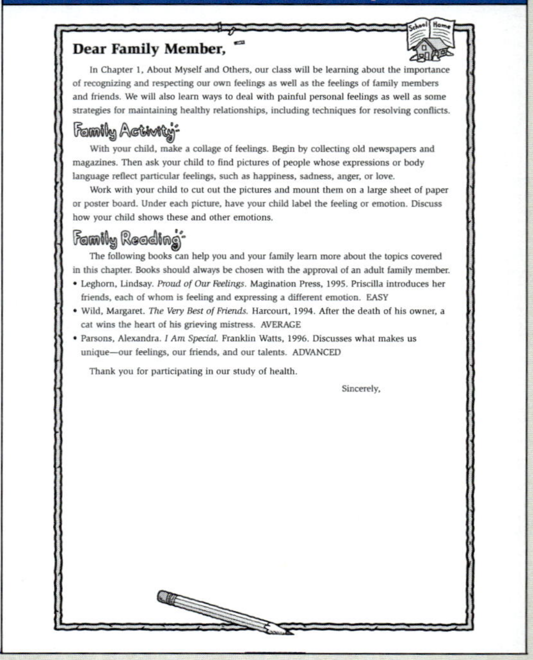

LIFE SKILLS Students practice *managing stress* and *resolving conflicts*.

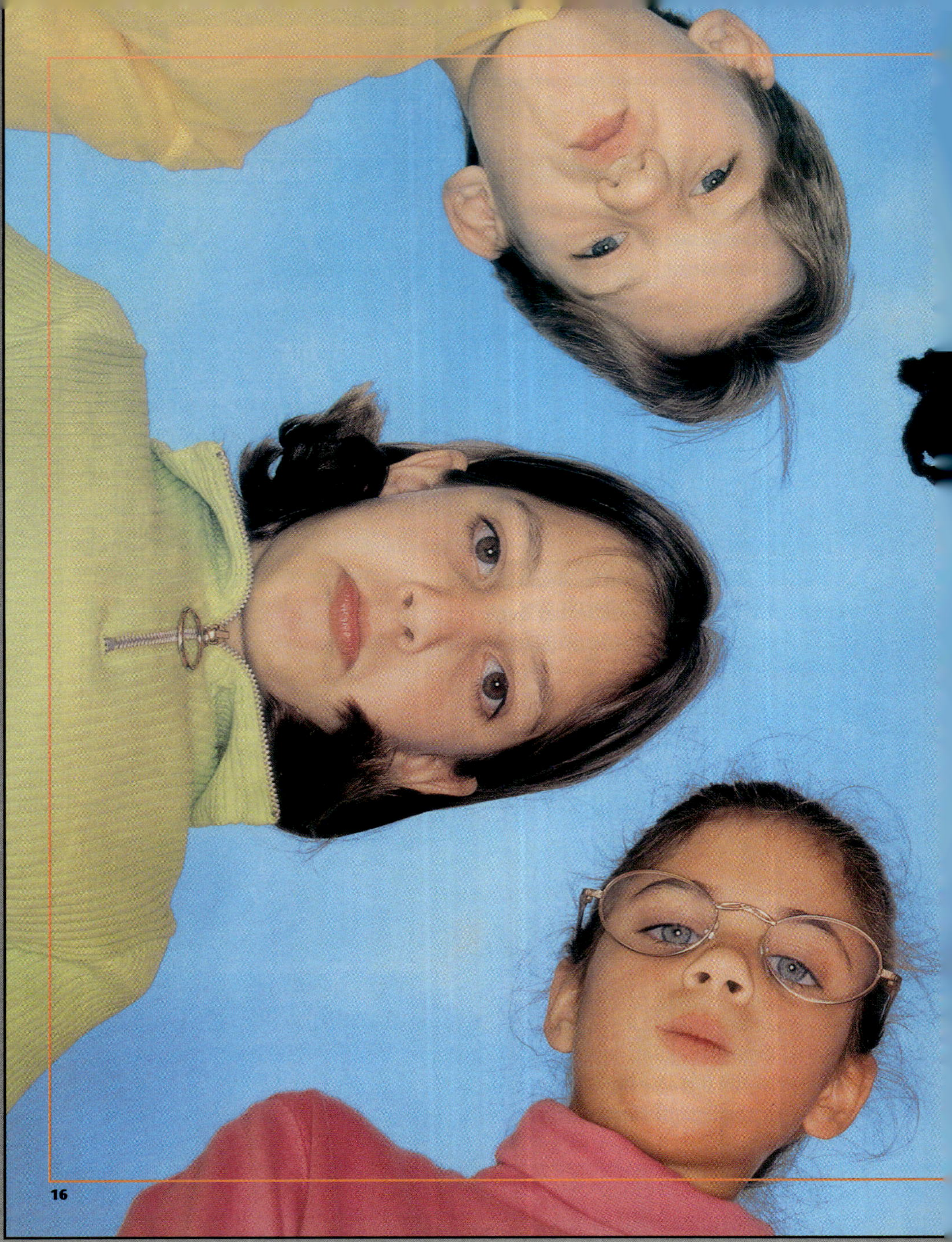

Literature Springboard

Use the poem *My Puppy* to spark interest in the chapter topic. See the Read-Aloud Anthology on page RA-2 of this Teacher's Edition.

16

School-Home Connection

Distribute copies of the School-Home Connection (in English or Spanish), TR page 33. Have students take the page home to share with their families as you begin this chapter.

Follow Up Have volunteers share their collages with the class.

Alternative Use the School-Home Connection page as a classroom resource for enrichment activities.

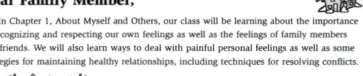

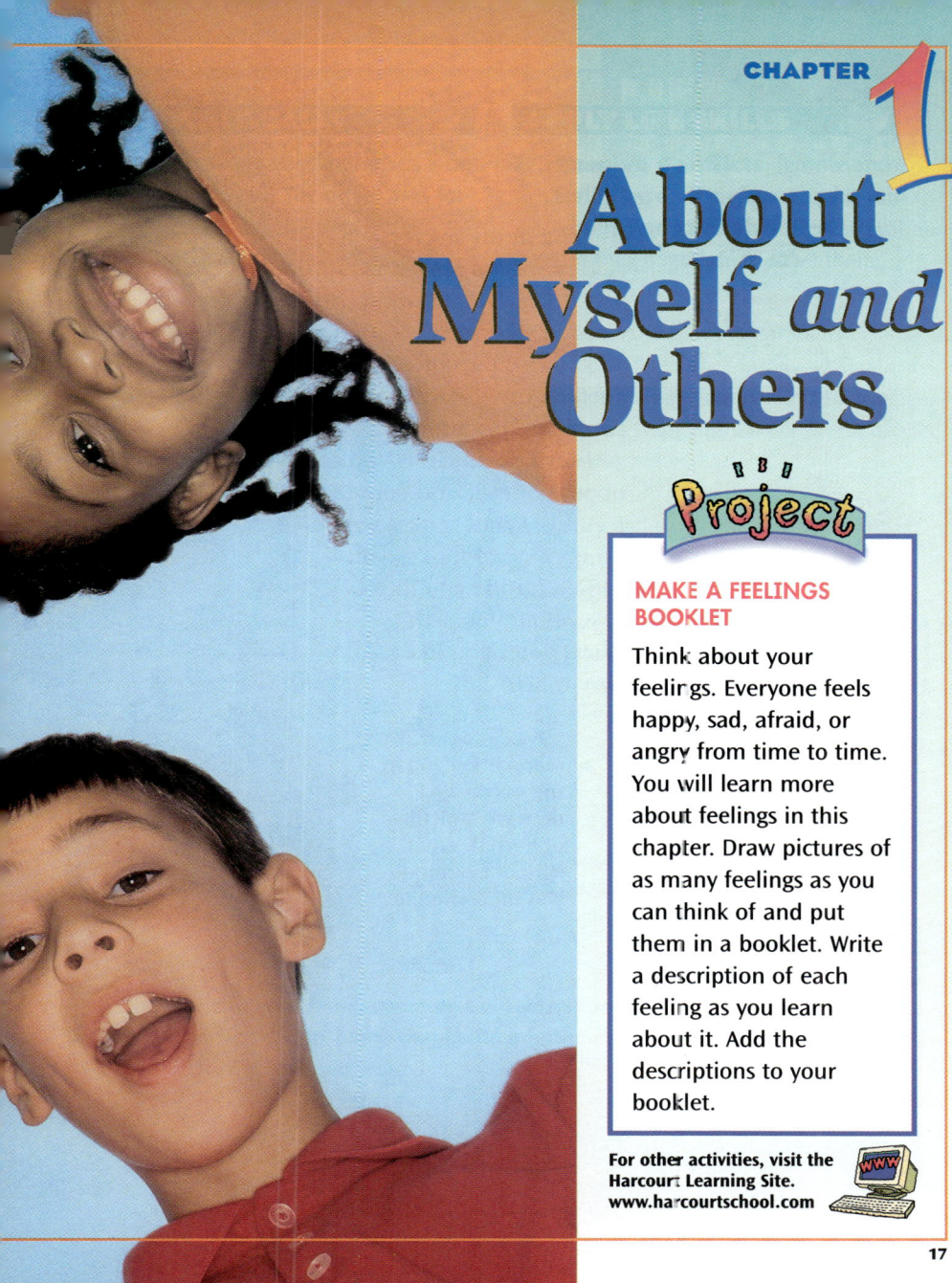

CHAPTER 1

About Myself and Others

MAKE A FEELINGS BOOKLET

Think about your feelings. Everyone feels happy, sad, afraid, or angry from time to time. You will learn more about feelings in this chapter. Draw pictures of as many feelings as you can think of and put them in a booklet. Write a description of each feeling as you learn about it. Add the descriptions to your booklet.

For other activities, visit the Harcourt Learning Site. www.harcourtschool.com

17

Teaching Transparency 1—Graphic Organizer

1 Chapter 1 Graphic Organizer

About Myself and Others

Taking Care of Yourself
1. _Respect_ yourself.
2. Be _responsible_ and honest.

Unpleasant Feelings
1. _fear_
2. stress
3. _anger_
4. grief

Relationships
1. family
2. _friends_

Ways Feelings Are Expressed
1. words
2. _actions_
3. _body_ language

Good Communication Skills
1. _speaking_ skills
2. _listening_ skills

Project

MAKE A FEELINGS BOOKLET

Access Prior Knowledge Discuss the various emotions the children pictured on pages 16 and 17 might be experiencing. Encourage students to draw upon their own knowledge and experiences, as well as on the factual information provided in the chapter, as they complete their projects. You might use the project as a baseline assessment of students' understanding of human emotions.

Performance Assessment The project can be used for performance assessment. Before students begin, explain how you will evaluate their performance. (See the Project Evaluation Sheet, Assessment Guide, p. 21.)

Prereading Strategies

Scan the Chapter Have students preview the chapter content by scanning the titles, headings, pictures, and charts. Ask volunteers to speculate on what they will learn.

Preview Vocabulary As students scan the chapter, point out the vocabulary words listed at the beginning of each lesson. As students work through the chapter, have them reinforce their understanding of these key words by completing the graphic organizer.

Visualize Key Concepts Display the Graphic Organizer Transparency. You may also wish to distribute photocopies to students. Have students complete the organizer as they work through the chapter. Suggested concepts for students to fill in are shown.

Follow Up Review the completed organizer with students as preparation for the Chapter Review and Chapter Tests.

OBJECTIVES

- Recognize the importance of respecting and taking care of oneself.
- Describe ways to exhibit responsible behavior.

PROGRAM RESOURCES

- Growth, Development, and Reproduction, pp. 20–25

VOCABULARY

- feelings (p.18)
- responsible (p. 19)
- respect (p. 19)
- honest (p. 19)

Daily Safety Tip

Students of this age may be encouraged by older siblings to do things they know they shouldn't. Tell them that respecting yourself and your feelings and being your own best friend will help give you the ability to say *no*.

1 Motivate

Direct students' attention to the group photograph on pages 16 and 17. Discuss what feelings the children might have, what their interests and talents might be, and how they might be alike in some ways and different in others. Lead students to understand that each child, like each student in the class, is different and special. Then read the following poem aloud.

Look in the Mirror

When you look in a mirror, what do you see?

An artist, an athlete, a climber of trees?

A singer, a dancer, who loves dogs and cats?

A rider of bikes, and a wearer of hats?

A list of your talents goes on without end!

Oh, look in a mirror,

And see your best friend!

Point out to students that in this lesson, they will learn some important tips on how to be their own best friend.

18

MAIN IDEA
Treating yourself like a good friend is a way to respect yourself.

WHY LEARN THIS? When you feel good about who you are, it is easier to be happy and get along better.

VOCABULARY
- feelings
- respect
- responsible
- honest

Feeling Good About Myself

Look in the mirror. Whose face do you see? A very special person is looking back at you. In the whole world there is no one else just like you.

Your feelings make you special. **Feelings** are the way you react to people and events.

Learn as much as you can about yourself and your feelings. What makes you happy? What makes you sad? What do you like best about yourself? What don't you like very much?

► Maria is looking in the mirror and drawing a picture of herself. What kind of person do you think she sees?

18

 MULTILEVEL ACTIVITIES

EASY **Draw Self-Portraits** Have students draw self-portraits by looking in mirrors. Suggest that they give themselves a quiet space and some uninterrupted time to complete their drawings. Have volunteers explain their drawings to the class. **INTRAPERSONAL/KINESTHETIC**

AVERAGE **Write Poems** Have students use the word RESPONSIBILITY to write acrostic poems about what being responsible means. Display poems in the classroom. **VERBAL/LINGUISTIC**

ADVANCED **Make Posters** Have students work with partners to make posters containing words and pictures that will help younger students understand the importance of feeling good about themselves. Make arrangements with a first or second grade teacher to provide time for the students to present their completed work to his or her students. **VISUAL/INTERPERSONAL**

It is important to treat yourself like the special person you are. Treat yourself the same way you would treat a good friend. This means you feel proud of yourself when you do something well.

Being a friend to yourself also means you respect yourself. If you **respect** (rih•SPEKT) yourself, you believe in yourself. You stand up for yourself. You listen to your feelings and take good care of yourself.

Taking care of yourself shows you are learning to be responsible. Being **responsible** (rih•SPAHNT•suh•buhl) means that other people can count on you. It also means that you are **honest**—you tell the truth. Being responsible is a sign of growing up.

LESSON CHECKUP

Check Your Facts
1. What are feelings?
2. What can you do to be a good friend to yourself?
3. CRITICAL THINKING Give an example of something you could do that shows you respect yourself.

Set Health Goals
4. Name one way you have been responsible at school today. Name another way you can be responsible today.

19

---

2 Teach

Discuss

Critical Thinking What does it mean to "stand up for yourself"? Possible answer: to defend your thoughts and actions to others. What are some examples of ways in which you could show others that you are responsible? Possible answers: be on time, respect other people's property and opinions.

3 Wrap Up

Lesson Checkup

1. Feelings are the way you react to people and events.
2. Possible answers: be proud when you do something well; forgive yourself when you make a mistake; respect yourself.
3. Answers will vary.
4. Have students record their answers in their Health Journals.

GROWTH, DEVELOPMENT, AND REPRODUCTION

Optional lessons on Body Image and Appropriate Clothing (pages 20–25) are provided in this supplement. Use this component in compliance with state and local guidelines.

DEVELOP READING SKILLS

Identify Important Words

Provide students with an opportunity to identify the ways in which vocabulary words are identified in their textbooks. Challenge them to scan this lesson and one or two others in Chapter 1, as well as the Chapter Review page. Then ask them to refer to the back matter of the book to find a section that relates to vocabulary words. Have students list four ways in which the book identifies or defines vocabulary words.

1. Vocabulary words are listed at the beginning of each lesson.
2. Words are highlighted in yellow when they are defined in the text.
3. Words are listed and reviewed in the Chapter Review.
4. Words are listed alphabetically and defined in the glossary.

After the list is completed, remind students that identifying the vocabulary words is a reading strategy that they can use at the beginning of each lesson to aid in their understanding of the text.

OBJECTIVES

- Recognize that feelings are expressed by words, actions, and body language.
- Identify effective ways to change or cope with unpleasant feelings.

PROGRAM RESOURCES

- Activity Book, pp. 6–7

VOCABULARY

- body language (p. 21)
- emotions (p. 22)
- self-control (p. 22)

Daily Safety Tip

Students may have the misconception that feelings such as anger or sadness are "bad," and that the only way to deal with "bad" feelings is to pretend you don't have them. Encourage students to think of negative feelings as normal, although uncomfortable. Point out that learning to deal with unpleasant feelings is an important skill they will use all their lives.

1 Motivate

Draw two large circles on the board. Label one circle *Pleasant Feelings,* and label the other circle *Unpleasant Feelings.* Call on students to suggest feelings to write in each circle. For each feeling suggested, ask volunteers to suggest an event or situation that might cause a person to have the feeling. Call on other volunteers to use facial expressions or body language to show how people having each feeling might look.

LESSON **2**

Understanding My Feelings

MAIN IDEA
You can choose how to show your feelings. You can also decide how to express what you are feeling.

WHY LEARN THIS? Knowing as much as you can about your feelings is an important part of growing up.

VOCABULARY
- body language
- emotions
- self-control

Your feelings are a part of what makes you a special person. You choose when and how to express your feelings. Learning to name your feelings and express them in a safe way shows that you are growing up.

Where do my feelings come from?

Sometimes feelings come from an event. You are happy working on a project with friends. Feelings also come from thinking about an event in the past. You feel sad thinking back to the day you moved. You also have feelings about events to come. You are excited for winter vacation to arrive.

▼ Working in a group can be a lot of fun. How do you think these children feel as they practice their math skills together?

20

 ## MULTILEVEL ACTIVITIES

EASY **Draw Emotions** Have students draw five circles and use the "happy face" design to show five different emotions. Ask them to label each emotion. Have students share their work and compare the emotions they portrayed with those that others chose. **VISUAL/INTERPERSONAL**

AVERAGE **Play Charades** Have student pairs act out feelings as other class members guess what the feelings are. You may wish to make a list of feelings, put them on small pieces of paper, and have students draw them "out of a hat" rather than have students generate ideas themselves. **KINESTHETIC/INTERPERSONAL**

ADVANCED **Write Similes** Explain to students that a simile is an expression comparing one thing to another. Examples are "as quick as a fox" and "as pretty as a peacock." Have students generate a list of possible emotions and then write a simile for each one. **LINGUISTIC/LOGICAL**

How do I show feelings?

You show your feelings in different ways. One way is through your words. Actions are another way to show feelings. When you cry, you may be saying you are sad, hurt, or angry. When you pet your dog, you are showing how much you care. Writing a thank-you note expresses your feelings in actions *and* in words!

Did you know that your body helps you show your feelings? Your face often tells others how you are feeling. A big smile lets people know that you are happy. Other parts of your body express your feelings, too. Your **body language** is how your body shows your feelings.

When your face gets red, your body is saying you are embarrassed or shy. If you say you aren't afraid, but your hands are shaking, your body is telling the truth for you.

When you know and can name a feeling, it is easier to choose how to express it. When feelings take you by surprise, they can explode out of you in words or actions. They can make you feel uncomfortable or not in control. This can be scary.

JOURNAL

In your Health Journal describe a time when you felt happy. How did you express it in words, in your actions, and in body language?

21

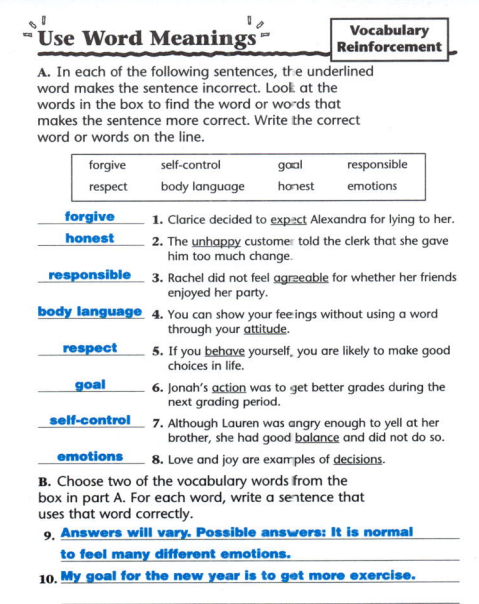

ACTIVITY BOOK, p. 6

Use Word Meanings | Vocabulary Reinforcement

A. In each of the following sentences, the underlined word makes the sentence incorrect. Look at the words in the box to find the word or words that makes the sentence more correct. Write the correct word or words on the line.

forgive	self-control	goal	responsible
respect	body language	honest	emotions

__forgive__ 1. Clarice decided to <u>expect</u> Alexandra for lying to her.

__honest__ 2. The <u>unhappy</u> customer told the clerk that she gave him too much change.

__responsible__ 3. Rachel did not feel <u>agreeable</u> for whether her friends enjoyed her party.

__body language__ 4. You can show your feelings without using a word through your <u>attitude</u>.

__respect__ 5. If you <u>behave</u> yourself, you are likely to make good choices in life.

__goal__ 6. Jonah's <u>action</u> was to get better grades during the next grading period.

__self-control__ 7. Although Lauren was angry enough to yell at her brother, she had good <u>balance</u> and did not do so.

__emotions__ 8. Love and joy are examples of <u>decisions</u>.

B. Choose two of the vocabulary words from the box in part A. For each word, write a sentence that uses that word correctly.

9. __Answers will vary. Possible answers: it is normal to feel many different emotions.__

10. __My goal for the new year is to get more exercise.__

MEET INDIVIDUAL NEEDS

Kinesthetic Learners Point out that body language includes posture (slouching to show disappointment), head gestures (nodding), and hand gestures (pointing, waving, clapping). Have students take turns exhibiting examples of body language people might use to show emotions such as pride, respect, agreement, disagreement, and boredom.

---

2 Teach

Learn from Pictures

Direct students' attention to the picture on page 20. Call on volunteers to suggest answers to the caption question. **Do you think different students in the photo may have different feelings? How can you tell?** Answers will vary.

Discuss

After reading the final paragraph on page 20, call on volunteers to suggest other events or situations that might make them happy, sad, or excited.

Project Checkup

Make a Feelings Booklet (p. 17) Encourage students to incorporate ideas and facts from this lesson into their feelings booklets. Some students may want to draw self-portraits showing a particular feeling to add to their booklets.

Learn from Pictures

Point out that the soccer players in the picture are using a combination of words ("All right!"), actions (hands), and body language (smiles) to express their feelings. Ask students to suggest other words, actions, and examples of body language they might use to express similar feelings.

Health Journal

Encourage students to use specific words such as *proud, excited,* or *surprised* to further define their "happy" event. This feature is designed to provide students with an opportunity to reflect on health decisions they are making in their personal lives. The journal should *not* be used to evaluate or assess students, nor do the results need to be shared among students.

Discuss

Problem Solving In what ways is making a choice to change unpleasant feelings an important part of taking care of yourself and being your own best friend? You are taking control of an unpleasant situation and learning how to deal with it as effectively as possible.

Learn from Pictures

Have students describe the feelings that each baby might be experiencing. Have other students suggest additional ways in which babies might express different feelings. How does your knowledge and use of language help you express your feelings in different ways now than you did when you were a baby? What other skills do you have now that help you get along with people and express your feelings to them? Accept any reasonable answers, including more self-control and the ability to listen, to think about options, or to compromise.

Health Background

Survival Skill Unlike most other mammals, human babies are defenseless and totally dependent on caregivers for survival. Point out to students that crying is the baby's only tool for communicating serious needs or pain. Without the ability to cry, babies could not signal their needs. Encourage students to remember to respect this communication tool in their baby sisters and brothers. When they hear a baby crying, they must provide, or summon, assistance.

For more background, visit the **Webliography** on the Teacher Resources page at:
www.harcourtschool.com/health
Keyword family life

How can I control my feelings?

Everybody has a wide range of **emotions** (ih•MOH•shuhnz), or strong feelings. Emotions such as love and joy are nice to have. But emotions such as sadness and anger don't feel so comfortable.

When you have **self-control**, or power over your emotions, you can usually deal with unpleasant emotions. If you pay attention to your unpleasant emotions, they may go away faster.

The first step to self-control is finding the best word to describe the way you're feeling. You may be sad but an even better word might be lonely. When you know that you are lonely, you can make choices about how to express that feeling.

▼ **People of all ages have feelings. How do babies show that they are hungry, tired, or bored? As children get older, they learn words to tell how they feel. They also begin to find ways to control their feelings.**

22

LANGUAGE ARTS

More Than Crying Reiterate to students that infants cry to show all their needs. Have students list needs an infant might have. Then ask them to write paragraphs or poems to tell how they meet similar needs now that they are older.

ACTIVITY BOOK, p. 7

Use Context Clues
Reading Skills

A. Look at the words in the box. Choose the word that best completes each sentence. Write your answers on the lines. Use each word only once.

| forgive | self-control | exercise |
| emotions | describe | unpleasant |

Dear Sam,

Today Ginny took my new bracelet without asking me. When she came home, it was gone. She said she lost it. I was so mad at her I screamed. Then Ginny started to cry.

My mom said I lost my ____self-control____. She said I had to start doing a better job of controlling my ____emotions____. She also said that everyone has trouble with their sisters and brothers sometimes.

Mom said the next time I got that angry, or had other ____unpleasant____ feelings, I should try new ways of dealing with them. First, she said it might help to get some ____exercise____ and give myself time to calm down. Then I should talk to Ginny and ____describe____ how I was feeling. My mom said I could also ask her if I needed an adult to help. She said it was important, in the end, to ____forgive____ my little sister. What do you think?

Becky

B. Write your own letter to a friend that uses all the words in the box.

_____
_____
_____
_____

You may decide to go to your room and feel lonely for a while. You might want to talk to a family member or close friend. You may want to write in your journal.

After a while you may be tired of feeling lonely. You might be ready to do something about how you are feeling.

There are many ways to let go of emotions of all kinds. You can forgive yourself or someone else for what happened. You can get some exercise. You can read a book that makes you laugh. You can think of something new to do. You can call a friend. What do you do to let go of an unpleasant feeling?

 Activity **Do Something About Your Feelings** Make a list of all the ways you can do something about unpleasant feelings such as boredom, anger, loneliness, and sadness. Draw a picture to show your best idea.

LESSON CHECKUP

Check Your Facts

1. What are three different ways you show your feelings?
2. What is self-control?
3. Give three examples of expressing yourself through body language.
4. CRITICAL THINKING Imagine that you are feeling sad. What is something you could do to make that feeling go away?

Set Health Goals

5. Imagine that you are angry with a friend because she didn't return a book she borrowed. You are not in control of your emotions. What could you do to control the way you're feeling?

23

OBJECTIVES

- List situations involving fear that require immediate help from a trusted adult.
- Identify effective strategies for dealing with fear, stress, anger, and grief.

VOCABULARY

- fear (p. 24)
- stress (p. 25)
- anger (p. 26)
- grief (p. 27)

Daily Safety Tip

Students may have difficulty distinguishing between common fears (being late, giving an incorrect answer) and very serious fears (being bothered by a stranger). As this lesson states, such serious fears require them to seek immediate help from a trusted adult. Discuss and emphasize important safety rules, such as never approaching a car driven by a stranger. Additionally, emphasize to students that trusted adults to whom they can go for help include parents or guardians, teachers, counselors, and other school personnel.

1 Motivate

Optional Materials photographs of a bright, sunny day and a dark, stormy day

Display the pictures, one at a time. (Alternatively, have students close their eyes and imagine each type of day.) Ask students to describe what feelings each scene brings to their minds, leading them to associate sunshine with pleasant feelings and lack of sunshine with unpleasant feelings. Point out that the natural world needs rainy days for plants and animals to survive. Then point out that life, like nature, contains good days and bad days, and that in this lesson they will learn some effective ways to deal with such "bad day" feelings as anger, fear, and sadness.

LESSON **3**

MAIN IDEA You can learn how to deal with unpleasant feelings such as fear, stress, anger, and grief.

WHY LEARN THIS? When you know about unpleasant feelings, you can make wise choices about how to deal with them.

VOCABULARY
- fear
- stress
- anger
- grief

Dealing with Fear, Stress, Anger, and Grief

It is important to learn as much as you can about unpleasant feelings. Understanding them will make it easier to help yourself or a friend deal with one of these feelings.

How can I deal with fear?

There are many reasons you might feel **fear**, or be scared.

- You are in a new school or class.
- You are alone in your house.
- Some older children bully you.

When you feel afraid, your heart beats faster. You are nervous and upset. It is important to trust how you feel and to do something about it. It is part of being a good friend to yourself.

You can deal with some fears by yourself. If you are afraid of missing the school bus, you can set your alarm so you get up earlier. Other fears may be much more serious. Sometimes you need to talk to a trusted adult right away.

I'm afraid!

WHEN TO ASK FOR HELP
• Something makes you feel uncomfortable or scared.
• You are afraid to go to school.
• You have trouble sleeping.
• Someone touches you in a way you don't like.

MULTILEVEL ACTIVITIES

EASY **Paint Feelings** Have each student paint or draw two pictures, one that is happy and one that is sad. Challenge them to show the feelings without using people in their pictures. **VISUAL/INTRAPERSONAL**

AVERAGE **Generate Strategies** Have students list things that cause stress in their lives, such as too many things to do in one afternoon or making difficult choices. After they have made a list, have them brainstorm ways in which they could avoid having those kinds of stress. Encourage students to listen to everyone's ideas without making judgments. **VERBAL/INTERPERSONAL**

ADVANCED **Exercise to Reduce Stress** Have students find some simple exercises, involving stretching and deep breathing, that help the body relax. Tell them such exercises have been used since ancient times by people all over the world and modern physicians have found them very useful. Have students present the exercises to the class. **KINESTHETIC/VERBAL**

I'm stressed!

How can I deal with stress?

When you feel **stress**, you may have butterflies in your stomach. Your hands may sweat. Your heart may even beat fast.

It is important to know why you are feeling stress. Are you afraid of a bully? Is there not enough time to finish your homework? If you have felt stress for a long time, you should talk to a parent or a trusted adult. He or she may have ideas to help you.

There are many ways to deal with stress. One way is to manage your time. First, make a list of what you have to do. Then, write down how long each task will take. Other ways to deal with stress are listed in the table.

DEAL WITH STRESS
- Talk to a family member or an adult.
- Plan your time wisely.
- Set goals you can reach.
- Get some exercise or work on a hobby.

CONSUMER FOCUS

Making Buying Decisions

Sometimes you can deal with stress by working on a hobby. Think of a hobby you have or would like to have, such as painting or fishing. Make a list of the items you would need to work on or start your hobby. Use the steps on page xiv to help you to find the best prices for these items.

• • •

25

2 Teach

Learn from Charts

Discuss each bulleted situation on the charts on pp. 24–25, stressing the importance of seeking help on these occasions.

Project Checkup

Make a Feelings Booklet (p. 17) Encourage students to incorporate information about feelings provided in this lesson into their feelings booklets.

Learn from Pictures

What is the boy in this photo experiencing stress about? having to wash a lot of dishes What advice would you have for him? Accept all reasonable answers.

Consumer Focus

Making Buying Decisions To help students get started you might want to provide an example of a hobby you enjoy, and then as a class have the students list items that would be needed for this hobby. Discuss with students that not all hobbies need to be expensive, and sometimes working on a hobby with a friend can be enjoyable.

DEVELOP READING SKILLS

Use Context Clues Remind students that by reading the words that come before or after the highlighted vocabulary, they can get important clues to the terms' meanings. Often, such clues might come after the word *or*. As an example, direct their attention to the sentence on page 24 that contains the highlighted word *fear*. Point out the word *or*, and call on students to identify the clue that follows it. Based on the clue, have students suggest the meaning of *fear* (being scared). Then point out that other clues are sometimes in the form of examples. Use the sentences containing the words *stress, anger,* and *grief* as examples. As you discuss each sentence, have students identify the clue and provide a definition for the highlighted term. Explain to students that they can use this technique to learn the meaning of many new words.

Health Background

Symptoms of Stress When the brain is stimulated by a stressful event, it causes the heart to beat faster to increase the flow of blood to the brain and muscles. This increased flow causes the muscles to tighten. Also breathing becomes more rapid, allowing more oxygen to enter the body. "Butterflies" in the stomach often occur because the stomach and intestines slow down their digestive activities to allow the body to respond to stress. Many people experience "dry mouth," because the moisture in the mouth and air passages temporarily dries up. Point out to students that although these symptoms may feel unpleasant, they are part of a process the body uses to protect itself.

Teach *continued*

Discuss

Students may have the misconception that feeling angry is "wrong." Point out that anger is a common feeling.

Critical Thinking Why is managing anger an important life skill? Managing anger helps people remain balanced, safe, and in control.

Life Skills Focus

Communicate Have students "put themselves in the shoes" of Murray, and describe how they might follow each step of anger management. Compare and contrast the effectiveness of "You are so stupid" and an alternative I-message, pointing out that the first message might turn into a heated argument, whereas the second message describes personal feelings that are factual.

Learn from Pictures

Ask students to extend each picture caption, improving each I-message so that it explains, in clear words, why the girl might feel each emotion.

Health Background

Recognizing Signs of Depression It was once thought that only adults became depressed. Now depression is being recognized in children. The warning signs of depression include:

- persistent sadness;
- an inability to enjoy formerly pleasurable activities;
- frequent complaints of physical illness such as headaches and stomach aches;
- frequent absences from school or poor performance in school;
- persistent boredom, low energy, poor concentration;
- a major change in eating and/or sleeping patterns.

For more background, visit the **Webliography** on the Teacher Resources page at:
www.harcourtschool.com/health
Keyword emotional health

How can I deal with angry, hurt, or sad feelings?

LIFE SKILLS FOCUS

Communicate

Murray feels angry because his brother left the tops off his colored markers. He feels like telling his brother, "You are so stupid." Suggest a better way for Murray to tell his brother how he feels. Use the steps for communicating shown on page *xii*. What if he began by saying "I feel . . ."?

• • •

When you feel **anger**, you are very mad. It is all right to be angry. Everyone gets angry sometimes. You may get angry if you don't get your way or if someone teases you. Hurt and sadness are other common feelings. You may feel hurt if you are blamed for something you didn't do. You may feel sad if your best friend moves away.

You can learn to manage your anger in ways that keep you safe and in control. You can learn to make wise choices about how you show your anger. Then you can decide what you want to do.

MANAGE ANGER

1. Stop what you are doing.
2. Count to ten to cool down or take three long, slow breaths.
3. Think about what is happening.
4. Take action. Either walk away or tell the person what you are feeling.
5. Use messages that tell how you feel. Begin with "I feel . . ."

I'm angry!
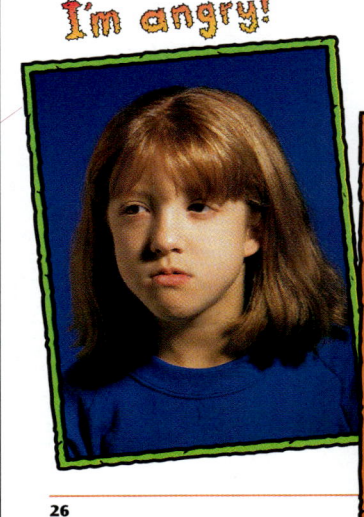

I'm hurt!

I'm sad

26

DRAMA

Role-Play Help students understand the importance of using I-messages by calling on volunteers to act out a scene in which two third graders disagree. Have one student in each pair respond first with an accusatory statement and then with an I-message. Have the other student describe the different feelings he or she experienced hearing each response. Use the demonstration(s) to stress the peacekeeping benefits of I-messages.

TEACHER TIP

Coping with Embarrassment Discuss what it feels like to be embarrassed. Share an embarrassing moment you have endured and encourage volunteers to share also. Brainstorm a list of methods of coping with embarrassing moments and record them on the chalkboard. Some of the coping methods might include using humor, apologizing, or changing the subject.

How can I deal with grief?

When you feel **grief** you feel a deep sadness. This sadness may last for a while.

You may feel grief when a person or a pet dies. You may feel like being alone, or you may feel like crying. It is important to find a way to express your feelings.

Talking about how you feel is another way to express your grief. Family members, a teacher, and a member of the clergy are people who will listen to you. You can also take care of yourself by exercising, eating well, and getting enough sleep.

You can write a poem in your journal or draw a picture that expresses your sadness. Did you know that many famous artists express their feelings of grief and sadness in their artwork?

► Visual artists express their feelings through art.

Career

Visual Artist

What They Do

Visual artists include painters, illustrators, photographers, and sculptors. Visual artists express many different ideas and feelings in their artwork. A painter may express grief by doing a painting in memory of a person who died.

Education and Training

Some visual artists go to art school. Others learn and practice on their own. Some visual artists teach art classes for children or adults.

LESSON CHECKUP

Check Your Facts

1. When should you ask for help if you are scared?
2. CRITICAL THINKING How can planning ahead help you feel less stress?
3. How can you express your anger but stay in control?
4. Who can help you deal with grief?

Use Life Skills

5. COMMUNICATE Pretend that you are angry with a friend who broke your favorite toy. How could you manage your anger in a way that keeps you in control?

27

MATH

Make Bar Graphs Have each student make a list of strategies for dealing with one of the emotions discussed in this lesson. Then have each student survey at least five people, asking which strategy they feel is most effective. Have students demonstrate their survey results by constructing bar graphs.

MULTICULTURAL LINK

An Artist Speaks Native Hawaiian artist Bryant Lagmay is only 18 years old, but already his paintings have won a prestigious Congressional Art Award and the Scholastic Art Award. Bryant took his first art course in the seventh grade, after a childhood that he describes as "not that great. I kept everything to myself. I felt no one really understood me." He found his teacher's encouragement to express his feelings in his art "very therapeutic. I realized art doesn't have to be realistic or even pretty. You can express yourself with a blotch of paint."

Discuss

Many counselors and therapists who work with grieving children often encourage these children to draw pictures or use puppets to help them express their very sad feelings. Ask students to suggest why such methods might be helpful. Lead them to understand that although young children may not have as sophisticated language skills to express themselves as do older children, their feelings and responses to a death, for example, are no less deep.

Career

For more information on careers in the visual arts, contact a local art association or

The National Endowment for the Arts 1100 Pennsylvania Avenue, NW Washington, D.C. 20506

202-682-5400

Or visit the **Webliography** on the Teacher Resources page at:
www.harcourtschool.com/health
Keyword health careers

3 Wrap Up

Lesson Checkup

1. Possible answers: if someone touches you in a way you don't like, if something makes you feel uncomfortable and scared, if you are afraid to go to school, if you have trouble sleeping.
2. Planning ahead enables you to manage your time more efficiently and set reasonable goals.
3. Use the steps for anger management: stop what you are doing, count to ten, think about what is happening, take appropriate action, use I-messages to explain how you feel.
4. family members, a teacher, a counselor, or a member of the clergy
5. Encourage students to include specific, realistic tips for using the steps for anger management.

LIFE SKILLS

OBJECTIVES

- Identify ways to manage stress.
- Apply stress-management skills to situations at school.

PROGRAM RESOURCES

- Activity Book, p. 8

1 Motivate

Divide the class into pairs. Supply each pair with stacking materials (blocks, craft sticks, sugar cubes, or any other manipulative). Instruct the students to take turns stacking the items, one on top of the other. The first person to make the stack fall over loses the game. **How did you feel as the stack grew taller? Can you describe your feelings as you began to place another item on the stack? What physical symptoms did you experience?** Write student answers on a chart. Explain that these feelings are a part of stress.

2 Teach

Learn from Pictures

Have students look at the picture of Tran in bed. Have a student tell what Tran may be thinking or feeling.

Step 1

Review the chart of the feelings students had when they did the stacking activity. Have them add any additional feelings Tran may be having.

Critical Thinking **Why is it important to know how stress feels?** so you will know when you are feeling stress and can help yourself take care of it

MANAGE STRESS at School

Everyone faces stress from time to time. Learning the following steps will help you handle your stress in a healthful way.

Learn This Skill

Tran's class is having a spelling bee next week. He is worried that he will be one of the first students to miss a word. How can Tran handle the stress he feels?

1. Know what stress feels like and what causes it.

Tran cannot fall asleep. He can feel his heart pounding and his muscles tightening. He is worried about the spelling bee.

2. When you feel stress, think about ways to handle it.

"My dad says I should make a list of what I need to do to get ready for the spelling bee."

28

ART

Stress Drawings Supply each student with a large sheet of drawing paper. Instruct students to draw a picture of themselves in the center showing how they look and feel when they are stressed. Encourage them to add symptoms such as "butterflies" in the stomach. Then, around the edges, have them draw five things they could do to help manage the stressful feelings. Have the students share their pictures and solutions.

MEET INDIVIDUAL NEEDS

Visual and Auditory Learners
Divide the class into groups of four. Have the groups write and perform skits showing how a famous movie star uses stress-management skills to handle her stress as she gets ready to appear on a talk show. She is really stressed because she does not have a script, and she is afraid she will not know what to say.

3. Focus on one step at a time.

"Dad and I made a list of the words I still need to work on."

4. Learn to relax.

Tran takes a deep breath. "I am prepared, and I know that I will do my best!" he tells himself.

Practice This Skill

Use this summary to help you solve the problems below.

Steps for Managing Stress

1. Know what stress feels like and what causes it.
2. When you feel stress, think about ways to handle it.
3. Focus on one step at a time.
4. Learn to relax.

A. Sara is joining a Little League team. She has heard people say mean things to players who make mistakes. What can Sara do to deal with her fear about making a mistake?

B. Luis didn't do his homework because he left his math book at school. He is worried that his teacher will call on him. What should Luis do?

29

ACTIVITY BOOK, p. 8

Manage Stress
Life Skills

Lee has a big social studies project due on Friday. She is worried that she will not be finished on time. Her stomach is upset, and she doesn't feel like eating. Use the Steps for Managing Stress to help Lee handle the stress she is feeling.

1. Know how stress feels and what causes it.
   What does Lee's stress feel like?
   Possible answers: Lee's stomach is upset; she doesn't feel like eating; she is worried that she will not get her project done on time.

2. When you feel stress, think about ways to handle it.
   How can Lee handle her stress?
   When Lee is upset, it usually helps to talk with someone. She decides to talk with her teacher. Other answers might include parents, older siblings, counselor, grandparent.

3. Focus on one step at a time.
   What plan could Lee follow?
   Lee decides to make a plan to complete each step of her project. She lists what she needs to complete each day. She works on each part every night after dinner and at school when she has extra time.

4. Learn to reduce tension.
   How can Lee reduce tension?
   Lee takes a brisk walk after dinner. She knows that by following her plan, she will be finished on time. She feels good about the plan she has made.

SOCIAL STUDIES

Pioneer Stress Talk to the class about what it would have been like to be a pioneer traveling west. Have students brainstorm some situations that may have caused the pioneers stress, such as lack of food or water, fear of attack, and broken wagon wheels. Talk about ways the pioneers might have dealt with the stress, and have each student write a story about it. Allow students to share their stories.

Step 2

Have students brainstorm other ways that Tran could handle the stress he is feeling about the spelling bee. Possible answers: practicing the words with someone so he feels more confident; breathing exercises to help keep him calm.

Step 3

If you focus on each step as you do it, it doesn't seem like such a big job. Have students help Tran make a plan of action to prepare for the spelling bee. List the steps on the board. Students may suggest writing the words five times each, posting words on the bathroom mirror or refrigerator, having parents quiz him nightly, practicing with a friend during lunch time. Then have students organize the ideas into a daily plan for Tran to put into action.

Step 4

Ask students to look at the picture of Tran at the class spelling bee. Have the students practice breathing in slowly through their noses and exhaling slowly through their mouths. Are there other things Tran might do to relieve his tension before the spelling bee? Possible answers: exercise, stretching, and relaxation breaks.

3 Wrap Up

A. Answers should include recognizing the stress, thinking of ways to handle it, and focusing on one step at a time. They should also include specific suggestions for reducing tension, such as deep breathing exercises.

B. Answers should include: recognizing stress, thinking of ways to handle it, taking one step at a time, and reducing tension.

29

OBJECTIVES

• Describe practical methods for establishing and building healthful relationships.

• Recognize the importance of standing up for personal values when faced with negative peer pressure.

PROGRAM RESOURCES

• Activity Book, p. 9

HEALTH VIDEO:
The Cleanup Kids

VOCABULARY

• relationship (p. 30)
• peers (p. 33)
• peer pressure (p. 33)

Daily Safety Tip

Even in third grade, the desire to be accepted and liked by peers can lead to negative experiences involving peer pressure. Remind students that they have learned the importance of being a good friend to themselves, including taking good care of themselves. Stress that if someone asks them to do something that doesn't seem right or safe, they must trust their own feelings and say *no*.

1 Motivate

Write the terms *family members* and *friends* on the board. Ask students to suggest words that describe what each of these groups of people can offer to someone. Write all answers under each term, pointing out that both groups can often offer similar things, such as understanding, fun, support, and love. Point out that developing protective factors can aid in resiliency. Participating in activities that promote development of bonds with peers and other adults in the school community helps to provide a positive support network.

Relationships with Family and Friends

MAIN IDEA
Having good relationships with family and friends helps you have healthy relationships with other people.

WHY LEARN THIS? Getting along with family members and friends makes you feel good about yourself.

VOCABULARY
• relationship
• peers
• peer pressure

A **relationship** (rih•LAY•shuhn•ship) is the way you get along with someone. You spend a lot of time with your family and friends. It is important to get along well. When you have good relationships with your family and friends, it makes you feel good about yourself.

What makes good relationships with family?

Each person in a family has a special role. It is important to respect everyone in your family—from the youngest to the oldest. Talking and listening to all family members are ways of showing respect.

▼ How would you describe the relationships of the family members in these four photos?

30

MULTILEVEL ACTIVITIES

EASY Make Cards Have each student select a family member or other member of their support system for whom to make a special friendship card. Encourage students to use pictures, sentences, or short poems to express their feelings. Encourage students to deliver or mail their cards. **VISUAL/INTERPERSONAL**

AVERAGE Make Chore Lists Have students list as many household chores as they can, put a check beside the ones they think they could do, and explain why they could not do each of the other chores. **LOGICAL/VERBAL**

ADVANCED Make Family Totem Poles Tell students that many Native American families of Alaska and the Pacific Northwest carved huge totem poles to represent the humans, animals, plants, and birds they considered to be their mythical ancestors. Have each student make a family totem pole on paper. Encourage them to include all family members represented in ways that show their strongest traits. **VISUAL/INTRAPERSONAL**

Families work together better when family members respect and trust each other. When you tell the truth, you let your family members know they can trust you.

Being a responsible family member makes you feel good about yourself. It also lets your family know that they can depend on you to do your part. It means you are growing up. Some people your age do the dishes, set the table, take out the trash, or care for a pet. What chores do you do at home?

Families need time to play together, too. When you and your family have a good time together, it reminds you of how special it is to be a family. Some families like to ride bikes, make pizza, play games, or plan surprises together.

All families have problems at times. That's when family members need to work together and support each other. Taking time to talk together about what each family member can do helps families feel close. It's another way for family members to show they care about each other.

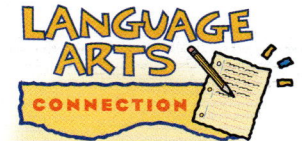
What do you like to do with your family?

31

What can each of us do to take care of these important relationships with family and friends? Accept all reasonable answers. Tell students that this lesson will provide them with other useful tips for getting along with family members and friends.

2 Teach

Discuss

Ask students to identify the roles they play in their families, such as son or daughter, big sister, or little brother. Have them describe what responsibilities they feel they have in each of these roles.

Critical Thinking Do you talk and listen to different family members and friends in different ways? If so, in what ways, and why? Answers will vary, but students may say yes, because of age, because of how well I know the person or how close we are, or because some people are easier to talk to and listen to than others.

Language Arts Connection

Gaining Attention Have students share their lists with other classmates, and make a combined list. Then make a class list, and discuss acceptable ways to gain attention.

Learn from Pictures

Discuss each picture and have students suggest answers to the caption question on page 30. Lead students to understand that each different relationship involves learning, sharing, fun, and a chance to be together and talk.

Project Checkup

Make a Feelings Booklet (p. 17) Direct students' attention to the caption question on this page. Encourage them to include in their booklets at least one picture of a favorite family activity and to describe the feelings they associate with that activity.

31

Discuss

What are some other ways to meet and enjoy being with friends? Accept any reasonable answers.

What things do you have in common with your friends? Students will have different things in common with different friends. Encourage them to realize that they have many different kinds of friends.

Do you think all your friends would get along well with each other? Answers will vary but some students will realize that all their friends would not get along because they would have nothing in common.

Learn from Pictures

Direct attention to the photograph and have students suggest answers to the caption question. Lead them to understand that common interests and values often bind good friends together.

Ask students to list two things these friends might have in common and two things that make them different from each other. **Which do you think is more important, the things you have in common with your friends or the things that make you different?** Answers will vary. Encourage students to realize that both are important.

What makes good relationships with friends?

Roller skating, birthday parties, school projects, and playing sports are fun ways to be with friends. Even doing a chore such as raking leaves is more fun with a friend!

Do you like to swim or build models? It's fun to find friends who like the same things you do. School clubs, neighborhood centers, and church groups can be good places to see old friends and make new friends.

Sometimes, however, even best friends disagree. When you and a friend don't agree, try to listen and talk things over. Say you're sorry if you do something that hurts a friend. Be ready to forgive your friend if he or she hurts you. Sometimes others do not know that their actions affect you.

Myth and **Fact**

Myth: Your friends will like you better if you always go along with them.

Fact: Your true friends will respect you for standing up for what you believe in.

• • • • • • •

► How are these children enjoying their friendship?

32

ACTIVITY BOOK, p. 9

Relationships with Family — Critical Thinking

A. Complete the chart below.

Sample answers are given. Accept reasonable answers.
Good Relationships with Family

Ways To Show Respect
1. Talk to all family members.
2. Listen to all family members.

Ways To Be Responsible
3. Do the dishes.
4. Care for a pet.

Ways To Play Together
5. Go for a bike ride together.
6. Play games together.

Ways To Help When There Are Problems
7. Support each other.
8. Talk with each other.

B. Write a paragraph describing a time your family worked together to complete a project. Be sure to discuss how family members felt and how they showed respect for each other.

◄ Friends can have differences and still have many things in common.

It's important to have **peers**—friends your age—who share your interests. However, if some of your friends want you to do something just because "everyone is doing it," they are using **peer pressure**. If it doesn't feel right to you, or it is against your family rules, stand up for yourself and make another choice. When you do that, you can be proud of yourself. It's a sign that you respect yourself and your family. You are also setting a good example for your peers.

LESSON CHECKUP

Check Your Facts

❶ How can you show respect for each member of your family? How can family members show respect for you?

❷ What jobs can children your age do to be responsible family members?

❸ What are some ways to meet new friends?

❹ **CRITICAL THINKING** Why is it important to be able to talk over problems with your friends?

Set Health Goals

❺ Give an example of peer pressure. Describe what you could do to stand up for yourself.

33

Discuss

Critical Thinking Tell students that younger sisters and brothers, and younger students at school, probably look up to them as the "big kids." **What can you do to set a good example for younger children on how to get along with friends?** Accept all reasonable answers. (See "Role-Model" activity suggested on page 16C. Following this discussion, have students complete their role-model profiles as suggested.)

3 Wrap Up

Lesson Checkup

1. Family members can show respect for each other by talking and listening carefully to each other, by telling the truth, and by being dependable and responsible.

2. Possible answers: do the dishes, set the table, take out the recycling, care for a pet, make the beds.

3. Possible answers: join a club or team, go to a neighborhood center, participate in religious activities.

4. Talking with friends can help you work out your problems in a positive way.

5. Have students record their responses in their Health Journals.

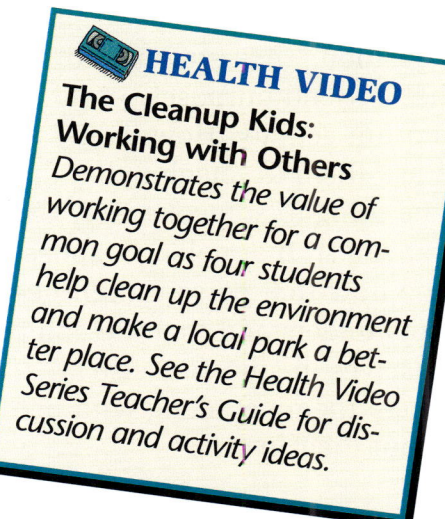

HEALTH VIDEO

The Cleanup Kids: Working with Others Demonstrates the value of working together for a common goal as four students help clean up the environment and make a local park a better place. See the Health Video Series Teacher's Guide for discussion and activity ideas.

OBJECTIVES

- Recognize that effective communication skills include both speaking and listening skills.
- Realize the importance of compassion, kindness, apology, and forgiveness.

PROGRAM RESOURCES

- Activity Book, p. 10

VOCABULARY

- communicate (p. 34)
- compassion (p. 34)
- apologize (p. 35)

Daily Safety Tip

Determined often to do "perfect" work, children are not always willing or able to apologize for mistakes or wrongs. When apologies do occur, they may include excuses or the blaming of others. Stress that everyone makes mistakes. Being able to face those mistakes and make sincere, honest apologies—without making excuses or blaming someone else—are important parts of being a responsible person.

1 Motivate

Write on the board *Put yourself in someone else's shoes.* Explain that this saying means "trying to understand how someone else feels inside; putting yourself in his or her position." Ask students to imagine that a friend purposely excluded them from a fun activity. **How would you feel?** Then ask them to imagine that they did the same thing to someone else. **Can you put yourself in that person's shoes and describe how that person might feel?** Help students understand that the ability to put themselves in someone else's shoes will help them get along with people throughout their lives.

Communicating Well with Others

MAIN IDEA
Speaking and listening respectfully to others helps you understand yourself and others better.

WHY LEARN THIS? You can use what you learn to improve your listening and communication skills.

VOCABULARY
- communicate
- compassion
- apologize

To **communicate** (kuh•MYOO•nuh•kayt) means to share information. You can learn to communicate in a way that helps you understand yourself and others better.

Using I-messages helps communicate your feelings. "I feel bad when you don't keep a promise" is an I-message. It helps others understand your feelings. It gives them a chance to respond.

It is important to take turns listening and speaking. When others are speaking, listen carefully so you can understand them. Listening carefully, even when you disagree, is a way to respect other people.

If you have **compassion** (kuhm•PA•shuhn), you can feel what others feel. You treat people in a kind and caring way. You don't use put-downs or act like a bully, because you want to show respect and communicate well.

▶ There are many ways for friends to communicate.

34

 MULTILEVEL ACTIVITIES

EASY Review Vocabulary To review all the Chapter 1 vocabulary terms, write each one on an index card. Have students form small teams. Have a volunteer select a card and use body language, clue words, and other "charade" elements to enable teammates to guess the term. **VERBAL/KINESTHETIC**

AVERAGE Design Apologies Have students imagine that they didn't complete their chores at home. Have them design cards that apologize to their parents or other family members. Tell them that many approaches may be effective—the apology could be straightforward or they could use humor. **VISUAL/INTERPERSONAL**

ADVANCED Graph Electronic Communications Have students survey classmates to find out what types of electronic devices they use to communicate with friends and family that are far away. Have them make bar graphs of their results to share with the class. **VERBAL/MATHEMATICAL**

▲ These brothers are communicating with a friend who lives far away. How else could they communicate with him?

LIFE SKILLS FOCUS

Communicate

A friend told someone else something about you that is not true. Tell how you can communicate your feelings by using I-messages. Use the steps for communicating shown on page *xii*.

• • •

When you are wrong, you should **apologize** (uh•PAH•luh•jyz)—say you are sorry. You are asking the other person to forgive you. When people tell you they are sorry, you can forgive them.

Using words to communicate your feelings and listening respectfully to other people are signs that you are becoming more responsible.

Activity **Use Communication Skills** Choose one of the pictures on these pages. Write a paragraph about the picture. Include how these friends are using good communication skills.

LESSON CHECKUP

Check Your Facts

❶ Name four helpful communication skills.

❷ CRITICAL THINKING Why might you apologize to a friend?

Set Health Goals

❸ Which communication skill is easiest for you? Which communication skill is the hardest for you? Describe a time when communication skills might come in handy.

35

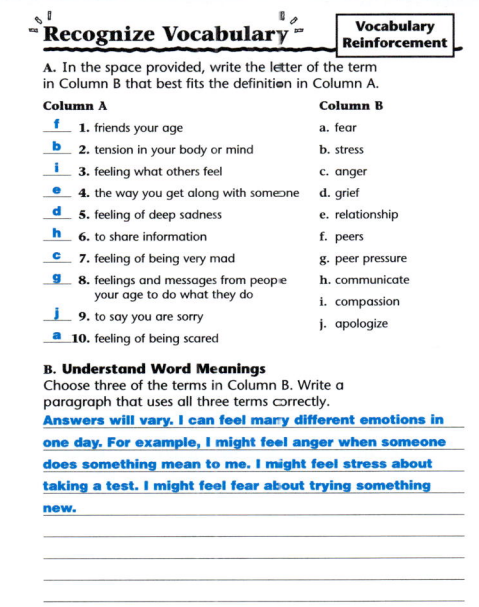

 **SCIENCE**

Do Animals Communicate?

Have students work in teams to research specific animals, such as birds, whales, dogs, cats, and porpoises, to learn how such animals communicate with each other. Do the animals use specific sounds? What types of body language might they use?

---

② Teach

Discuss

Critical Thinking What saying might mean the same thing as "having compassion"? putting yourself in someone else's shoes Why might compassion help someone remember not to use put-downs or to act like a bully? The person would feel how such actions would hurt another person.

Life Skills Focus

Communicate Encourage students to express complete I-messages, such as "I feel bad when . . .," supported by facts and reasons. Stress the importance of complete I-messages in contrast to statements such as "I'm mad at you." Then encourage students to put themselves in the position of the friend who made an untrue statement. **How might the friend phrase his or her apology without making excuses or blaming someone else? How might the other person respond to show forgiveness?**

Activity

Use Communication Skills Students should include writing, speaking, and listening skills in their paragraphs.

③ Wrap Up

Lesson Checkup

1. use I-messages, take turns listening and speaking, listen carefully, develop compassion

2. Possible answer: when you make a mistake or do something hurtful, you should apologize.

3. Have students record their responses in their Health Journals. Encourage them to practice the skill they find most difficult.

35

OBJECTIVES

- Identify strategies for resolving conflicts.
- Use negotiation to resolve conflicts with friends and peers.

PROGRAM RESOURCES

- Activity Book, p. 11

1 Motivate

Assign half the class a math practice page with lots of problems. Allow the other half to draw pictures for the bulletin board. When protests arise from the math group, pretend you do not hear them at first. Continue to encourage the drawing group with praise, and urge the math group to get to work. List some of the math group's protests on the board. Tell the class that ignoring how people feel can lead to conflicts. Practice turning each of the protests into an "I feel" statement. Ask students how such statements might make it easier to solve conflicts.

2 Teach

Learn from Pictures

Direct students' attention to the pictures of Martha and her situation. **Why are the kids making fun of Martha?** because she is wearing glasses; because she is new **Can Martha change either of these things?** no **What choice does Dennis have to make in this situation?** whether to go along with his friends or stand up for what he believes is right

Step 1

What are some I-messages that Dennis could use in this situation? I don't feel good about teasing Martha; I feel sad when you tease Martha about things she can't help.

RESOLVE CONFLICTS with Friends

Ignoring how other people feel can lead to conflicts. Learning how to resolve conflicts will help you have more healthful relationships.

Learn This Skill

Some of the students are making fun of Martha, the new girl, because she wears glasses. When Dennis arrives, they expect him to join in. Dennis wants to go along with his friends, but he knows that teasing is wrong. What should Dennis do?

1. Use I-messages to tell how you feel.

"I feel sad when Martha is teased," says Dennis.

2. Listen to each other.

"You may think what you are saying is funny, but it isn't funny if it makes someone sad." "We weren't trying to be mean," the group replies.

MULTICULTURAL LINK

Understand Differences Read or tell the students a story about a child from a different culture. Examine the similarities and differences of things such as dress, language, food, and religion. Have students imagine that a child from another culture is coming to your classroom today. Ask them to write stories or create skits describing a conflict that might arise because of the cultural differences. Students should explain how the steps for resolving conflicts could be used in the situation.

TEACHER TIP

Anger Remind students that emotions are a normal and healthful part of life. Sometimes children feel that anger is not an acceptable emotion because they get in trouble when they express it. Reinforce that it is normal to feel anger and important to learn safe ways to express it so that it doesn't build up inside. Allow students to role-play situations showing safe ways to express anger.

3. Think of the other person's point of view.

"Look—Martha's new. That's hard enough. Let's include her in our group."

4. Decide what to do.

"Dennis is right—let's all try to get to know each other."

Practice This Skill

Use this summary to help you solve the problems below.

Steps for Resolving Conflicts

1. Use I-messages to tell how you feel.

2. Listen to each other.

3. Think of the other person's point of view.

4. Decide what to do.

A. Your friend's parents say it's OK to walk to the store. You want to go, but you know your parents wouldn't want you to. Explain how you feel and why you can't go.

B. You are the youngest one on a family vacation. Your parents want you to go to bed earlier than everyone else. Write down why your parents might think you need to go to bed early.

37

ACTIVITY BOOK, p. 11

Resolve Conflicts
Life Skills

Haley and Sandra are walking home from school. They are hungry, but they don't have any money to buy a snack. Sandra suggests that they take a candy bar from the shelf and share it. Haley knows that stealing is wrong, but she is afraid that Sandra will not be her friend anymore unless she goes along with the idea. Write a dialog that shows how Haley can use the conflict resolution steps to deal with this problem.

1. Use I-messages. **Possible answers are shown.**

Haley — I don't feel comfortable taking a candy bar without paying for it.

Sandra — I think it's okay this time because we are really hungry.

2. Listen to each other.

Haley — But stealing is always wrong; we could get into trouble.

Sandra — We won't get caught; I am really hungry.

3. Think of the other person's point of view.

Haley — Look, I know you are hungry. We can go to my house and get something to eat.

Sandra — I know that you are worried about getting in trouble. But I want to eat now.

4. Decide on a way to act.

Haley — Come on Sandra, let's hurry to my house.

Sandra — You're right, Haley. We shouldn't steal even if we are hungry. Let's go to your house and get something to eat now!

Critical Thinking Why is it important for Dennis to think for himself? Possible answers: If Dennis does something he knows is wrong, he will feel bad about himself. He may lose the chance to develop a new friendship.

Step 2

What does the group say about the teasing? Encourage students to role-play or to suggest possible answers that the students in the picture might make.

Critical Thinking Why is it important to listen to each other? You need to know how other people are feeling and what they are thinking; it helps you understand someone else's point of view.

Step 3

How do you think Martha is feeling? Possible answers: upset, lonely, sad, angry. What do you think she wants the kids to do? Possible answers: leave her alone, make her a part of the group.

Step 4

Critical Thinking Why is it important to get to know someone before you make judgments about him or her? Possible answers: Without getting to know someone, you have no way to know what she or he is really like. You may find that you have many things in common, but you will never know that just by looking at the person.

3 Wrap Up

A. Students should use I-messages. Possible answers: I would like to walk to the store with you, but it's against my family's rules. I know you really want to walk to the store, but I want to obey my family's rules.

B. Look for the use of I-messages to tell how they feel and for their ability to think of their parents' points of view.

Review

Use Vocabulary 2 pts. each

1. peers
2. communicate
3. Emotions
4. angry
5. apologize
6. responsible
7. stress
8. compassion
9. Feelings
10. honest
11. Grief
12. relationship
13. respect
14. body language
15. Peer pressure
16. self-control
17. fear

Check Your Facts 6 pts. each

18. An I-message is the way you tell people how you feel about something.

19. Possible answer: you can forgive yourself or someone else, you can get some exercise, you can read a book.

20. Possible answer: you can treat yourself as someone special, you can respect yourself.

21. Possible answers: you can listen and talk things over, you can say you're sorry, you can forgive your friend.

22. You can plan your time wisely, set goals you can reach, get some exercise, and take time to have fun.

Review

USE VOCABULARY

anger (p. 26)
apologize (p. 35)
body language (p. 21)
communicate (p. 34)
compassion (p. 34)

emotions (p. 22)
fear (p. 24)
feelings (p. 18)
grief (p. 27)
honest (p. 19)

peer pressure (p. 33)
peers (p. 33)
relationship (p. 30)
respect (p. 19)
responsible (p. 19)

self-control (p. 22)
stress (p. 25)

Use the terms above to complete the sentences. Page numbers in ( ) tell you where to look in the chapter if you need help.

1. Friends your own age are ____.

2. To ____ means to share information.

3. ____ are strong feelings.

4. If you feel ____, you are very mad.

5. When you say you are sorry, you ____.

6. Being ____ means that other people can count on you.

7. When you feel ____, you may have butterflies in your stomach.

8. If you have ____, you can feel what others feel.

9. ____ are the way you react to people and events.

10. When you are ____, you tell the truth.

11. ____ is a deep sadness.

12. A ____ is the way you get along with someone.

13. If you ____ yourself, you believe in yourself.

14. Your ____ is how your body shows your feelings.

15. ____ may cause you to do something because "everyone is doing it."

16. If you have power over your emotions, you have ____.

17. If you feel ____, you are afraid.

CHECK YOUR FACTS

Page numbers in ( ) tell you where to look in the chapter if you need help.

18. What is an I-message? (p. 34)

19. What are three ways to let go of emotions? (p. 23)

20. Name two things you can do to be a good friend to yourself. (p. 19)

21. What are two things you can do when you and a friend disagree? (p. 32)

22. Name four things you can do to deal with stress. (p. 25)

THINK CRITICALLY

23. Describe three things you do that make you a responsible member of your family.

24. Pretend that you are sad because your best friend is moving away. How would you express your sadness in your words, actions, and body language?

APPLY LIFE SKILLS

25. **Manage Stress** Suppose you are worried about a math test you will have tomorrow. Write the steps for managing stress and tell how you can deal with the stress you feel.

26. **Resolve Conflicts** Suppose you and a friend have a disagreement because he wants you to play baseball instead of finishing your homework. Write the steps for resolving conflicts and tell how you can work out your disagreement.

Think Critically 8 pts. each

23. Answers will vary but could include doing chores, listening to other members of the family, and caring for a younger member of the family.

24. Answers will vary but could include telling your friend you will miss him or her, writing your friend a letter, being more quiet than usual, or being angry.

Apply Life Skills 10 pts. each

25. Know what stress feels like and what causes it. When you feel stress, think about ways to handle it. Focus on one step at a time. Learn to relax. Ways to deal with stress will vary but should include the steps above.

26. Use I-messages to tell how you feel. Listen to each other. Think of the other person's point of view. Decide what to do. Ways to resolve the conflict will vary but should include the steps above.

PERFORMANCE ASSESSMENT

Project—Make a Feelings Booklet

The chapter project (introduced on page 17) can be used for individual or team performance assessment. Allow students the opportunity to revise and complete their projects before submitting them for evaluation. Students can use the Project Summary Sheet (Assessment Guide, p. 17) to tell about their projects. You can use the rubric provided on the Project Evaluation Sheet (Assessment Guide, p. 21) to evaluate student performance.

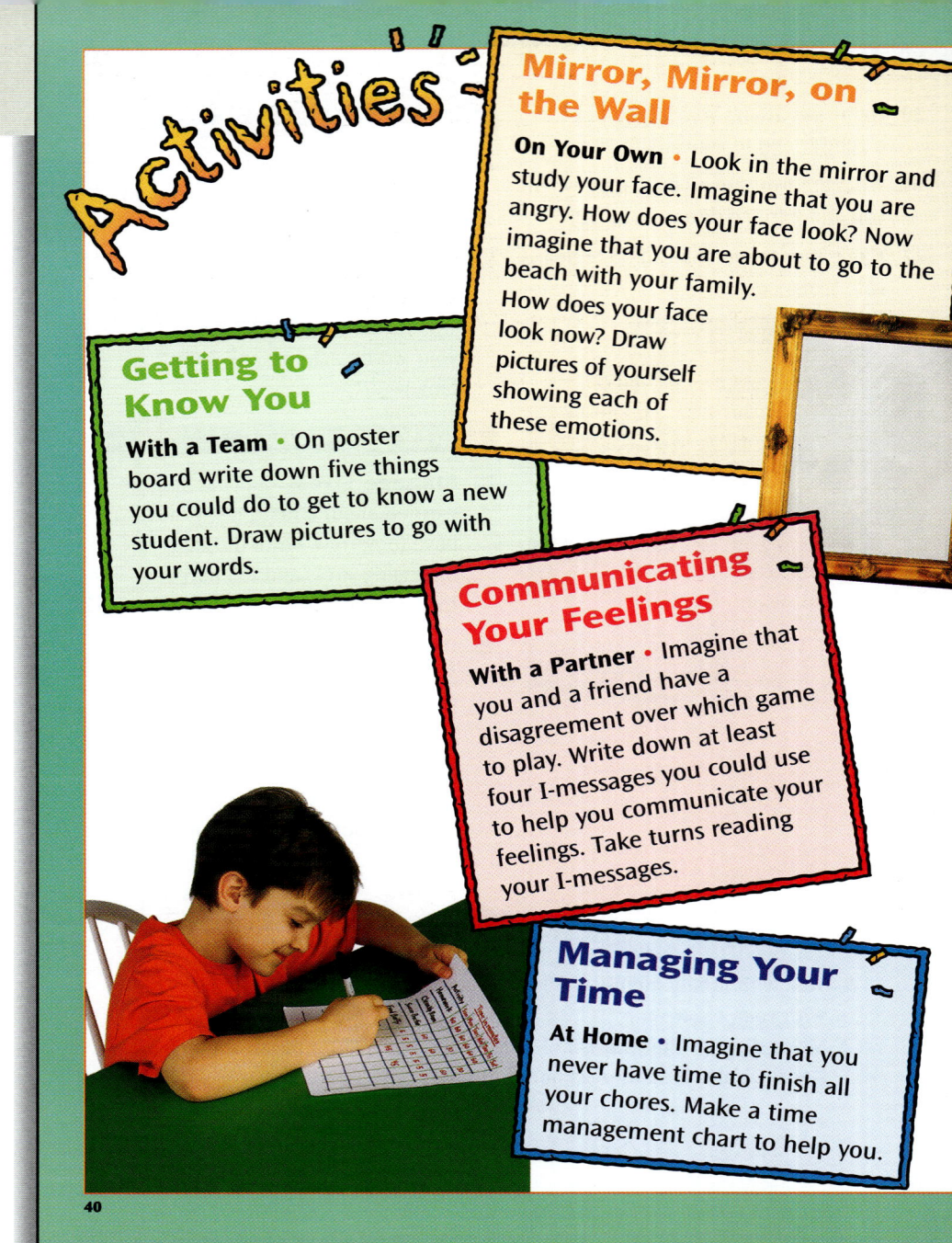

Activities

Mirror, Mirror, on the Wall

On Your Own • Look in the mirror and study your face. Imagine that you are angry. How does your face look? Now imagine that you are about to go to the beach with your family. How does your face look now? Draw pictures of yourself showing each of these emotions.

Getting to Know You

With a Team • On poster board write down five things you could do to get to know a new student. Draw pictures to go with your words.

Communicating Your Feelings

With a Partner • Imagine that you and a friend have a disagreement over which game to play. Write down at least four I-messages you could use to help you communicate your feelings. Take turns reading your I-messages.

Managing Your Time

At Home • Imagine that you never have time to finish all your chores. Make a time management chart to help you.

40

Chapter Test

ASSESSMENT GUIDE, p. 18

About Myself and Others — Chapter 1 Test

Write *T* or *F* to show if the sentence is true or false.

T 1. If you respect yourself, you believe in yourself.

F 2. Being responsible means that others cannot count on you.

T 3. Being honest means to tell the truth.

T 4. One way we show feelings is through words.

F 5. No one shows feelings through actions.

T 6. Body language helps us show our feelings to others.

F 7. Emotions are strong feelings that few people have.

F 8. When we have self-control, we cannot control our unpleasant feelings.

T 9. One way of letting go of emotions is by forgiving yourself or others for what happened.

T 10. There is no one else in the whole world just like you.

Match a strong emotion listed below with the story that best describes what that person is feeling. Write the name of the emotion on the line at the left.

fear	stress
grief	anger

anger 11. Beth is not speaking to her best friend, Toni, because Toni is telling lies about Beth. Beth found out about the lies, and doesn't want to be friends with Toni anymore.

fear 12. Pedro plays alone in his yard most days after school. Sometimes the neighbor's dog runs over to him, barking and growling. Pedro doesn't like this dog, and wishes that his neighbor would keep it tied up.

ASSESSMENT GUIDE, p. 19

stress 13. Lauren's teacher told her class about an important spelling test coming up at the end of the week. Lauren forgot about it, and now it's the night before the big test. Lauren is not a good speller, and should have been studying the spelling list all week. She is very worried about the test.

grief 14. Jaime's cat was 18 years old and had been sick for awhile. The medicine the veterinarian gave the sick cat no longer worked. The cat died last night. Jaime loved his cat very much.

15. Name one time when you should ask for help.
Possible answers: when you have trouble sleeping; when you are afraid to go to school; when something makes you feel uncomfortable and scared; when someone touches you in a way you don't like.

16. Name one good way of dealing with stress.
Possible answers: plan your time wisely; set goals you can reach; get some exercise; take time to have fun.

17. Name one step to take to help manage anger.
Possible answers: stop what you are doing; count to ten to cool down; think about what is happening; take action; use "I-messages."

18. Draw a picture that shows that you and a friend using good communication skills.

19. Draw a picture that shows what it means to have compassion.

Drawing should show words or actions, as well as body language, to display communication.

Drawing should show student saying or doing something that shows that he or she shares the same feelings as the person who is experiencing a hardship or other trouble.

ASSESSMENT GUIDE, p. 20

Write the letter of the best answer on the line at the left to complete the sentence.

a 20. When you have good relationships with your family and friends, it makes you _____.
a. feel good about yourself b. get better grades in school
c. make more friends d. feel bad about yourself

c 21. Families work together better when family members _____.
a. do their own thing b. have lots of arguments
c. respect and trust each other d. own lots of things

b 22. When you and a friend disagree, you should _____.
a. never speak to each other again
b. try to listen and talk things over
c. find a new friend
d. say mean things and walk away

a 23. When friends want you to do something just because "everyone is doing it," they are using _____.
a. peer pressure b. peer teasing
c. peer example d. peer fun

d 24. If you have compassion, you _____.
a. have a disease b. dislike most people
c. think only of yourself d. can feel what others feel

25. Write an "I-message" about how you feel when someone in your family hurts your feelings.
Possible answers: "I feel bad when you say those words to me"; "I feel angry when you talk to me like that"; "I feel hurt when you use those words."

Multiple Choice

Choose the letter of the correct answer.

1. You can show your feelings through _____.
   a. actions
   b. words
   c. body language
   d. all of these

2. You're feeling _____ when you have butterflies in your stomach and your hands are sweaty.
   a. stress
   b. grief
   c. anger
   d. sadness

3. It's important to have good _____ with family members and friends.
   a. responsibility
   b. emotion
   c. relationships
   d. feeling

4. Using I-messages helps you _____ your feelings.
   a. respect
   b. communicate
   c. forgive
   d. apologize

Modified True or False

Write *true* or *false*. If a sentence is false, replace the underlined term to make the sentence true.

5. Taking care of yourself shows that you are learning to be <u>responsible</u>.

6. Having <u>self-control</u> over your emotions can help you deal with unpleasant feelings.

7. Families work together better when family members <u>respect</u> each other.

8. It is <u>not all right</u> to feel angry.

9. Your <u>feelings</u> are the way you respond to people and events.

10. Using <u>you-messages</u> is a good way to communicate your feelings.

11. Talking and listening to others is a way of showing <u>respect</u>.

Short Answer

Write a sentence to answer each item.

12. What are two things families might do when they have problems?

13. Name two things you do for yourself when you respect yourself.

14. Give an example of something you could do to show compassion.

15. Name three types of visual artists.

16. What are three things you can do to improve your communication?

Writing in Health

Write a paragraph to answer each item.

17. Luis feels lonely. What are three things he could do to let go of that feeling?

18. Roberta is feeling stress because she doesn't think she can finish her social studies project on time. How could she deal with her stress?

41

Two options are provided for Chapter Tests—the in-book test and the reproducible test in the Assessment Guide. In addition to providing students with the opportunity to show what they have learned, both tests provide practice in taking standardized tests.

Multiple Choice (3 pts. each)

1. d   3. c
2. a   4. b

Modified True or False (5 pts. each)

5. true
6. true
7. true
8. false; all right
9. true
10. false; I-messages
11. true

Short Answer (7 pts. each)

Sample answers are shown; accept other reasonable answers.

12. They can work together and support each other.

13. Treat yourself as you would a good friend; forgive yourself when you make a mistake.

14. I could make friends with a new student at school.

15. Three types of visual artists are painters, photographers, and sculptors.

16. I can listen better, use I-messages, and use self-control when I am angry.

Writing in Health (9 pts. each)

Sample answers are shown; accept other reasonable answers.

17. Luis can think about how he is feeling, figure out why he feels that way, and do something to change the way he feels.

18. Since she already knows what is causing the stress, she needs to find out how to finish her project on time. She could break the project down into small steps and work on one step at a time.

Chapter Organizer

Lesson	Objectives	Vocabulary	Program Resources
Introduce the Chapter pp. 42–43	• Preview the chapter. • Begin chapter project.		• School-Home Connection, TR p. 35 • Assessment Guide, p. 25 • Read-Aloud Anthology, p. RA–3 ✏️ Teaching Transparency 2— Graphic Organizer
Lesson 1 **What Is a Family?** pp. 44–47 Pacing: 1 class period ✓ 3•4•7	• Describe different kinds of families and the basic needs that families of all kinds attempt to meet. • Describe ways family members can work and play together.	family values	• Activity Book, p. 12
Lesson 2 **Changes in Families** pp. 48–51 Pacing: 1 class period ✓ 3•5•7	• Describe some of the big changes that can affect the members of a family. • Identify ways that family members can help each other when big changes happen.	divorce sibling	• Activity Book, p. 13
Life Skills **Communicate with Family Members** pp. 52–53 Pacing: 1 class period ✓ 5•7	• Identify communication skills. • Use communication skills to get along with family members.		• Activity Book, p. 14
Lesson 3 **Everyone Grows and Changes** pp. 54–57 Pacing: 1 class period ✓ 1•2•5	• Describe each stage of the human life cycle. • Compare the four stages of the human life cycle.	life cycle	• Activity Book, p. 15 • Growth, Development, and Reproduction pp. 2–10 and 16–19
Lesson 4 **People Grow at Different Rates** pp. 58–61 Pacing: 1 class period ✓ 1•7	• Describe how growth occurs. • Compare kinds of cells and how they are designed to do special jobs. • Describe one kind of growth in addition to physical growth and the changes that occur as a result.	cell tissues organs organ system growth rate	💻 Computer Graphing Activity, TR p. 54 ✏️ Teaching Transparency 22
Lesson 5 **Taking Care of My Body** pp. 62–63 Pacing: 1 class period ✓ 1•3•7	• Identify ways to care for your body.	private	• Activity Book, pp. 16–17 • Growth, Development, and Reproduction p. 32
Chapter Review and Test pp. 64–67 ✓ 1•5•7	• Assess chapter objectives and project. • Provide extension activities.		• Assessment Guide, pp. 22–25

 National Health Education Standards
A complete list of the Standards is provided on the next page.

Key: TR = Teaching Resources

National Health Education Standards

1. Comprehend concepts related to health promotion and disease prevention.
2. Access valid health information and health-promoting products and services.
3. Practice health-enhancing behaviors and reduce health risks.
4. Analyze the influence of culture, media, technology, and other factors on health.
5. Use interpersonal communication skills to enhance health.
6. Use goal-setting and decision-making skills to enhance health.
7. Advocate for personal, family, and community health.

Art
- Teamwork Mobiles, p. 50

Drama
- Decision: Role-Play, p. 42C

Math
- Family Time Book, p. 42C
- Communicate to Solve a Math Problem, p. 52
- Activity Cycles, p. 55

Curriculum Integration

Use these topics to integrate health into your daily planning.

Social Studies
- The Basics of Egg Care, p. 42C
- Your New Home, p. 46

Science
- Life Cycles, p. 56

Language Arts
- Truth or Fiction, p. 42C
- I'll Never Forget the Time . . ., p. 45
- Write About Feelings, p. 51

ASSESSMENT OPTIONS

Portfolio Assessment
Have students select their best work from the following suggestions:
- **I'll Never Forget the Time . . .**, p. 45
- **Movin' On**, p. 66
- **Picture Perfect**, p. 66

Student Self-Assessment
- **Journal Notes**, pp. 50, 57;
- **Set Health Goals**, pp. 47, 51, 57, 61
- **Use Life Skills**, p. 63

Daily Assessment
- **Check Your Facts**, pp. 47, 51, 57, 61, 63

Performance Assessment
- **Chapter Project:** Make a Family Book, pp. 43, 46, 57, 65
- **Project Evaluation Sheet**, Assessment Guide, p. 25

Formal Assessment
- **Chapter Review**, pp. 64–65
- **In-Book Test**, p. 67
- **Chapter Test**, Assessment Guide, pp. 22–24

Cross-Curricular Activities

Social Studies

The Basics of Egg Care

To help students better understand what providing basic needs entails, have students care for an egg for one week.

- Give each student an egg. Allow a few students to have twins.

- Have students name, weigh, and measure their eggs. Each student should then make a home to protect it, create a simple menu of meals for it, and bathe it daily. They should carry it with them everywhere they go or arrange for someone to care for it for brief periods.

- After one week, hold a class discussion of the students' experiences.

Language Arts

Truth or Fiction

Have students discuss whether they think the following statements are true or false. Discuss why these statements might have been created. What purpose do they serve?

- Spinach builds strong muscles. (F)

- Carrots make you see better. (T) Beta carotene is converted to vitamin A by the body. It is needed for the retina to function.

- Cigarettes stunt your growth. (F)

Ask students to talk with their parents and grandparents if possible. What statements can they think of to add to the list? Compile them into an illustrated class book.

Math

Family Time Book

Have students make a book by logging times spent with family members for one week.

- Students should identify the day of the week and the amount of time spent with each family member.

- Have students describe who they spent time with and what they did.

Examples might include eating breakfast with the whole family, reading with dad, doing dishes with a sister, and so on.

- Who would they like to spend more time with next week?

- Have students create a modest goal and then try to arrange a date with that family member, if possible.

Drama

Decision: Role-Play

Discuss ways to make good decisions regarding situations that could affect students' personal health.

- Have students identify situations when they must make choices that could affect their health.

- Discuss the options that are available and the best choice to make.

- Ask volunteers to role-play the situations, demonstrating the process of making healthful decisions.

Bulletin Board

Create a bulletin board titled "Everyone Grows and Changes."

- Have students bring in a photo of themselves as babies. Explain that they should not show their photos to anyone.

- Collect photos and randomly affix them to the bulletin board around a subtitle, "Guess Who!"

- You may number the photos and allow students to submit a list attempting to identify each picture, or allow time in class for students to guess who is pictured.

Resources

Books for Students

Rogers, Fred. *Let's Talk About It: Divorce.* G.P. Putnam's Sons, 1998. Simple, honest discussion about divorce. **EASY**

Girard, Linda Walvoord. *My Body Is Private.* Albert Whitman & Company, 1999. Teaches children about privacy at all levels. **AVERAGE**

Clifford, Eth. *Family for Sale.* Houghton Mifflin, 1996. Middle reader's novel about family life. **ADVANCED**

Books for Teachers and Families

Teyber, Edward. *Helping Children Cope with Divorce.* John Wiley & Sons, 2001. A good support book for parents and teachers in aid of troubled youth.

Erikson, Joan M. *Wisdom and the Senses: The Way of Creativity.* W.W. Norton & Company, 1991. The focus here is on the physical senses and their role in each stage of growth and development.

Videos

All About the Senses. Schlessinger Media, 2001. (23 minutes) Viewers will learn that we receive information from the outside world through our sense organs.

Everyday Etiquette. Rainbow Educational Media, 1996. (15 minutes) A live-action video that provides a good overview of basic etiquette.

Amazing Mallika. MarshMedia, 1997. (15 minutes) Tells about Mallika, a tiger with a bad temper who learns how to deal with her anger and take charge of her feelings.

Let's Get A Move On! Kidvidz, 1990. (25 minutes) Families are moving more frequently today. Watch students experience the adventure of moving.

Your Health Webliography

The **Webliography** provides links to the Health Background and teaching resources that will support you as you teach the topics in *Your Health*. Simply choose a keyword and you will be taken to a page of links with descriptions of the content you can obtain at each site. The **Webliography** is located on the Teacher Resources page at **www.harcourtschool.com/health** Please review websites before referring your students to them.

Organizations and Agencies

Administration on Aging
330 Independence Ave., SW
Washington, DC 20201
Provides comprehensive information and resources on aging.

The National Center For Missing And Exploited Children
699 Prince Street
Alexandria, VA 22314
Provides information on child sexual abuse and exploitation.

For more information about health organizations and agencies, please see the *Teaching Resources* book.

Community Health

Dental Hygienist Invite a dental hygienist—perhaps a parent—from a local dentist office (someone who is a particularly engaging speaker) to talk about teeth and gum care. If possible, have the dental hygienist bring in a model of the teeth to show proper brushing and flossing techniques. Request that the hygienist also bring in toothbrushes and tablets that expose areas of plaque left after brushing. Provide a time for students to check the effectiveness of their brushing techniques.

Note that information, while correct at time of publication, is subject to change.

Visit **The Harcourt Learning Site** for related links, activities, resources, and the health **Webliography**.

www.harcourtschool.com

"Positive interpersonal relationships are essential to a person's health."

—Comprehensive School Health Education

CHAPTER SUMMARY

In this chapter students
- are introduced to the ways families meet the needs of their members.
- examine the process of growth.
- learn ways to care for their bodies.

LIFE SKILLS Students practice *communication* within the family.

HUMAN BODY Students investigate the body's structure including cells, tissues, organs, and organ systems. They then examine various organ systems and describe what the systems do.

Literature Springboard

Use the poem *Mark's Fingers* to spark interest in the chapter topic. See the Read-Aloud Anthology on page RA-3 of this Teacher's Edition.

42

School-Home Connection

 Distribute copies of the School-Home Connection (in English or Spanish), TR page 35. Have students take the page home to share with their families as you begin this chapter.

Follow Up Discuss the positive things that family members do for one another.

Alternative Use the School-Home Connection page as a classroom resource for enrichment activities.

Dear Family Member,

In Chapter 2, Me and My Family, our class will be learning that there are many types of families and that all families experience change in the form of major life events. We will also learn about the physical changes that make up the human life cycle. Taking care of one's body and respecting one's privacy are important parts of growing and maturing.

Family Activity

There are many types of families. Some families consist of people related by blood, such as one or two parents raising children. Other families are made up of people whose members are not all related, such as families raising adopted or foster children.

Help your child identify at least three different types of families that exist in your neighborhood or community. Enter your findings in the following chart. In the first column, identify the type of family, such as single-female parent family. In the second column, list the members of the family, such as a mother and son. Discuss the chart with your child. How are the families alike? How are they different?

Types of Families in My Community

Type of Family	Family Members

Family Reading

The following books can help you and your family learn more about the topics covered in this chapter. Books should always be chosen with the approval of an adult family member.

- Rogers, Fred. *Let's Talk About It: Divorce.* G.P. Putnam's Sons, 1998. Simple, honest discussion about divorce. EASY
- Girard, Linda Walvoord. *My Body Is Private.* Albert Whitman & Company, 1999. Teaches children about privacy at all levels. AVERAGE
- Clifford, Eth. *Family for Sale.* Houghton Mifflin, 1996. Middle reader's novel about family life. ADVANCED

Thank you for participating in our study of health.

Sincerely,

2

Me and My Family

MAKE A FAMILY BOOK

Make a book titled "Things Families Do Together." Include fun things as well as jobs families might work on together, such as making meals.

For other activities, visit the Harcourt Learning Site. www.harcourtschool.com

43

Teaching Transparency 2—Graphic Organizer

2 Chapter 2 Graphic Organizer

Me and My Family

Teach Values	Play Together	Work Together	Grow Together
1. honesty	1. play games	1. set the table	1. cell
2. caring about others	2. watch videos	2. carry in firewood	2. tissues
	3. read aloud	3. wash dishes	3. organs
	4. play sports	4. care for a pet	4. organ system
		5. take out recycling	5. growth rate

© Harcourt

Introduce the Chapter

MAKE A FAMILY BOOK

Access Prior Knowledge Use this activity as a baseline assessment of students' understanding of the importance of family relationships.

Performance Assessment The project can be used for performance assessment. Before students begin, explain how you will evaluate their performance. (See the Project Evaluation Sheet, Assessment Guide, p. 25.)

Prereading Strategies

Scan the Chapter Have students preview the chapter content by scanning the titles, headings, and pictures. Ask volunteers to speculate on what they will learn.

Preview Vocabulary Have each student fold a sheet of legal-sized paper in half three times to form eight squares. As students preview the vocabulary terms in each lesson, ask them to consider how they could illustrate the meaning of each term. Have them choose one term to write and illustrate for each square.

Visualize Key Concepts Display the Graphic Organizer Transparency. You may also wish to distribute photocopies to students. Have students complete the organizer as they work through the chapter. Suggested concepts for students to fill in are shown.

Follow Up Review the completed organizer with students as preparation for the Chapter Review and Chapter Tests.

OBJECTIVES

- Describe different kinds of families and the basic needs that families of all kinds attempt to meet.
- Describe ways family members can work and play together.

PROGRAM RESOURCES

- Activity Book, p. 12

VOCABULARY

- family (p. 44)
- values (p. 44)

Daily Safety Tip

Learning responsibility is an important part of growing older. Helping out at home is one way to show responsibility. Remind students that they should attempt to do only those jobs that have the approval of an adult family member. Certain jobs like cooking require that students know how to use cooking utensils, cook foods, and use a stove or oven safely.

1 Motivate

Tell students that everyone is a part of a family, but that families can differ in many ways. Ask students to take a few minutes to draw or list their family members. Then, allow several volunteers to talk about the members of their families.

From what we heard from these few volunteers, what differences in families can we already see? Possible answers: number of adults in the family; number of children in the family; the make-up of a family (number of boys, number of girls); extended family members.

MAIN IDEA
Families enjoy working and playing together.

WHY LEARN THIS? When family members play and work well together, they learn to respect each other.

VOCABULARY
- family
- values

What Is a Family?

Your **family** is the group of people you live with. There are many kinds of families. Some families have children and two parents. Other families have one parent, a grandparent, or another adult. A stepparent or stepchildren may be part of a family. Who is in your family?

Your family makes sure your basic needs are met. They give you food, a place to sleep, and clothes to wear. They love you, help you when you are ill or scared, and make rules to keep you safe.

Families also teach values. **Values** (VAL•yooz) are strong beliefs, such as honesty and caring about others. Children first learn about right and wrong in their families.

Most parents love their children. They try hard to give their children what they need to grow up strong and healthy.

▼ There are many kinds of families.

44

 MULTILEVEL ACTIVITIES

EASY Make Posters Have students form small groups. Ask students to cut out from magazines pictures of families spending time together. Then have the groups make posters as a reminder to families to take time to play together. **VISUAL**

AVERAGE Make Coats of Arms Family symbols have existed for hundreds of years. Called by various names, such as a coat of arms, or a mon, these symbols represent the qualities or interests of the families. Have students think about the qualities of their families and make coats of arms showing those qualities. **VISUAL/INTRAPERSONAL**

ADVANCED Learn Stories Many cultures have oral traditions, where stories are passed down through generations. Have each student ask a family member to tell him or her a story from when that person was young. When students learn their stories have them tell them to the class as dramatically as they can using props or simple costumes. **VERBAL/AUDITORY**

▲ Family members can have fun together.

How does a family play together?

Family members can play together in many ways. Some families like to play sports or go hiking. Other families choose books to read out loud. Some work on jigsaw puzzles. Others play games or watch videos. How do the people in your family play together?

Playing together can make everyone in a family feel good. You laugh together as you plan a special surprise. You talk as you put together a puzzle. You have a chance to relax together as you ride bikes or walk the dog.

Playing together gives family members a chance to talk and listen to each other. You get to know each other better. You talk about what you are feeling. You learn to respect each other.

When members of a family have fun together, it makes everyone happy. It makes everyone glad to be part of the family.

"I'll Never Forget the Time . . ."

On Your Own Write a story about a funny or exciting time with your family that you will never forget. Tell what you liked best about the event.

○ ○ ○

45

2 Teach

Discuss

Have students read page 45. As they read, ask them to think about what they most like to do with their families.

Critical Thinking Why is playing together so important? What would it be like to not have any play time with your family or friends? Possible answers: everything would be serious, we would only be working, no one would laugh.

Language Arts Connection

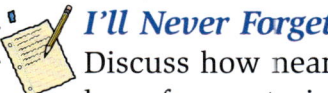

I'll Never Forget the Time . . ." Discuss how nearly all families have funny stories to tell. You might share a funny or exciting story that happened in your own family when you were a child. Give students time to think of the best funny or exciting true story they can remember about their family. Have them write it in first person. Ask for volunteers to read their stories aloud to the class.

DEVELOP READING SKILLS

Identify Important Words
Provide students with an opportunity to identify the ways in which vocabulary words are identified in their textbooks. Ask them to scan their books and see if they can list four ways that each word is identified or defined.

1. Vocabulary words are listed at the beginning of the lesson.

2. Words are highlighted in yellow when they are defined in the text.

3. Words are listed and reviewed in the Chapter Review.

4. Words are listed alphabetically and defined in the glossary.

Remind students that identifying the important words is a reading strategy they can use at the beginning of each lesson.

Discuss

How many different places to live can you name? Possible answers: house, trailer, apartment, city, farm. Write the list on the board.

Critical Thinking How might the chores children do at home differ for children living in these different situations? Answers should reflect that jobs around a house would involve inside and outside chores. Jobs around an apartment might involve only inside chores. Farm jobs would be like those of a family living in a house, only there might be additional chores to care for animals or crops.

Critical Thinking What might your chores be if you lived on a boat or in another environment very different from the one you now live in? Answers will vary.

Project Checkup

Make a Family Book (p. 43) As students create their family books, they may want to add a page describing examples of what they learn from family members and of duties different family members perform. Encourage students to set a goal and develop a plan for their responsibilities within the family.

How does a family work together?

It's important for family members to work together. When people in a family work together, it makes everyone in the family feel proud.

In some families the children are responsible for certain jobs. One child may always set the table, carry in firewood, or take care of a pet. In other families parents and children take turns doing some jobs, such as washing the dishes or taking out the trash.

You may have different jobs depending on where your family lives. If you live in a city apartment, you will have different jobs from someone who lives on a farm.

Taking Care of Maggie

1. Feed her. ✓
2. Give her clean water. ✓
3. Pet her. ✓
4. Brush her for 10 minutes. ○
5. Keep her litter box clean. ✓

◀ **Taking care of a pet is a good way to show responsibility.**

46

 SOCIAL STUDIES

Your New Home Ask students to imagine themselves living in a *really* different environment. Ask them to pretend that their families will soon be moving to live on a space station! Have students do a little research on space stations. What do they look like? Have students design the inside of a space station, including what their room might look like and what other rooms there would be. Would they have any pets in space? Then ask students to list the kinds of jobs they might be responsible for doing in their new home in space.

TEACHER TIP

Affirm Differences You can help students relax and generally feel better if you make the point in the beginning that differences in families are wonderful. Many students believe that their family is not a "real" family, because it looks different from other families they know. Remind students that, just as every person is different, every family is also different. There is not one "right" way to look like or to be a family.

I'll help!

→ **Activity** **Think of New Jobs** List the ways you help your family. What three new ways could you add to your list?

It feels good to be a responsible member of your family. You are being responsible when you do a job without waiting to be asked. For example you can keep your room clean or offer to help with big jobs.

When everyone in a family works together, no one person has to do all the work. Jobs get done more quickly. And that leaves more time for play!

LESSON CHECKUP

Check Your Facts

❶ How does your family meet your basic needs?

❷ Name three reasons it's important for family members to play together.

❸ CRITICAL THINKING What jobs could people in your family take turns doing?

Set Health Goals

❹ Think of three things you would like to do with your family. Give other family members a chance to add to the list. With your family, choose an activity from the list, and make a plan for doing it.

47

Discuss

Talk with students about chores and how children can help around the house by picking up their toys, hanging up their clothes, and cleaning up after themselves. **What are some jobs that you do around your house?** Possible answers: care for pet, take out trash and recycling materials, clean room, make the bed, pick up toys, wash or dry dishes

→ **Activity**

Think of New Jobs After surveying the long list of things that need to be done around a house, ask students to list any of those jobs that they already routinely do. Have them put a *D* by the ones they do daily, a *W* for weekly, and an *N* for now and then. Then, ask them to think of three new ways they could help out at home. In each case, have students indicate whether it is on a D, W, or N basis.

③ Wrap Up

Lesson Checkup

1. They provide food, clothing, shelter, love, and protection.

2. Playing together can make you feel good, give you time to talk to each other, and teach you to respect each other more.

3. Answers will vary but should indicate an understanding that many simple jobs, such as drying dishes or taking out the garbage, can be done by everyone in the family.

4. Students' activities and plans will vary.

TEACHER TIP

Receiving Help Students need to know that they are worthy of receiving help. Talk with students about the ways they appreciate being helped by family members, and have them discuss the kind of help they would like to receive more often. What common ideas are expressed? In some cases, help students see how they can help themselves. In other cases, help them brainstorm ways that they can get the help they need and deserve.

OBJECTIVES
- Describe some of the big changes that can affect the members of a family.
- Identify ways that family members can help each other when big changes happen.

PROGRAM RESOURCES
- Activity Book, p. 13

VOCABULARY
- divorce (p. 49)
- sibling (p. 49)

Daily Safety Tip

Big changes in families can affect individual family members differently. Some changes, like a divorce or the death of a family pet, can cause considerable emotional trauma for children. Remind students that everything they feel is OK. Help students understand that sometimes it helps to talk about their feelings with an adult. It can be a family member, or it can be another trusted adult. Explain that finding someone to talk to is a good way for them to take care of themselves.

1 Motivate

Ask students if they have seen a snow globe. Bring one to class if you can. Have students describe the snow globes they are familiar with. **Why is a snow globe a good image for how a person might feel when big changes happen in a family? What big changes can you think of?** Answers will vary and may include: it feels like you are turned upside down or tossed around; changes might include a death, family illness, a new sibling, or a move.

LESSON  2

Changes in Families

MAIN IDEA All families go through changes. Some changes are harder than others.

WHY LEARN THIS? It helps to know ways that family members can help each other during good times and bad times.

VOCABULARY
- divorce
- sibling

Have you ever seen a snow globe—a glass ball that "snows" when you turn it upside down? When big changes happen in a family, you may feel as if you're inside a snow globe. Everything may suddenly seem to be turning upside down.

What happens when families change?

Changes happen all the time. Many changes are fun, but some are hard. Moving, divorce or remarriage, a new baby, and the death of a pet are all big changes. Everyone in the family will need time to get used to changes like these.

Moving to a new place can feel confusing. If you move, you may feel sad about leaving your old friends and your old home. But you may also feel excited about going to a new school.

Moving day can bring mixed feelings.

48

 MULTILEVEL ACTIVITIES

EASY **Identify Main Ideas** Have students read page 48 and then write in their own words three main ideas on this page. Have them include any examples they find. **LOGICAL**

AVERAGE **Perform a Puppet Show** Have students create and present a puppet show that demonstrates how siblings interact when they have a problem. The show could portray poor behavior by two young children and then show an older sibling intervening and helping the children solve the conflict peacefully. **VISUAL/KINESTHETIC**

ADVANCED **Find Books About Change** Sometimes when students are going through stressful changes, it helps if they can read a book about a character that went through something similar. Have students consult the media specialist and make a bibliography for the class on topics such as divorce, remarriage, death, illness, and moving. Display the bibliography in the classroom. **VISUAL/INTERPERSONAL**

Activity **Write About Change** These snow globes show big changes that can turn a family upside down for a time. Choose one, or think of another big change. Write about all the feelings you might have as you get used to the change.

When parents **divorce** (duh•VORS), it means they are no longer married to each other. If parents divorce or remarry, it is normal to feel sad, scared, and confused for a while.

When a pet dies, you may feel sad a long time. Even if you get another pet, you will always remember the pet that died.

When a new baby joins your family, you have a new brother or sister, or **sibling**. You may feel excited but also jealous of the time your parents spend with the baby. It may take some time for you to get to know your new brother or sister.

If a big change happens in your family, it's all right to feel whatever you are feeling. Be patient with yourself and with other family members.

49

ACTIVITY BOOK, p. 13

Use Vocabulary | **Vocabulary Reinforcement**

Find the word in Column B that best fits the definition in Column A. Then write the letter of the word on the line at the left. Use each word only once.

Column A

b 1. when two people decide not to be married any longer

c 2. honesty, helpfulness

d 3. a brother or sister

a 4. the group of people who live with you

Column B

a. family

b. divorce

c. values

d. sibling

In the space below, write a new sentence using each word in Column B correctly.

5. family: **Accept reasonable answers.**

6. divorce:

7. values:

8. sibling:

TEACHER TIP

Acknowledge Change Remind students that not all big changes are bad. Help students see that our lives are full of change, and most of them are probably good. In fact, even changes that are difficult in the beginning may turn out to be good. Give students time to share examples from their own lives. Encourage them to be detectives on the lookout for all the changes that are constantly happening around them.

---

2 Teach

Discuss

Explain that big changes often cause mixed feelings. For example, remind students that when they started school, they were probably excited, but also a little scared. They may have missed being at home until they got used to being at school.

Critical Thinking **How do you and members of your family deal with change?** Possible answers: talk about the situation; allow the change to occur over time, little by little; cry together; laugh together; spend time together; hug each other; try to be patient.

Discuss

Talk about patience. **What is patience? How would you define it? Can you give some examples?**

Critical Thinking **Why do you think patience is important when dealing with change? Can you give an example from your own life?** Answers will vary but may include the idea that things continue to change in ways you can't predict in the beginning, and that sometimes these changes can even surprise you in a good way.

Activity

Write About Change Discuss with students what changes could be taking place in each of the snow globes pictured. Before students begin writing, have them imagine themselves in each situation and think about the different feelings they might have. After they have written, ask volunteers to share and discuss their answers. Students may also want to illustrate other snow globes with different situations pictured in them. Have volunteers share their illustrations with the class.

49

Teach *continued*

Discuss

Have students read the text and caption on this page. **What do you think are the most important ideas on this page? Are any of these ideas new to you? Have you ever thought of you and your family as a team?**

Critical Thinking **If all of us in this classroom wanted to act more like a team, what might we do?** Possible answers: solve problems peacefully, be friendlier, listen to each other, respect classroom and school rules.

Another way in which family members can help and support one another is in making choices about family health behaviors. **How does your family influence your health behaviors? What kind of decisions do different family members make about family health?**

Emphasize to students that parents make most of the decisions about the health of the family. These include nutrition, medical attention, and vaccinations. However, the students also make desicions about their health, such as how much physical activity they get and what types of snacks they eat. Further, students can influence the health of the entire family with suggestions about family activities and meals.

Health Journal

 Discuss the team concept, where each person's job contributes to the overall success of the group. Have students think of ways their family works as a team. Ask students to consider new ways that they could help their "home team."

This feature is designed to provide students with an opportunity to reflect on health decisions they are making in their personal lives. The journals should *not* be used to evaluate or assess students, nor do the results need to be shared among students.

Make notes in your Health Journal about how you and your family work as a team. How can you help your family in new ways? Remember that your journal is private. You do not have to share it with classmates.

How can family members help each other?

When you were little, your parents did everything for you. Now that you are older, you can begin to help them. When family members help each other, they feel as if they're part of the same team.

It's easier for a family to be a good team when family members share the same values. If all the people in your family speak politely to each other and tell the truth, it helps your family stay strong.

Family rules also help family members work as a team. When all the people in your family respect the rules, family members argue less often and have more fun together.

Team members help each other. You may help by reading stories to a younger sibling. Sometimes the whole family might pitch in for a big project such as painting the house. By helping, you are being a responsible member of your family.

◄ Reading a book out loud is a good way to spend time with a younger sibling.

50

 **TEACHER TIP**

Brainstorm Teams Teams exist in many places besides sports. Brainstorm with students other places they might find teams, such as education (team teaching), medicine, science, and publishing. After listing several examples on the board, ask students who the members of each team might be, and what the common goal or purpose might be. Finally, ask students to think carefully about what all these teams have in common.

ART

Teamwork Mobiles Provide students with coat hangers, string or yarn, and construction paper. Have students identify and represent the ways that members of their family work together to get things done around the house. Allow students to explain and display their mobiles.

▲ Mealtime is a good time for family members to listen to each other's ideas and feelings.

LIFE SKILLS FOCUS

Resolve Conflicts

Your younger brother and sister always interrupt when you are talking. This makes you angry. How can you help them learn to listen politely and wait their turn to speak? Use the steps for resolving conflicts shown on page *xiii*.

• • •

For a family to be a good team, family members need to communicate. It takes practice to learn to talk and listen respectfully to each family member. Some families spend time talking while eating meals, riding in the car, or making breakfast.

When family members can talk to each other, work together, and have fun together, they feel like a team. They feel close to each other. Feeling close makes it easier for family members to help each other when big changes happen.

LESSON CHECKUP

Check Your Facts

❶ Name some times when all the members of a family can talk together.

❷ What kinds of feelings might you have when a new sibling is born?

❸ **CRITICAL THINKING** How are family team rules like a sports team's rules?

❹ Why are family rules important?

Set Health Goals

❺ Write one goal you would like your family to work toward. What could each family member do to help?

51

LANGUAGE ARTS

Write About Feelings There are many ways to express feelings. One of these is through poetry. Have students think of a time they were sad, angry, or very happy and ask them to write poems about how they felt and why they felt that way. Remind them that not all poems have to rhyme.

LIFE SKILLS FOCUS

Resolve Conflicts Have students review the steps for resolving conflicts before they complete this activity. You may wish to encourage interested students to complete this activity as a skit, which they could present to the rest of the class. They may even wish to show several different "endings" for the conflict and have the class vote on which one was the best.

③ Wrap Up

Lesson Checkup

1. Possible answers: during meal times, when riding in a car, when preparing a meal.

2. Possible answers: excitement and jealousy. Accept all reasonable answers.

3. Rules help members of teams and families accomplish things, stay safe, and respect each other.

4. When family members respect family rules, arguments are less likely to happen and everyone gets along better. It helps everyone when the family feels like a team, because they have things in common that they all agree on.

5. Answers will vary.

Health Background

Family Communication For effective family communication to take place, the family has to provide a safe environment, emotionally and physically. In healthy families the conversation is spontaneous, meaningful, and clear. Ideas and emotions are freely expressed, because each person knows that other family members will listen and respond appropriately.

For more background, visit the **Webliography** on the Teacher Resources page at:
www.harcourtschool.com/health
Keyword family life

LIFE SKILLS

OBJECTIVES

- Identify communication skills.
- Use communication skills to get along with family members.

PROGRAM RESOURCES

- Activity Book, p. 14

1 Motivate

Have students list each member of their families on a sheet of paper. Have them write each person's favorite hobbies, sports, or activities under her or his name. Tell students they are going to plan an activity for their family. Ask them to think of an activity that everyone will want to do based on the things they have listed. Once they have finished the task, ask for volunteers to tell what activity they have selected and how it will satisfy each member of the family.

2 Teach

Learn from Pictures

Direct students' attention to the situation listed on this page. **How is this like the activity you just completed?** Jenny's family wants to go out to dinner. Each one gets to suggest a place, but they will only be able to go to one. They need to find a place everyone will accept. Discuss the process the family used.

Step 1

How can you tell this family is ready to communicate? Possible answers: they are seated around the table facing each other; they look as if they are ready to talk.

COMMUNICATE with Family Members

Even when planning fun activities, family members need to communicate with each other. This skill will help you do just that.

Learn This Skill

Jenny's family is planning which restaurant to go to on Friday night. Each family member gets to present an idea.

1. Understand your audience.

Jenny knows each family member has certain likes and dislikes. They will have to work together to choose a restaurant all will accept.

2. Give a clear message.

Jenny says that she loves Mexican food and that she'd like to go to the Mexican Fiesta.

MATH

Communicate to Solve a Math Problem Divide students into groups of four. Tell them they will be using the communication steps to solve a math problem.

- Ask each group to divide a sheet of paper into four parts and label each section with a step in the model. Pass out a word problem to each group.
- Have groups read the problems and discuss how they will solve them. Tell groups to record their ideas in box 1 on the paper they

labeled with the communication steps.
- Let each person in the group tell what he or she thinks is the best way to solve the problem. Record those ideas in box 2.
- Have the group tell which idea they think will work best. Record that idea in box 3.
- Have the students solve the problem and record the answer in box 4.

When the process is complete, have each group tell what compromises they had to make and how their group communicated to solve the problem.

3. Listen.

Jenny listens to the rest of the family. Her brother says they eat Mexican food too often. He wants to go to the Little Italy restaurant.

4. Gather feedback.

Everyone talks and listens. They decide to go Italian this Friday and Mexican next Friday.

Practice This Skill

Use the steps to help you solve the problems.

Communicating with Family Members

1. Understand your audience.
2. Give a clear message.
3. Listen.
4. Gather feedback.

A. Kathy gets angry when her brother borrows her bike without asking. How can Kathy communicate her feelings to her brother?

B. Larry is upset. His sister promised to help him clean the kitchen, and then she forgot. How can Larry communicate how he feels?

53

Step 2

What is Jenny's message? She wants to go eat Mexican food.

Critical Thinking What might happen if Jenny just shrugged her shoulders or said, "I don't know." Possible answers: she wouldn't have given her family any ideas; she might not like the place they choose; she would not be giving a clear message to her family.

Step 3

Critical Thinking Why is it important to listen to everyone's input? so everyone will feel they had a part in making the decision

Step 4

What decision did the family make? to have Italian food this Friday and Mexican next Friday

3 Wrap Up

A. Students should explain how Kathy could use the steps for communicating with family members to talk to her brother. Look for a clear message, such as "I feel angry when you borrow my bike without asking. I want you to ask me first." Students should also include the "listen" and "gather feedback" steps.

B. Students should explain how Larry can use the communication steps to tell his sister how he feels, including understanding his audience, giving a clear message, listening to his sister's response, and gathering feedback.

OBJECTIVES

- Describe each stage of the human life cycle.
- Compare the four stages of the human life cycle.

PROGRAM RESOURCES

- Activity Book, p. 15
- Growth, Development, and Reproduction, pp. 2–10 and 16–19

VOCABULARY

- life cycle (p. 54)

Daily Safety Tip

As children grow and develop greater abilities, they also take greater risks. In activities that they may presently engage in, like riding a bike or skateboard, speed and lack of proper safety equipment can be a dangerous combination. Remind students to wear protective gear in any activity that poses a risk, even when they become good at it.

1 Motivate

Explain to students that sometimes we forget all the changes we go through in the course of our lives. Even though they are not grown up yet, they have already experienced many changes from the time they were born until now. They have grown and developed in many ways. They have developed many new interests and abilities.

What are some of the changes you have experienced since you were born? Possible answers: grown, learned to walk, learned to talk, learned to read and write, learned to play certain sports.

Critical Thinking What changes do you think you will experience in the next ten years? Possible answers: learn to drive a car, learn to play a musical instrument, learn to speak a foreign language, have a part-time job.

Everyone Grows and Changes

MAIN IDEA As you develop from a baby into an adult, you go through four stages of growth.

WHY LEARN THIS? Learning about how people grow helps you understand the changes you will go through.

VOCABULARY
- life cycle

The Human Life Cycle

birth to two

two to ten

ten to adult

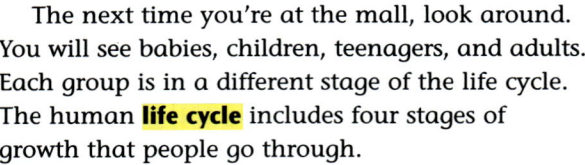
adult to senior

What is the human life cycle?

▲ Birth to two

The next time you're at the mall, look around. You will see babies, children, teenagers, and adults. Each group is in a different stage of the life cycle. The human **life cycle** includes four stages of growth that people go through.

Birth to Two During the first stage of growth in the human life cycle, you were a tiny, helpless baby. You were not able to care for yourself. To stay alive, you had to be cared for by your parents or other adults.

During this first stage of your life, you grew at an amazing rate. From before you were born until about age two, you grew faster than you ever will again. You changed from a baby into an active, more independent two-year-old.

54

MULTILEVEL ACTIVITIES

EASY Write Letters Have students write letters to their families explaining what they would like to do when they grow up. **VERBAL/LOGICAL**

AVERAGE Make Time Lines Have students make time lines that show the changes they have experienced since birth. When the time lines are finished, have students identify the experiences they have in common up to this point in their lives. **KINESTHETIC/SPATIAL**

ADVANCED Diagram Similarities and Differences Have students identify similarities and differences between themselves and a person who is in a different stage of growth. Provide students with Venn diagrams using two overlapping circles. In one circle, students should record things they like to do. In the other, they should record things the other person likes. The overlapping area should contain things both like. Ask students to predict how the overlap will change as they get older. **VERBAL/LOGICAL**

Two to Ten Between the ages of two and ten, you grow more slowly. You grow only about 2 or 3 inches a year.

Your language skills develop quickly during this stage. Now you can read and write. You can use your thinking skills to solve problems.

You can run faster and throw a ball farther than ever before. You can put your physical and mental skills together to learn a complex task, such as riding a bicycle.

▼ Two to ten

Career

Pediatrician

What They Do

Pediatricians are doctors who take care of babies and children. Your parents probably took you to a pediatrician for many checkups when you were a baby. You were measured and weighed to make sure you were healthy and growing normally. Pediatricians make sure children have their vaccinations. They also help children get better when they are ill. Pediatricians may see the same children from the time they are babies until they are adults.

Education and Training

Pediatricians go to college for four years and medical school for four more years. After they go through training in pediatrics for three more years, they can practice medicine.

MATH

Activity Cycles Another kind of cycle is an activity cycle. Activity cycles in pets are fun to observe and to map. Observe your pet at different times of the day. When does it eat? sleep? hunt? exercise by running from room to room or by chasing its tail? What other activities does your pet go through in the course of a day? Make an illustrated activity chart that maps your pet's daily activity cycle, hour by hour. Then, just for fun, calculate how many hours your pet spends on each activity. Compare data with other pet owners in the class.

2 Teach

Discuss

Explain that the word *cycle* refers to a set of events that continues to occur in the same order. A *life cycle* involves a sequence of changes in a living thing from birth to the development of the same form in another generation.

Discuss

Draw students' attention to the fact that the descriptions of the stages of the human life cycle involve more than just physical changes. How we *act* at different stages in our lives is a very distinctive and important part of the human life cycle.

Critical Thinking Why do the stages in the human life cycle involve more than just a change in size? What is responsible for the changes in actions and abilities we experience at different stages? Guide students to reason that it is the development of the human brain, along with the rest of our physical development, that makes it possible for us to change dramatically in many ways during the stages of growth.

Learn from Pictures

Have students look at the picture of the girl and the bicycle.

What is the girl doing in this picture that she could not do in the first stage of her life? figuring out how to fix her bicycle and then doing it

Career

For more information about careers in pediatrics, contact

American Academy of Pediatrics
141 Northwest Point Boulevard
Elk Grove Village, IL 60007-1098

Or visit the **Webliography** on the Teacher Resources page at:
www.harcourtschool.com/health
Keyword health careers

Teach *continued*

Learn from Pictures

Have students look at the pictures on this page. **What is the girl in the picture doing?** graduating from high school

Critical Thinking **What kinds of changes might this girl experience during the next few years?** Possible answers: leave home and go to college, get a job, get married, take a vacation, buy a car.

Life Skills Focus

 *Communicate* Discuss effective communication with students before they complete this activity. Emphasize that anger has no place in effective communication.

Critical Thinking **Why might Peggy's parents have given her sister more privileges than they gave to Peggy?** Possible answers: Peggy's sister is older than Peggy; Peggy's sister has proved to her parents that she is responsible.

Health Background

Erikson's Stages of Life Erik Erikson presented life as eight distinct stages with associated developmental tasks. Each stage can be characterized as follows: (1) Infancy (birth to 1 year) Child is completely dependent. (2) Early Childhood (1–3 years) Child is learning to do things independently. (3) Middle Childhood (3–5 years.) Child begins to make decisions and carry out projects. (4) Late Childhood (6–11 years.) Child investigates surroundings and develops complex skills. (5) Adolescence (12–18 years.) Personal search for identity. (6) Young Adulthood (19–30 years.) Person develops close relationships. (7) Middle Adulthood (31–60 years.) Person concentrates on work and the well-being of family and community. (8) Maturity and Old Age (61 years-to-death) Person tries to understand the meaning of life.

For more background, visit the **Webliography** on the Teacher Resources page at:
www.harcourtschool.com/health
Keyword growth and development

LIFE SKILLS FOCUS

Communicate

Peggy's teenage sister gets a bigger allowance and can stay up later than Peggy does. Peggy thinks this is unfair. Write a script for a conversation in which Peggy talks to her parents about her feelings. Use the steps for communicating shown on page *xii*.

• • •

▶ **Ten to adult**

Ten to Adult
At about age ten or twelve, you will enter the next stage of growth. You will begin to change from a child into an adult. As a teenager you will again grow very fast. Your body will become taller and heavier.

This growth stage usually happens sooner for girls than for boys, but boys catch up and often grow faster at about age fourteen or fifteen. Your body will grow and change when it is the right time for you.

Adult to Senior When you are an adult, you will stop growing taller. As an adult you will decide what kind of job you want to have, whether or not you will get married, and whether or not you will have children. As an older adult, or senior, you will have more free time to learn new things and to enjoy your family and friends.

◀ **Adult to senior**

SCIENCE

Life Cycles Investigate the life cycles of other living things, such as the monarch butterfly or the frog. In the most dramatic life cycle changes, both the physical body and the behavior change in a complete metamorphosis. What other examples of this kind of metamorphosis can you think of? Why aren't our physical changes as humans a true metamorphosis?

GROWTH, DEVELOPMENT, AND REPRODUCTION

Optional lessons on Stages of Growth (pages 2–10) and Physical Changes of Puberty (pages 16–19) are provided in this supplement. Use this component in compliance with state and local guidelines.

younger

older

younger

older

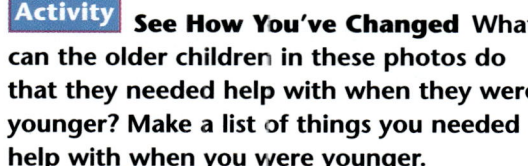

 **Activity** **See How You've Changed** What can the older children in these photos do that they needed help with when they were younger? Make a list of things you needed help with when you were younger.

Remember when you were a baby?

You probably don't remember yourself as a tiny baby, but this is what you were like. You had a large head and wobbly legs. You could grasp a finger and suck to get milk, but adults had to take care of you.

Your fastest growth period began before you were born and lasted until you were two. Your body and brain grew quickly. By the age of two, you could sit up, walk, and talk. Look at pictures of yourself as a baby. Think of all the ways you have changed since then!

JOURNAL

Ask family members to tell you their favorite stories about things you did when you were a baby. Choose your favorite story, and write it in your Health Journal.

LESSON CHECKUP

Check Your Facts

1. During which two stages of the human life cycle do you grow most quickly?

2. **CRITICAL THINKING** What kinds of decisions will you make when you are an adult? What do you think you'll decide to do?

3. What skills do you learn during your second stage of growth?

Set Health Goals

4. List three things you can do now that you couldn't do three years ago. Now list three things you hope to do three years from now.

57

Activity

See How You've Changed Have students recall things they needed help with when they were younger. When did you first learn to do those tasks without help? Have students create a THEN and NOW chart of their own. What new activities or skills might go in the NOW chart when you are older? Possible answers: driving a car, cooking meals.

Health Journal

Tell students to ask their parents to tell them stories about when they were babies. Explain that they should take careful notes, so they can learn the story about themselves to tell on their own.

Project Checkup

Make a Family Book (p. 43) As students create their family books, suggest that some of them may want to write and illustrate a Baby Me story to include in their books.

3 Wrap Up

Lesson Checkup

1. from birth to age two and from teen to adult

2. Possible answers: deciding on a type of job or whether to get married. Accept all reasonable answers.

3. You learn language skills, reading, writing, thinking skills, and more coordinated physical skills, including running and throwing a ball.

4. Answers will vary.

ACTIVITY BOOK, p. 15

Use a Flow Chart **Reading Skills**

Reread the lesson. Find facts to fill in the blanks in the chart below.

Life Cycle

Description	Stages	Growth
tiny, helpless baby cared for by parents	Birth to Two	grow faster than ever will again
become active, more independent		
1. develop language skills—reading, writing	A. Two to Ten	6. grow more slowly, 2 or 3 inches a year
2. can use thinking to solve problems		
3. can run faster		
4. can throw a ball farther		
5. can learn complex skills, such as riding a bicycle		
1. begin to change from child to adult	B. Ten to Adult	3. grow very fast—become taller, heavier
2. girls begin growing sooner than		
1. will decide what kind of job to do	C. Adult to Senior	3. stop growing
2. will decide whether or not to get married and have children		

MEET INDIVIDUAL NEEDS

Kinesthetic Learners Have students devise a trivia game about the human life cycle. Questions and facts about each life cycle stage can be written on index cards. A game board can be developed with spaces for each life cycle stage. Markers can be advanced by rolling a die and may be moved in any direction. The first person to land on and answer a question correctly from each stage wins.

OBJECTIVES

- Describe how growth occurs.
- Compare kinds of cells and how they are designed to do special jobs.
- Describe one kind of growth in addition to physical growth, and the changes that occur as a result.

PROGRAM RESOURCES

 Computer Graphing Activity, Teaching Resources p. 54

 Teaching Transparency 22

VOCABULARY

- cell (p. 58)
- tissues (p. 59)
- organs (p. 59)
- organ system (p. 59)
- growth rate (p. 60)

Daily Safety Tip

For growth to occur, the body needs extra energy. This energy is supplied through the nutrients in a child's diet. Remind students to eat three good meals a day and to choose healthful snacks in order to boost their growing power.

1 Motivate

Discuss with students how they have been growing for years. They have grown both taller and heavier. They have also grown smarter.

What is responsible for these changes? Possible answer: Height is a result of bone growth. Weight is a result of additional bone, muscle, and fat. An increase in the number of connections in the brain (along with experience) has enabled us to become smarter.

 LESSON 4

MAIN IDEA Cells have important jobs to do. When cells divide and multiply, you grow.

WHY LEARN THIS? Learning how you grow helps you understand why it is important to take care of your body.

VOCABULARY
- cell
- tissues
- organs
- organ system
- growth rate

People Grow at Different Rates

How do people grow?

Everything from your nose to your toes grows because of the tiny cells inside you. A **cell** is the smallest working part of your body. Your growth began with one cell. Now you have many cells. During periods of rapid growth, the cells inside your body multiply quickly.

Your bones, skin, blood, and muscles are all made up of cells. Cells contain information your body needs to be able to eat, breathe, and think. By taking good care of your body, you help your cells do their important work.

 Activity **List Differences** Each person starts out as one cell, yet no two people are alike. List ten ways you are different from the people in the photo and from anyone else you know.

58

 ## MULTILEVEL ACTIVITIES

EASY **Make Concept Maps** Have students make concept maps that show the body is made of specific types of cells. Have students refer to the lesson and pages 1–15 for help. VISUAL/LOGICAL

AVERAGE **Diagram the Skull** Tell students that the human skull changes dramatically as we age. Have them find out what their skull looked like when they were born, what it looks like now, and what it will look like when they have finished growing. Have them diagram each stage of growth on posters. Display the posters in the classroom. TACTILE/SPATIAL

ADVANCED **Draw Cartoons** Have students draw cartoons of cells, tissues, organs, and organ systems that include speech bubbles that add explanations. For example, a drawing of the heart could have a bubble saying "I'm all heart, but I started out as a single cell." LINGUISTIC/KINESTHETIC

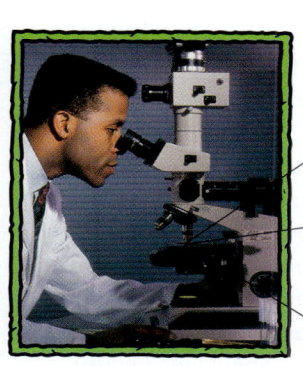

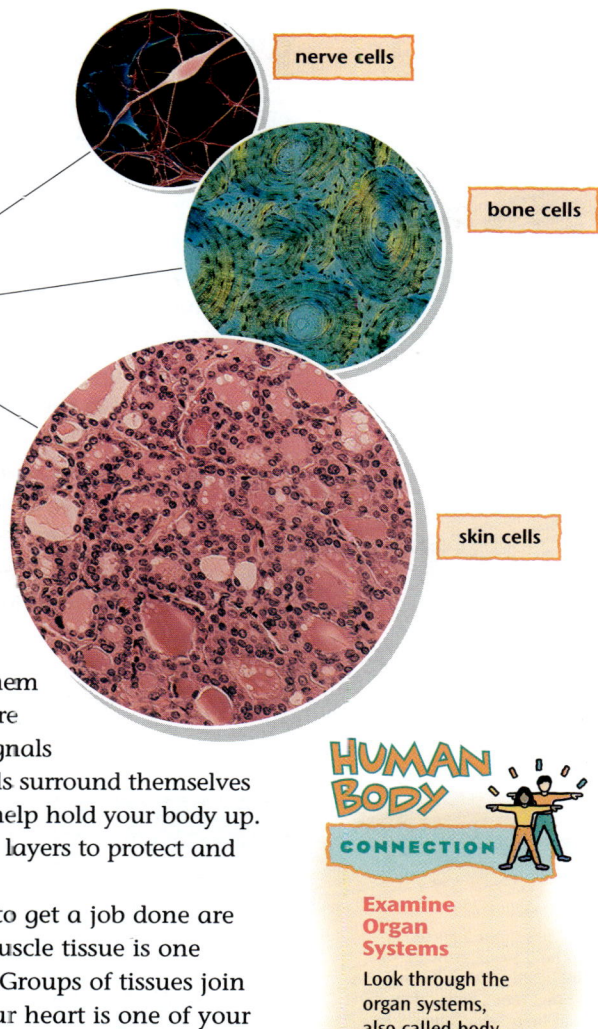

nerve cells

bone cells

skin cells

▲ You need a microscope to see most cells. Each cell's shape helps it do its job.

What do cells do?

Cells come in different shapes and sizes that help them do special jobs. Nerve cells are long and thin. They carry signals through your body. Bone cells surround themselves with a hard material. They help hold your body up. Skin cells are flat. They form layers to protect and cover your body.

Cells that work together to get a job done are called **tissues** (TIH•shooz). Muscle tissue is one kind of tissue in your body. Groups of tissues join together to form **organs**. Your heart is one of your organs. It is made up of different tissues that work together to pump blood through your whole body. Many organs work together in an **organ system**. Your blood, heart, and all your blood vessels together make up your circulatory system.

HUMAN BODY CONNECTION

Examine Organ Systems

Look through the organ systems, also called body systems, on pages 1–15. Pick one organ in each system, and tell what it does.

• • •

59

2 Teach

2 Teach

Activity

List Differences Remind students that it is not any one thing that makes one person different from another person. It is a combination of physical, mental, emotional, and social traits that combine to make each person unique and special. Have each student think of one "fascinating fact" about himself or herself to share with the class.

Discuss

Have students think of tools that are designed to do particular jobs. For example, a spatula's shape is designed to slide under foods, and a spoon is designed to scoop up foods. Explain that in the same way, cells are shaped to do their own special jobs.

Critical Thinking What shape are nerve cells? What does their shape remind you of? electrical wire How do you think their shape helps them do their special job? Possible answer: like electrical wire, nerve cells are thin and long in order to run through the body and carry signals. Ask students the same questions about bone cells and skin cells. Answers will vary, but, in general, students should begin to form analogies between the shapes of different kinds of cells and the jobs they do and the shapes and functions of objects they know.

Human Body Connection

Examine Organ Systems As you refer students to pages 1–15, you might assign organ systems to groups of students to research. Then, have them give oral presentations of their findings, complete with drawings to illustrate the system.

TEACHER TIP

Think in Analogies Thinking in analogies enables students to develop higher order thinking skills, creativity, and scientific literacy. Asking the question, *What else does it remind you of?* keeps students thinking and theorizing. Using this tool, students will come up with metaphors for poems and new raw material to keep them thinking and asking questions. The second question, *Why is it like that?* encourages students to search for patterns and build theories.

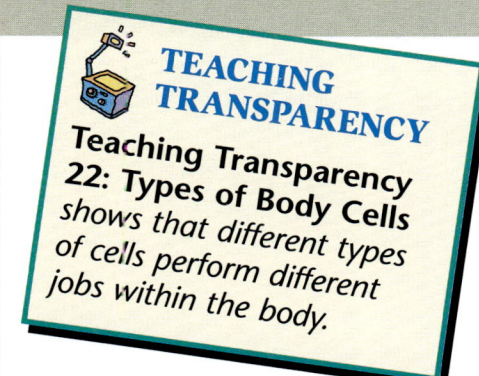

TEACHING TRANSPARENCY

Teaching Transparency 22: Types of Body Cells shows that different types of cells perform different jobs within the body.

Discuss

Ask students if they have ever wondered (or worried) about their own height. Explain that many students their age, and older, worry about their height. They wonder if they will grow or when they will stop growing. They think they are too tall or too short. Take a survey. Ask students to talk with their parents about how they felt about their height when they were children. Have students talk to seniors, other adults, teenagers, and other students their age or slightly older. **What did you find? How many teenagers were worried or upset about their height? What about students who are about your age? Are adults or seniors still worried about their height?**

Critical Thinking **What do you think happens to make most adults feel OK about their height, while many children and teenagers seem to be worried about how tall they are?** Students may reason that by the time you are an adult, you no longer wonder what will happen—you know. Since you can't change it, you get used to it. But when you are younger, you worry that you are not OK and that you will stand out because you are too short or too tall.

Consumer Focus

Access Valid Health Information Students should locate information stating that calcium helps keep bones strong. Explain that if a person doesn't provide the body with calcium the body will take calcium from the bones, which will make the bones weak. Discuss with the students that calcium can be found in other foods than dairy, such as oranges and broccoli.

"We all grow at our own rate."

▲ Have fun and don't worry! Your body is growing just the way it should.

What is the special way you grow?

Your **growth rate** is how quickly or slowly you grow. Everyone goes through the same basic periods of growth, but each person's growth rate is different.

From before birth to age two, you grew very quickly. Your family can tell you how much you changed in a short amount of time when you were a baby. As a teenager you will again grow quickly. In between, your growth rate will be very slow. By the time you are an adult of about age twenty, you will stop growing taller.

Sometimes you may compare yourself to your friends and wonder if you are normal. You may worry that you are growing too much or not enough. Remember, no two people are alike. And there is no one way to grow. You grow in your own time and at your own speed to the height that is right for you.

CONSUMER FOCUS

Access Valid Health Information

Sylvie's mom buys foods to help Sylvie grow up to be healthy. Sylvie's mom knows foods with calcium will help Sylvie's bones to be strong. Use the steps on page xvi to research what calcium is and why it helps Sylvie's bones grow strong.

• • •

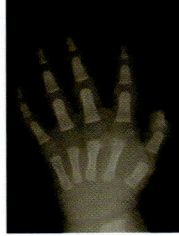
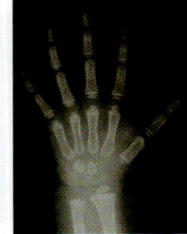

birth   twelve months   eighteen months

▲ Growth happens all through your body. When you were born, you had no wrist bones. But they developed by the time you were eighteen months (one and a half years) old.

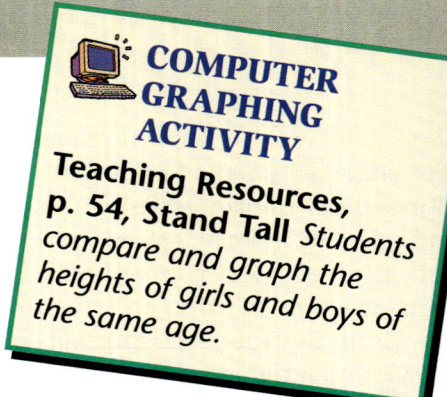

COMPUTER GRAPHING ACTIVITY

Teaching Resources, p. 54, Stand Tall Students compare and graph the heights of girls and boys of the same age.

six months   one year   three years   five years   seven years   ten years

▲ A newborn baby's head is very large. As a person grows, the body gets bigger, but the head size remains about the same.

You grow because the cells inside you divide to make many new cells. You add inches to your height as your bones get longer. You grow stronger as your muscles stretch to cover your growing bones. You also add weight to your body.

Your physical growth is easy to see, but you are growing in other ways, too. As your brain cells grow larger and make new connections, you learn new things. You can think about and solve harder problems. You can begin to be more responsible for yourself. People can count on you in new ways.

LESSON CHECKUP

Check Your Facts

❶ What happens when cells multiply and make many new cells?

❷ Why are cells different shapes?

❸ CRITICAL THINKING Do you ever stop growing?

❹ Tell how cells, tissues, organs, and organ systems are related.

Set Health Goals

❺ Name two ways your growth can let you be a more responsible family member.

61

Discuss

What are some examples of activities you can do and problems you can solve as your brain cells get larger and make new connections? Possible answers: learn a new language; do harder math problems; complete more complex mental tasks such as solving a puzzle and remembering a sequence of numbers or letters; perform more complex physical tasks such as jumping rope or playing string games.

3 Wrap Up

Lesson Checkup

1. Your body grows.

2. Cells have special shapes to help them do their special jobs.

3. Yes. Your body stops growing at about age 20, when you reach adulthood. (Students may also think of "growing" in terms of learning new things, in which case they might say no.)

4. Cells form tissues; tissues form organs; organs form organ systems.

5. Answers will vary, but should include the idea that as your body grows larger and stronger, your mental, emotional, and social abilities grow also.

Health Background

Cell Division Growth takes place in four stages. In stage one, the material in a cell nucleus makes an exact copy of itself. In stage two, the membrane that surrounds the nucleus disappears and the material lines up in the middle of the cell. In stage three, the material separates, half going to each side of the cell. In stage four, new membranes form around each set of nuclear material, forming two nuclei. The cell divides to form two new cells. These cells then divide to form four, then eight, and so on.

For more background, visit the **Webliography** on the Teacher Resources page at:
www.harcourtschool.com/health
Keyword human body

TEACHER TIP

Growing Differences Explain that growth rates differ not only between individuals, but also among the many parts of the body. During certain stages, individuals may appear more clumsy than during other stages. This may be due to one part of the body growing faster than another part. As the body evens out in its development, the individual becomes more coordinated and is able to develop more physical skills, such as dribbling a basketball.

OBJECTIVE

• Identify ways to care for your body.

PROGRAM RESOURCES

• Activity Book, pp. 16–17
• Growth, Devolopment, and Reproduction, p. 32

VOCABULARY

• private (p. 63)

Daily Safety Tip

Help students understand that maintaining good health habits is like putting together a jigsaw puzzle. Discuss with students how diet, exercise, rest, and hygiene are all parts of the health puzzle. If any one piece is missing, the picture is incomplete and good health may be hard to maintain.

1 Motivate

What needs do your body and a car share? Students may reply that they both need fuel, or energy, to work. A car needs gas and oil; the body needs food and water. (Neither cars nor people can run on empty.) Regular maintenance goes a long way toward keeping your car running smoothly; diet and exercise help keep your body healthy. When something is wrong, you take your car to the mechanic and your body to the doctor. They both need to be washed, and both cars and people need rest—they can't run all the time. Draw a chart on the board for students to further develop this analogy. Tell students that they will learn more about diet and exercise later in this book.

MAIN IDEA Your body has important jobs to do. When you take good care of your body, you can grow and develop in healthful ways.

WHY LEARN THIS? Taking good care of your body helps you grow strong and healthy.

VOCABULARY
• private

Taking Care of My Body

The best way to grow healthy and strong is to take good care of your body. When you feel well, your body is telling you that you are doing a good job of taking care of it. When you feel tired or weak, or if you are often ill, your body may be telling you to make some changes.

Getting regular exercise and eating a balanced diet are important. Your body also needs to rest. With enough sleep you will be ready for the day ahead. Keeping your body, hair, nails, and teeth clean is important, too. You will learn more about exercise and diet in Chapters 3 and 4 of this book.

MULTILEVEL ACTIVITIES

EASY **Make Posters** Have students make posters that show ways to care for their bodies in order to ensure healthy growth. Compare students' work. Display the posters in the classroom. **VISUAL/TACTILE**

AVERAGE **List Healthful Snacks** Explain to students that when choosing healthful snacks, it is important to choose snacks from different food groups. Have students come up with a classroom list of healthful snacks that students can use to improve their dietary choices. **LOGICAL/VISUAL**

ADVANCED **Set Exercise Goals** Most children benefit from participation in some kind of sports activities. Have students find out what sorts of teams are available to children their age and make a display for the classroom that shows what team sports they could choose from and how to get in touch with the adults in charge. **VISUAL**

You may have a box of special treasures that you keep **private**, which means they belong only to you. Each family member has a right to private things. You need to respect the privacy of others. Knock before entering a room. Ask before using things that belong to someone else.

Your body is special. There are parts of your body you have a right to keep private. It feels good to get a hug from someone you trust. A pat on the back for a job well done makes you feel great. But there are some touches that don't feel good. It is not proper for someone to touch you on a private part of your body or in a way that makes you feel uncomfortable. Talk to a trusted adult if this happens.

When You Need Help, Talk to a Trusted Adult
- Parent
- Teacher
- Doctor
- Religious leader
- Counselor
- Nurse
- Police officer

▶ A kind touch on the shoulder can make someone feel better.

LESSON CHECKUP

Check Your Facts

❶ Why is it important to take good care of your body?

❷ Tell where to get help with a problem.

Use Life Skills

❸ MAKE DECISIONS Imagine that your friend invites you over to have ice cream. You want to go, but you haven't eaten dinner yet. Use your decision-making skills to make a healthful choice.

63

---

2 Teach

Discuss

After students read page 63, ask them to think of something they own that is very special to them. **Where do you keep this special object? How do you take care of it?** Explain that their bodies are also very special and belong to them alone. Their bodies deserve the same care and respect as the objects mentioned earlier. Keeping your body clean, feeding it healthful food, and giving it plenty of rest are good ways to let your body know you care. Keeping parts of your body private is another way to keep it safe, just as you do your special possessions.

3 Wrap Up

Lesson Checkup

1. Taking good care of your body is the best way to grow healthy and strong so that you can do the things you want to do.

2. When you need help, talk to a trusted adult.

3. Answers will vary but should exhibit the knowledge that eating ice cream before dinner is a poor nutritional choice.

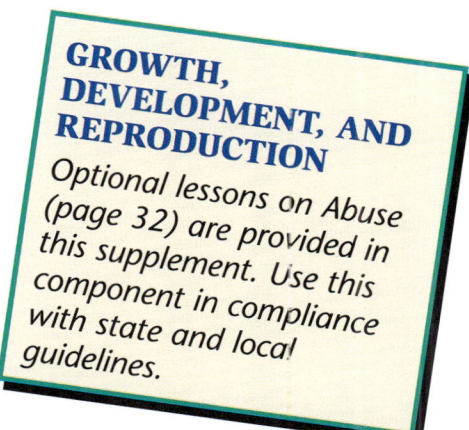

GROWTH, DEVELOPMENT, AND REPRODUCTION

Optional lessons on Abuse (page 32) are provided in this supplement. Use this component in compliance with state and local guidelines.

Use Vocabulary 4 pts. each

1. sibling
2. organs
3. growth rate
4. cell
5. life cycle
6. private
7. divorce
8. tissues
9. values
10. family
11. organ system

Check Your Facts 6 pts. each

12. Possible answers: set the table, take care of a pet, wash dishes.

13. moving, divorce or remarriage, a new baby, a death of a pet (or family member)

14. birth to two; two to ten; ten to adult; adult to senior

15. skin cells, nerve cells, bone cells

16. Possible answers: eat healthful foods, get regular checkups, get plenty of rest, exercise, keep the body clean, be vaccinated against disease.

CHAPTER 2 Review

USE VOCABULARY

cell (p. 58)	growth rate (p. 60)	organs (p. 59)	tissues (p. 59)
divorce (p. 49)	life cycle (p. 54)	private (p. 63)	values (p. 44)
family (p. 44)	organ system (p. 59)	sibling (p. 49)	

Use the terms above to complete the sentences. Page numbers in ( ) tell you where to look in the chapter if you need help.

1. Your brother or sister is called your _____.

2. Tissues work together to form _____.

3. Your _____ is very fast between birth and two years of age.

4. Your growth began with one _____.

5. Birth to age two is one stage in the human _____.

6. When you keep something _____, it belongs only to you.

7. When parents _____, they are no longer married to each other.

8. Cells that work together are called _____.

9. Strong beliefs taught in families are called _____.

10. Your _____ is the group of people you live with.

11. Many organs work together to form a(n) _____.

CHECK YOUR FACTS

Page numbers in ( ) tell you where to look in the chapter if you need help.

12. Name three jobs you can do to help as a member of your family. (p. 46)

13. Name four big changes that can happen in families. (pp. 48–49)

14. List the four stages of growth in the human life cycle. (pp. 54–56)

15. Name the types of cells in the pictures shown here. (p. 59)

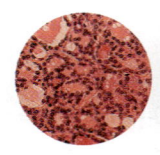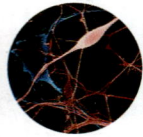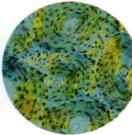

16. Name three good ways to take care of your body. (p. 62)

THINK CRITICALLY

17. How can you respect each family member's right to privacy? How can family members respect yours?

18. Study the photo below. Why is it important to understand that all people grow at their own rates and in their own time?

APPLY LIFE SKILLS

19. **Resolve Conflicts** Suppose a friend invites you over on the night your family has planned to do something together. What will you say to your friend, and why?

20. **Communicate** Suppose someone touches you in a way that does not feel comfortable to you. What would you say or do, and why?

Promote Health  Home and Community

1. In your school, take a survey of the chores children do around the house. Sort the chores by grade level. Design and make a poster to show your results.

2. Make a growth chart, and ask your family members to record their heights on the chart each month for a year. Be sure to record your height, too. As each month passes, notice how much some family members are growing taller. At the end of the year, add up the number of inches each person grew. Use the numbers to show which stage of the life cycle each person is in.

Think Critically 6 pts. each

17. Possible answer: I can respect other family members' right to privacy by knocking on doors before I enter and leaving other people's things alone. Other people could do the same for me.

18. Possible answer: A person may be a lot taller or shorter than his or her friends during some period of life. By looking at a wide range of people, you can see these growth differences and realize that most of them will even themselves out in time.

Apply Life Skills 7 pts. each

19. Possible answers: I would think about the situation from my family's point of view. I would tell my friend that, because my family had prior plans, those plans come first.

20. Possible answers: I would tell the person to stop and then tell a trusted adult about the incident.

PERFORMANCE ASSESSMENT

Project—Make a Family Book

The chapter project (introduced on page 43) can be used for individual or team performance assessment. Allow students the opportunity to revise and complete their projects before submitting them for evaluation. Students can use the Project Summary Sheet (Assessment Guide, p. 17) to tell about their projects. You can use the rubric provided on the Project Evaluation Sheet (Assessment Guide, p. 25) to evaluate student performance.

Activities

"When I Was Your Age . . . "

At Home • Interview older family members, and list the jobs they did when they were your age. Which jobs are the same as the ones you do? Which are different?

Circles of Life

With a Team • Find out about the life cycles of other living things. How are their stages of growth the same as the stages in the human life cycle? How are they different?

Picture Perfect

With a Partner • Make a poster of the human life cycle. Draw a big circle, and divide it into four parts to represent each stage. Then cut out pictures, and paste them in each section. Be sure your chart shows how humans may look and what they may do at each stage of life.

Movin' On

On Your Own • Imagine that you have moved several times and you have been asked to help other children your age who are moving. Make a booklet suggesting ways to help them deal with the move.

66

Chapter Test

"Me and My Family" — Chapter 2 Test

Write *T* or *F* to show if the sentence is true or false.

F 1. A family is a group of people you work with or go to school with.

T 2. Your family makes sure your basic needs are met.

T 3. Families also teach values.

F 4. Values are strong teachings about how to cheat other people.

F 5. All families look the same.

T 6. Every family member has responsibilities.

T 7. You are being responsible when you do a job without waiting to be asked.

T 8. Playing together as a family helps make everyone happy.

F 9. Respecting family members is not an important thing to do.

T 10. Children first learn about right and wrong in their families.

Choose the best words from the word bank to complete the story below.

| family rules | changes | family | divorce |
| communicate | remarriage | sibling | |

The Boyle family is going through some hard 11. **changes**. Mr. and Mrs. Boyle are getting a 12. **divorce**. They are worried about their children. Patrick is nine years old, and he has one 13. **sibling**, who is four years old. Mr. and Mrs. Boyle try to 14. **communicate** often with their children. They want the children to know that they will always be a 15. **family** even when big changes like this one happen.

Match the facts about the human life cycle with the correct stages of growth. Write the letter of the sentences on the lines at the left.

a 16. Birth to Two   **c** 17. Two to Ten

d 18. Ten to Adult   **b** 19. Adult to Senior

a. During this stage, a person grows at an amazing rate.

b. During this stage, a person decides whether or not to get married.

c. During this stage, a person's language skills develop quickly. The person can do complex tasks, such as riding a bicycle.

d. During this stage, a person changes from a child into an adult.

20. List three ways in which you have changed since you were a baby.
Possible answers: I can now do many things for myself; I can walk and talk and sit up; I have grown much larger; I can read and write.

Write the letter of the best answer on the line at the left.

b 21. What is the smallest working part of your body?
a. skin   b. cell   c. blood   d. organ

d 22. Cells that are long and thin and carry signals through your body are called _____ cells.
a. bone   b. heart   c. skin   d. nerve

a 23. Cells that work together to get a job done are called _____.
a. tissues   b. bone cells   c. organs   d. nerve cells

c 24. Groups of tissues join together to form _____.
a. organ   b. tissues   c. organs   d. muscles
systems

c 25. Your growth rate is _____.
a. how quickly you become an adult
b. how slow you are at learning new things
c. how quickly or slowly you grow
d. how you grew as a baby

26. Jose is worried about how he is growing. His twin sister is already four inches taller than he is. He is worried that his body might not be growing as it should. What could you tell Jose to help him feel better about his growth rate?
Possible answers: everyone grows at his or her own rate; his body is growing just as it should; growth spurts happen to children at different ages; he is unique—not even his twin is exactly like him.

27. Name three good health habits you and your classmates could practice to make sure your bodies stay healthy and grow strong.
Possible answers: eat healthful foods, get regular checkups, get plenty of rest, be vaccinated against disease, keep your body clean, exercise.

28. Sue Ann doesn't like the way an adult member of her family touches her. What should she do?
Sue Ann should tell the person to stop and then tell a trusted adult about what is happening.

29. What is wrong with comparing yourself to other people your age?
Comparing myself to others might make me feel as if I am not growing fast enough or big enough; I might feel something is wrong with me.

30. Name the parts of your body that work together to make up the circulatory system.
blood, heart, and blood vessels

Multiple Choice

Choose the letter of the correct answer.

1. Basic needs are met in your ____.
   a. club   b. family
   c. cells   d. life cycle

2. Your whole body is made up of ____.
   a. growth   b. cells
   c. organs   d. water

3. Cleaning your room shows you are ____.
   a. responsible   b. healthy
   c. honest   d. happy

4. When tired, your body needs ____.
   a. food   b. exercise
   c. rest   d. water

5. Your first stage of growth ended at ____.
   a. two   b. adulthood
   c. twelve   d. sixteen

Modified True or False

Write *true* or *false*. If a sentence is false, replace the underlined term to make the sentence true.

6. Listening respectfully is a good way to <u>communicate</u>.

7. A new <u>doctor</u> causes family changes.

8. Tissues that work together form <u>organs</u>.

9. During the <u>third</u> stage of growth, you are becoming a senior.

10. A pediatrician is a doctor who specializes in the care of <u>adults</u>.

11. Families teach <u>jobs</u>, like honesty.

12. It is important to respect other people's <u>privacy</u>.

13. Teenagers grow at <u>the same</u> rates.

14. As <u>an adult</u> you make lots of decisions.

15. Once you are about <u>twelve</u> years old, you will not grow any taller.

Short Answer

Write a complete sentence to answer each question.

16. What important jobs do cells do?

17. Who can you talk to if someone touches you in a way that makes you uncomfortable?

18. How can families help each other?

19. List two skills that develop between the ages of two and ten.

20. If a younger sibling is having a hard day, how can you show you care?

Writing in Health

Write paragraphs to answer each item.

21. Describe what it feels like when big changes happen in families.

22. During the two-to-ten stage, many children learn to ride a bicycle. List some skills needed to ride a bike.

67

Writing in Health (10 pts. each)

Sample answers are shown; accept other reasonable answers.

21. Answers should indicate that students understand that a wide range of feelings are possible when changes occur in families, and these feelings are normal.

22. Skills needed to ride a bike include having a good sense of balance, being able to look and listen for traffic and react to situations around you, being responsible to wear a helmet each time you ride.

Test

CHAPTER 2

Two options are provided for Chapter Tests—the in-book test and the reproducible test in the Assessment Guide. In addition to providing students with the opportunity to show what they have learned, both tests provide practice in taking standardized tests.

Multiple Choice (2 pts. each)

1. b   3. a   5. a
2. b   4. c

Modified True or False (3 pts. each)

6. true

7. false; sibling, brother, or sister

8. true

9. false; fourth

10. false; children

11. false; values

12. true

13. false; different

14. true

15. false; 20

Short Answer (8 pts. each)

Sample answers are shown; accept other reasonable answers.

16. Cells carry nerve signals throughout the body, hold the body up, and carry out all life processes.

17. Students may suggest a parent or other trusted adult.

18. Families can work together to do chores around the house and to meet goals that will let them have fun together.

19. reading, writing, riding a bike

20. Possible answers: read a book or play a game with the sibling, hug them, and so on.

Keeping My Body Fit

Chapter Organizer

Lesson	Objectives	Vocabulary	Program Resources
Introduce the Chapter pp. 68–69	• Preview the chapter. • Begin chapter project.		• School-Home Connection, TR p. 37 • Assessment Guide, p. 29 • Read-Aloud Anthology, p. RA-4 Teaching Transparency 3—Graphic Organizer
Lesson 1 ✓ 1·2·4 **Caring for My Skin** pp. 70–73 Pacing: 1 class period	• Explain how and why to keep skin clean. • Explain how and why to protect skin and eyes from the sun.	pores bacteria sunscreen	• Activity Book, p. 18

Lesson 2 ✓ 1·2·4
Caring for My Teeth and Gums pp. 74–77
Pacing: 1 class period
	• Explain how plaque can lead to cavities and loss of teeth.
	• Describe and demonstrate how to brush and floss correctly.
	• Explain how to protect teeth from injury.
		plaque
		cavity
		dental floss
		fluoride
			• Activity Book, p. 19
			  Teaching Transparency 23
			  Computer Graphing Activity, TR p. 55

Lesson 3 ✓ 1·2·4 **Caring for My Ears and Nose** pp. 78–81 Pacing: 1 class period	• Explain how the parts of the ear function. • Describe how to take good care of the ears and the nose.	ear canal eardrum	• Activity Book, p. 20 Teaching Transparency 11
Lesson 4 ✓ 1·3·6 **Exercise and Rest for Fun and Health** pp. 82–85 Pacing: 1 class period	• Describe different ways exercise helps the body. • Explain how and why to get aerobic exercise. • Explain why sleep is helpful.	exercise aerobic exercises	Computer Graphing Activity, TR p. 56
Life Skills ✓ 1·3·6 **Set Goals** pp. 86–87 Pacing: 1 class period	• Identify goal-setting steps. • Practice goal-setting steps to get enough rest.		• Activity Book, p. 21 HEALTH VIDEO: The Cleanup Kids
Lesson 5 ✓ 1·3·6 **Staying Safe While Exercising** pp. 88–91 Pacing: 1 class period	• Explain how to use safety gear, warm-ups, cool-downs, and water to stay safe during exercise. • Describe what to do in case of injury.	warm-up cool-down	• Activity Book, pp. 22–23
Chapter Review and Test ✓ 1·7 pp. 92–95	• Assess chapter objectives and project. • Provide extension activities.		• Chapter Test and Project Evaluation Sheet, Assessment Guide, pp. 26–29

 National Health Education Standards
A complete list of the Standards is provided on the next page.

Key: TR = Teaching Resources

National Health Education Standards

1. Comprehend concepts related to health promotion and disease prevention.
2. Access valid health information and health-promoting products and services.
3. Practice health-enhancing behaviors and reduce health risks.
4. Analyze the influence of culture, media, technology, and other factors on health.
5. Use interpersonal communication skills to enhance health.
6. Use goal-setting and decision-making skills to enhance health.
7. Advocate for personal, family, and community health.

Math
- Graph Exercise Favorites, p. 68C
- Acd Up Brushings, p. 76
- Add Up a Week's Exercise, p. 89

Art
- Wash-Hands Poster, p. 71
- Draw A Dream, p. 85

Physical Education
- Daily Fitness, p. 87

Curriculum Integration
Use these topics to integrate health into your daily planning.

Social Studies
- Dressing for the Sun, p. 68C
- Exercise Long Ago, p. 89

Drama
- Skits for Health, p. 68C

Science
- What Is Smell? p. 68C
- Research the Sun, p. 72
- Nocturnal Animals, p. 84

Language Arts
- A Dirty Day, p. 71
- Write a Story, p. 80
- A Pleasant Sound, p. 81
- Sleep Poems, p. 84
- Sleeping and Dreaming, p. 85

ASSESSMENT OPTIONS

Portfolio Assessment
Have students select their best work from the following suggestions:
- **Wash-Hands Posters,** p. 71
- **Sleepy Time,** p. 94
- **Warm-up and Cool-down Collage,** p. 94

Student Self-Assessment
- **Journal Notes,** p. 76
- **Set Health Goals,** pp. 73, 81, 91
- **Use Life Skills,** pp. 77, 85

Daily Assessment
- **Check Your Facts,** pp. 73, 77, 81, 85, 91

Performance Assessment
- **Chapter Project: Plan a Fitness Game,** pp. 69, 83, 91, 93
- **Project Evaluation Guide,** Assessment Guide, p. 29

Formal Assessment
- **Chapter Review,** pp. 92–93
- **In-Book Test,** p. 95
- **Chapter Test,** Assessment Guide, pp. 26–28

Cross-Curricular Activities

Math

Graph Exercise Favorites

Have students take a survey of ten people in a group, such as ten class members, team members, third graders, school personnel, relatives, or neighbors.

- Have students ask what healthful sport or activity is a person's favorite.
- Students should make a bar graph of the results. At the top of the graph, students should identify the group they interviewed (Ms. Smith's Class, Softball Team, and so on).
- Post the graphs on the board, and discuss similarities and differences among groups.

Science

What Is Smell?

Have students work in groups to research the sense of smell. Students can present their findings in reports with pictures and diagrams.

- Have them find out the different kinds of smells people can detect and provide an example of each one. (One system lists seven: camphoraceous, musky, floral, pepperminty, ethereal, pungent, putrid.)
- Tell students to explain exactly how smell travels from the source to the nose, and from the nose to the brain.
- Have them explore how the sense of smell differs among animals.

Social Studies

Dressing for the Sun

Provide students with books or access to the library for research.

- Have students find examples of traditional clothing people in different parts of the world wear (or wore) in the sun.
- Students may draw pictures or cut pictures from old magazines and newspapers to show the kinds of hats, shoes, shirts, pants, and so on that people use for comfort, protection, and style.

Drama

Skits for Health

Have groups of students think of a health issue suggested by the chapter, such as protecting the skin from sun or using safety gear in sports.

- Have them plan a short skit that demonstrates healthful choices or actions that relate to their health issue.
- They should use words and movement to get across their idea.

Bulletin Board

Set up the bulletin board with a central box labeled *Places to Exercise*. Draw four spikes with the labels *In Any Room, In a Special Room, Outside on a Field or Court, Somewhere Outside*.

- Have students gather pictures that show places people exercise. They can use old magazines, newspapers, and photographs, or make their own drawings.
- For each picture, have students make a label on an index card that tells what sport or sports take place here and what kind of exercise each sport provides.
- Have them place their pictures around the bulletin board title on the correct spokes of the web.

Resources

Books for Students

Sandeman, Anna. ***Body Books: Eating.*** Watts Publishing Group, 2000. Easy-to-read, colorful book packed with information to help children learn about themselves. **EASY**

Showers, Paul. ***Sleep is for Everyone.*** HarperCollins, 1997. Discusses the importance of sleep and what happens to our brains and bodies when we sleep. **AVERAGE**

Parsons, Alexandra. ***Fit for Life.*** Watts Publishing Group, 1996. Provides information on healthful living, eating, grooming habits, and fitness. **ADVANCED**

Books for Teachers and Families

Kalish, Susan. ***Your Child's Fitness: Practical Advice for Parents.*** Human Kinetics Publications, 1996. This book offers solid advice to adults as they work to make family fitness a priority.

Virgilio, Stephen J. ***Fitness Education for Children: A Team Approach.*** Human Kinetics Publications, 1997. This comprehensive resource includes more than 100 practical activities on good health and fitness.

Videos

Sun Sense. Marsh Media, 1997. (10 minutes) Helps children learn to enjoy the sunshine while protecting themselves from the harmful effects of UV rays.

My Body, My Buddy: Healthy Habits. Rainbow Educational Media, 1993. (15 minutes) Emphasizes that healthful habits that are learned early last a lifetime.

The Magic School Bus Flexes Its Muscles. Scholastic, Inc., 1997. (30 minutes) Ms. Frizzle's class learns the importance of how muscles and joints work together in this fun video.

Health Video Series by Harcourt
The Cleanup Kids
This video is referenced at point-of-use in this Teacher's Edition.

GO ONLINE Your Health Webliography

The **Webliography** provides links to the Health Background and teaching resources that will support you as you teach the topics in *Your Health.* Simply choose a keyword and you will be taken to a page of links with descriptions of the content you can obtain at each site. The **Webliography** is located on the Teacher Resources page at **www.harcourtschool.com/health** Please review websites before referring your students to them.

Organizations and Agencies

National Institute of Child Health and Human Development
Bldg. 31, Room 2A32, MSC 2425
31 Center Drive
Bethesda, MD 20892-2425
Conducts research on the processes that determine the health of children and their families.

Better Hearing Institute
515 King Street
Alexandria, VA 22314
Works to inform the hearing-impared public about hearing loss and rehabilitation.

For more information about health organizations and agencies, please see the ***Teaching Resources*** book.

Community Health

School Athletes Invite older students who participate in various school sports and activities to visit to discuss safety in their sports. Have the athletes bring in and show students some of the clothing and safety gear that are appropriate to their sports. Have them discuss any safety practices they follow when they prepare for or participate in games or competitions.

Free and Inexpensive Material

American Academy of Dermatology
930 North Meacham Road
Schaumburg, IL 60168-4014
847-330-0230
Their "Block the Sun, Not the Fun!" Program provides teachers with a guide and posters on sun safety.

Will Rogers Institute
1640 Marengo Street, Suite 406
Los Angeles, CA 90033
877-957-7575 ext. 208
Provides free educational booklets on walking for fun and fitness.

Note that information, while correct at time of publication, is subject to change.

Visit **The Harcourt Learning Site** for related links, activities, resources, and the health **Webliography**.

www.harcourtschool.com

"Wellness . . . is a way of living that stresses taking steps to prevent illness and prolong our lives."

—*The Wellness Encyclopedia*

CHAPTER SUMMARY

In this chapter students
- learn what can cause problems with and describe how to care for their skin, teeth, gums, ears, and nose.
- identify the importance of aerobic exercise, other types of exercise, rest, and sleep.
- learn how to exercise safely and what to do in case of injury.

LIFE SKILLS Students practice *setting goals* in order to get enough rest.

CONSUMER HEALTH Students investigate how the services of a physical therapist can help with healing.

 HUMAN BODY Students examine the structure of the skin and the function of the nose as a sense organ.

68

Literature Springboard

Use the poem "A Pig Is Never Blamed" to spark interest in the chapter topic. See the Read-Aloud Anthology on page RA-4 of this Teacher's Edition.

School-Home Connection

Distribute copies of the School-Home Connection (in English or Spanish), TR page 37. Have students take the page home to share with their families as you begin this chapter.

Follow Up Have volunteers share the information with the class about expiration dates. Help students draw conclusions about which foods stay fresh the longest.

Alternative Use the School-Home Connection page as a classroom resource for enrichment activities.

TEACHING RESOURCES, p. 37

Dear Family Member,

In Chapter 3, Keeping My Body Fit, our class will learn healthful habits for protecting skin, teeth, gums, hearing, and vision. In addition, we will learn the importance of exercise in staying healthy as well as some techniques for exercising safely.

Family Activity

People use a variety of products each day to protect and care for their skin, teeth, hearing, and vision. With your child, make an inventory of the health care products currently found in your home.

Help your child record the results of the inventory in the following chart. What does the chart tell you about your family? For example, if your family includes elderly persons, then the chart might include products for cleaning dentures. If your family includes teenagers, then the chart might have many skin-care products.

My Family's Health-Care Products

Skin	Teeth/Gums	Ears/Hearing	Eyes/Vision

Family Reading

The following books can help you and your family learn more about the topics covered in this chapter. Books should always be chosen with the approval of an adult family member.
- Sandeman, Anna. *Body Books: Eating.* Watts Publishing Group, 2000. Easy-to-read, colorful book packed with information to help children learn about themselves. EASY
- Showers, Paul. *Sleep Is for Everyone.* HarperCollins, 1997. Discusses the importance of sleep and what happens to our brains and bodies when we sleep. AVERAGE
- Parsons, Alexandra. *Fit for Life.* Watts Publishing Group, 1996. Provides information on healthful living, eating, grooming habits, and fitness. ADVANCED

Thank you for participating in our study of health.

Sincerely,

Keeping My Body Fit

PLAN A FITNESS GAME

Running, swimming, riding a bike, jumping rope, and even walking are different kinds of exercise. As you read through this chapter, you will learn that exercise is an important part of taking care of your body. Plan a fitness game for your class to play. Be sure your game includes several kinds of exercise that will help your body in different ways.

For other activities, visit the Harcourt Learning Site. www.harcourtschool.com

69

Teaching Transparency 3—Graphic Organizer

3 Chapter 3 Graphic Organizer

Keeping My Body Fit

Caring for My Skin
1. _wash_ hands
2. bath or _shower_
3. protect _skin_ from sunburn

Caring for My Ears and Nose
1. _noise_ can hurt
2. _protect_ ears
3. _wash_ outside of ears
4. _blow_ nose gently

Exercise and Rest for Fun and Health
1. _aerobic exercise_
2. _rest_
3. _sleep_

Caring for My Teeth and Gums
1. _floss_
2. _brush_
3. _protect_

Staying Safe While Exercising
1. _safety gear_
2. _warm-up_
3. _cool-down_

Introduce the Chapter

PLAN A FITNESS GAME

Prior Knowledge Use this activity as a baseline assessment of students' understanding of personal health and fitness. Have students keep track of different types of exercise as they plan their games.

Performance Assessment The project can be used for performance assessment. Before students begin, explain how you will evaluate their performance. (See the Project Evaluation Sheet, Assessment Guide, p. 29.)

Prereading Strategies

Scan the Chapter Have students preview the chapter content by scanning the titles, headings, pictures, and charts. Ask volunteers to speculate on what they will learn.

Preview Vocabulary As students scan the chapter, point out the vocabulary words listed at the beginning of each lesson and pronounce each word. Have students sort the words into two groups: familiar words and unfamiliar words. Ask volunteers for definitions of words familiar to them. Discuss these for accuracy. If some words still remain unfamiliar, students can find out more about them in the glossary.

Visualize Key Concepts Display the Graphic Organizer Transparency. You may also wish to distribute photocopies to students. Have students complete the organizer as they work through the chapter. Suggested concepts for students to fill in are shown.

Follow Up Review the completed organizer with students as preparation for the Chapter Review and Chapter Tests.

OBJECTIVES

- Explain how and why to keep skin clean.
- Explain how and why to protect skin and eyes from the sun.

PROGRAM RESOURCES

- Activity Book, p. 18

VOCABULARY

- pores (p. 70)
- bacteria (p. 70)
- sunscreen (p. 73)

Daily Safety Tip

Students may not be aware that even if their hair is clean and well kept, they can get lice. Lice are tiny arachnids that lay eggs along hair shafts. Lice can make the scalp itchy and red. Tell students that they should not use someone else's comb, brush, pillow, or hat. Washing with a special shampoo can kill lice, and combing with a special comb removes nits, or lice eggs.

1 Motivate

Optional Materials **hand lens**

Have students examine their hands with a hand lens. Suggest they look for dirt, dry skin, or any foreign objects on the skin. (As an alternative, students can look closely at their hands.) Tell them to think about when they last washed their hands. Lead students to understand that their hands might be dirty even though their hands look clean. Tell them that there are thousands of kinds of very, very small organisms called bacteria that live on their hands all the time.

As a footnote, let students know that over-washing their hands can dry out the skin and damage it. Stress the times they should wash their hands: after using the bathroom, before eating or handling food, and before putting your hands in your mouth.

70

LESSON 1

MAIN IDEA Caring for your skin helps you stay healthy.

WHY LEARN THIS? You can use what you learn to practice good skin care.

VOCABULARY
- pores
- bacteria
- sunscreen

Caring for My Skin

Have you ever had an itchy rash? If so, you know skin problems can be annoying. You can't stop all skin problems. But you can stop many of them. Caring for your skin helps you stay healthy and look good too.

How can I keep my skin clean?

Do you know your skin has holes in it? These tiny holes are called **pores** (POHRZ). Sweat comes up through your pores. Sweat helps cool your body. Oil comes up to the surface of the skin along hairs. Oil helps keep your skin soft.

Oil, sweat, and dirt collect on your skin. Bacteria grow on your skin too. **Bacteria** (bak•TIR•ee•uh) are living things that are so tiny you cannot see them. Some bacteria cause illness. Washing with soap and warm water is the best way to get rid of oil, sweat, dirt, and bacteria on your skin.

HUMAN BODY CONNECTION

Under Your Skin

Your skin is more than a simple covering for your body. Turn to page 3 of The Amazing Human Body to find out what lies beneath the surface of your skin.

▶ It's a good idea to wash your hands several times a day.

70

MULTILEVEL ACTIVITIES

EASY **Make a List** Provide a sheet of poster board, and have students make an illustrated list of the items they need to spend a safe day in the sun. Students should tell the purpose of each item. Display the poster in the classroom. **VISUAL/LOGICAL**

AVERAGE **Prepare a Demonstration** Have students bring in squares of many kinds of material. Test each square by holding it in front of a lightbulb. Rank the materials in order from the one that lets through the least light to the one that lets through the most light. Based on their findings, ask students to prepare a demonstration about the material that best protects you from the sun. **KINESTHETIC/LOGICAL**

ADVANCED **Research Bacteria** Provide students with resource materials to research bacteria. Encourage them to draw pictures of the different-shaped bacteria: rod-shaped, spiral-shaped, and round. Have students find an example of each shape and tell what that bacterium does. **VISUAL**

Washing your hands is very important. When your hands are clean, you are less likely to catch or spread illnesses such as colds. Always wash your hands before you eat. Wash your hands after using the bathroom. Wash your hands right away if you sneeze or cough into them. If you touch an animal, wash your hands soon afterward.

To clean your whole body, take a bath or shower. Bathe whenever you are dirty or sweaty. Some people need to bathe every day. Others can skip a day if they don't get too dirty or sweaty.

▼ Bath time can be relaxing and fun. A back brush helps you wash hard-to-reach spots.

2 Teach

Discuss

Explain that the word *pore* means "a tiny opening."

What are pores and what do they do? tiny holes in skin that let sweat come to the surface

Critical Thinking **What is the main difference between bacteria and the other things that collect on your skin?** Bacteria are living things.

Human Body Connection

Under Your Skin As students study the diagram, point out that the skin consists of two main layers, the top layer, or epidermis, and the bottom layer, or dermis.

Discuss

Explain to students that viruses, such as those that cause colds can easily pass from unwashed hands to the mouth. But that is not the most likely way to catch a cold. Touching your eyes can bring the virus to the tear ducts, which are connected directly to the nose—a place where cold viruses grow well.

Learn from Pictures

Have students look at the picture and tell why bathing or showering is important. Discuss how to decide how often to wash (when you are dirty or sweaty, when you've been playing very hard, and so on).

LANGUAGE ARTS

A Dirty Day Have students write short stories describing someone's activities during a particular dirty day. The main character can be the student, another person, an imaginary creature, or an animal.

ART

Wash-Hands Posters Have students draw and color posters that show a time you should wash your hands. Students should include information explaining why you should wash your hands at that time.

Health Background

Bacteria are one-celled organisms, so small that 25,000 of them could be lined up to make 1 inch (2.5 cm). Even though they are tiny, they share all the characteristics of other living things: they grow and change, they move, they reproduce. Bacteria live everywhere and on everything, often getting the food they need from what they live on.

Discuss

A sunburn causes the same reactions in the skin as a burn from a hot object.

Critical Thinking Why should you avoid a sunburn? It can be painful now, and later it can cause tough or wrinkled skin or even skin cancer.

Problem Solving Some of your friends think having tanned skin looks great. They want you to get a tan too. **Should you listen to them? Why or why not?** No; because even though a tan doesn't cause your skin to hurt the way a sunburn does, it causes skin damage.

Learn from Pictures

Have students look at the picture and read the caption question. List students' answers on the board. wearing hats and sunglasses, using sunscreen Ask volunteers to suggest other ways they protect themselves from the sun.

Health Background

Sunscreens contain chemicals that absorb, but don't block, ultraviolet light. By absorbing some of the light, they allow a person to extend time in the sun. All sunscreens are marked with a numerical sun protection factor, or SPF. The SPF represents the ratio of the time a person would have to be in the sun with the sunscreen on to get a slight redness of the skin versus the time a slight redness would occur without the sunscreen. Thus, an SPF of 15 (15:1) means that a person would have to be in the sun 15 times longer than normal to be affected harmfully.

PABA, or paraaminobenzoic acid, causes allergic reactions in some people. Children should avoid sunscreens with PABA.

For more background, visit the **Webliography** on the Teacher Resources page at:
www.harcourtschool.com/health
Keyword personal care

Myth: A tan is a sign of good health.

Fact: There is no such thing as a "healthful tan." A tan means your skin has been in the sun's harmful rays.

• • • • • • •

How can I protect my skin from the sun?

The sun gives off harmful rays. You cannot see the rays, but they can burn you. This kind of burn is called a sunburn. A sunburn goes away in a few days. The real harm from too much sun shows up years later. Skin may get tough. It may get very wrinkled. Skin cancer, a disease that can be deadly, may occur.

Skin damage can happen even if you never get a sunburn. It can happen if you get a tan. Everyone needs protection from the sun.

Everyone needs to use sunscreen!

▼ How are these children protecting themselves from the sun?

72

SCIENCE

Research the Sun Have students research the sun and list ways sunlight is helpful—such as for photosynthesis, as a source of natural light and heat, and for solar energy—and ways it can be harmful. Suggest students find out why the sun's rays are more of a danger now than in the past.

TEACHER TIP

Skin Color and Sun Damage Students with darkly pigmented skin may feel that they do not have to worry about sun damage to their skin. Remind all students that no matter what color skin they have, they can get a sunburn. Everyone needs protection from damaging sun rays.

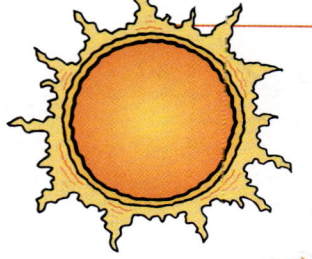

The sun is strongest in the middle of the day. So try to limit your time outdoors to early morning, late afternoon, or evening. If you do go out in the middle of the day, cover up. Your clothes will help protect you from the sun. Wear long sleeves and long pants. If it is hot, wear loose clothes that are light in weight and light colored. They will help you stay cool. Wear a hat to shade your face.

Rub sunscreen on any uncovered skin. **Sunscreen** is a lotion or cream that can protect you from the sun's harmful rays. Some sunscreens block almost all harmful rays. Other sunscreens give you just a little protection. Before you go outside, ask an adult in your family which sunscreen is best for you.

Your eyes also need protection from the sun. Over time the sun's rays can harm your eyes. Wearing sunglasses is the best way to protect them. Never look right at the sun, even if you're wearing sunglasses. With sunglasses, sunscreen, and the right clothing, you can have fun in the sun and still be safe.

CONSUMER FOCUS

Making Buying Decisions

How can you choose the best sunscreen? Find out what SPF means and choose the best SPF for you. Then compare several different sunscreen brands to decide which one is best for you and your family. Use page *xiv* to help you make your decision.

- - -

LESSON CHECKUP

Check Your Facts

1. Why is it important to wash your hands often?

2. CRITICAL THINKING Think about what oil does for your skin. What do you think might happen if you used harsh soap or bathed too often?

3. List three ways to protect your skin from the sun.

Set Health Goals

4. Think back over the past two days. How many times did you go outside, and how long did you stay out each time? Write down the different ways you protected yourself from the sun. Then think of ways you could do even better next time. Write these ideas down too.

73

TEACHER TIP

Living with Smog Since children spend more time outdoors than adults, they are exposed to more pollutants overall than adults. Children have respiratory systems that are still developing and breathe about 50% more air per body weight than adults. Discuss with children ways they can protect themselves when air quality is poor or when the sun and heat are at their strongest, such as in the middle part of the day.

Discuss

When is the sun strongest? in the middle of the day

Problem Solving Imagine you do not know what time it is, and no one has a watch. **How can you tell whether the sun is at its strongest?** If the sun is overhead, high in the sky, it is at its strongest and you should stay inside.

Critical Thinking **What are four ways you can protect yourself from the sun?** Wear long sleeves and long pants. Wear a hat. Use a sunscreen. Wear sunglasses.

Consumer Focus

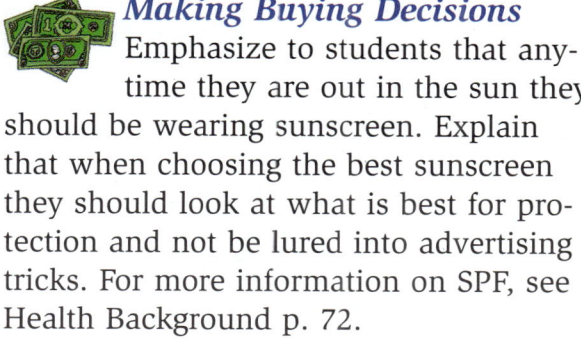

Making Buying Decisions Emphasize to students that anytime they are out in the sun they should be wearing sunscreen. Explain that when choosing the best sunscreen they should look at what is best for protection and not be lured into advertising tricks. For more information on SPF, see Health Background p. 72.

3 Wrap Up

Lesson Checkup

1. Clean hands are less likely to spread illnesses to yourself and others.

2. You would wash away the oil, and your skin could become rough and dry.

3. Wear long pants and a long-sleeved shirt; wear a hat; and use sunscreen.

4. Have students set up in their Health Journals a section for each day and write the date. Tell them to list times they went outside and about how long they stayed. For each time, have them tell how they protected themselves from the sun and how they might do better. Remind students that even in winter, their eyes need protection.

OBJECTIVES

- Explain how plaque can lead to cavities and loss of teeth.
- Describe and demonstrate how to brush and floss correctly.
- Explain how to protect teeth from injury.

PROGRAM RESOURCES

- Activity Book, p. 19

 Teaching Transparency 23

 Computer Graphing Activity, Teaching Resources p. 55

VOCABULARY

- plaque (p. 74)
- cavity (p. 74)
- dental floss (p. 75)
- fluoride (p. 76)

Daily Safety Tip

Students may not realize that biting down on hard foods can harm teeth. Tell students that they should not bite hard candies, ice, or other very hard items. Biting these can crack tooth enamel, making teeth more likely to stain or decay. Biting hard things can also chip or fracture teeth.

1 Motivate

Have pairs of students stand and face each other with their mouths closed. On sheets of paper, each student should write what they think the partner might be feeling or thinking about. Ask students to repeat the exercise with the pairs smiling at each other.

What is different about a person with a closed mouth and a person with a smile? Possible answer: A person seems happier or friendlier when smiling. Remind students that a nice smile depends on keeping teeth healthy.

MAIN IDEA You can take good care of your teeth and gums by learning how to floss and brush and how to protect your teeth from injury.

WHY LEARN THIS? Caring for your teeth and gums helps you stay healthy.

VOCABULARY
- plaque
- cavity
- dental floss
- fluoride

Caring for My Teeth and Gums

Some of your adult teeth may grow in this year. You will need them for biting, chewing, and even talking. These teeth will last for the rest of your life if you take good care of them.

What can cause problems with teeth and gums?

Plaque (PLAK) is a sticky coating that is always forming on teeth. Plaque has bacteria that break down bits of food and give off acids. These acids can make a hole called a **cavity** (KA•vuh•tee) in a tooth.

Look at the diagram below. A cavity can grow through the enamel, into the dentin, and even into the pulp. A deep cavity can even kill the tooth.

When plaque stays on a tooth and hardens, it can make the gum weak. If the gum gets very weak, teeth may fall out.

▼ You can protect your teeth by flossing and brushing away plaque. Chewing a *disclosing tablet* makes areas with plaque dark red.

The Parts of a Tooth

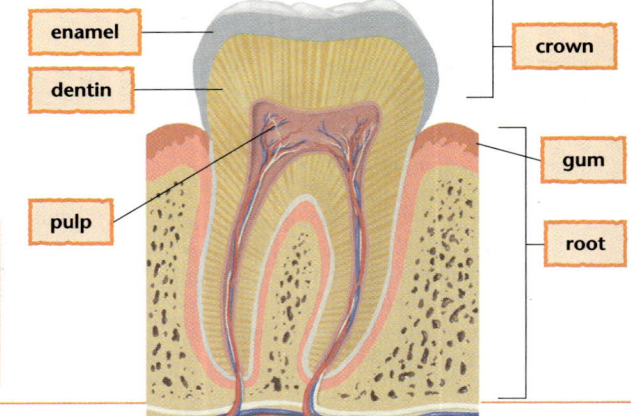

enamel · dentin · pulp · crown · gum · root

74

MULTILEVEL ACTIVITIES

EASY **Write a Song** Have students work together to write song lyrics that describe how to brush and floss your teeth. Encourage them to use a familiar tune so they can teach their song to the rest of the class. **VERBAL/MUSICAL**

AVERAGE **Define Tooth Terms** Have students draw diagrams of a tooth, labeling each part. Then ask them to use a dictionary to find alternate meanings of the words for tooth parts, such as crown. Students should write the alternate meanings on their diagrams and tell how the definition is related to the tooth term. **LINGUISTIC/LOGICAL**

ADVANCED **Investigate Teeth** Have students interview a dentist and find out the difference between the structures of baby teeth and permanent teeth. Have them share their findings in a diagram or other visual presentation. **AUDITORY/INTERPERSONAL**

How can I floss my teeth?

Plaque can build up on all the surfaces of your teeth. It can also build up between your teeth. To remove plaque from between your teeth, you need a special thread called **dental floss**. Using this thread is called flossing.

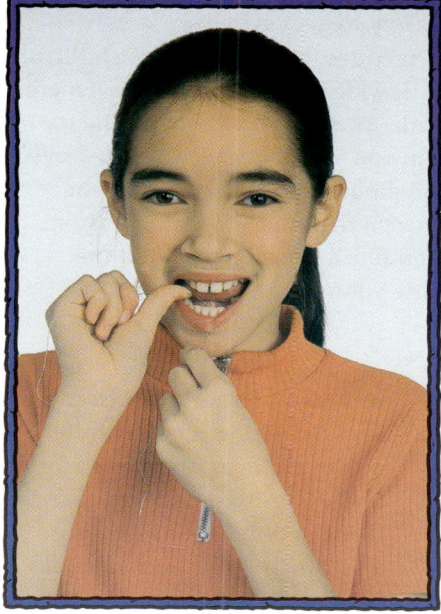 

Look at the pictures to see how to floss. Break off about 18 inches of dental floss. Wrap one end of it around the middle finger of one hand. Guide the floss with your thumbs and index fingers. Push the floss gently between two teeth. Rub gently back and forth as you move the floss toward the gum. Also rub near the gum line of one tooth and then the other. Remove the floss. Unwind it a bit to reach a clean part. Repeat for each tooth.

▲ Plan to floss once a day. It's a good idea to floss just before you brush your teeth.

75

2 Teach

Discuss

Remind students that bacteria are living things that can reproduce, or make, more bacteria.

Critical Thinking **Why is it doubly important to brush away bacteria?** Bacteria make acids that cause cavities, and if you don't brush, more and more bacteria can grow in your mouth.

Learn from Diagrams

Ask students to point to each layer of the tooth: enamel, dentin, pulp. Have them tell in their own words what the crown is the part that shows, and what the root is the part below the gums.

Discuss

A toothbrush should have soft nylon bristles with rounded or tapered ends. Some flexible nylon bristles are thin enough to fit between some teeth.

Critical Thinking **Why doesn't brushing remove all the plaque from between teeth?** because the brush can't get in between all the teeth the way floss can

Problem Solving **You have something caught between your teeth, and you have no floss. A friend says you can use any thread. Do you use the thread? Explain.** No; floss is a special thread; a regular thread would not be clean and is not made for use on teeth.

Learn from Pictures

Have students look at the pictures and explain the part of the flossing process shown in each picture. Then review as a class the steps for flossing teeth.

Critical Thinking **Why should you push the floss gently between teeth?** If you force it, you can hurt your gums.

Teach *continued*

Discuss

Fluoride is a mineral that aids bone formation. The forms commonly used in toothpaste are sodium fluoride or sodium monofluorophosphate.

Why should your toothpaste have fluoride in it? Fluoride makes teeth stronger and harder so they are less likely to develop cavities.

Why should you use a toothbrush with soft bristles? Soft bristles clean your teeth without hurting your gums.

Problem Solving A friend tells you that you should brush your teeth hard to make them clean and shiny. **Will you follow this advice? Why or why not?** No; you should brush gently to avoid hurting the gums.

Activity

Practice Flossing and Brushing Have students work in pairs to review how to brush and floss teeth. They should show the actual movements without putting anything in their mouths.

Health Journal

Have students list in their Health Journals the days of the week and record for one week how they care for teeth and gums each day. Suggest they review their record to see if they are brushing and flossing as recommended (brushing at least twice a day and flossing at least once before brushing). If they need improvement, have them list what they should do.

This feature is designed to provide students with an opportunity to reflect on health decisions they are making in their personal lives. The journal should *not* be used to evaluate or assess students, nor should the results be shared among students.

How can I brush my teeth?

Brushing gets rid of plaque on the front, back, and top of each tooth. Use a toothbrush with soft bristles. Soft bristles will clean your teeth without hurting your gums. Use a toothpaste that has **fluoride** (FLAWR•yd). Fluoride is a chemical that makes teeth stronger and harder. Strong, hard teeth are less likely to get cavities.

Look at the pictures to see how to brush. Brush with short, tooth-wide back and forth movements on all your teeth. Brush along the gum line too. Spend extra time on your back teeth. They have deep pits where plaque can collect. Turn your toothbrush to reach the inner sides of your front teeth. When you finish brushing, spit out the toothpaste. Rinse your mouth with water.

JOURNAL

Keep a record of how you care for your teeth and gums every day for a week. Then look over your journal to make sure you're taking good care of your teeth and gums.

▶ Brush your teeth at least twice a day, once in the morning and again at night.

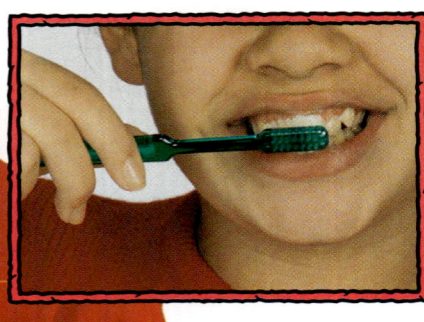

Activity **Practice Flossing and Brushing** Look carefully at the pictures on pages 75 and 76. With a partner, take turns acting out how to floss and brush your teeth. Explain each step as you act it out.

 MATH

Add Up Brushings Ask students to note how many times they usually brush their teeth each day. At that rate, how many times will they brush in a week, a month, and a year? If they began brushing when they were six months (one-half year) old, and they live until they are seventy years old, how many times will they brush their teeth? (You may wish to do the last part of this activity as a class.)

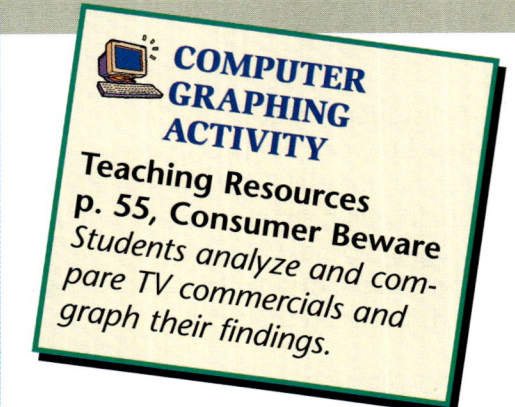 **COMPUTER GRAPHING ACTIVITY**

Teaching Resources p. 55, Consumer Beware Students analyze and compare TV commercials and graph their findings.

How can I protect my teeth from injury?

Your teeth are very strong and hard. But if you use them for cutting or tearing things other than food, you can harm the tooth enamel. For example, you should never open food packages with your teeth.

If you play sports, wear a mouth guard to protect your teeth from being hit or injured in a fall. A mouth guard is made of plastic. You can buy one at a store, or a dentist can make one for you.

If a tooth gets knocked out, put it back in place. If it is dirty, lightly rinse it first in a little milk or water. Hold it, and go right to the dentist. The dentist may be able to save the tooth.

LIFE SKILLS FOCUS

Make Decisions
Alan plays roller hockey. His coach recommends that all players wear mouth guards, but his friends say they aren't going to wear them. Use the decision-making steps shown on page *ix* to help Alan decide what to do.

● ● ●

◄ Dentists recommend mouth guards for football, baseball, basketball, hockey, and soccer players.

LESSON CHECKUP

Check Your Facts

① **CRITICAL THINKING** How do you help your gums when you remove plaque from your teeth?

② When should you floss your teeth? When should you brush?

③ What kind of toothbrush and toothpaste should you use? Why?

Use Life Skills

④ **MAKE DECISIONS** Make a list of your favorite activities. Circle the activities you need a mouth guard for. Make up your own list of rules to help you decide when to use your mouth guard.

77

TEACHER TIP

Care of a Knocked-Out Tooth
Remind students that a knocked-out tooth should never be washed with soap. It should not be wrapped in a tissue. If you can't get it back into the mouth, keep it in water or milk until you reach the dentist.

Discuss

Critical Thinking Why shouldn't you use your teeth to open packages? You can harm tooth enamel.

What should you do if a tooth gets knocked out? If it is dirty, lightly rinse it first in a little milk or water. Hold it in place, and go to the dentist right away.

Problem Solving A friend wants to borrow your mouth guard. What would you say? Why? No; because it is an item you use in your mouth so sharing it would spread germs.

Life Skills Focus

Make Decisions Review the steps in the decision-making process. Then have groups work through the situation and reach a decision for Alan. Allow groups to share results and discuss any differences of opinion.

3 Wrap Up

Lesson Checkup

1. If plaque stays on your teeth, it can harden and make gums weak, so removing it helps gums as well as teeth.

2. You should floss at least once a day before you brush. You should brush twice a day, once in the morning and once at night.

3. You should use a toothbrush with soft bristles so you don't damage your gums; use toothpaste with fluoride because fluoride strengthens tooth enamel.

4. Have students write the list in their Health Journals. Remind them to circle each activity that they would use a mouth guard for and to write their own rules to obey.

OBJECTIVES

- **Explain how the parts of the ear function.**
- **Describe how to take good care of the ears and the nose.**

PROGRAM RESOURCES

- Activity Book, p. 20

 Teaching Transparency 11

VOCABULARY

- ear canal (p. 78)
- eardrum (p. 79)

Daily Safety Tip

A small insect can fly into the ear canal, causing a very loud buzz. Remind students not to panic and reach inside the ear with a finger. Many times the insect will fly out on its own. If not, they should get the help of an adult, who can use drops of vegetable or mineral oil to help bring the insect out. If it stings or doesn't come out, they should see a doctor.

1 Motivate

Tell students to gently put a finger on their necks below their chins, on their voice boxes, and to breathe gently. Do they feel anything? Then have them say their names in a normal voice. They should feel a sensation in their fingers and an up and down movement. Have them experiment in the same way with other sounds, such as loud and soft, high and low, short and long, and different letter sounds. Discuss the differences.

What are you feeling with your finger?
sound vibrations Explain that when you talk, air moves from the lungs over the vocal cords—in the voice box, or larynx—making them vibrate. The vibrations make sounds.

MAIN IDEA
Caring for your ears and nose helps you stay healthy.

WHY LEARN THIS? Learning
about your ears and nose will help you take good care of them.

VOCABULARY
- ear canal
- eardrum

Caring for My Ears and Nose

You go for a walk after it rains. You hear splashes as you walk through a puddle. Everything smells clean and damp. Your ears and nose help you enjoy the things around you, so take good care of them.

What can cause problems with hearing?

Your ear has three main parts—the outer ear, the middle ear, and the inner ear. The diagram below shows the three parts. Sound enters your ear through your **ear canal**. This is part of your outer ear. The opening you can see in your ear is the beginning of your ear canal.

▶ The part of the ear you can see collects sound waves and channels them into your ear canal.

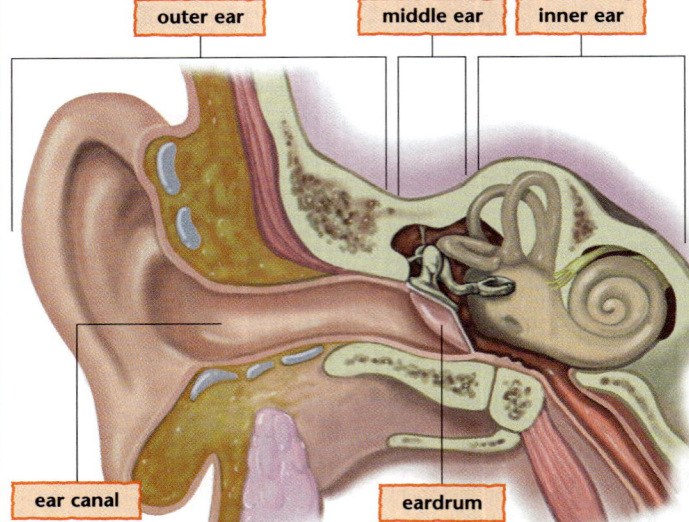

outer ear middle ear inner ear

ear canal eardrum

 MULTILEVEL ACTIVITIES

EASY **Draw a Warning Poster** Have students choose an event that makes a loud noise that might damage hearing. Students should draw the event and add a child wearing ear protection. Ask them to insert a caption that explains why the ear protection is necessary. For example, "Keep Your Hearing Safe!" or "Protect Your Ears, They Last a Lifetime." **VISUAL**

AVERAGE **Listen to Sounds** Have students sit quietly in the classroom for five minutes and then list all the sounds they heard. Encourage them to repeat this activity outside and at home. Ask volunteers to make an audio tape of sounds for other students to identify. **AUDITORY**

ADVANCED **Make a Word Game** Have students brainstorm a list of words that contain "ear"—eardrum, earring, and so on. Ask them to use these words to make a word puzzle, such as a word search, a crossword, or a word scramble. Help them duplicate the game and share it with the rest of the class. **LINGUISTIC/LOGICAL**

Noise can hurt!

Your **eardrum** is at the other end of your ear canal. Sound waves make the eardrum move back and forth. This movement sends the waves on to the inner ear. The inner ear turns the waves into nerve signals. These signals travel to your brain, and you hear a sound.

Some things can harm your ears. Bacteria in your ear can give you an ear infection. An ear infection can make your ear hurt. You may also have trouble hearing. If this happens, tell an adult. The adult may take you to a doctor. The doctor may give you medicine to help your ear heal.

Loud sounds also can harm your ears. Over time such sounds can cause you to have trouble hearing. Loud music, loud machines, and loud traffic all can cause hearing problems. You may not notice these problems for many years. By then it will be too late to correct the harm to your ears.

▲ Noise from these things can cause hearing problems over time. What are some other sounds that might harm your hearing?

79

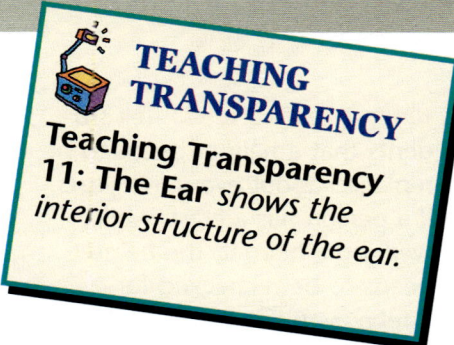

TEACHING TRANSPARENCY

Teaching Transparency 11: The Ear shows the interior structure of the ear.

2 Teach

Discuss

The ear canal leads from the pinna, or outer ear, through the skull bones to the eardrum. The eardrum is a tightly stretched piece of skin at the end of the ear canal.

Critical Thinking **How is an eardrum like a drum?** It has tightly stretched skin on it, and it vibrates when struck.

Critical Thinking **What happens to the sound waves after they reach the eardrum?** The movement of the eardrum sends vibrations to the middle and inner ear; the inner ear turns the vibrations to nerve signals that travel to the brain.

Learn from Pictures

Have students identify the items shown in the picture and then answer the caption question. Possible answers: traffic, construction equipment.

Discuss

What actions can you take to avoid things that might hurt your hearing? Stay away from noisy places; turn the sound down when you listen to TV, radio, or boom box; keep the sound low when you play video games; and keep the sound low when you use head-phones.

Many helmets are constructed with a hard outer shell and a liner made from polystyrene foam which absorbs energy. Pads should make it fit snugly on the head. A buckle or D-ring chin strap keeps it on.

Critical Thinking **What would happen to the energy of a hard hit if you did not have a helmet on?** It would be absorbed by the skull, so it could harm the head and the ears.

Why should you avoid sticking anything into the ear canal? You can poke a hole in your eardrum.

Learn from Pictures

Have students look at the picture and read the caption. Have them suggest other times they wear helmets, such as when biking or in-line skating.

Language Arts Connection

 *Write a Story* Have students brainstorm a list of ways to keep ears safe by telling things they should or should not do in specific situations. Suggest that students use some of these and other ideas to help focus their stories. When stories are finished, have students share them in groups.

How can I take care of my ears?

LANGUAGE ARTS CONNECTION

Write a Story

On Your Own Think about ways to keep your ears safe. Think about things you should and should not do. Write a story about what you can do to have a safe hearing day.

You cannot stop all the things that might hurt your hearing, but you can avoid most of them. Stay away from noisy places. Turn the sound down when you listen to the TV, radio, or CD player. Also keep the sound low when you play video games. When you use headphones, you should still be able to hear sounds around you. If you can't, you may be hurting your ears.

Getting hit on your ears also can hurt your hearing. Wear a helmet when you play rough sports. This will help protect your ears.

You can wash the outsides of your ears with a washcloth. But do not stick anything into the ear canal. Doing this can poke a hole in the eardrum and damage hearing.

◄ Wearing a helmet will help protect your ears when you play hockey, baseball, or football.

80

TEACHER TIP

Helmet Replacement Tell students that a helmet needs to be replaced about every five years. If a person has a crash while wearing a helmet, the helmet needs to be rechecked for safety, even if it seems undamaged. The helmet can be sent back to the manufacturer for testing or replacement. For more information about bike safety, see pages 268–269.

How can I protect my nose?

Have you ever had a hard bump to your nose? If you have, you know how much it can hurt. Injuries to the nose usually heal quickly. Still, you need to take care of your nose to feel your best.

Taking care of your nose is especially important when you have a cold. Always blow your nose gently. Keep both nostrils and your mouth open. If you blow your nose too hard, you can send bacteria from your throat through a tiny tube into your middle ear. This can give you an earache.

Blowing your nose too hard also can break blood vessels. When that happens, your nose may bleed. If you get a nosebleed, stand or sit up and lean forward. Gently pinch your nose. Breathe through your mouth. The bleeding should stop soon.

HUMAN BODY CONNECTION

The Sense Organs

When your nose feels stuffed up, what happens to your senses of smell and taste? Turn to pages 2 and 3 of The Amazing Human Body to learn more about the nose and your senses.

▶ If bleeding from your nose doesn't stop after a short time, visit your doctor for help.

LESSON CHECKUP

Check Your Facts

1. Explain how your eardrum helps you hear.
2. What can happen if you listen to loud sounds over a period of years?
3. CRITICAL THINKING Why might spicy foods taste good to you when you have a cold?
4. What should you do if you get a nosebleed?

Set Health Goals

5. Make a list of common noises that could hurt your hearing over time. Next to each noise, write one or more ways you could protect your ears from that noise. Share your list with your family. Make plans to put your ideas into action.

81

Discuss

Sitting up when you have a nosebleed helps lower the pressure of blood in the veins. Leaning forward keeps blood from running down the throat.

Problem Solving You have a nosebleed and someone tells you to lie down. What should you do? Why? Possible answer: Sit down or stand up because if you lie down, more blood will flow to your head.

Learn from Pictures

Have students explain in their own words what the girl is doing, and then suggest they try out the position. Read the caption.

Human Body Connection

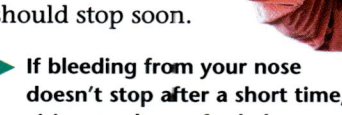

The Sense Organs Have students look at the diagram of the nose and study the information about senses. Help them see how the nose contributes to both smell and taste.

3 Wrap Up

Lesson Checkup

1. Sound enters through the ear canal and makes the eardrum move back and forth. This movement is passed on to the middle and inner ear.

2. You can damage your hearing.

3. When you have a cold and can't smell what you are eating, things don't taste as good. A spicy food has a stronger taste, so you might be able to taste it even though you can't smell it.

4. Sit or stand, and lean forward. Gently pinch your nose, and breathe through your mouth.

5. Have students work in groups to list noises that could hurt hearing over time. They can start with situations that involve music, machines, and traffic. After students finish lists, ask them to write how they could protect their ears from each sound.

OBJECTIVES

- Describe different ways exercise helps the body.
- Explain how and why to get aerobic exercise.
- Explain why sleep is helpful.

PROGRAM RESOURCES

 Computer Graphing Activity, Teaching Resources p. 56

VOCABULARY

- exercise (p. 82)
- aerobic exercises (p. 82)

Daily Safety Tip

Most children have probably experienced muscle cramps, which can occur at rest or during exercise. Tell students that when a cramp, or muscle spasm, occurs, they should stretch the muscle and gently massage the area to relax the muscles. If they get a cramp during hard exercise, they should drink more water. Water helps balance certain minerals in the blood that can cause cramping.

1 Motivate

Explain to students that you can count the number of times your heart beats in a minute by using your pulse. Your pulse is pressure you can feel each time your heart pumps blood. Have students use a finger to find a pulse on the back side of the wrist, below the thumb. Direct them to count the pulses as you time them for a minute. Ask them to take their pulses again after running outside or in place for several minutes.

How does your pulse rate compare before and after exercise? Students will have a faster pulse rate after exercise.

What does your heart do when you exercise? Your heart pumps blood more often when you exercise.

LESSON 4

MAIN IDEA
You need a balance of exercise, rest, and sleep to be physically fit.

WHY LEARN THIS? Learning about exercise, rest, and sleep can help you plan ways to feel and be fit.

VOCABULARY
- exercise
- aerobic exercises

Exercise and Rest for Fun and Health

You come in from playing outside. You are laughing and have lots of energy. In fact, you feel great. That's because you have good physical fitness.

How can I exercise for fitness?

Exercise helps you become and stay physically fit. **Exercise** (EK•ser•syz) is any activity that makes your body work hard. Running games and sports are exercise. Swimming is exercise. Jumping rope is exercise. Riding a bike is exercise. Even walking is exercise.

Different kinds of exercise help your body in different ways. Some exercises make your muscles strong. For example, bicycling uphill strengthens your leg muscles. Some exercises stretch your muscles. Doing gymnastics stretches your arm, leg, and back muscles.

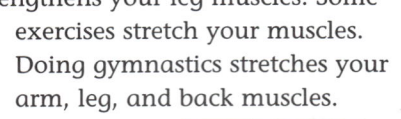

Aerobic exercises (air•OH•bik EK•ser•sy•zuhs) strengthen your heart and lungs by making them work harder.

82

MULTILEVEL ACTIVITIES

EASY **Keep an Exercise Diary** Have students make lists of the different kinds of exercise they do in a week. Suggest they include physical education classes, team sports or athletic classes, other classes, and home activities. Have them put checks next to exercises they think strengthen their hearts and lungs. Call on volunteers to share their exercise diaries with the class. **KINESTHETIC/VISUAL**

AVERAGE **Exercise to Music** Have students find a song that would work well for an aerobic exercise, such as jumping rope or dancing. Encourage them to design an exercise routine to go with the music and demonstrate it to the class. **KINESTHETIC/MUSICAL**

ADVANCED **Demonstrate Safety Equipment** Tell students that many sports and aerobic activities require special safety equipment. Have pairs of students choose a sport and find out what safety equipment is suggested. Ask students to prepare a demonstration or diagrams of the equipment showing how it helps prevent injury. **VERBAL/VISUAL**

Activity **Choose Exercises** Look at the exercises in the pictures. Which ones do you already like to do? Which ones would you like to try? Tell which exercises you will do this week to be fit.

Aerobic exercise helps your whole body work better. The activities in the pictures can be aerobic exercises. They are aerobic if you do them hard enough to speed up your heart and breathing rates. But you should not exercise so hard that you can't talk with a friend. Also, you must exercise for at least twenty minutes.

You can exercise by yourself or with friends or family. Exercise can be fun. It can cheer you up if you feel angry, sad, or stressed.

◀ There are many different kinds of aerobic exercise. Try to do aerobic exercise at least three times each week.

83

MULTICULTURAL LINK

World of Dancing Have students research and learn about dances from around the world. Some of these dances will be good aerobic activities. Others will provide stretching or strengthening of muscles. Have students share pictures and music of the dances, and teach a dance if they can.

COMPUTER GRAPHING ACTIVITY
Teaching Resources p. 56, Keep at It Students graph increases in endurance and plan ways to improve their own endurance.

2 Teach

Discuss

Three possible results of exercise include stronger muscles; stretched, or flexible, muscles; or muscles that can work hard for a long time.

Critical Thinking How is bicycling uphill different from doing gymnastics? Bicycling uphill makes muscles strong and able to work a long time; gymnastics stretches muscles.

What kind of exercise strengthens the heart and lungs? aerobic exercise

Activity

Choose Exercises Have students look at the exercises shown in the pictures and tell which ones they already like to do. Discuss which ones students would like to try. Encourage them to choose one or two new activities, such as the ones shown, to try this week.

Critical Thinking Swimming and biking aren't always aerobic exercises. **What makes the difference?** You need to do them hard enough and for at least twenty minutes.

Problem Solving Imagine you are feeling so sad that you don't feel like doing anything. **What could you do that might help you feel better as well as improve your fitness?** Possible answer: Do some exercise, especially aerobic exercise.

Critical Thinking Why might it be better to exercise with others rather than alone? Accept reasonable answers, such as it's more fun, it's safer, you can play games you wouldn't be able to do alone.

Project Checkup

Plan a Fitness Game (p. 69) Encourage students to use information from this lesson to help them plan their fitness game.

Discuss

When you sleep, many of the nerve cells that you use when you are awake rest too. But the nerves that control breathing, heartbeat, and digestion always continue to work.

Critical Thinking **What would happen if these nerves didn't keep working when you sleep?** You would stop breathing; your heart would stop beating; you would stop digesting food; you could die.

What happens to your body when you sleep? Your body slows down; senses become dull; you breathe slowly and deeply; your muscles relax; your body repairs itself by making new blood cells and bone cells.

Problem Solving **Imagine that you do not sleep well one night and feel tired the next day. What can you do the following night to help you feel better?** Get some extra sleep.

Learn from Pictures

Have students look at the picture and read the caption. Ask students to share experiences they have had or heard about involving animals that are awake at night.

Health Background

Getting to Sleep Part of the brain, called the reticular-activating system, governs waking and sleeping. It sends "wake-up" messages to other areas of the brain. When it sends fewer messages, people get drowsy. With even fewer messages, people begin to fall asleep. But the reticular-activating system still receives signals from organs, so people can be awakened by movement, noise, or lights. People can also keep themselves awake by continuing to think, which sends "stay-awake" messages back to the reticular-activating system.

For more background, visit the **Webliography** on the Teacher Resources page at:
www.harcourtschool.com/health
Keyword human body

Did you know?

You dream for several hours every night. When you dream, your eyes dart back and forth. Your eyelids may flutter. But your arms and legs probably don't move much at all.

How do rest and sleep help me stay fit?

Exercise is good for your body. Rest is also good for you. After exercise your body needs to rest. When you rest, you breathe more slowly. Your heart beats more slowly too. Your muscles have a chance to relax. After resting, you may have more energy. You may want to do something active again.

Sleep is an important way to rest. When you sleep, your whole body slows down. Your senses become dull. You breathe slowly and deeply. Your heart beats slowly. Your muscles relax. Your body repairs itself during sleep. It makes new blood cells and bone cells.

Sleep gives your brain a chance to rest too. If you do not sleep much one night, you may have trouble thinking the next day. You may have a hard time remembering things. Extra sleep the next night will help you think better and feel better.

▶ Sleep is your body's deepest form of rest. People naturally sleep at night. But many animals, including cats, spend all or part of the night awake.

84

SCIENCE

Nocturnal Animals Ask students to research animals that stay awake at night, or are nocturnal. Have them draw a picture of each animal and tell what it does at night. Encourage interested students to find out what unique features nocturnal animals have that make them able to move around at night.

LANGUAGE ARTS

Sleep Poems Have students write poems about resting, sleeping, or dreaming. Have them illustrate their poems in a way that makes them look restful or "dreamy."

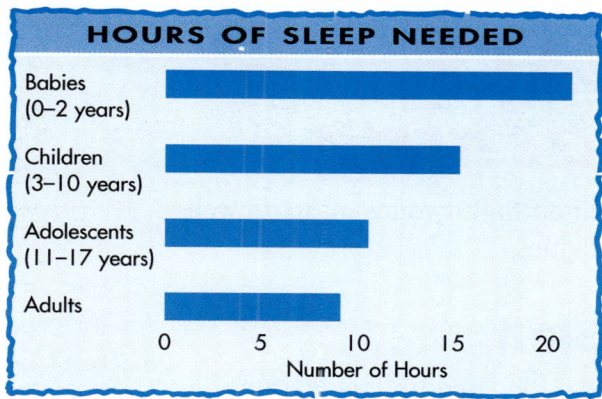

HOURS OF SLEEP NEEDED

▲ At different ages, people need different amounts of sleep. How much sleep do you need to feel your best?

As you grow, the amount of sleep you need changes. Right now you need ten to fourteen hours of sleep every night to stay healthy. Babies need more sleep than you do. Most adults need less.

LESSON CHECKUP

Check Your Facts

1. What are two ways exercise can help your body?
2. CRITICAL THINKING Of the exercises you do, which are aerobic exercises?
3. CRITICAL THINKING Why do you think babies need so much more sleep than adults do?
4. Why is sleep important?

Use Life Skills

5. REFUSE Imagine that you are spending the night at a friend's home. Your friend wants you to stay up late and play games. You know you need your sleep. Write down three ways you could politely say *no* to your friend.

85

 LITERATURE

Sleeping and Dreaming Help students find folk tales, myths, stories, or poems that involve or describe sleeping or dreaming. Ask students to read the literature and report on the importance of sleep or provide a description of sleeping or dreaming found in the literature.

 **ART**

Draw a Dream Have students draw or paint pictures of imagined dream scenes. Remind them that dream scenes are not necessarily realistic or logical.

Learn from Graphs

Have students look at the graph and answer these basic questions: Which group of people needs the most sleep? Which two groups of people need equal amounts of sleep? Then have students answer these math questions.

• What is the difference in hours between the sleep needs of babies and the sleep needs of adolescents?

• How many more hours than adults do children need to sleep?

• Do babies need one time, two times, or three times more sleep than adolescents?

Life Skills Focus

Make Decisions Have students use the decision-making model to decide what will satisfy both of Amber's needs. Discuss how students can use what they have learned to change their own relationships with friends.

3 Wrap Up

Lesson Checkup

1. Make muscles stronger, stretch muscles, strengthen heart and lungs. Students may also mention relieving anger, tension, or sadness.

2. Answers will vary but should include activities done hard enough and long enough to be of aerobic value.

3. Accept any logical answers. Possible answer: Babies' bodies are growing rapidly.

4. It gives your body, senses, and muscles a chance to relax. It lets your heart and breathing slow down, and it gives your body time to repair itself.

5. Have students write their own answers to the question. Then allow them to work in groups to decide on the three answers they feel are most polite and effective.

OBJECTIVES

- Identify goal-setting steps.
- Practice goal-setting steps to get enough rest.

PROGRAM RESOURCES

- Activity Book, p. 21
- HEALTH VIDEO: The Cleanup Kids

1 Motivate

Ask for five volunteers. Tell one volunteer to stand in the middle at the front of the room, with two of the other volunteers on each side. Instruct the four students on the sides to make noise, move around, talk softly into the middle person's ear, and generally be disruptive. Tell the student in the middle to listen carefully to a selection you are about to read. Tell him or her there will be questions at the end. Read in a quiet, steady voice. When you have finished, instruct the four to sit down. Direct the other student to try to answer questions. Ask the class why it is hard to answer the questions. Discuss conditions that may be necessary in order to learn.

2 Teach

Learn from Pictures

Direct students' attention to the situation on these pages. Tell them goal setting is a way to help them learn.

Step 1

How can you tell Lisa is having a hard time concentrating? Her desk is disorganized. She is not focused. She looks tired.

SET GOALS for Learning

Getting enough rest is important if you want to do well in school and other activities.

Learn This Skill

Lisa was very sleepy today. She had trouble learning. She could not pay attention and had trouble sitting still and listening.

1. Set a goal.

Lisa wanted to feel more awake in class.

2. Plan steps to help you meet the goal.

Lisa's dad suggested she go to bed earlier so she could get the rest she needed.

86

HEALTH VIDEO

The Cleanup Kids: Working with Others
Demonstrates the value of working together for a common goal. See the Health Video Series Teacher's Guide for discussion and activity ideas.

TEACHER TIP

Practice Setting Goals Have students set short-term goals for one week, such as to turn in all their work on time. Ask them to make plans and think of ways to monitor progress. At the end of the week, students should evaluate their goals. Remind them that they can always monitor and adjust goals if needed. They can set new goals when they reach the ones on which they have been working.

3. Monitor progress toward the goal.

Lisa and her dad made a chart she could fill in. Each night she went to bed on time, she gave herself a star.

4. Evaluate the goal.

When Lisa got the sleep she needed, she felt better at school. She could pay attention in class.

Practice This Skill

Use the steps to help you solve the problems.

Steps for Setting Goals

1. Set a goal.

2. Plan steps to help you meet the goal.

3. Monitor progress toward the goal.

4. Evaluate the goal.

A. Gene wants to spend more time reading. Use the goal-setting steps to help Gene find time to read.

B. Carrie wants to exercise at least three times each week. Use the goal-setting steps to help her.

87

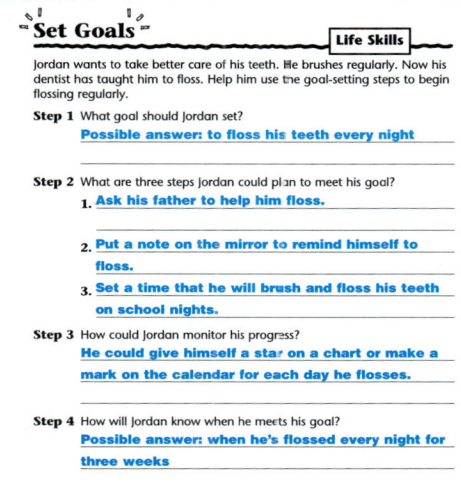

Set Goals — Life Skills

Jordan wants to take better care of his teeth. He brushes regularly. Now his dentist has taught him to floss. Help him use the goal-setting steps to begin flossing regularly.

Step 1 What goal should Jordan set?
Possible answer: to floss his teeth every night

Step 2 What are three steps Jordan could plan to meet his goal?
1. Ask his father to help him floss.
2. Put a note on the mirror to remind himself to floss.
3. Set a time that he will brush and floss his teeth on school nights.

Step 3 How could Jordan monitor his progress?
He could give himself a star on a chart or make a mark on the calendar for each day he flosses.

Step 4 How will Jordan know when he meets his goal?
Possible answer: when he's flossed every night for three weeks

---

PHYSICAL EDUCATION

Daily Fitness Discuss with children ways they can increase their daily exercise by changing some of their regular activities. Have them share ways they can modify activities to increase daily exercise. Make a wall chart listing changes they have suggested. At the end of the week, review the chart with the children and ask them to evaluate their results.

What is the problem that is making it hard for Lisa to learn? not enough rest

What kind of goal statement could Lisa make? Possible answer: to get more sleep so I can concentrate in class, feel more awake in class, and have more energy for my studies.

Step 2

What could Lisa do to feel more rested? Possible answers: go to bed earlier; take a nap after school; eat a balanced diet; eat breakfast; exercise.

Step 3

Critical Thinking Why is it important to monitor progress toward a goal? Possible answers: so you can tell if you are making progress, so you remember to keep working on it, so you won't give up, so you can feel positive about the changes on which you are working.

Step 4

How can you tell that Lisa made progress toward her goal? She is smiling; she looks as if she has more energy; she has stars on her chart.

3 Wrap Up

Practice This Skill

A. Students' answers should include each of the goal-setting steps, with specific suggestions for Gene. His goal would be to find time to read. He could make a variety of plans, such as making time to read just before bedtime. He could monitor his progress on a calendar and evaluate the goal in one week.

B. Students' answers should include a plan for Carrie to meet her goal of exercising at least three times a week, a way to monitor progress, and an evaluation of the goal, such as Carrie's feelings of improved well-being when she exercises regularly.

OBJECTIVES

- Explain how to use safety gear, warm-ups, cool-downs, and water to stay safe during exercise.
- Describe what to do in case of injury.

PROGRAM RESOURCES

- Activity Book, pp. 22–23

VOCABULARY

- warm-up (p. 89)
- cool-down (p. 89)

Daily Safety Tip

Safe exercising involves more than putting on the right safety gear. Students need to learn what is important for each exercise. For example, for biking,

- wear a helmet.
- choose a bike with a frame that fits in such a way that when you straddle the tube, the groin is about an inch above it.
- wear bright, reflective clothing when visibility is poor.
- don't wear headphones because you need to hear cars.
- don't wear a heavy backpack because it will throw off your balance.

1 Motivate

Optional materials: **pictures of people taking part in different sports and activities**

Have students look at the pictures and list all the choices the athletes made that might affect the safety of their performance. For example, students might note safety gear, safety features of the equipment, the type of clothing, and the location. (As an alternative, make the list with students remembering activities they have seen or taken part in.)

LESSON 5

MAIN IDEA
Exercising safely means following some simple safety rules.

WHY LEARN THIS? Most injuries can be prevented. But if you are injured, you should know what to do.

VOCABULARY
- warm-up
- cool-down

Staying Safe While Exercising

You are playing soccer with your friends. One by one your friends stop playing. One has a bruised shin. Another has a pulled muscle. One is thirsty and has a headache. The game would still be going on if everyone had followed simple safety rules.

How can I exercise safely?

Putting on safety gear before you start exercising is important. Soccer players should protect their legs with shin guards. They also need special shoes and mouth guards. Look through this chapter for pictures of different kinds of safety gear.

▶ Doing a warm-up before hard exercise and a cool-down afterward can help keep you from getting hurt. Both your warm-up and your cool-down should include stretching activities.

 MULTILEVEL ACTIVITIES

EASY **Identify Cause and Effect** Have students create charts of causes and effects for injuries or other safety problems. **VISUAL/LOGICAL**

AVERAGE **Write Safety Tips** Have students pick a sport or activity that has not been discussed in class. Ask them to write sentences describing all the safety tips they can think of for the sport. **VERBAL/LOGICAL**

ADVANCED **Demonstrate Treatment for an Injury** Tell students that the treatment for a sudden injury is sometimes represented by the acronym RICE—*r*est the injured part; apply *i*ce; *c*ompress, or gently press down on the area; and *e*levate, or hold the injured part above the level of the heart. Have students make four cards, each with a letter and description of the step. Allow students to present the steps by holding up each card in order, reading the step, and showing how the step could be done for a particular injury. **VERBAL/KINESTHETIC**

Warming up your muscles gets them ready for hard exercise. During your **warm-up**, stretch and do slow exercises for about five minutes. This helps prevent pulled muscles. After hard exercise, do slow exercise and stretching again. This is called a **cool-down**. A five minute cool-down helps prevent muscle soreness later.

Your body loses a lot of water during exercise. You see this when you sweat. Drinking water before, during, and after exercise can help prevent discomfort and illness.

▲ During exercise you can take small sips of water. This will cool you and replace some of the water you lose.

Work out!

Cool down!

89

 **SOCIAL STUDIES**

Exercise Long Ago Have students research how children exercised long ago. They may want to look at different time periods, such as colonial times in the United States, or different cultures, such as Mayan, Iroquois, and Egyptian.

 MATH

Add Up a Week's Exercise
Remind students that aerobic exercise requires twenty minutes to be effective. Ask students how long a safe and effective exercise session needs to be (five minutes warm-up + twenty minutes hard exercise + five minutes cool-down). Have students total up the time they would need to exercise three times (four times, five times) a week.

2 Teach

Discuss

Point out that safety gear depends on the type of sport and on individual needs. For example, students who wear glasses may need to wear contact lenses.

Critical Thinking What should you do before you begin any exercise? have the right safety gear on

What safety gear do soccer players need? shin guards, special shoes, mouth guards

Learn from Pictures

Have students describe what the girl is doing in each of the pictures on these pages. Then have them read the caption on page 88, then explain why the terms *warm-up* and *cool-down* fit what they describe. Warming up gets your body ready for exercise; cooling down helps prevent muscle soreness later.

Direct students to the picture at the top of this page. Read the caption. **Explain why sipping water might be better than drinking a whole glass at once during exercise.** to replace water lost in sweat

Health Background

Stretching Three major types of stretching are static, contract-relax, and ballistic. Ballistic stretching, as the name suggests, is not gentle; it involves bouncing and forcing muscles to move quickly, which can easily harm muscles and does not provide an effective stretch. Tell students to avoid ballistic stretching. Static and contract-relax stretching are helpful because they are gentle and slow. A static stretch is a gradual movement until resistance is met, a holding at that point, and a gradual return to a starting position. For contract-relax stretching, muscle groups are contracted, held, and then relaxed.

For more background, visit the **Webliography** on the Teacher Resources page at:
www.harcourtschool.com/health
Keyword physical fitness

Teach *continued*

Discuss

Broken bones are a potential sports injury. Muscles and other soft tissues, such as tendons, ligaments, and cartilage, can also be injured.

Some soreness after exercise is natural. Exercise will actually help ease soreness and speed recovery of this natural soreness. If students are unsure about any pain, they should talk to a trusted adult before exercising.

Critical Thinking **Why should you avoid exercising if your muscles are painful?** You could injure the muscles, and recovery time would be prolonged.

Problem Solving Imagine you are in a softball game and you fall on your arm. The game is still going on, but your arm is very painful. **What should you do?** Stop playing right away and tell an adult.

Learn from Pictures

Ask students what they think happened to the boy in the picture. Then have them read the caption. Emphasize the need to use a towel or other wrap to avoid freezing the skin.

What should I do if I get injured while exercising?

A little muscle soreness is normal after certain exercises. However, if you feel more than a mild soreness when you exercise, tell an adult. The adult will probably tell you to stop exercising for a while. You can see how you feel the next day. If you still feel sore, you can try a different exercise. Or you can do light exercise to give your muscles a chance to recover.

If you feel pain while exercising, you may have an injury. Stop right away. Tell an adult. The adult may give you an ice pack to keep the injury from swelling. Hold the ice on the injured spot for about fifteen minutes two or three times a day.

If you have a serious injury, the adult may take you to the doctor. The doctor may give you medicine or put a bandage or cast on the injured area. The doctor may decide you need extra help to heal. If so, he or she will send you to a physical therapist. A physical therapist helps people regain movement and strength so they can become active again soon.

▼ If you put ice on an injury, wrap the ice in a towel or other cloth so it will not freeze your skin. The picture shows a reusable frozen gel pack.

Health Background

Steps in Muscle Healing Once a muscle has been injured, blood vessels in the area grow larger. At the same time white blood cells rush in to fight infection and remove dead cells. These changes cause redness, heat, and swelling. Movement becomes painful, which is the body's sign to let the area rest. In a day or two, the body begins manufacturing a protein called collagen, which makes up muscle tissue. Additional small blood vessels develop and bring more oxygen and nutrients to feed the new cells. The collagen covers the injury site. As collagen forms, it needs to be gently stretched and strengthened so that it does not leave a scar that can't be stretched. It may take months for the muscle to gain normal or close-to-normal flexibility and strength.

ACTIVITY BOOK, p. 22

Use Word Meanings — Vocabulary Reinforcement

The following vocabulary terms are not correctly defined. Write the correct meaning for each term.

1. *warm-up*—harder exercise done to prepare your body for easier exercise
   slow exercise done to prepare your body for harder exercise
2. *aerobic exercises*—exercises that make your leg muscles strong
   exercises that strengthen your heart and lungs
3. *eardrum*—part of the ear that turns sound waves into nerve signals
   part of the ear that moves back and forth and is at the end of the ear canal
4. *cool-down*—a cold shower after hard exercise
   slow exercise and stretching that helps prevent muscle soreness
5. *exercise*—any kind of sitting or standing
   any activity that makes your body work hard
6. *ear canal*—a combination of the middle ear and the inner ear
   the part of your outer ear through which sounds enter

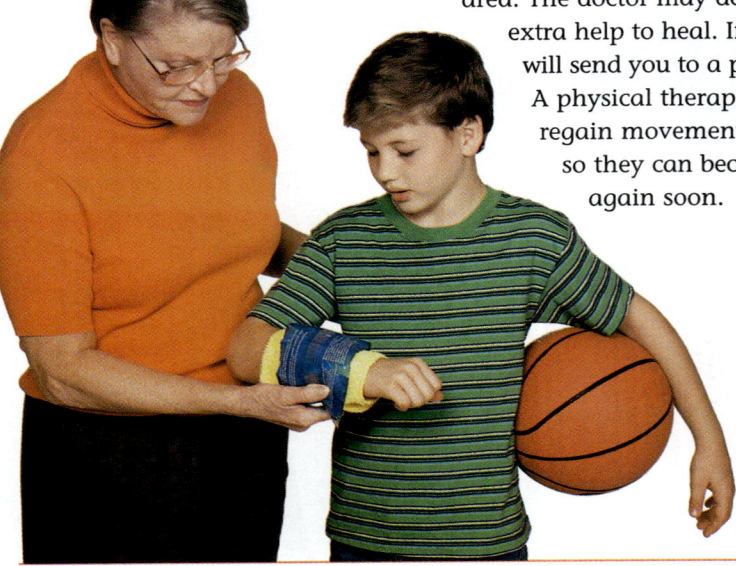

Career

Physical Therapist

What They Do

Physical therapists work in hospitals or clinics. Some have their own offices. They help people with injuries or disabilities learn or relearn to move. They also encourage people to do exercises on their own between therapy sessions.

Education and Training

Physical therapists can get degrees in physical therapy from four-year colleges. People who studied other subjects in college can enroll in master's degree programs in physical therapy. To get licenses to practice, therapists must pass tests given by their states.

▶ If you need a cast, you may also need a physical therapist to help you strengthen your muscles after the cast comes off.

LESSON CHECKUP

Check Your Facts

❶ CRITICAL THINKING List the safety gear for your favorite sport. Tell how each item helps keep players safe.

❷ Why is it important to do a warm-up and a cool-down when exercising?

❸ Why is it important to drink water before, during, and after exercising?

❹ CRITICAL THINKING You fall while jumping rope. Your ankle hurts. What should you do?

Set Health Goals

❺ Plan a weekly exercise program. Write which activity or activities you will do for aerobic exercise. Describe the warm-up and cool-down you will do during each exercise session. Try your plan for a week. Then write how you could make it better.

91

ACTIVITY BOOK, p. 23

Predict Outcomes | Reading Skills

Read the paragraphs. After each paragraph, predict what might happen next. **Possible answers are shown.**

1. Sam loves to play soccer. When the other children put on their shin guards, soccer shoes, and mouth guards, Sam just laughs. He plays a lot of games and doesn't get hurt. He says this proves he doesn't need safety gear. Then one day Sam
is kicked in the mouth. Sam's front tooth is loose.

2. Lauren swims 20 laps at the pool every day. She exercises hard and does not stop. Before exercising, Lauren does warm-up exercises. After swimming, she does cool-down exercises. As a result, Lauren
does not get sore muscles.

3. While running the bases, Sally hurts her ankle. She doesn't tell anyone though, and she keeps playing the game. Later that day Sally
is in a lot of pain from her injury.

4. Tranh thinks he hurt his elbow during a fall while playing basketball. His coach, Ms. Kopeck, puts ice on it. Later
Tranh has far less swelling than he might have had.

5. Amy often plays basketball with her family. Amy's family stops playing every thirty minutes to take a water break. As a result, Amy and the other family members
don't feel discomfort or get ill while they play.

MULTICULTURAL LINK

Famous Athletes Have students research the names of famous athletes and the countries they come from or from which their ancestors came. Post a list of names and the countries or cultural backgrounds to emphasize that famous athletes come from all different backgrounds.

Career

For more information on careers in physical therapy, contact

American College of Sports Medicine
401 W. Michigan St.
Indianapolis, IN 46202-3233
317-637-9200

Or visit the **Webliography** on the Teacher Resources page at:
www.harcourtschool.com/health
Keyword health careers

Learn from Pictures

Have students explain what is happening in the picture and tell who the two people are patient, physical therapist. Tell them to read the caption and infer why the girl may need the help of a physical therapist.

Project Checkup

Plan a Fitness Game (p. 69) Encourage students to include information about safety when planning their fitness game.

3 Wrap Up

Lesson Checkup

1. Students' answers will vary. Check answers to be sure that students have listed all safety gear for their sport and have explained the function of each piece.

2. You need to do a warm-up to avoid hurting muscles and a cool-down to avoid muscle soreness.

3. You lose water by sweating during exercise, so drinking before, during, and after helps replace the water.

4. Stop jumping, keep weight off the ankle, and tell an adult.

5. Tell students to write their plans in their Health Journals. Remind them that the warm-up and cool-down can include stretching and slower movement similar to the hard exercise. After a week, encourage them to note in their journals possible improvements.

Use Vocabulary 3 pts. each

1. pores
2. plaque
3. ear canal
4. exercise
5. bacteria
6. cavity
7. eardrum
8. aerobic exercises
9. dental floss
10. warm-up
11. sunscreen
12. fluoride
13. cool-down

Check Your Facts 5 pts. each

14. Brush with short, tooth-wide back and forth movements. Brush along the gum line.

15. Wear safety gear; warm up and cool down.

16. Stay away from noisy places; turn the sound down when you listen to the TV, radio, or CD player; use equipment to protect your ears when you play sports.

17. The sun gives off harmful rays that can damage your skin.

18. Babies need about twenty hours of sleep; children need about fifteen hours; adolescents need about ten hours; adults need about eight hours.

USE VOCABULARY

aerobic exercises (p. 82)	dental floss (p. 75)	exercise (p. 82)	pores (p. 70)
bacteria (p. 70)	ear canal (p. 78)	fluoride (p. 76)	sunscreen (p. 73)
cavity (p. 74)	eardrum (p. 79)	plaque (p. 74)	warm-up (p. 89)
cool-down (p. 89)			

Use the terms above to complete the sentences. Page numbers in ( ) tell you where to look in the chapter if you need help.

1. Sweat comes to the surface of your skin through tiny holes called ____.

2. The sticky coating that forms on your teeth is called ____.

3. The opening that you can see in your ear is the beginning of your ____.

4. Any activity that makes your body work hard is ____.

5. Certain tiny living things that may cause illness are called ____.

6. When acids make a hole in a tooth, the hole is called ____.

7. The part that moves back and forth at the end of the ear canal is the ____.

8. Exercises that strengthen your heart and lungs by making them work harder are called ____.

9. The special thread you use to remove plaque between teeth is ____.

10. Stretching and slow exercise that you do before hard exercise is a ____.

11. A cream or lotion that can protect skin from the sun's harmful rays is called ____.

12. A chemical that makes teeth stronger and harder is ____.

13. Stretching and slow exercise that you do after hard exercise is a ____.

CHECK YOUR FACTS

Page numbers in ( ) tell you where to look if you need help.

14. Describe the correct way to brush your teeth. (p. 76)

15. Tell two things you can do to exercise safely. (pp. 88–89)

16. List three ways to take good care of your ears and prevent hearing problems. (p. 80)

17. Explain why you need to protect your skin from the sun. (p. 72)

18. Use the bar graph to tell the greatest number of hours of sleep needed by people in each age group. (p. 85)

HOURS OF SLEEP NEEDED

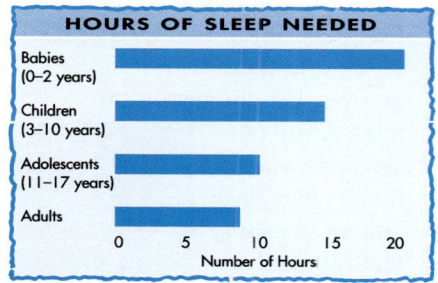

APPLY LIFE SKILLS

21. Manage Stress Imagine that you are feeling stressed or angry about something that happened at school. What could you do for half an hour when you get home that would help you feel happier and build your fitness? Give details.

22. Make Decisions Imagine that you are spending the night at a friend's house. When you unload your backpack, you realize that you forgot your toothbrush. Decide what you would do. Tell how you made your decision.

THINK CRITICALLY

19. Why might someone who seldom washes his or her hands be likely to get or spread a cold?

20. Would it be a good idea to clean the inside of your ears with cotton swabs? Explain.

Promote Health  **Home and Community**

1. Talk to family members about what you have learned in this chapter. Together, make a plan for taking care of yourselves. For example, you might go to the store together to choose a good sunscreen or toothpaste. Or you might come up with a family exercise program that everyone can enjoy.
2. Make posters about exercise safety. Get permission to display them at places in your community where people play sports or do other kinds of exercise.

93

Think Critically 8 pts. each

19. Your hands are covered with bacteria and viruses. When you wash your hands, you remove these pathogens. People who don't wash their hands, especially before they handle food or eat, are likely to get ill more often than others.

20. No, you should never put anything in your ears; you could damage your eardrum or push earwax farther into your ear and harm your hearing.

Apply Life Skills 10 pts. each

21. Possible answers: I could play outside with some friends or go for a walk; exercise would reduce my stress and improve my fitness.

22. I know that I need to brush my teeth every night to keep them healthy. I could ask my friend's parents if they have an unused toothbrush, or I could call an adult family member and ask him or her to bring me my toothbrush.

PERFORMANCE ASSESSMENT

Project—Plan a Fitness Game

The chapter project (introduced on page 69) can be used for individual or team performance assessment. Allow students the opportunity to revise and complete their projects before submitting them for evaluation. Students can use the Project Summary Sheet (Assessment Guide, p. 17) to tell about their projects. You can use the rubric provided on the Project Evaluation Sheet (Assessment Guide, p. 29) to evaluate student performance.

Activities

Teeth of Different Sorts

With a Partner • Look for pictures that show the teeth of different animals. Find animals that have sharp teeth, large flat teeth, and teeth with holes or grooves. Use the pictures to tell a group of classmates or friends how each animal uses its teeth to catch or eat its food.

Warm-up and Cool-down Collage

With a Team • Brainstorm good ways to warm up before and cool down after different kinds of hard exercise. A warm-up and a cool-down should use the same muscles that the hard exercise does. Make a collage using pictures of the exercises you brainstormed.

Sleepy Time

On Your Own • Keep track of your sleep for a week. Write down the time you go to sleep each night and the time you wake up each morning. Make a bar graph that shows how long you slept each night.

The Nose Knows

At Home • Ask an adult to help you gather some "mystery foods" for family members to sample. Have those family members put on blindfolds, hold their noses, and try to identify the foods by taste. Then have them try to identify the foods without holding their noses. Talk about how the nose affects taste as well as smell.

94

Chapter Test

Keeping My Body Fit

Chapter 3 Test

Write *T* or *F* to show if the sentence is true or false.

T **1.** Tiny holes in your skin are called pores.
F **2.** Sweat helps warm your body.
T **3.** Bacteria are living things that are so tiny you cannot see them.
T **4.** Some bacteria cause illness.
T **5.** Washing one's hands often is an important way of stopping the spread of illnesses.
F **6.** You need protection from the sun only if your skin does not tan.
T **7.** The sun is strongest in the middle of the day.
F **8.** Sunscreen does not protect you from the sun's harmful rays.
F **9.** Only your skin needs protection from the sun.
T **10.** Never look right at the sun, even if you're wearing sunglasses.

Use the words below to fill in the blanks.

mouth guard	cavity	fluoride
dental floss	plaque	

Ben had an appointment with the dentist. The last time that Ben went to the dentist, the dentist reminded him to brush his teeth twice a day with a toothpaste that has 11. __fluoride__ and to use

12. __dental floss__ once a day. The dentist said that by doing these two things every day, Ben could reduce the amount of

13. __plaque__ on his teeth. Ben also learned that it was important for him to wear a 14. __mouth guard__ when he played soccer. When the dentist finished examining Ben's teeth, he told Ben that he was doing a great job of caring for his teeth. Ben did not have a single

15. __cavity__! Ben was very glad that he had done all the things the dentist had told him to do.

Look carefully at the diagram below. Then label each part of the ear. Use the words below to help you.

ear canal	eardrum	middle ear
inner ear	outer ear	

16. **outer ear**
17. **ear canal**
18. **middle ear**
19. **inner ear**
20. **eardrum**

21. Susan plays baseball. She wants to protect her ears while she's playing this game. What could she do? **Wear a helmet.**

22. Mike sometimes gets nosebleeds. When he gets a nosebleed, he tips his head backward. What is Mike doing wrong? **He should sit or stand up straight and tip his head forward, while pinching his nose.**

Write the letter of the best answer on the line at the left.

b **23.** Any activity that makes your body work hard is called ____.
a. stretching   b. exercising
c. strengthening   d. aerobic exercise

d **24.** This kind of exercise speeds up your heart and breathing and helps your whole body work better.
a. warm-up exercise   b. cool-down exercise
c. stretching exercise d. aerobic exercise

a **25.** Rest is important because it helps your muscles ____.
a. relax   b. stretch
c. become more flexible d. work better

26. Kenny woke up late for soccer practice. He hurried over to the field to meet his coach and teammates. Kenny went straight out on the field and started playing. He soon got a bad cramp in his leg muscles. What did Kenny forget to do before playing?
Kenny forgot to warm up his muscles.

27. Marta felt pain in her ankle when her physical education class was running the track. She kept running. What should Marta have done immediately?
Marta should have stopped running and told her teacher.

28. Brad and Ted went bike riding together. They rode for three hours and were very tired when they got home. The boys got off their bikes and sat on Brad's front steps for an hour. When they tried to stand up, their leg muscles were very stiff and sore. What did the boys forget to do after bike riding?
They forgot to cool down their muscles.

29. Meg fell and broke her arm. She now has the cast off but she is having trouble using her arm. Her mother took her to a physical therapist. What kind of help will the physical therapist give Meg?
The physical therapist will help her regain movement and strength in her arm.

30. Louis twisted his knee while playing football with his friends. His friends took him home. Louis's dad knew what to do to help Louis's sprained knee. What did Louis's dad do?
Louis's dad put ice on the injured knee.

Multiple Choice

Choose the letter of the correct answer.

1. What should you do before you eat?
   a. apply sunscreen   b. bathe
   c. wash hands   d. floss

2. Brushing gets rid of ____.
   a. minerals   b. plaque
   c. cavities   d. fluoride

3. Avoiding loud sounds is one way to protect your sense of ____.
   a. hearing   b. smell
   c. sight   d. taste

4. Bicycling uphill ____ leg muscles.
   a. speeds up   b. stretches
   c. strengthens   d. slows down

5. If you get hurt while exercising, ____ is the best thing to help stop the swelling.
   a. hot water   b. bandages
   c. cold water   d. ice

Modified True or False

Write *true* or *false*. If a sentence is false, replace the underlined term to make the sentence true.

6. Washing with soap is <u>a poor way</u> to get rid of bacteria on your hands.

7. One way to protect uncovered skin from the sun is to put <u>sunscreen</u> on.

8. Remove plaque from between teeth by <u>rinsing your mouth</u>.

9. Baseball players should wear <u>mouth guards</u> to protect their ears.

10. Blowing your nose too hard can give you an <u>earache</u>.

11. You should do aerobic exercise for <u>at least twenty minutes</u> at a time.

12. People your age need <u>seven to nine hours</u> of sleep each night to stay healthy.

13. Drinking <u>water</u> before, during, and after exercising can help prevent discomfort and illness.

Short Answer

Write a complete sentence to answer each question.

14. How can the sun harm you?

15. Tell what to do if a tooth is knocked out.

16. How can you protect your hearing when listening to music at home?

17. Tell what to do to stop a nosebleed.

18. When you exercise, how should you warm up and cool down?

Writing in Health

Write paragraphs to answer each item.

19. Describe a perfect "healthful habits day."

20. Someone doesn't want to exercise because it's "boring." Tell how you would change his or her mind.

95

Writing in Health 9 pts. each

Sample answers are shown; accept other reasonable answers.

19. Answers will vary. Accept reasonable answers.

20. I'd tell the person that lots of exercises can be fun. It is important to try lots of different kinds of sports and exercises before you decide that all of them are boring.

Two options are provided for Chapter Tests—the in-book test and the reproducible test in the Assessment Guide. In addition to providing students with the opportunity to show what they have learned, both tests provide practice in taking standardized tests.

Multiple Choice 4 pts. each

1. c   3. a   5. d
2. b   4. c

Modified True or False 4 pts. each

6. false; a good way
7. true
8. false; flossing your teeth
9. false; helmets
10. true
11. true
12. false; ten to fifteen
13. true

Short Answer 6 pts. each

Sample answers are shown; accept other reasonable answers.

14. It can damage your skin and your eyes.

15. If it's dirty, rinse the tooth off and put it back in place. Then see a dentist immediately.

16. Keep the sound low.

17. Stand or sit so that your head is above your heart; lean forward; gently pinch your nose until the bleeding stops.

18. Warm up by walking and stretching; cool down by doing an exercise similar to what you were doing but slower, also stretch your muscles to prevent soreness.

Food *for a* Healthy Body

Chapter Organizer

Lesson	Objectives	Vocabulary	Program Resources
Introduce the Chapter pp. 96–97	• Preview the chapter. • Begin chapter project.		• School-Home Connection, TR p. 39 • Assessment Guide, p. 33 • Read-Aloud Anthology, p. RA-5 ✎ Teaching Transparency 4— Graphic Organizer
Lesson 1 ✓ 1·3 **Why My Body Needs Food** pp. 98–101 Pacing: 2 class periods	• Identify healthful food choices. • Explain why eating healthful foods is important to good health. • Describe where food comes from.	nutrients nutrition diet fiber	✎ Teaching Transparency 17
Lesson 2 ✓ 1·2·3 **The Food Guide Pyramid and Healthful Meals** pp. 102–105 Pacing: 2 class periods	• Explain how to use the Food Guide Pyramid to plan a healthful diet. • Describe how people get the water they need to stay healthy. • Explain why food is needed at regular intervals.	Food Guide Pyramid serving fluoride balanced diet	💻 Computer Graphing Activity, TR p. 57 ✎ Teaching Transparency 24 • Activity Book, pp. 24–25
Lesson 3 ✓ 3·5·6 **Healthful Snack Choices** pp. 106–107 Pacing: 1 class period	• Describe how to choose healthful snacks.	snacks	💻 Computer Graphing Activity, TR p. 58
Life Skills ✓ 3·5·6 **Make Decisions** pp. 108–109 Pacing: 1 class period	• Identify steps for making decisions. • Use the decision-making steps to make healthful snack choices.		• Activity Book, p. 26 📼 HEALTH VIDEO: International Food Fare
Lesson 4 ✓ 2·4·6 **Being a Wise Food Shopper** pp. 110–113 Pacing: 2 class periods	• Define **ingredients** and tell how to use labels to choose foods with the most nutritious ingredients. • Explain why a food's price varies.	ingredients food label	• Activity Book, p. 27 ✎ Teaching Transparency 25 📼 HEALTH VIDEO: The Good Health Game Show
Lesson 5 ✓ 3·4·7 **Handling Food Safely** pp. 114–115 Pacing: 2 class periods	• Explain why it is important to store foods properly. • Describe ways to handle foods safely.	spoiled pathogens	• Activity Book, pp. 28–29
Chapter Review and Test ✓ 1·7 pp. 116–119	• Assess chapter objectives and project. • Provide extension activities.		• Assessment Guide, pp. 30–33

 National Health Education Standards
A complete list of the Standards is provided on the next page.

Key: TR = Teaching Resources

National Health Education Standards

1. Comprehend concepts related to health promotion and disease prevention.
2. Access valid health information and health-promoting products and services.
3. Practice health-enhancing behaviors and reduce health risks.
4. Analyze the influence of culture, media, technology, and other factors on health.
5. Use interpersonal communication skills to enhance health.
6. Use goal-setting and decision-making skills to enhance health.
7. Advocate for personal, family, and community health.

Drama and Art
- Cooking with the Master, p. 96C
- Write an Ad, p. 112

Science
- Research Grains, p. 100

Math
- Estimate and Measure Temperatures, p. 96C
- How Much Is Really Juice?, p. 107
- Compare Prices, p. 113
- Figure Per-Unit Cost, p. 113

Curriculum Integration
Use these topics to integrate health into your daily planning.
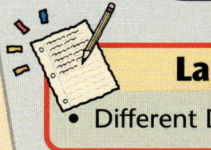

Social Studies
- Research and Map Foods, p. 96C
- Snacks from Around the World, p. 109
- Influences in Food Selections, p. 113

Language Arts
- Different Diets, p. 96C

ASSESSMENT OPTIONS

Portfolio Assessment
Have students select their best work from the following suggestions:
- **Write an Ad**, p. 112
- **Local Foods**, p. 118
- **Make Your Own Food Guide Pyramid**, p. 118

Student Self-Assessment
- **Journal Notes**, p. 115
- **Set Health Goals**, pp. 101, 105, 115
- **Use Life Skills**, pp. 107, 113

Daily Assessment
- **Check Your Facts**, pp. 101, 105, 107, 113, 115

Performance Assessment
- **Chapter Project: Make a Food Display**, pp. 97, 99, 103, 107, 117
- **Project Evaluation Guide**, Assessment Guide, p. 33

Formal Assessment
- **Chapter Review**, pp. 116–117
- **Chapter Test**, Assessment Guide, pp. 30–32

Cross-Curricular Activities

Social Studies

Research and Map Foods

Students should use maps and information in their social studies books, encyclopedia, or other resources to find out where major farm products are grown or raised in the United States.

- They can look for products such as irrigated and non-irrigated fruits and vegetables; sheep, hogs, and cows; and corn, wheat, and other grains.

- Have students present their findings on a map with symbols and a key for the different farm products.

Language Arts

Different Diets

Have students write a day-in-the-life story about twins—one who eats a healthful diet and one who does not. Students should describe the meals and snacks each twin eats and contrast the effects of the opposite diets on the twins' activity levels, mental abilities, and emotional states.

Drama

Cooking with the Master

Have students work in groups to plan an episode of a television program called "Cooking with the Master."

- Students may first want to discuss similar shows they have seen on television.

- Each group needs to decide what dish or dishes they will prepare and how they will show the preparation. Remind them to show safe handling of food.

- After students present their skits, have viewers list all the ways the players modeled safe food handling.

Math

Estimate and Measure Temperatures

Assign this activity to be done at home.

- Have students estimate the temperatures of their refrigerators and freezers at home.

- Students should then use thermometers to measure the actual temperatures of the compartments. Students should use indoor/outdoor thermometers, as those designed to read body temperature will not register.

- Have students compare their results and then determine what the ideal refrigerator and freezer temperatures are (refrigerator—not more than 40°F or less than 32°F; freezer—about 0°F).

Bulletin Board

Set up two sections on the bulletin board for students to use. Label one section *Foods from Plants* and the other *Foods from Animals*.

- Have students collect from magazines or draw and color pictures of foods from plants and foods from animals (animals that are eaten or food products that animals make).

- Tell students to pin their pictures under the correct headings on the bulletin board.

- After students have collected a number of pictures on the board, suggest that they reorganize the pictures into groups under the main head. Ask questions such as the following to help them discover groups. **How could you regroup foods from plants?** Vegetables, Fruits, Grains **How could you regroup foods from animals?** Animals We Eat, Animal Products We Eat Under *Animals We Eat* students might write the divisions *Meat, Poultry, Fish.*

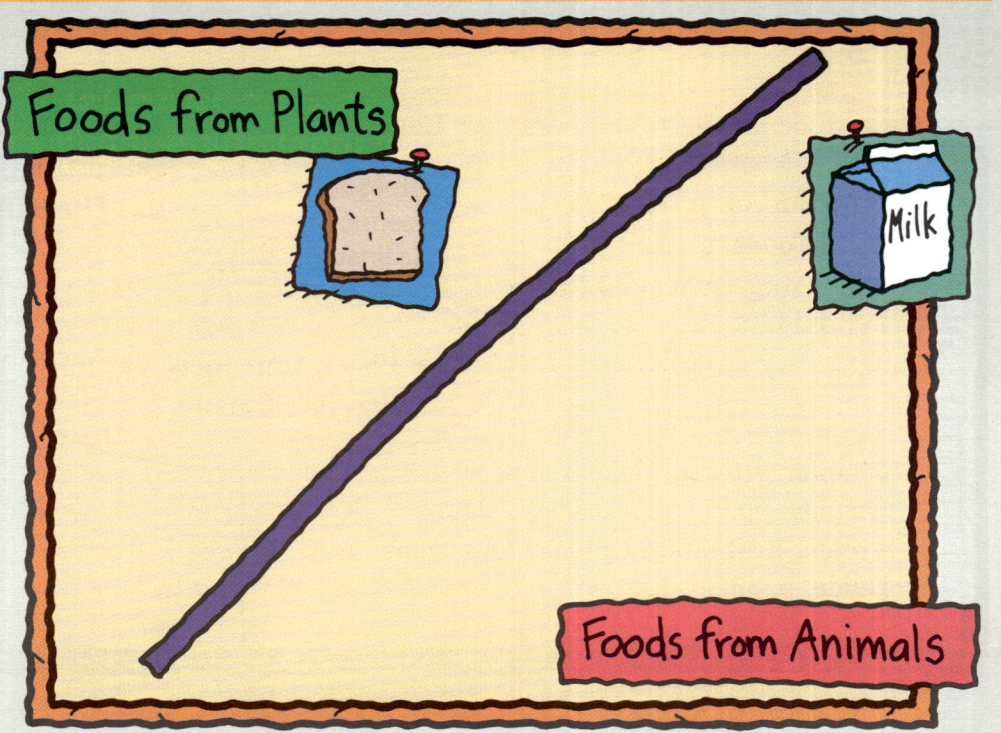

Resources

Books for Students

Sweet, Julia E. *Activities for Fitness, Food, and Fun for the Whole Family.* McGraw Hill, 2001. Features activities to get children active and provides healthy recipes. **EASY**

Dooley, Norah. *Everybody Bakes Bread.* Carolrhoda Books, Inc., 1996. Presents bread-making as routine family time; presents bread as a basic food found in many cultures, represented here in one neighborhood. **AVERAGE**

Lambourne, Mike. *Down the Hatch—Find Out About Your Food.* Millbrook Press, 1992. Good information, child-friendly format, almost comic book-like illustrations and activities. **ADVANCED**

Books for Teachers and Families

Balch, Phyllis A., C.N.C. and James F. Balch, M.D. *Prescription for Nutritional Healing.* Avery Penguin Putnam, 2000. The power of good nutrition is shown in a helpful body of information.

Ewin, Jeanette. *The Plants We Need to Eat: Discover the Power of Nature's Miracle Nutrients.* Thorsons Publishing, 1997. An interesting look at natural supplements and the effect they may have on daily nutrition.

Videos

The Good Food Diner. United Learning, 1995. (14 minutes) Explains the digestive system and the importance of eating healthful meals.

The Magic School Bus for Lunch. Scholastic Productions Inc., Warner Vision Entertainment, 1995. (30 minutes) When Arnold accidentally swallows his miniature classmates, the class takes a firsthand look at the human digestive system.

My Body, My Buddy: Healthy Food. Rainbow Educational Media, 1993. (16 minutes) Provides up-to-date information on healthful food choices and explains the role of advertising.

Health Video Series by Harcourt
International Food Fare
The Good Health Game Show
These videos are referenced at point-of-use in this Teacher's Edition.

Your Health Webliography

The **Webliography** provides links to the Health Background and teaching resources that will support you as you teach the topics in *Your Health*. Simply choose a keyword and you will be taken to a page of links with descriptions of the content you can obtain at each site. The **Webliography** is located on the Teacher Resources page at **www.harcourtschool.com/health** Please review websites before referring your students to them.

Organizations and Agencies

American School Health Association
7263 State Route 43
P.O. Box 708
Kent, OH 44240
330-678-1601
Provides information about school lunch programs and classroom-based nutrition programs.

Center for Science in the Public Interest
1875 Connecticut Avenue N.W.
Suite 300
Washington, D.C. 20009
A consumer advocacy organization that offers several publications on nutrition topics. Small fee for publications; catalog available free.

For more information about health organizations and agencies, please see the *Teaching Resources* book.

Community Health

Local Farm Operator or Food Store Owner Invite a farm operator or food store owner to discuss with the class how he or she ensures that food stays safe for the people who eat it. Ask the visitor to discuss any precautions or procedures used to keep food fresh and safe. Encourage students to ask questions about the safe handling of food.

Free and Inexpensive Material

National Cattlemen's Beef Association
1301 Pennsylvania Avenue, Suite 300
Washington, DC 20004
Provides resources to teach lessons about the Food Guide Pyramid.

North Dakota Wheat Commission
4023 State Street
Bismarck, ND 58501-0690
701-328-5111
Offers a sixteen-page booklet explaining how wheat is produced.

Note that information, while correct at time of publication, is subject to change.

Visit **The Harcourt Learning Site** for related links, activities, resources, and the health **Webliography**.

www.harcourtschool.com

WELCOME TO THE LEARNING SITE

"Educating school age children about nutrition is important to establishing healthy eating habits early in life."

—*Healthy People 2010*

CHAPTER SUMMARY

In this chapter students
- recognize the importance of healthful food choices and use the Food Guide Pyramid to make a balanced diet.
- learn the importance of reading and comparing food labels.
- discuss how to keep foods safe to eat.

LIFE SKILLS Students practice *making decisions* about snack foods.

CONSUMER HEALTH Students use food labels to compare foods and food prices.

HUMAN BODY Students investigate the role of the intestines in digestion.

96

Literature Springboard

Use the poem "Greedy Mable" to spark interest in the chapter topic. See the Read-Aloud Anthology on page RA-5 of this Teacher's Edition.

School-Home Connection

Distribute copies of the School-Home Connection (in English or Spanish), TR page 39. Have students take the page home to share with their families as you begin this chapter.

Follow Up Have volunteers share their meal charts and answers to the questions. Did they discover they are eating balanced diets? What suggestions did their families have for eating balanced diets?

Alternative Use the School-Home Connection page as a classroom resource for enrichment activities.

Dear Family Member,

In Chapter 4, Food for a Healthy Body, our class will be learning the importance of planning healthful meals and choosing healthful snacks. We will also learn how to read food labels and how to safely store, handle, and prepare food.

Family Activity

One way to ensure a healthful diet is to eat three meals a day. In the space provided, ask your child to record what he or she eats on a particular day. Then, use the questions that follow as a springboard for discussing whether or not your child is eating a balanced diet.

What I Ate Today

| Breakfast: |
| Lunch: |
| Dinner: |
| Snacks: |

Questions
1. What vegetables and fruits did you eat today?
2. Did you drink milk or eat yogurt or cheese?
3. Did you have bread, cereal, rice, or pasta?
4. Did you eat meat, fish, dried beans, eggs, or nuts?

Family Reading

The following books can help you and your family learn more about the topics covered in this chapter. Books should always be chosen with the approval of an adult family member.
- Sweet, Julia E. *365 Activities for Fitness, Food, and Fun for the Whole Family.* McGraw Hill, 2001. Features activities to get children active and provides healthy recipes. EASY
- Dooley, Norah. *Everybody Bakes Bread.* Carolrhoda Books, Inc., 1996. Presents bread-making as routine family time; shows bread as a basic food found in many cultures, represented here in one neighborhood. AVERAGE
- Lambourne, Mike. *Down the Hatch—Find Out About Your Food.* Millbrook Press, 1992. Good information, child-friendly format, almost comic book-like illustrations and activities. ADVANCED

Thank you for participating in our study of health.

Sincerely,

Food *for* *a* Healthy Body

MAKE A FOOD DISPLAY

As you work through this chapter, think about which foods you need to eat to stay healthy. Cut out pictures from magazines and food labels, and arrange them on paper plates. Include information about each food, and explain why it is healthful. Put your food display in the school cafeteria.

For other activities, visit the Harcourt Learning Site. www.harcourtschool.com

97

Teaching Transparency 4—Graphic Organizer

4 Chapter 4 Graphic Organizer

Food for a Healthy Body

Why My Body Needs Food
1. _nutrients_
2. energy
3. _nutrition_

Healthful Snack Choices
1. low in _fat_
2. low in _oil_
3. low in _sweets_

Handling Food Safely
1. _Spoiled_ food is unsafe.
2. _Pathogens_ can spoil food.

The Food Guide Pyramid and Healthful Meals
1. food groups
2. _water_
3. _balanced diet_

Being a Wise Food Shopper
1. _ingredients_
2. _food labels_
3. _prices_
4. size

Introduce the Chapter

Project

MAKE A FOOD DISPLAY

Access Prior Knowledge Poll students about foods they think are healthful and not healthful. Ask what makes foods healthful or not. Use this activity as a baseline assessment of students' understanding of which foods are needed to stay healthy.

Performance Assessment The project can be used for performance assessment. Before students begin, explain how you will evaluate their performance. (See the Project Evaluation Sheet, Assessment Guide, p. 33.)

Prereading Strategies

Scan the Chapter Have students preview the chapter content by scanning the titles, headings, pictures, and charts. Ask volunteers to speculate on what they will learn.

Preview Vocabulary As students scan the chapter, have them write the vocabulary words listed at the beginning of each lesson. Tell them to cross out words they know, make a box around words they think they know, and circle words they don't know. Have them cross out words they have boxed or circled as they confirm or learn them.

Visualize Key Concepts Display the Graphic Organizer Transparency. You may also wish to distribute photocopies to students. Have students complete the organizer as they work through the chapter. Suggested concepts for students to fill in are shown.

Follow Up Review the completed organizer with students as preparation for the Chapter Review and Chapter Tests.

OBJECTIVES

- Identify healthful food choices.
- Explain why eating healthful foods is important to good health.
- Describe where food comes from.

PROGRAM RESOURCES

 Teaching Transparency 17

VOCABULARY

- nutrients (p. 98)
- nutrition (p. 98)
- diet (p. 99)
- fiber (p. 99)

Daily Safety Tip

Many illnesses, such as colds and flu, are spread by hands that have not been properly washed. Remind students to wash their hands well with soap and warm water before eating or handling food to kill germs that could get into the food and make them or someone else sick.

1 Motivate

Optional Materials **two identical sheets of paper and crayons**

On one sheet of paper, draw (or have volunteers draw) several colored shapes to make a varied and interesting pattern. Repeat a single shape on the second sheet. Hold up both sheets and have students describe how they are different. (As an alternative, you can use the board and colored chalk.) Tell students to imagine that the marks on the papers represent foods people eat. Ask students which group they would choose to eat. Most will choose the paper with the varied pattern. Explain that people need to eat a variety of healthful foods each day.

MAIN IDEA Eating healthful foods from plants and animals is important to good health.

WHY LEARN THIS? In order to eat a healthful diet, you need to understand which foods are good for you.

VOCABULARY
- nutrients
- nutrition
- diet
- fiber

Why My Body Needs Food

When you eat, does it matter whether you eat bananas or potato chips? Yogurt or french fries? Carrots or cookies? You bet it does! Some foods are more healthful than others. Eating healthful foods is important in keeping your body healthy.

Why is food important?

You cannot live without food. Food gives your body energy. You need energy to grow. You need energy to be active. You need energy to read, write, and think. You even need energy to sleep!

Nutrients (NOO•tree•uhnts) are the parts of food that help your body grow and get energy. There are many different kinds of nutrients. You get all the nutrients you need by eating different kinds of foods.

Nutrition (nu•TRIH•shuhn) is the study of food and how it affects the body. Knowing about nutrition can help you stay healthy.

◀ What are some ways people use energy? ▼

98

 MULTILEVEL ACTIVITIES

EASY **Using Energy** Ask students to list the ways they use energy. Remind them to include processes carried out by their bodies as well as day-to-day activities. **INTRAPERSONAL**

AVERAGE **Food Songs** Encourage groups of students to write songs about where foods come from or how a food is processed between harvest and store. They can use a common melody or make up their own. **MUSICAL**

ADVANCED **Farm Lands** Have students research the locations of major farm lands in the United States. Have them present their findings on maps. **SPATIAL/VISUAL**

These foods help you grow.

These foods give you energy and help you grow.

These foods help your body work as it should.

Why should you eat different kinds of foods?

Loni eats leftover pizza for breakfast. Ali snacks on popcorn and pretzels. Cathy often has rice and vegetables for dinner. The foods a person usually eats and drinks make up his or her **diet** (DY•uht). What foods are a part of your diet?

Some diets are more healthful than others. For you to stay healthy, your diet must give your body all the nutrients it needs. Your diet also must include **fiber**, the woody part of plants. Fiber helps keep you healthy. Many fruits and vegetables contain fiber. Grains, such as brown rice, and foods made from grains, such as oatmeal and bread, also contain fiber.

Variety is important in a diet. Some foods give your body energy. Some foods help you grow. Other foods help parts of your body work well. The photograph shows some healthful foods that do these jobs. Which of these foods do you eat?

HUMAN BODY CONNECTION

The Intestines
Fiber helps keep food moving through your small and large intestines. Look at the digestive system on page 8 at the front of the book. Trace the intestines from one end to the other.

• • •

99

DEVELOP READING SKILLS

Identify Sequence In this lesson, students read steps for making bread and for how milk gets from farms to grocery stores. Have students use the following words and signal words to describe one of the processes. Write the words on the board and have volunteers suggest sentences, or have students write paragraphs on their own.

Making Bread	Getting Milk
second	first
ground	heated
finally	second
baked	last
wrapped	milked
first	containers
next	
harvest	

2 Teach

Learn from Pictures

Ask students to look at the pictures on page 98 and describe what is happening in each. Encourage students to answer the caption question by identifying other ways in which people use energy.

Discuss

The nutrients people need to stay healthy include proteins, carbohydrates, and fats as well as vitamins, minerals, and water. How do you get all the nutrients you need? by eating different kinds of foods

Learn from Pictures

Ask students to look at the picture on this page. Have volunteers identify the foods shown. Ask students questions such as the following to help them read the caption blocks. **What kinds of foods give you energy? What kinds of foods help your body work properly?**

Human Body Connection

The Intestines Have students look at the diagram of the digestive system on page 8. Ask them to find the intestines and follow their routes with a finger. Explain that their paths are curved to allow a longer time for digestion and absorption of nutrients.

Project Checkup

Make a Food Display (p. 97) Encourage students to use the information they have learned to help them with their displays.

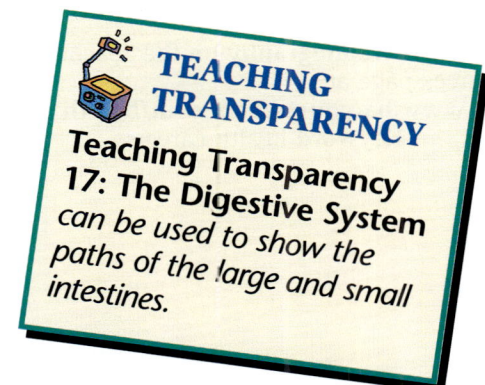

TEACHING TRANSPARENCY
Teaching Transparency 17: The Digestive System can be used to show the paths of the large and small intestines.

Learn from Pictures

Have students look at the series of pictures on pages 100 and 101. Ask volunteers to read aloud each of the four captions. Ask students questions such as the following to help them understand the captions. **What does each picture show? What happens before the wheat is harvested?** It is planted and grown. **What happens after the bread arrives in stores?** It is purchased and eaten.

Discuss

Critical Thinking **What are some common fruits and vegetables?** Possible answers: fruits—strawberries, apples, watermelon; vegetables—carrots, lettuce, squash.

Ask volunteers to identify the kinds of produce grown in your region. In many parts of the country, it is not possible to grow fruits and vegetables year-round because of the weather.

Problem Solving **How do we get fresh fruits and vegetables in the winter?** They are shipped from where they are grown and delivered by trucks to grocery stores.

Critical Thinking **Why are some plant foods canned, packaged, or frozen?** to keep them fresh and edible longer

Career

For more information on careers in farming, contact the

U.S. Department of Agriculture
14th Street and Independence Ave., SW
Washington, D.C. 20250

Or visit the **Webliography** on the Teacher Resources page at:
**www.harcourtschool.com/health
Keyword** health careers

▲ Wheat is needed to make bread. Wheat is a grain that is harvested in mid- or late summer.

▲ The wheat is taken to a factory to be ground into a fine powder called flour.

Where does food come from?

Many of the foods we eat come from plants. Fruits and vegetables come from plants. So do beans, nuts, and seeds. Grains used to make cereals and breads also come from plants. Some common grains are corn, wheat, oats, and rice. Look at the pictures to see how bread is made.

When plant crops are ripe, they are harvested. Some plant foods are sold fresh. Others are sent to factories where they are canned, packaged, or frozen.

Career

Farm Operator

What They Do
Farm operators raise grains, fruits, vegetables, livestock, and dairy cows. They plan, plant, and care for crops. They care for animals. They harvest crops and send foods to market.

Education and Training
Many farm operators grow up on farms. Farm operators need strong science and math skills. Some may use computers. People without farming experience can go to college to learn how to grow crops or raise animals.

100

SCIENCE

Research Grains Students should research grains, such as wheat, oats, barley, rice, rye, corn, millet, buckwheat, and amaranth. Ask them to investigate where these plants grow, what they look like, and how they are used as food or nonfood products.

MULTICULTURAL LINK

Fruits of the World Have students work in groups to find pictures or samples of fruits common to different parts of the world. Ask them to label each picture or fruit with the fruit's name and where it comes from. Invite students who have tasted any of the fruits to share descriptions of what they taste like. Fruits to research include Asian pear, carambola, cherimoya, chayote, fig, guava, loquat, litchi, mango, persimmon, prickly pear, and sapodilla.

▲ At large bakeries wheat flour is made into loaves of bread. The loaves are packaged in plastic bags.

▲ Trucks bring loaves of fresh bread to grocery stores every day.

Most of the other foods people eat come from animals. We eat meat from cows, sheep, pigs, chicken, and fish. Most of the eggs we eat come from chickens. Most of the milk we drink comes from cows. After the cows are milked, the milk is heated to make it safe to drink. Then it is put into containers. Some milk is made into cheeses, butter, ice cream, or yogurt.

All kinds of plant and animal foods come from farms across the United States. Some foods even come from other countries. When ready for sale, fresh and prepared foods are sent to markets. They may be sent by truck or train. Inside the market, food is placed on shelves or in cold storage. Finally, it ends up on your table.

LESSON CHECKUP

Check Your Facts

1. Why are nutrients important to good health?
2. What is nutrition?
3. Where does food come from?
4. Describe how wheat becomes the bread you eat.

Set Health Goals

5. What kinds of foods make up your diet? List the foods you eat often. Tell which are plant foods and which are animal foods. What can you do to make your diet more healthful?

101

Discuss

Most of the meat people buy in grocery stores comes from cows, sheep, pigs, chickens, and fish.

Critical Thinking Which other animals provide meat for humans to eat? Possible answers: deer, elk, antelope, rabbits, ducks, and frogs.

What are two ways we get foods from animals? We eat animal meat and we eat products made by animals, such as milk and eggs. Explain that the reason animals make things like milk and eggs is not to provide people with food. These products are made for the survival of the animal species. For example, a cow's milk is made to feed the cow's young.

3 Wrap Up

Lesson Checkup

1. Nutrients give the body energy, help the body grow, and help some parts of the body work.

2. the study of food and how it affects the body

3. plants and animals

4. Wheat is grown and harvested on farms. It is ground into flour at a factory. The flour is then made into bread at a bakery. The bread is packaged and sent to grocery stores.

5. Help students develop a format for the information. This might be a chart with columns for symbols and a key to show plant foods and animal foods. After students have made the lists and noted ways they might make their diets more healthful, suggest that they try out each idea for a week to see how it works.

OBJECTIVES

- Explain how to use the Food Guide Pyramid to plan a healthful diet.
- Describe how people get the water they need to stay healthy.
- Explain why food is needed at regular intervals.

PROGRAM RESOURCES

 Computer Graphing Activity, Teaching Resources p. 57

 Teaching Transparency 24

- Activity Book, pp. 24–25

VOCABULARY

- Food Guide Pyramid (p. 102)
- serving (p. 102)
- fluoride (p.104)
- balanced diet (p. 105)

Daily Safety Tip

One way students can make sure the food they eat is safe is to pay attention: check for mold on breads and cheeses; make sure wrappers on unopened goods are not broken; don't drink milk that doesn't taste right.

1 Motivate

Optional Materials a dozen or more index cards or slips of paper with one healthful food written on each

Place the cards in a box and have volunteers pick four cards for each meal. List the menus for the meals on the board. (As an alternative, have students name foods and write them in random groups of four on the board.) Then discuss what seems wrong or right about each meal. Help students realize this activity shows what might happen if meals are not planned.

MAIN IDEA The Food Guide Pyramid shows how many servings from each food group you need to eat each day to have a healthful diet.

WHY LEARN THIS? You can use what you learn to make sure you eat a balanced diet.

VOCABULARY
- Food Guide Pyramid
- serving
- fluoride
- balanced diet

LIFE SKILLS FOCUS

Make Decisions One of the Dietary Guidelines for Americans is to let the Food Guide Pyramid guide your food choices. Make a list of your favorite foods. Sort each food into its food group. Use some of your favorite foods and the steps on page *ix* to help plan a balanced diet for at least one day. Make sure you're getting the correct number of servings from each group.

• • •

The Food Guide Pyramid and Healthful Meals

The Cortéz family wants to be healthy. Every Sunday they sit down and plan their meals for the week. They plan for three meals and two snacks each day. The family chooses a variety of foods. They want to make sure everyone gets all the nutrients he or she needs.

What makes a meal healthful?

By itself a potato is not a healthful meal. But if you eat it with salad, chicken, and a glass of milk, you will have a healthful meal. A healthful meal includes a variety of foods. Eating a variety of foods gives your body the nutrients it needs.

The **Food Guide Pyramid** (FOOD GYD PIR•uh•mid) is a tool to help you choose foods for a healthful diet. It has six groups. The Food Guide Pyramid tells how many servings you should eat from each group each day. A **serving** is the measured amount of a food you would probably eat during a meal or as a snack.

The bread group is the largest group in the Food Guide Pyramid. It includes bread, pasta, rice, and cereal. The smallest section of the pyramid is the fats, oils, and sweets group. You don't need to eat many of these foods.

Fruits are one group. Vegetables are another. Milk products make up a group. Meat, fish, poultry, eggs, nuts, and dried beans make up another group.

MULTILEVEL ACTIVITIES

EASY **Describe Foods** Ask each student to think of three foods he or she likes and write a sentence for each food, using at least three adjectives that describe the food. Example: I like milk because it is cool, smooth, and refreshing. **LINGUISTIC**

AVERAGE **Jumping Jacks** Have students demonstrate how they might do 20 jumping jacks if they had recently eaten a healthful meal and if they had not eaten for several hours. **KINESTHETIC/LOGICAL**

ADVANCED **Measure Your Water Intake** Suggest students bring in glasses from home. Use a measuring cup to measure the amount of water held by each glass. Students should multiply that number by the number of glasses they drink each day to estimate water intake. **MATHEMATICAL**

Fats, oils, and sweets group Eat very little from this group each day.

Meat, poultry, fish, dry beans, eggs, and nuts group Eat 2–3 servings from this group each day.

Milk, yogurt, and cheese group Eat 2–3 servings a day.

Fruit group Eat 2–4 servings each day.

Vegetable group Eat 3–5 servings each day.

Bread, cereal, rice, and pasta group Eat 6–11 servings from this group each day.

2 Teach

Life Skills Focus

Make Decisions Invite each student to keep a notebook for one day to list what he or she eats and drinks. Then have students organize the lists into food groups. Review the decision-making model to help students consider possible changes to their diets.

For a complete list of all the Dietary Guidelines for Americans see pages 286–287.

Learn from Diagrams

Direct attention to the Food Guide Pyramid. Ask volunteers to read aloud the caption boxes. **What are the six groups of the Food Guide Pyramid? What kinds of foods should you eat the most of? The least of?**

Discuss the foods included in each group. Ask students to try to name other foods they commonly eat that might be included in each group. Then discuss the shape of the pyramid. Help them understand that the decreasing size of sections moving from the base to the top reflects the number of servings needed from each group, not the importance of the foods. Tell students that a serving is about as much as they would eat at one sitting.

Project Checkup

Make a Food Display (p. 97)
Encourage students to use the information on the Food Guide Pyramid to help them plan displays that contain foods from all of the important food groups.

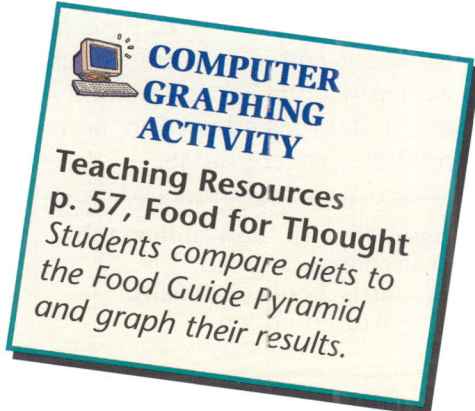

COMPUTER GRAPHING ACTIVITY

Teaching Resources p. 57, Food for Thought Students compare diets to the Food Guide Pyramid and graph their results.

DEVELOP READING SKILLS

List, Group, and Code Vocabulary Words Have students complete the following to help them understand the Food Guide Pyramid and link the concepts associated with it.

• Students should brainstorm words that relate to the Food Guide Pyramid. List the words on the board.

• Read the list as a class, having students look for words that are alike or have something in common with each other.

• Have students use a code to link related words, such as a circle for all food-group words (bread, fats, vegetables, milk products), a square for words that tell the results of using the pyramid (balanced diet, health), and an underline for words that tell how to use the pyramid (tool, serving).

▼ All these foods contain water. Which foods do you eat? What other foods might have water in them?

Discuss

Water regulates body temperature, helps carry nutrients throughout the body, helps protect the body's organs, and cushions joints. One way to drink more water every day is to drink a glass of water with every meal and snack.

Critical Thinking **What are other ways to drink more water every day?** Possible answer: Drink a glass of water every morning as soon as you get up. Accept all reasonable answers.

Beverages that have caffeine in them, such as iced tea and some soft drinks, make the body lose water. So even though they have water in them, they do not count toward daily water intake.

Learn from Pictures

Have students look at the picture and identify the foods. Then ask the caption questions. Other foods that might have water in them would be dairy products, other fruits and vegetables, rice and pasta, and prepared foods. The amount of water in each food varies. Remind students that eating these foods should not replace drinking six to eight glasses of water daily.

Where do you get your water?

Did you know your skin contains water? So do your bones and muscles. Water is everywhere in your body. You need water to stay healthy.

You get some water from the foods you eat. Fruits such as apples, peaches, and melons contain water. Vegetables such as lettuce and carrots also have water. But to get enough water, you need to drink six to eight glasses of water each day.

Fluoride (FLAWR•yd) is a nutrient your body needs in small amounts. It helps keep your teeth healthy. Fluoride is often added to the water that is piped to homes. If you get your water from a water company, you may get some of this fluoride each time you drink water from your faucet.

Some people don't drink water that is piped to their homes. They buy bottled water to drink or get their water from a well.

Sometimes fluoride and other chemicals are removed from bottled water. People who drink water without fluoride, such as bottled water or water from private wells, may need to get fluoride in other ways. Sometimes they get fluoride treatments from a dentist.

Did you know?

More than half the weight of your body is made up of water. There is water everywhere in your body. Even your bones are one-fifth water!

104

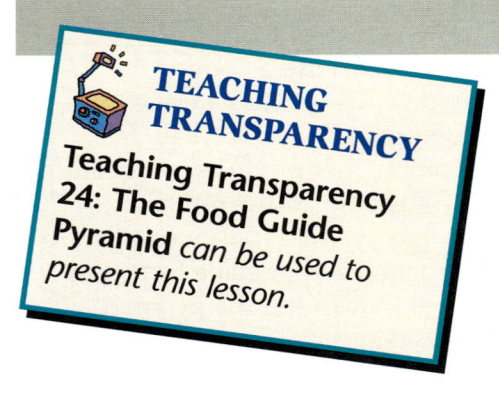

TEACHING TRANSPARENCY

Teaching Transparency 24: The Food Guide Pyramid *can be used to present this lesson.*

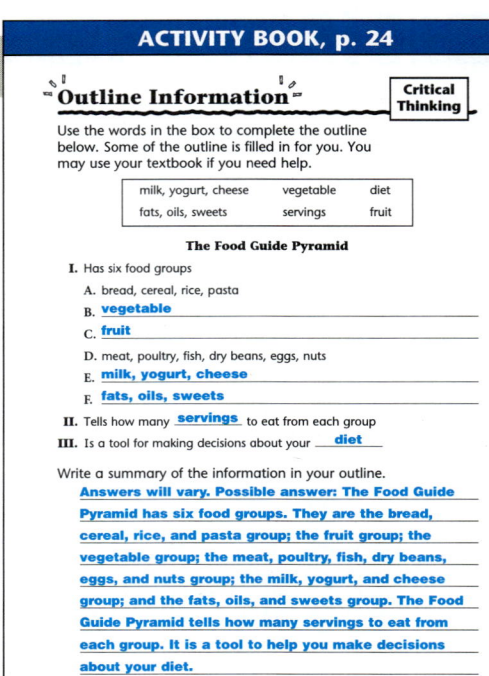

ACTIVITY BOOK, p. 24

Outline Information
Critical Thinking

Use the words in the box to complete the outline below. Some of the outline is filled in for you. You may use your textbook if you need help.

| milk, yogurt, cheese | vegetable | diet |
| fats, oils, sweets | servings | fruit |

The Food Guide Pyramid

I. Has six food groups
  A. bread, cereal, rice, pasta
  B. **vegetable**
  C. **fruit**
  D. meat, poultry, fish, dry beans, eggs, nuts
  E. **milk, yogurt, cheese**
  F. **fats, oils, sweets**
II. Tells how many **servings** to eat from each group
III. Is a tool for making decisions about your **diet**

Write a summary of the information in your outline.

Answers will vary. Possible answer: The Food Guide Pyramid has six food groups. They are the bread, cereal, rice, and pasta group; the fruit group; the vegetable group; the meat, poultry, fish, dry beans, eggs, and nuts group; the milk, yogurt, and cheese group; and the fats, oils, and sweets group. The Food Guide Pyramid tells how many servings to eat from each group. It is a tool to help you make decisions about your diet.

Why eat three meals a day?

Everything you do uses energy. Even when you are not doing anything, your body is using energy. Your body needs energy all day.

Different activities use different amounts of energy. When you ride your bike, your body uses a lot of energy. When you sit and read, it uses less.

All the energy your body uses comes from the food you eat. Your body uses energy throughout the day. The Food Guide Pyramid can help you eat foods to provide your energy needs. If you use the guide to eat foods from each food group every day, you will have a **balanced diet** (BA•luhnst DY•uht).

Suppose you ate all the foods you need each day at one meal. Your body could not use all that food at once. It's important to eat meals throughout the day. Spacing meals gives your body the energy and nutrients it needs all day.

▶ What provided these boys with the energy they need to play their favorite sport?

LIFE SKILLS FOCUS

Make Decisions
Kim is always late. She often skips breakfast so she won't miss the bus. This makes Kim tired and cranky. Use the steps for making decisions on page ix to help Kim get the energy she needs and still catch the bus.

LESSON CHECKUP

Check Your Facts

❶ What is the Food Guide Pyramid?

❷ What are the food groups in the Food Guide Pyramid?

❸ How can you make sure you get enough water?

❹ CRITICAL THINKING How can you eat a balanced diet?

Set Health Goals

❺ Think back over what you've eaten for lunch the last three days. Did you eat foods from every food group in the Food Guide Pyramid? How many things did you eat from each group? How can you make your lunches more healthful?

105

ACTIVITY BOOK, p. 25

Use Word Meanings — Vocabulary Reinforcement

In the space provided, write the letter of the vocabulary term in Column B that best fits the definition in Column A. Use each term only once.

Column A

_g_ 1. the woody parts of plants

_d_ 2. a tool to help you choose foods for a healthful diet

_a_ 3. the study of food and how it affects the body

_h_ 4. the measured amount of food you would probably eat during a meal or as a snack

_e_ 5. a diet based on the Food Guide Pyramid

_c_ 6. a nutrient your body needs in small amounts

_f_ 7. parts of food that help your body grow and get energy

_b_ 8. the foods a person usually eats and drinks

Column B

a. nutrition

b. diet

c. fluoride

d. Food Guide Pyramid

e. balanced diet

f. nutrients

g. fiber

h. serving

In the space below, write a short paragraph using three vocabulary terms from above. In your paragraph, explain the term *balanced diet*.

Answers will vary. Possible answer: A balanced diet is a diet based on the Food Guide Pyramid. A balanced diet has all the nutrients a person needs. These nutrients include water, fiber, and fluoride.

MEET INDIVIDUAL NEEDS

Visual Learners Invite groups of students to come to the board, draw the shape of the Food Guide Pyramid, and draw or write the name of at least one food for each group in the diagram. Then have students compare the results.

Learn from Pictures

Have students look at the photograph and tell what the children are doing. Point out that food gave them the energy they needed to play football.

Critical Thinking What other important thing do they need while they play? water

Life Skills Focus

Make Decisions Review the decision-making model and ask students for suggestions about how Kim could solve her problem. Write the suggestions on the board. Then have students vote on which suggestion they would choose if they were Kim and which one they think is most healthful. Discuss any differences.

3 Wrap Up

Lesson Checkup

1. a guide to help people choose foods for a healthful diet

2. bread, cereal, rice, and pasta group; vegetable group; fruit group; meat, poultry, fish, dry beans, eggs, and nuts group; milk, yogurt, and cheese group; fats, oils, and sweets group

3. Drink six to eight glasses of water each day.

4. Eat foods from each group in the amounts suggested in the Food Guide Pyramid.

5. Suggest students list in their Health Journals all the foods they ate and drank at lunch each day. They can identify and label the foods by group or make three blank pyramids—one for each lunch—and write the foods in the proper places. Remind them to evaluate their diets and note suggestions for changes. After several weeks, remind them to evaluate the success of any changes they made.

OBJECTIVE

- Describe how to choose healthful snacks.

PROGRAM RESOURCES

 Computer Graphing Activity, Teaching Resources p. 58

VOCABULARY

- snacks (p. 106)

Daily Safety Tip

Children sometimes do not use common sense about food cleanliness. Explain that when food is dropped on the floor or ground, it is exposed to dirt and germs carried on people's and animals' feet. Tell students to discard any unwrapped food that is dropped on the floor.

1 Motivate

Share and discuss the following poem with students.

When you are very hungry
And it isn't time to eat
Breakfast, lunch, or dinner,
What's your favorite treat?

When you are very hungry,
As hungry as a bear,
Do you find some berries,
Or an apple or a pear?

When you are very hungry,
As hungry as a mouse,
Do you find cheese and nuts
In a cupboard in your house?

When you are very hungry,
As hungry as a rabbit,
Do you nibble carrot sticks?
That's a very healthful habit!

How are all the snacks mentioned in the poem alike? They are all healthful foods.

MAIN IDEA
Snacks are an important part of a healthful diet.

WHY LEARN THIS? You can use what you learn to help you choose healthful snacks.

VOCABULARY
- snacks

Healthful Snack Choices

Seth gets home from school every day at three o'clock. He heads straight for the refrigerator. He's starving! Milk, cheese, crackers, grapes, apples, carrots, celery. What will Seth choose today?

Like most children, Seth eats a few snacks—food between meals—every day. Snacks are a part of a healthful diet. They keep you from getting too hungry. They also give you the energy and nutrients you need. Snacks are especially important if you are active.

People eat snacks for many reasons. You might be hungry. You may eat snacks when you are with friends. You may want a snack when you are tired. You may have a snack to celebrate a happy time, such as a birthday.

A quick snack gives me energy!

106

MULTILEVEL ACTIVITIES

EASY **Substitute Snacks** Have students list their five favorite snack foods. Have them put a star by those that are healthful and write healthful substitutes for the others. **INTRAPERSONAL**

AVERAGE **Invent a Snack Food** Ask students to invent a healthful snack food. They should describe what the food has in it and, if applicable, how it is made. **LOGICAL/LINGUISTIC**

ADVANCED **Class Favorites** Invite pairs of students to interview classmates about their favorite fruits. Tell students to use the information to make tables or graphs. **INTERPERSONAL/MATHEMATICAL**

What makes a snack healthful?

As you use the Food Guide Pyramid, remember to include snacks in your diet. Snacks help you get nutrients you may not get during meals. A plum or pear as a snack gives you a fruit serving. A granola bar or half a bagel gives you a serving from the bread, cereal, rice, and pasta group.

Some snacks are not healthful. They don't give you the nutrients you need most. Potato chips and chocolate bars are mostly fats and sweets. You should eat these foods only in small amounts.

Healthful snacks don't contain a lot of fats, oils, or sweets. Some healthful snacks are listed below.

This snack counts as a serving of fruit.

- fresh fruit
- raw vegetables
- whole grain cereal
- orange juice
- milk
- raisins
- lowfat yogurt
- unbuttered popcorn
- whole wheat crackers
- cheese
- peanut butter sandwich

Which foods in the healthful snacks list do you like? Remember these foods the next time you race for the kitchen. Find yourself a healthful snack!

LESSON CHECKUP

Check Your Facts

1. What is a snack?
2. CRITICAL THINKING What are two reasons snacks are important?
3. What are two unhealthful snacks?
4. Give four examples of healthful snacks.

Use Life Skills

5. COMMUNICATE Write a letter to an adult family member. Explain why you like to eat healthful snacks. Include suggestions for five healthful snacks that you would eat. Ask if you might help shop for these foods.

107

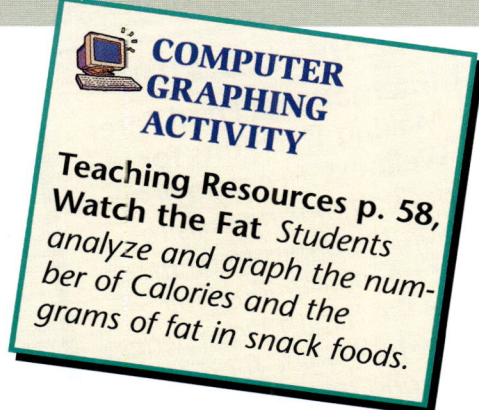
---

2 Teach

Discuss

Snacks such as candy bars and soft drinks are like rocket fuel: they provide a quick burst of energy that gets burned up quickly. That is because they contain mostly sugar.

Critical Thinking What happens if you eat only sweets for snacks? You will be energetic for short periods of time, but you might feel tired later. You probably won't get all the nutrients you need to stay healthy.

Discuss

Critical Thinking Why should you eat only small amounts of foods that are mostly fats and sweets? They do not give you the nutrients you need most; they are at the top of the Food Guide Pyramid.

Project Checkup

Make a Food Display (p. 97)
Encourage students to include pictures of healthful snacks in their displays.

3 Wrap Up

Lesson Checkup

1. a food eaten between meals

2. they provide energy; they provide nutrients

3. Possible answers: candy, chocolate, potato chips. Accept all reasonable answers.

4. Possible answers: peanut butter sandwich, celery sticks, fruit, low-fat yogurt. Answers may include foods from the list on this page but also can include foods that are low in fats and sweets. Accept all reasonable answers.

5. Have each student write a rough draft of the letter to revise and copy in final form. Volunteers may want to share their letters in small groups.

LIFE SKILLS

OBJECTIVES

- Identify steps for making decisions.
- Use the decision-making steps to make healthful snack choices.

PROGRAM RESOURCES

- Activity Book, p. 26
- HEALTH VIDEO: International Food Fare

1 Motivate

Optional Materials **chart paper, self-stick notes**

Prepare a large diagram of the Food Guide Pyramid on a sheet of chart paper. Have groups choose their four favorite snacks and write the name of each snack on a self-stick note. Stick the notes on the appropriate sections of the Food Guide Pyramid. (As an alternative, draw the pyramid on the board and write the items in the appropriate sections.) Which section has most of their favorite snacks? Which snacks are the most healthful? Which snacks are the least healthful? Which snacks are easiest to prepare?

2 Teach

Learn from Pictures

Draw students' attention to the pictures of Belinda making a decision about a snack. Why is it important for Belinda to make a healthful choice for her snack? She will need energy in order to skate.

Step 1

What choices are available to Belinda? piece of cake, peanut butter and jelly sandwich, milk, orange juice, apple, carrot

---

MAKE DECISIONS About Snacks

Choosing snacks is something most people do every day. This skill will help you make healthful choices.

Learn This Skill

Belinda has a skating lesson in thirty minutes. Her friends are ready to go, but she wants to eat a healthful snack that will give her energy during her lesson.

1. **Find out about the choices you could make.**

Belinda opens the refrigerator to check out her choices. What will she choose?

2. **Imagine the possible result of each choice.**

Belinda thinks about what would taste good. She also thinks about how long each snack will take to fix and eat.

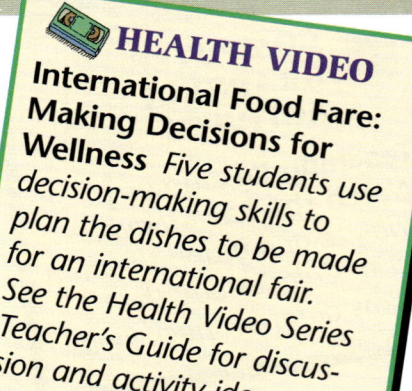

HEALTH VIDEO

International Food Fare: Making Decisions for Wellness *Five students use decision-making skills to plan the dishes to be made for an international fair. See the Health Video Series Teacher's Guide for discussion and activity ideas.*

TEACHER TIP

Fun with Fruit Have a fruit-tasting party. Write the names of fruits on slips of paper. Use fruits that are not commonly eaten but are available in your area, such as kiwis, papayas, mangos, star fruits, tangelos, figs, and plantains. Have each student draw a slip and bring that fruit to class. Let students taste and rate the fruits. Have students make a graph showing how the fruits rated. A local grocery might sponsor this project and donate fruit for your party. NOTE: Check for food allergies before allowing students to eat any foods.

3. Make what seems to be the best choice.

Belinda chooses an apple because it's her favorite fruit. It's also ready to eat!

4. Think about the result of your choice.

Belinda got a healthful snack and didn't keep her friends waiting.

Practice This Skill

Use this summary as you solve the problems below.

Steps for Making Decisions

1. **Find out about the choices you could make.**
2. **Imagine the possible result of each choice.**
3. **Make what seems to be the best choice.**
4. **Think about the result of your choice.**

A. Howard is bringing drinks for the baseball team. He may bring cola, fruit juice, or water. Use the steps to help Howard make his choice.

B. Ann is planning a snack for a hike. She needs a healthful snack she can carry easily. What are some possible choices? What is the best choice? Why?

109

Step 2

Refer students to the Food Guide Pyramid activity you just completed. **Where would the foods Belinda is choosing from fit on the pyramid?** All groups are represented. **Which foods would be healthful and provide energy for skating?** milk, apple, carrot, bread, peanut butter, juice **Which would be easiest to eat so she wouldn't keep her friends waiting?** apple, carrot, milk, juice

Step 3

Do you think Belinda made a healthful choice? yes

Critical Thinking **Why is it important to make the most healthful choice instead of the one that would be the quickest to fix and eat?** It might make a difference in Belinda's ability to skate well.

Step 4

Did Belinda's choice work for her? Why or why not? Yes, it was healthful and quick to fix and eat. **Could Belinda have made other choices that would have worked well?** She also could have chosen the carrots or a glass of milk or juice.

3 Wrap Up

A. Students should use the decision-making steps to suggest a healthful choice, such as juice or water. Be sure students consider the consequences of the choices.

B. Students should use the decision-making steps to consider a variety of healthful choices, such as fruit, unsalted nuts or pretzels, or carrot or celery sticks. Their choices and explanations should be based on the consequences of several choices.

ACTIVITY BOOK, p. 26

Make Decisions   **Life Skills**

Janette and Sonja are planning a sleep-over for Friday night. They want to have some snacks while they watch movies. Janette wants to buy soda and candy for munching, but Sonja knows she will feel better if she eats healthful snacks. Use the decision-making steps to help Janette and Sonja decide which snacks would be healthful and easy to fix and taste great too.

Step 1 Find out the choices you could make. Possible answers: popcorn, fruit, vegetables, peanut butter with celery.

Step 2 Imagine the possible result of each choice. Possible answers: popcorn would be good as long as it doesn't have too much butter or salt; fruit, vegetables, and peanut butter with celery are all good choices. They are easy to fix and eat. They would be easy to eat while watching a movie.

Step 3 Make what seems to be the best choice. Accept any reasonable answer. Possible answer: Janette and Sonja decide to buy apples, celery, and peanut butter for their snack. They choose these foods because they are good for them, and they like them. They can use the peanut butter on both the celery and apples.

Step 4 Think about the result of your choice. Janette and Sonja are happy with the choice. They have a great snack that is healthful and easy to fix.

SOCIAL STUDIES

Snacks from Around the World
Have students use ethnic cookbooks to find snack foods that are popular in other countries. Have them analyze the ingredients and decide if the snacks would be healthful choices. Encourage them to classify the snacks using the Food Guide Pyramid or other cultural food guide pyramids. See pages 284–285 for different food guide pyramids.

109

OBJECTIVES

- Define *ingredients* and tell how to use labels to choose foods with the most nutritious ingredients.
- Explain why a food's price varies.

PROGRAM RESOURCES

- Activity Book, p. 27

 Teaching Transparency 25

 HEALTH VIDEO:
The Good Health Game Show

VOCABULARY

- ingredients (p. 110)
- food label (p. 111)

Daily Safety Tip

Many third graders help in the kitchen. Remind students that kitchen tools and appliances can be dangerous if not used correctly. Some should be used only with adult supervision. Children should be especially careful around knives, electric appliances, and the stove and oven.

1 Motivate

Optional Materials **containers of foods**

Hold up each food container and ask students to identify the food. Then have pairs of students list ingredients they think are in each food. Tape paper over the ingredients list if you want students to look more closely at the packaging. Check the lists against the products. (As an alternative, have student pairs think of a canned, packaged, or boxed food and list its ingredients.) Point out that students might not be aware of all the ingredients in the foods they eat.

MAIN IDEA
Foods vary in their ingredients and prices.

WHY LEARN THIS? You can use what you learn to make wise choices when shopping for food.

VOCABULARY
- ingredients
- food label

Being a Wise Food Shopper

Sabrena and her father go shopping together every week. By shopping together, they each get a variety of foods they like. As they shop, Sabrena and her father carefully look at all the labels. They want to be sure the foods they buy are healthful.

How can you choose among food products?

Many foods are packaged. Packaged foods include cake mixes, canned fruits, and bread. These foods are made of more than one thing. The things that go into a food are its **ingredients** (in•GREE•dee•uhnts).

▶ There are so many different cereals! What do you think helped Sabrena and her father make their choice?

110

MULTILEVEL ACTIVITIES

EASY Research Cans Have students research the invention of cans, the initial problems scientists found, and how the problems were solved. They should also make posters displaying these facts. **VISUAL**

AVERAGE History of Food Packaging Ask students to give short speeches explaining how and why canned and packaged foods have changed the way most modern families eat. They can discuss how people obtained and preserved food hundreds of years ago and the advantages and disadvantages of packaged foods. **VERBAL**

ADVANCED Look Up Meanings Encourage students to look up the definitions of words from the ingredients lists on food labels. Students will find chemical names of natural ingredients as well as names of manufactured chemicals added to color, flavor, or preserve the food. **LINGUISTIC**

Activity **Compare Soups** Compare the ingredients in the canned and dried chicken noodle soup. See what is listed first and second in each food. How many ingredients does each have? Look for ingredients that are in both soups. Which soup do you think is more healthful? Why?

Dry Chicken Noodle Soup
INGREDIENTS: enriched egg noodles, salt, sugar, chicken meat, chicken fat, chicken flavoring, and onion.

Condensed Chicken Noodle Soup
INGREDIENTS: chicken stock, enriched egg noodles, carrots, water, salt, margarine, onion powder, garlic, and spice.

Corn, water, and salt may be the only ingredients in a can of corn. Other foods, such as rice mixes or frozen dinners, have many ingredients.

A **food label** can be found on every packaged food. It gives information about how nutritious a food is. The information is called Nutrition Facts.

A food label also lists the ingredients in a food. You can use food labels to compare the ingredients in different foods. The ingredients are listed in order of amount. The first ingredient is the one used most in the food. The last ingredient is the one used least.

Food labels also show the amounts of different nutrients. Similar foods may have different nutrients. They may also have different amounts of each nutrient.

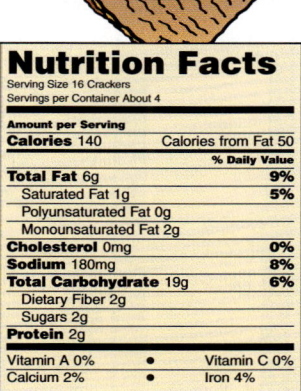

Nutrition Facts
Serving Size 16 Crackers
Servings per Container About 4

Amount per Serving	
Calories 140	Calories from Fat 50
	% Daily Value
Total Fat 6g	9%
Saturated Fat 1g	5%
Polyunsaturated Fat 0g	
Monounsaturated Fat 2g	
Cholesterol 0mg	0%
Sodium 180mg	8%
Total Carbohydrate 19g	6%
Dietary Fiber 2g	
Sugars 2g	
Protein 2g	
Vitamin A 0%	Vitamin C 0%
Calcium 2%	Iron 4%

111

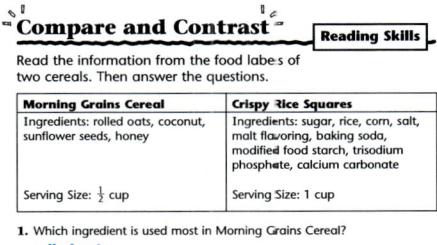
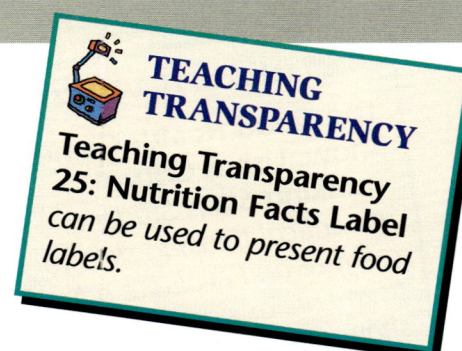

TEACHING TRANSPARENCY
Teaching Transparency 25: Nutrition Facts Label can be used to present food labels.

---

2 Teach

Learn from Pictures

Ask students to describe what is happening in the picture on page 110. Elicit that Sabrena and her father use labels to make their food choices. Have volunteers share how they help their families shop.

Discuss

It is a law that the label of a food with more than one ingredient must list all the ingredients in the food.

Critical Thinking Why do you think the government made it a law to list the ingredients? so people buying products have information about all the products and can compare them

Critical Thinking What does knowing the ingredients tell you about the food? how healthful it is

Activity

Compare Soups Help students see the similarities and differences by copying the ingredients in vertical lists on the board. Place the lists side by side, so that the ingredients line up. Note that salt and sugar usually are not main ingredients in healthful foods.

Health Background

Federal Food Regulations During the early 1800s states had control over foods, and laws were haphazard and inconsistent. By the mid-1800s the federal government saw the need to step in to prevent the sale of adulterated and harmful foods. The Pure Food and Drug Act, passed in 1906, defined adulteration and prohibited misbranding and interstate commerce of adulterated foods. The Gould Amendment, passed in 1913, required quantity labels on all packaged foods. In 1938 the Pure Food, Drug, and Cosmetic Act helped in many ways. One change it provided was factory inspections.

For more background, visit the **Webliography** on the Teacher Resources page at:
www.harcourtschool.com/health
Keyword food safety

111

Teach *continued*

Learn from Pictures

Have students look at the illustrations on pages 112 and 113. Have volunteers suggest why an individual might choose one type of packaging over another.

Critical Thinking **Why are foods sold in different amounts?** because people have varying needs

Which package of juice has the highest price? the 64-ounce carton

Critical Thinking **Why might the 64-ounce carton have the highest price?** It is bigger. It might be a brand name. It might be fresh juice.

Discuss

Nutritional value causes some people to choose more expensive foods. Frozen fruits and vegetables are more nutritious than canned. Fresh fruits and vegetables might be most nutritious, unless they have been shipped long distances. Since foods are frozen soon after picking, the amount of vitamins and minerals in frozen food may be higher than in older fresh produce.

Critical Thinking **Is buying the least costly food always the best choice? Why or why not?** Not necessarily; you need to consider nutritional value, freshness, personal taste, how soon you will use the food, and how much of the food you need.

Consumer Focus

Analyze Advertisements and Media Messages Students might notice "tricks" such as using a famous person to sell the item, bright pictures and colors, or an unrealistic outcome from the food item. Discuss how "tricks" are used and how being aware of them can help students become better consumers.

CONSUMER FOCUS

Analyze Advertising and Media Messages
Some ads use "tricks" to get you to buy the product. Find an ad for a popular drink, such as juice or a sports drink. Use the steps on page *xv* to figure out what "tricks" are being used to help sell the drink.

• • •

▼ Orange juice comes in many different packages.

112

Why the price difference?

Kito and his brother need to buy orange juice. They can buy fresh juice, canned juice, or frozen juice. They can buy a big package or a small package. They can buy juice in cartons, cans, bottles, or boxes.

The boys want to get the best deal. But each package of juice has a different price. They are so confused!

One kind of food may have many different prices. Fresh foods are often most expensive. Frozen foods may cost more than canned foods.

Some foods cost more because they carry brand names. You know these names because you see them in ads. The ads cost a lot of money to make. But you help pay for the ads each time you buy the food.

HEALTH VIDEO

The Good Health Game Show: Using Critical Thinking Skills Students use critical thinking skills to analyze and evaluate advertisements as part of a game show. See the Health Video Series Teacher's Guide for discussion and activity ideas.

ART

Write an Ad Discuss some ways advertisers use scenes, people, and ideas to promote products. Have students work in groups to write a magazine advertisement for orange juice. Invite each group to share its ad with the class and tell why they designed it the way they did.

A large supermarket may have its own store brand. You do not see many ads for these foods. So store brand foods are usually cheaper than brand-name foods.

Foods are sold in different amounts. A small can of juice costs less than a large can. But be careful. The juice in the small can may really be more expensive! You must compare the cost by weight or unit. The cost per ounce of the small can is probably higher than that of the large can. You can often find the unit cost on tags near the food on the store shelf.

Sometimes foods are packaged together. You can buy packages of boxed juice. Each box is a single serving. This type of package is expensive. You can save money by buying the juice in larger packages and using a clean, tightly closed jar to carry it in your lunch.

LESSON CHECKUP

Check Your Facts

❶ What are ingredients?

❷ How are food labels useful?

❸ What are three things that can affect the cost of food?

❹ **CRITICAL THINKING** Why do you have to be careful when comparing the prices of small and large packages?

Use Life Skills

❺ **RESOLVE CONFLICTS** Tess wants the small boxes of orange juice. Her sister wants to buy the frozen juice. Why might Tess want the small boxes? Why do you think her sister wants the frozen juice? How might they resolve their conflict?

113

SOCIAL STUDIES

Influences in Food Selections
Invite students to volunteer to share information about any celebrations or special family gatherings where food is served. Ask volunteers to discuss some of the food selections that are available at these celebrations or gatherings. Children might want to bring in food samples from family recipes to share. NOTE: Check for food allergies before allowing students to eat foods. Be sensitive to those students who might not be involved in celebrations.

MATH

Figure Per-Unit Cost Ask students which operation they need to perform to figure out how much an item costs per unit, such as per ounce or per gram. Then have them divide to find some simple costs per unit. Use situations such as the following: if 10 ounces cost $1.00; if 100 grams cost $1.00; if 5 ounces cost $2.00.

Discuss

Television is a powerful and effective tool for advertisers. Ask students to volunteer names of food products they like or would like to try. Ask them where they first heard about these products.

Critical Thinking **What is the main purpose of many advertisements?** to get people to buy something so that the company selling the product makes money

Critical Thinking **If a television advertisement says a food is healthful, what is one way to see if that is true?** Read the ingredients list on the label.

Math Connection

Compare Prices Encourage students to take notebooks with them the next time they go with their families to the grocery store. Tell them to copy the names of two or more peanut butter choices and write down information about each one. Have students compare their findings in class.

3 Wrap Up

Lesson Checkup

1. things that go into a food

2. Food labels tell the ingredients of a food, size of the product, how nutritious the product is, and other information about the product.

3. Possible answers: preparation of the food, brand, size, packaging.

4. The product in the small package might really be more expensive; you need to compare the cost by weight or unit.

5. Have students suggest reasons for the girls' choices and possible solutions to resolve the conflict. Write the proposed solutions on the board. Take a hand-raise vote to determine which solution the class thinks is best. Then have volunteers tell why.

OBJECTIVES

- **Explain why it is important to store foods properly.**
- **Describe ways to handle foods safely.**

PROGRAM RESOURCES

- Activity Book, pp. 28–29

VOCABULARY

- **spoiled** (p. 114)
- **pathogens** (p. 115)

Daily Safety Tip

Bacteria that cause food-borne illnesses are almost everywhere. Therefore students who help in the kitchen should help keep all kitchen surfaces meticulously clean. It is especially important to clean cutting boards after using them for raw meat and poultry.

1 Motivate

Optional Materials **sets of cards, one per group, with the following foods listed on them: frozen whole turkey, frozen fish, frozen fruit bars, eggs, milk, whole chicken, broccoli, raspberries, canned soup, boxed cereal, spaghetti**

Divide the class into groups and give each group a set of cards. Have them put the cards in three groups showing the order (first, middle, last) in which they think the foods should be put away after grocery shopping. They should show an order for the items in each group if they think order is important. (As an alternative, place the list on the board and have groups list the foods as per the suggestion above.)

Which foods need to be put away first? Why? frozen foods, because they can melt or thaw

Why is it important to store foods properly? They can spoil and become unsafe.

LESSON 5

MAIN IDEA
Foods need to be stored and handled correctly to keep them safe to eat.

WHY LEARN THIS? You can use what you learn to stay well.

VOCABULARY
- spoiled
- pathogens

Handling Food Safely

Jen is helping unload groceries. First, she quickly places the frozen foods in the freezer. Next, she puts the meat, chicken, and eggs in the refrigerator. She puts some of the fruits and vegetables in the refrigerator, too. Finally, Jen stacks the canned and dry foods in the cupboard.

Which foods need refrigerating?

Some foods spoil. A **spoiled** food is one that is unsafe to eat. Some foods spoil quickly. These foods usually need to be kept cold or frozen. You should store meat, milk, eggs, and leftovers in the refrigerator. This helps keep these foods from spoiling.

Foods such as meats, milk, and some fresh fruits and vegetables need to be refrigerated. Unopened canned foods do not.

114

MULTILEVEL ACTIVITIES

EASY Food Safety Announcement Have students write public service announcements for radio or television about properly handling food. **LINGUISTIC**

AVERAGE Food Storage Posters Suggest students use photos of food cut out of magazines to make posters showing where foods should be stored. **VISUAL**

ADVANCED Helpful Bacteria Ask students to find out how some bacteria are used to make food products such as yogurt, some cheeses, and vinegar. Ask students to give short reports about their findings. **VERBAL**

Some foods need to go into the freezer. Already frozen foods, such as frozen vegetables, must stay frozen to be safe. Foods that are not bought frozen, such as meats, can be kept longer in the freezer.

What are some safety tips for preparing a meal?

Pathogens (PA•thuh•juhnz), or germs, in food can cause illness. If a food with pathogens touches another food, the pathogens can spread.

You can help keep pathogens from spreading. Before and after handling food, wash your hands with soap and warm water. Also wash and keep your work areas clean.

Meat and poultry can carry pathogens. You should not cut other foods on a surface that raw meat and poultry have touched. Cutting boards must be washed with soap and hot water.

Wrapping foods keeps out air and pathogens. It helps keep food safe. Always wrap foods before putting them away.

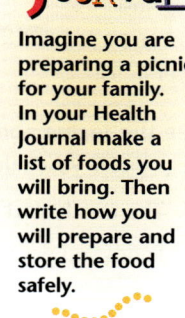

JOURNAL

Imagine you are preparing a picnic for your family. In your Health Journal make a list of foods you will bring. Then write how you will prepare and store the food safely.

▶ Wrapping your food helps keep it fresh.

LESSON CHECKUP

Check Your Facts
1. Why shouldn't you eat spoiled food?
2. Name four foods that must be kept in the refrigerator.
3. CRITICAL THINKING Why might you want to store meat in the freezer instead of the refrigerator?

Set Health Goals
4. When should you wash your hands throughout the day? When do you wash your hands? Set goals for keeping your hands cleaner. Try to meet your goals.

115

---

2 Teach

Discuss

You can't always tell if a food is spoiled by looking at or smelling it. Never taste a food to see if it is spoiled. Remember this rule: when in doubt, throw it out.

Health Journal

When recording how to prepare and store foods students would bring on a picnic, students might find it helpful to make a chart with three columns showing the food item, how it is prepared, and how it is stored. For more information about preparing food and food safety tips, see pages 252-253.

3 Wrap Up

Lesson Checkup

1. Spoiled food is unsafe to eat.
2. Possible answers: meat, poultry, eggs, milk, some fruits. Accept all reasonable answers.
3. Foods keep longer when they are frozen.
4. Suggest that students begin checklists in their Health Journals, noting when they *should* wash their hands and when they actually *do* wash their hands. As they note differences, they should set goals to wash their hands frequently.

Health Background

Food Safety Following are important food safety tips for the home.

- Refrigeration—below 40°F—significantly slows the growth of bacteria, the most common pathogen affecting foods. Freezing stops bacteria growth but does not kill most bacteria. Heating food to a temperature of 160°F destroys bacteria.
- Always wash hands before handling foods, and wash dishes in hot, soapy water.
- Refrigerate foods as quickly as possible.

115

Review

Use Vocabulary 3 pts. each

1. fiber
2. snacks
3. Food Guide Pyramid
4. food label
5. nutrients
6. balanced diet
7. diet
8. spoiled
9. Ingredients
10. nutrition
11. serving
12. pathogens
13. Fluoride

Check Your Facts 5 pts. each

14. Possible answer: A farm operator grows grains, fruits, or vegetables; raises and takes care of animals; and harvests crops to send to market.

15. six to eight

16. Snacks provide the body with nutrients it doesn't get during regular meals.

17. It is used the most (in the greatest amount) in the food.

18. Washing hands removes pathogens.

Review

USE VOCABULARY

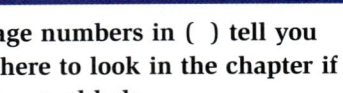

balanced diet (p. 105)	fluoride (p. 104)	ingredients (p. 110)	serving (p. 102)
diet (p. 99)	Food Guide Pyramid (p. 102)	nutrients (p. 98)	snacks (p. 106)
fiber (p. 99)	food label (p. 111)	nutrition (p. 98)	spoiled (p. 114)
		pathogens (p. 115)	

Use the terms above to complete the sentences. Page numbers in ( ) tell you where to look in the chapter if you need help.

1. The woody part of plants is ____.

2. Foods you eat between meals are ____.

3. The ____ is a tool to help you choose foods for a healthful diet.

4. A ____ gives you information about a food.

5. Parts of a food that help your body grow, get energy, and work well are ____.

6. When you have a ____, you eat foods from each food group every day.

7. The foods you usually eat or drink make up your ____.

8. A food that is unsafe to eat has ____.

9. ____ are the things that go into a food.

10. The study of food and how it affects the body is ____.

11. A ____ is the measured amount of a food you would probably eat during a meal or as a snack.

12. Germs in food that can cause illness are ____.

13. ____ is a nutrient that helps keep your teeth healthy.

CHECK YOUR FACTS

Page numbers in ( ) tell you where to look in the chapter if you need help.

14. What are some jobs of a farm operator? (p. 100)

15. How many glasses of water do you need each day? (p. 104)

16. How do snacks help you get the nutrients you need? (p. 107)

17. What does listing an ingredient first on a food label tell you about the ingredient? (p. 111)

Cholesterol	Less Than	300mg	300mg
Sodium	Less Than	2,400mg	2,400mg
Total Carbohydrate		300g	375g
Dietary Fiber		25g	30g

Calories per gram:
Fat 9 • Carbohydrate 4 • Protein 4

INGREDIENTS: Unbleached wheat flour, water, salt, yeast and soda.

18. Why is it important to wash your hands before eating? (p. 115)

THINK CRITICALLY

19. Name four plant foods and four animal foods.

20. What are three things you can do at home to help keep foods safe?

APPLY LIFE SKILLS

21. **Make Decisions** Imagine you are going to the movies with friends. They want to share hot buttered popcorn. You are trying to eat healthful snacks. Use the steps for making decisions to choose a more healthful snack you could have with your friends.

22. **Make Decisions** You go shopping with your parents. They want to buy the same kind of macaroni and cheese they usually get but they think the store brand, which comes in a larger box, is cheaper. How can you use the steps for making decisions to help your parents decide which product is a better buy?

Promote Health — Home and Community

1. Sit down with your family to discuss what healthful snacks the whole family can enjoy. Make a shopping list that includes the snacks you agree on.
2. Talk with a farmer or a gardener who grows plants for food. Find out what kinds of things plants need to grow well. Share what you learn with your class.

117

Think Critically 8 pts. each

19. Possible answers: plant foods—fruits, vegetables, grains, nuts; animal foods—meat, poultry, eggs, milk.

20. Possible answers: Wash hands before and after working with foods; store foods in the proper place; wash counters, and keep work spaces clean; wash cutting boards after using them to prepare raw meat or poultry.

Apply Life Skills 10 pts. each

21. Possible answer: Find out what healthful choices are available. Ask the friends if they would mind sharing a more healthful snack. If not, order a healthful snack for yourself.

22. Possible answer: Compare the per-unit prices of the two choices. Consider that even if the store brand is less expensive, the family might not like it as well as their regular brand. Choose to try the less expensive brand. Discuss with the family if you like the new brand.

PERFORMANCE ASSESSMENT

Project—Make a Food Display

The chapter project (introduced on page 97) can be used for individual or team performance assessment. Allow students the opportunity to revise and complete their projects before submitting them for evaluation. Students can use the Project Summary Sheet (Assessment Guide, p. 17) to tell about their projects. You can use the rubric provided on the Project Evaluation Sheet (Assessment Guide, p. 33) to evaluate student performance.

Activities

Make Your Own Food Guide Pyramid

With a Team • Use boxes to make a model of a Food Guide Pyramid. Use pictures cut from food labels or magazines to show which foods belong in each part of the pyramid. Add labels to the pyramid that name each food group and tell how many servings a person should eat from the group each day.

Choosing Healthful Foods

On Your Own • Being safe in the kitchen is important for you and anyone else that might use the kitchen. Use pages 252–253 as a guide to make a kitchen safety checklist. You might want to place your checklist on the refrigerator so that everyone may use it.

cereal
pizza
popcorn
cheese
apple
animal crackers
corn

Local Foods

With a Partner • Find out what kinds of plant and animal foods are raised in your state. Draw a map of your state, and include pictures of the different types of foods.

Select Your Snacks

At Home • Look through your kitchen to see what kinds of snack foods are there. Make a list of the foods you find. Place a check beside each food you think makes a healthful snack.

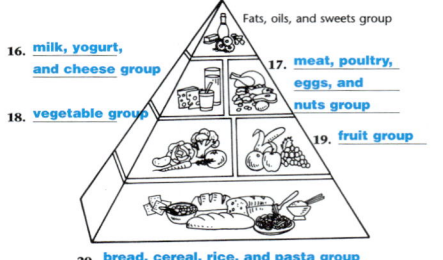

118

Chapter Test

118

Multiple Choice

Choose the letter of the correct answer.

1. _____ helps keep food moving through the digestive system.
   a. Nutrition   b. Fiber
   c. Fat   d. Cheese

2. Fluoride is a nutrient you may get from _____.
   a. juice   b. water
   c. fiber   d. vegetables

3. Snacks help you get the _____ you may not get during meals.
   a. nutrients   b. oils
   c. fats   d. nutrition

4. Your _____ is what you eat each day.
   a. serving   b. snack
   c. nutrition   d. diet

5. Foods such as _____ need to be refrigerated.
   a. canned fruit   b. chips
   c. meats   d. bread

Modified True or False

Write *true* or *false*. If a sentence is false, replace the underlined term to make the sentence true.

6. Nutrition is the study of <u>fiber</u> and how it affects the body.

7. Fruits and vegetables come from <u>animals</u>.

8. The <u>fruit</u> group is the largest group in the Food Guide Pyramid.

9. You need to drink extra <u>water</u> when you exercise.

10. You should eat fats and sweets in <u>large</u> amounts.

11. Fresh foods are usually <u>less</u> expensive than canned foods.

12. The first ingredient on a food label is the one used <u>least</u> in the food.

13. Some foods cost more because they carry <u>brand</u> names.

14. A spoiled food is <u>safe</u> to eat.

15. Wrapping foods helps keep <u>pathogens</u> from spreading.

Short Answer

Write a complete sentence to answer each question.

16. Why should you wash your hands before and after handling food?

17. How can you compare the costs of foods sold in different amounts?

18. Name two things on a food label.

19. Name three healthful snacks.

20. Name three foods that contain water.

21. Name a food that comes from animals.

22. List three common grains.

Writing in Health

Write paragraphs to answer each item.

23. Why should you eat a variety of foods?

24. Explain some safety tips for preparing a meal.

Writing in Health (10 pts. each)

Sample answers are shown; accept other reasonable answers.

23. The nutrients in foods give your body the energy it needs to grow. There are many kinds of nutrients. To get all the nutrients you need, you must eat a variety of foods.

24. Wash your hands before and after handling or eating food. Wash cutting boards or utensils after using them to prepare raw meat or poultry. Keep kitchen surfaces clean.

Two options are provided for Chapter Tests—the in-book test and the reproducible test in the Assessment Guide. In addition to providing students with the opportunity to show what they have learned, both tests provide practice in taking standardized tests.

Multiple Choice (3 pts. each)

1. b	3. a	5. c
2. b	4. d	

Modified True or False (3 pts. each)

6. false; food

7. false; plants

8. false; bread, cereal, rice, and pasta

9. true

10. false; small

11. false; more

12. false; most

13. true

14. false; unsafe

15. true

Short Answer (5 pts. each)

Sample answers are shown; accept other reasonable answers.

16. You wash your hands to get pathogens off them.

17. You compare the costs of foods by weight or by unit.

18. The ingredients list and the size of the product are on a food's label.

19. Apples, oranges, and carrot sticks are healthful snacks.

20. Broccoli, celery, and apples contain water.

21. Eggs come from animals.

22. Wheat, oats, and rice are common grains.

Preventing Disease

Chapter Organizer

Lesson	Objectives	Vocabulary	Program Resources
Introduce the Chapter pp. 120–121	• Preview the chapter. • Begin chapter project.		• School-Home Connection, TR p. 41 • Assessment Guide, p. 37 • Read-Aloud Anthology, p. RA–6 Teaching Transparency 5— Graphic Organizer
Lesson 1 **What Is Disease?** pp. 122–123 Pacing: ½ class period 1•3•7	• Define **symptom** and **disease**, and list some common symptoms of disease. • Explain what a disability is, and discuss how to treat a person with a disability.	symptom disease	
Lesson 2 **Some Diseases and Their Causes** pp. 124–127 Pacing: 1 class period 1•3•4	• Define **infectious disease**. • Compare and contrast bacteria and viruses. • List some infectious diseases and their symptoms.	infectious disease pathogens bacteria virus fever	• Activity Book, pp. 30, 31 • Growth, Development, and Reproduction, pp. 58–65
Lesson 3 **Fighting Disease** pp. 128–131 Pacing: 1 class period 1•3•6	• Explain two ways a person can become immune to a disease. • Define **medicine**, and explain the importance of taking all medicines only as directed.	immune vaccine medicine	• Activity Book, p. 32 Computer Graphing Activity, TR p. 59 Teaching Transparency 26
Lesson 4 **Diseases You Can't Catch** pp. 132–135 Pacing: 1 class period 1•2	• Define **noninfectious diseases**, and list three examples. • Compare and contrast allergies and asthma. • Explain what happens to sugar in a person with diabetes.	noninfectious diseases allergy asthma diabetes	• Activity Book, p. 33 Teaching Transparencies 18, 20
Lesson 5 **Fighting Disease with a Healthful Lifestyle** pp. 136–139 Pacing: 1 class period 1•3•7	• Explain how a healthful lifestyle reduces a person's chances of getting certain diseases.	abstinence	• Activity Book, p. 34 Computer Graphing Activity, TR p. 60
Life Skills **Manage Stress** pp. 140–141 Pacing: ½ class period 3•5•6	• Identify ways to manage stress. • Apply stress-management skills to help control disease.		• Activity Book, p. 35
Chapter Review and Test pp. 142–145 2•7	• Assess chapter objectives. • Provide extension activities.		• Chapter Test and Project Evaluation Sheet, Assessment Guide, pp. 34–37

 National Health Education Standards
A complete list of the Standards is provided on the next page.

Key: TR = Teaching Resources

National Health Education Standards

1. Comprehend concepts related to health promotion and disease prevention.
2. Access valid health information and health-promoting products and services.
3. Practice health-enhancing behaviors and reduce health risks.
4. Analyze the influence of culture, media, technology, and other factors on health.
5. Use interpersonal communication skills to enhance health.
6. Use goal-setting and decision-making skills to enhance health.
7. Advocate for personal, family, and community health.

Art
- Pop Art, p. 120C
- Building the Pyramid, p. 137

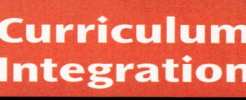
Math
- Exercise Your Rights! p. 138
- Smoking Makes No Cents! p. 139

Music
- Does Music Soothe the Savage Beast? p. 120C

Curriculum Integration

Use these topics to integrate health into your daily planning.

Social Studies
- Pima Indians, p. 120C

Drama
- Just Say *No!* p. 131

Physical Education
- Pulse Rates, p. 120C
- Exercise Options, p. 120C

Science
- Teeny, Tiny Germs, p. 120C
- Breaking Down Barriers, p. 125
- Body Temperature, p. 130

Language Arts
- Success Story, p. 120C
- Make a Game of It, p. 140

ASSESSMENT OPTIONS

Portfolio Assessment
Have students select their best work from the following suggestions:
- **Building the Pyramid,** p. 137
- **Gathering Cheer,** p. 144
- **Health Collage,** p. 144

Student Self-Assessment
- **Journal Notes,** pp. 123, 138
- **Set Health Goals,** pp. 123, 127, 139
- **Use Life Skills,** pp. 131, 135

Daily Assessment
- **Check Your Facts,** pp. 123, 127, 131, 135, 139

Performance Assessment
- **Chapter Project: Make a Germ-Fighter Bulletin Board,** pp. 121, 127, 129, 143
- **Project Evaluation Sheet,** Assessment Guide, p. 37

Formal Assessment
- **Chapter Review,** pp. 142–143
- **In-Book Test,** p. 145
- **Chapter Test,** Assessment Guide, pp. 34–36

Cross-Curricular Activities

Physical Education

Pulse Rates

Show students how to take their pulse rates. Have students record their resting pulses. Then have them hypothesize how exercise might affect pulse rate. Instruct students to run in place for two minutes and then retake and record their pulses. Some students might be surprised to find out that aerobic exercise increases pulse rate.

Exercise Options

Suggest that students make a chart of all the exercises they can think of. Have them indicate on the chart which exercises they would like to do to accomplish the following: strengthen the heart and lungs, strengthen muscles, increase energy, relieve stress, maintain a healthful weight. Students can refer to the chart when they are looking for an exercise that will help achieve a desired outcome.

Art

Pop Art

Have students research the work of pop artist Andy Warhol, who is probably most well known for his Campbell's® soup can work. Have pairs of students draw a piece of pop art that stresses the importance of daily exercise, managing stress, or eating a healthful diet. Provide students with various media to decorate their pieces. Invite other classes in the school to viewings of the artwork.

Science

Teeny, Tiny Germs

Obtain some prepared slides of bacteria that cause various infectious diseases. Demonstrate how to use a microscope and have students use a microscope to observe the pathogens. Have students record their observations as detailed, colored illustrations. Remind students to label each drawing with the name of the bacteria represented.

Social Studies

Pima Indians

Have students research to find out why this group of Native Americans has a higher than normal prevalence of diabetes.

Music

Does Music Soothe the Savage Beast?

Play some segments of different kinds of music for students and have them describe how each makes them feel. Be sure to include classical, hip-hop, rock n' roll, rap, country and western, soul, rhythm and blues, and jazz. Have students relate their feelings to managing stress.

Language Arts

Success Story

Invite students to write a fictional story about a disabled person who overcomes a challenge.

Bulletin Board

What's My Disease?

Divide the class into small groups. Assign each group a disease discussed in the chapter and allow students an hour or so to research their assigned diseases in the library. Instruct students to take notes on their assigned diseases.

- Make a silhouette of a third-grade boy named Sick Sammy and a third-grade girl named Ill Isabel. Post these silhouettes in the center of the bulletin board.

- Have students use colored markers and strips of butcher paper to compose short statements/clues that describe the disease they researched, its cause, its symptoms, and its treatment. For example, suppose the disease was diabetes. Statements might include *It's not sweet to have this disease!*, *It's a pain in the pancreas!*, and *I'm so thirsty I could drink a gallon of water.*

- After you have completed the chapter, allow each group 10 minutes to place their statements in place around either Sammy or Isabel. Challenge the rest of the class to identify the disease based on the clues.

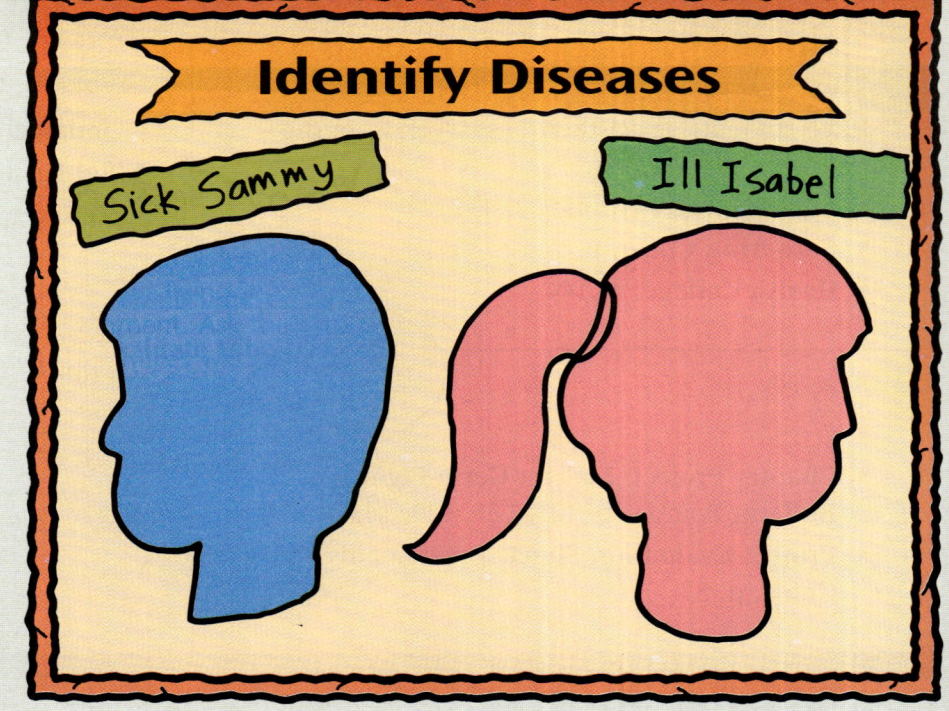

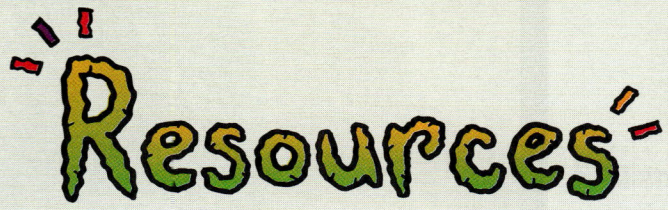

Resources

Books for Students

Gosselin, Kim. *Zoo Allergy.* JayJo Books LLC, 1996. Explains allergies and conditions that can trigger asthma attacks. **EASY**

Silverstein, Alvin; Virginia Silverstein and Laura Silverstein Nunn. *Common Colds.* Franklin Watts, 1999. Explains how people catch colds, and the precautions people can take against them. **AVERAGE**

Landau, Elaine. *Allergies (Understanding Illness Series.)* Twenty-First Century Books, 1995. Complete information on a common human affliction. Honest and appropriately in-depth. **ADVANCED**

Books for Teachers and Families

Clayman, Charles B. M.D., Ed. *The American Medical Association Family Medical Guide.* Random House, 1994. An excellent reference book for families and educators.

Willingham, Theresa. *Food Allergy Field Guide.* Savory Palate, 2000. A lifestyle manual for families with children who have food sensitivities.

Videos

Morris Has a Cold. Churchill Media, 1997. (14 minutes) Viewers see how Morris and Boris learn about colds and how to treat them.

The Magic School Bus Inside Ralphie. Scholastic Productions Inc., Joanna Cole and Bruce Degen, 1995. (30 minutes) The magic school bus takes a journey through the immune system.

Head Lice: Dealing, Destroying & Preventing. United Learning, 1994. (10 minutes) Teachers and children learn what lice are and are given instructions on how to prevent the spread of lice as well as ways to eliminate lice.

GO ONLINE Your Health Webliography

The **Webliography** provides links to the Health Background and teaching resources that will support you as you teach the topics in *Your Health.* Simply choose a keyword and you will be taken to a page of links with descriptions of the content you can obtain at each site. The **Webliography** is located on the Teacher Resources page at **www.harcourtschool.com/health** Please review websites before referring your students to them.

Organizations and Agencies

American School Health Association
7263 State Route 43
P.O. Box 708
Kent, OH 44240
330-678-1601

Centers for Disease Control
1600 Clifton Road NE
Atlanta, GA 30333
404-639-3311
Offers information on stopping the spread of diseases.

For more information about health organizations and agencies, please see the *Teaching Resources* book.

Community Health

Home Health Aide Invite a home health aide to speak to the class about the work he or she does in your community.

Free and Inexpensive Material

Will Rogers Institute
1640 Marengo Street
Suite 406
Los Angeles, CA 90033
Offers brochures that describe what happens during a heart attack and preventative measures that can be taken.

Pharmacia Corporation
100 Route 206, North
Peapack, NJ 07977
Distributes brochures to educate young children and parents to the importance of antibiotic compliance.

Note that information, while correct at time of publication, is subject to change.

Visit **The Harcourt Learning Site** for related links, activities, resources, and the health **Webliography**.

www.harcourtschool.com

WELCOME TO THE LEARNING SITE

"In the United States, ensuring clean water, safe food, and effective waste management has contributed greatly to a declining threat from many infectious diseases; however, there is still more that can be done."

—*Healthy People 2010*

CHAPTER SUMMARY

In this chapter students
- differentiate between infectious and noninfectious diseases.
- identify ways to prevent the spread of pathogens.
- learn how a healthful lifestyle can reduce the risk of some diseases.

LIFE SKILLS Students practice *managing stress* to control disease.

HUMAN BODY Students identify the parts of the digestive, respiratory, and circulatory systems that help fight disease. Students also use information presented in the text to identify the body systems affected by allergies and asthma. Finally, students identify body systems that benefit from exercise.

Literature Springboard

Use the excerpt from *No Measles, No Mumps* to spark interest in the chapter topic. See the Read-Aloud Anthology on page RA-6 of this Teacher's Edition.

120

School-Home Connection

 Distribute copies of the School-Home Connection (in English or Spanish), TR page 41. Have students take the page home to share with their families as you begin this chapter.

Follow Up Have volunteers share the information they gathered from their families about strategies for staying healthy. Discuss how family members can help each other stay healthy.

Alternative Use the School-Home Connection page as a classroom resource for enrichment activities.

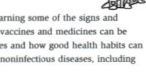

TEACHING RESOURCES, p. 41

Dear Family Member,

In Chapter 5, Preventing Disease, our class will be learning some of the signs and symptoms of infectious diseases. We also will learn how vaccines and medicines can be used to prevent and cure many types of infectious diseases and how good health habits can help the body fight infection. The chapter also discusses noninfectious diseases, including allergies, asthma, and diabetes.

Family Activity

Good health is affected by many factors, including exercise, rest, a healthful diet, and the avoidance of tobacco. Have your child ask family members to identify one strategy the family member pursues or would like to pursue to stay healthy. Discuss the survey with your child. Ask your child how he or she might help a family member make a commitment to staying healthy.

Family Wellness Survey

Family Member	Wellness Strategy

Family Reading

The following books can help you and your family learn more about the topics covered in this chapter. Books should always be chosen with the approval of an adult family member.
- Gosselin, Kim. *Zoo Allergy*. JayJo Books LLC, 1996. Explains allergies and conditions that can trigger asthma attacks. EASY
- Silverstein, Alvin; Virginia Silverstein and Laura Silverstein Nunn. *Common Colds*. Franklin Watts, 1999. Explains how people catch colds, and the precautions people can take against them. AVERAGE
- Landau, Elaine. *Allergies (Understanding Illness Series)*. Twenty-First Century Books, 1995. Complete information on a common human affliction. Honest and appropriately in-depth. ADVANCED

Thank you for participating in our study of health.

Sincerely,

CHAPTER 5

Preventing Disease

MAKE A GERM-FIGHTER BULLETIN BOARD Make a bulletin board with pictures that show things you can do to avoid spreading germs. Make your own drawings, and cut out or copy pictures from magazines and newspapers. For each picture, include a short sentence telling how the activity shown prevents the spread of germs.

For other activities, visit the Harcourt Learning Site.
www.harcourtschool.com

121

Teaching Transparency 5—Graphic Organizer

5 Chapter 5 Graphic Organizer

Preventing Disease

What is Disease?
1. symptoms
2. disease

Fighting Disease
1. immune
2. vaccine
3. medicine

Diseases You Can't Catch
1. noninfectious diseases
2. allergies
3. asthma
4. diabetes

Some Diseases and Their Causes
1. infectious disease
2. Two kinds of pathogens:
   bacteria
   viruses

Fighting Disease with a Healthful Lifestyle
1. healthful food choices
2. exercise
3. abstinence

Introduce the Chapter

MAKE A GERM-FIGHTER BULLETIN BOARD

Access Prior Knowledge Use this activity as a baseline assessment of students' understanding as to how people catch and spread infectious diseases. Allow each student to contribute an item to the bulletin board.

Performance Assessment The project can be used for performance assessment. Before students begin, explain how you will evaluate their performance. (See the Project Evaluation Sheet, Assessment Guide, p. 37.)

Prereading Strategies

Scan the Chapter Have students preview the chapter content by scanning the titles, headings, pictures, and charts. Ask volunteers to speculate on what they will learn.

Preview Vocabulary Have students preview the chapter vocabulary and sort the words into two lists—familiar words and unfamiliar words. Have students look up unfamiliar words in the glossary and record their definitions before they begin reading the chapter.

Visualize Key Concepts Display the Graphic Organizer Transparency. You may also wish to distribute photocopies to students. Have students complete the organizer as they work through the chapter. Suggested concepts for students to fill in are shown.

Follow Up Review the completed organizer with students as preparation for the Chapter Review and Chapter Tests.

121

OBJECTIVES

- Define *symptom* and *disease*, and list some common symptoms of disease.
- Explain what a disability is, and discuss how to treat a person with a disability.

VOCABULARY

- symptom (p. 122)
- disease (p. 122)

Daily Safety Tip

Many infectious diseases, such as the common cold, are spread by direct contact. Remind students to cough and sneeze into tissues when they have colds. Stress the importance of quickly discarding used tissues and washing your hands frequently with soap when you have a cold, the flu, or any other infectious disease.

1 Motivate

Optional Materials index cards identifying behaviors that help prevent the spread of diseases (cough and sneeze into a tissue, wash your hands after coughing or sneezing, wipe your nose with a tissue) or spread disease (cough and sneeze into your hands, wipe your nose with your hand, share drinks or eating utensils).

Have volunteers pretend they have colds and act out the behaviors on the index cards. (As an alternative, describe the behaviors to the class.) For each behavior, ask

Why should this behavior be carried out (or avoided) when you have a cold? Answers should indicate how the behavior helps prevent the spread of disease or helps spread disease.

LESSON

MAIN IDEA
Diseases keep the body from working normally.

WHY LEARN THIS? What you learn can help you understand what is happening when you feel ill.

VOCABULARY
- symptom
- disease

JOURNAL

In your Health Journal, describe how you felt the last time you had a cold or the flu. What were your symptoms? How long did you feel ill? Remember that your journal is private.

What Is Disease?

Patty was not eating her favorite meal. "Don't you feel well?" her father asked. Patty said her head and throat hurt. Her father knew she was ill because of her symptoms. A **symptom** (SIMP•tuhm) is a sign that something is wrong in the body. A headache and sore throat are common symptoms of a cold or flu.

How do you feel when you are ill? Like Patty, you probably don't feel very well. An illness is a disease. A **disease** (dih•ZEEZ) is something that causes the body not to work normally.

There are many kinds of diseases. Some diseases spread from one person to another. Sneezing without covering your mouth is one way to spread diseases such as a cold or the flu. Some other diseases can't be spread to other people.

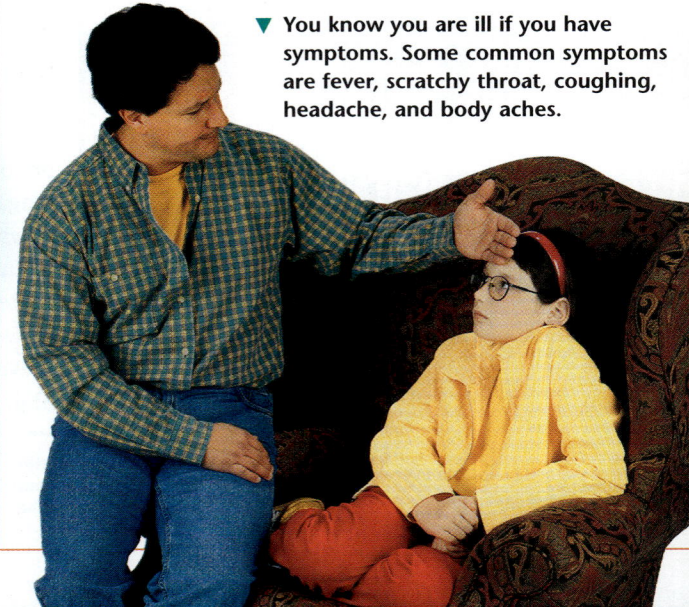

▼ You know you are ill if you have symptoms. Some common symptoms are fever, scratchy throat, coughing, headache, and body aches.

MULTILEVEL ACTIVITIES

EASY **How Pathogens Spread** Have pairs of students demonstrate how pathogens are spread. Direct one student to put finger paint on his or her hands and handle several items (a straw, a paper cup, a sheet of paper). Then ask the other student to handle the items. Like pathogens, the paint will be transferred to the hands of the second student.
TACTILE/KINESTHETIC

AVERAGE **Making Life Easier** Have groups of students research and report about aids used by people with disabilities—wheelchairs, hearing-ear dogs, Braille books, and so on. **INTERPERSONAL/VERBAL**

ADVANCED **Record Temperatures** Ask each student to have an adult in the house take the oral temperature of several family members. Direct students to record and bring the values to class. Have students work in groups to display the combined data in a bar graph or tally chart.
INTERPERSONAL/MATHEMATICAL

▶ People with disabilities might not be able to do some things. But there are many other things they *can* do.

How should you act toward people who are ill?

When friends have diseases that can spread, you should know how you can keep the disease from spreading to you. Different diseases spread in different ways.

Sometimes people have diseases or health problems that you cannot catch. Stacy has an illness that keeps her from walking. She uses a wheelchair to get around. Stacy's illness can't be spread to others, but it has caused her to have a disability. A disability is a physical or mental problem. You can't catch a disability.

People with illnesses and disabilities may feel bad because their bodies aren't working normally. You should treat people with diseases and disabilities the same way you treat your other friends. Imagine how you would feel if you were that person. Think about how an illness or a disability would affect you and how you would want to be treated.

LESSON CHECKUP

Check Your Facts
1. What is a disease?
2. How do you know if you have a disease?
3. CRITICAL THINKING Suppose a student in your class is home with a cold. Should you visit him? If not, what could you do instead?

Set Health Goals
4. Think about a time when you were ill. How did you feel? What made you feel better? List some ways to help a person with an illness feel better.

123

2 Teach

Discuss

Critical Thinking **How is a disease similar to and different from a disability?** Both are conditions in which the body is not working as it should. Unlike some diseases, a disability can't be spread to others.

Problem Solving **How could you include a student who uses a wheelchair in PE games?** Possible answer: PE games could be designed so strategy and skill rather than speed determine the winner. Also, the student who uses a wheelchair might be asked to keep score or watch the timer.

Health Journal

Symptoms of a cold include a scratchy throat, a runny nose, coughing, and congestion. Symptoms of flu include body aches, a fever, vomiting, diarrhea, and fatigue. Both viruses last about a week. This feature is designed to provide students with an opportunity to reflect on health decisions they are making in their personal lives. The journal should *not* be used to evaluate or assess students, nor do the results need to be shared among students.

3 Wrap Up

Lesson Checkup

1. something that causes the body not to work normally

2. if you have symptoms such as a fever, a scratchy throat, coughing, a headache, and body aches

3. No; you can cheer him up with phone calls and get-well cards.

4. Possible answers: Rest and medications often make people feel better; ways to make people who have noninfectious diseases such as cancer feel better include talking to them and listening to them talk about their feelings.

OBJECTIVES

- Define *infectious disease*.
- Compare and contrast bacteria and viruses.
- List some infectious diseases and their symptoms.

PROGRAM RESOURCES

- Activity Book, pp. 30–31
- Growth, Development, and Reproduction, pp. 58–65

VOCABULARY

- infectious disease (p. 124)
- pathogens (p. 124)
- bacteria (p. 124)
- virus (p. 125)
- fever (p. 126)

Daily Safety Tip

Cold sores are infectious. Remind students not to share lip balms, straws, cups, cans, or glasses with others. Also remind students not to share eating utensils or foods that have been in contact with another person's mouth or hands.

1 Motivate

Optional Materials **piece of moldy bread, cheese, or fruit in a sealed plastic bag**

Have students examine mold on bread, cheese, or fruit and list adjectives that describe it, such as *fuzzy, green, black, white*. Explain that many molds grow deep into the food, where they can't be seen or cut away. (As an alternative, ask students to describe foods on which they have seen mold growth, and elicit what the mold looked like.)

Why should you not eat a food on which you can see mold, even if someone cuts away the mold? Eating such foods can cause illness. Parts of the mold that are not visible might still be on the food.

MAIN IDEA
Bacteria and viruses are two kinds of pathogens that cause disease.

WHY LEARN THIS? You can use what you learn to keep from getting a disease.

VOCABULARY
- infectious disease
- pathogens
- bacteria
- virus
- fever

Some Diseases and Their Causes

A friend at school gets a cold. She sniffles and sneezes all day Monday. By Friday several people in your class are ill. A cold is an infectious disease. An **infectious disease** (in•FEK•shuhs dih•ZEEZ) is a disease that can spread from one person to another. Infectious diseases are caused by pathogens. **Pathogens** (PA•thuh•juhnz) are germs that cause disease. When your friend sneezed, she spread the pathogens that caused her disease to others.

What are some kinds of pathogens?

Two main kinds of pathogens cause infectious diseases. One kind is bacteria. **Bacteria** (bak•TIR•ee•uh) are very simple living things. They are each made of just one cell. They are so small that you can see them only with a microscope.

Activity **Find the Ways Pathogens Spread** How are these students spreading pathogens? List other ways that pathogens can be spread.

MULTILEVEL ACTIVITIES

EASY **Starve a Cold, Feed a Fever?** Have pairs of students use information in this lesson to compose songs that compare and contrast colds and flu. **MUSICAL**

AVERAGE **Tiny Food Processors** Have students research the roles of bacteria and fungi in making foods such as vinegar, sauerkraut, pickles, yogurt, Swiss cheese, soy sauce, olives, and butter. Ask students to diagram the process of fermentation in the making of one of these foods. **LOGICAL/SPATIAL**

ADVANCED **You Can Stop the Spread of Head Lice** Have students write public service announcements about preventing the spread of head lice. Allow them to read their announcements in class. **VERBAL**

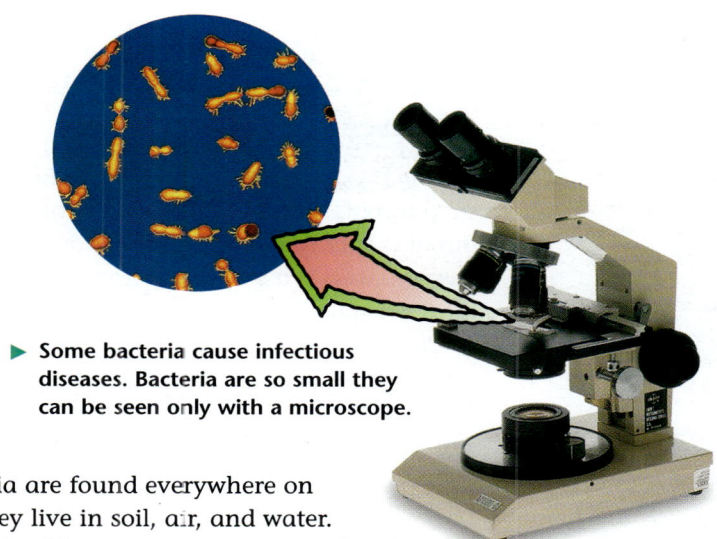

▶ Some bacteria cause infectious diseases. Bacteria are so small they can be seen only with a microscope.

Bacteria are found everywhere on Earth. They live in soil, air, and water. Some kinds of bacteria grow on or inside other living things. Not all of these bacteria cause disease. Some bacteria even help your body work normally.

However, a few kinds of bacteria *do* cause disease. When they get into your body, they can begin to multiply. They can grow into such large groups that your body cannot work normally. Then you become ill.

Another kind of pathogen is a virus. A **virus** (vy•ruhs) is one of the tiniest pathogens that cause disease. Viruses are even smaller than bacteria. Viruses must use cells in other living things to make more viruses. Viruses cause disease by destroying the cells they use.

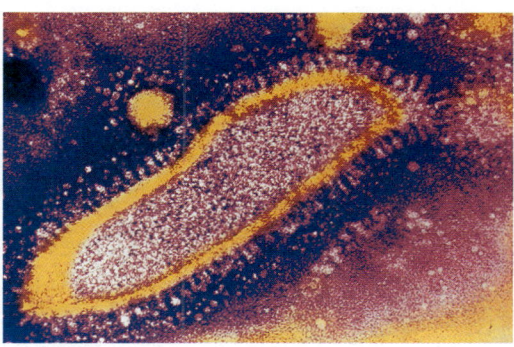

▲ Viruses also cause some infectious diseases. Viruses are even smaller than bacteria. Special microscopes must be used to see them. This virus has been magnified many hundreds of times.

125

SCIENCE

Breaking Down Barriers Many bacteria are decomposers—organisms that break down living or once-living matter to obtain energy. Have students use two small apples, a plastic knife, and two small self-sealing bags to show how bacteria can break down apple tissues. Instruct students to place one apple into a bag and seal it. Ask them to make cuts into the other apple, place it in the second bag, and seal it. Lead a discussion encouraging the class to account for the differences in appearance of the apples after a few days.

2 Teach

Activity

Find the Ways Pathogens Spread One boy is sneezing onto the food of others. Two students are spreading pathogens by sharing a drink from the same straw.

Learn from Pictures

What are some ways not shown in the photograph on page 124 that pathogens can be spread from person to person? Possible answers: sharing the same eating utensils, not washing your hands before eating, not washing your hands after going to the bathroom, putting things such as pencils and pens into your mouth.

Discuss

How do bacteria and viruses cause disease? Bacteria multiply and grow into such large groups that the body cannot work normally. Viruses cause disease by destroying the cells they use to reproduce.

Critical Thinking **How are bacteria and viruses similar?** Both are tiny pathogens that may cause diseases in humans. Both kinds of pathogens can only be seen with a microscope.

Learn from Pictures

Direct students to look at and compare the photographs of the bacteria and the virus. Tell students that the small, hair-like projections surrounding each bacterium are called flagella.

Health Background

Bacteria and Floods *Escherichia coli* is a type of bacteria found in the intestines of humans and other animals. During floods human wastes containing *E. coli* can enter a community's drinking water system and make people ill. Boiling contaminated water kills the bacteria and makes the water safe to drink.

125

Discuss

Diagnosis of common infectious diseases such as colds and flu is based on symptoms exhibited by the ill person. When making a diagnosis, doctors sometimes consider the presence of other cases in the community. It is usually not necessary to do blood tests to confirm these diagnoses. However, sometimes blood tests are done and results are shared with public health officials.

Critical Thinking **Why would public health officials be interested in the results of blood tests diagnosing colds and flu?** to determine the nature and extent of the illness in the community **What might public health officials do with the information?** advise the public to take precautions

Critical Thinking **What symptoms do colds, flu, and strep throat have in common?** sore throat and fever **How do causes of these illnesses differ?** Colds and flu are caused by viruses; strep throat is caused by bacteria.

Did you know?

Fall marks the start of cold and flu season. Even though cold, wet weather doesn't cause colds and influenza, these diseases are much more common in fall and winter. This may be because people spend more time inside, where viruses can spread more easily.

What are some infectious diseases?

One infectious disease that bacteria cause is strep throat. When you have strep throat, your throat is very sore and you may have a fever. A **fever** (FEE•ver) is a body temperature that is higher than normal.

Colds and flu are two kinds of infectious diseases viruses cause. When you have a cold, you may have a stuffy nose, a scratchy throat, and a cough. You may even have a fever. Colds usually last about a week.

The flu has many of the same symptoms as a cold. You also may have chills, fever, and body aches. The flu can make you feel very tired. The flu usually lasts one day to a week.

▼ If you have a very sore throat, your doctor may take a swab of your throat. The doctor will try to grow what's on the swab. If certain bacteria grow, you may have strep throat.

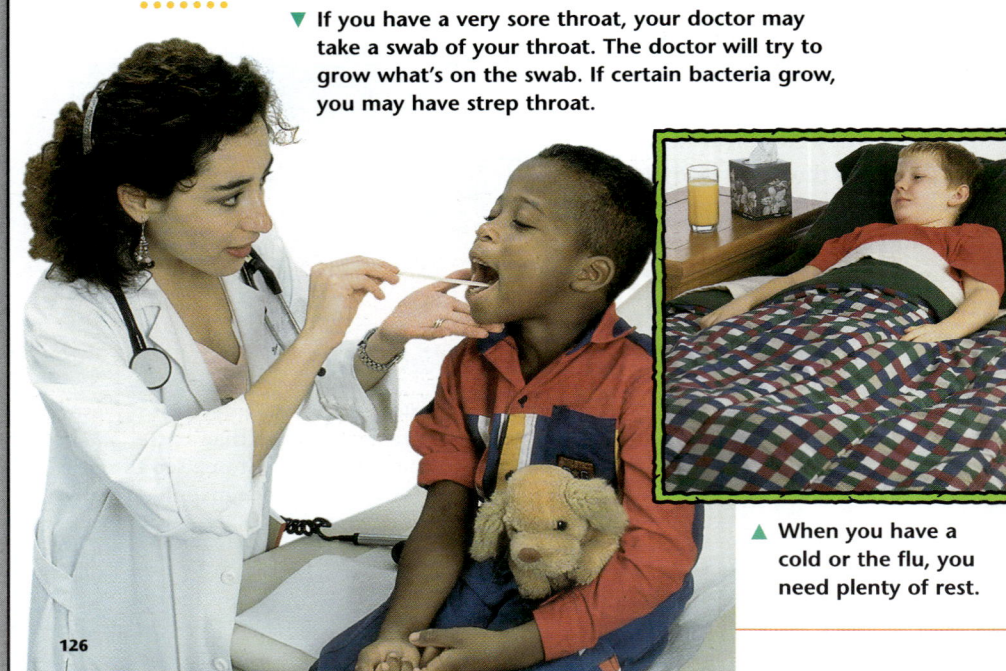

126

▲ When you have a cold or the flu, you need plenty of rest.

Health Background

Flu Shots Scientists have determined that the influenza, or flu, virus changes constantly. Over the period of a few years, the virus changes slightly. A slightly modified vaccine to prevent the disease is formulated each year. However, every few decades, the virus changes so much that a completely new vaccine must be developed.

For more background, visit the **Webliography** on the Teacher Resources page at:
www.harcourtschool.com/health
Keyword diseases

GROWTH, DEVELOPMENT, AND REPRODUCTION

Optional Lessons on Sexually Transmitted Diseases (pages 58–65) are provided in this supplement. Use this component in compliance with state and local guidelines.

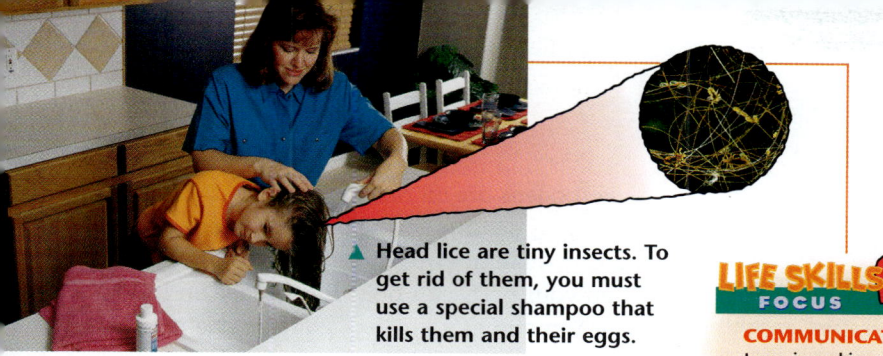

▲ Head lice are tiny insects. To get rid of them, you must use a special shampoo that kills them and their eggs.

What are other health problems that can spread?

Another common problem that can spread is head lice. People who have head lice can spread the lice by being near other people or by sharing things like combs, brushes, and hats.

Head lice are very small insects that crawl on skin and hair and feed on blood. As the lice feed, the head becomes very itchy. Other symptoms of head lice are tiny red bumps near the root of the hair on the head.

People who have head lice must use a special shampoo that kills the insects. The eggs in the hair must be removed with a fine comb or tweezers. All combs, brushes, clothing, and bed linens must be washed in very hot water to kill the lice and their eggs.

LIFE SKILLS FOCUS

COMMUNICATE

Joyce is making a picture book to help a kindergarten class learn how infectious diseases spread. What should Joyce think about while she's planning her book? How can she communicate her message clearly? Use the steps for communicating shown on page *xii*.

LESSON CHECKUP

Check Your Facts

❶ What are pathogens?

❷ How do pathogens cause infectious diseases?

❸ **CRITICAL THINKING** Is it a good idea to share a cup with a friend who doesn't seem ill? Why or why not?

Set Health Goals

❹ Think of a time when you caught an infectious disease from a friend or relative. How do you think you got the disease? Write down some things you might have done to keep from getting the disease.

127

ACTIVITY BOOK, p. 31

Recognize Vocabulary | Vocabulary Reinforcement

On each line write the letter for the word that best completes each sentence.

_d_ **1.** A _____ is a condition that prevents the body from working normally.
 a. symptom b. virus
 c. pathogen d. disease

_c_ **2.** A _____ is a sign of an illness.
 a. lifestyle b. medicine
 c. symptom d. pathogen

_d_ **3.** A disease that can be spread from one person to another is a(n) _____ disease.
 a. lifestyle b. vaccine
 c. noninfectious d. infectious

_b_ **4.** Germs that cause diseases are called _____.
 a. symptoms b. pathogens
 c. diabetes d. allergies

_b_ **5.** Some _____ are very simple living things that causes disease.
 a. viruses b. bacteria
 c. head lice d. vaccines

_a_ **6.** A _____ is one of the smallest pathogens that causes diseases.
 a. virus b. fever
 c. symptom d. vaccine

_b_ **7.** A _____ is a symptom in which the body temperature is higher than normal.
 a. virus b. fever
 c. rash d. cough

Explain how infectious diseases are spread.

8. Infectious diseases are spread from person to person by pathogens. Sneezing, coughing, or sharing food are just some of the ways pathogens are spread.

Life Skills Focus

Communicate Possible answer: Joyce should use infectious diseases with which the younger students are most familiar such as colds, flu, strep throat, and pinkeye. She might use pairs of pictures to show students what to do and what not to do to prevent spreading certain diseases. Joyce could use and explain the universal symbol for "no" (a red circle with a diagonal slash through it) to indicate which pictures represent poor health practices.

Project Checkup

Make a Germ-Fighter Bulletin Board (p. 121) Some students may wish to include in their chapter projects the information about how pathogens are passed from one person to another.

3 Wrap Up

Lesson Checkup

1. germs that cause disease

2. Some pathogens that enter the body multiply quickly and keep the body from working properly. Other pathogens destroy cells.

3. No; the friend might be infectious even though he or she doesn't show symptoms.

4. Answers should reflect the knowledge that infectious diseases can be transmitted by direct contact or when pathogens are sprayed into the air by coughing and sneezing. Washing your hands often with antibacterial soap, keeping your hands and other objects out of your mouth and away from your face, and having an ill person use tissues when he or she coughs or sneezes may prevent the spread of disease.

OBJECTIVES

- Explain two ways a person can become immune to a disease.
- Define *medicine*, and explain the importance of taking all medicines only as directed.

PROGRAM RESOURCES

 Teaching Transparency 26

 Computer Graphing Activity, Teaching Resources p. 59

- Activity Book, p. 32

VOCABULARY

- immune (p. 129)
- vaccine (p. 129)
- medicine (p. 130)

Daily Safety Tip

Skin is often the body's first line of defense against disease because it prevents pathogens from entering the body. Stress the importance of cleaning a cut or scrape with soap or an antiseptic and covering it with a clean bandage until a scab forms.

1 Motivate

Optional Materials **hand vacuum, handkerchief, rubber band, small amount of dust**

Secure the handkerchief over the vacuum cleaner nozzle with the rubber band. Sprinkle dust on a desktop. Turn on the vacuum and hold it above, but not touching, the dust. (As an alternative, elicit from students what happens to dust on a carpet when a vacuum is passed over it.)

How does this demonstrate the function of the nose? As a person inhales, he or she may inhale tiny particles present in the air. The handkerchief prevented dust from entering the vacuum cleaner.

Fighting Disease

MAIN IDEA
Most diseases can be prevented and treated.

WHY LEARN THIS? You can use what you learn to help keep yourself and others healthy.

VOCABULARY
- immune
- vaccine
- medicine

Pathogens are all around us. Sometimes pathogens get into your body and cause disease. Luckily, there are ways to treat most diseases. Often your body can fight the disease on its own. Sometimes you need a doctor's help.

How can you prevent disease?

Reggie wants Juan to come outside and play. Juan's mom says that Juan has the flu. He can't play with other children until he is well. She tells Reggie that she doesn't want him to catch the flu from Juan.

Staying away from people who are ill is only one way to prevent disease. A very important way to prevent disease is by washing your hands with soap and water. Many objects that people touch a lot, such as doorknobs and handrails, have pathogens on them. Washing with soap and water helps get rid of the pathogens on your hands. Keeping your hands clean helps prevent disease.

► Reggie can't play with Juan because Juan is ill. Learning how diseases are spread helps you know how to stay healthy.

MULTILEVEL ACTIVITIES

EASY **Write a Poem** Have students write a poem about how they feel when they are ill. Encourage them to use words they have learned in this chapter. **VERBAL/LINGUISTIC**

AVERAGE **Make a Word Puzzle** Have students use the vocabulary words in this lesson to make a word puzzle. They can make a word search; they can make an acrostic; or they can write riddles. **VERBAL/LINGUISTIC**

ADVANCED **Smallpox** Have groups of students research smallpox to find out when a vaccine for this disease was first developed and when the disease was considered eradicated. Suggest that students summarize their findings in a time line. **SPATIAL/INTERPERSONAL**

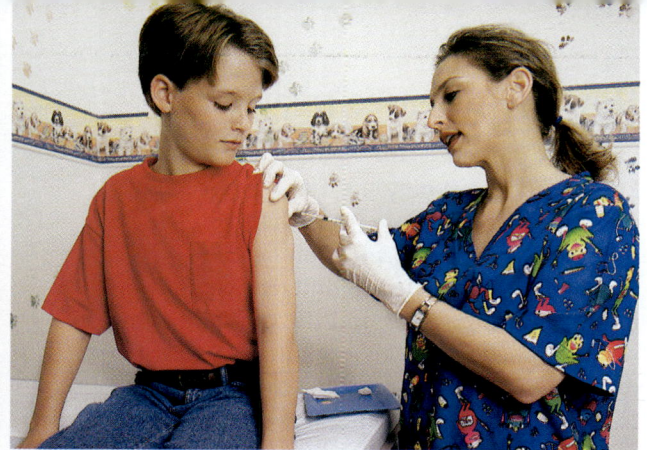

◀ A vaccine is usually given by injection. It will prevent one specific disease.

You can also prevent diseases by becoming immune to them. A person is **immune** (ih•MYOON) when a pathogen that causes a disease cannot make that person ill. People often become immune to a disease after they have had that disease. They also become immune when they get a vaccine for that disease. A **vaccine** (vak•SEEN) is a substance given to keep you from getting a certain kind of disease.

When you get a vaccine, a pathogen for a disease is put into your body. The pathogen has been weakened or killed so it can't make you ill. But it does cause your body to make a substance to fight the pathogen. If that pathogen gets in your body again, this substance will destroy it right away. You won't become ill.

When you are ill, you must also keep from spreading the disease to others. There are several easy things you can do. Wash your hands often. Cover your mouth and nose with a tissue when you cough or sneeze. Don't share anything that you have put in your mouth or near your nose. Doing these things will help keep others from catching your disease.

Some Diseases for Which There Are Vaccines

- Chicken pox
- Diphtheria
- Haemophilus Type B
- Hepatitis B
- Measles
- Mumps
- Pertussis
- Pneumonia
- Polio
- Rubella
- Tetanus

129

In the same way, a person's nose is lined with tiny hairs that trap particles and pathogens, preventing them from entering the lungs.

2 Teach

Project Checkup

Make a Germ-Fighter Bulletin Board (p. 121) The information presented on this page regarding the importance of hand washing could be included in the chapter project.

Discuss

Antibodies, substances the body produces in response to a foreign substance, or antigen, provide immunity. There are two types of immunity. Passive immunity develops when you receive antibodies from your mother during her pregnancy or through breast milk. Active immunity develops when you are actively exposed to antigens, which, in turn, stimulate the formation of antibodies.

Critical Thinking What kind of immunity does an injected vaccine give? active immunity Which type of immunity do you develop before you are born? passive immunity

Human Body Connection

Immune System The immune system is made of organs, tissues, and cells that usually belong to other body systems as well. Some parts of the body's immune system include bone marrow, the skin, and white blood cells. Challenge students to use pages 1–15 to locate the body system to which each of these defenses against disease belongs. Bone marrow is part of the skeletal system. Skin is a sense organ. White blood cells are in the body's circulatory system.

Teach *continued*

Discuss

Name some medicines you have taken or been given recently, and explain why you were given them. Answers will vary but might include antibiotics for strep throat, pinkeye, or ear infections; acetaminophen to reduce fever or control pain; cough syrups or lozenges to control coughing; and decongestants and antihistamines to relieve allergy symptoms.

Science Connection

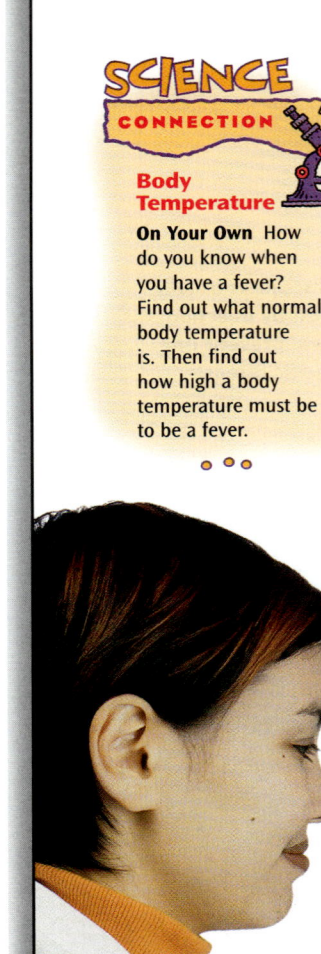

Body Temperature Normal body temperature is 98.6 degrees F. Generally, any value above 99 degrees is considered a sign of a fever. Young children can run fevers of 102 degrees or more when they are ill.

Learn from Pictures

Direct students' attention to the photograph. Based on the information given in the Science Connection tip above, pose these questions.

Critical Thinking What is the boy's temperature? 99.1 degrees Is he running a fever? yes

---

SCIENCE CONNECTION

Body Temperature

On Your Own How do you know when you have a fever? Find out what normal body temperature is. Then find out how high a body temperature must be to be a fever.

○ ○ ○

How are diseases treated?

Before a disease can be treated, you must know what the symptoms are. Always tell a parent, teacher, or caregiver when you feel ill. Then you will get the care you need.

Diseases are treated in different ways. Many diseases, such as colds and flu, are treated by resting in bed and drinking liquids. Sometimes diseases are treated with medicines. A **medicine** (MEH•duh•suhn) is a liquid, powder, cream, spray, or pill used to treat illness.

Not all medicines work alike. Some medicines kill the pathogen causing the disease. Medicines for strep throat and ear infections work like this. Other medicines treat the symptoms of a disease to make the person feel better. Cold medicines work like this. These medicines can help clear a stuffy nose and soothe a sore throat. But they cannot cure a cold.

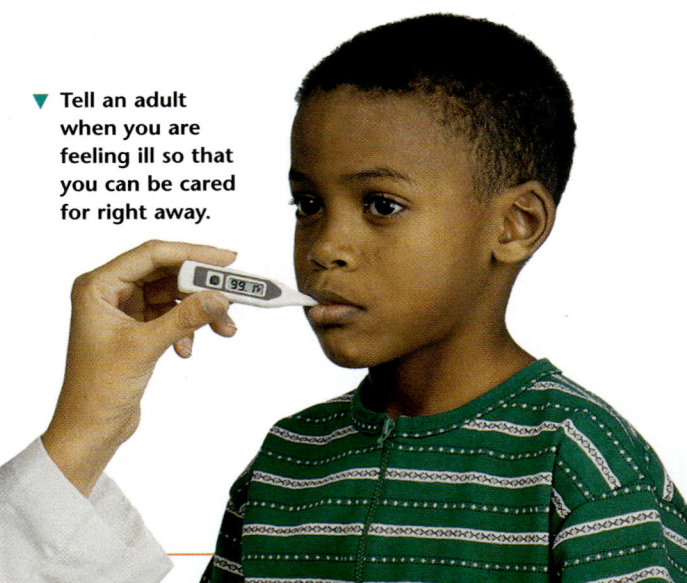

▼ Tell an adult when you are feeling ill so that you can be cared for right away.

130

Health Background

Reye Syndrome Reye syndrome is an acute illness that develops in children under the age of twenty who are recovering from a minor viral infection such as chicken pox or the flu. The cause of the illness is unknown, but its occurrence has been associated with the use of aspirin or other medications containing salicylates during the viral infection. Symptoms of the illness include drowsiness, disorientation, seizures, respiratory arrest, and ultimately, coma.

For more background, visit the **Webliography** on the Teacher Resources page at:
www.harcourtschool.com/health
Keyword diseases

COMPUTER GRAPHING ACTIVITY

Teaching Resources p. 59, Causes of Death. Students investigate the leading causes of death in the United States and use their data to predict future trends.

ACTIVITY BOOK, p. 32

Using Medicines Safely

Critical Thinking

Read each medicine warning label. Then answer the questions.

Medicine A
WARNING: Do not eat cheese or other dairy products for two hours after taking this medicine. Do not take this medicine with milk.

Medicine B
WARNING: Use this medicine for only temporary relief of pain. If symptoms continue for more than two days, call your physician.

Medicine C
WARNING: Take this medicine with food to avoid stomach upset.

Medicine D
WARNING: This medication may cause drowsiness.

1. Which medicine is best taken at bedtime? Explain your choice.
Medicine D should be taken at bedtime because it causes a person to become drowsy.

2. Which medicine should be taken right after you eat a meal? Explain.
Medicine C; because it can upset an empty stomach, it should be taken right after a meal.

3. When would be the best time to take Medicine A? Why?
It would be best to take this medicine two or three hours before a meal since the warning states not to take it with dairy products. It also could be taken before or after a meal that contains no dairy products.

4. How long should a person use Medicine B? Explain.
Because the warning states that this medicine should be used only temporarily, a person should use this medicine for no more than two days in a row.

Fever is a symptom of many diseases. To bring your temperature back to normal, an adult can give you a fever medicine. Some fever medicines are very safe for children to take. However, one kind—aspirin—is not safe for children. It can cause a serious illness in children. For this reason, take medicine only when a trusted adult gives it to you. The adult should read the labels or consult a doctor to decide which medicine to use, how much to give you, and how often you need it.

Take medicine only from a parent or other trusted adult.

▶ This child is getting fever medicine. Fever medicines help the body temperature return to normal.

LESSON CHECKUP

Check Your Facts

❶ What are two ways to prevent disease?

❷ What does it mean to be immune to a disease?

❸ CRITICAL THINKING If you feel ill, should you take medicine that another student gives to you? Why or why not?

Use Life Skills

❹ COMMUNICATE List three ways to keep from spreading or getting disease. Post your list where family members can see it.

131

Discuss

Problem Solving While you are spending the night with a friend, you realize you don't feel well. You think you might have a fever. Your friend offers you some aspirin because the label says it reduces fever. **What should you do, and why?** Don't take the aspirin because aspirin can be dangerous to children and you should only take medicine from a trusted adult. Instead, tell your friend's parent how you feel.

3 Wrap Up

Lesson Checkup

1. Possible answers: staying away from people with infectious diseases, washing your hands regularly with soap and water, covering your mouth when you sneeze or cough, and not sharing anything you've put in your mouth or near your nose.

2. If you are immune to a disease, a pathogen that causes the disease cannot make you ill.

3. No; medicines should be administered only by trusted adults.

4. Possible answers: cleaning common objects, such as telephones, doorknobs, and light switch panels, with disinfectants; using separate cups in the bathroom; staying away from people who have infectious diseases; washing hands regularly with antibacterial soap and water; covering the mouth when sneezing or coughing; and not sharing drinks or food.

LESSON 4

Pages 132–135

OBJECTIVES

- Define *noninfectious diseases*, and list three examples.
- Compare and contrast allergies and asthma.
- Explain what happens to sugar in a person with diabetes.

PROGRAM RESOURCES

Teaching Transparencies 18, 20

- Activity Book, p. 33

VOCABULARY

- noninfectious diseases (p. 132)
- allergy (p. 132)
- asthma (p. 134)
- diabetes (p. 135)

1 Motivate

Act out a scenario in which you sneeze repeatedly, making sure to cover your mouth and nose as you do.

What conditions might cause a person to sneeze a lot? Possible answers: colds, flu, allergies.

Use answers to introduce the subject of allergies. Invite volunteers who suffer from allergies to tell what causes their allergic reactions and what they do to prevent or control them.

LESSON 4

MAIN IDEA
Some diseases are not spread by pathogens.

WHY LEARN THIS? You may know people who have diseases that cannot be spread.

VOCABULARY
- noninfectious diseases
- allergy
- asthma
- diabetes

Diseases You Can't Catch

You have been learning about infectious diseases. Infectious diseases are spread from one person to another by pathogens. Other diseases are not spread by pathogens. **Noninfectious diseases** cannot be caught from or spread to other persons. Some examples of noninfectious diseases are allergies, asthma, and diabetes.

What is an allergy?

One common noninfectious disease is an allergy. An **allergy** (A•ler•jee) is the body's reaction to some substance. People with allergies are not all allergic to the same things. Some people are allergic to just one thing. Other people are allergic to many things.

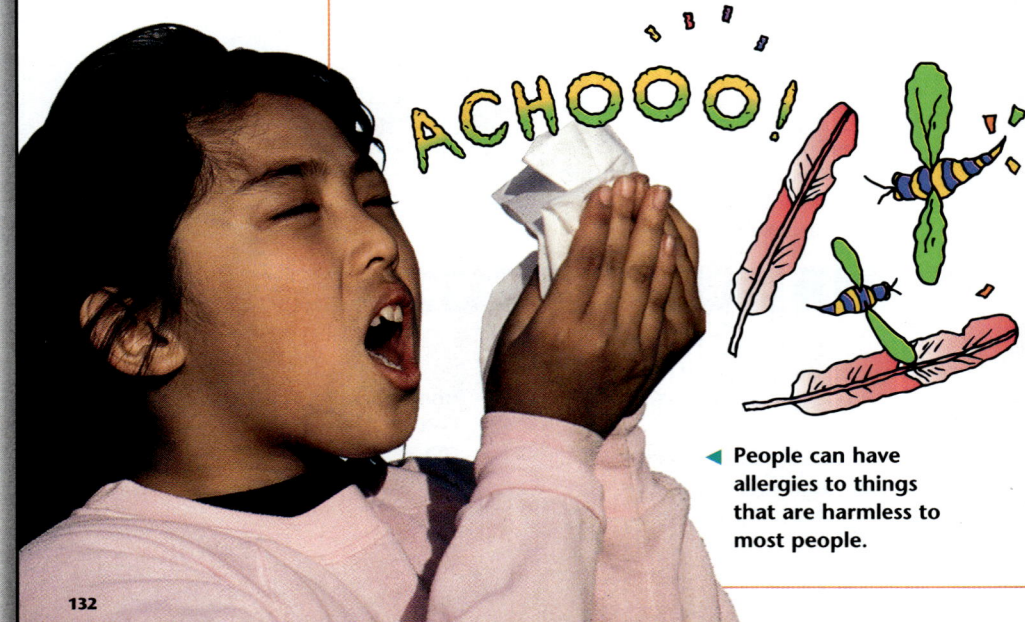

ACHOOO!

◄ People can have allergies to things that are harmless to most people.

132

MULTILEVEL ACTIVITIES

EASY **Allergies in Your School** Have students survey the student body to find out how many students have allergies. Ask them to make tally charts to summarize their findings. Charts could include the number of students who react to each allergen. **INTERPERSONAL/MATHEMATICAL**

AVERAGE **Allergy Bulletin Board** Have students work in groups to find out the allergic reactions associated with various allergens, such as dust, bee stings, milk, chocolate, and nuts. After each group has devised its list, have the class work together to create a bulletin board showing the allergens and their effects. The bulletin board can be illustrated with pictures of the items that cause allergies. **SPATIAL/INTERPERSONAL**

AVERAGE **Take a Deep Breath** When at rest, the average person inhales about 12 times per minute. Have students compute the number of times they inhale in one day. (17,280 times in a twenty-four-hour period) **MATHEMATICAL**

Animals, plants, medicines, dust, bee stings, and foods can all cause allergies. Some foods that can cause allergies include eggs, peanuts, strawberries, wheat, and milk.

Not all people have allergies. Those who do have allergies have symptoms like sneezing, itchy and watery eyes, a runny nose, or an itchy skin rash. Some people have only mild symptoms. Others react strongly and may need to see a doctor right away. A very serious allergic reaction can cause death.

Doctors can help people with allergies. If you have an allergy to something, your doctor may tell you to stay away from it. Doctors can give medicine to help symptoms go away. They use skin tests to find out what things cause allergies. Sometimes people get allergy shots to reduce their symptoms.

Myth and **Fact**

Myth: Hay fever is a hay allergy.

Fact: Hay fever is an allergic reaction in the nose to pollen, animal skin, feathers, and molds carried in the air.

133

2 Teach

Learn from Pictures

Have students study the illustration on this page as you ask these questions.

What insect stings or bites, other than a bee sting, might cause allergic reactions? wasp, hornet, yellow jacket, mosquito **What other dairy products might cause allergic reactions?** yogurt, sour cream, cheeses

Discuss

Remind students how the body's immune system works. Then explain that allergies occur when the body's immune system perceives a substance, such as a food or a medicine, as potentially dangerous to the body—an allergen.

Problem Solving A friend who is allergic to strawberries is eating dinner with your family. Your mother doesn't know about your friend's allergy and serves strawberry shortcake for dessert. **What can you do so your friend can have dessert without having an allergic reaction?** Possible answers: Suggest that your friend have the shortcake without strawberries; ask your mother if there is another dessert your friend could eat.

DEVELOP READING SKILLS

Identify Cause and Effect
Have students make a table listing the noninfectious diseases mentioned in this lesson. In subsequent columns students should list the cause(s) of each disease and the effects each disease has on the human body. An example is given below.

Effects	Cause(s)	Disease
allergies	animals, plants, foods, dust, medicines, bee stings	sneezing, itchy and watery eyes, runny nose, itchy skin rash
asthma	allergies, exercise, lung diseases	difficulty breathing, tightness in chest, wheezing
diabetes	malfunctioning pancreas	too much sugar stays in the blood, making the person thirsty and tired

Health Background

Anaphylaxis Anaphylaxis is a rare, but severe reaction to an allergen. Left untreated it can result in death. Anaphylaxis is most common in people with a history of allergies.

For more background, visit the **Webliography** on the Teacher Resources page at:
www.harcourtschool.com/health
Keyword diseases

Human Body Connection

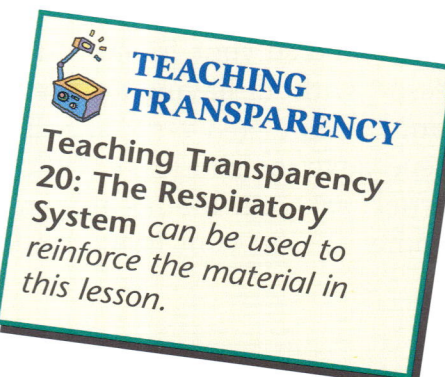

Respiratory System During an asthma attack the tubes leading to the lungs become narrow, making it difficult for air to move freely into and out of the lungs. This restricted air flow can cause a tightness in the chest, making it difficult for a person to breathe.

Discuss

Critical Thinking How are asthma and respiratory allergies alike? How are they different? Both are noninfectious diseases of the respiratory system. Asthma is a disease of the lungs in which it is difficult for a person to breathe. Most respiratory allergies, on the other hand, affect only the nose and throat.

TEACHING TRANSPARENCY

Teaching Transparency 20: The Respiratory System *can be used to reinforce the material in this lesson.*

Health Background

Asthma Treatments Two kinds of medicines are commonly used to treat asthma. Bronchodilators relax the muscles that tighten around the airways during an asthma attack. Anti-inflammatory medicines prevent, reduce, or reverse the swelling in the air sacs that cause asthmatic symptoms. Often a combination of both kinds of medicines is needed to control asthma. Asthma inhalers should be used only under a doctor's supervision and by the person for whom it is prescribed.

What is asthma?

Another noninfectious disease is asthma. **Asthma** (AZ•muh) causes people to have difficulty breathing. During an asthma attack, airways in the lungs become very narrow. This makes it hard for air to move in and out of the lungs. Compare the pictures below of the healthy airway and airway with asthma.

People who have asthma do not feel ill all the time. Their attacks are usually set off by allergies, exercise, or diseases that affect the lungs. Symptoms include tightness in the chest, difficulty breathing, and coughing and wheezing. Wheezing can be very loud and sometimes sounds squeaky.

Doctors can give medicine to help the symptoms of asthma go away. If you have asthma, your doctor may tell you to avoid the things that cause your asthma attacks.

HUMAN BODY CONNECTION

The Respiratory System

Study the respiratory system found on pages 12 and 13 of The Amazing Human Body. Find the lungs in the picture. How does asthma affect these organs?

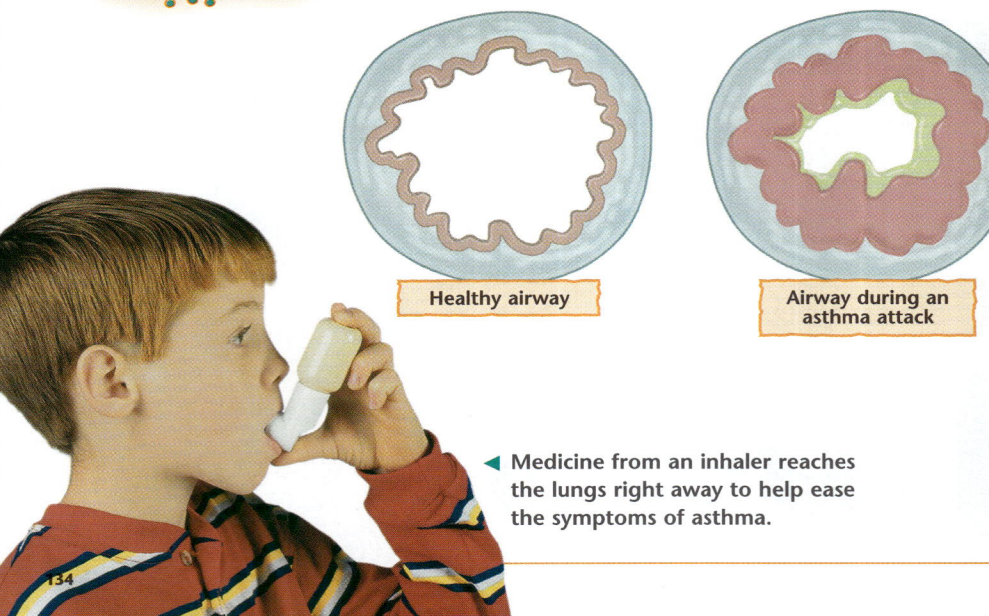

Healthy airway

Airway during an asthma attack

◄ Medicine from an inhaler reaches the lungs right away to help ease the symptoms of asthma.

134

MEET INDIVIDUAL NEEDS

Kinesthetic Learners Use a small soft plastic drink bottle to demonstrate how air moves into and out of the lungs. Have a volunteer hold his or her hand over the mouth of the bottle to feel the air leaving the bottle as you gently squeeze the bottle. Explain that this action simulates exhaling. Again with a volunteer's hand over the mouth of the bottle, release the pressure on the bottle to simulate inhaling. Explain that when you release the pressure, air rushes into the bottle.

ACTIVITY BOOK, p. 33

Identify the Main Idea and Important Details   Reading Skills

Read the paragraph below about asthma. Then on the lines below write the three most important details that support the main idea.

Asthma is a lung disease that has no cure. It is characterized by swelling of the passageways that carry air to the lungs. When the passageways swell, they prevent air from moving from the nose and mouth to the lungs. Because the air can't move freely, the lungs are unable to remove poisonous gases from the blood and replace these gases with oxygen. The swelling also causes the passageways to produce mucus, a substance that is about as thick as honey or maple syrup. The mucus can clog the airways even more, making breathing very difficult.

Main Idea: Asthma is a lung disease.

Important Details: Details can be listed in any order. Possible details include:

1. Swelling of airways prevents air from moving from the nose and mouth to the lungs.

2. Swelling prevents the lungs from getting oxygen.

3. Swelling causes mucus to form, which further clogs the airways.

Use information from your textbook to explain why asthma is a noninfectious disease.

4. Asthma is not spread by pathogens. It cannot be caught from or spread to other people.

What is diabetes?

Your digestive system changes some of the food you eat to a kind of sugar. The blood carries this sugar to the body cells. The cells use the sugar to make energy. **Diabetes** (dy•uh•BEE•teez) is a noninfectious disease that prevents the body from using sugar properly. The sugar doesn't go into the cells. Instead, it stays in the blood. Too much sugar in the blood can make people ill. They may feel very thirsty and tired and lose weight.

A doctor uses a blood test to find out if someone has diabetes. People with diabetes must eat a special diet. Often they must also take medicine. The medicine helps the body use the sugar from food.

Jill has just learned that she has diabetes. A home health nurse has come to help Jill and her mother. He shows them how to check the amount of sugar in Jill's blood. He talks to them about Jill's diet. He also shows Jill's mother how to give Jill medicine for her diabetes.

Career

Home Health Nurse

What They Do

Home health nurses go to patients' homes to observe their health, give medicines, give baths, and prepare meals. They may tell patients how to take medicine. They also may tell or show a patient's family how to take care of the patient.

Education and Training

Home health nurses must have some college education and training in nursing. Many states also require them to pass a special test. Home health nurses must have good communication skills, a desire to help others, and good judgment.

LESSON CHECKUP

Check Your Facts

1. What is an allergy?
2. What are some symptoms of asthma?
3. CRITICAL THINKING Why would someone with diabetes feel tired?

Use Life Skills

4. COMMUNICATE Choose one of the diseases described in the lesson. Imagine that you have this disease. Tell how it might affect your life.

135

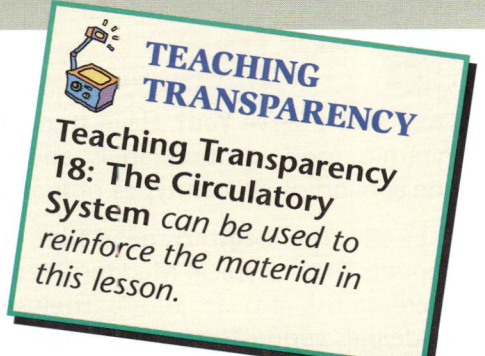

Discuss

People with Type 1 diabetes receive daily injections of insulin to prevent damage to body organs caused by excess glucose in the blood. Type 1 diabetes often "runs in families." That means that it may be inherited, like hair color or freckles. More common is Type 2 diabetes. The pancreas of a person with this type of diabetes often produces enough insulin, but his or her body does not use it properly. Type 2 diabetes can often be controlled with exercise and diet. If this isn't enough, various medicines help the body use insulin more efficiently. Some people with Type 2 diabetes must also use insulin.

Career

For more information on careers in home health care, contact:

National Home Caring Council
513 C Street, NE
Washington, D.C. 20002

Or visit the **Webliography** on the Teacher Resources page at:
**www.harcourtschool.com/health
Keyword** health careers

3 Wrap Up

Lesson Checkup

1. the body's reaction to some substance

2. tightness in the chest, difficulty breathing, and wheezing

3. In a person with diabetes, sugars from foods are not transported to the body's cells. Cells need this sugar for energy. Thus, a diabetic can often feel tired.

4. Answers will vary but should include both physiological as well as psychological and emotional effects.

OBJECTIVE

• Explain how a healthful lifestyle reduces a person's chances of getting certain diseases.

PROGRAM RESOURCES

 Computer Graphing Activity, Teaching Resources p. 60

• Activity Book, p. 34

VOCABULARY

• abstinence (p. 139)

Daily Safety Tip

More than three-fourths of all cases of lung cancer are due to smoking or exposure to environmental tobacco smoke. Encourage students to say *no* to all tobacco products because tobacco contains nicotine, an addictive and harmful drug, which makes it hard for a person to stop smoking once they have started.

---

1 Motivate

List on the board activities or behaviors students say they do every day.

Which activities help you stay healthy?
Possible answers: bathing or showering, brushing your teeth, exercising, not eating too many "junk" foods, and getting enough sleep.

2 Teach

Activity

Identify Healthful Foods The lunch on the left is the more healthful choice. Other healthful choices for lunch include a slice of cheese pizza; a pita sandwich with cheese, lettuce, and tomato; a fresh fruit salad; a chicken and vegetable stir-fry with rice; pasta with tomato sauce; and a salad with low-fat or fat-free dressing.

136

MAIN IDEA
Having a healthful lifestyle can help you fight disease.

WHY LEARN THIS? You can use what you learn to keep your body well.

VOCABULARY
• abstinence

Fighting Disease with a Healthful Lifestyle

You can do many things every day to keep your body healthy. Your lifestyle can make a difference in your health. *Lifestyle* refers to the choices a person makes about how to live his or her life. If you make healthful choices, then you have a healthful lifestyle. A healthful lifestyle helps your body fight disease.

How does the food you eat help you stay healthy?

Every morning for breakfast, Paul has orange juice and oatmeal with milk. Paul never feels tired during the school day. Lucas likes to have doughnuts and a soft drink for breakfast. Lucas is often sleepy at school.

Activity Identify **Healthful Foods** Compare these lunches. Which lunch is more healthful? Make a list of other healthful lunches.

Which is healthful?

136

MULTILEVEL ACTIVITIES

EASY May I Serve You? Have students use an illustration of the Food Guide Pyramid, food nutrition labels, and reference books to determine the size of one serving of various types of foods. **KINESTHETIC/LOGICAL**

AVERAGE The Mediterranean Diet Have pairs of students find out the components of the typical Mediterranean diet, which has been found to decrease risk of heart attack. They should compare this diet with the dietary guidelines suggested in the Food Guide Pyramid. **INTERPERSONAL**

ADVANCED Words to Live By Have students write and share with the class poems about how living a healthful lifestyle helps fight disease. **LINGUISTIC/VERBAL**

Always read labels.

◄ Check the amounts of fat, sugar, and salt in foods. Eating less of these can help reduce your risk for some noninfectious diseases.

The foods you choose to eat are important to your health. Food gives your body energy. Food also gives your body the things it needs to grow and fight disease.

Every day you should eat a variety of healthful foods. Use what you know about the Food Guide Pyramid to make smart choices about the foods you eat. When you make smart choices, your body gets the right amounts of nutrients and fiber.

If you choose foods that are not healthful, your body doesn't get the things it needs. You may have less energy, gain extra weight, and catch infectious diseases easily. If you eat a lot of foods low in fiber and high in fats, sugar, and salt, you may increase your risk of developing some noninfectious diseases, too.

At the grocery store you may have noticed foods labeled "fat-free," "sugar-free," or "low in salt." Are these foods really more healthful? The only way to know for sure is to read the labels on the food packages. Each food package is labeled with the amounts of fat, sugar, and salt in that food. By reading and comparing labels, you can find out which foods are more healthful.

CONSUMER FOCUS

Analyze Advertising and Media Messages

Some packages might have bright colors, star characters, or certain words like "fat free" to try to get you to buy the product. Choose one of your favorite packaged foods. Look at the package, and list all the ways the package is being used to try to sell the food. Then read the label and decide if the food is healthful for your body. Use the steps on page xv to help you.

• • •

137

Discuss

Nutrition experts recommend that 30 percent or less of a person's daily Calorie intake should be from fats. Unfortunately in the United States, most people obtain about 40 percent of their total Calories from fat.

What are some foods that contain a lot of fat? margarine, butter, cheeses, sour cream, whole milk, oils, poultry skin, peanut butter, ice cream, nuts, milk chocolate, coconut, avocados, and many meats

Nutrition labels tell the number of grams of fat in a food and the percentage of Calories in the food that are from fat.

Problem Solving **How could you make sure 30 percent or less of your daily Calories are from fat?** Eat only foods in which 30 percent or fewer of the Calories are from fat.

Fiber aids in the digestive process and may decrease the risk of heart disease.

What are some sources of fiber? celery, carrots, and members of the cabbage family; prunes, oranges, and other fruits; and whole grains, lentils, and beans

Consumer Focus

Analyze Advertising and Media Messages You might want to have available packages of foods for students that might not have access to bringing in a package. Make a class tally list to compare how often certain advertising tricks are used.

 **ART**
· ·

Building the Pyramid To help them learn the divisions of the Food Guide Pyramid, have students make drawings of entrées for breakfast, lunch, and dinner that illustrate the requirements suggested in the pyramid. Direct students to arrange the food items as they appear in the pyramid. For example, a breakfast possibility might be toast topped with apple slices and a little peanut butter. The lunch choice might be half a bagel topped with lettuce, tomato, onion, a slice of cheese, a slice of turkey, and a small dollop of mayonnaise. For dinner students might show a bed of rice topped with stir-fried vegetables, a small amount of chicken, and perhaps some tofu.

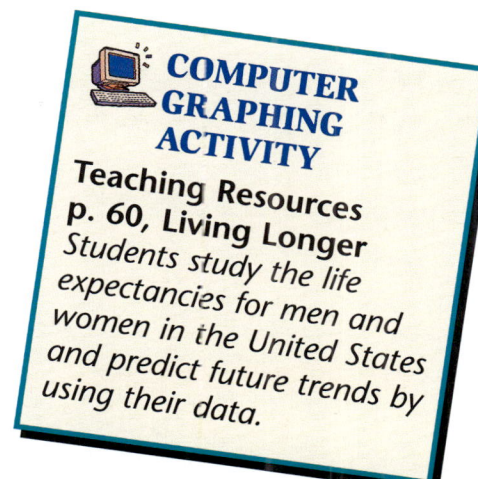

COMPUTER GRAPHING ACTIVITY
Teaching Resources p. 60, Living Longer Students study the life expectancies for men and women in the United States and predict future trends by using their data.

Human Body Connection

Skeletal, Circulatory, and Respiratory Systems After students have read the second paragraph on this page, challenge them to use pages 1–15 to determine to which body system their muscles, heart, and lungs belong.

Discuss

Name at least five benefits of exercise. Exercise helps make your muscles, heart, and lungs stronger. Exercise also allows your body to use the foods you eat for energy. Exercise helps you maintain your weight and helps fight certain diseases. Finally, exercise helps you manage stress and can make you feel calmer.

Health Journal

Favorite exercises will vary but may include organized sports, gymnastics, running or jogging, and street hockey. Students' rates of participation will vary as well. Most students will probably say that they feel tired but relaxed after most forms of exercise.

How does exercise help you stay healthy?

Jane's gym teacher always has the class begin with a jog around the playground. At first Jane couldn't make it all the way around. Now she can always finish. And she seems to have more energy.

Exercise is important to good health. It makes your muscles, heart, and lungs stronger. It helps your body use food and keeps you at a healthful weight. Exercise also helps your body fight disease.

JOURNAL

In your Health Journal, describe your favorite kinds of exercise. Tell when, where, and how often you do them. How do you feel after exercising? Remember that your journal is private.

Exercise helps you manage stress, too. You may be stressed when something makes you worried, nervous, angry, sad, or tired. You may also be stressed when things around you change or when you begin something new. Symptoms of stress include headache, stomachache, and trouble sleeping. Stress also can make your heart pound and your muscles feel tight. Too much stress can make you ill.

Exercise can help you feel calmer. It can help make the symptoms of stress go away. If you exercise regularly, your body will also handle stress better.

138

MATH

Exercise Your Rights! Have each student survey ten people to find out favorite exercises. Invite students to work together to compile the results and display the data in either a tally chart or a bar graph.

MULTICULTURAL LINK

Acupuncture Have students research acupuncture, an Asian form of medicine that treats and prevents various diseases as well as relieves stress.

How does tobacco use affect a person's health?

Using tobacco is not a healthful lifestyle choice. When people smoke, they breathe tobacco smoke into their mouths, noses, throats, and lungs. Tobacco smoke has many harmful substances.

Smoking weakens the body. People who smoke are more likely to catch diseases such as colds and flu than those who don't smoke. People who use chewing tobacco usually have problems with their teeth and gums. Over time any kind of tobacco use may cause cancer, lung disease, and heart disease.

To have a healthful lifestyle, you must practice abstinence from tobacco. **Abstinence** (AB•stuh•nuhnts) means avoiding a behavior that will harm your health. Choosing not to use tobacco is one of the best things you can do for your health.

LIFE SKILLS
FOCUS

Refuse
Deborah's mom has asthma. A neighbor who is visiting asks Deborah's mom if she can smoke in the house. Use the steps for refusals shown on page xi to help Deborah's mom respond.

• • •

◀ When you breathe in other people's smoke, you get the same harmful substances that smokers breathe in. Many public places have made special areas for smokers. This helps keep the smoke away from nonsmokers.

LESSON CHECKUP

Check Your Facts
1. List two healthful lifestyle choices.
2. Why is it important to eat healthful foods?
3. CRITICAL THINKING If you feel worried about a test that's coming up, what might make you feel better?

4. CRITICAL THINKING Some of your friends think that smoking is cool. What should you tell them?

Set Health Goals
5. Joe gets exercise one day a week. How can he change his lifestyle to make it more healthful?

139

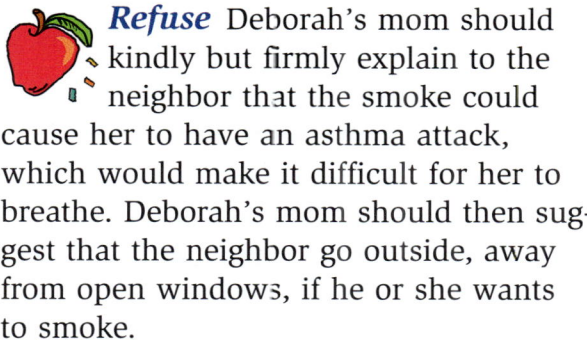

MATH

Smoking Makes No Cents!
Have students calculate how much money a person will spend if he or she starts smoking at age eighteen and smokes one pack of cigarettes a day (at $2.00 per pack) until age 65. For one year, 365 days × $2.00 per day = $730 in one year. For 47 years, the cost is $34,310. *Advanced*

Discuss

According to the U.S. surgeon general, more than 3 million teenagers under the age of eighteen smoke. Some started smoking as early as age eight or nine.

Problem Solving **What might you say to someone who is trying to get you to smoke?** Answers will vary. Encourage students to be firm and direct in their responses.

Life Skills Focus

Refuse Deborah's mom should kindly but firmly explain to the neighbor that the smoke could cause her to have an asthma attack, which would make it difficult for her to breathe. Deborah's mom should then suggest that the neighbor go outside, away from open windows, if he or she wants to smoke.

3 Wrap Up

Lesson Checkup

1. Possible answers: eating a healthful diet, exercising, abstaining from tobacco.

2. Eating a well-balanced diet gives you the energy your body needs to grow and to fight disease.

3. allowing enough time to study and relax before the test, getting enough sleep the night before the test, eating a healthful breakfast the morning of the test, exercising

4. Answers should be firm but constructive.

5. Answers may include eating a more healthful diet, allowing more time for exercise, getting enough sleep each night, or not smoking or using other drugs.

OBJECTIVES

- Identify ways to manage stress.
- Apply stress-management skills to help control disease.

PROGRAM RESOURCES

- Activity Book, p. 35

1 Motivate

Optional Materials **a jar containing folded slips of paper, musical instrument**

Bring a musical instrument to class. Announce that you will select one student's name from a jar containing folded strips of paper. As an alternative, say you will select one of the students. This student will play the instrument and be graded on how well she or he plays. Tell the class that while only one person will be chosen, they all need to be ready. At this point students probably will tell you they don't know how to play the instrument. Hold the jar of names high and choose a slip. Slowly open it. Instead of saying a name, ask students to name the physical symptoms they are experiencing. List these symptoms on the board. Explain that these are all symptoms of stress.

2 Teach

Learn from Pictures

Direct students' attention to the pictures of Marcy. Discuss some ways Marcy can handle her stress.

MANAGE STRESS to Control Disease

We all feel stress sometimes. Learning to manage stress will help keep you healthy.

Learn This Skill

Marcy has to give an oral report tomorrow, and she is feeling a lot of stress. She is sitting quietly, but her muscles feel tight, her heart is pounding, and her head hurts. Here are four things Marcy can do to manage her stress.

Exercise.

"Maybe I'll feel less tense if I go for a walk."

Imagine yourself doing well in the situation.

"I've had to give oral reports before. I'm usually nervous at first, but I always get through them."

140

LANGUAGE ARTS

Make a Game of It Organize students into groups of four. Have groups design game boards for stress management games. Direct them to include on their boards squares that show stressors in their lives and to decorate their boards with pictures of ways to manage stress. To play the game, students roll number cubes or spin a spinner and advance the indicated number of spaces. Then they state the stressor in that square and give an idea to manage that type of stress. If they cannot manage that stress, they move back two spaces. Players cannot repeat ideas for stress managers during the game.

Find a way to relax.

"Maybe I'll finish that book I was reading."

Talk to someone about how you're feeling.

"Maybe I'll call Maria. She always knows just what to say to make me feel better."

Practice This Skill

Here are some ways to help you solve the problems.

Ways to Manage Stress
- Exercise.
- Imagine yourself doing well in the situation.
- Find a way to relax.
- Talk to someone about how you're feeling.

A. Ann is worried about her first visit to the hospital to see her grandfather. She can feel her heart pounding. Use what you know about managing stress to help Ann.

B. Clay has a big math test tomorrow, and he can't get to sleep. Use what you know about managing stress to help Clay.

141

ACTIVITY BOOK, p. 35

"Manage Stress" ・ ・ Life Skills

Instructions: Think of things in life that can cause stress. Write at least eight ideas inside the balloon. Think of ways you have learned to manage stress. Write at least five ideas around the outside of the balloon. Draw a small picture of yourself doing each activity that helps you manage stress.

Answers may include: too many things to do at once; an upcoming test; an argument with a friend or family member; and so on.

Step 1

Critical Thinking How does exercise help manage stress? Possible answers: makes you feel calmer, relaxes tense muscles, reduces the tense feelings that stress brings.

Step 2

Critical Thinking How can picturing yourself doing something successfully be helpful? Possible answers: It gives you confidence; if you can picture yourself doing something well, you will be less afraid to try it, you will feel as if you can do it.

Step 3

What are some things you like to do to relax? Answers will vary.

Step 4

Critical Thinking Why is it important to share your feelings when you feel stress? Possible answers: lets you express your feelings, helps find out if other people feel the same way and what they do when they feel that way.

With whom could you talk? Possible answers: a parent, friend, teacher, counselor, pastor, brother, sister.

3 Wrap Up

Practice This Skill

A. Students may suggest a variety of ways to help Ann manage her stress, such as finding a way to relax, perhaps by taking some deep breaths. Look for students to suggest that talking to someone about her feelings would be helpful in this situation.

B. Students might suggest that Clay find a way to relax, perhaps by reading. He also could imagine himself doing well on the test.

141

Use Vocabulary 3 pts. each

1. immune
2. fever
3. allergy
4. virus
5. disease
6. medicine
7. bacteria
8. diabetes
9. pathogens
10. symptom
11. noninfectious diseases
12. asthma
13. vaccine
14. infectious disease
15. abstinence

Check Your Facts 5 pts. each

16. A disease is something that causes the body not to work normally. When the body doesn't work normally, you usually have symptoms that keep you from feeling well.

17. The top photo is of bacteria and the bottom photo is a virus. Bacteria cause infectious diseases by growing into large groups in your body causing your body not to work normally. Viruses cause infectious diseases by destroying the cells they use for reproduction.

18. You can't catch an allergy, asthma, or diabetes. The symptoms for an allergy are sneezing, itchy and watery eyes, a runny nose, or an itchy rash. The symptoms for asthma include tightness in the chest, difficulty breathing, coughing, and wheezing. The symptoms of diabetes are feeling thirsty and tired and losing weight.

19. Eating right and getting exercise are parts of a healthful lifestyle. Eating right helps you have energy and ensures you have the things you need to grow and to fight disease. Getting exercise gives you energy; helps you fight disease; makes your muscles, heart, and lungs stronger; helps you use food and keep a healthful weight; and helps you manage stress.

USE VOCABULARY

abstinence (p. 139)	diabetes (p. 135)	infectious disease (p. 124)	pathogens (p. 124)
allergy (p. 132)	disease (p. 122)	medicine (p. 130)	symptom (p. 122)
asthma (p. 134)	fever (p. 126)	noninfectious diseases	vaccine (p. 129)
bacteria (p. 124)	immune (p. 129)	(p. 132)	virus (p. 125)

Use the terms above to complete the sentences. Page numbers in ( ) tell you where to look in the chapter if you need help.

1. When a pathogen cannot make a person ill, that person is ____.

2. A body temperature that is higher than normal is called a ____.

3. The body's bad reaction to some substance is an ____.

4. One of the tiniest pathogens that cause diseases such as colds is a ____.

5. Something that causes the body not to work normally is a ____.

6. A liquid, powder, cream, spray, or pill used to treat illness is called ____.

7. ____ are simple living things made of just one cell.

8. A disease that prevents the body from using sugar properly is ____.

9. Germs that cause disease are called ____.

10. A sign such as a headache that something is wrong in the body is a ____.

11. Diseases, such as diabetes or asthma, that cannot be caught are ____.

12. A disease that causes people to have difficulty breathing sometimes is ____.

13. A substance given to keep you from getting a certain kind of disease is a ____.

14. A disease that can spread from one person to another is an ____.

15. You practice ____ when you avoid a behavior that will harm your health.

CHECK YOUR FACTS

Page numbers in ( ) tell you where to look in the chapter if you need help.

16. Tell what disease is. How do you know if you have a disease? (p. 122)

20. Possible answers: keeping people who are ill away from those who are well, keeping hands clean, being immune to a disease, covering mouth and nose with a tissue when coughing and sneezing, and not sharing anything put into the mouth or near the nose.

17. Name the two kinds of pathogens in the photos below, and tell how they cause infectious diseases. (p. 125)

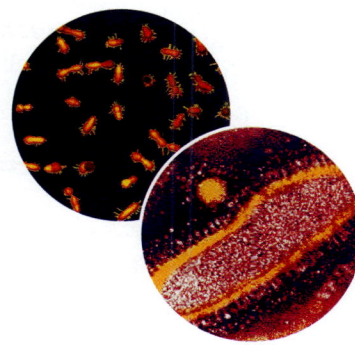

18. List three diseases that you can't catch. What are their symptoms? (pp. 132–135)

19. List two things that are part of a healthful lifestyle. Tell how they help you stay healthy. (pp. 136–138)

20. Name three ways you can prevent a disease from spreading. (pp. 128–129)

THINK CRITICALLY

21. Mike has the chicken pox. A virus causes chicken pox. Could Mike spread chicken pox to others? Explain.

22. Jenny eats many high-fat foods and rarely exercises. Explain how and why Jenny should change her lifestyle.

APPLY LIFE SKILLS

23. **Manage Stress** Suppose you will be playing soccer on a new team this year. How can you manage your stress to help you feel comfortable about playing on the new team?

24. **Communicate** Suppose your friend begins to feel ill at school. She wants to stay because there is a special program today. What would you tell her? How could you help her get care for her illness?

Promote Health

1. **Explain to your family what you have learned about how important exercise is for good health. Think of some ways family members can exercise together.**
2. **Make an advertisement that describes the importance of getting vaccines. Display the ad someplace in your school.**

Think Critically 7 pts. each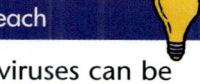

21. Yes, diseases caused by viruses can be spread to others.

22. Jenny should eat more healthfully (foods low in fat, sugar, and salt and high in fiber) and get regular exercise. Eating healthfully and getting regular exercise will increase her ability to fight diseases, give her more energy, ensure she has the things she needs to grow, make her stronger, help her use her food and keep a healthful weight, and help her manage stress.

Apply Life Skills 8 pts. each

23. Possible answer: You can manage your stress by getting regular exercise; not only does exercise reduce stress, but keeping in top form will help ensure you are playing at your best and will increase your self confidence. You can reduce your stress by imagining yourself doing well in the situation, finding a way to relax, and talking to someone about how you are feeling.

24. Possible answer: You should tell her that she needs to go to the nurse's office. She could spread her illness to everyone else if she stays, and the sooner she gets care the sooner she will recover. You can help her get care by telling an adult that she is ill.

PERFORMANCE ASSESSMENT

Project—Make a Germ-Fighter Bulletin Board

The chapter project (introduced on page 121) can be used for individual or team performance assessment. Allow students the opportunity to revise and complete their projects before submitting them for evaluation. Students can use the Project Summary Sheet (Assessment Guide, p. 17) to tell about their projects. You can use the rubric provided on the Project Evaluation Sheet (Assessment Guide, p. 37) to evaluate student performance.

Activities

Health Collage

With a Partner • Look through old magazines to find pictures that show healthful lifestyle choices. Cut out these pictures. Use them to make a collage about healthful lifestyles. Be sure to give your collage a title.

Gathering Cheer

With a Team • Make a list of things other than medicine that would help an ill person feel better. If possible, gather these items together to make a "cheer-up kit." Send your kit to someone who is in the hospital or at home with an illness.

Disease Search

On Your Own • Find out more about smallpox. It is a dangerous infectious disease that many people died from until about 200 years ago. Write a paragraph about smallpox. Tell what causes it, what its symptoms are, and how it was stopped.

Germ Stoppers

At Home • Ask a family member to help you find items in the house that are used to kill pathogens. Find out how they are used to keep pathogens from spreading.

144

Chapter Test

144

Multiple Choice

Choose the letter of the correct answer.

1. To treat a disease, your doctor might give you ____.
   a. diabetes   b. viruses
   c. medicine   d. pathogens

2. A fever is a ____, or a sign that something is wrong in the body.
   a. disease   b. pathogen
   c. lifestyle   d. symptom

3. Which health problem can be spread from one person to another?
   a. allergies   b. head lice
   c. asthma   d. diabetes

4. Choosing not to smoke is an example of ____.
   a. exercise   b. abstinence
   c. diet   d. studying

5. A disease that causes people to have difficulty breathing is ____.
   a. strep throat   b. diabetes
   c. asthma   d. cancer

Modified True or False

Write *true* or *false*. If a sentence is false, replace the underlined term to make the sentence true.

6. You are immune to a disease when its pathogen <u>cannot</u> make you ill.

7. <u>Food</u> gives your body things it needs to grow and fight disease.

8. <u>Asthma</u> is a disease that prevents the body from using sugar properly.

9. A <u>disease</u> is something that causes the body not to work normally.

10. Using tobacco is a <u>healthful</u> lifestyle choice.

11. A <u>pathogen</u> is given to keep you from getting a certain kind of disease.

12. An <u>allergy</u> is the body's reaction to some substance.

13. An infectious disease <u>can</u> be spread from one person to another.

Short Answer

Write a complete sentence to answer each question.

14. Name two ways to prevent disease.

15. What are some ways that infectious diseases are spread?

16. What does exercise do for the body?

17. Describe how smoking affects the body.

18. Why should you tell an adult when you are feeling ill?

Writing in Health

Write paragraphs to answer each item.

19. Samantha is going to perform in her first play. Describe how she can manage her stress and relax.

20. Explain why living a healthful lifestyle helps prevent disease.

Two options are provided for Chapter Tests—the in-book test and the reproducible test in the Assessment Guide. In addition to providing students with the opportunity to show what they have learned, both tests provide practice in taking standardized tests.

Multiple Choice (3 pts each)

1. c   **3.** b   **5.** c

2. d   **4.** b

Modified True or False (4 pts each)

6. true

7. true

8. false; Diabetes

9. true

10. false; harmful or unhealthful

11. false; vaccine

12. true

13. true

Short Answer (7 pts each)

Sample answers are shown; accept other reasonable answers.

14. Eating healthfully and getting regular exercise help prevent disease.

15. Infectious diseases are spread through breathing in or touching pathogens from infected people.

16. Exercise gives you energy; helps you fight disease; makes your muscles, heart, and lungs stronger; helps you use food and keep a healthful weight; and helps you manage stress.

17. Smoking weakens the body.

18. You should tell an adult when you feel ill so you can be cared for right away.

Writing in Health (9 pts. each)

Sample answers are shown; accept other reasonable answers.

19. She can manage her stress and relax by getting regular exercise, being prepared for her performance, and having confidence in her abilities. She can also imagine herself doing well in the performance, find a way to relax (her drama teacher may know techniques especially effective for actors), and talk to someone about how she is feeling.

20. Living a healthful lifestyle, which includes eating healthfully and getting regular exercise, helps prevent disease by giving your body the things it needs to fight diseases, keeping you strong, and reducing your stress.

Chapter Organizer

Lesson	Objectives	Vocabulary	Program Resources
Introduce the Chapter pp. 146–147 — 3·5	• Preview the chapter. • Begin chapter project.		• School-Home Connection, TR p. 43 • Assessment Guide, p. 41 • Read-Aloud Anthology, p. RA-7 Teaching Transparency 6—Graphic Organizer
Lesson 1 Learning About Drugs pp. 148–149 **Pacing: 1 class period** — 1·2·4	• Explain what drugs are. • Distinguish between drugs that help the body and drugs that harm the body.	drug	
Lesson 2 Medicines and Their Uses pp. 150–153 **Pacing: 1 class period** — 1·2·4	• Differentiate between OTC medicines and prescription medicines. • Describe ways medicines can help people and how medicines are taken or applied.	over-the-counter medicine prescription medicine	• Activity Book, p. 36
Lesson 3 How Can Medicines Be Used Safely? pp. 154–155 **Pacing: 1 class period** — 3·5	• Understand that medicines can be helpful only if they are used correctly. • List the rules for using medicines safely.	side effects	• Activity Book, pp. 37–38
Lesson 4 What Is Caffeine? pp. 156–157 **Pacing: 1 class period** — 4·6	• Explain what caffeine is and what it does to the body. • Suggest ways to avoid foods and drinks with caffeine.	caffeine	Computer Graphing Activity, TR p. 61 Teaching Transparency 19
Lesson 5 Inhalants and Other Drugs pp. 158–161 **Pacing: 2 class periods** — 1·2·4	• List the dangerous physical effects of using inhalants, marijuana, or cocaine, and tell why these drugs should be avoided. • Describe how to avoid breathing inhalants.	inhalants marijuana cocaine	• Activity Book, p. 39 Teaching Transparencies 20 and 27 Computer Graphing Activity, TR p. 62
Lesson 6 How Can I Say *No* to Drugs? pp. 162–163 **Pacing: 1 class period** — 3·5·6	• Emphasize the importance of saying **no** to drugs. • Suggest ways to avoid dangerous drugs.	refuse	• Activity Book, p. 40
Life Skills REFUSE Inhalants pp. 164–165 **Pacing: 1 class period** — 3·5·6	• Identify refusal skills. • Use refusal skills to say **no** to drug use.		• Activity Book, p. 41 HEALTH VIDEO: The "No!" Video
Chapter Review and Test pp. 166–169 — 1·7	• Assess chapter objectives and project. • Provide extension activities.		• Assessment Guide, pp. 38–41

National Health Education Standards
A complete list of the Standards is provided on the next page.

Key: TR = Teaching Resources

National Health Education Standards

1. Comprehend concepts related to health promotion and disease prevention.
2. Access valid health information and health-promoting products and services.
3. Practice health-enhancing behaviors and reduce health risks.
4. Analyze the influence of culture, media, technology, and other factors on health.
5. Use interpersonal communication skills to enhance health.
6. Use goal-setting and decision-making skills to enhance health.
7. Advocate for personal, family, and community health.

Art
- A Drug-Free Playground, p. 146C
- "Just Say *No*" Buttons, p. 163

Math
- Medicine Frequency Tally, p. 146C

Science
- The Discovery of Antibiotics, p. 152
- The Immune System, p. 153

Curriculum Integration

Use these topics to integrate health into your daily planning.

Social Studies
- Community Trust Reference File, p. 146C
- Ancient Medicines, p. 149

Drama
- Refusals Puppet Show, p. 164

Language Arts
- Write to a Role Model, p. 146C
- Understand Tolerance, p. 161

ASSESSMENT OPTIONS

Portfolio Assessment

Have students select their best work from the following suggestions:
- **"Just Say *No*" Buttons**, p. 163
- **Drug Messages**, p. 168
- **Safety Cartoons**, p. 168

Student Self-Assessment
- **Journal Notes**, p. 152
- **Set Health Goals**, pp. 149, 155, 157
- **Use Life Skills**, pp. 153, 161, 163

Daily Assessment
- **Check Your Facts**, pp. 149, 153, 155, 157, 161, 163

Performance Assessment
- **Chapter Project:** Make Drug Posters, pp. 147, 152, 161, 167
- **Project Evaluation Sheet**, Assessment Guide, p. 41

Formal Assessment
- **Chapter Review**, pp. 166–167
- **In-Book Test**, p. 169
- **Chapter Test**, Assessment Guide, pp. 38–40

Cross-Curricular Activities

Math

Medicine Frequency Tally

- Have students keep a record of the OTC and prescription medicines that they and their family members take over a one-week time period. To avoid issues of privacy, just have students note whether the drug is an OTC medicine or a prescription medicine.

- Have students tally their own results and then add them to the tallies of other students to get total results.

- Have students illustrate the results in a chart or graph that shows how many people used OTC drugs and how many used prescription drugs.

Art

A Drug-Free Playground and Activity Center

Have students design a playground and activity center that promotes exercise and fun in a drug-free environment.

- Brainstorm a variety of activities that young people might enjoy participating in at the center, indoors and outdoors.

- Together plan how the center will accommodate these activities. For example, one room might be for basketball and indoor soccer; another might be for arts and crafts or music; an outside area may be designed for tennis.

- Assign one or two students the task of drawing and labeling a design plan for the center.

- Display the design plan, and, as a class, think of an appropriate name for the center.

Language Arts

Write to a Role Model

Have students choose real-life role models for leading healthy, drug-free lives. Then encourage students to write letters to the persons they chose, describing why they chose them and how they plan to model their own lives after those of the role models.

Social Studies

Community Trust Reference File

Have students create a reference file of adults in the community that they could turn to for help with a problem related to health issues or drug abuse.

- Assign pairs of students a name from the list, and have them find the address, telephone number, and, if possible, the e-mail address of the assigned person.

- Ask students to write the information on an index card.

- Have students organize the cards in a file box, alphabetically and according to a particular group. For example, students might group pharmacists; doctors and nurse practitioners; teachers; clergy; and so on.

- Place the file in the classroom or school library.

Bulletin Board

Cut out letters to spell the headings and text as shown here. Under *Yes*, cut out and paste a square piece of cardboard to represent the inside of a medicine cabinet and show a safety lock on the side. Add medicine bottle shapes in rows to the medicine cabinet. Under *No*, provide space for photos or drawings of caffeine products, inhalants, marijuana, and a coca plant or cocaine.

- Have students form two groups: *Yes* (to using medicines safely) and *No* (to drugs that harm the body).

- Give each student in the *Yes* group a medicine bottle cut-out and ask them to write and illustrate one safety rule for medicine use on it.

- Assign students in the *No* group one of the harmful drug categories and have them cut out or draw and label pictures for each category.

- Have the *Yes* group paste their medicine bottles in neat rows in the medicine cabinet shape. Have the *No* group arrange their pictures and labels in a pattern of their choice.

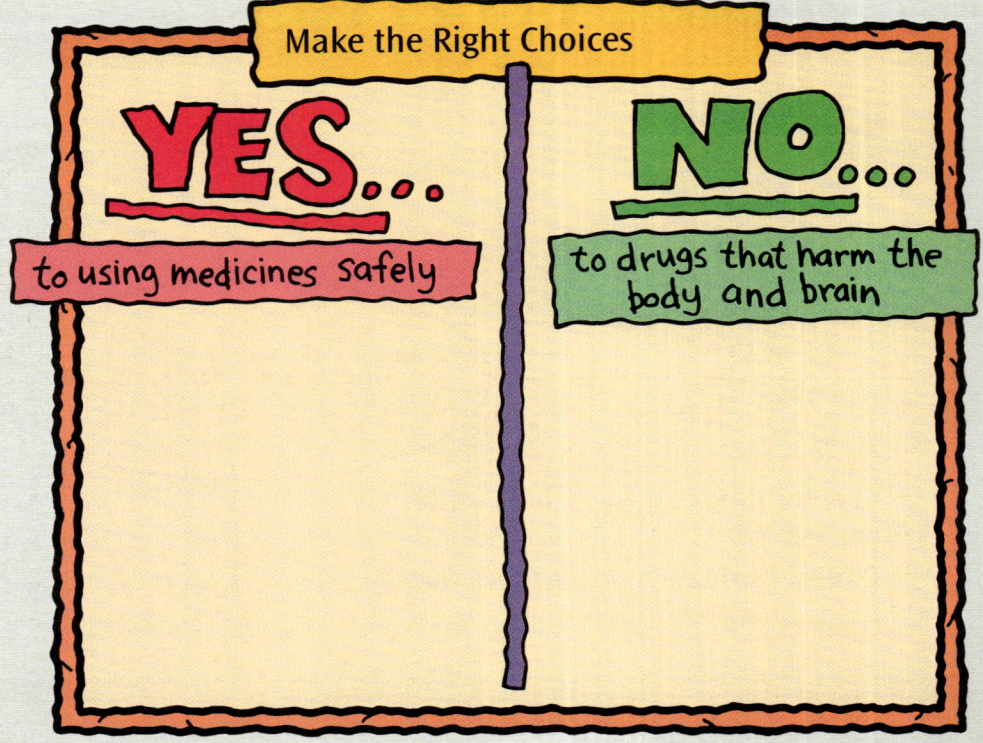

Make the Right Choices

YES... to using medicines safely

NO... to drugs that harm the body and brain

Resources

Books for Students

Taylor, Clark. **The House That Crack Built.** Chronicle Books, 1992. Uses rhyme to teach about cocaine. **EASY**

Powell, Jillian. **Drugs and Your Health (Health Matters).** Raintree Steck–Vaughn Publishers, 1998. Discusses drug benefits and problems and how to become more knowledgeable about each. **AVERAGE**

Sanders, Pete and Steve Myers. **What Do You Know About Drugs?** Gloucester Press, 2000. Uses cartoon storyline and color photos to discuss the dangers of drug use. **ADVANCED**

Books for Teachers and Families

Rybacki, James J. and James W. Long, M.D. **The Essential Guide to Prescription Drugs: Everything You Need to Know for Safe Drug Use.** Harper Resource, 2001. This book offers a helpful guide through the many prescription drugs available.

Graedon, Joe and Theresa Graedon, Ph.D. **The People's Pharmacy.** St. Martin's Press, 1998. A very comprehensive guide to prescription drugs, OTC medications, and other drug products.

Videos

The Boy Who Was Swallowed by the Drug Monster. STARS, 1994. (13 minutes) A powerful, animated, true story of a lifetime addiction to drugs leading up to jail time.

Happy, Healthy, Drug-Free Me, Part 1. Rainbow Educational Media, 1997. (10 minutes) Explains to students that medicines are drugs and incorrect consumption is dangerous.

Happy, Healthy, Drug-Free Me, Part 2. Rainbow Educational Media, 1997. (10 minutes) This video explains that stress is a natural part of life but drugs and alcohol are poor choices for stress relief.

Health Video Series by Harcourt **The "No!" Video** This video is referenced at point-of-use in this Teacher's Edition.

Your Health Webliography

The **Webliography** provides links to the Health Background and teaching resources that will support you as you teach the topics in *Your Health.* Simply choose a keyword and you will be taken to a page of links with descriptions of the content you can obtain at each site. The **Webliography** is located on the Teacher Resources page at **www.harcourtschool.com/health** Please review websites before referring your students to them.

Organizations and Agencies

Drug Abuse Resistance Education (DARE)
P.O. Box 2090
Los Angeles, CA 90051-0090
800-223-DARE
Provides information and programs to help keep children off drugs.

National McGruff House Network
1879 South Main
Suite 180
Salt Lake City, UT 84115
801-486-8768
Provides information on the McGruff program for violence and drug-abuse prevention.

For more information about health organizations and agencies, please see the **Teaching Resources** book.

Community Health

Physician/Physician's Assistant Invite a local physician or physician's assistant to the class to discuss the safe use of medicines. Ask the doctor or the PA to be prepared to discuss how some medicines work to relieve symptoms that accompany certain illnesses and how some cure illnesses. He or she should also provide information about side effects from commonly prescribed medicines. Beforehand, you might ask children to prepare questions related to the safe use of medicines to ask the invited guest.

Free and Inexpensive Material

Non-Prescription Drug Manufacturers Association
Publications Department
1150 Connecticut Ave., N.W.
Washington, D.C. 20036
Distributes brochures describing tips for taking OTC drugs safely.

Note that information, while correct at time of publication, is subject to change.

Visit **The Harcourt Learning Site** for related links, activities, resources, and the health **Webliography**.

www.harcourtschool.com

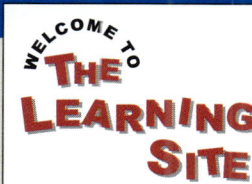

WELCOME TO **THE LEARNING SITE**

"The prevention and treatment of substance abuse require that all abused substances be addressed—from tobacco and alcohol to marijuana and other illicit drugs."

—*Healthy People 2010*

CHAPTER SUMMARY

In this chapter students
- learn that drugs can be both helpful and harmful to the body.
- learn that over-the-counter and pre-scription medicines are helpful drugs that must be used safely.
- learn about harmful drugs, including inhalants, marijuana, and cocaine, and how to avoid them.

LIFE SKILLS Students practice *refusing* to use an inhalant to get high.

 HUMAN BODY Students deter-mine how inhalants affect various organs of the body.

146

Literature Springboard

Use the Selection from *Circle of Thanks—Native American Poems and Songs of Thanksgiving* to spark interest in the chapter topic. See the Read-Aloud Anthology on page RA-7 of this Teacher's Edition.

School-Home Connection

Distribute copies of the School-Home Connection (in English or Spanish), TR page 43. Have students take the page home to share with their families as you begin this chapter.

Follow Up Have students bring in the charts they completed with their families. Using classroom volunteers, review how to distinguish OTC drugs from prescription drugs.

Alternative Use the School-Home Connection page as a classroom resource for enrichment activities.

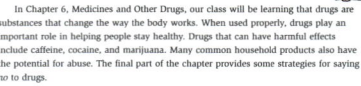 **TEACHING RESOURCES, p. 43**

Dear Family Member,

In Chapter 6, Medicines and Other Drugs, our class will be learning that drugs are substances that change the way the body works. When used properly, drugs play an important role in helping people stay healthy. Drugs that can have harmful effects include caffeine, cocaine, and marijuana. Many common household products also have the potential for abuse. The final part of the chapter provides some strategies for saying no to drugs.

Family Activity

Most families have a variety of prescription and over-the-counter medicines in their homes. Locate two prescription medicines and two over-the-counter medicines. Show these medicines to your child and then work with your child to complete the following chart. In the first column, write the name of the medicine. In the second column, write whether the medicine is prescription or over-the-counter.

When the chart is completed, discuss with your child how he or she can tell the difference between over-the-counter medicines and prescription medicines.

Medicines in My Home

Name of Medicine	Prescription or Over-the-Counter

Family Reading

The following books can help you and your family learn more about the topics covered in this chapter. Books should always be chosen with the approval of an adult family member.

- Taylor, Clark. *The House That Crack Built.* Chronicle Books, 1992. Uses rhyme to teach about the harmful effects of cocaine. EASY
- Powell, Jillian. *Drugs and Your Health (Health Matters).* Raintree Steck-Vaughn Publishers, 1998. Discusses drug benefits and problems. AVERAGE
- Sanders, Pete and Steve Myers. *What Do You Know About Drugs?* Gloucester Press, 2000. Uses cartoon story line and color photos to discuss the dangers of drug use. ADVANCED

Thank you for participating in our study of health.

Sincerely,

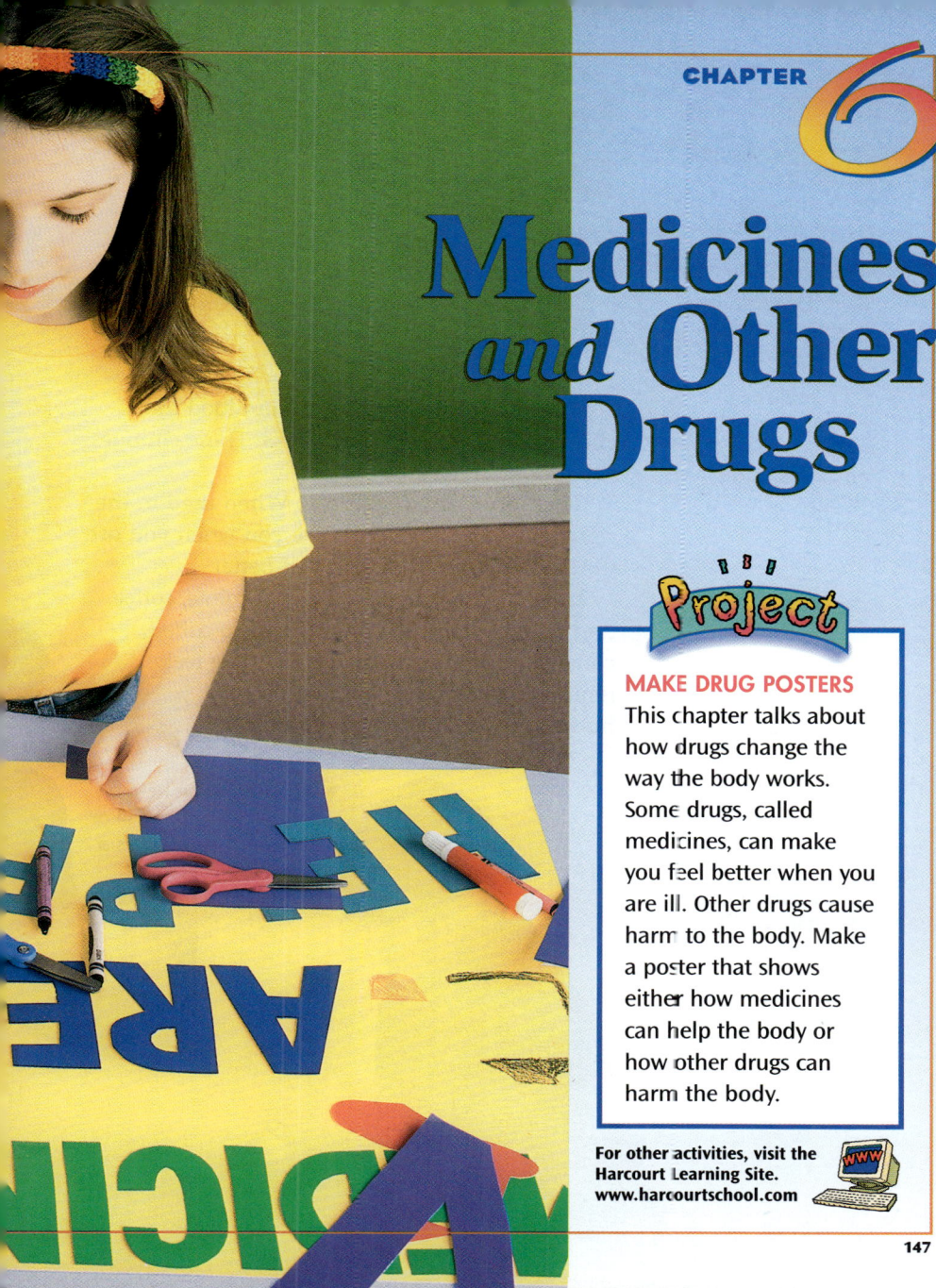

Medicines and Other Drugs

MAKE DRUG POSTERS

This chapter talks about how drugs change the way the body works. Some drugs, called medicines, can make you feel better when you are ill. Other drugs cause harm to the body. Make a poster that shows either how medicines can help the body or how other drugs can harm the body.

For other activities, visit the Harcourt Learning Site. www.harcourtschool.com

147

Introduce the Chapter

MAKE DRUG POSTERS

Access Prior Knowledge Use this activity as a baseline assessment of students' understanding of how medicines and harmful drugs can affect the body.

Performance Assessment The project can be used for performance assessment. Before students begin, explain how you will evaluate their performance. (See the Project Evaluation Sheet, Assessment Guide, p. 41.)

Prereading Strategies

Scan the Chapter Have students preview the chapter content by scanning the titles, headings, pictures, and charts. Ask volunteers to speculate on what they will learn.

Preview Vocabulary As students scan the chapter, invite them to sort vocabulary words into two groups—familiar and unfamiliar words. Have students look up unfamiliar words in the glossary.

Visualize Key Concepts Display the Graphic Organizer Transparency. You may also wish to distribute photocopies to students. Have students complete the organizer as they work through the chapter. Suggested concepts for students to fill in are shown.

Follow Up Review the completed organizer with students as preparation for the Chapter Review and Chapter Tests.

Teaching Transparency 6—Graphic Organizer

6 Chapter 6   Graphic Organizer

Medicines and Other Drugs

Medicines	Safe Drug Use	Avoiding Harmful Drugs
1. Some ___drugs___ are medicines.	1. Medicines can be helpful only if used ___correctly___.	1. Do not breathe the fumes of an ___inhalant___.
2. Two kinds of medicines are: ___over-the-counter medicines___ ___prescription medicines___	2. ___Caffeine___ is a drug that speeds up the heart.	2. ___Refuse___ illegal drugs like marijuana and cocaine.

OBJECTIVES

- **Explain what drugs are.**
- **Distinguish between drugs that help the body and drugs that harm the body.**

VOCABULARY

- **drug (p. 148)**

Daily Safety Tip

All drugs, including medicines, can sometimes cause harmful, even severe reactions in the body. Remind students to be prepared for such emergencies by posting near the telephone a list of emergency phone numbers, including the number for the Poison Control Center. Remind students that people under twenty should not use aspirin or other medicines that contain aspirin. Also, children should not take more acetaminophen, the drug in Tylenol® and many other medicines, than is appropriate for their age and size.

1 Motivate

Optional Materials **small, closed box with prescription medicine container, OTC pain reliever, and packet of instant coffee**

Explain that the box contains drugs. Have students pass the box around and tell what should be done with it. Elicit that the box should be given to a parent or other trusted adult. Then reveal the contents of the box. (As an alternative, write on the board a list of items that are drugs or contain drugs, such as a common antibiotic, a name-brand pain reliever, coffee or tea, and an illegal drug. Ask students to talk about which of the items are drugs.) With either activity, reinforce the idea that not all drugs are illegal. However, stress that students should never take any kind of drug, even if legal, on their own.

MAIN IDEA Drugs change the way the body works. They can help you or harm you.

WHY LEARN THIS? Knowing the difference between helpful and harmful drugs will help keep you healthy.

VOCABULARY
- drug

Learning About Drugs

Some drugs can help you when you are ill. Other drugs can make you ill. Do you know which drugs are helpful and which are harmful?

What are drugs?

A **drug** is something other than food that changes the way the body works. These changes can be helpful or harmful.

Some drugs are medicines. When used in the right way, medicines can cure you when you are ill. They can also help you feel better.

Some foods and drinks, like chocolate, coffee, and some soft drinks contain a drug called caffeine. Caffeine makes some people feel more awake. But caffeine can also be harmful if you have too much.

SOCIAL STUDIES CONNECTION

Ancient Medicines

On Your Own Long ago Native Americans found that drinking tea made from the bark of a willow tree took away pain. The bark contains the same chemical that is in aspirin. Find out about other ancient medicines.

• • •

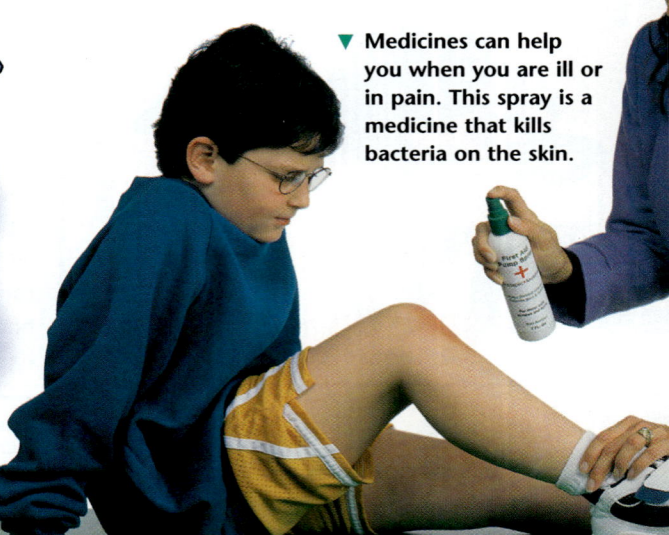

▼ Medicines can help you when you are ill or in pain. This spray is a medicine that kills bacteria on the skin.

148

MULTILEVEL ACTIVITIES

EASY **Make Lists** Have students fold sheets of paper in half lengthwise. On the left side, have them list illnesses or injuries they have had. On the right side, have them list the corresponding medicines they were given. **INTRAPERSONAL**

AVERAGE **Design Stickers** Have students design stickers to apply to household products that contain dangerous substances. Describe or show them the "Mr. Yuk" symbol as an example. **VISUAL**

ADVANCED **Research Drug Actions** Have students research how messages normally are sent to and from the brain and how drugs such as alcohol, cocaine, and marijuana change the way these messages are transmitted. Ask them to share their findings with the class. **VERBAL**

◄ Many products around the home contain dangerous substances. The warning labels on these containers warn the products should only be used as directed.

Some drugs, like marijuana and cocaine, are harmful. They change the way people think, feel, and act. They can also make people very ill. Because they are so harmful, marijuana and cocaine are illegal. It is against the law for anyone to buy, sell, have, or use them.

Many household products give off dangerous fumes. Some people use the fumes as a drug. They sniff the fumes to get high. A "high" is a common way of describing how people feel when they use drugs. But the fumes are poisons that can cause illness, brain damage, or even death.

LESSON CHECKUP

Check Your Facts

❶ What do drugs do to the body?

❷ CRITICAL THINKING All medicines are drugs. But are all drugs medicines? Explain your answer.

❸ How can household products be dangerous?

Set Health Goals

❹ Make a list of items in your home that might contain warnings on the label. Why do you think it is important for warnings to be listed on the items?

149

DEVELOP READING SKILLS

Make a Concept Map Help students make concept maps like the one shown below. Write the word *drug* in the center of the concept map. As students read the lesson, have them provide a definition for *drug*, topics related to the term *drug*, and details to go with each topic.

What are helpful drugs? medicines	How do helpful drugs change the body? They cure you when you are ill. They kill germs.

DRUG
Something other than food that changes the way the body works. The changes may be helpful or harmful.

What are harmful drugs? marijuana, cocaine	How do harmful drugs hurt the body? They change people's behavior. They can make people ill.

2 Teach

Learn from Pictures

Point out the picture on page 148, and ask students to name other topical medicines and what they are used for. Answers could include sunburn, itch, burns, or aching muscles.

Social Studies Connection

Ancient Medicines Direct students to reference materials related to the sources and uses of ancient medicines. Encourage students to incorporate what they discover into a poster that identifies each medicine, its source, and its use.

Discuss

The container of a dangerous household substance must have a warning label that explains how the product can be harmful and what to do in an emergency.

Problem Solving How can you tell that household products such as the ones pictured on this page might be harmful? by reading the warning labels How would you know what to do in an emergency? Again, read the warning label.

3 Wrap Up

Lesson Checkup

1. Drugs change the way the body works.

2. All drugs are not medicines. Some drugs, such as cocaine and marijuana, can hurt the body and make it ill.

3. Many household products give off dangerous fumes. People sometimes use these fumes to get "high." The fumes are poisons that can cause illness or even death.

4. Answers will vary depending on the products examined. Warnings are important so the user knows correct usage, possible harmful effects, and first-aid treatment.

LESSON 2

Pages 150–153

OBJECTIVES

• Differentiate between over-the-counter medicines and prescription medicines.

• Describe ways medicines can help people and how medicines are taken or applied.

PROGRAM RESOURCES

• Activity Book, p. 36

VOCABULARY

• over-the-counter medicine (p. 150)

• prescription medicine (p. 151)

Daily Safety Tip

Over-the-counter medicines can be dangerous if used incorrectly. Remind students that adults should read the entire label when using or administering a medicine for the first time. If they do not understand something, they should consult a doctor or pharmacist.

1 Motivate

Write *medicine* vertically on the board. Then ask students to think of diseases and symptoms beginning with the letters found in the word *medicine*. Write the words next to each letter. Accept all reasonable answers. For example, students might suggest: m—mumps, measles; e—earache, eye drops; d—diabetes, diarrhea, disease; i—indigestion, infection; c—cold, cough, cancer, constipation; i—illness, itch, insulin; n—nose drops, nosebleeds, numbness, nausea; e—ear infection.

LESSON 2

Medicines and Their Uses

MAIN IDEA
Medicines can help you get well when you use them correctly.

WHY LEARN THIS? You can find out how different medicines can help you.

VOCABULARY
• over-the-counter medicine
• prescription medicine

When you get ill, an adult may give you medicine to help you get better. How do grown-ups know what kind of medicine you need? Where does it come from?

What are the different kinds of medicine?

There are two kinds of medicines. An <mark>over-the-counter medicine</mark> (OTC medicine) is a medicine that an adult can buy without a doctor's order. Drugstores and grocery stores sell OTC medicines. OTC medicines are for minor health problems, such as sore throats, colds, and headaches. Cough syrups, pain relievers, and first-aid sprays are all OTC medicines. The label on an

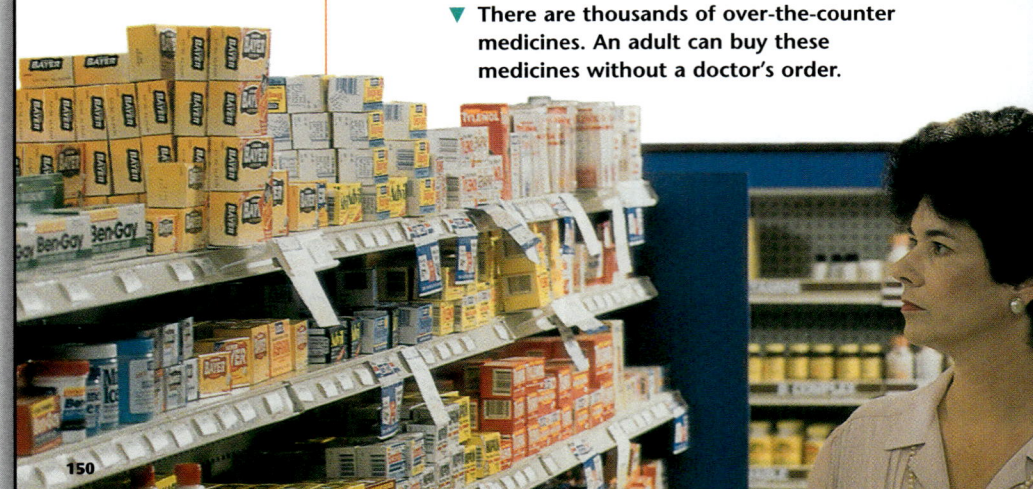

▼ There are thousands of over-the-counter medicines. An adult can buy these medicines without a doctor's order.

150

MULTILEVEL ACTIVITIES

EASY Design Labels Tell students the pertinent facts about the use of a medicine, and have them design labels for it. **AUDITORY/KINESTHETIC**

AVERAGE Evaluate Labels Provide pairs of students with packaging for several OTC medicines, and have them evaluate how easy or difficult it is to read and understand the labels. **VISUAL/INTERPERSONAL**

ADVANCED Calculate Dosage Give students directions for using a medicine that include how often the medicine can be taken and how much medicine should be taken each time. Have students calculate how much medicine could be taken in a twenty-four-hour period and indicate times the doses could be taken. **MATHEMATICAL**

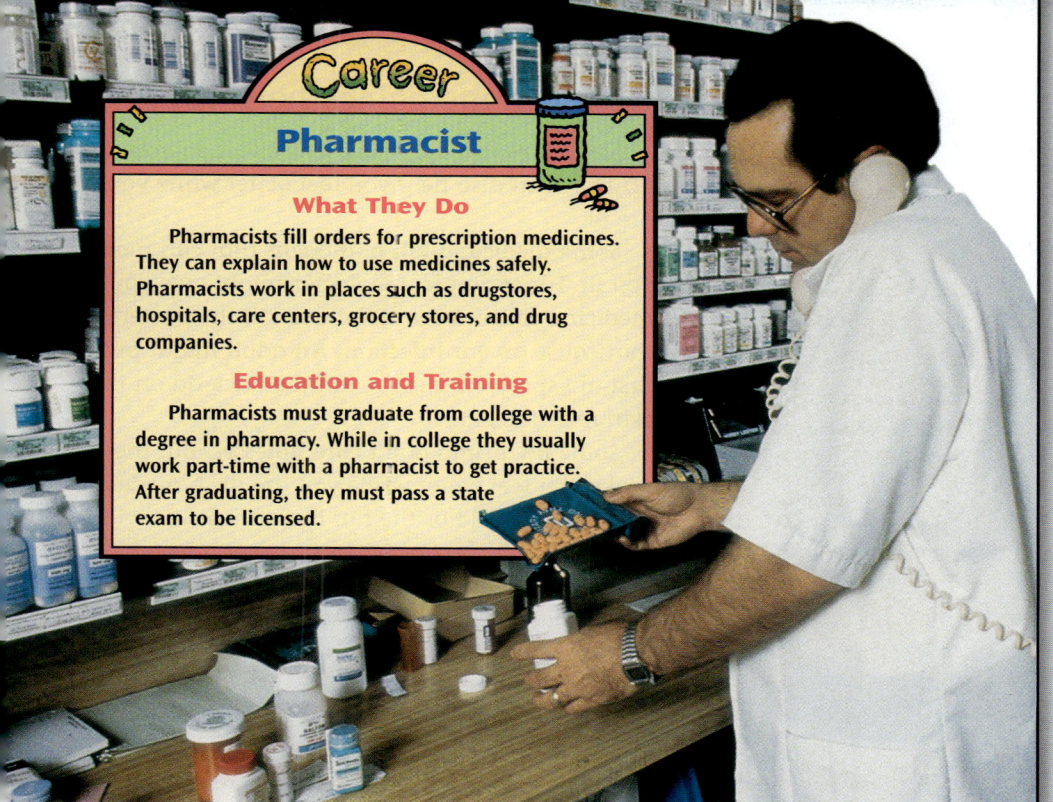

▲ This pharmacist is filling a prescription.

OTC medicine tells what the medicine treats. It also gives directions for using the medicine. Adults must always follow these directions exactly so the medicine will be used safely.

A **prescription medicine** (prih•SKRIP•shuhn MEH•duh•suhn) is a medicine that must be ordered by a doctor. A doctor writes the order, called a prescription. Then a pharmacist fills the order.

Prescription medicines are strong and must be used correctly. That is why a doctor must order them. A doctor or pharmacist can explain exactly how to use them.

151

DEVELOP READING SKILLS

Compare Terms Recognizing the similarities and differences between related terms can help students recall and understand them more easily. As students read this lesson, ask them to complete charts like the one shown to compare the related terms *over-the-counter medicine* and *prescription medicine*.

Kinds of medicines	over-the-counter medicine	prescription medicine
How they are bought	without doctor's orders	with doctor's orders/prescription
Ways in which an adult knows how to use them	read label directions	read label directions
What they treat	colds, headaches, etc.	ear infections, strep throat
Examples	cough syrup, pain relievers, first-aid sprays	antibiotics

2 Teach

Discuss

The label on an OTC medicine has information on the conditions for which the medicine is indicated, how much to use, how often and how long to use it, and precautions to take.

Problem Solving How can the woman in the photo on page 150 figure out which over-the-counter medicine she should buy? She should think about the symptoms she or someone else has and read the label to see if a particular medicine treats those symptoms. She also can ask a pharmacist which OTC medicine is best for certain symptoms.

Learn from Pictures

Ask students to look at the picture of the pharmacist on this page.

Critical Thinking Why is it important for a pharmacist to fill a prescription carefully? Possible answers: because prescription medicines are strong; if the prescription is not filled correctly, it could harm instead of help the person taking it.

Careers

For more information on a career in pharmacy, contact:

American Association of Colleges
of Pharmacy
1426 Prince Street
Alexandria, VA 22314

Or visit the **Webliography** on the Teacher Resources page at:
www.harcourtschool.com/health
Keyword health careers

151

Health Journal

Discuss common illnesses among children, such as strep and ear infections. Encourage students to think about times when they had these or other illnesses. How did they know they were getting sick? How did they find out what the sickness was? What kind of medicine did they take? How did they know the medicine was working? This feature is designed to provide students with an opportunity to reflect on health decisions they are making in their personal lives. Be sensitive to children who might not take medicines for religious or personal reasons. The journals should *not* be used to evaluate or assess students, nor should the results be shared among students.

Learn from Pictures

Ask students to examine the pictures on the bottom of the page and read the caption.

Critical Thinking How does this mother know how often to give the medicine and how much medicine to give? by reading the label on the bottle, by talking to a physician or pharmacist

How will the mother and child know if the medicine is working? The ear pain will go away; the child will feel better.

Project Checkup

Make Drug Posters (p. 147) Students who are making a poster about how medicines help the body will find the information in this lesson useful.

How can medicines help you?

Write about a time you took a medicine that helped you get well or feel better. First write down your health problem. Then tell which medicine you took and describe how it helped you.

Medicines can help you get well when you are ill. They can also help you feel better while you are ill.

Some medicines kill pathogens that can make you ill. For example, the doctor might give you a medicine called an antibiotic to kill the bacteria that cause an ear infection. An adult might put a first-aid spray on a cut to kill the bacteria on the skin near the cut.

Some medicines don't cure illnesses. But they make you feel better while you are ill. A medicine won't cure a cold or the flu. But a medicine will make a headache feel better or lower a fever caused by the flu. One medicine children your age should *not* take is aspirin. Aspirin is only safe for adults. Aspirin can cause an illness in children that can lead to death.

▼ Antibiotics are prescription medicines that kill bacterial pathogens. This mother is giving her child an antibiotic to help cure an ear infection.

152

SCIENCE

The Discovery of Antibiotics It might be difficult for students to imagine a world without antibiotics. However, it wasn't until 1928 that Alexander Fleming discovered penicillin. Encourage students to find out how Fleming learned he had discovered the first antibiotic.
Fleming unintentionally discovered penicillin when he noticed that mold growing in a culture plate had destroyed the bacteria around it.

ACTIVITY BOOK, p. 36

Medicine Labels | Critical Thinking

Read the paragraph. Then answer the questions.

OTC drugs must have labels that tell people how to use them safely. But people must be able to read the labels and understand what they are reading. Many people cannot read medicine labels because the print is too small. Sometimes there is so much information on a label that the important information is difficult to find. Also, some of the information on medicine labels is difficult to understand.

What is the solution? The government is proposing that medicines should have simpler labels. They should be in simpler words. For example, a label could read, "Keep out of reach of children," instead of "Keep this and all drugs out of the reach of children." The words should be in large print. There also should be a package insert with information in even larger print for people who cannot see well. Important information, such as side effects and warnings, should be in bolder print so that it clearly stands out.

1. What do labels on OTC drugs do? tell people how to use the drugs safely

2. Why can't some people read medicine labels? because the type is too small

3. Why can't some people understand medicine labels? because important information can be difficult to find; because the wording is too difficult

4. What are examples of important information on a medicine label? side effects and warnings

5. What are some solutions to these problems? use larger print and simpler language on labels; make important information stand out

◄ Some OTC medicines can help when you are in pain. There are many different kinds of pain relievers.

Medicines come in many different forms. There are pills, liquids, sprays, and creams. Some pills can be chewed. Other pills are swallowed whole. Some liquid medicines are meant to be swallowed. Other liquids, creams, and sprays are put directly on the area being treated. All medicines should always be given by an adult.

LESSON CHECKUP

Check Your Facts

1. Name the two kinds of medicines.
2. Which kind of medicine can an adult buy without a doctor's prescription?
3. CRITICAL THINKING Why must a pharmacist be able to read a doctor's prescription?
4. CRITICAL THINKING Can a medicine help you even if it does not cure you? Give an example.

Use Life Skills

5. MAKE DECISIONS Often OTC medicines help a person feel better. Sometimes a prescribed medicine is more helpful. Make a list of reasons why a doctor might decide to write an order for a prescription.

153

Learn from Pictures

Invite a volunteer to read the caption accompanying the pictures on this page.
Critical Thinking Why might the child in the picture need a pain reliever? A broken arm can be painful. Have you ever broken a bone or sprained or strained a muscle? What medicines made you feel better? Answers will vary.

3 Wrap Up

Lesson Checkup

1. over-the-counter and prescription
2. over-the-counter medicine
3. The pharmacist must be able to read the prescription in order to fill it correctly, which is important because prescription drugs are strong and can be harmful if not used correctly.
4. Yes. No medicine can cure the flu, but medicines can reduce the fever, which will make you feel better.
5. Accept all reasonable answers. Possible answers: there is not an OTC medicine strong enough or a stronger dosage is needed.

SCIENCE

The Immune System Point out to students that the body has its own defense system that works to fight off pathogens and the symptoms of disease. It is called the immune system. When the immune system is not successful on its own, people need to take medicines. Ask groups of students to work together to research and design posters illustrating how the body's immune system works to fight off pathogens.

Health Background

How Medicines Enter the Body Medicines can enter the body in several ways. Many pills and liquids are swallowed and enter the bloodstream through the small intestine. The fastest way to get a medicine into the bloodstream is by injection with a hypodermic needle. Some medicines must be administered in this way because the digestive system would destroy them if they were taken orally.

For more background, visit the **Webliography** on the Teacher Resources page at:
www.harcourtschool.com/health
Keyword medicines

OBJECTIVES

- Understand that medicines can be helpful only if they are used correctly.
- List the rules for using medicines safely.

PROGRAM RESOURCES

- Activity Book, pp. 37–38

VOCABULARY

- side effects (p. 155)

Daily Safety Tip

Some people are allergic to certain medications. If a student has a reaction to a medicine, he or she should tell an adult. The doctor might be able to prescribe a different medicine that will make the student feel better without adverse side effects.

1 Motivate

Do a skit in which you break several medicine safety rules. For example, you have a stomachache. You find medicine for an upset stomach, but it is a prescription medicine for someone else. The directions say to take one teaspoon; instead you take two big gulps. Ask students if you have shown how to use medicines safely, and if not, what you did wrong.

Health Background

Drug Interaction Some medicines when used together may have harmful or fatal results. Before giving any combination of prescription or OTC medicines to children or before combining medicines themselves, adults should ask a doctor or a pharmacist about any interaction between the drugs.

For more background, visit the **Webliography** on the Teacher Resources page at:
**www.harcourtschool.com/health
Keyword** medicines

MAIN IDEA Medicine can harm the body if it is used in the wrong way.

WHY LEARN THIS? Using medicine correctly will help you stay healthy.

VOCABULARY
- side effects

How Can Medicines Be Used Safely?

Medicines can help you when you are ill. But they can also be harmful if used in the wrong way. Always remember to follow the rules when you must use a medicine.

LIFE SKILLS FOCUS

Refuse

Bryan started sneezing while he was playing at Linda's home. Linda offered Bryan some of her prescription allergy medicine. Tell ways that Bryan could refuse this offer. Use the steps for refusing shown on page *xi*.

• • •

OPEN
PUSH DOWN & TURN
CLOSE

Safety Rules for Medicine Use

Be careful! Medicines can be dangerous.

- Only an adult should give you medicine. Never take a medicine on your own.
- Always follow the directions on the medicine label.
- Never take someone else's prescription medicine.
- Don't use old medicines. They can change when they get old and make you ill. Look at the date on the label.
- Leave the labels on all medicines.
- Keep medicines on high shelves in locked cabinets.
- Keep medicines away from small children.

154

 MULTILEVEL ACTIVITIES

EASY **Perform Skits** Have groups of three students write and perform skits in which a doctor or pharmacist explains to a parent and child how to use a medicine safely. **KINESTHETIC/VERBAL**

AVERAGE **Make a Diagram** Have students make diagrams showing where medicines should be stored in their homes. **SPATIAL/LOGICAL**

ADVANCED **Find Out About Side Effects** Have students research side effects of common medicines and make charts presenting their findings. If possible, information should include how prevalent and serious each side effect is. **VISUAL**

◄ Medicines on store shelves have safety seals. The seals keep the medicines clean. They also stop other people from opening the medicine before someone buys it. Never buy medicine with a broken safety seal.

What should you do when you think you need a medicine? Tell a trusted adult! An adult can help you. Before buying a medicine, an adult should check the safety seal. The seal should not be broken. An adult should give you the correct amount listed on the label, not more and not less. Watch for any side effects. **Side effects** are unwanted changes in the body caused by a medicine. If you feel any side effects, such as dizziness, itching, or a headache, tell a trusted adult.

Activity **Follow Medicine Safety Rules**
Read the safety rules on page 154. Then look at the pictures on pages 152 and 153. How are the people in the pictures following the safety rules? What are some other safety rules you should follow?

LESSON CHECKUP

Check Your Facts
1. What does the label on a medicine do?
2. Why should you never use old medicines?
3. **CRITICAL THINKING** Why should you be careful when taking medicines?
4. What are side effects?

Set Health Goals
5. Make a small poster listing the safety rules for medicine. Put it up at home where medicines are kept. How can the poster help you use medicines safely?

155

ACTIVITY BOOK, p. 37

Identify Cause and Effect | Reading Skills

Read each sentence. Find the cause and effect in each sentence. Then, in the spaces provided, write the cause and the effect.

1. Because it was too old, Jim's prescription medicine was no longer effective.
   Cause: The prescription medicine was too old.
   Effect: It was no longer effective.

2. Mrs. Chin locked the medicine in the cabinet. As a result, her small children could not get it.
   Cause: Mrs. Chin locked the medicine in the cabinet.
   Effect: Her small children could not get it.

3. Mr. O'Hara always follows the directions on medicine labels so that he does not harm himself.
   Cause: Mr. O'Hara always follows the directions on medicine labels.
   Effect: He does not harm himself.

4. Because she took medicine that was not prescribed for her, Marlene got very sick.
   Cause: Marlene took medicine not prescribed for her.
   Effect: She got very sick.

5. Carla took her antibiotics exactly as prescribed, so they cured her ear infection.
   Cause: Carla took her antibiotics exactly as prescribed.
   Effect: They cured her ear infection.

ACTIVITY BOOK, p. 38

Define Vocabulary | Vocabulary Reinforcement

Complete the chart below.

Word	What is it?	What is it like?	What are some examples?
drug	something other than food that changes the way the body works	can be helpful or harmful, legal or illegal	medicines, caffeine, marijuana, cocaine
over-the-counter medicine	a medicine that an adult can buy without a doctor's order	available in stores; gives directions for treatment; should be given by an adult	pain relievers, cough syrups, first-aid sprays
prescription medicine	medicine that must be ordered by a doctor	strong, must be used correctly, should be given by an adult	antibiotics, insulin, anticancer drugs
side effects	unwanted changes in the body caused by a medicine	physical feelings	dizziness, headaches

---

2 Teach

Discuss

In 1982 an OTC pain reliever was pulled from shelves when someone poisoned the contents of several packages. Safety seals are now required for OTCs.

Critical Thinking Why is it never safe to buy a medicine with a broken safety seal? The medicine might have been tampered with or affected in some way.

Life Skills Focus

Refuse Possible answer: Bryan can say *no*. He can explain that it is unsafe to take someone else's medicine and that he might suffer side effects from it. If Linda insists, Bryan should say *no* again emphatically.

Activity

Follow Medicine Safety Rules The woman on page 152 is reading the label and following the directions before giving the medicine to her child. The child is waiting for an adult to give the medicine. The medicines on page 153 are out of reach of children.

3 Wrap Up

Lesson Checkup

1. It gives the name, dosage, and directions for the medicine; prescription medicine labels also include the pharmacy's name, address, and phone number and the doctor's name and number.

2. They can change when they get old and could make a person ill.

3. Medicines are drugs; all drugs are dangerous if not taken properly.

4. Side effects are unwanted changes in the body caused by a medicine.

5. by reviewing the rules on the poster before taking any medicine

155

OBJECTIVES

- Explain what caffeine is and what it does to the body.
- Suggest ways to avoid foods and drinks with caffeine.

PROGRAM RESOURCES

 Computer Graphing Activity, Teaching Resources p. 61

 Teaching Transparency 19

VOCABULARY

- caffeine (p. 156)

Daily Safety Tip

Twenty ounces of cola has the same amount of caffeine as a cup of coffee. A cup of cocoa can have up to half the caffeine found in a cup of coffee. Students should learn what drinks contain caffeine so they can avoid taking in too much caffeine.

1 Motivate

Invite students to name items people eat and drink for breakfast. Each time a student mentions a caffeine product, write it on the board. These might include coffee, cocoa, tea, chocolate cereal, and chocolate-flavored instant breakfast drinks. **Then ask students if they know what all the items listed on the board have in common.** caffeine Discuss that many people use caffeine to perk up in the morning.

2 Teach

Learn from Pictures

Call the students' attention to the photograph. **Which of the drinks and foods contain caffeine?** all of them

---

MAIN IDEA
Caffeine is a drug that speeds up the heart. It is in many common drinks and foods.

WHY LEARN THIS? Learning which foods have caffeine and what it does to the body will help you stay healthy.

VOCABULARY
- caffeine

What Is Caffeine?

Do you enjoy iced tea, chocolate, and soft drinks? Many people do. But watch out! Some of these items contain caffeine. **Caffeine** (ka•FEEN) is a drug that speeds up the heart. Some OTC medicines contain caffeine, too.

It is not harmful to take in a small amount of caffeine. Many adults drink coffee in the morning. It helps them feel more awake. But large amounts of caffeine can make adults feel jittery. Smaller amounts of caffeine can keep children from sleeping. Too much caffeine also can strain the heart and upset the stomach.

It is hard for people who take in a lot of caffeine to stop using it. When they don't have caffeine, they can get tired and upset. They might also get headaches.

▼ Caffeine is in many drinks and foods, such as coffee, tea, and chocolate. Colas and fruit-flavored soft drinks often contain caffeine, too.

156

 MULTILEVEL ACTIVITIES

EASY **Breakfast Plan** Have students devise a menu for a healthful, caffeine-free breakfast. **LOGICAL**

AVERAGE **Plan a Menu** Have students plan a day's worth of healthful meals, beverages, and snacks that are all caffeine free. Copy the plans, and distribute them to the class. Have students answer questions about their plans. **AUDITORY/INTERPERSONAL**

ADVANCED **Research Stimulants** Caffeine belongs to the category of drugs known as stimulants. Have students work in pairs to find out what stimulants do to the body and to brainstorm other ways to get energy in the morning. **VERBAL/INTERPERSONAL**

◀ Does your favorite drink have caffeine? Look for drinks that are labeled "caffeine-free."

CONSUMER FOCUS

Access Valid Health Information
Use the Internet or other sources to find out how much caffeine is in soft drinks. Make a list of at least five different soft drinks. Next to each one, write how many milligrams of caffeine the soft drink contains. Use the steps on page *xvi* to help you decide whether the sources are reliable.

• • •

How can you avoid caffeine?

Many people drink a lot of soft drinks filled with caffeine or eat a lot of chocolate. They may not even know that they are taking in caffeine. If you know which foods have caffeine, you can avoid letting caffeine become a habit.

Chocolate, coffee, tea, and soft drinks often have caffeine. If you often eat or drink foods with caffeine, try to find foods without caffeine instead.

LESSON CHECKUP

Check Your Facts
1. List four sources of caffeine.
2. Why should people limit caffeine?
3. CRITICAL THINKING Name four drinks that don't have caffeine.

Set Health Goals
4. Cola drinks and many other soft drinks contain caffeine. Think about the drinks you've had in the last two days. List the ones that contain caffeine. If you drank several drinks with caffeine, think about what you can do to cut back on the amount of caffeine you take in each day.

157

MULTICULTURAL LINK

The Caffeine Culture Coffee and tea play important roles in the customs of many cultures. For example, in Arabic countries guests are expected to accept at least one cup of Arabic coffee from their host. This offering is a sign of hospitality, so it would be disrespectful to decline. Encourage students to investigate customs related to coffee and caffeine products in other cultures. Have them find out if the people of these cultures are concerned about caffeine-related health problems.

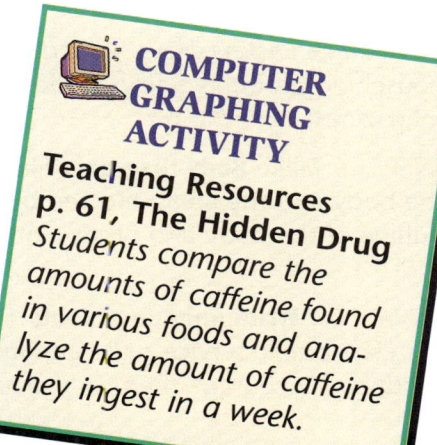

COMPUTER GRAPHING ACTIVITY
Teaching Resources p. 61, The Hidden Drug Students compare the amounts of caffeine found in various foods and analyze the amount of caffeine they ingest in a week.

Discuss

Caffeine is listed as an ingredient only when it is added to a product, such as a soft drink. However, the amount does not have to be indicated. Coffee, tea, and chocolate naturally contain caffeine; it is not added to these items.

Critical Thinking What do you drink or eat that might contain caffeine even though it is not listed on the label?
Possible answers: candy bars, hot chocolate, chocolate milk, and iced tea.

3 Wrap Up

Lesson Checkup

1. Possible answers: coffee, tea, colas and other soft drinks, chocolate, OTC medicines.

2. Caffeine is a drug that speeds up the heart. Too much caffeine can strain the heart and upset the stomach.

3. Possible answers: water, milk, orange juice, apple juice, caffeine-free sodas.

4. Before having students write their responses in their Health Journals, have small groups of students brainstorm ways to cut back on caffeine.

Consumer Focus

Access Valid Health Information Have students put the soft drinks in order from the ones that contain the least caffeine to the ones that contain the most. Discuss side effects that might occur with the intake of too much caffeine.

TEACHING TRANSPARENCY
Teaching Transparency 19: The Heart emphasizes the function and importance of a healthy heart.

OBJECTIVES

- List the dangerous physical effects of using inhalants, marijuana, or cocaine, and tell why these drugs should be avoided.
- Describe how to avoid breathing inhalants.

PROGRAM RESOURCES

 Computer Graphing Activity, Teaching Resources p. 62

 Teaching Transparencies 20 and 27

- Activity Book, p. 39

VOCABULARY

- inhalants (p. 158)
- marijuana (p. 160)
- cocaine (p. 161)

Daily Safety Tip

Using inhalants even once can result in death by asphyxia—suffocating on the bags used for inhaling, choking on vomit; dangerous behavior; or cardiac arrest. Students should be cautioned against any use, even first-time use, of inhalants. Tell students that over time people who use inhalants can become psychologically dependent on them.

1 Motivate

List important organs and body systems on the board. Discuss the effects of inhalants, marijuana, and cocaine on these areas of the body. As you identify each organ or system that is affected by one of these drugs, erase it from the board. Point out that few major organs and body systems are not affected by drugs.

MAIN IDEA There are many harmful drugs. Some are household products that can be misused.

WHY LEARN THIS? Knowing the effects of dangerous drugs will help you avoid them.

VOCABULARY
- inhalants
- marijuana
- cocaine

Inhalants and Other Drugs

You probably know about harmful drugs such as marijuana and cocaine. But did you know that some household products are also dangerous drugs?

What are inhalants?

You walk into the bathroom and know right away that it has been cleaned recently. How do you know? You smell the fumes from the cleaning products. You can also smell fumes at a gas station.

Some people breathe in fumes from products such as spray paints, glues, markers, cleaners, and nail polish remover. These people are trying to get high. This can be very dangerous. The fumes are poisons. Substances that give off fumes are **inhalants** (in•HAY•luhnts). Labels on inhalants warn people to avoid breathing them.

► You must use some glues only where there is a lot of fresh air. Look at the label for warnings when you use glue.

158

 ## MULTILEVEL ACTIVITIES

EASY Make Posters Have students make safety posters listing ways to use household products safely. Students may wish to cut product pictures out of magazines. **KINESTHETIC/SPATIAL**

AVERAGE Make Body Diagrams Have students make a textural diagram of the body and the areas affected by drugs. They can use yarn to form the outline of the body and other materials to pinpoint each affected area. **VISUAL/TACTILE**

ADVANCED Write Announcements Have students write, record, and play for the class public service radio announcements about safe use of household products. Encourage them to include jingles in the announcements. **VERBAL/MUSICAL**

nosebleed

confusion

hearing loss

brain damage

upset stomach

sneezing

coughing

violent behavior

headaches

slowed heart rate

death

WARNING!

▶ Inhalants have many side effects.

slowed breathing rate

Inhalants distort how you see, hear, and feel. Yet many people do not think of inhalants as drugs because many inhalants are sold as common household products.

Inhaling the fumes can cause nosebleeds and headaches. Inhalants can cause brain damage. Inhalants can also slow your heart and breathing rates, which can kill you. Many people have died instantly by breathing in too much of the poisonous fumes at one time.

HUMAN BODY

CONNECTION

Inhalants

Study the picture showing how inhalants affect the body. List all the organs of the body that inhalants affect. Find these organs in the human body diagrams on pages 1–15 at the front of the book.

159

---

2 Teach

Learn from Pictures

Call attention to the picture on page 158.

Critical Thinking How are these children using glue safely? They have a fan going to circulate fresh air. An adult is present in case a problem occurs.

Human Body Connection

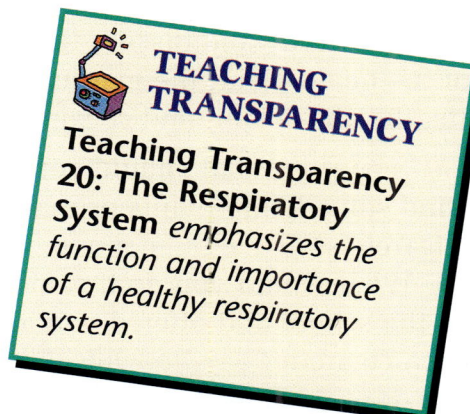

Inhalants Ask volunteers to tell which parts of the body are most likely to be affected by each of the side effects shown. Students should note that the brain, heart, lungs, digestive system, nasal passages, and ears are all affected by inhalants.

TEACHING TRANSPARENCY

Teaching Transparency 20: The Respiratory System emphasizes the function and importance of a healthy respiratory system.

Health Background

History of the Abuse of Inhalants As early as the 1800s, people in Europe and North America inhaled ether or nitrous oxide to get high. Many young people of the 1960s sniffed the solvents in nail polish remover and airplane glue. Soon after, young people sniffed the fluorocarbons in aerosol containers. Partly in reaction to this abuse, which resulted in the death of many abusers, and partly in reaction to further damage to Earth's ozone layer, manufacturers replaced the fluorocarbons in aerosols with hydrocarbons.

For more background, visit the **Webliography** on the Teacher Resources page at:
www.harcourtschool.com/health
Keyword drug abuse

DEVELOP READING SKILLS

Use Semantic Clues to Identify Important Words Remind students that by reading the sentences that precede, include, and follow highlighted vocabulary words, they can find clues to the terms' meanings. Copy on the board the chart shown at the right. Ask volunteers to locate each listed term where it appears in yellow highlight in this lesson. Have them read each word in context and then write in the second column of the chart their own definitions, based on their understanding of the word from the text. Have them complete the third column by listing each term's meaning as it appears in the glossary.

Highlighted term	What I think it means	What it does mean
inhalants		
marijuana		
cocaine		

Teach *continued*

Discuss

Researchers believe marijuana is especially harmful to the lungs because users inhale deeply and hold the smoke in their lungs for a prolonged period of time. Habitual marijuana users often suffer the same types of illnesses as smokers, such as lung cancer and emphysema.

Critical Thinking **What would you say to someone who says marijuana is not a dangerous drug?** Possible answer: Marijuana is dangerous because it can cause serious heart problems and lung disease.

Learn from Pictures

Have students study and discuss the features of the hemp plant, the marijuana cigarette, the coca plant, and cocaine.

Problem Solving **What should you do if you find some hemp plants or marijuana cigarettes?** Leave them alone; tell an adult. **What would you do if someone came to the school and offered you a marijuana cigarette?** Say *no.* Quickly tell a teacher or other adult.

Review with students school rules prohibiting the use of drugs.

For more information about a drug-free school, see page 281.

What are some illegal drugs?

Do you know the facts about marijuana and cocaine? Why should you avoid these drugs?

Marijuana

Marijuana (mair•uh•WAH•nuh) is an illegal drug that comes from the hemp plant. Users smoke or eat the dried leaves and flowers of the plant.

Marijuana contains more than 400 substances. One substance is called THC. THC is a drug that changes the way the brain works. THC can make it hard to remember things or to learn.

Marijuana can speed up the heart. It can cause breathing problems. Because marijuana makes it hard for the body to fight infections, users get ill more often than nonusers. Marijuana can also make users nervous. When it is smoked, it can cause cancer, just as cigarettes do.

▼ Marijuana (left) is made from the leaves of the hemp plant. Cocaine (right) is made from the leaves of the coca plant.

160

COMPUTER GRAPHING ACTIVITY
Teaching Resources p. 62, Dangerous Drugs
Students analyze marijuana use by eight and twelfth graders and evaluate trends in drug use.

TEACHING TRANSPARENCY
Teaching Transparency 27: The Brain and Skull emphasizes the function and importance of a healthy brain.

▲ It is against the law to have, use, sell, or buy cocaine or marijuana. People who use these drugs can go to jail.

Cocaine

Cocaine (koh•KAYN) is an illegal drug made from the leaves of the coca plant. Most users sniff powdered cocaine. Some users inject it with a needle. Others smoke a strong form of cocaine, called "crack."

Cocaine can make people feel good for five to forty minutes. Then users often feel sad, nervous, confused, angry, or tired. They want to use more and more of the drug to get the same feeling back.

Cocaine users may get dizzy. Cocaine can also cause lung or brain damage. Even one use of cocaine can cause a stroke, heart attack, or death.

Myth: Most kids smoke marijuana. So what's the big deal?

Fact: Most kids have *never* used marijuana or other dangerous drugs. They know that illegal drug use is dangerous.

LESSON CHECKUP

Check Your Facts

❶ CRITICAL THINKING Why is it a good idea to turn on a fan when using certain types of glue?

❷ List two products that people misuse as inhalants.

❸ What are the harmful effects of marijuana?

❹ What are the harmful effects of cocaine?

Use Life Skills

❺ REFUSE Make a list of the harmful effects of inhalants. Keep this list in mind if anyone asks you to try an inhalant.

161

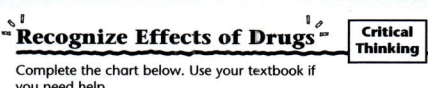

LANGUAGE ARTS

Understand Tolerance People who use inhalants and other drugs often develop a tolerance for the drugs. Explain that the word *tolerance* has a special meaning when used in reference to drug abuse. Encourage students to look in a dictionary or in a drug reference book to learn the meaning of this word. Have them share what they learn with the class.

Discuss

Crack cocaine, named for the crackling sound it makes as it is smoked, reaches the brain in less than ten seconds. According to users, the high that comes from using crack is a super high that lasts from five to twenty minutes; but the crash—the sick feeling users get when the high wears off—is extremely bad. To avoid this crushing low and to experience the high again, crack users take the drug over and over. This pattern of repeated use is why crack users get addicted so quickly.

Project Checkup

Make Drug Posters (p. 147) Students who are making a poster about how drugs can harm the body will find the information in this lesson useful.

3 Wrap Up

Lesson Checkup

1. to circulate the air so that people do not breathe the fumes

2. Possible answers: spray paints, glues, markers, cleaners, and nail polish removers.

3. It can make it hard to remember things or learn; it can speed up the heart and cause breathing problems; it can make it hard for the body to fight infections so users get ill more often than nonusers; it can make users nervous; it can cause cancer.

4. Users feel sad, nervous, confused, angry, or tired; they get dizzy and have sore throats and coughs. Cocaine can cause lung or brain damage, a stroke, heart attack, or death.

5. Students should list the following bad effects: violent behavior, upset stomach, nosebleed, hearing loss, confusion, brain damage, coughing, sneezing, headaches, slowed heart rate, slowed breathing rate, death.

OBJECTIVES

- Emphasize the importance of saying *no* to drugs.
- Suggest ways to avoid dangerous drugs.

PROGRAM RESOURCES

- Activity Book, p. 40

VOCABULARY

- refuse (p. 162)

Daily Safety Tip

Most offers of drugs to students come from people about their own age in friendly social situations. Have students think about what it would be like to be offered a drug in this type of situation and how and why they would refuse to use it.

1 Motivate

Provide students with several decision-making scenarios. Examples are given below. Ask students to explain what they would decide in each circumstance and why.

- You get up for school and have to decide what to wear.
- Your friends are going to the movies Saturday and want you to come along. You have a science project due Monday.
- You are at a party, and someone you know offers you marijuana.

Are all decisions you make as important as others? no What kinds of things do you have to think about when you make decisions? what will make you happy and keep you safe and healthy If you have trouble making an important decision, what should you do? Talk to a parent or family member or a trusted friend.

LESSON

MAIN IDEA If someone asks you to use drugs, you must know how to say *no*.

WHY LEARN THIS? Learning how to say *no* to drugs will help you stay healthy.

VOCABULARY
- refuse

How Can I Say *No to Drugs?*

Sometime someone may ask you to try a drug. It is important to decide ahead of time how to refuse. To **refuse** is to say *no*.

You can practice ways to refuse with your family or friends. You might say something like, "I want to have fun, not hurt my body" or "I can have fun without it." Think of something that feels right for you. Then you will be ready if someone asks you to use drugs.

▶ Avoid dangerous drugs. Get involved in an activity you enjoy instead, like sports, music, or art.

162

 MULTILEVEL ACTIVITIES

EASY **Make "No" Cards** Have students make small cards they can carry in their pockets or book bags that list five ways to say *no* to someone offering them drugs. Encourage students to write a pledge not to use or distribute drugs on the back of their cards. **TACTILE/INTRAPERSONAL**

AVERAGE **Draw a Comic** Invite students to think of a time when they or someone they know had to resist pressure from their friends to do something wrong. Have them illustrate this event in a comic strip format. **INTRAPERSONAL/VISUAL**

ADVANCED **Invent a Game** Have students design a board game that illustrates the importance of saying *no* to drugs. As an example, the game could have spaces describing positive and negative scenarios. When players land on positive spaces, they move ahead; on negative spaces, they move back. **KINESTHETIC/MATHEMATICAL**

▲ More and more kids are saying *no* to drugs.

LIFE SKILLS
FOCUS

Communicate

Cathy's friend told her that someone on the playground had drugs. Cathy's friend said she might like to try the drugs. What should Cathy say to her friend? Use the steps for communicating shown on page *xii*.

• • •

If you have doubts about saying *no*, remember how harmful drugs can be. A person can go to jail for using drugs. Drugs can change the way the brain works so a person cannot think well. They can cause illness and even death.

Some people use drugs to get high or to escape from their problems. But the high feeling doesn't last long. When that feeling wears off, users feel very low. And their problems are still there.

If someone asks you to use drugs, say *no*. Then talk to a trusted adult about it. That adult can be a family member, teacher, or doctor. You do not have to face the problem alone.

LESSON CHECKUP

Check Your Facts

1. **CRITICAL THINKING** Why should you choose friends who don't use drugs?

2. What should you remember if you have doubts about saying *no* to drugs?

3. Whom can you talk to for help if someone asks you to try drugs?

Use Life Skills

4. **REFUSE** Make a list of three ways you can say *no* to drugs.

163

ACTIVITY BOOK, p. 40

Analyze Vocabulary — Vocabulary Reinforcement

Read the descriptions at the top of the chart. Then read each word at the side of the chart. If the words at the top correctly describe the word at the side, write +. If the words at the top do not correctly describe the word at the side, write −. If you are unsure, write ?.

	drug	illegal	gives off fumes	can be breathed in or smoked	is contained in common drinks	speeds up the heart	slows down the heart	can harm you
caffeine	+	−	−	−	+	+	−	+
inhalant	+	−	+	+	−	−	+	+
marijuana	+	+	−	+	−	+	−	+
cocaine	+	+	−	+	−	+	−	+

Explain how you could say *no* to the use of inhalants, marijuana, or cocaine. Use the word *refuse* in your response.

Answers will vary. I could say *no* to the use of inhalants by explaining that they are harmful. I also could *refuse* by just walking away from anyone who offered them.

ART

"Just Say *No*" Buttons Provide students art materials, and have them design and make buttons or pins that reflect the theme of Lesson 6: saying *no* to drugs. Refer students to the antidrug slogans in the above picture on this page for ideas. Students may choose to display their buttons during the Antidrug Party activity, described on page 168.

---

2 Teach

Learn from Pictures

Point out the picture on page 162, and invite a volunteer to read the caption.

How are these children avoiding drugs and staying healthy at the same time? They are having fun playing funnel ball and getting exercise and fresh air.

What activities can you do to avoid drugs? Accept all reasonable answers.

Life Skills Focus

Communicate Have students explain what Cathy needs to do. Encourage them to apply the steps in the communication process. Possible answer: Cathy knows drugs are harmful and illegal. In a clear firm voice, Cathy can tell her friend that they both should leave the playground and go tell an adult. If Cathy's friend does not want to leave, Cathy should leave anyway and tell an adult. Cathy should not return to that playground.

3 Wrap Up

Lesson Checkup

1. so you can avoid situations in which your friends try to pressure you to use drugs

2. Remember how harmful drugs can be, that a person can go to jail for using drugs, that drugs can change the way the brain works so a person cannot think well, and that they can cause illness and death.

3. a trusted adult, such as a parent, teacher, family member, or doctor

4. Monitor small groups of students as they discuss ideas about how they can say *no* to drugs. Then have them write in their Health Journals three ways they would choose to say *no*.

LIFE SKILLS

OBJECTIVES

- Identify refusal skills.
- Use refusal skills to say *no* to drug use.

PROGRAM RESOURCES

- Activity Book, p. 41
  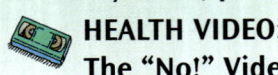 HEALTH VIDEO:
  The "No!" Video

1 Motivate

Form groups of four. Give each group a large sheet of butcher paper. Ask students to think of as many ways as they can to say *no*, such as "No way!" "Forget it!" "Why would I want to do that?" Ask them to record their ideas on the paper. Allow groups five minutes to come up with as many responses as possible. Then ask groups to tape their lists to the board. Have one member of each group read the responses. Comment on how many different ways there are to say *no*.

2 Teach

Direct students' attention to this page. Tell them they are going to learn a skill that will help them say *no*.

Learn from Pictures

Read and discuss the situation. **Is Roger using a drug?** Yes, when you sniff glue, it becomes an inhalant. Inhaling glue can be dangerous to your health. It can damage your brain and respiratory system.

Step 1

Are there other ways that Kamil could say *no*? Check the posted lists to see if any of the suggestions would work in this situation. Point out that certain phrases are more appropriate in specific situations.

REFUSE Inhalants

There may be a time when someone asks you to use drugs. Know ahead of time how to refuse.

Learn This Skill

Kamil went shopping with his friend Roger. They were looking at art supplies. Roger opened a tube of glue and started sniffing it. He wanted Kamil to try it.

1. Say *no*.

"Try it. It will make you feel really weird," Roger says.
"No," says Kamil.

2. State your reasons for saying *no*.

Warning—Sniffing glue can cause brain damage.

"I don't want to fry my brain!" says Kamil.

164

TEACHER TIP

Home Drug Use Be sensitive to the fact that some children may live in homes where illegal drugs are used. Information in this lesson may be uncomfortable for them, especially if this is the first time they are making the connection between what is going on at home and what they are learning in the classroom. Be sure to set some ground rules for talking about sensitive issues that include not using names of people. If students are going to share specific information, instruct them to say, "I know of someone who . . ."

DRAMA

Refusals Puppet Show Have students create a puppet show using refusal skills. Have them brainstorm problems about drugs kids their age might face. being offered a cigarette, a beer, a pinch of chewing tobacco; being asked to sniff nail polish remover Have them write a script that follows the refusal steps. Allow them to present their shows to the class.

LIFE SKILLS

3. Suggest something else to do.

"I want to look for some new paintbrushes," Kamil says.

4. Repeat *no*; walk away.

"I don't want to be anywhere near that stuff!" Kamil says as he walks away.

Practice This Skill

Use the steps to help you solve the problems below.

> ### Steps for Refusing
>
> **1.** Say *no*.
>
> **2.** State your reasons for saying *no*.
>
> **3.** Suggest something else to do.
>
> **4.** Repeat *no*; walk away.

A. Marta is visiting her cousin Jane. Jane has found some pills in her mother's purse. She wants Marta to try them with her. How can Jane refuse?

B. Tara's older brother Mike wants her to try some pills that will give her more energy. How can Tara say *no*?

165

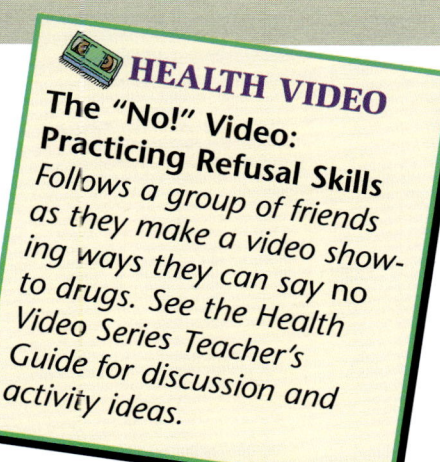

HEALTH VIDEO

The "No!" Video: Practicing Refusal Skills

Follows a group of friends as they make a video showing ways they can say no to drugs. See the Health Video Series Teacher's Guide for discussion and activity ideas.

Critical Thinking What are some reasons you would not want to use drugs? Possible answers: They harm your body; they can affect your brain; you might lose interest in school; you can get into trouble.

Step 3

Have students name some things they like to do after school. These are the activities that work well in Step 3.

Step 4

How does walking away help in this situation? It gets you away from the problem and the pressure to do something you don't want to do.

Critical Thinking Why is it important to stand up for what you believe when someone is trying to pressure you? Possible answers: If you don't follow what you believe, you might do something with which you are not comfortable. You would not feel very good about yourself. You might lose the respect of others.

3 Wrap Up

A. Students' responses should include all the steps for refusing, including saying *no* and giving a reason, such as "My parents told me never to take any medicines without an adult," and suggesting something else to do, such as playing a game, and walking away.

B. Students' responses should include all the steps for refusing. Reasons for saying *no* might be "I don't want to take any medicine without Mom and Dad's permission," or "I have plenty of energy—I don't need pills." Suggestions for other things to do might include eating healthful foods for energy or getting plenty of sleep. If Tara needs to walk away, she might go to her room or go visit a friend.

Use Vocabulary 2 pts. each

1. side effects
2. cocaine
3. drug
4. caffeine
5. prescription medicine
6. refuse
7. marijuana
8. Inhalants
9. over-the-counter medicine

Check Your Facts 6 pts. each

10. Medicines are drugs that can cure you when you are ill. They also can help you feel better.

11. what the medicine treats, directions for using the medicine

12. a medicine that must be ordered by a doctor

13. Answers could include dizziness, itching, a headache.

14. Answers could include tea (iced or hot), coffee, chocolate, soft drinks.

15. Answers could include nosebleed, hearing loss, confusion, brain damage, sneezing, coughing, slowed heart rate, slowed breathing rate, headaches, upset stomach, violent behavior, death.

16. THC

17. Answers could include sports, music, art.

CHAPTER 6 Review

USE VOCABULARY

caffeine (p. 156)   inhalants (p. 158)   prescription medicine (p. 151)
cocaine (p. 161)   marijuana (p. 160)   refuse (p. 162)
drug (p. 148)   over-the-counter medicine (p. 150)   side effects (p. 155)

Use the terms above to complete the sentences. Page numbers in ( ) tell you where to look in the chapter if you need help.

1. The unwanted changes in the body caused by a medicine are ____.

2. An illegal drug made from the leaves of the coca plant is ____.

3. Something other than food that changes the way your body works is a ____.

4. Coffee and chocolate contain ____, a drug that speeds up the heart.

5. A medicine that an adult can get only with a doctor's order is a ____.

6. To say *no* is to ____.

7. An illegal drug that comes from the hemp plant is ____.

8. ____ are substances that give off dangerous fumes and are sometimes used as drugs.

9. A medicine that an adult can buy without a prescription is an ____.

CHECK YOUR FACTS

Page numbers in ( ) tell you where to look in the chapter if you need help.

10. What are medicines? (p. 148)

11. What does the label on an OTC medicine tell you? (pp. 150–151)

12. What is a prescription medicine? (p. 151)

13. List two possible side effects of medicine. (p. 155)

14. List two foods that contain caffeine. (p. 156)

15. List four side effects people may develop if they misuse the products shown here. (p. 159)

16. Which substance in marijuana changes the way the brain works? (p. 160)

17. Name a fun activity that does not include the use of drugs. (p. 162)

THINK CRITICALLY

18. Why is it important to read the labels on over-the-counter medicines?

19. Illegal drugs, such as marijuana and cocaine, are dangerous. Why do some people use them anyway?

20. Why should you read warning labels on substances such as glue?

APPLY LIFE SKILLS

21. **Refuse** You go to a party at a friend's house. After a while many of the people go into the basement to sniff glue. They tell you to try it. Everyone is looking at you, waiting for your answer. How would you refuse?

22. **Communicate** You can refuse drugs when someone offers them to you. But how can you communicate to others that they should never offer drugs to you?

Promote Health **Home and Community**

1. Look at the place where your family stores medicines. Is it safe, according to the Safety Rules for Medicine Use? If so, why? If not, where can your family store the medicine more safely?
2. Make a poster that tells other kids to stay off drugs. Hang your poster up in the classroom.

167

Think Critically 6 pts. each

18. Medicines can be harmful if used in the wrong way.

19. Some people use drugs to get high or to escape their problems.

20. Fumes from substances such as glue are poisonous. They can be dangerous. The label tells how to use the substance safely.

Apply Life Skills 8 pts. each

21. Answers will vary. Students should include the steps for refusing in their answers.

22. Answers will vary. Students should include the steps for communicating in their answers.

PERFORMANCE ASSESSMENT

Project—Make Drug Posters

The chapter project (introduced on page 147) can be used for individual or team performance assessment. Allow students the opportunity to revise and complete their projects before submitting them for evaluation. Students can use the Project Summary Sheet (Assessment Guide, p. 17) to tell about their projects. You can use the rubric provided on the Project Evaluation Sheet (Assessment Guide, p. 41) to evaluate student performance.

Activities

Safety Cartoons

At Home • Look at the Safety Rules for Medicine Use shown here. Pick one. Then draw a cartoon to illustrate the rule. Print the rule at the bottom of the drawing. Display your cartoon with those of your classmates.

Drug Messages

With a Partner • How do ads and TV programs show the use of alcohol and other drugs? Watch several TV programs and ads. Take notes. What messages do these shows and ads send to kids about alcohol and other drugs? Report to your class.

Antidrug Party

With a Group • Plan a party or rally at your school to celebrate saying *no* to drugs. Think of fun activities for the celebration. Include music and food. Ask speakers to take part. Make posters and buttons with antidrug messages. Show that you can have lots of fun without drugs—and that most kids don't want to use them.

OPEN
PUSH DOWN & TURN
CLOSE

Safety Rules for Medicine Use

- Only an adult should give you medicine. Never take a medicine on your own.
- Always follow the directions on the medicine label.
- Never take someone else's prescription medicine.
- Don't use old medicines. They can change when they get old and make you ill. Look at the date on the label.
- Leave the labels on all medicines.
- Keep medicines on high shelves in locked cabinets.
- Keep medicines away from small children.

Talk to Your Pharmacist

On Your Own • Talk with a pharmacist about his or her job. What do pharmacists do each day? Is the work fun? How did he or she become a pharmacist? Write down what the pharmacist says, or record the interview. Share what you find out with your class.

168

Chapter Test

ASSESSMENT GUIDE, p. 38

Medicines and Other Drugs | Chapter 6 Test

Write the letter of the correct term in the space.

a. drug
b. over-the-counter medicine
c. prescription medicine
d. side effects
e. caffeine

Dana was feeling ill, so her mother took her to see Doctor Chu. Doctor Chu examined Dana and said she needed medicines to help her get well. He wrote an order for a 1. __c__ and asked Dana's mom to also buy a bottle of 2. __b__ at the pharmacy. Doctor Chu told Dana not to drink anything that has 3. __e__ in it, such as some sodas. He said that caffeine is a 4. __a__ that can interact with the medicines and could cause some 5. __d__ .

Write *T* or *F* to show if the sentence is true or false.

__T__ 6. A drug is something other than food that changes how the body works.

__T__ 7. Caffeine makes people feel more awake.

__F__ 8. Drugs can never be harmful.

__T__ 9. Many household products give off dangerous fumes.

__F__ 10. "High" is a common way of describing people who take medicine ordered by a doctor.

__F__ 11. Over-the-counter medicines cannot be bought without an order from a doctor.

__T__ 12. OTC medicines are for minor health problems like sore throats, colds, and headaches.

__F__ 13. It is not important for adults to follow the directions on OTC medicines.

__T__ 14. A prescription medicine is a medicine that must be ordered by a doctor.

__F__ 15. The order a doctor writes for a medicine is called a pharmacist.

168

ASSESSMENT GUIDE, p. 39

Choose the sentences below that are good safety rules for using medicines. Write their letters on the lines.

a. Only an adult should give you medicine.
b. It's OK to take the labels off medicines.
c. Never take someone else's prescription medicine.
d. Always follow the directions on a medicine.
e. Children should take medicines on their own.
f. Keep medicines away from small children.
g. Keep medicines on high shelves or in locked cabinets.

__a__ 16.
__c__ 17.
__d__ 18.
__f__ 19.
__g__ 20.

21. List some ways to avoid taking in caffeine.
Know which foods and drinks have caffeine. Do not eat chocolate. Drink soft drinks that do not contain caffeine.

22. Name three harmful reactions a person could have from inhaling fumes from dangerous products.
Possible answers: nosebleed, confusion, hearing loss, upset stomach, violent behavior, headache, sneezing, coughing, slowed breathing rate, death.

ASSESSMENT GUIDE, p. 40

23. Lexie's older brother uses marijuana and cocaine. What could Lexie tell her brother about these two dangerous drugs that might get him to stop using them?
Possible answers: These drugs can speed up the heart; make it hard for the body to fight infections; cause cancer; make users feel nervous, sad, confused, angry, or tired; lead to brain or lung damage; make users need more and more of the drugs.

24. Kevin doesn't want to take illegal drugs. What does Kevin know about illegal drugs that might make him feel this way? **Possible answers: Kevin knows that a person can go to jail for using illegal drugs. He also knows that illegal drugs can change the way the brain works so a person cannot think well. Drugs also can cause illness or death.**

Some older kids at Melissa's school use drugs. Today they will ask Melissa to use drugs. Draw two ways Melissa can say *no* to drugs.

25.

26.

Students' art might show Melissa saying, "No thanks," and walking away; saying, "I want to have fun, not hurt my body"; or saying, "I can have fun without drugs."

Multiple Choice

Choose the letter of the correct answer.

1. Drugs change the way the body ____.
   a. looks   b. works
   c. tastes   d. smells

2. Pharmacists prepare ____ medicines.
   a. no   b. OTC
   c. prescription   d. all

3. Caffeine is a drug that ____ the heart.
   a. speeds up   b. destroys
   c. slows down   d. copies

4. The fumes that come from inhalants are ____.
   a. poisons   b. medicines
   c. safe   d. air

5. It is important to decide ahead of time how to ____ drugs.
   a. accept   b. buy
   c. try   d. refuse

Modified True or False

Write *true* or *false*. If a sentence is false, replace the underlined term to make the sentence true.

6. Drugs can change the way people <u>think</u>, feel, and act.

7. A <u>doctor</u> uses a prescription to fill a medicine order.

8. Some over-the-counter medicines <u>relieve pain</u> or stop coughs.

9. Never take someone else's <u>medicine</u>.

10. Always read the <u>safety seal</u> on a medicine.

11. Caffeine is in coffee and some <u>soft drinks</u>.

12. Marijuana is an illegal drug that comes from the <u>corn</u> plant.

13. Cocaine use can cause <u>brain</u> damage.

Short Answer

Write a complete sentence to answer each question.

14. What kinds of health problems do over-the-counter medicines treat?

15. Why should you always leave the labels on medicines?

16. How can you cut down the amount of caffeine in your diet?

17. List some of the harmful effects that marijuana can have on the body.

18. How can inhalants harm the body?

Writing in Health

Write paragraphs to answer each item.

19. What is the safe way to take medicine?

20. What could happen to someone who uses drugs?

Writing in Health (10 pts. each)

Sample answers are shown; accept other reasonable answers.

19. The safe way to take medicine is to follow the safety rules. Take medicine only from an adult. Leave the labels on all medicines, and always follow the directions on the medicine label. Never take someone else's prescription medicine. Don't use old medicines.

20. A person who uses drugs could go to jail. The person's brain could be damaged by using the drugs. The person could get ill or die.

Two options are provided for Chapter Tests—the in-book test and the reproducible test in the Assessment Guide. In addition to providing students with the opportunity to show what they have learned, both tests provide practice in taking standardized tests.

Multiple Choice (3 pts. each)

1. b   3. a   5. d
2. c   4. a

Modified True or False (5 pts. each)

6. true
7. false; pharmacist
8. true
9. true
10. false; label
11. true
12. false; hemp
13. true

Short Answer (5 pts. each)

Sample answers are shown; accept other reasonable answers.

14. Over-the-counter medicines treat minor health problems, such as sore throats, colds, headaches, cough, and pain.

15. The label tells what the medicine treats and gives directions for using the medicine.

16. You can cut down on the amount of caffeine in your diet by reading food and drink labels and choosing things without caffeine.

17. Marijuana can make it hard to remember things or learn, speed up the heart, cause breathing problems, make it hard for the body to fight infections, make users nervous, and cause cancer.

18. Inhalants can distort how a person sees, hears, and feels. They can cause brain damage, nosebleeds, confusion, hearing loss, sneezing, coughing, slowed heart rate, slowed breathing rate, headache, upset stomach, violent behavior, and death.

Avoiding Alcohol and Tobacco

Chapter Organizer

Lesson	Objectives	Vocabulary	Program Resources
Introduce the Chapter pp. 170–171	• Preview the chapter. • Begin chapter project.		• School-Home Connection, TR p. 45 • Assessment Guide, p. 45 • Read-Aloud Anthology, p. RA-8 Teaching Transparency 7—Graphic Organizer
Lesson 1 1•2•4 **Learning About Tobacco and Alcohol** pp. 172–173 Pacing: 1 class period	• Describe the harmful effects of nicotine and alcohol on the body. • Identify products that contain tobacco or alcohol.	nicotine alcohol	• Activity Book, p. 42
Lesson 2 1•7 **How Tobacco Affects the Body** pp. 174–177 Pacing: 2 class periods	• Identify the effects of tobacco on specific human body parts. • Describe the hazards of environmental tobacco smoke.	addiction chewing tobacco smokeless tobacco tar cancer environmental tobacco smoke	• Activity Book, p. 43 Teaching Transparencies 20 and 28 Computer Graphing Activity, TR p. 63
Lesson 3 1•4 **How Alcohol Affects the Body** pp. 178–181 Pacing: 2 class periods	• Describe some effects of alcohol on specific body organs and on behavior. • Identify safety risks associated with alcohol use.	bloodstream alcoholism	• Activity Book, p. 44 Computer Graphing Activity, TR p. 64 Teaching Transparency 18
Lesson 4 1•3•5 **Refusing to Use Alcohol and Tobacco** pp. 182–185 Pacing: 1 class period	• Describe some laws regarding the sale, use, and packaging of alcohol and tobacco products. • Explain reasons for refusing and demonstrate ways to refuse tobacco and alcohol.		• Activity Book, pp. 45–46
Life Skills 1•3•5 **Refuse** pp. 186–187 Pacing: 1 class period	• Identify skills for refusals. • Use refusal skills to say **no** to alcohol and tobacco.		• Activity Book, p. 47
Chapter Review and Test pp. 188–191	5•7 • Assess chapter objectives and project. • Provide extension activities.		• Chapter Test and Project Evaluation Sheet, Assessment Guide, pp. 42–45

 National Health Education Standards
A complete list of the Standards is provided on the next page.

Key: TR = Teaching Resources

National Health Education Standards

1. Comprehend concepts related to health promotion and disease prevention.
2. Access valid health information and health-promoting products and services.
3. Practice health-enhancing behaviors and reduce health risks.
4. Analyze the influence of culture, media, technology, and other factors on health.
5. Use interpersonal communication skills to enhance health.
6. Use goal-setting and decision-making skills to enhance health.
7. Advocate for personal, family, and community health.

Science
- What's Your Reaction Time? p. 170C
- Animal Peer Pressure, p. 185

Drama
- Role-Play Refusals, p. 170C
- Handling ETS, p. 177

Art
- Refusals Comic Strips, p. 187

Math
- Make a Picture Graph, p. 170C

Curriculum Integration

Use these topics to integrate health into your daily planning.

Social Studies
- Smoke-Free Pledge, p. 184

Language Arts
- Peer Pressure Poems, p. 170C

ASSESSMENT OPTIONS

Portfolio Assessment
Have students select their best work from the following suggestions.
- **Refusals Comic Strips,** p. 187
- **Have a Heart,** p. 190
- **Know the Rules,** p. 190

Student Self-Assessment
- **Journal Notes,** p. 177
- **Set Health Goals,** pp. 173, 177
- **Use Life Skills,** pp. 181, 185

Daily Assessment
- **Check Your Facts,** pp. 173, 177, 181, 185

Performance Assessment
- **Chapter Project: Make a Model,** pp. 171, 175, 179, 184, 189
- **Project Evaluation Sheet,** Assessment Guide, p. 45

Formal Assessment
- **Chapter Review,** pp. 188-189
- **In-Book Test,** p. 191
- **Chapter Test,** Assessment Guide, pp. 42-44

Cross-Curricular Activities

Math

Make a Picture Graph

Have each student survey ten other people, getting yes or no answers to the following question: Does any adult who lives in your home smoke? Students should total the yes and no answers they receive. Then ask them to make a symbol for nonsmokers and a symbol for smokers. Students can display their survey results on bar graphs using their picture symbols.

Science

What's Your Reaction Time?

Reaction time is how long it takes a person's body to react when something happens to it or near it. Alcohol slows a person's reaction time, increasing the danger of mistakes while driving, for example. Have students make five attempts with each hand for both of the following tests. Discuss how their reactions might be different if they had consumed alcohol.

- **Grab the Coin** Provide a coin for each student. Demonstrate how to hold one arm out, palm down, place a coin on the center of the back of the hand, then slowly tilt the hand so that the coin begins to slide off. Once the coin starts to slide, have students try to flip their hands over to catch the coins. After five attempts with each hand, ask the following questions: How many times did you catch the coin? Do you get better with practice? Is one hand faster than the other?

- **Hand Slap** Have students remove any rings or bracelets, then pair students. Direct one student in each pair to hold out his or her right hand, palm up. Have the partners lightly rest their left hands, palms down, on top of the first students' palms. Instruct the first students to turn over their hands and lightly slap the back of their partners' hands before they can pull their "at-risk" hands away.

Drama

Role-Play Refusals

Have groups of students make up skits to practice the refusal skills presented in the chapter. They may use the following scenario suggestions or think up their own.

- You and your friends find a package of unopened cigarettes at the mall.

- A friend offers you a beer after you have been playing hard.

Language Arts

Peer Pressure Poems

Sometimes humor can be used to relieve tension in peer-pressure situations. Have students work in pairs to write clever poems or limericks they can recite when confronted with peer pressure to use alcohol or tobacco. They can practice by reading their poems in class.

Bulletin Board

Place large *No Drinking* and *No Smoking* symbols in the center of the bulletin board, as shown. Place the following words as a large banner or title at the top of the bulletin board: *Instead of Choosing Tobacco or Alcohol, I'll Choose . . .*

- Have students cut out magazine pictures, draw pictures, or bring photos from home showing themselves or others doing enjoyable activities that do not involve tobacco or alcohol.

- Have students print large, colorful captions naming the activities illustrated. Remind them to sign their names to their captioned pictures.

- Have students place their captioned and signed pictures on the bulletin board in a collage around the center graphic.

Instead of choosing tobacco or alcohol, I'll choose...

Resources

Books for Students

Hastings, Jill M. *Elephant in the Living Room: The Children's Book.* Hazelden Foundation, 1994. Written for children who are living in families where drinking is or was a problem. **EASY**

Haughton, Emma. *Drinking, Smoking, and Other Drugs (Health and Fitness).* Raintree Steck-Vaughn, 2000. Explains the nature of both legal and illegal drugs, how they can affect the body, and how they can help or harm users. **AVERAGE**

Berry, Joy. *Substance Abuse: (Good Answers to Tough Questions).* Gold Star Publishing, 2000. A self-help book for children that discusses using illegal substances, what risks are involved in using them, and solutions to avoid substance abuse. **ADVANCED**

Books for Teachers and Families

Schaefer, Dick and Johnson Institute Staff. *Choices and Consequences: What to do When a Teenager Uses Alcohol/Drugs.* Johnson Institute, 1996. Offers tools for adults concerned with teenage alcohol and drug abuse.

Haughton, Emma. *A Right to Smoke? (Viewpoints.)* Franklin Watts Inc., 1997. While this is geared to a middle school readership, this book provides a valuable resource for educators working with the topic of smoking.

Videos

Not Just Blowing Smoke. GTR Productions, 1998. (10 minutes) Explains to students why smoking is a poor choice and how they can be pressured to smoke.

Tobacco Free—You & Me. Durrin Productions, 1997. (19 minutes) Points out to students how tobacco products are sold to children. Explains effects of environmental tobacco smoke. Contains footage of mouth cancer.

Your Health Webliography

The **Webliography** provides links to the Health Background and teaching resources that will support you as you teach the topics in *Your Health.* Simply choose a keyword and you will be taken to a page of links with descriptions of the content you can obtain at each site. The **Webliography** is located on the Teacher Resources page at **www.harcourtschool.com/health** Please review websites before referring your students to them.

Organizations and Agencies

Action on Smoking and Health
2013 H St., NW
Washington, D.C. 20006
This organization works for the rights of nonsmokers.

Alcohol and Drug Abuses Services Administration
Department of Human Services
1300 1st St., NE
Suite 300
Washington, D.C. 20002
202-727-9393
This government agency provides information on alcohol and drugs.

For more information about health organizations and agencies, please see the *Teaching Resources* book.

Community Health

Local Cancer, Heart, or Lung Health Resources Invite a representative of the local American Lung Association, American Heart Association, or Cancer Society of America to talk about the effects of smoking.

- Prior to the speaker's visit, prompt students to prepare three-column charts and label the columns "What I Know About _____ (e.g., Smoking and Lung Health)," "What I Want to Know," and "What I Learned." Have them complete the first two columns before the talk and the third after the speaker presents his or her information.

Free and Inexpensive Material

Americans for Nonsmokers' Rights
2530 San Pablo Ave.
Suite J
Berkeley, CA 94702
510-841-3032
Provides educational materials on the health hazards of exposure to secondhand smoke.

Note that information, while correct at time of publication, is subject to change.

Visit **The Harcourt Learning Site** for related links, activities, resources, and the health **Webliography**.

www.harcourtschool.com

WELCOME TO THE LEARNING SITE

CHAPTER

Pages 170–191

"The use of alcohol, tobacco, and other drugs ... has major implications in the lifelong health of individuals."

—Page 43, *California Health Framework*

CHAPTER SUMMARY

In this chapter students
- are introduced to tobacco and alcohol as harmful drugs.
- learn to recognize various types of alcohol and nicotine products.
- examine the harmful effects of alcohol, the nicotine and tar in tobacco, and environmental tobacco smoke.

LIFE SKILLS Students practice ways to *refuse* the use of tobacco, exposure to environmental tobacco smoke (ETS), and alcohol.

CONSUMER HEALTH Students learn about laws concerning the purchase, use, and advertising of alcohol and tobacco products.

HUMAN BODY Students investigate the effects of alcohol and tobacco on various body systems.

Literature Springboard

Use the story excerpt *Where There's Smoke* to spark interest in the chapter topic. See the Read-Aloud Anthology on page RA-8 of this Teacher's Edition.

170

School-Home Connection

Distribute copies of the School-Home Connection (in English or Spanish), TR page 45. Have students take the page home to share with their families as you begin this chapter.

Follow Up Have students make a list of the claims implied by the alcohol ads. Then review the true effects of alcohol.

Alternative Use the School-Home Connection page as a classroom resource for enrichment activities.

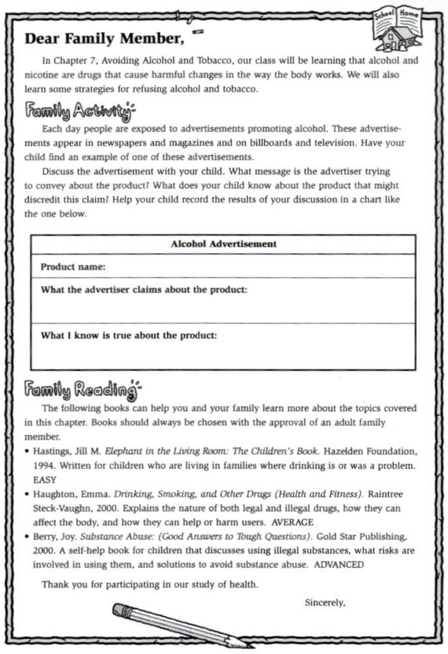

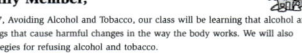

Dear Family Member,

In Chapter 7, Avoiding Alcohol and Tobacco, our class will be learning that alcohol and nicotine are drugs that cause harmful changes in the way the body works. We will also learn some strategies for refusing alcohol and tobacco.

Family Activity

Each day people are exposed to advertisements promoting alcohol. These advertisements appear in newspapers and magazines and on billboards and television. Have your child find an example of one of these advertisements.

Discuss the advertisement with your child. What message is the advertiser trying to convey about the product? What does your child know about the product that might discredit this claim? Help your child record the results of your discussion in a chart like the one below.

Alcohol Advertisement
Product name:
What the advertiser claims about the product:
What I know is true about the product:

Family Reading

The following books can help you and your family learn more about the topics covered in this chapter. Books should always be chosen with the approval of an adult family member.
- Hastings, Jill M. *Elephant in the Living Room: The Children's Book.* Hazelden Foundation, 1994. Written for children who are living in families where drinking is or was a problem. EASY
- Haughton, Emma. *Drinking, Smoking, and Other Drugs (Health and Fitness).* Raintree Steck-Vaughn, 2000. Explains the nature of both legal and illegal drugs, how they can affect the body, and how they can help or harm users. AVERAGE
- Berry, Joy. *Substance Abuse: (Good Answers to Tough Questions).* Gold Star Publishing, 2000. A self-help book for children that discusses using illegal substances, what risks are involved in using them, and solutions to avoid substance abuse. ADVANCED

Thank you for participating in our study of health.

Sincerely,

CHAPTER 7

Avoiding Alcohol and Tobacco

MAKE A MODEL With a small group, make a life-size model of the human body on cardboard or drawing paper. On the model, draw the body organs that are affected by alcohol and tobacco.

For other activities, visit the Harcourt Learning Site. www.harcourtschool.com

171

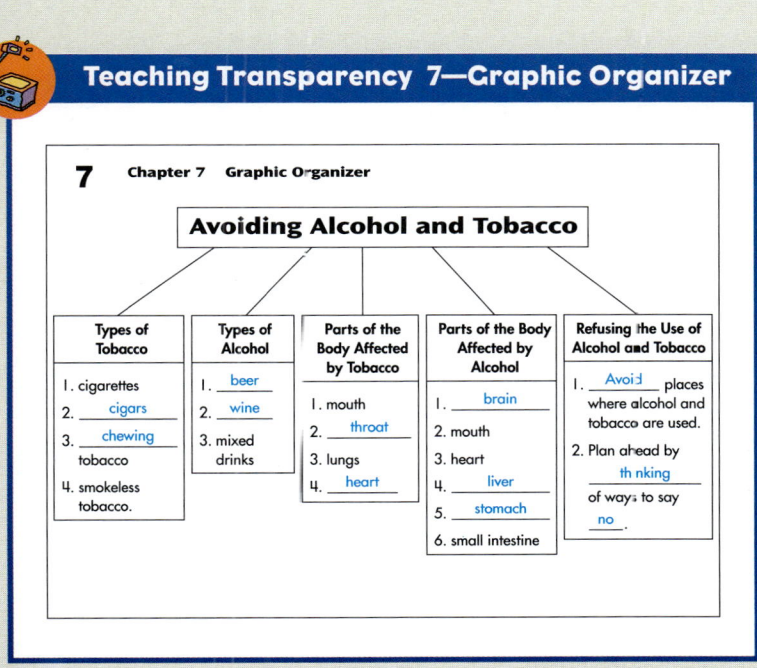

Teaching Transparency 7—Graphic Organizer

7 Chapter 7 Graphic Organizer

Avoiding Alcohol and Tobacco

Types of Tobacco	Types of Alcohol	Parts of the Body Affected by Tobacco	Parts of the Body Affected by Alcohol	Refusing the Use of Alcohol and Tobacco
1. cigarettes	1. beer	1. mouth	1. brain	1. Avoid places where alcohol and tobacco are used.
2. cigars	2. wine	2. throat	2. mouth	2. Plan ahead by thinking of ways to say no.
3. chewing tobacco	3. mixed drinks	3. lungs	3. heart	
4. smokeless tobacco.		4. heart	4. liver	
			5. stomach	
			6. small intestine	

Introduce the Chapter

MAKE A MODEL

Access Prior Knowledge Use this activity as a baseline assessment of students' understanding of the bodily effects of alcohol and tobacco. Encourage students to note in their journals the organs that the group drew, along with any personal observations.

Performance Assessment The project can be used for performance assessment. Before students begin, explain how you will evaluate their performance. (See the Project Evaluation Sheet, Assessment Guide, p. 45.)

Prereading Strategies

Scan the Chapter Have students preview the chapter content by scanning the titles, headings, pictures, and charts. Ask volunteers to speculate on what they will learn.

Preview Vocabulary As students scan the chapter, point out the vocabulary words listed at the beginning of each lesson. Pronounce each word. Invite volunteers to offer meanings for words they recognize. Have students locate each word in bold in context, or in the glossary, to learn its meaning.

Visualize Key Concepts Display the Graphic Organizer Transparency. You may also wish to distribute photocopies to students. Have students complete the organizer as they work through the chapter. Suggested concepts for students to fill in are shown.

Follow Up Review the completed organizer with students as preparation for the Chapter Review and Chapter Tests.

OBJECTIVES

- Describe the harmful effects of nicotine and alcohol on the body.
- Identify products that contain tobacco or alcohol.

PROGRAM RESOURCES

- Activity Book, p. 42

VOCABULARY

- nicotine (p. 173)
- alcohol (p. 173)

Daily Safety Tip

Alcohol and tobacco products are both dangerous and illegal for students to use. Remind students that for safety, adults should keep alcohol, tobacco products, and matches out of the reach of children. Also, adults should never ask children to handle, serve, or pour alcohol at parties. Remind students that they can refuse such requests.

1 Motivate

Optional Materials photo of a child; magazine advertisements for foods, non-foods, and tobacco and alcohol products

Have students imagine that they are parents and are responsible for helping the child in the picture grow up safe and healthy. Show pictures of various foods, nonfoods, and toxic substances, having students classify each one as safe or harmful for the child to eat or drink. (As an alternative, name the substances.)

What did this activity show? Some products help the body grow, and others can harm it.

MAIN IDEA Alcohol and tobacco are harmful drugs.

WHY LEARN THIS? Knowing the dangers of alcohol and tobacco will help you avoid using them.

VOCABULARY
- nicotine
- alcohol

Learning About Tobacco and Alcohol

You may have seen adults using tobacco (tuh•BA•koh) or alcohol (AL•kuh•hawl) products. You may think these products are safe to use. But did you know that tobacco and alcohol are drugs? Drugs change the way a person's body works. Tobacco and alcohol can harm a person who uses them.

Why are tobacco and alcohol drugs?

The tobacco in cigarettes and cigars comes from the leaves of the tobacco plant. Tobacco that is smoked in pipes is made from the same leaves. Other tobacco products are chewed or sucked. These products look different, but they all contain tobacco.

Types of Tobacco

snuff

smoking tobacco

chewing tobacco

► Smoking tobacco includes cigarettes, cigars, and loose tobacco smoked in pipes. Snuff and chewing tobacco are smokeless tobacco products.

172

 MULTILEVEL ACTIVITIES

EASY Make a Tobacco Bulletin Board Have students find pictures of tobacco products, tobacco plants, warning labels, and so on. Suggest they put together a bulletin board display showing the information they have gathered. **VISUAL/SPATIAL**

AVERAGE Make Concept Maps Have students form two groups. Direct each group to make a concept map—one for alcohol and one for nicotine. Have them include facts such as what it is, what it does to the body, and what harm it causes. Display the maps. **LOGICAL/INTERPERSONAL**

ADVANCED Make Alcohol Webs Tell students that many alcohol products are made from plants. Many students will know that wine, for instance, is made from grapes. Suggest they find out what other types of plants alcohol is made from (grains, berries, and potatoes). Have them make concept webs that show all the beverages made from each source. **VERBAL/VISUAL**

All tobacco products have nicotine. **Nicotine** (NIH•kuh•teen) is a drug in tobacco. People who use tobacco products are putting this drug into their bodies. Like other drugs, nicotine causes changes in the body. Some drugs, such as the medicines a doctor gives, cause good changes. The changes nicotine causes are not good.

Nicotine is a poison. Farmers and gardeners use it to kill insects on plants. Nicotine can kill people, too. A small amount of pure nicotine—about a tablespoonful—can kill an adult. Smaller amounts harm the body. Many tobacco users know that tobacco can make them ill. But the nicotine also makes them keep wanting tobacco.

Alcohol is also a drug. Like nicotine, alcohol causes changes in the user's body. Alcohol is found in drinks such as beer, wine, and mixed drinks. Some adult liquid medicines also have alcohol. Most children's medicines are made so that they have no alcohol.

Drinking alcohol is harmful, especially for children. Using alcohol for many years also causes health problems. Some people who use alcohol can't stop using it without help. They can get the help they need at programs in local clinics, hospitals, and treatment centers. Alcoholics Anonymous, Rational Recovery, and Al-Anon are also places they and their families can go for help.

Types of Alcohol

beer

wine

mixed drinks

LESSON CHECKUP

Check Your Facts
1 What drug is found in beer, wine, and mixed drinks?

2 **CRITICAL THINKING** Most people know that tobacco and alcohol can harm the body. Why do people still use these drugs?

3 Name a drug found in tobacco.

Set Health Goals
4 List three reasons to avoid using tobacco and alcohol. Then write ways you can keep from using these drugs.

173

---

2 Teach

Learn from Pictures

Have volunteers identify the tobacco plant and the three types of tobacco products pictured on page 172. Have volunteers also identify the three alcohol products pictured on this page. Then ask students to point to each picture as you name the products in random order.

Discuss

Invite volunteers to name other tobacco and alcohol products they might know. Before reading, have students discuss how they think these products are used and how they might be harmful.

Critical Thinking **Are all tobacco products harmful?** Yes; because they all contain the drug nicotine.

Some adults can safely drink small amounts of alcohol, but are alcoholic products harmful to children? Yes; because alcohol is a drug and causes changes in the body. Because children's bodies are much smaller than adults' bodies, even a tiny amount of alcohol can be dangerous for children.

3 Wrap Up

Lesson Checkup

1. alcohol

2. Possible answer: Some of the changes caused by alcohol and tobacco make it hard for people to stop using these products.

3. nicotine

4. Have students write their experiences and suggestions in their Health Journals. Accept reasonable answers.

TEACHER TIP

Home Use of Tobacco and Alcohol Many children live in homes where tobacco and alcohol are used. Remind students that these substances are legal for adults to use, and their use does not imply that an adult is a bad person. Tell students that smoking can be addictive and difficult to stop. Emphasize that they cannot change the behavior of others, but that they can make their own choices not to use tobacco or alcohol.

173

OBJECTIVES

- Identify the effects of tobacco on specific human body parts.
- Describe the hazards of environmental tobacco smoke.

PROGRAM RESOURCES

- Activity Book, p. 43

 Teaching Transparencies 20 and 28

 Computer Graphing Activity, Teaching Resources p. 63

VOCABULARY

- addiction (p. 174)
- chewing tobacco (p. 174)
- smokeless tobacco (p. 174)
- tar (p. 175)
- cancer (p. 175)
- environmental tobacco smoke (p. 176)

Daily Safety Tip

Killer smoke! Besides tar and nicotine, cigarette smoke contains many other poisons, such as arsenic, formaldehyde, ammonia, and carbon monoxide. Explain that carbon monoxide has no color or smell and is especially dangerous because it takes up the space in the blood where oxygen belongs.

1 Motivate

In a safe area, have students spin 10–20 times in one direction Then ask them to describe what happens when they try to stand still and walk in a straight line.

What did you learn from this experiment? Dizziness causes the body to feel odd and behave strangely. Explain that dizziness is one of the effects of drugs or poisons.

 **LESSON**

MAIN IDEA Many things in tobacco harm the user.

WHY LEARN THIS? Knowing how dangerous tobacco is will help you refuse to use it.

VOCABULARY
- addiction
- chewing tobacco
- smokeless tobacco
- tar
- cancer
- environmental tobacco smoke

How Tobacco Affects the Body

All kinds of tobacco have nicotine in them. Nicotine can get into the body through smoke or through juice from the tobacco.

Nicotine can cause addiction. **Addiction** (uh•DIK•shuhn) is a constant need that makes people keep using drugs even when they want to stop. Nicotine affects the way the brain works. It also makes the heart beat faster and harder and can cause heart disease.

How do people use tobacco?

Most people who use tobacco smoke it. Some smoke it in a pipe or cigar. Most smoke it in cigarettes. To make smoking tobacco, the green leaves of the tobacco plant are dried. Then the dried tobacco leaves are shredded. Pipe tobacco and the tobacco in cigars look similar to the tobacco in cigarettes. The outside of a cigar is made from tobacco leaves that have not been shredded.

Some people chew small wads—or plugs—of moist tobacco. This moist tobacco for chewing is called **chewing tobacco**.

Some people put clumps of powdered or shredded tobacco between their cheeks and gums and suck it. This tobacco is called **smokeless tobacco**, or snuff.

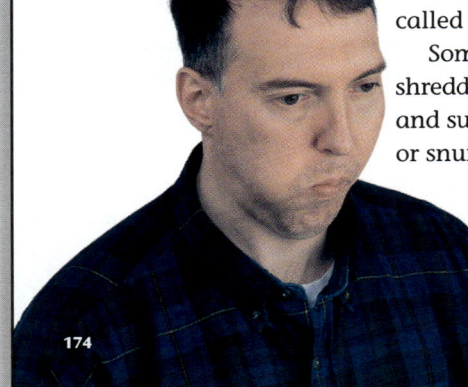

◀ Some people think chewing tobacco is safer than smoking it. It's not! Nicotine in the tobacco still gets into the body.

174

MULTILEVEL ACTIVITIES

EASY **Make a Puzzle** Have students use the vocabulary terms to make a fill-in word puzzle. Duplicate the puzzle, and let the rest of the students complete it. **VERBAL/SPATIAL**

AVERAGE **Interview a Dentist** When adults go to the dentist, the dentist checks for mouth cancers that may be caused by tobacco use. He or she also cleans stains on the teeth caused by tobacco use. Have students talk to a dentist to find out what he or she would suggest to smokers to improve their dental health. **VERBAL/INTERPERSONAL**

ADVANCED **Investigate Tobacco Plants** Tell students that much of the tobacco used in tobacco products is grown in the United States. Have them research where tobacco is grown and show the locations on a map of the United States. **VISUAL/SPATIAL**

How does tobacco affect the body?

Tobacco smoke has more than 4,000 different things in it. Many of these things can harm a person's body. You have already learned how harmful nicotine is. Tobacco smoke also contains tar. **Tar** is a dark, sticky substance. It coats the lungs and air passages of people who breathe in tobacco smoke. Tar makes breathing hard. It can also lead to lung diseases and **cancer** (KAN•ser), a disease that makes cells grow wildly. Other problems that tobacco causes are shown in the diagram below.

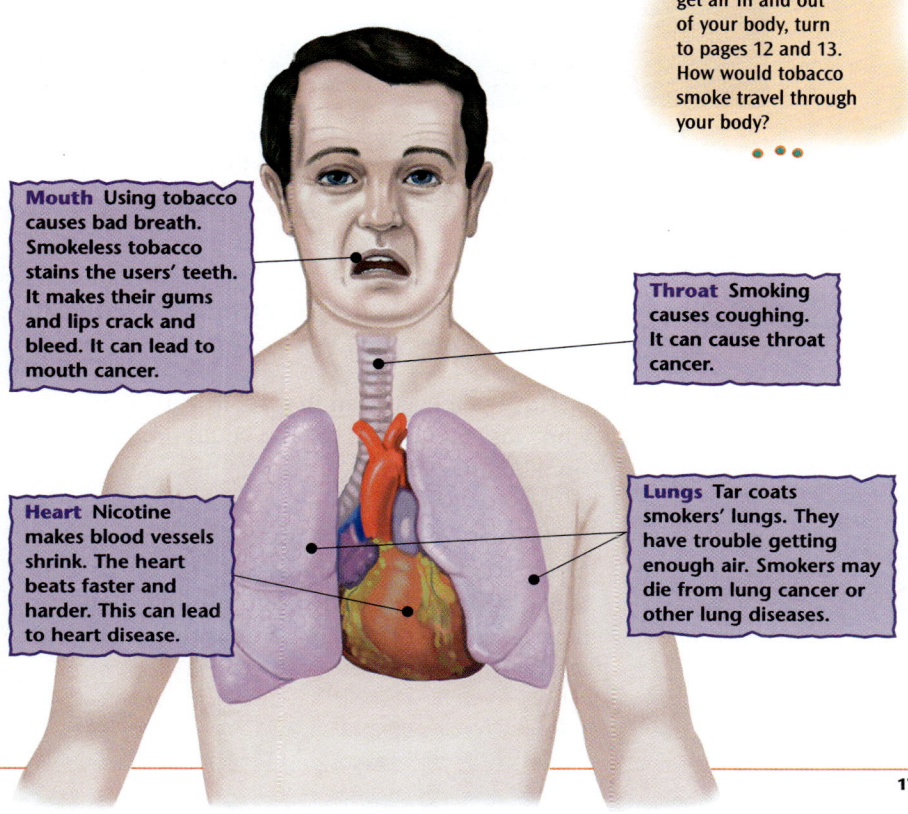

HUMAN BODY CONNECTION

Your Lungs
Your lungs are part of your respiratory system. To learn more about how your lungs get air in and out of your body, turn to pages 12 and 13. How would tobacco smoke travel through your body?

• • •

Mouth Using tobacco causes bad breath. Smokeless tobacco stains the users' teeth. It makes their gums and lips crack and bleed. It can lead to mouth cancer.

Throat Smoking causes coughing. It can cause throat cancer.

Heart Nicotine makes blood vessels shrink. The heart beats faster and harder. This can lead to heart disease.

Lungs Tar coats smokers' lungs. They have trouble getting enough air. Smokers may die from lung cancer or other lung diseases.

175

2 Teach

Learn from Pictures

Have students point to the picture of the person on page 174.

What kind of tobacco is this person using? How can you tell? The person is using chewing tobacco. The wad of tobacco shows as a bump in the cheek.

Human Body Connection

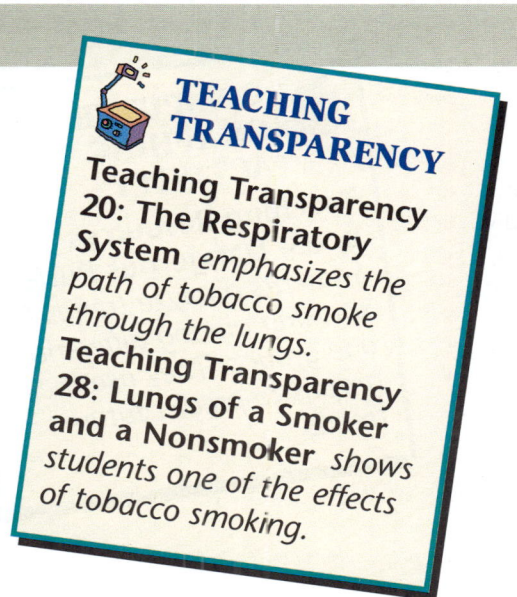

Your Lungs Point out to students the diagram of the lungs on pages 12 and 13. Have them trace with their fingers the path of the air into and out of the lungs. Then ask students to place their hands on the front lower parts of their rib cages. Point out how the lungs are protected by the bones that make up the rib cage. Instruct students to inhale as slowly and deeply as possible so they can feel how the lungs expand and contract as air enters and exits.

PROJECT CHECKUP

Make a Model (p. 171) Point out to students that the information on body parts that are affected by tobacco can help them complete part of their human body model project.

Health Background

Leading Cause of Death One of every five deaths in the United States has to do with smoking. The American Lung Association reports that smoking kills more people in this country every year than drug abuse, alcohol abuse, motor vehicle crashes, and intentional deaths combined. Most of these deaths are from cancers or lung diseases.

Smokeless Tobacco The use of smokeless tobacco, also called "moist snuff," is on the rise in the United States, while other forms of tobacco use are generally declining. Users "dip" out a "quid" of snuff from a bag or packet, put it in their mouths, and suck on the tobacco. Each quid contains the nicotine of two cigarettes, making snuff use more addictive than smoking.

TEACHING TRANSPARENCY

Teaching Transparency 20: The Respiratory System *emphasizes the path of tobacco smoke through the lungs.*
Teaching Transparency 28: Lungs of a Smoker and a Nonsmoker *shows students one of the effects of tobacco smoking.*

MEET INDIVIDUAL NEEDS

Kinesthetic Learners Allow students the opportunity to interpret the effects of tobacco on each body part, as described in the captions surrounding the body diagram, by acting out each of the descriptions.

Teach *continued*

Learn from Pictures

Help students describe what is taking place in the photo. Before having a volunteer read the caption, ask the following questions.

Who is smoking? the adults

What are they smoking? a pipe and a cigar

What is the girl doing? reading

Who is breathing the smoke? the girl and the adults

Discuss

Help students understand that the girl is not smoking, but she is endangered by the smoke.

Problem Solving If you were the girl in the picture, what would you say to the adults if you didn't want them to smoke near you? Discuss appropriate ways to call the smokers' attention to the dangers of ETS.

Life Skills Focus

Communicate Students may enjoy writing the poem as an acrostic, by listing each letter of "ENVIRONMENTAL TOBACCO SMOKE" vertically, and beginning each line with the letters, in order.

▲ This girl isn't smoking. But smoke from the pipe and cigar in the room is affecting her. The ETS harms her eyes, nose, throat, and lungs.

Communicate
Martha knows that tobacco can harm her body. She wants to write a poem to tell others about the dangers of tobacco. How can Martha use her communication skills to write this poem? Use the steps for communicating shown on page *xii*.

• • •

How is tobacco harmful to people who don't use it?

Have you ever been in a room with someone who was smoking? If so, you could probably see smoke in the air.

The smoke that fills a room when someone is smoking is called **environmental tobacco smoke** (in•vy•ruhn•MEN•tuhl tuh•BA•koh SMOHK), or *ETS*. Some ETS comes directly from burning cigarettes, pipes, or cigars. The rest is smoke that is breathed out by smokers.

176

Health Background

ETS Environmental tobacco smoke was classified by the Environmental Protection Agency as a Group A carcinogen, the category of the most dangerous cancer-causing agents in humans. More than 40 compounds in tobacco smoke are carcinogens, including tar, carbon monoxide, hydrogen cyanide, phenols, ammonia, formaldehyde, benzene, nitrosamine, and nicotine.

For more background, visit the **Webliography** on the Teacher Resources page at:
www.harcourtschool.com/health
Keyword tobacco

TEACHER TIP

Parents Who Smoke Keep in mind that some students may have family members who smoke, thus repeatedly exposing those students to ETS. Help prevent them from feeling singled out. Remind students that some children may not be able to completely avoid ETS if they live in a family of smokers. However, they may be able to help educate household members about the dangers of ETS, state how they feel about breathing smoke, and request that others refrain from smoking near them.

COMPUTER GRAPHING ACTIVITY

Teaching Resources p. 63, Dangerous Puffs Students analyze trends in smoking among different age groups. They use their graphs to predict future trends.

ETS carries poisons that can hurt people who breathe it—even if they don't smoke themselves. Some people live or work in places filled with ETS. These people may become ill more often than people who live and work in smoke-free places.

Adults and children who live in homes with ETS may get more colds, coughs, and sore throats than those who do not live with smokers. Nonsmokers who breathe ETS for many years may get the same diseases as smokers. They have a higher risk of getting lung diseases, heart diseases, and cancer than people who live or work in smoke-free places.

One way you can avoid ETS is to sit in the nonsmoking section of a restaurant. You can have an adult politely ask people sitting near you not to smoke. If necessary, leave a room where many people are smoking.

JOURNAL

Have you ever been in a room where ETS bothered you? In your Health Journal, write about ways other people's smoke has affected you. Tell what you might have done to solve the problem.

Cough! Cough! Please don't smoke!

Activity **Avoid ETS** Imagine you are in a place where people are smoking. Suggest ways you could protect your health from ETS. Tell what you might do or say. Be sure your suggestions are polite!

LESSON CHECKUP

Check Your Facts

1. List four products that have tobacco in them.
2. Name two substances in tobacco smoke that can harm you.
3. **CRITICAL THINKING** How can you be harmed by tobacco even if you don't smoke?

4. How does nicotine affect the heart of a tobacco user?

Set Health Goals

5. List three things you like to do that require a strong heart and lungs. How would smoking affect your ability to do these activities?

177

DRAMA

Handling ETS Give students the opportunity to locate information about environmental tobacco smoke. Then have them role-play situations in which they might encounter environmental tobacco smoke. Direct them to act out ways they might react to the situations.

Health Journal

Encourage students to write as if they were able to speak without fear of retaliation and directly to the person(s) involved, to say exactly how they felt about the smoke.

This feature is designed to provide students with an opportunity to reflect on health decisions in their personal lives. The journal should *not* be used to evaluate or assess students, nor should the results be shared among students.

Activity

Avoid ETS Possible answers: "I learned recently that tobacco smoke is very dangerous. Would you mind smoking outside?" "I'm sorry to bother you, but the smoke really makes my eyes, nose, and throat hurt. Would it be possible for you to smoke somewhere else?" Remind students to speak respectfully to others. Accept all reasonable answers.

3 Wrap Up

Lesson Checkup

1. Answers may include cigarettes, cigars, pipe tobacco, smokeless tobacco, or chewing tobacco.

2. nicotine and tar

3. Possible answer: ETS can cause heart diseases, lung diseases and cancer.

4. Possible answer: Nicotine causes the heart to beat faster, stressing the circulatory system, and sometimes causing heart disease.

5. Remind students to list activities they enjoy. Best answers will relate smoking to difficulty getting enough breath and straining the heart, thus decreasing enjoyment or performance levels.

OBJECTIVES

- Describe some effects of alcohol on specific body organs and on behavior.
- Identify safety risks associated with alcohol use.

PROGRAM RESOURCES

- Activity Book, p. 44
- Computer Graphing Activity, Teaching Resources p. 64
-  Teaching Transparency 18

VOCABULARY

- bloodstream (p. 178)
- alcoholism (p. 181)

Daily Safety Tip

Students may be confronted with situations in which they see friends or underage siblings using alcohol or tobacco. They can encourage the person to quit, but they also need to tell a responsible adult about the problem.

1 Motivate

Optional Materials chalk or 20-foot piece of yarn, string, or masking tape

Mark out a 20-foot line. Have students try to walk the line without losing their balance. Then engage them in a quick game of Simon Says to perform a few coordination exercises, such as "Touch your right index finger to your nose," "Touch your left hand to the top of your head."

Explain that when you are coordinated, you have balance and steadiness, and you can talk, think, and act clearly. Under the influence of alcohol, you lose these abilities, because alcohol affects the brain's control centers.

MAIN IDEA Any amount of alcohol is dangerous for young people.

WHY LEARN THIS? Knowing how dangerous alcohol is will help you refuse it.

VOCABULARY
- bloodstream
- alcoholism

How Alcohol Affects the Body

Drinking alcohol regularly can be harmful. An adult who drinks too much alcohol can have serious health problems. Alcohol is especially harmful to young people, because they are still growing.

What happens when a person drinks alcohol?

Most food you eat has to be digested. It takes several hours for food to travel through your digestive system. Chemicals there break food into nutrients. Nutrients move from your digestive system to your bloodstream. Your **bloodstream** is the blood flowing through your body. Look on pages 10–11 to see how your bloodstream carries nutrients to all parts of your body.

Alcohol doesn't need to be digested. It begins to enter the bloodstream as soon as it reaches the stomach and small intestine. Just minutes after a person drinks alcohol, the alcohol has traveled to all parts of the body.

Alcohol slows down the brain's ability to collect information. It also slows down the messages the brain sends to other parts of the body. After drinking alcohol, the user might find it hard to walk or speak. He or she cannot see clearly. Making decisions isn't easy. Paying attention or remembering things becomes hard, too.

Alcohol can even change the user's personality. Different people change in different ways. Some people get silly when they drink alcohol. Others feel sad. Still others become loud or angry.

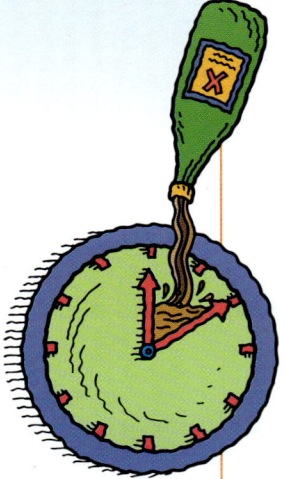

▲ Alcohol enters the bloodstream from the stomach and small intestine. Within a few minutes it reaches the brain and other parts of the body.

178

 MULTILEVEL ACTIVITIES

EASY Talk to Nondrinkers Have students talk with an adult who has chosen not to drink alcohol to find out what reasons that person has for his or her choice. Ask students to share what they learn with the class. **VERBAL**

AVERAGE Make Transparencies Have students make transparencies showing topics such as what happens when alcohol enters the body, how alcohol affects the body, why some people begin using alcohol, or what problems are experienced by problem drinkers. Students may include other concepts from the chapter. Allow students to share the transparencies with the rest of the class. **VISUAL/VERBAL**

ADVANCED Define FAS Mothers who drink alcohol when they are pregnant may have babies with fetal alcohol syndrome (FAS). Ask students to find out what FAS is and how it affects the baby. Have them prepare a short presentation for the rest of the class. **VISUAL/VERBAL**

Often people who drink too much feel sleepy. People who drink too much may also get dizzy. Sometimes the dizziness is so bad it makes them ill. They may still feel ill the next day. Many people get headaches after they drink. These headaches can last a few hours or a whole day.

Alcohol in the Body

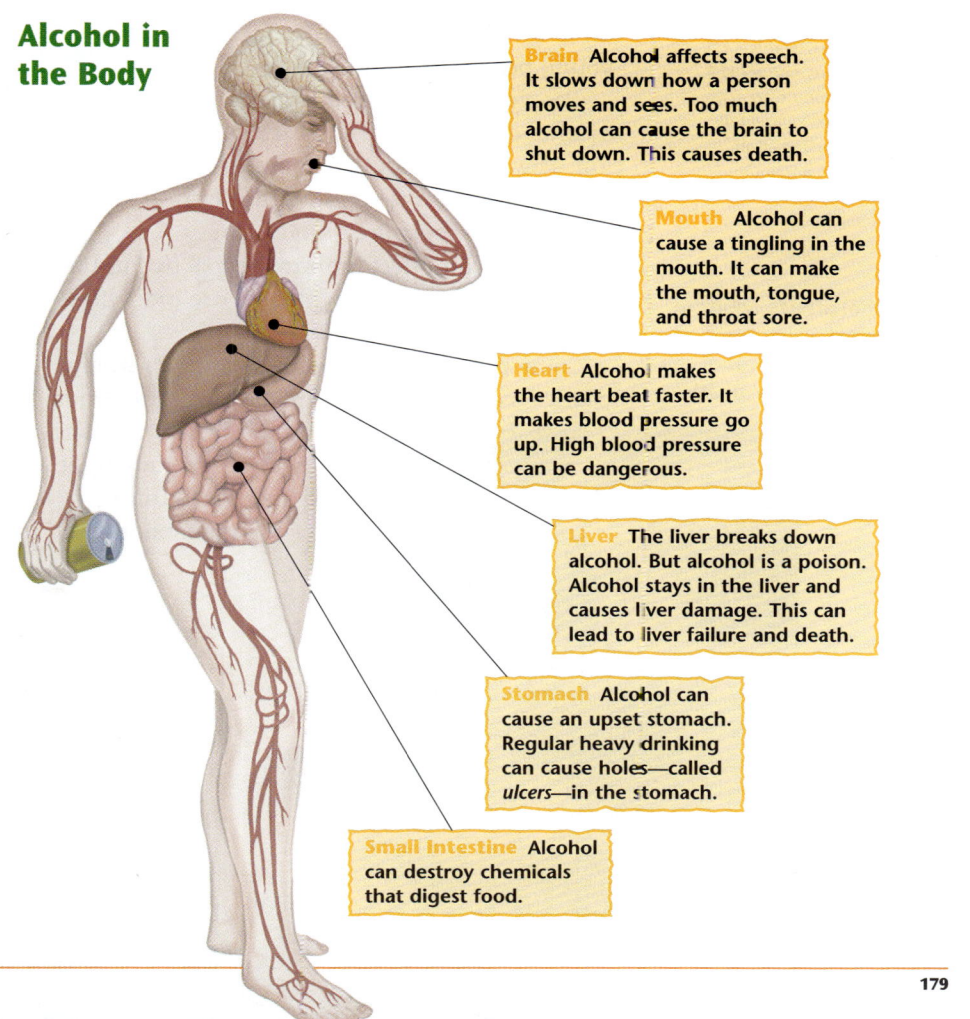

Brain Alcohol affects speech. It slows down how a person moves and sees. Too much alcohol can cause the brain to shut down. This causes death.

Mouth Alcohol can cause a tingling in the mouth. It can make the mouth, tongue, and throat sore.

Heart Alcohol makes the heart beat faster. It makes blood pressure go up. High blood pressure can be dangerous.

Liver The liver breaks down alcohol. But alcohol is a poison. Alcohol stays in the liver and causes liver damage. This can lead to liver failure and death.

Stomach Alcohol can cause an upset stomach. Regular heavy drinking can cause holes—called *ulcers*—in the stomach.

Small Intestine Alcohol can destroy chemicals that digest food.

179

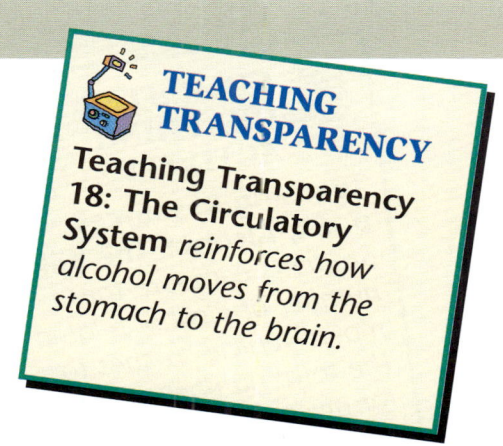

TEACHING TRANSPARENCY

Teaching Transparency 18: The Circulatory System *reinforces how alcohol moves from the stomach to the brain.*

2 Teach

Learn from Diagrams

Draw students' attention to the human body diagram. Have students point to and identify the brain, mouth, heart, liver, stomach, and small intestine. Before discussing the harmful effects of alcohol, you may wish to ask volunteers to recall the function of each organ from earlier study, or have students consult pages 1–15. Then invite volunteers to read the captions. Point out that the effects shown in the illustration are only some of the effects alcohol can cause in the body.

Critical Thinking If a person's stomach has food in it when the alcohol arrives, will alcohol still reach the bloodstream? Yes. It may be slowed by the food, but eventually all of the alcohol will reach the bloodstream.

Discuss

Point out that while some alcohol (about 20 percent) enters the bloodstream through the stomach, most of the alcohol (80 percent) will be absorbed through the small intestine. Meanwhile, the alcohol irritates the inside of the stomach as it passes through. Have students trace on the illustration the path of alcohol through the mouth, stomach, small intestine, and into the bloodstream.

Project Checkup

Make a Model (p. 171) Remind students that the information on how alcohol affects the body can help them complete their human body models. As an extension, suggest that students record details about the effects of alcohol on or near each organ or system. Point out that not only the diagram but also the text on these and the following pages can provide facts and details for their projects.

Teach *continued*

Learn from Pictures

Before reading the captions or text on these pages, ask volunteers to describe what is taking place in each picture on these pages. For each picture, ask "What do you think just happened?" Students may infer that alcohol can cause people to feel unhappy or angry or to like fighting, or it can cause crashes. Then have volunteers read the captions.

Discuss

After reading, have students discuss the ways that alcohol might have influenced each situation pictured. Help students relate each effect to the bodily effects described on pages 178–179.

Critical Thinking **Why do you think some people feel sad or angry after drinking alcohol?** Possible answer: Alcohol slows down the brain and keeps a person from thinking clearly.

Life Skills Focus

Communicate Some students might feel that if they talk to someone they would be tattling. Explain to students the difference between talking to trusted adults to receive help and tattling. Giving examples might be helpful.

For more information about what to do in situations with Alcohol, Tobacco, and Other Drugs, see page 280.

Communicate
Some people might have problems refusing alcohol. You might be concerned that a family member or close friend is having this type of problem. If this happens, use your communicating skills on page *xii* and talk to a trusted adult, such as a school counselor, about your feelings.

▼ Alcohol affects adults in different ways. Some of the effects of alcohol can lead to injury or death.

How is alcohol harmful?

Even a small amount of alcohol can be harmful—especially for young people. Alcohol prevents normal brain and body growth. That's one reason why it is against the law for young people to buy or drink alcohol. A young person will feel the effects of alcohol more quickly than an adult. No amount of alcohol is safe for a young person to drink.

People who drink even small amounts of alcohol are at risk for injuries. Sometimes they fall. They might run into things. Alcohol users who drive can cause crashes that hurt or kill themselves or people around them.

Alcohol can affect the way people act and treat others. People who drink alcohol are more likely to feel angry and cause fights.

Some people drink a lot of alcohol for many years. Over time heavy drinking can hurt almost every part of the body. Alcohol can kill brain cells, making it hard for the user to think clearly or to remember things.

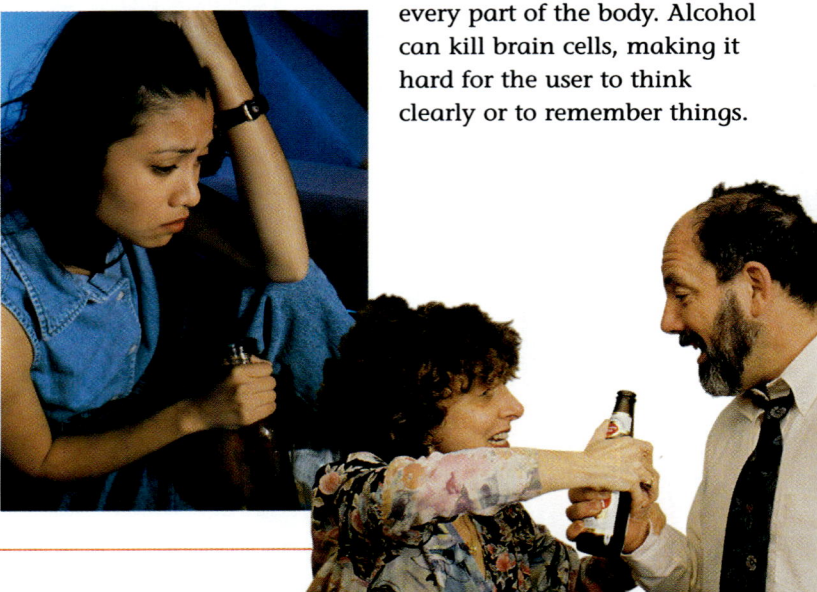

180

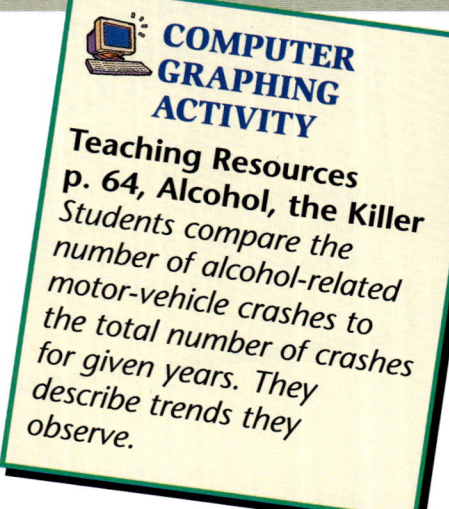

COMPUTER GRAPHING ACTIVITY
Teaching Resources p. 64, Alcohol, the Killer Students compare the number of alcohol-related motor-vehicle crashes to the total number of crashes for given years. They describe trends they observe.

The liver is an organ that is often damaged by alcohol. The liver removes poisons from the blood. It does other jobs as well. Alcohol can scar the liver. Then the liver can't clean the blood. The liver may stop working. This can cause death.

Finally, for some people, drinking alcohol can lead to a disease called **alcoholism** (AL•kuh•haw•lih•zuhm). Alcoholics, or people with alcoholism, can't stop using alcohol. They know alcohol causes problems for them and for people they care about. But they still need to drink it. If they don't, they become nervous and ill.

Myth: Alcoholics wear dirty clothing and drink in alleys.

Fact: Only about 6 out of 100 alcoholics in the United States are like this. Most alcoholics appear to live normal lives.

▼ **People who drink and then drive are responsible for many car crashes.**

LESSON CHECKUP

Check Your Facts

❶ Why is alcohol especially dangerous for young people?

❷ Why is drinking alcohol a safety risk?

❸ CRITICAL THINKING Why might a person who uses alcohol have trouble learning?

❹ List three organs that are affected by alcohol use.

Use Life Skills

❺ MANAGE STRESS Some adults drink alcohol because they don't know other ways to relax. List three healthful things you do to relax.

181

3 Wrap Up

Lesson Checkup

1. It affects the way the body and brain grow.

2. Alcohol can cause people to become violent, and its use increases the risk of car crashes.

3. Alcohol slows the ability of the brain to collect information.

4. Answers may include brain, mouth, heart, stomach, small intestine, or liver.

5. Remind students that when you do something to relax, it can be any activity you enjoy or do just for fun. It can also be a quiet activity that helps calm you, such as just before sleep. Accept all reasonable answers.

ACTIVITY BOOK, p. 44

Identify a Sequence | Reading Skills

How Alcohol Moves Through the Body
Read the following sentences about how alcohol moves through the body. The sentences are in the wrong order. Write the letters of the sentences in the correct order on the numbered lines. The first one is done for you.

a. The bloodstream picks up the rest of the alcohol from the small intestine.

b. In the stomach some of the alcohol passes into the bloodstream.

c. Most of the alcohol finally passes through the liver, where it may cause permanent scarring.

d. A very small amount of alcohol leaves the body through breath, sweat, and urine.

e. When a person swallows alcohol, it can cause a burning feeling in the mouth, throat, food tube, and stomach.

f. The blood carries the alcohol throughout the body, including the brain and heart.

g. Most of the alcohol leaves the stomach and enters the small intestine.

h. Alcohol in the brain and heart causes changes in a person's body and behavior.

1. e   5. f
2. b   6. h
3. g   7. d
4. a   8. c

TEACHER TIP

More Myths & Facts You might share this information with students.

• *Myth:* Drinking alcohol can warm you up.
Fact: Alcohol dilates blood vessels, so it can give a person a temporary feeling of warmth as more blood rushes toward the skin; however, this draws blood and therefore heat away from the internal organs, resulting in a cooling of the body. The risk of hypothermia increases when a person drinks alcohol.

OBJECTIVES

- Describe some laws regarding the sale, use, and packaging of alcohol and tobacco products.
- Explain reasons for refusing and demonstrate ways to refuse tobacco and alcohol.

PROGRAM RESOURCES

- Activity Book, pp. 45–46

Daily Safety Tip

The following are some warning signs of a drunk driver: wide turns; driving on the center line; weaving or zig-zagging; driving too slowly, too close to things, or off the road. Remind students that people shouldn't try to stop a drunk driver. Instead, they should call local law enforcement officers immediately and tell them the color and type of car, the license number, the street, and the direction the driver was headed.

1 Motivate

Optional Materials **clear glass or plastic container, dropper, clean water, small amount of milk**

Pour water into a clear container. Explain that the clean, clear water is like a person's blood when it is healthy and has no alcohol, nicotine, or other drugs or poisons in it—it is pure. Then use a dropper to add one drop of milk to the water. Explain that this is like taking a sip of alcohol, because the alcohol enters the blood quickly.

Is the blood still pure? How do you know? No; the water looks a little cloudy.

Continue adding drops of milk into the water, up to a dropperful or so. Elicit student observations as the purity of the "blood" becomes more contaminated. (As an alternative, describe this demonstration.)

MAIN IDEA
To stay safe from alcohol and tobacco, avoid places where people use these drugs. Plan ahead by thinking of ways to say *no*.

WHY LEARN THIS? Avoiding alcohol and tobacco is an important skill that will protect your health and safety.

Refusing to Use Alcohol and Tobacco

You may hear people say "Just say *no* to drugs!" Maybe you think it's not always that easy—especially when friends pressure you to smoke or drink. But saying *no* is important. That little word could save your life!

What are some laws about the use of alcohol and tobacco?

It is against the law for young people to buy or receive from others alcohol and tobacco. You must be at least 21 years old to buy alcohol. In most places you must be 18 years old or older to buy tobacco products. It is against the law for anyone your age to buy alcohol or tobacco.

Laws also protect people from the harmful effects of ETS. Most government buildings are smoke-free. Many other places, such as restaurants, have nonsmoking areas.

The government requires warning labels on alcohol and tobacco packaging that tell about the dangers of using these products. The government hopes warnings will help people avoid the dangers of these products.

◀ **You can choose many healthful drinks.**

 MULTILEVEL ACTIVITIES

EASY **Make a Collage** Have students write at the top of a sheet of poster board one of the steps for acting against peer pressure. Then they can add pictures of young people in group situations in which they would resist peer pressure. Students can use magazine photos, or they can draw their own pictures. **VISUAL**

AVERAGE **Draw Cartoons** Ask students to recall the steps they can take to resist peer pressure. Have students work with partners to draw cartoon strips in which they show themselves or imaginary characters using the steps to act against peer pressure. **VISUAL**

ADVANCED **Write a Script** Direct students to write short scripts in which a young person says *no* to an offer to use alcohol. Allow students to share their scripts by reading them aloud in small groups. Have students lead their groups in a discussion about why it might be difficult to resist peer pressure. **VERBAL/INTERPERSONAL**

How can you stay safe from alcohol and tobacco?

Many adults use more alcohol and tobacco than they really want to. Using these drugs has become a habit they can't quit. Understanding why people use these drugs can help you decide never to start using them.

Many people first try alcohol and tobacco when they are young. They think it will make them look grown up, but many adults don't use these drugs. You may be afraid to say *no* if your friends urge you to try them. To stay safe from alcohol and tobacco, stay away from places where people use them. Find friends who don't want to use these products.

Some people use alcohol and tobacco because ads make using alcohol and tobacco products look fun. The truth is that these products are dangerous.

LIFE SKILLS FOCUS

Refuse Bill and his friend, Lyle, find an open bottle of alcohol at Lyle's house. Lyle tells Bill he has heard it is fun to drink alcohol. Lyle wants to try the alcohol. He wants Bill to try it too. How can Bill use what he knows about alcohol to refuse to try it? Use the steps for refusing shown on page *xi*.

• • •

Career

Health Spokesperson

What They Do
Community health spokespersons get information about health-care groups. They tell the public about health information by sending it to newspapers and to TV and radio stations. They also hold events such as health fairs to make people aware of health-care information.

Education and Training
Some community health spokespersons earn college degrees in public relations or health education. Others start as journalists. Some train by getting jobs with public health departments.

183

What did this demonstration show? Even a small amount of alcohol in the blood affects its purity.

2 Teach

Life Skills Focus

Refuse You may wish either to have small groups role-play the Skills Focus scenario or to pose it as a class activity, having volunteers take turns playing the role of Bill.

Career

You may wish to invite a community health spokesperson to speak to the class on alcohol or tobacco. In addition to local health department or hospital personnel, you may contact one of these sources for more information.

- American Lung Association 1-212-315-8700
- MADD (Mothers Against Drunk Driving) 1-800-GET-MADD

Or visit the **Webliography** on the Teacher Resources page at:
www.harcourtschool.com/health
Keyword health careers

DEVELOP READING SKILLS

Identify the Main Ideas and Supporting Details Have students locate the section heading on page 182 "What are some laws about the use of alcohol and tobacco?" and have a volunteer read it aloud. Help students identify the two categories in this main idea. (laws about alcohol and laws about tobacco)

Copy on the board the chart below. Demonstrate how to turn the question into a heading for the chart. Then have volunteers locate details in the text to fill in under each category.

Laws About the Use of Alcohol and Tobacco	
Laws About Alcohol	Laws About Tobacco

Health Background

Bans on Smoking Laws protecting non-smokers have been passed in almost every state and in more than 560 local governments. Also all interstate bus travel and airline flights inside the United States are smoke-free by law.

Bans on Tobacco Advertising Many state and local governments have banned tobacco advertising in public transit vehicles, in stadiums, and on public property.

For more background, visit the **Webliography** on the Teacher Resources page at:
www.harcourtschool.com/health
Keyword tobacco

Discuss

Explain that the information on this page suggests some ideas for how to practice saying *no* when invited to use alcohol and tobacco. After students read the text, you might want to have students work in pairs or small groups to role-play each suggestion in the list.

Invite students to think up additional ways to say *no* and to share their ideas with the class.

Project Checkup

Make a Model (p. 171) Students should be working to finalize their human body models.

Consumer Focus

Analyze Advertising and Media Messages Some ads might use more than one trick. Discuss the ads' influences. Have volunteers read the refusal comments for the ad that they chose.

How can you say *no* to alcohol and tobacco?

It's important to decide ahead of time that you don't want to use alcohol and tobacco. Then you'll be ready if someone pressures you to try them.

skate   read   sing

Think of some ways you can say *no*. Here are ideas you might try.

CONSUMER
FOCUS

Analyze Advertising and Media Messages
Most ads use "tricks" to sell a product. Being able to identify these "tricks" could help you plan ways to refuse alcohol and tobacco. Find an alcohol or tobacco ad. Use page *xv* to figure out a "trick" being used in the ad. Then write a way to refuse the product the ad is trying to sell.

- Say *no*, and walk away. You don't have to explain why.
- Make a face. Say, "It doesn't taste good."
- Look surprised. Say, "That's against the law."
- Say, "It's against my family's rules."
- Say, "No, thanks." Then change the subject.
- Laugh and say, "I want to have fun, not hurt my body."
- Look at a clock. Say, "I have to get going."
- Say, "I can have fun without it."
- Say, "I need to be at my best for sports"— or for whatever activities you enjoy.

184

SOCIAL STUDIES

Smoke-Free Pledge Your students might want to sign pledges to be smoke-free for life or to write letters to local businesses or lawmakers to encourage smoke-free environments, the removal of cigarette vending machines, or a ban on tobacco advertising in public areas.

ACTIVITY BOOK, p. 45

My Reasons Not to Smoke   Critical Thinking

Read the paragraph. Then read the reasons that someone might use to start using tobacco. Write one or two sentences that give your reasons for not using tobacco. **Possible answers are shown.**

Most young people do not use tobacco. But some do start smoking or using smokeless tobacco. Someday you may need to choose whether or not to use tobacco. Choosing to use tobacco can cause harm to you and to others. Choosing to be tobacco-free helps protect you and others. Choosing to be tobacco-free sets a good example and helps others say *no*. If you are prepared to say *no* ahead of time, you can make wiser choices.

1. I want to know what smoking is like.
   I know that smoking is harmful. I have made up my mind not to try it.

2. I want to know what smokeless tobacco is like.
   Smokeless tobacco can cause addiction and diseases, so I will never use it.

3. I saw a cartoon character smoking in an advertisement.
   Advertisers don't fool me. I know that tobacco is dangerous, and I will always be tobacco-free.

4. My parents use tobacco.
   My parents might be addicted. I don't want to be addicted to nicotine. I don't want to get cancer.

5. I will seem more grown-up if I use tobacco.
   Being grown-up means making smart choices. Using tobacco is not a smart choice because it does harm.

Practice with your family ways to say *no*. Or practice with a friend who has also decided not to use alcohol or tobacco. Try out different ways. Choose the ways you are most comfortable with. When the time comes to say *no*, one of them is sure to feel right. Remember, when you say *no*, you might be saving your health—or your life!

Activity **Say *Yes* to Good Health** When you say *no* to alcohol and tobacco, you can say *yes* to the many activities you enjoy. Without alcohol or nicotine your mind and body work at their best. What activities would you like to say *yes* to? List five things you like to do. Then list ways in which using alcohol or tobacco could affect these activities.

LESSON CHECKUP

Check Your Facts

1. What are two laws about alcohol and tobacco?
2. How can you avoid people who want you to use alcohol and tobacco?
3. CRITICAL THINKING Why is it important to say *no* to alcohol and tobacco?

Use Life Skills

4. REFUSE Think of a time when you refused to do something a friend wanted you to do. How did you say *no*? What did you think about when you said it? How was that situation like saying *no* to alcohol and tobacco?

185

 SCIENCE

Animal Peer Pressure Animals react to the actions of other animals in ways that are similar to the ways humans react to peer pressure. Tell students that lemmings (small Arctic rodents) follow each other over cliffs to their deaths. Sheep are also known for "following the leader." Have students think of sayings they may have heard that relate to these animal behaviors. (Students may need to ask adult family members about these sayings.)

Learn from Pictures

Have students describe what the children in the pictures are doing. Explain that the pictures show activities that the children in the pictures have said *yes* to; that is, what they choose to do instead of using tobacco or alcohol.

Activity

Say *Yes* to Good Health Invite volunteers to name at least five activities that they would like to say *yes* to. Discuss how the activities can help students stay away from alcohol and tobacco use.

3 Wrap Up

Lesson Checkup

1. Possible answers: It's against the law for anyone to drive after drinking more than a small amount of alcohol; it's against the law for young people to buy or use alcohol or tobacco; companies that sell tobacco and alcohol have to put warning labels on these products.

2. Possible answers: Stay away from places where young people use these products; find friends who don't use them.

3. Answers may include: They are illegal; they are dangerous to health and safety; it is easier not to start using them than to try to quit.

4. Experiences will vary. Best answers will respond to all three questions and may point out that saying *no* was like practice for saying *no* to tobacco or alcohol or that it required going against a friend's wishes.

LIFE SKILLS

OBJECTIVES

- Identify skills for refusals.
- Use refusal skills to say *no* to alcohol and tobacco.

PROGRAM RESOURCES

- Activity Book, p. 47

1 Motivate

Optional Materials **handful of thumb tacks**

Tell students to imagine that a friend has asked them to eat a handful of thumb tacks. Ask for a show of hands of students who would eat the tacks. **Why would you not eat the tacks?** Possible answers: they would harm your mouth and digestive system; they would taste bad; it would be stupid to eat the tacks. **What would you say to your friend who asked you to eat the tacks?** that it would be stupid to eat the tacks because they wouldn't taste good and they would harm you **Would you feel embarrassed or bad about telling your friend you would not eat the tacks? Why, or why not?** No; because there is no reason to feel embarrassed or bad about refusing to do something you don't want to do or something you know will harm you.

2 Teach

Step 1

Remind students that tobacco and alcohol are illegal for young people to use. These substances also are unhealthful.

Step 2

Review some of the reasons students gave for refusing to eat the thumb tacks. Then have them brainstorm additional reasons to refuse tobacco and alcohol.

REFUSE ALCOHOL and Tobacco

What will you do if someone asks you to use alcohol or tobacco? Practice learning how to say *no*. Then you'll be ready to refuse to use these drugs.

Learn This Skill

Amy is at Pam's house. Pam's big sister smokes cigarettes. Pam thinks it looks cool. She wants Amy to try it with her. How can Amy say *no*?

Say, "It's against the law."

"This is against the law," Amy tells Pam, "and it's bad for us!"

Say, "I don't want to get into trouble or get sick."

"It won't hurt us," says Pam. "We'll be in big trouble if we get caught," Amy says. "We could get really sick."

TEACHER TIP

Positive Peer Pressure Tell students that peer pressure can be negative, involving situations that are harmful, dangerous, or illegal. It can also be positive– for example, one student might encourage another to volunteer for a service project, learn the rules of a game, or refuse harmful substances. Have students brainstorm ways they could influence their peers in positive ways. Then have them role play situations in which they could use those skills.

Suggest something else to do.

"Why don't you come outside with me to skate?" Amy asks.

Walk away.

"Just try one," Pam says. "I am not going to try cigarettes," Amy says. "I'm going skating."

Practice This Skill

Use these ideas to help you solve the problems.

Ways to Refuse

- Say, "It's against the law."
- Say, "I don't want to get into trouble or get sick."
- Suggest something else to do.
- Walk away.

A. Derrel's friends say that the tobacco some baseball players chew doesn't hurt the lungs. Help Derrel use refusal skills to end this discussion.

B. Cheryl's friends want to go to a park to play. Cheryl knows that people who use drugs hang out there. How could Cheryl say she doesn't want to go?

187

Step 3

Critical Thinking Why is it a good idea to suggest another activity? Possible answers: to switch the focus away from using tobacco or alcohol, to give the other person a chance not to use tobacco or alcohol, to give you a place to go or a reason to leave if your friend still insists on using tobacco or alcohol.

Step 4

Critical Thinking Why is it important to walk away? Possible answers: to get away from a situation that might get you in trouble, to show you mean what you are saying and do not intend to use tobacco or alcohol, to get you away from someone who might start calling you names or trying to make you feel bad about your decision.

3 Wrap Up

A. Students should suggest a variety of things Derrel could say, such as "Chewing tobacco can make you sick. It can really harm your mouth." He also can just walk away from the discussion.

B. Students should suggest an effective refusal for Cheryl, such as "I don't want to be near people who use drugs." She can also suggest an alternative activity.

ACTIVITY BOOK, p. 47

**Refuse** | Life Skills

Tyler and Madison are at Robin's house after school. No one else is home. They find an opened pack of cigarettes on the coffee table where Robin's dad left them. Madison and Robin want to try one to see what it is like to smoke. Tyler knows that smoking is harmful to one's health and that it is addictive. Help Tyler brainstorm some ideas that will make using refusal skills easier. **Possible answers are shown.**

1. Make a list of five reasons showing why smoking is not a good idea. **It is bad for your lungs, it is addictive, it is bad for your heart, it gives you bad breath, it is illegal for people under eighteen, it is against my family rules.**

2. Make a list of five activities Tyler could suggest to do instead of smoking. **ride a bike, go in-line skating, watch TV, do homework, play a computer game**

3. Think of three things that Tyler could say as he walks away from the friends who are smoking. **I'm not going to smoke. I'm leaving now. I don't want to smoke; I'd rather watch TV.**

4. Which of these strategies would you use if you were in this situation? Explain. **Accept all reasonable answers.**

**ART**

Refusals Comic Strips Have students make comic strips showing the different ways to refuse. They can make original characters or cut characters out of the newspaper comic pages. Emphasize the importance of dialogue and body language for this skill. Allow students to share their comics in small groups or in a bulletin board display.

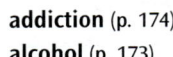

Use Vocabulary 5 pts. each

1. addiction
2. Alcoholism
3. Nicotine
4. alcohol
5. environmental tobacco smoke
6. Tar
7. chewing tobacco
8. bloodstream
9. Smokeless tobacco
10. cancer

Check Your Facts 5 pts. each

11. Students should choose any three of the organs shown on page 179 and describe the effects listed there.

12. Possible answers: Nicotine is an addictive poison that harms the body of a tobacco user. It makes the blood vessels shrink, causing the heart to beat faster. This can lead to heart disease.

13. ETS carries poisons that can hurt people who breathe it and can cause lung diseases, heart diseases, and cancer in a nonsmoker. It also might increase the number of colds, coughs, and sore throats in nonsmokers.

14. Alcohol and tobacco are illegal for young people to use.

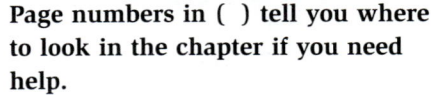

USE VOCABULARY

addiction (p. 174)
alcohol (p. 173)
alcoholism (p. 181)
bloodstream (p. 178)
cancer (p. 175)
chewing tobacco (p. 174)
environmental tobacco smoke (p. 176)
nicotine (p. 173)
smokeless tobacco (p. 174)
tar (p. 175)

Use the terms above to complete the sentences. Page numbers in ( ) tell you where to look in the chapter if you need help.

1. It is hard to quit using tobacco because the nicotine in tobacco causes ____.

2. ____ is a disease in which people "need" alcohol.

3. ____ is a poisonous substance found in all tobacco products.

4. The drug ____ is found in beverages such as beer, wine, and whiskey.

5. The smoke in the air that comes from burning cigarettes is ____.

6. ____ is a dark, sticky substance that coats the lungs of smokers.

7. People who put moist tobacco in their mouths are using ____.

8. Alcohol is carried through the ____ to the brain and the heart.

9. ____ is a dry, powdered form of tobacco that is held between the cheek and gum.

10. A disease that makes cells grow wildly is ____.

CHECK YOUR FACTS

Page numbers in ( ) tell you where to look in the chapter if you need help.

11. Using the diagram, choose three organs that are affected by alcohol and describe the effects. (p. 179)

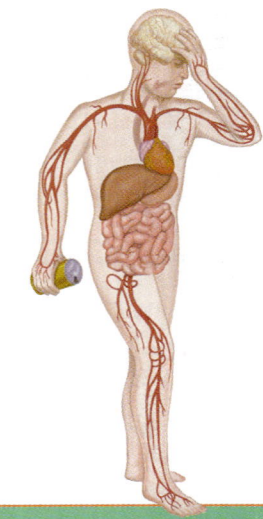

12. How is nicotine harmful to the body? (pp. 173, 175)

13. How does ETS affect nonsmokers? (pp. 176–177)

14. What law about alcohol and tobacco is the most important for young people? (p. 182)

THINK CRITICALLY

15. You hear someone say, "People who don't like alcohol and tobacco shouldn't use them. But they shouldn't try to stop others from using them." Do you agree or not? Explain why.

16. Why do you think advertisers make ads for alcohol and tobacco that show people using these products while having fun?

APPLY LIFE SKILLS

17. **Refuse** A good friend of yours is excited. She has met some older students she really likes. She wants you to go to the mall with her to meet these older students. You go, but as you get near the mall entrance, you see that they are smoking. What would you do?

18. **Communicate** You're at a friend's house after school one day. Your friend's parents aren't home, and your friend says, "Want to try something?" He goes into the refrigerator and takes out a beer. He tells you, "Drink it. It will make you feel great." What would you say?

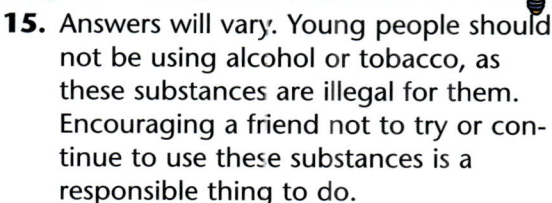

Promote Health *Home and Community*

1. Is there a place your family goes to, such as a favorite restaurant, that has environmental tobacco smoke? Discuss ETS with your family. Think of ways your family can avoid ETS there and at other places.

2. A federal law says alcohol can not be sold to anyone under 21 years old. However, states, towns, and counties can have other laws about selling and using alcohol. Make a poster showing local alcohol laws. Display the poster someplace where people in your community can see it.

189

Think Critically 6 pts. each

15. Answers will vary. Young people should not be using alcohol or tobacco, as these substances are illegal for them. Encouraging a friend not to try or continue to use these substances is a responsible thing to do.

16. Answers will vary. Advertisers want people to purchase their products. They try to make them as appealing as possible so that people will purchase them.

Apply Life Skills 9 pts. each

17. Answers will vary. Students should pick a strategy as outlined in Life Skills. Suggesting not meeting the students or calling a trusted adult to pick them up would be two options.

18. Answers will vary. Students should pick a strategy as outlined in Life Skills. Saying *no*, reminding the friend of consequences, walking away, or suggesting other things to do are possibilities.

PERFORMANCE ASSESSMENT

Project—Make a Model

The chapter project (introduced on page 171) can be used for individual or team performance assessment. Allow students the opportunity to revise and complete their projects before submitting them for evaluation. Students can use the Project Summary Sheet (Assessment Guide, p. 17) to tell about their projects. You can use the rubric provided on the Project Evaluation Sheet (Assessment Guide, p. 45) to evaluate student performance.

Activities

Conduct an Interview

At Home • With your family's permission, talk with some people who use tobacco. Ask them how and when they started using tobacco. Ask whether they would like to change the way they use it. Ask them what advice they would offer to someone your age who wants to try tobacco.

Please Don't Smoke

With a Partner • Find out school rules about using alcohol and tobacco. Make a poster for each rule. Display your posters.

Have a Heart

On Your Own • Cut a large heart shape from construction paper. Use it to record all the activities you do in a day. At the end of the day, list the ways your heart helped you. Write what you have learned about decisions you can make that will help keep your heart healthy.

Body Parts Skit

With a Team • Put on a body parts skit. Have people in the skit play different body parts. Each character can explain how alcohol and tobacco affect the body part.

190

Chapter Test

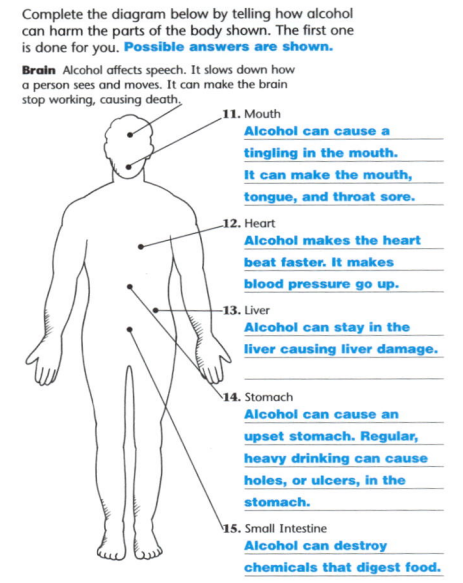

Multiple Choice

Choose the letter of the correct answer.

1. Nicotine is found in _____ products.
   a. tar
   b. alcohol
   c. tobacco
   d. drug

2. Nonsmokers can get ill by breathing _____.
   a. ETS
   b. nicotine
   c. alcohol
   d. oxygen

3. Alcohol makes the brain _____.
   a. more alert
   b. slow down
   c. speed up
   d. bigger

4. Alcoholism is _____.
   a. a disease
   b. a drug
   c. fear of drinking
   d. dislike of alcohol

5. If offered tobacco, _____.
   a. pretend to smoke, but don't
   b. give it a try
   c. impress people with how much you can smoke
   d. say *no* and leave

Modified True or False

Write *true* or *false*. If a sentence is false, replace the underlined term to make the sentence true.

6. Nicotine and alcohol are both <u>drugs</u>.

7. Nicotine causes <u>addiction</u>.

8. ETS affects <u>nonsmokers</u>.

9. Alcohol reaches the heart through the <u>bloodstream</u>.

10. A person's ability to speak and walk are affected by <u>tobacco</u> products.

11. The <u>liver</u> can be scarred by alcohol.

12. <u>A small</u> amount of alcohol is safe for adults to drink.

13. It is harder to <u>keep</u> using alcohol and tobacco than it is to never start at all.

Short Answer

Write a complete sentence to answer each question.

14. What are three tobacco products?

15. What are some health risks caused by smokeless and chewing tobacco?

16. How does alcohol affect the actions of people who drink it?

17. Why can even small amounts of alcohol be harmful to young people?

18. Why is it against the law for people to drive after they drink more than a small amount of alcohol?

Writing in Health

Write paragraphs to answer each item.

19. Explain why using tobacco in ANY form is harmful.

20. Explain why young people who refuse to use drugs are more grown up than those who use them.

191

Two options are provided for Chapter Tests—the in-book test and the reproducible test in the Assessment Guide. In addition to providing students with the opportunity to show what they have learned, both tests provide practice in taking standardized tests.

Multiple Choice (3 pts. each)

1. c
3. b
5. d
2. a
4. a

Modified True or False (4 pts. each)

6. true
7. true
8. true
9. true
10. false; alcohol
11. true
12. true
13. false; stop

Short Answer (7 pts. each)

Sample answers are shown; accept other reasonable answers.

14. cigarettes, chewing tobacco, smokeless tobacco

15. bleeding gums and lips, mouth cancer

16. Alcohol slows down how a person moves and sees. It affects speech. It may cause the brain to shut down, causing death.

17. Alcohol prevents normal brain and body growth; a young person will feel the effects of alcohol more quickly than an adult.

18. Alcohol slows down the brain. This can cause people who drink and drive to have car crashes.

Writing in Health (9 pts. each)

Sample answers are shown; accept other reasonable answers.

19. Tobacco contains many chemicals that can harm the body. In any form it is addictive and can cause cancer and heart diseases.

20. Refusing to use alcohol and tobacco shows that you have taken responsibility for your own actions. You have enough self-respect to know what you want to do and to follow family rules.

Keeping Safe

Chapter Organizer

Lesson	Objectives	Vocabulary	Program Resources
Introduce the Chapter pp. 192–193	• Preview the chapter. • Begin chapter project.		• School-Home Connection, TR p. 47 • Assessment Guide, p. 49 • Read-Aloud Anthology, p. RA-9 • Teaching Transparency 8— Graphic Organizer
Lesson 1 **Being Responsible for Your Safety** pp. 194–197 *Pacing: 1 class period* ✓ 1•3•7	• Recognize that there are people who are responsible for keeping children safe. • Practice safety rules on the way to and from school and at school.	safety rules injury hazard limit passenger	• Activity Book, p. 48
Lesson 2 **Safety Around Strangers and Bullies** pp. 198–201 *Pacing: 2 class periods* ✓ 3•5•7	• Describe how to stay safe around strangers. • Explain how to avoid conflicts and get along with bullies.	stranger trusted adult bully	• Activity Book, p. 49
Life Skills **Resolve Conflicts** pp. 202–203 *Pacing: 1 class period* ✓ 3•5	• Identify steps to resolve conflicts. • Use negotiation to handle conflicts with friends.		• Activity Book, p. 50
Lesson 3 **Safety at Home—Fire, Electricity, and Poisons** pp. 204–207 *Pacing: 2 class periods* ✓ 3•7	• Make a home fire escape plan. • Describe how to safely escape a home fire. • List safety rules for using electricity and household products.	emergency poison	• Activity Book, p. 51 • Teaching Transparency 26 • Computer Graphing Activity, TR p. 65
Lesson 4 **Safety for Sports and Bicycling** pp. 208–211 *Pacing: 2 class periods* ✓ 3•7	• Identify safety gear. • Explain safety rules for bicycling. • Know what features to look for when purchasing a helmet.	safety gear mouth guard	• HEALTH VIDEO: The Good Health Game Show • Teaching Transparency 27
Life Skills **Make Decisions** pp. 212–213 *Pacing: 1 class period* ✓ 3•6•7	• Identify steps to make decisions. • Use decision-making steps to stay safe.		• Activity Book, p. 52 • HEALTH VIDEO: International Food Fare
Lesson 5 **Getting Help and Giving First Aid** pp. 214–215 *Pacing: 1 class period* ✓ 1•3	• Learn how to get emergency assistance when someone has been injured or accidentally poisoned. • Describe first aid for cuts, scrapes, insect bites, and stings.	first aid	• Activity Book, p. 53
Chapter Review and Test pp. 216–219 ✓ 1•7	• Assess chapter objectives and project. • Provide extension activities.		• Assessment Guide, pp. 46–49

 National Health Education Standards
A complete list of the Standards is provided on the next page.

Key: TR = Teaching Resources

National Health Education Standards

1. Comprehend concepts related to health promotion and disease prevention.
2. Access valid health information and health-promoting products and services.
3. Practice health-enhancing behaviors and reduce health risks.
4. Analyze the influence of culture, media, technology, and other factors on health.
5. Use interpersonal communication skills to enhance health.
6. Use goal-setting and decision-making skills to enhance health.
7. Advocate for personal, family, and community health.

Science
- Brain Protection, p. 210

Art and Drama
- Safety First Drama, p. 192C
- Sports Catalog, p. 192C
- Playground Cartoons, p. 202

Curriculum Integration

Use these topics to integrate health into your daily planning.

Physical Education
- Protective Sports Equipment, p. 212

Social Studies
- Stormy Weather Warning Posters, p. 192C

Math
- To Follow or Not to Follow Safety Rules, p. 196
- Compare Helmet Costs, p. 211

Language Arts
- Letter to the Editor, p. 192C
- Clever Sayings, p. 206
- Safety Announcements, p. 210
- First-Aid Book, p. 215

ASSESSMENT OPTIONS

Portfolio Assessment
Have students select their best work from the following suggestions:
- **Letter to the Editor,** p. 192C
- **A Safer Bicycle,** p. 218
- **Know the Rules,** p. 218

Student Self-Assessment
- **Journal Notes,** p. 197
- **Set Health Goals,** pp. 207, 211, 215
- **Use Life Skills,** pp. 197, 201

Daily Assessment
- **Check Your Facts,** pp. 197, 201, 207, 211, 215

Performance Assessment
- **Chapter Project,** Safety Collage, pp. 193, 207, 217
- **Project Evaluation Sheet,** Assessment Guide, p. 49

Formal Assessment
- **Chapter Review,** pp. 216–217
- **In-Book Test,** p. 219
- **Chapter Test,** Assessment Guide, pp. 46–48

Cross-Curricular Activities

 ### Drama

Safety First Drama
Have students write a play for younger students that dramatizes choices students have to make to stay safe.

- As a class, brainstorm a list of emergency situations that students may find themselves in if they ignore safety rules at home, at school, at play, in vehicles, while playing sports, and when bicycling.

- Assign teams to one of the situations discussed. Have each team write a scene that shows what could happen if safety rules are ignored and what usually happens when safety rules are followed.

- Have students rehearse and perform their play for younger students in the school and community.

 ### Social Studies

Stormy Weather Warning Posters
- Ask partners to research different types of weather emergencies that are common to the region, such as hurricanes, lightning storms, tornadoes, and blizzards.

- Have students find out how to prepare for one of these storms and how to stay safe during and after the storm.

- Invite students to make posters that illustrate and explain what to do to stay safe in case of a weather emergency.

 ### Art

Sports Catalog
Suggest students work together to design a line of bright, colorful sports equipment to include in a sports catalog aimed at people their age.

- Brainstorm a list of equipment to include in the catalog, such as mouth guards, helmets, shin guards, face guards, gloves, and shoes.

- Organize the students into groups and assign each group a piece of safety gear. Have group members decide on a unique design for their product.

- Ask each group to make a catalog page advertising their product. Each page should include a colorful illustration of the product, a description of its safety features, and a price.

- Assemble the pages into a catalog and have students work together to name the catalog and design a cover.

 ### Language Arts

Letter to the Editor
Discuss safety hazards in the community that put young people at risk, such as a neglected playground site that attracts bullies and gangs, a bicycle path with bumpy pavement and potholes, or a busy intersection that has no traffic light or stop sign. Have students choose a topic and write a letter to the editor of the local paper that explains the problem and suggests a solution. If necessary, review correct letter and envelope format with students and mail the letters to the paper.

 ### Bulletin Board

Place the drawing of a child in the center of the bulletin board beneath the heading *Safe Kids Think Safety First.* (As an alternative, you could place photographs of students in the center of the board.) Add thought balloons labeled *At Home; On Bikes; In Sports; In an Emergency; Around Bullies and Strangers*

- Organize students into five groups. Assign each group a safety topic.

- The groups should work together to illustrate with drawings or words how children can follow safety rules to stay safe in each situation.

- Have groups use string or yarn to connect the ideas illustrated in their thought balloons to the picture of the child (or children).

Resources

Books for Students

Rathmann, Peggy. **Officer Buckle and Gloria.** Putnam's Sons, 1995. Caldecott Medal book describes Officer Buckle's attempts to provide safety education to students. Filled with safety tips and illustrated with Gloria's antics. **EASY**

Schulson, Rachel Ellenberg. **Guns: What You Should Know.** Albert Whitman and Company, 1999. Colorful drawings warn of the danger of guns and of playing with them. **AVERAGE**

Girard, Linda Walvoord. **Who Is a Stranger and What Should I Do?** Concept Books, 1993. Explains how to deal with strangers in public places, on the telephone, at home, and in cars. **ADVANCED**

Books for Teachers and Families

Jones, Craig. **Pet First Aid for Kids!** Rescue Critters LLC, 2000. An indispensable reference that encourages both child and adult to learn pet first-aid skills together.

Flegel, Melinda J. **Sport First Aid.** Human Kinetics Publications, 1996. A helpful reference for anyone working with kids and sports.

Videos

Bully Dance. Bullfrog Films, 2000. (10 minutes) This ALA video is a non-verbal film containing a strong message about bullies.

Bicycle Safety: Zone of Danger. Altschul Group, 1994 (14 minutes) A talking bicycle and a delivery girl teach bicycle safety by showing kids unsafe and safe actions.

Water Safety for Kids. Swim Safe Fundamentals, 1994. (15 minutes) This video provides water safety rules that are understandable to students.

Health Video Series by Harcourt
The Good Health Game Show
International Food Fare
These videos are referenced at point-of-use in this Teacher's Edition.

Your Health Webliography

The **Webliography** provides links to the Health Background and teaching resources that will support you as you teach the topics in *Your Health.* Simply choose a keyword and you will be taken to a page of links with descriptions of the content you can obtain at each site. The **Webliography** is located on the Teacher Resources page at **www.harcourtschool.com/health** Please review websites before referring your students to them.

Organizations and Agencies

California Department of Boating and Waterways
Education Unit
2000 Evergreen Street, Suite 100
Sacramento, CA 95815
888-326-2822
Provides tips on water rescues and water safety as well as lesson plans and situational stories for teachers.

National Highway Traffic Safety Administration
400 Seventh Street, SW
Room 5119
Washington, D.C. 20590
Distributes a leaflet presenting tips for safe bicycle riding.

National Rifle Association
11250 Waples Mill Road
Fairfax, VA 22030
800-231-0752
Promotes gun safety.

For more information about health organizations and agencies, please see the *Teaching Resources* book.

Community Health

Missing Children Officer Invite a representative of the police department's missing children's bureau to talk about the importance of following safety rules around strangers. Ask the guest to discuss methods strangers use to lure children away from neighborhoods and homeland to suggest ways students should respond to these tactics.

Free and Inexpensive Material

Air Bag Safety Campaign
National Safety Council
1019 19th Street, NW
Suite 401
Washington, D.C. 20036-5101
202-625-2570
Provides free information about air bag safety.

School Age Child Care Project
Center for Research on Women
Wellesley College
106 Central Street
Wellesley, MA 02481
Offers safety tips for children who come from school to empty homes.

Note that information, while correct at time of publication, is subject to change.

Visit **The Harcourt Learning Site** for related links, activities, resources, and the health **Webliography**.

www.harcourtschool.com

CHAPTER 8

Pages 192–219

"In fact, many injuries are not 'accidents,' or random, uncontrollable acts of fate; rather, most injuries are predictable and preventable."

—*Healthy People 2010*

CHAPTER SUMMARY

In this chapter students
- learn how to take responsibility for their own safety at home, in school, in vehicles, and at play.
- learn safety rules about strangers and bullies.
- learn how to get help in emergency situations and how to give first aid.

LIFE SKILLS Students practice resolving conflicts using negotiation and making decisions with safety in mind.

CONSUMER HEALTH Students learn important safety features of a safety helmet.

 **HUMAN BODY** Students study the human respiratory system to determine what parts of the body are affected when smoke from a fire is inhaled.

Literature Springboard

Use the poem *I Need My Knees* to spark interest in the chapter topic. See the Read-Aloud Anthology on page RA-9 of this Teacher's Edition.

192

School-Home Connection

Distribute copies of the School-Home Connection (in English or Spanish), TR page 47. Have students take the page home to share with their families as you begin this chapter.

Follow Up Have volunteers share the information they found about hazards in their homes with the class. Have them discuss ways to reduce the hazards.

Alternative Use the School-Home Connection page as a classroom resource for enrichment activities.

TEACHING RESOURCES, p. 47

Dear Family Member,

In Chapter 8, Keeping Safe, our class will be learning how to stay safe—at home, at school, in the car, and in the neighborhood. We will learn that distinguishing between a stranger and a trusted adult is an important part of staying safe. We will also learn about home health hazards, such as fire and poison, as well as the usefulness of safety gear during sports and when biking. Finally, the chapter provides some first-aid strategies.

Family Activity:

Home hazards are a major cause of injury. Work with your child to survey your home for hazards. Help your child record in the chart below any hazards you find. Talk about the hazards that can be easily remedied, such as toys on stairs or dangerous items within the reach of small children.

Hazards in My Home

Fire and Electric Hazards	Poison Hazards	Other Hazards

Family Reading:

The following books can help you and your family learn more about the topics covered in this chapter. Books should always be chosen with the approval of an adult family member.
- Rathmann, Peggy. *Officer Buckle and Gloria*. Putnam's Sons, 1995. This Caldecott Medal award-winner describes Officer Buckle's attempts to provide safety education to students. Filled with safety tips and illustrated with Gloria's antics. EASY
- Schulson, Rachel Ellenberg. *Guns: What You Should Know*. Albert Whitman & Company, 1999. Colorful drawings warn of the danger of guns and of playing with them. AVERAGE
- Girard, Linda Walvoord. *Who Is a Stranger and What Should I Do?* Concept Books, 1993. Explains how to deal with strangers in public places, on the telephone, at home, and in cars. ADVANCED

Thank you for participating in our study of health.

Sincerely,

Keeping Safe

SAFETY COLLAGE As you read through this chapter, you will learn tips to help keep you safe at home, at school, and at play. Make a collage showing ways to stay safe. You can use photos, draw pictures, or cut out pictures from magazines.

For other activities, visit the Harcourt Learning Site.
www.harcourtschool.com

193

Introduce the Chapter

Project

SAFETY COLLAGE

Access Prior Knowledge Use this activity as a baseline assessment of students' understanding of injury prevention and first aid.

Performance Assessment The project can be used for performance assessment. Before students begin the project, explain how you will evaluate their performance. (See the Project Evaluation Sheet, Assessment Guide, p. 49.)

Prereading Strategies

Scan the Chapter Have students preview the chapter by scanning the titles, headings, pictures, and charts. Ask volunteers to speculate on what new information they will learn.

Preview Vocabulary As students scan the chapter, point out the vocabulary words listed at the beginning of each lesson. Invite students to make up a riddle card for each word with a riddle on one side of a card and the word *answer* on the other. An example is, "Watch out. This means danger ahead." hazard Partners can take turns reading a riddle and trying to guess the word.

Visualize Key Concepts Display the Graphic Organizer Transparency. You may also wish to distribute photocopies to students. Have students complete the organizer as they work through the chapter. Suggested concepts for students to fill in are shown.

Follow Up Review the completed organizer with students as preparation for the Chapter Review and Chapter Tests.

Teaching Transparency 8—Graphic Organizer

8   Chapter 8   Graphic Organizer

Keeping Safe

Being Responsible for Your Safety
1. Safety ___rules___ help protect you from ___injury___.
2. A ___hazard___ is a danger.

Safety at Home
1. Make an ___escape___ plan and ___practice___ fire drills.
2. A ___poison___ causes illness or death.

Safety for Sports and Bicycling
1. Safety ___gear___ protects players from injury.
2. Mouth ___guards___ protect teeth.

Safety Around Strangers and Bullies
1. Be careful around ___strangers___.
2. If you need help look for a ___trusted adult___.

Getting Help and Giving First Aid
1. Dial ___911___ for emergencies.
2. Use ___first aid___ for small injuries.

OBJECTIVES

- Recognize that there are people who are responsible for keeping children safe.
- Practice safety rules on the way to and from school and at school.

PROGRAM RESOURCES

- Activity Book, p. 48

VOCABULARY

- safety rules (p. 195)
- injury (p. 195)
- hazard (p. 195)
- limit (p. 195)
- passenger (p. 196)

Daily Safety Tip

Air bags have saved hundreds of lives but have also caused injuries and deaths because of the power and speed at which they are deployed. Drivers and passengers are advised to sit so that their chests are positioned at least 10 inches from air bags; they should also wear safety belts, of course. Children should sit in the back seat.

1 Motivate

Explain that you are going to read a story about a third-grade boy named Willy. Whenever they think Willy is in danger, they should call out: "Watch Out, Willy!" As you read, pause at the brackets [] to allow students time to react to the text.

On Monday, Willy walked home alone from school. All the way down the busy road, Willy walked with one foot on the street and one on the sidewalk. [] Before he got to the crosswalk, Willy dashed between two parked cars and ran across the street without looking. [] Then he took a shortcut to his street through a dark alley. [] He wasn't paying attention.

LESSON

MAIN IDEA Following safety rules helps keep you and others safe.

WHY LEARN THIS? What you learn can help protect you and others from harm.

VOCABULARY
- safety rules
- injury
- hazard
- limit
- passenger

Being Responsible for Your Safety

Who is responsible for your safety?

Many people help protect you and keep you safe. At home your family watches over you. Family members have a responsibility, or duty, to protect you.

At school the principal and teachers share the duty of keeping the students safe. Others may also help. The bus driver and the crossing guard help you get safely to school. A hall monitor may help keep the school hallways safe and peaceful. All these people help protect you from harm.

You also have a duty. Your important job is to keep yourself safe. The person most responsible for your safety is **YOU**.

Who is most responsible for your safety? You!

family

bus driver

194

MULTILEVEL ACTIVITIES

EASY **Hazards Role-Play** Have students work in small groups to role-play a safety hazard and how to avoid injury. When groups are ready, have them show their role-play to the class. **KINESTHETIC**

AVERAGE **Draw Your Responsible Self** Have students draw pictures of themselves taking responsibility for their own safety. Display students' drawings in the classroom. **VISUAL**

ADVANCED **Family Limits** Have students write two or three sentences about a limit set by their families. Have students state the limit and write a brief explanation about how this limit helps them stay safe. **VERBAL/LINGUISTIC**

What does it mean to be careful?

Being careful means that you know and follow safety rules. **Safety rules** are rules that help protect you from injury. An **injury** (INJ•ree) is harm done to a person's body.

One safety rule is to watch out for hazards wherever you are. A **hazard** (HA•zerd) is a danger, like broken glass on a playground, that could lead to an injury. Another safety rule is to obey the limits set by adults. A **limit** (LIH•muht) is a point at which you must stop. Your family probably sets limits by letting you play only in places that are safe.

▼ The pictures show some of the people who help you stay safe. How does each person help protect you? Who is missing? (**Hint**: Who is most responsible for your safety?)

coach

principal

crossing guard

teacher

195

He almost tripped over a pile of rotten wood and old bricks. [] When Willy reached his building, he walked up the stairs backward, with his eyes closed. []

Do you think Willy was lucky to get home without getting hurt? Why or why not? Elicit through discussion that Willy was certainly lucky to reach home unharmed because he was not careful and did not follow basic safety rules.

2 Teach

Learn from Pictures

Focus students' attention on the pictures at the bottom of pages 194 and 195 and read the captions. Invite volunteers to identify the people pictured and explain how each person helps keep children safe. After reading the text on page 194, students should understand that *they* are most responsible for keeping themselves safe.

Discuss

After students have read the text on this page, ask them to close their eyes and visualize themselves at a local playground or park playing with friends. **What hazards or dangers do you see?** Accept all reasonable answers. Remind students that some situations are not hazards themselves but become hazards when other people or objects are involved. For example, swinging on a swing becomes a hazard when someone walks too close to the person swinging.

Problem Solving What can you do to avoid these dangers and take responsibility for your own safety? Answers will vary depending on hazards identified.

195

Learn from Pictures

Have students read the labels as they examine the pictures that show ways to stay safe on the road and at school. Invite them to point out the pictures that show the safety rules they always follow.

Discuss

Ask students to think about the safety rules that are pictured and those that are explained in the text on these pages. Encourage students to focus on the rules they sometimes forget or neglect to follow.

Critical Thinking Why do you think you forget or neglect to follow certain safety rules? Reasons may include being unaware a rule existed or carelessness.

Critical Thinking Why is it important that you know and follow all these safety rules? to avoid getting hurt while doing everyday activities

Discuss

Other tips for school bus safety are

- stand at least 6 feet from where the bus stops.
- make sure you are always in sight of the bus driver.
- if you must cross in front of the bus, walk about 10 feet up from the bus so the driver can see you.
- be careful that book-bag straps, drawstrings, or other loose-fitting items do not catch on handrails as you enter or exit the bus.

Critical Thinking What other bus safety rules can you think of? Possible answers: do not walk behind the bus; if you drop something near the bus, tell the driver; get on the bus when the driver says it is OK.

How can you stay safe on the way to and from school?

These safety rules can help keep you safe.

When riding the bus,
- do not bother the driver.
- stay in your seat.
- talk quietly—never yell.

When riding in a car,
- always buckle your safety belt.
- sit in the backseat. It is the safest place for passengers. A **passenger** (PA•suhn•jer) is someone riding in a car or bus with a driver.

When walking,
- stay on the sidewalk.
- walk with others, not alone.
- cross streets only at corners or crosswalks. Before crossing, STOP, LOOK, and LISTEN. THINK about what might be a hazard.

▼ The pictures show ways to keep safe on the road and at school. Which safety rules do you follow?

Talk quietly.

Use safety belts.

 **196**

MATH

To Follow or Not To Follow Safety Rules Have students write a safety rules checklist using the bulleted items on these pages. Have them use their checklists to record how often people at school follow or ignore safety rules. At the end of a week, have students gather to tally their results and determine which rules are followed most often and which are followed least often.

How can you stay safe at school?

At school everyone must obey the safety rules. Otherwise, both you and others could get injured.

- Never run in the hallways.
- Don't stand on chairs or other furniture.
- Follow game rules on the playground.
- Don't push or shove.

Sometimes the best safety rule is to get help. Here are two times to get adult help.

- If you see a fight, tell an adult.
- If you see a weapon, such as a gun or a knife, get an adult right away.

JOURNAL

In your Health Journal, write about how you go to and from school. What are the hazards along the way? What safety rules can you follow to make your trip safer?

Use sidewalks.

Walk in school.

LESSON CHECKUP

Check Your Facts

1. Who is most responsible for your safety?
2. Why do you need to watch out for hazards?
3. **CRITICAL THINKING** What are five safety rules that you follow at school? Name at least two that are not mentioned in this lesson.

Use Life Skills

4. **MAKE DECISIONS** Imagine that you walk to school with two friends who don't follow safety rules. How could you use the decision-making steps to help them make safer choices? Look on page *ix* if you need help.

197

Health Journal

Encourage students to visualize their journey from home to school each day and focus on hazardous areas. This feature is designed to provide students with an opportunity to reflect on health decisions they are making in their personal lives. The journals should *not* be used to evaluate or assess students, nor do the results need to be shared among students.

For more information about safety during extreme weather conditions and fire safety, see pages 272–273.

3 Wrap Up

Lesson Checkup

1. I am.

2. Hazards are dangers that can lead to injuries.

3. Answers will vary but might include don't run, don't fight, look out for hazards, play in groups, tell a teacher or principal if there's a problem.

4. Students' answers should reflect the decision-making process. These steps are about the choices you could make; imagine the possible result of each choice; make what seems to be the best choice; think about what happened as a result of your choice.

OBJECTIVES

- Describe how to stay safe around strangers.
- Explain how to avoid conflicts and get along with bullies.

PROGRAM RESOURCES

- Activity Book, p. 49

VOCABULARY

- stranger (p. 198)
- trusted adult (p. 198)
- bully (p. 200)

Daily Safety Tip

Just as sinister strangers can wander into neighborhoods to prey on innocent children, so can they wander about the Internet with the same intent. Warn children never to write to strangers on the Internet; never to give their name, address, or phone number to strangers on the Internet; and to tell a trusted adult if anyone they encounter on the Internet suggests meeting in person.

---

1 Motivate

Share this retelling of the classic fairy tale, "Little Red Riding Hood."

One day Mother asked Red to take a basket of goodies to Grandma. "Stay on the path, don't talk to strangers, and wait for your sister to go with you," Mother said. Red grew impatient and decided to deliver the basket herself. She left the path and took a shortcut through the forest. Suddenly, she spotted Wolf leaning against a giant oak. "Hey, Red," Wolf said, guessing her name because of her flaming red hair. Red thought Wolf was a friend since he knew her name. "Hi," she said. "I'm going to Grandma's." "It will be faster if I carry you," Wolf said. "Gee, thanks," Red said. "What are friends for?" the hungry Wolf chuckled.

LESSON 2

MAIN IDEA You can take steps to keep safe around strangers and bullies.

WHY LEARN THIS? What you learn can help protect you from strangers and bullies.

VOCABULARY
- stranger
- trusted adult
- bully

Safety Around Strangers and Bullies

What should you do if you are approached by a stranger?

You need to be very careful around strangers. A **stranger** (STRAYN•jer) is someone you don't know well. You must stay away from people you don't know because some strangers are not safe to be around.

If a stranger approaches, or comes near you, look for a trusted adult to help you. A **trusted adult** is a grown-up you know well or an adult in a responsible position. Usually your family members, teachers, good neighbors, security people, and police officers are adults you can trust.

Strangers in Cars Suppose someone in a car stops next to you and calls to you. What should you do? Follow the rules listed here to be safe.

- Ignore him or her.
- Leave the area. Keep walking, cross the street, or change directions.
- If the stranger gets out of the car or follows you, run away, and yell, "I don't know you!"

Four Safety Rules About Strangers

1. Stay more than an arm's reach away from a stranger.
2. Don't talk to a stranger.
3. Don't take anything from a stranger—not even your own things.
4. Don't go anywhere with a stranger.

 Activity **Review Safety Rules** Read this list of safety rules about strangers. What other rules can you add to the list?

MULTILEVEL ACTIVITIES

EASY **Bully Posters** Have students discuss and draw pictures of what bullies do. Then encourage them to make "No Bullying" posters from their pictures. Display the posters throughout the school to discourage bully behavior. **VISUAL**

AVERAGE **Dramatic Reenactment** Encourage partners to write a scene in which a stranger tries unsuccessfully to entice a child their age to go with him or her. Have students rehearse and present their scenes to the class. Did the child use the safety rules? **VERBAL**

ADVANCED **No Bullying** Have a group of four students role-play a scene in which one of them is a bully and one is getting picked on. Have the two who watch evaluate the role-play in terms of using the safety rules if one has to face a bully. **INTERPERSONAL/KINESTHETIC**

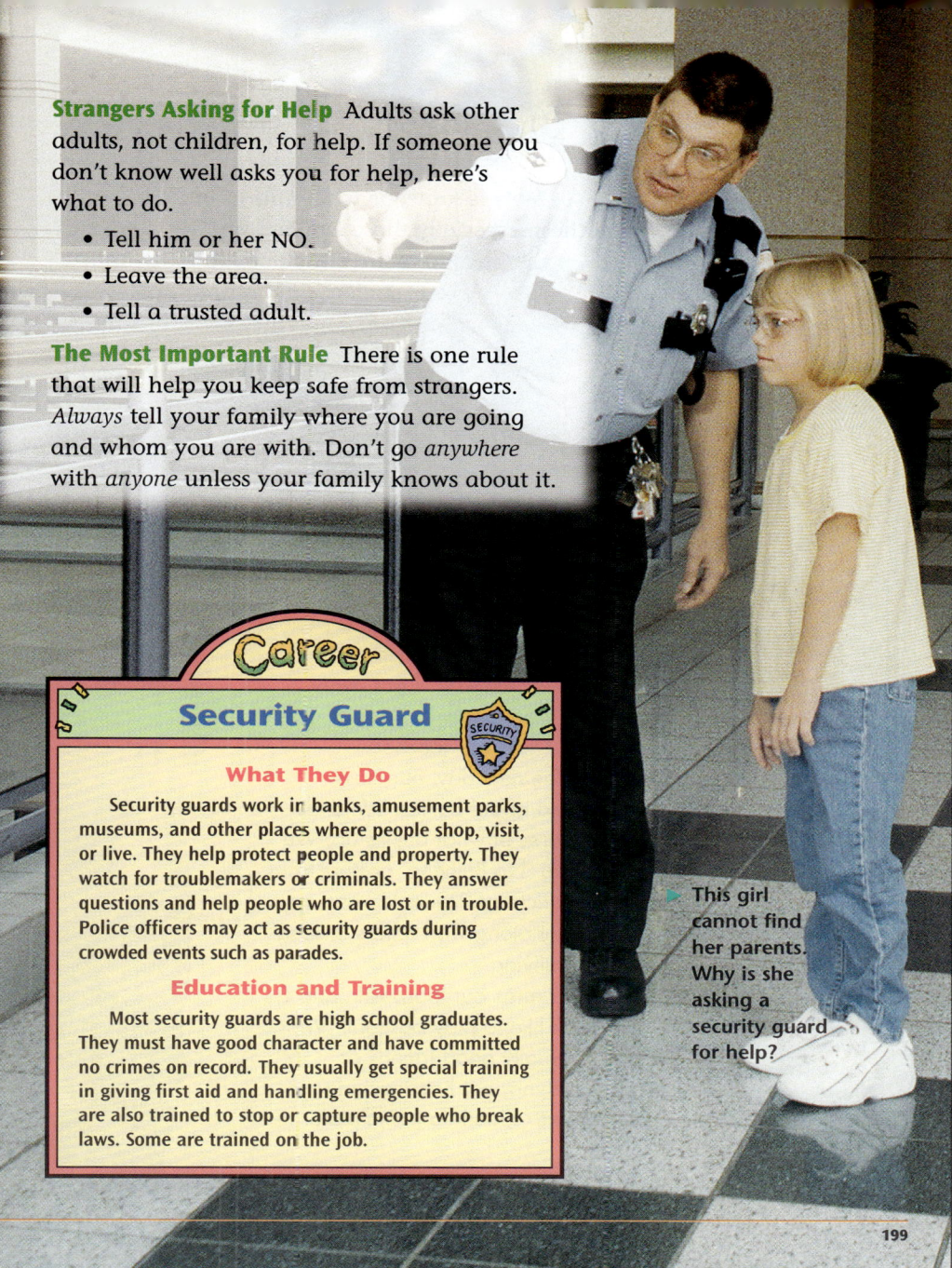

Strangers Asking for Help Adults ask other adults, not children, for help. If someone you don't know well asks you for help, here's what to do.

- Tell him or her NO.
- Leave the area.
- Tell a trusted adult.

The Most Important Rule There is one rule that will help you keep safe from strangers. *Always* tell your family where you are going and whom you are with. Don't go *anywhere* with *anyone* unless your family knows about it.

Career

Security Guard

What They Do

Security guards work in banks, amusement parks, museums, and other places where people shop, visit, or live. They help protect people and property. They watch for troublemakers or criminals. They answer questions and help people who are lost or in trouble. Police officers may act as security guards during crowded events such as parades.

Education and Training

Most security guards are high school graduates. They must have good character and have committed no crimes on record. They usually get special training in giving first aid and handling emergencies. They are also trained to stop or capture people who break laws. Some are trained on the job.

▶ This girl cannot find her parents. Why is she asking a security guard for help?

199

Would you go with Wolf if you were Red? Why or why not? *Most students will guess that he wants to eat her.*

How did Red put herself in danger? *She didn't wait for her sister or stay on the path. She talked to Wolf, a stranger.*

2 Teach

Activity

Elicit other safety rules about strangers, and list them on the board. Rules might include the following:

- Don't answer the door for strangers, even if they say other family members know who they are.

- Don't tell a telephone caller you are home alone. Explain that a parent or an older sibling is busy and can't come to the phone.

- Always call home when you reach a friend's house to let parents know you arrived safely.

- Don't believe a stranger who says, "Your parents sent me to pick you up."

Discuss

Have students name trusted adults in their lives, such as parents, guardians, grandparents, aunts, uncles, adult siblings, teachers, principal, school nurse, and counselor.

Career

For more information on a career as a security guard, contact the following organization or visit the Web site address provided:

Pinkerton's Inc.
4330 Park Terrace Drive
Westlake Village, CA 91361

Or visit the **Webliography** on the Teacher Resources page at:
**www.harcourtschool.com/health
Keyword** health careers

DEVELOP READING SKILLS

Identify Related Concepts Write the term *trusted adult* on the board. On either side, write the terms *stranger* and *bully* as shown in the diagram. Next, have students brainstorm words and ideas related to *stranger* and *bully*. For example, they might list words used to describe strangers or bullies, ideas related to where they encounter strangers or bullies, and feelings that these encounters might arouse. List students' suggestions next to the appropriate terms. Then ask students to explain how a trusted adult might help with strangers and bullies, and have them brainstorm a list of people they think of as trusted adults.

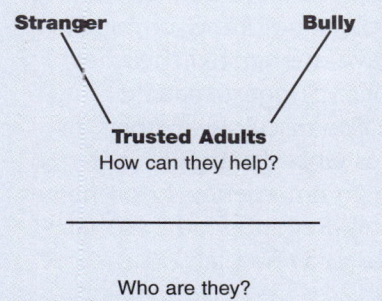

Stranger   Bully

Trusted Adults
How can they help?

_____

Who are they?

_____

Discuss

Focusing on the problem of a classroom bully without confronting the bully can be a wise strategy. It provides a healthful environment for a bully to question and evaluate his or her behavior without having to assume a defensive position. Equally important, it provides bullied students with ways to deal with bully tactics and helps them better understand the bully's motivation.

Critical Thinking Why did Ms. Díaz have the class talk about bullies without pointing out Justin as a bully? Possible answer: with the class talking about bullying in general, Justin could relax and think about his behavior; if he had been accused he might have been embarrassed and then acted even worse.

Life Skills Focus

Communicate Have students apply the steps in the communication process as they role-play what Helen should do. Students might suggest that Helen try to ignore Laura's remarks and think about something that makes her feel happy.

Health Background

Teaching Bullies Research indicates that bullies grow up in families where power is equated with violence and aggressive, harsh, inconsistent methods of discipline are frequently applied. Early intervention programs that teach young bullies to cooperate with others, to share, and to solve problems through negotiation provide bullies with life skills that some cannot learn at home but that are necessary for dealing with the problems of everyday life.

For more background, visit the **Webliography** on the Teacher Resources page at:
www.harcourtschool.com/health
Keyword violence prevention

What can you do if someone tries to bully you?

A **bully** is someone who hurts or frightens others, especially those who are smaller or weaker. Here is a story about a bully from one student's journal.

One day a new boy named Justin came to school. He looked mad and did not smile. He was bigger than all the other boys.

The trouble started after school. Justin started calling me names. He pushed me against the wall. I got away. My friends saw it. We told Ms. Díaz, our teacher.

The next day, our class talked about bullies. We drew pictures of what bullies do. We made "No Bullying" posters from our pictures. We acted out ways to get along with others instead of bullying.

It turns out that Justin and I both like to play baseball. We're not really good friends or anything, but he's teaching me how to slide into home plate.

LIFE SKILLS FOCUS

Communicate
Laura teases Helen because she has freckles and red hair. Helen feels sad when someone teases her. Role-play with a partner to show how Helen could handle how she feels about being teased. Use the steps for communicating shown on page *xii*.

200

TEACHER TIP

Important Telephone Numbers
Check to see that all students know their telephone numbers. Students who are new to the area might not know or might not have memorized their new numbers. Suggest that students also discuss with their families who else they might call in an emergency if no one is home. Remind students that they can always dial 911.

ACTIVITY BOOK, p. 49

Analyze Vocabulary   Vocabulary Reinforcement

Use the words in the word box to answer each question below. You will write some words more than once.

| passenger | stranger | injury | limit |
| safety rules | trusted adult | bully | hazard |

Write four words that name people.
1. **passenger**   2. **stranger**
3. **trusted adult**   4. **bully**

Write three words that name people or things that could be dangerous to you.
5. **hazard**   6. **stranger**
7. **bully**

Write three words that name people or things that are likely to protect you.
8. **safety rules**   9. **limit**
10. **trusted adult**

Write the word that names a possible result of not following a safety rule.
11. **injury**

The word *limit* comes from a Latin word that means "boundary." Explain how a limit is like a boundary.
12. **Answers will vary. Possible answer: A boundary is a line showing where to go and not to go. It tells you where to stop.**

Remember the following safety rules if you have to face a bully.

- Ignore mean remarks. You are not the problem. The bully's problems are causing his or her actions.
- Don't talk back or fight. Walk away.
- Get help if the bully follows you.
- Stay with others. Bullies pick on people who are alone.
- Choose friends who stay away from bullies.

▶ Finding common interests is one way to get along with a bully.

LESSON CHECKUP

Check Your Facts

1. What should you do if a stranger approaches you?
2. CRITICAL THINKING Why should you always tell your family where you are going and whom you are with?
3. What should you do if someone tries to bully you?

4. CRITICAL THINKING Describe a situation in which you should ask a trusted adult for help.

Use Life Skills

5. REFUSE Suppose you see an adult stranger looking for a lost dog. The adult asks you to help find the dog. What should you do?

201

Discuss

Read and discuss the safety rules for dealing with bullies.

Critical Thinking Which of these safety rules do you think is the most difficult to follow? Why? Answers will vary.

Problem Solving Who might you ask for help if a bully followed you on the street? Near school? Near home? Possible answers: a police officer; a teacher or older student; a family member or trusted neighbor.

Critical Thinking Where are you likely to run into bullies? Possible answers: at the playground or mall where groups of students tend to gather.

3 Wrap Up

Lesson Checkup

1. Stay away from the person, and look for a trusted adult.

2. Answers will vary but should suggest it is important that they know where to find you and who to call if there is a problem.

3. Ignore mean remarks. Don't talk back or fight; just walk away. Stay with others, choose friends who stay away from bullies. Don't go where bullies go.

4. Possible answers: if a stranger approaches, if a bully threatens you.

5. Say *no*. Leave the area quickly, and tell a trusted adult what happened.

MEET INDIVIDUAL NEEDS

Learners Acquiring English Students who are learning English might be teased about their accents, incorrect use of idioms, or other characteristics of speech associated with learning a second language. One way to combat this is to turn learners into teachers. Invite students who are learning English to teach the rest of the class each day one new word or phrase in the student's first language. All students may then come to appreciate the difficulty as well as the fun of learning a new language.

OBJECTIVES
- Identify steps to resolve conflicts.
- Use negotiation to handle conflicts with friends.

PROGRAM RESOURCES
- Activity Book, p. 50

1 Motivate

Divide the class into groups of four. Give each group two wrapped candies (or a nonfood item) and ask them to come up with the best way to decide who should get the candies in their group. Ask them to discuss the problem, list possible solutions, and then decide. Tell them not to eat the candy until they have reported their solution to the whole class. When the groups have finished, ask them to share their lists of possible solutions and their decisions. Then supply each of the group members with a piece of candy. Check for food allergies before giving any food to students.

2 Teach

Explain that the exercise they just participated in provided practice using negotiation skills. "Negotiation" means being able to work together to work out problems.

Learn from Pictures

What is the conflict? Three people want to play table tennis, but there are only two paddles.

Critical Thinking Why is it important to understand what the conflict is? You need to know what the problem is before you can think of ways to solve it.

RESOLVE CONFLICTS
Using Negotiation

Conflicts happen, even among friends. Knowing ways to work things out will help you get along better.

Learn This Skill

Pascal, Susan, and Keith want to play table tennis. There are only two paddles. They argue about who gets to play. How can they negotiate, or work together, to resolve their conflict?

1. Agree that you disagree.

"Wait, this isn't getting us anywhere."

2. Listen to each other.

"Let's face it—we can't all play at once. We need a fair way to decide who gets to play."

202

TEACHER TIP

Classroom Conflicts When students have conflicts in the classroom or on the playground, remind them of the conflict resolution steps. Encourage them to use the steps to handle their issues.

ART

Playground Cartoons Have students draw cartoons showing the four steps to resolve conflicts. Have them depict a conflict they have had on the playground. They can divide a sheet of paper into four sections and use the Life Skills pages in the book as a model. Encourage students to label each step and show the choices being made in the pictures.

3. Negotiate.

"We could flip a coin, and the winner will play first."
"We could draw names from a hat."
"We could go in alphabetical order."

4. Compromise on a solution.

"Let's take three pieces of paper and write our names on them. Keith can mix them up, and Pascal will pick two names to play first."

Practice This Skill

Use this summary to help you solve the problems below.

> **Resolve Conflicts**
> 1. Agree that you disagree.
> 2. Listen to each other.
> 3. Negotiate.
> 4. Compromise on a solution.

A. You and a friend decide to play a game. You both want to go first. Use what you know about resolving conflicts to solve this problem.

B. Your friend comes home with you after school. You want to play outside, but your friend would rather play computer games. What do you do?

203

Step 1

What does it mean to agree that you disagree? You admit there is a conflict that you need to solve.

Step 2

How can you tell these students are really listening to each other? They are looking at the person who is speaking; only one person is talking; they look interested in what the speaker is saying.

Critical Thinking Why is listening to each other so important? You need to understand each person's point of view. When you know what each person feels, it will be easier to come up with a solution.

Step 3

Critical Thinking Why is it important to think of several solutions to the problem? To negotiate well, you need to come up with several choices. Each person should have a chance to express ideas. This will make it easier to find one on which everyone can agree.

Step 4

What does compromise on a solution mean? It means that all of the people agree on the solution that is made. It might not be the one you suggested, or it might be parts of several choices that were suggested, but each person agrees to go along with the choice.

3 Wrap Up

A. Students should indicate that they would listen to each other, negotiate, and suggest a compromise.

B. Students should indicate how they would use the conflict resolution steps to compromise on a solution, such as playing outside for a certain amount of time and then playing computer games for the same amount of time.

OBJECTIVES

- Make a home fire escape plan.
- Describe how to safely escape a home fire.
- List safety rules for using electricity and household products.

PROGRAM RESOURCES

- Activity Book, p. 51

 Teaching Transparency 26

 Computer Graphing Activity, Teaching Resources p. 65

VOCABULARY

- emergency (p. 204)
- poison (p. 206)

Daily Safety Tip

Students may be in the habit of stacking extension outlets when adding video game players to already busy outlets supplying power for television, VCR, and stereo equipment. Suggest that students and their parents check the outlets near TVs and computers to make sure that they are not overloaded and that cords are not tangled, pulled, or frayed.

---

1 Motivate

Have students divide a sheet of paper in half. On one side of the paper, they should draw a picture that shows how fire can help people; on the other side, they should draw a picture that shows how fire can be dangerous. Invite students to display and explain their pictures.

When is fire helpful? Possible answers: when it is used to cook food or to warm rooms (fireplace or wood stove).

When is fire dangerous? Possible answers: when it is burning out of control, as in a house fire; when it burns skin.

MAIN IDEA You and your family can take steps to protect yourselves from fire, electricity, and poisons.

WHY LEARN THIS? What you learn can help keep you and your family safe at home.

VOCABULARY
- emergency
- poison

HUMAN BODY CONNECTION

Smoke Alarm
Look at the human respiratory system on pages 12 and 13. Find out where smoke goes in your body if you breathe it in during a fire. Make a list of the organs that are affected by smoke.

Safety at Home—Fire, Electricity, and Poisons

How can you stay safe in a fire?

The smoke alarm beeps. You smell smoke. Someone yells, "Fire!" A house fire is an **emergency** (ih•MER•juhnt•see)—a situation in which help is needed right away. To be prepared, you and your family can work together to make an escape plan and practice fire drills.

Make an Escape Plan Draw a map of your home. Draw arrows to show two ways to escape from each room. Windows or doors may be used. Make sure everyone knows both ways to escape. Choose a place outdoors to meet after you escape. The meeting place could be a tree or a neighbor's house.

Practice Fire Drills Here's how to escape a fire.

- **Crawl out quickly.** If you notice fire or smoke, drop down and stay low. Keep below the smoke so you don't breathe it. As you crawl, hold a damp cloth over your mouth and nose. Breathe through the cloth.
- **Warn others.** Shout or blow a whistle loudly to alert your family.
- **Follow the escape paths.** Crawl along the walls if the smoke is too thick to see through. If you come to a closed door, feel it with your hand. If the door is cool, you may open it.

MULTILEVEL ACTIVITIES

EASY **Electricity Rules** Have students work as partners to illustrate and label a *Do* poster and a *Don't* poster about electricity. Suggest they model their posters on the pictures in the chart on page 206. **VISUAL**

AVERAGE **Fire Escape Plans** Ask students to make escape plans for their homes, with at least two exits from each room. Students should practice their escape plans with their parents. Then have students write out the rules for escaping a fire and post them in their kitchens for everyone to review. **KINESTHETIC**

ADVANCED **Stop, Drop, and Roll** Have students work in small groups to illustrate the method of putting out a fire that involves a person's clothing. Display the posters or graphics in a prominent place in the classroom. **TACTILE**

If it is warm, stop. Do not open the door. Escape using a different path.

- **Go to the meeting place.** This is very important. If you don't come, your family may think you are trapped inside the house.

- **Call 911 or the fire department.** You need to know your address to tell the 911 operator. The operator may also ask how big the fire is, what is burning, and whether anyone is trapped inside. Don't hang up before the operator does.

- **Stop, drop, and roll.** If your clothing catches fire, stop and drop to the ground. Roll slowly back and forth to smother the fire.

▶ Smoke, heat, and dangerous gases rise and reach the smoke detector. The smoke sets off a loud alarm signal. When you hear the alarm, get low and crawl. Cover your mouth and nose with a damp cloth. The cloth helps keep out the smoke.

205

2 Teach

Human Body Connection

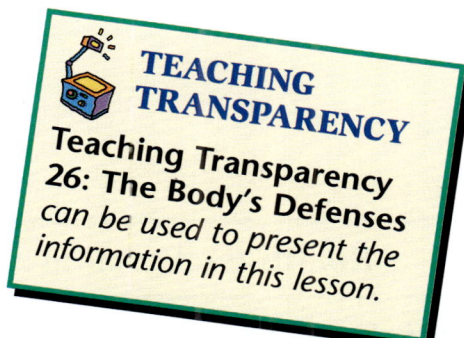

Smoke Alarm Refer students to the diagram of the human respiratory system on pages 12 and 13. Ask students to trace the path smoke takes through the body once it is breathed in and to identify the body organs it might damage.

Learn from Pictures

Point out the picture of the boy in the illustration and read the caption.

Critical Thinking What else should this boy do as he crawls out of the house? Warn other people in the house, continue to follow along the escape route made by his family, go to the outside meeting place (should be at least 30 feet from the home) and stay there, call 911 or the fire department from a neighbor's house to report the fire.

DEVELOP READING SKILLS

List, Group, and Label Vocabulary
Write the word *emergency* on the board. Have students find in the text and think about the definition for *emergency*. Then have students brainstorm and list all the words they can think of that relate to *emergency*. When lists are complete, help students group words that have something in common and record the responses in a web or chart. Common labels might be *Causes of an Emergency*

(fire, poison, lightning, falls); *Types of Emergencies* (poisoning, home fires, drowning); and *People Who Respond to an Emergency* (police officers, firefighters, EMTs).

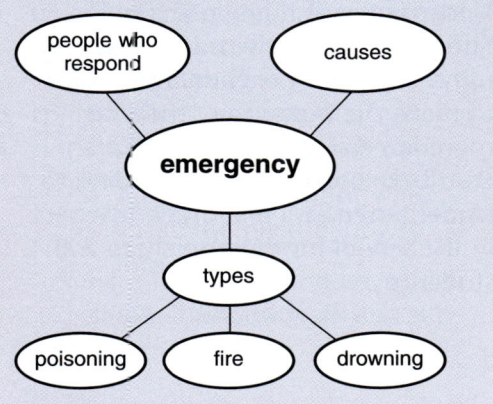

Health Background

Smoke Detector Smoke detectors reduce the chances of a person dying in a fire by 50 percent. Smoke detectors should be installed on every level of the home and in or near all the bedrooms. Families should be sure that every member of the family can hear and recognize the sound of a smoke detector. Also, parents should test detectors frequently, preferably once a month, to be sure they are working. Batteries should be replaced at least once a year.

205

Discuss

Tell students that carbon monoxide is a colorless, odorless, poisonous gas. It is produced by burning fuels in furnaces and engines. It is important to have a source of fresh air available at all times.

For more information about safety in and near water, see pages 270–271.

Activity

Have students identify the safe and unsafe practices related to electricity that are pictured in the *Do* and *Don't* chart. Then help students develop a list of additional safety rules about electricity. Write students' suggestions on the board.

DO	DON'T
DO hold the plug.	DON'T hold the cord.
DO use only one plug in each outlet.	DON'T overload extension cords.
DO use wall outlets properly.	DON'T poke things into outlets.

 Activity **Identify Safety Rules** The pictures in the chart show some ways to be safe or unsafe with electricity. What other safety rules can you add?

How can you stay safe around electricity?

Lighting rooms. Drying hair. Keeping food cold. Electricity is very useful. But it also can be dangerous. Practice the safety rules shown and listed here when you use electricity.

- Electrical cords are safe to use only when they aren't cracked or frayed. If you can see the wires inside a cord, don't use it.
- Hold the plug, not the cord, when plugging or unplugging things.
- If there are young children in your home, an adult may want to put covers over the outlets that are not in use.
- Use only one plug in each outlet.
- Never run cords under a carpet.
- To prevent a shock, never plug in or turn on electrical things when you have wet hands.
- NEVER touch outdoor power lines, especially fallen power lines.

How can you stay safe around poisons?

A **poison** (POY•zuhn) is a substance that causes illness or death when it gets in the body. Many useful home products become poisons if they are not used in the right way.

206

Health Background

Electric shock Electric shock, which occurs when a jolt of electricity passes through the body, can interrupt the heartbeat, make it stop, and, in the worst cases, cause death. Rubber and plastic are not good conductors of electrical current, which is why manufacturers cover cords and plugs with rubber or heavy plastic. On the other hand, electricity passes easily through metal and water. People should never touch water while using an electrical appliance. They also should avoid water during a lightning storm.

For more background, visit the **Webliography** on the Teacher Resources page at:
www.harcourtschool.com/health
Keyword injury prevention

LANGUAGE ARTS

Clever Sayings Encourage students to make up clever sayings about the safe use of electricity that are aimed at a kindergarten and first-grade audience. Suggest students record their sayings, using cartoonish or humorous voices to make the message of their sayings more appealing to young children. Distribute copies of the recording to kindergarten and first-grade teachers in the school for them to share with students.

MULTICULTURAL LINK

Respect for Fire Among Different Cultures The reverence of fire is common to a variety of ancient mythologies. Most include an explanation of how fire was presented to humans. Encourage partners to research the significance of fire in the early mythologies of the world. Students can share what they learn in oral reports, or they may wish to write brief essays to share with the class.

Many products must not be breathed, swallowed, or touched. Even medicines become poisons if too much is taken. These rules will help you stay safe.

- Keep household cleaning products locked up where small children cannot reach them.
- Keep all medicines, even vitamins, locked up and out of the reach of small children.

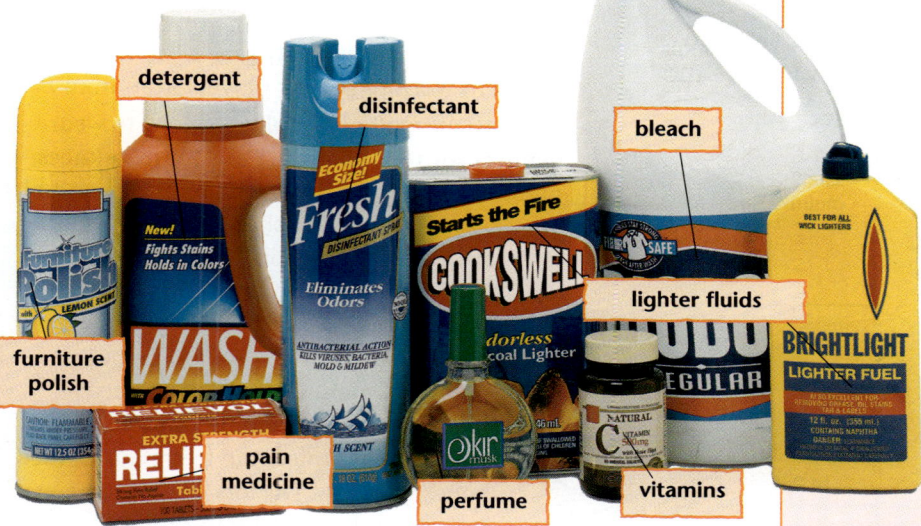

detergent
disinfectant
bleach
lighter fluids
furniture polish
pain medicine
perfume
vitamins

▲ These products can be poisons if not used correctly. Most families keep products like these in their homes. How is each one normally used? Which ones are in your home?

LESSON CHECKUP

Check Your Facts

1 When a fire breaks out, what information does the 911 operator need?

2 CRITICAL THINKING Think about the household products in your home. Name four products other than those pictured on this page that could be poisons if used in the wrong way.

3 List five electricity safety rules.

Set Health Goals

4 Make a map or floor plan of your home. Draw arrows to show the fire escape paths. Make sure each room has two escape paths such as a door and window. Show where your family members can meet after they escape.

207

TEACHER TIP

Some Chemicals Don't Mix Adults and older children do not usually ingest poisonous products accidentally as young children do. However, adults and older children put themselves at risk of being poisoned when they mix two chemical products, such as bleach and ammonia. This creates potentially deadly gas fumes. Warn students about this problem and advise them never to combine two cleaning products unless package directions and parents indicate it is acceptable and safe to do so.

Learn from Pictures

Focus students' attention on the picture of household products. Point out the picture labels and invite a volunteer to read the caption. Then have students answer the caption questions. Most students should be able to identify the common uses of each product, but be prepared to offer help when necessary.

Project Checkup

Safety Collage (p. 193) Students may wish to look for pictures related to the safety tips presented in this lesson to add to their collages.

3 Wrap Up

Lesson Checkup

1. address of the fire, how big the fire is, what is burning, if anyone is trapped

2. Possible answers: dishwashing liquid, hair spray, paint, glue.

3. Possible answers: Don't use cracked or frayed extension cords. Hold the plug, not the cord, when plugging in and unplugging something. Stick only plugs into outlets. Use only one plug in each outlet. Never run cords under a carpet. Cover outlets when young children are in the home. Do not touch plugs or appliances with wet hands. Do not use electric appliances near water. Never touch outdoor power lines, especially fallen power lines.

4. Plans should clearly indicate two escape routes from each room and an outdoor meeting place for the family.

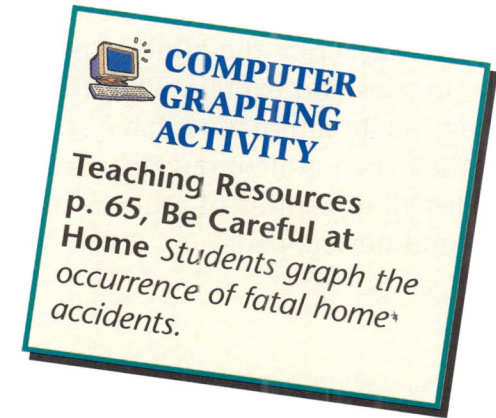

COMPUTER GRAPHING ACTIVITY
Teaching Resources p. 65, Be Careful at Home Students graph the occurrence of fatal home accidents.

OBJECTIVES

- Identify safety gear.
- Explain safety rules for bicycling.
- Know what features to look for when purchasing a helmet.

PROGRAM RESOURCES

Teaching Transparency 27

HEALTH VIDEO:
The Good Health Game Show

VOCABULARY

- safety gear (p. 208)
- mouth guard (p. 208)

Daily Safety Tip

While protective gear can help young athletes avoid serious injury while participating in sports, some simple warm-up exercises before a sporting event can help prevent many of the aches and pains people often suffer during and after the game. Suggest that students ask athletic trainers and coaches to recommend warm-up programs for their specific sport.

---

1 Motivate

Optional Materials pictures of professional and amateur athletes in protective sports gear pasted to stiff paper or cardboard and cut into pieces to form jigsaw puzzles (place each puzzle in its own small paper bag)

Pair students, and give each pair a jigsaw puzzle. Allow partners several minutes to put their puzzles together. Then invite students to describe the athletes pictured in the puzzles and explain what they're wearing. As an alternative, have students make their own athlete puzzles, or have them describe pictures of athletes in magazines and newspapers.

Safety for Sports and Bicycling

MAIN IDEA Wearing the proper safety gear helps prevent injuries.

WHY LEARN THIS? What you learn can help keep you safe when you play a sport, skate, ride a bicycle, or ride a scooter.

VOCABULARY
- safety gear
- mouth guard

How can you stay safe when playing on a team?

In many team sports, players must wear safety gear in order to play. **Safety gear** is clothing or equipment worn to protect players from injury.

Football In football all players need to wear helmets with face guards. Pads for legs, knees, and shoulders protect players from falls and hits. Players also wear shoes that have small pegs called cleats on the bottom. Cleats help keep players from slipping on wet grass.

Football players also wear mouth guards. A **mouth guard** is a protective plastic shield worn in the mouth. Mouth guards help protect the teeth, gums, face bones, and jaw. Doctors and dentists recommend wearing mouth guards for most team sports.

Hockey Hockey players are likely to fall or get hit by the sticks or puck. Players wear padding, helmets, and face guards as safety gear. Players also should wear mouth guards.

Softball Softball safety gear includes cleated shoes and padded gloves. However, players are most likely to get injured when batting or running to a base. Batting helmets with ear guards protect batters and runners. A mouth guard also can protect a player.

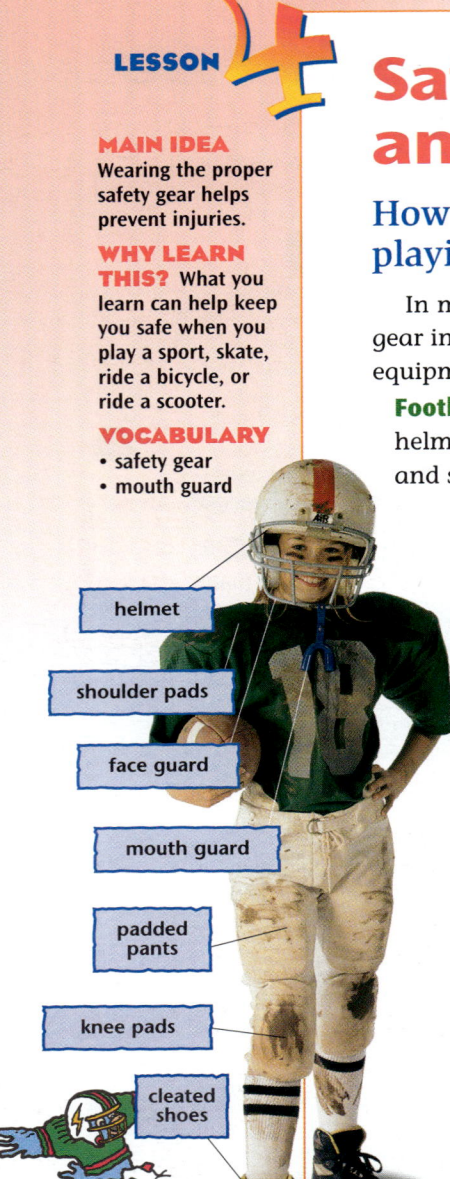

helmet
shoulder pads
face guard
mouth guard
padded pants
knee pads
cleated shoes

Always wear your safety gear!

MULTILEVEL ACTIVITIES

EASY Proper Stretching Techniques Have students work in small groups to demonstrate proper stretching exercises. Ask them to contact the physical education instructor for help with their demonstrations. Warm-up and cool-down exercises should be done before and after participating in sports or other physical activities. **KINESTHETIC/INTERPERSONAL**

AVERAGE Sports History and Safety Issues Have students research a sport. Ask them to find out when and where the sport was invented and how the rules and equipment have changed over the years to increase the safety of the players. Invite students to share their findings with the class. **VERBAL**

ADVANCED Make Bicycle Rules Murals Have small groups of students draw murals illustrating the bicycle safety rules. Have the class play the "Can You Find It?" game: Each student should state his or her rule and have classmates find it in the mural. **VISUAL**

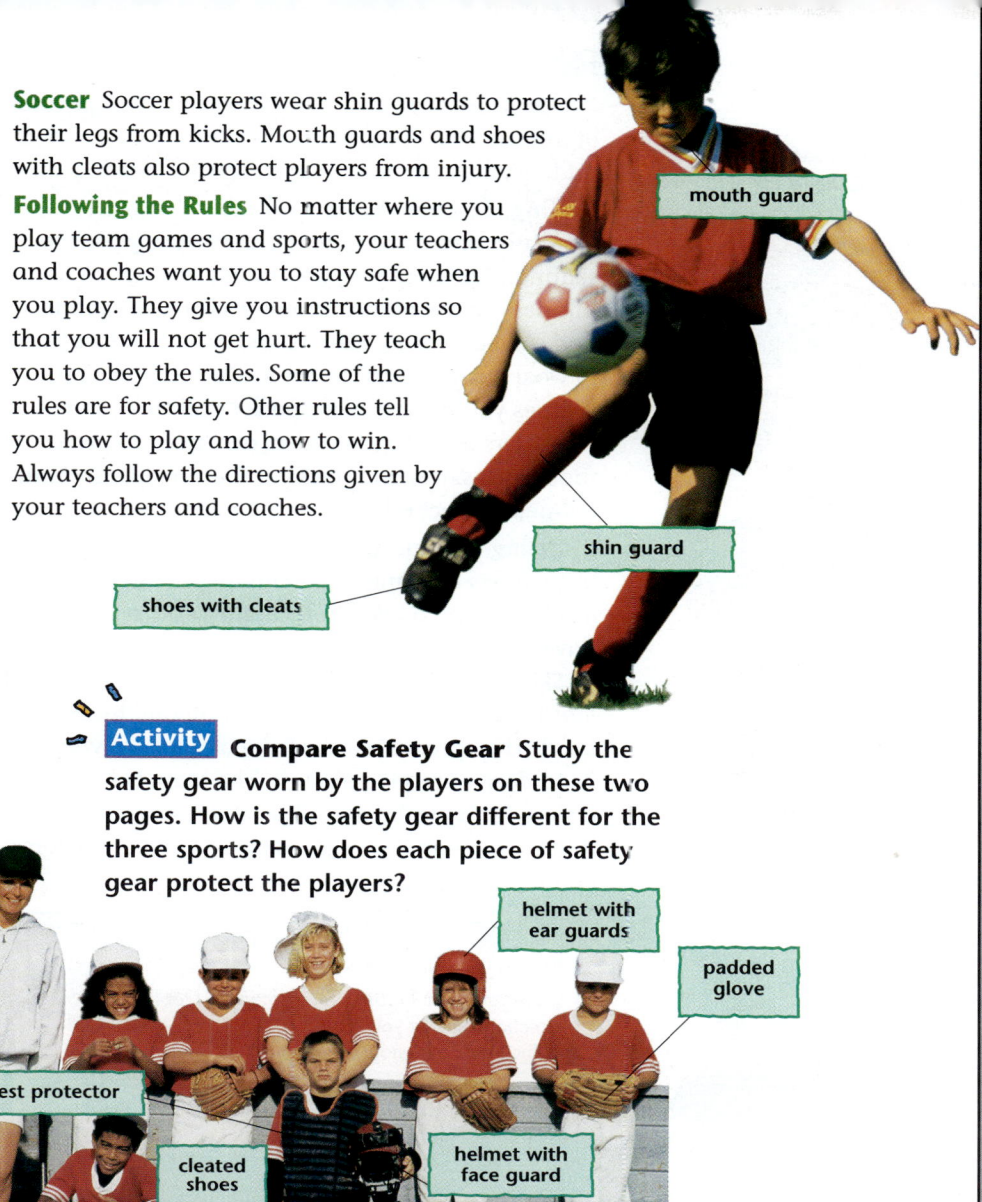

Soccer Soccer players wear shin guards to protect their legs from kicks. Mouth guards and shoes with cleats also protect players from injury.

Following the Rules No matter where you play team games and sports, your teachers and coaches want you to stay safe when you play. They give you instructions so that you will not get hurt. They teach you to obey the rules. Some of the rules are for safety. Other rules tell you how to play and how to win. Always follow the directions given by your teachers and coaches.

mouth guard

shin guard

shoes with cleats

Activity **Compare Safety Gear** Study the safety gear worn by the players on these two pages. How is the safety gear different for the three sports? How does each piece of safety gear protect the players?

helmet with ear guards

padded glove

chest protector

cleated shoes

helmet with face guard

209

2 Teach

Discuss

Even when all preventative measures are taken, sports injuries still occur. These injuries should be attended to as quickly as possible. If left untreated, injuries to growing bones, muscles, ligaments, and tendons can affect a child's growth and might result in a permanent injury.

Critical Thinking Why are children more likely than adults to suffer sports-related injuries? because children's bones, muscles, ligaments, and tendons are still growing

Problem Solving What should you do if you feel sore or in pain during or after a game? Why? Possible answer: tell the coach or a parent so that injury can be treated quickly.

Activity

Compare Safety Gear Have students study the pictures and equipment labels. You may wish to help students compare safety gear among the three sports by listing similarities and differences in a chart.

Learn from Pictures

Focus students' attention on the skating equipment, and have students explain in their own words how each item can help protect them while skating. Students can read the text to confirm their responses. You might also have students share personal experiences about skating injuries that might not have happened if they had been wearing proper safety gear.

Learn from Charts

Invite volunteers to read the items in the Safety Rules for Bicycling chart.

Problem Solving **What would you say to someone who says wearing a helmet is for babies?** Help students devise comebacks that use facts and humor to explain the importance of wearing helmets.

Critical Thinking **Why is it important to obey traffic signs when bicycling?** to avoid accidents with other vehicles on the road **Why should you ride your bicycle only in bright daylight?** to avoid accidents with car drivers who might not see you in the dark

Problem Solving **How can bicycle riders make themselves more visible to car drivers?** Possible answers: wear light-colored clothing; make sure bicycles have front and rear reflectors.

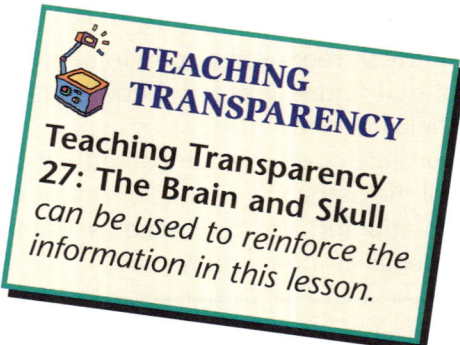

TEACHING TRANSPARENCY

Teaching Transparency 27: The Brain and Skull can be used to reinforce the information in this lesson.

How can you stay safe on wheels?

People playing sports on wheels have high rates of injuries. Skaters, skateboard riders, scooter riders, and bicyclists all need to wear special safety gear.

Skating, Skateboarding, and Riding Scooters The first three pictures on the left show safety gear for skating, skateboarding and riding scooters. Wrist injuries are the most common injuries in skating and skateboarding. Skaters and skateboarders need to wear wrist guards. To avoid elbow and knee injuries you need to wear pads in all three sports.

Skaters and skateboarders also need to protect the fronts, sides, and backs of their heads. Skating helmets protect all sides of the head.

Bicycling The most important safety gear for bicycling is a helmet. Head injuries are likely when a rider falls off a bike. In fact, many states and cities have laws that require bicyclists to wear helmets.

Skate and bicycle helmets are made of thick, hard foam. The foam will crush if you fall and hit your head. This spreads out the force of a fall, so your head doesn't receive all of it. The foam is covered by a slick, hard plastic shell. The slick shell slides when it hits the ground. This takes away some of the force of a fall.

▼ What safety gear do you need for skating?

helmet

knee pads

elbow pads

wrist guards

SAFETY RULES FOR BICYCLING

- Always wear your helmet.
- Walk your bike across streets. Stop and look in all directions before you cross. Listen for traffic. Obey all traffic lights and stop signs.
- Carry only one person—YOU!
- Be careful around driveways and parked cars. Watch for cars that might be backing out or car doors that might be opening.
- Ride only in daylight. Use reflective clothes if you must ride in cloudy or rainy weather.
- Avoid wearing heavy backpacks—use a basket.

210

 LANGUAGE ARTS

Safety Announcements Have students write brief public service announcements to remind young people of the importance of wearing protective gear while participating in sports and other leisure activities, such as bicycling, skateboarding, riding scooters, and skating. Suggest that students incorporate humor, rhyme, or any creative device of their choice to make their announcements interesting and informative. Invite students to share their announcements with the class. Students can also read their announcements at school-wide safety-awareness programs.

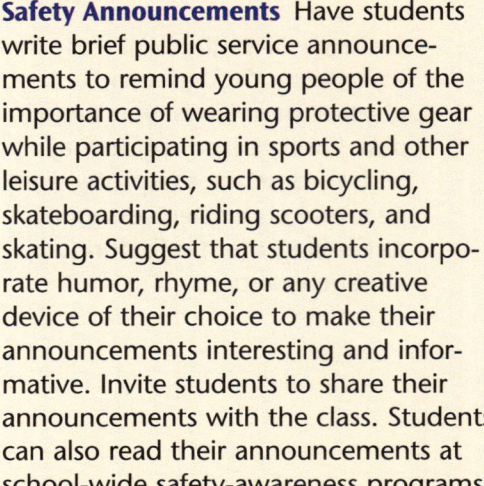 **SCIENCE**

Brain Protection Have students study the Skeletal System on pages 4 and 5 and the Nervous System on pages 14 and 15 to determine how helmets protect the brain from injury. Students can also research the types of temporary and permanent injuries people sustain when they fall or are thrown from bikes and hit their heads while *not* wearing helmets.

What should you look for when buying a helmet?

There are many important things to consider when buying a helmet.

- Look for a hard shell and an approval sticker that shows the helmet meets safety standards.
- Buy a bright color to help others see you.
- Wear the helmet level on your head. Make sure it sits evenly between your ears and low on your forehead.
- Make sure the helmet fits. Take the time to fit all the pads and straps. Adjust them so that the helmet is snug but not too tight. Try hard to pull the helmet off. If it comes off, adjust the straps again. If it still comes off, try another helmet.

After buying a helmet, the most important thing to do is to wear it every time you ride. The best helmet in the world won't help you if it's not on your head while you ride.

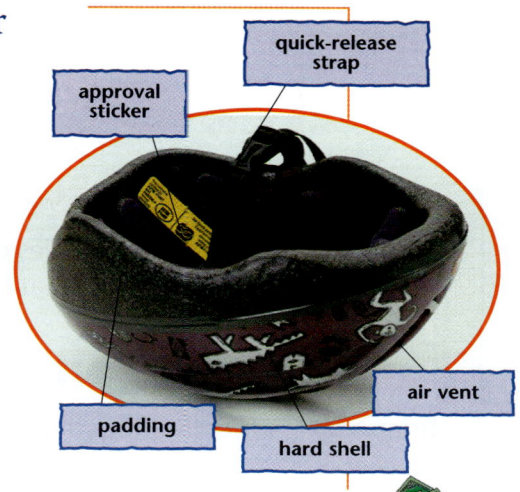

quick-release strap

approval sticker

air vent

padding

hard shell

CONSUMER FOCUS

Making Buying Decisions

Wearing a helmet for activities such as biking or skating helps keep your head safe from injury. If your helmet doesn't fit anymore, or if you have had an accident with your helmet, you will need to buy a new one. Use the steps on page xiv and compare different helmets to decide which helmet is best for you.

• • •

LESSON CHECKUP

Check Your Facts

1. Tell what a mouth guard protects and when you should wear one.
2. CRITICAL THINKING How does following the rules of a game help protect the players?
3. What safety gear should be worn while skating and skateboarding?
4. CRITICAL THINKING Why do you think it is important to fit a bicycle helmet properly before buying it?

Set Health Goals

5. List the sports you like to play. Make a chart or drawing that shows the safety gear you need to wear for each sport.

211

HEALTH VIDEO

The Good Health Game Show: Using Critical Thinking Skills Helps students understand how to analyze and evaluate advertisements for sports equipment. See the Health Video Series Teacher's Guide for discussion and activity ideas.

MATH

Compare Helmet Costs

Encourage students to visit area sporting goods stores with older family members to find the costs of several bicycle helmets. Have them make charts that compare the costs and features of the different models. Then have them determine which model offers the most safety features for the least amount of money.

Learn from Pictures

Point out the picture of the helmet and read the labels. Invite volunteers to explain in their own words the safety features they would look for when buying a helmet.

For more information about bike safety, see pages 268–269.

Consumer Focus

Making Buying Decisions
Emphasize to students the importance of a good fitting helmet. If students are purchasing a bicycle helmet they should look for helmets with the ANSI (American National Standards Institute) or The Snell Memorial Foundation label. These stickers ensure that the helmet has been stringently tested to protect against head injuries.

3 Wrap Up

Lesson Checkup

1. Mouth guards help protect teeth, gums, face bones, and jaw; they should be worn for playing most team sports.
2. Some of the rules are for keeping players safe. Other rules tell how to play the game. If players follow the rules, there is less chance someone will get injured.
3. helmet, knee pads, elbow pads, wrist guards
4. Possible answers: so that it stays in place and does not slip off the head while riding; so that it is comfortable to wear.
5. Have students make their charts or drawings in their Health Journals. You may wish to make a model chart on the board for students to copy.

OBJECTIVES

- Identify steps to make decisions.
- Use decision-making steps to stay safe.

PROGRAM RESOURCES

- Activity Book, p. 52

 HEALTH VIDEO:
International Food Fare

1 Motivate

Optional Materials **ladder, mobile**

Have a ladder handy, but don't draw students' attention to it. Tell students you need to stick a mobile to the ceiling. While they watch, stack two chairs. Add an overturned trash can to the top of the chairs, and stack a few dictionaries on top of that. Pretend you are going to climb up on this stack. Stop at the last moment, and ask the students to decide if you are making a safe choice. Ask them for other choices you could make. Think about each possible choice and make a decision. Place the mobile on the ceiling. Thank students for helping you make a safe and healthful choice.

2. Teach

Tell students that every day they make choices that affect their safety. Many accidents can be avoided if we make safe decisions.

Learn from Pictures

Direct attention to Brian's situation. **What is the problem?** Brian left his shin guards at home. **How might this affect his safety during the game?** He might be injured because he doesn't have the right equipment.

MAKE DECISIONS with Safety in Mind

Staying safe and avoiding injuries doesn't just happen. The decisions you make are what keep you safe.

Learn This Skill

Brian met his friends after school to play soccer. When he checked his gear, he saw he had left his shin guards at home. How can the steps for making decisions help Brian make a choice for safety?

1. Find out about the choices you could make.

What are Brian's choices?

2. Imagine the possible result of each choice.

What does Brian think might happen?

212

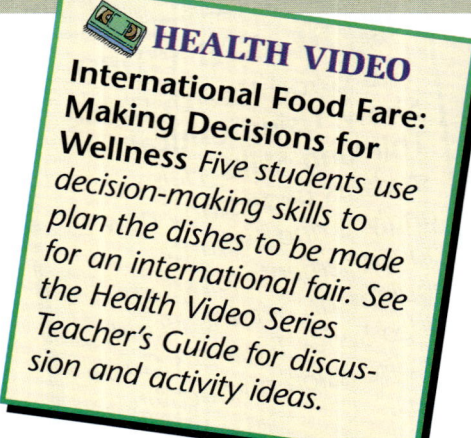

3. Make what seems to be the best choice.

"I live only two blocks away. I'll ask my friends to wait for me."

4. Think about what happened as a result of your choice.

Being safe is being smart.

Practice This Skill

Now it's your turn to use your decision-making skills.

Steps for Making Decisions

1. Find out about the choices you could make.

2. Imagine the possible result of each choice.

3. Make what seems to be the best choice.

4. Think about what happened as a result of your choice.

A. You ride your bike to school. When it is time to go home, you can't find your helmet. Decide what to do.

B. An adult you don't know stops his car and offers you a ride. Decide what to do.

213

ACTIVITY BOOK, p. 52

Make Decisions | Life Skills

Sarita was late for school. She rushed out to the garage and jumped on her bike. Just as she was leaving the driveway, she realized she had forgotten her helmet. Sarita wants to be safe, but she doesn't want to be late for school. Help Sarita use the decision-making steps to make a choice for safety. **Possible answers are shown.**

Step 1 Find out about the choices you could make.

What are Sarita's choices?
go back and get her helmet; keep riding to school and not use her helmet this time; ask her dad to drive her to school; leave her bike and run to school

Step 2 Imagine the possible result of each choice.

List a possible result for each choice you listed in Step 1.
If she gets her helmet, she might be late. If she doesn't use a helmet, she might get hurt and might be breaking the law. If her dad drives her, she won't be late. If she runs to school, she might not be late, but she might not be safe.

Step 3 Make what seems to be the best choice.

What do you think is the best choice for Sarita?
She decides to get her helmet, even if it makes her late.

Step 4 Think about what happened as a result of your choice.

What do you think would happen for the choice you suggested?
Sarita got to school safely. She wasn't even late! She made a healthful choice.

TEACHER TIP

Staying Safe Emphasize that most injuries people suffer are preventable. People need to think ahead and practice safety in everyday situations to prevent injury. Brainstorm ways to stay safe in everyday situations, such as riding a bike, using a stairway, and getting something from a high cupboard.

Step 1

What are some possible choices Brian could make? playing without the guards or running home to get them

Step 2

Critical Thinking Why is it important to think about the possible results of each choice before making a decision? Each choice will have both good and bad results. To make a good choice, you need to think about all of the results beforehand.

Step 3

Critical Thinking Why was going home to get the shin guards the better choice? He will be able to play safely and protect himself from injury. He didn't live very far away, so his friends didn't have to wait very long.

Step 4

What happened as a result of Brian's choice? He was safe.

- **NOTE:** Shinguards are worn underneath socks.

3 Wrap Up

A. Students should indicate how they would use the decision-making steps to make a safe choice, such as calling a family member to explain what happened and possibly getting a ride home.

B. Students should use the decision-making steps to conclude that accepting a ride from a stranger could have dangerous results, and would not be a safe choice.

213

OBJECTIVES

- Learn how to get emergency assistance when someone has been injured or accidentally poisoned.
- Describe first aid for cuts, scrapes, insect bites, and stings.

PROGRAM RESOURCES

- Activity Book, p. 53

VOCABULARY

- first aid (p. 214)

Daily Safety Tip

Suggest that students post the names and telephone numbers of two trusted adults (other than immediate family members) by the telephone along with the numbers of family doctors and dentists, 911, and other emergency numbers.

1 Motivate

Share this poem with students:

When you fall
and stub your toes
or cut your arm
or scrape your nose,
you may want to holler, "Ouch!"
or sit and cry
or pout and slouch.
That's okay, I understand;
but it won't help
to heal your hand,
or your arm,
or your nose—
heaven knows.
Since that won't do,
take this advice:
call for help,
give first aid, too!
Sooner and not later.

LESSON 5

MAIN IDEA You can take steps to help when someone gets injured.

WHY LEARN THIS? What you learn can help you treat small injuries and get help in an emergency.

VOCABULARY
- first aid

Getting Help and Giving First Aid

You see a friend trip and fall on the playground. You find your little brother playing with an open bottle of pain killers. Your parent suddenly becomes very ill. What should you do? Get help! At home, tell your family or the baby-sitter. At school, tell a teacher or another adult.

Calling 911 If you can't find an adult, use a telephone to get help. Dial 911 or the emergency number for your area. Tell the operator
- where you are.
- your name and phone number.
- what happened and who needs help.

Calling the Poison Control Center If someone has been poisoned, call the Poison Control Center. Look for the number on the first page of the telephone book, and keep the number handy. Different poisons need different treatments. The people at the Poison Control Center know what to do for each kind of poison.

First Aid No matter how careful you are, you may get small injuries from time to time. Caring for them is called **first aid**. Here are some first-aid tips. Remember, the first thing you should do is tell an adult about the injury, no matter how small. First aid that is properly given can keep a person's injury from getting worse.

214

MULTILEVEL ACTIVITIES

EASY **Call 911** Have students work in pairs to role-play making an emergency call to 911. Be sure they include all of the information the operator will need and stay on the line until they are told to hang up. **VERBAL**

AVERAGE **Help! I'm Hurt** Have students work in pairs to role-play what to do when a friend falls and scrapes his or her elbow. Stress cleanliness. **KINESTHETIC**

ADVANCED **Cuts and Scrapes** Give students two sheets of drawing paper. Have them draw several pictures showing the basic first-aid steps for treating minor cuts and scrapes. Students should label their illustrations with a sentence or two describing each procedure. **VISUAL/LOGICAL**

First Aid for Cuts and Scrapes

- Wash your hands. Put on gloves to keep the other person's blood off your skin. Blood can carry pathogens.
- Run water over the injury. Rinse away any dirt. Then wash the injury with soap and water.
- Dry the area and put on a clean bandage. Change the bandage every day and when it gets wet or dirty. Keeping the injury clean will help it heal.

First Aid for Insect Bites or Stings

- Find out what kind of insect made the sting or bite.
- Scrape any stinger out. Don't pull it out because more venom may get squeezed into the skin.
- Wash the injury and put ice or a cold pack on it for a few minutes.

LANGUAGE ARTS CONNECTION

First-Aid Book

With a Team On index cards, write the steps to care for small injuries, such as sunburn, insect bites and stings, blisters, scrapes, cuts, and bruises. Look up any steps you don't know.

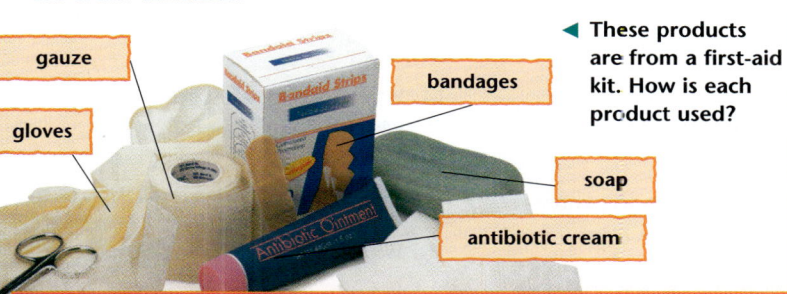

◄ These products are from a first-aid kit. How is each product used?

gauze

gloves

bandages

soap

antibiotic cream

LESSON CHECKUP

Check Your Facts

1. What should you do if someone is badly injured?
2. **CRITICAL THINKING** If someone has been poisoned, should you give first aid or call the Poison Control Center first? Why?

3. Why is it important not to touch other people's blood?

Set Health Goals

4. Look up the emergency phone numbers on the first page of your local telephone book. Make a card that lists the numbers, such as 911 and the Poison Control Center.

215

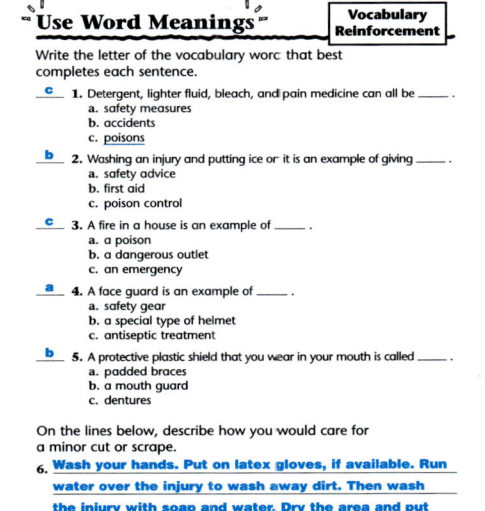

ACTIVITY BOOK, p. 53

Use Word Meanings | Vocabulary Reinforcement

Write the letter of the vocabulary word that best completes each sentence.

c 1. Detergent, lighter fluid, bleach, and pain medicine can all be _____.
   a. safety measures
   b. accidents
   c. poisons

b 2. Washing an injury and putting ice on it is an example of giving _____.
   a. safety advice
   b. first aid
   c. poison control

c 3. A fire in a house is an example of _____.
   a. a poison
   b. a dangerous outlet
   c. an emergency

a 4. A face guard is an example of _____.
   a. safety gear
   b. a special type of helmet
   c. antiseptic treatment

b 5. A protective plastic shield that you wear in your mouth is called _____.
   a. padded braces
   b. a mouth guard
   c. dentures

On the lines below, describe how you would care for a minor cut or scrape.

6. Wash your hands. Put on latex gloves, if available. Run water over the injury to wash away dirt. Then wash the injury with soap and water. Dry the area and put on a clean bandage. Change the bandage every day or if it gets wet or dirty.

---

2 Teach

Discuss

Critical Thinking Why might you want to apply an antiseptic ointment to a cut? to kill pathogens that might cause the cut to become infected; to soothe or alleviate the pain

Language Arts Connection

First-Aid Book Assign each team a small injury to research. Refer students to print and on-line reference materials that will help them identify usual first-aid steps for the assigned injuries. Collect index cards in a binder and place in the school library reference section.

Learn from Pictures

Focus students' attention on the picture of the first-aid kit. Invite volunteers to explain how each first-aid product is used. If necessary, have students reread the text to determine the answers.

For more information about first aid, see pages 276–279.

3 Wrap Up

Lesson Checkup

1. Tell an adult, and call 911 or an emergency number for your area.
2. Call the Poison Control Center because different poisons need different treatments.
3. Blood can carry pathogens.
4. Students can ask their parents for the numbers of their family doctors and dentists so they can add them to the list. Suggest students put the list near the telephone at home.

TEACHER TIP

Allergic Reactions Determine if any students in your class are allergic to insect bites or stings, and know what to do in case one of these students suffers an allergic reaction from a bite or sting. You can also invite students to explain in as much detail as they wish what happens to them when they get bit or stung and what emergency first-aid treatment is necessary to prevent them from becoming very sick.

Use Vocabulary 3 pts. each

1. injury
2. hazard
3. safety rules
4. limit
5. passenger
6. stranger
7. trusted adult
8. bully
9. poison
10. safety gear
11. mouth guard
12. emergency
13. first aid

Check Your Facts 5 pts. each

14. always buckle your safety belt; sit in the back seat

15. Some strangers are not safe to be around.

16. your address, how big the fire is, what is burning, if anyone is trapped inside

17. Mouth guards help protect the teeth, gums, face bones, and jaw when you play team sports.

18. Possible answers: soap to clean the area, bandages to cover the area, gloves to protect the first-aid giver from blood from the injury, antiseptic cream to aid in killing pathogens, gauze to clean the wound or to stop the bleeding.

USE VOCABULARY

bully (p. 200)	**injury** (p. 195)	**passenger** (p. 196)	**safety rules** (p. 195)
emergency (p. 204)	**limit** (p. 195)	**poison** (p. 206)	**stranger** (p. 198)
first aid (p. 214)	**mouth guard** (p. 208)	**safety gear** (p. 208)	**trusted adult** (p. 198)
hazard (p. 195)			

Use the terms above to complete the sentences. Page numbers in ( ) tell you where to look in the chapter if you need help.

1. An ____ is harm done to the body.

2. A danger that could lead to an injury is called a ____.

3. Rules to keep you from injury are called ____.

4. A ____ is a point at which you must stop.

5. A person who rides in a car or bus with a driver is a ____.

6. A ____ is someone you don't know well.

7. A ____ is a grown-up you know well or someone who is responsible for you.

8. Someone who hurts or frightens others is called a ____.

9. A substance that causes illness or death can be called a ____.

10. Clothing or equipment that can help protect you from injury is ____.

11. A protective shield you wear in your mouth is called a ____.

12. An ____ is a situation in which help is needed right away.

13. The care given to small injuries is ____.

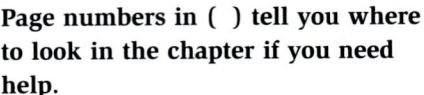

CHECK YOUR FACTS

Page numbers in ( ) tell you where to look in the chapter if you need help.

14. What are two safety rules to follow when riding in a car? (p. 196)

15. Why should you stay away from strangers? (p. 198)

16. What might a 911 operator need to know about a fire emergency? (p. 205)

17. Why do dentists recommend that people wear mouth guards for most team sports? (p. 208)

18. Name four things you need to have in a first-aid kit, and tell how each is used. (p. 215)

THINK CRITICALLY

19. You are walking to school when a car stops beside you. The driver asks for directions to school. What should you do?

20. Your mom is driving you to school. You want to be safe in the car. Name two things you should do and two things you shouldn't do.

APPLY LIFE SKILLS

21. **Resolve Conflicts** Jerome and Carlos are on the playground when a bully starts to bother them. How can they negotiate to solve their problem?

22. **Make Decisions** Janine is shopping with her family when she becomes lost. What should she do? Use the steps for making decisions in your answer.

Promote Health **Home and Community**

1. With your family, plan an outdoor hazard hunt. Look for places around your home that could be hazardous. Then discuss ways to correct the hazards.
2. On cards, list emergency numbers for your community. Hand the cards out at school or at a community event.

217

Think Critically 8 pts. each

19. ignore him or her; leave the area, keep walking, cross the street, or change directions; run away, or yell "I don't know you!"

20. Possible answers: wear a safety belt, sit in the back seat, don't put your hands out the window, don't disturb the driver, don't yell or talk loudly, don't eat or drink.

Apply Life Skills 10 pts. each

21. Accept all reasonable answers. Possible answers: They can agree that they disagree and ignore mean remarks, listen to the bully and don't talk or fight back, think of alternatives to the problem, try to reach a compromise. They can also get help from a trusted adult, stay with others, and choose friends who stay away from bullies.

22. Accept all reasonable answers that include the decision-making steps: find out about the choices she could make, imagine the possible result of each choice, make what seems the best choice, and think about what happened as a result. Possible choices include staying where she last saw her parent, going to the store manager or a clerk, telling a security guard, or meeting at a prearranged place in the store.

PERFORMANCE ASSESSMENT

Project—Safety Collage

The chapter project (introduced on page 193) can be used for individual or team performance assessment. Allow students the opportunity to revise and complete their projects before submitting them for evaluation. Students can use the Project Summary Sheet (Assessment Guide, p. 17) to tell about their projects. You can use the rubric provided on the Project Evaluation Sheet (Assessment Guide, p. 49) to evaluate student performance.

Activities

A Safer Bicycle

On Your Own • Find out what kind of safety gear bicycles need to have. Then make a poster showing safety gear on bicycles.

Know the Rules

With a Partner • Make a list of different places at your school that you and your classmates use, such as the cafeteria, library, and playground. Make a chart comparing the rules for each of the places you have chosen. List reasons you think some places might need different rules.

First-Aid Kit

With a Team • Visit the school nurse or office and make a list of the first-aid supplies the school has. Make a booklet for a kindergarten class explaining how each item is used.

Safety Search

At Home • Look up *safety* and *fire* in an encyclopedia or in library books. Make a list of fire hazards that are common in homes. Talk about them with your family. Help an adult in your family correct the fire hazards that you find.

218

Chapter Test

ASSESSMENT GUIDE, p. 46

Keeping Safe

Chapter 8 Test

Write *T* or *F* to show if the statement is true or false.

- **T** 1. Family members have a responsibility to protect you.
- **F** 2. You have no duty to help protect yourself.
- **F** 3. Safety rules are rules that can be dangerous.
- **T** 4. An injury is harm done to a person's body.
- **F** 5. A hazard is a rule that helps protect you from injury.
- **T** 6. A limit is a point at which you must stop.
- **T** 7. A passenger is someone riding in a car or bus.
- **F** 8. The safest place for children in a car is in the front seat.
- **F** 9. It's safe to walk on the road.
- **F** 10. Crossing a street in the middle of the block is as safe as crossing at a corner.

11. Cross out the one thing you should *never* do when a stranger approaches you.

Ignore him or her.

~~Go in a car with him or her.~~

Leave the area.

Run away and yell, "I don't know you."

12. Cross out the person below who would *not* be thought of as a trusted adult.

a grandparent

a teacher

a good neighbor

a police officer

a security guard

~~a stranger on the street~~

ASSESSMENT GUIDE, p. 47

13. Circle the safety rules you *could* follow when faced with a bully.

(Ignore mean remarks.)

(Don't talk back or fight.)

Yell something mean back at the person.

(Get help if the bully follows you.)

(Stay with others.)

(Choose friends who stay away from bullies.)

Keep running if the bully follows you.

14. Cross out the sentences below that are *not* emergencies.

Your house is on fire.

Your mother has fallen and is injured.

~~Someone is knocking on your front door.~~

~~The wind has blown over your patio furniture.~~

Your younger brother has swallowed poison.

A storm has blown off part of your roof.

15. Draw a picture of yourself escaping a fire. Be sure that your picture shows you practicing something that you learned about safely escaping a fire.

The picture should show one of the following: child crawling out of a room; warning others; following an escape route; meeting family outside; calling 911 or the fire department; stop, drop, roll.

ASSESSMENT GUIDE, p. 48

Write the letter of the best answer on the line in front of the sentence.

- **b** 16. When unplugging a lamp, hold the ___.
  - a. cord
  - b. plug
  - c. lamp
  - d. shade
- **a** 17. Never plug in or turn on electrical things when you have ___.
  - a. wet hands
  - b. eyeglasses on
  - c. dry hands
  - d. a book in your hand
- **d** 18. A substance that causes illness or death when it gets into the body is called a ___.
  - a. medicine
  - b. cover
  - c. home product
  - d. poison
- **d** 19. Clothing or equipment worn to protect players from injury is called ___.
  - a. safety net
  - b. safety belt
  - c. safety guard
  - d. safety gear
- **c** 20. The most important safety gear to wear while bicycling ___.
  - a. is a mouth guard
  - b. are wrist guards
  - c. is a helmet
  - d. are elbow pads
- **d** 21. When you buy a helmet, you should look for ___.
  - a. the price tag
  - b. a helmet that fits loosely
  - c. your favorite color
  - d. a hard shell and an approval sticker
- **a** 22. If someone has been poisoned, call ___.
  - a. the Poison Control Center
  - b. 911
  - c. your neighbor
  - d. your local police
- **a** 23. If someone is very ill and there is no adult to tell, call ___.
  - a. 911
  - b. the Poison Control Center
  - c. your local police
  - d. your teacher
- **b** 24. Caring for small injuries is called ___.
  - a. dangerous
  - b. first aid
  - c. an emergency
  - d. an antiseptic
- **c** 25. The first thing you should do about an injury is ___.
  - a. call 911
  - b. call the Poison Control Center
  - c. tell an adult
  - d. tell a friend

Multiple Choice

Choose the letter of the correct answer.

1. The person most responsible for your safety is _____.
   a. your mom　　b. your brother
   c. you　　d. your teacher

2. Cross a street _____.
   a. at a crosswalk　　b. on the left
   c. in the middle　　d. on the right

3. If a bully follows you, _____.
   a. turn and talk　　b. tell a friend
   c. yell　　d. get help

4. If you are trying to escape a fire, _____.
   a. run　　b. find water
   c. crawl　　d. hide

5. A bicycle helmet should _____.
   a. not have straps　　b. fit properly
   c. be black　　d. be loose

Modified True or False

Write *true* or *false*. If a sentence is false, replace the underlined term to make the sentence true.

6. Before crossing the street, STOP, LOOK, <u>BLINK</u>, and THINK.

7. The safest place for car passengers to sit is in the <u>front</u> seat.

8. Stay <u>a hand's</u> reach from a stranger.

9. When bullied, <u>stay and fight</u>.

10. One piece of safety gear hockey players wear is a <u>mouth guard</u>.

11. A bicycle helmet should fit <u>loosely</u> on your head.

12. In a fire the cleanest air is <u>up high</u>.

13. Hold the <u>cord</u> when you unplug something.

14. A 911 operator <u>should</u> hang up first.

15. You should put <u>ice</u> on an insect bite.

Short Answer

Write a complete sentence to answer each question.

16. Describe a limit set by an adult.

17. How does a safety belt protect you?

18. Why is safety gear important when you play sports?

19. How could medicine be a poison?

20. Tell what you should do after you escape from a fire.

21. Why shouldn't you plug in a toaster when you have wet hands?

22. Tell why a helmet is important safety gear.

23. What are two safety rules for crossing the street?

Writing in Health

Write paragraphs to answer each item.

24. Give an example of an emergency. Tell what safety steps should be followed in the emergency.

25. What should you look for when you shop for a bicycle helmet?

Writing in Health (10 pts. each)

Sample answers are shown; accept other reasonable answers.

24. A fire is an emergency. If there is a fire you should crawl out quickly, warn others, follow an escape path, go to your family's meeting place, and call 911 or the fire department. If your clothes catch on fire, you should stop, drop, and roll.

25. When you shop for a bicycle helmet, you should look for one with a hard shell and an approval sticker that shows it meets safety standards; one that is brightly colored; and one that fits snug but not tight when sitting evenly between your ears, low on your forehead, and with straps tightened.

Two options are provided for Chapter Tests—the in-book test and the reproducible test in the Assessment Guide. In addition to providing students with the opportunity to show what they have learned, both tests provide practice in taking standardized tests.

Multiple Choice (2 pts. each)

1. c	3. d	5. b
2. a	4. c	

Modified True or False (3 pts. each)

6. false; listen

7. false; back

8. false; more than an arm's

9. false; walk away

10. true

11. false; snug but not tight

12. false; near the floor

13. false; plug

14. true

15. true

Short Answer (5 pts. each)

Sample answers are shown; accept other reasonable answers.

16. A limit set by an adult is a rule that sets boundaries, such as places where you are allowed to play.

17. A safety belt keeps you in place, minimizing injuries.

18. Safety gear helps prevent injuries during sports.

19. A medicine could be a poison if it is used improperly.

20. After escaping a fire, you should meet in your family's meeting place and call 911 or the fire department.

21. If you plug in a toaster with wet hands, you could receive a shock.

22. A helmet is important safety gear because it takes away the force of a fall and helps protect your head from injury.

23. You should cross streets only at corners or crosswalks, and before crossing you should stop, look, listen, and think.

CHAPTER 9 Health *in the* Community

Chapter Organizer

Lesson	Objectives	Vocabulary	Program Resources
Introduce the Chapter pp. 220–221	• Preview the chapter. • Begin chapter project.		• School-Home Connection, TR p. 49 • Assessment Guide, p. 53 • Read-Aloud Anthology, p. RA-10 • Teaching Transparency 9— Graphic Organizer
Lesson 1 ✓ 1·2·7 **Health Departments, Hospitals, and Clinics** pp. 222–225 **Pacing: 1 class period**	• Define **community**. • Explain some of the responsibilities of people who work to promote public health. • Compare and contrast hospitals and clinics.	community health department hospital clinic	• Activity Book, p. 54
Lesson 2 ✓ 1·2·6 **Keeping the Environment Healthful** pp. 226–229 **Pacing: 1 class period**	• Define **pollution**. • List several sources of air pollution. • Explain how noise pollution can be harmful to humans.	environment pollution air pollution pollution control technician noise pollution	• Activity Book, p. 55 Computer Graphing Activity, TR p. 66 Teaching Transparency 11
Lesson 3 ✓ 1·6·7 **Controlling Water Pollution** pp. 230–233 **Pacing: 1 class period**	• List several sources of water pollution. • Describe how water is treated so that it is safe for human consumption. • Explain how groundwater becomes polluted.	water pollution groundwater	• Activity Book, p. 56
Life Skills ✓ 1·5·6 **Set Goals** pp. 234–235 **Pacing: 1 class period**	• Identify steps in the goal-setting process. • Use goal-setting skills to protect the environment.		• Activity Book, p. 57 HEALTH VIDEO: The Cleanup Kids
Lesson 4 ✓ 1·6·7 **Reduce, Reuse, and Recycle** pp. 236–239 **Pacing: 1 class period**	• Discuss how to prevent litter from becoming an unsightly part of the community. • List ways to reduce, reuse, and recycle.	littering reduce reuse recycle	• Activity Book, pp. 58–59 Computer Graphing Activity, TR p. 67
Chapter Review and Test ✓ 1·7 pp. 240–243	• Assess chapter objectives and project. • Provide extension activities.		• Chapter Test and Project Evaluation Sheet, Assessment Guide, p. 50–53

 National Health Education Standards
A complete list of the Standards is provided on the next page.

Key: TR = Teaching Resources

National Health Education Standards

1. Comprehend concepts related to health promotion and disease prevention.
2. Access valid health information and health-promoting products and services.
3. Practice health-enhancing behaviors and reduce health risks.
4. Analyze the influence of culture, media, technology, and other factors on health.
5. Use interpersonal communication skills to enhance health.
6. Use goal-setting and decision-making skills to enhance health.
7. Advocate for personal, family, and community health.

Art
- Recycled Robots, p. 220C
- Before-and-After Posters, p. 235

Math and Science
- Pollution Problems in Your Community, p. 220C
- Cave Icicles, p. 220C

Drama
- General Hospital, p. 224

Curriculum Integration
Use these topics to integrate health into your daily planning.

Social Studies
- The American Red Cross, p. 220C
- Locate Water Sources, p. 232

Physical Education
- Goal Posters, p. 234

Language Arts
- Letter Writing, p. 220C
- Pollution Speech, p. 233

ASSESSMENT OPTIONS

Portfolio Assessment
Have students select their best work from the following suggestions:
- **Pollution Speech**, p. 233
- **Save the Groundwater**, p. 242
- **Checking Up**, p. 242

Student Self-Assessment
- **Journal Notes**, p. 224
- **Set Health Goals**, pp. 229, 239
- **Use Life Skills**, pp. 225, 233

Daily Assessment
- **Check Your Facts**, pp. 225, 229, 233, 239

Performance Assessment
- **Chapter Project: Reuse Classroom Items**, pp. 221, 238, 241
- **Project Evaluation Sheet**, Assessment Guide, p. 53

Formal Assessment
- **Chapter Review**, pp. 240–241
- **In-Book Test**, p. 243
- **Chapter Test**, Assessment Guide, pp. 50–52

Cross-Curricular Activities

Art

Recycled Robots

Have students collect recyclable items around the house that can be used to make life-sized robots. Items could include empty paper towel, toilet tissue, and wrapping paper rolls; cardboard boxes from crackers, cereals, and other such products; old buttons; paper plates and cups; clean jar lids; and so on. Divide the class into groups of three or four. Provide each group with poster paints, glue, string, scissors, and tape to decorate and assemble their robots.

Social Studies

The American Red Cross

Have pairs of students find out about the American Red Cross and its role in keeping communities healthy and safe and their role following disasters such as floods, fires, and earthquakes. Students can display their findings as posters or brochures.

Language Arts

Letter Writing

Have pairs of students compose letters to local businesses and industries—factories, grocery stores, dry cleaners, clothing stores, offices, and so on—asking how each limits the pollutants that result from its operation, or how the business reduces and recycles the materials it uses.

Math

Pollution Problems in Your Community

Have each student in your classroom survey ten adults to find out what each adult feels is the most critical pollution problem in your community. Have the class compile the results and make a bar graph to display the data. If time permits, have students brainstorm a list of ways that these problems can be prevented or lessened.

Science

Cave Icicles

Groundwater plays an important role in the formation of stalactites, or cave icicles. Have students simulate the formation of stalactites.

What you need
glass jar, cotton string, granulated sugar, hot water, spoon, pencil

What to do
- In the jar, have students make a concentrated solution of $1\frac{1}{2}$ cups of hot water and 1 cup of sugar.

- Have students tie a piece of string to the pencil and place the pencil over the mouth of the jar. The string should dangle into the solution.

- The jar should be put on a window sill and left undisturbed. After a week or so, students will observe sugar crystals that have formed on the string. Explain that minerals precipitate, or come out of solution, from groundwater to form stalactites.

Bulletin Board

Divide the bulletin board in half vertically. Title the left-hand side *Sources of Pollution* and the right-hand side *Solutions to Pollution*.

- Divide the class into two groups. One group should make sketches or find pictures in old magazines, newspapers, and catalogs of sources of pollution. (Note that sources include motor vehicles, fertilizers, paints, pesticides, household cleaning products, cigarettes, trash, and motor oil.)

- Challenge the second group to sketch or cut out pictures of solutions to the first group's sources of pollution. (Solutions to the examples listed above include biking or walking to reduce air pollution, using organic gardening and cleaning products, not smoking, not littering, reducing the amount of trash generated, recycling, and disposing of used motor oil properly—i.e., not dumping it down the drain or into a sewer.)

- Midway through the chapter, have the groups exchange roles and repeat the activity.

Resources

Books for Students

Bowman-Kruhm, Mary. *A Day in the Life of a Police Officer.* PowerKids Press, 1998. Describes a day in the life of a police officer and his police dog. **EASY**

Showers, Paul. *Where Does the Garbage Go?* HarperCollins, 1994. Discusses wastes and recycling using a school classroom and a field trip to the landfill. **AVERAGE**

Markle, Sandra. *After the Spill: The Exxon Valdez Disaster, Then and Now.* Walker and Co., 1999. Describes how the oil spill occured and the environmental disaster it caused. **ADVANCED**

Books for Teachers and Families

Dadd-Redalia, Debra. *Home Safe Home: Protecting Yourself and Your Family From Everyday Toxics and Harmful Household Products.* Putnam, 1997. Contains valuable information about household chemicals.

Lawson, Lynn. *Staying Well in a Toxic World.* Lynnwood Press, 2000. Practical information about the little understood illnesses caused by exposures to modern chemicals.

Videos

Keeping Your Community Clean. Rainbow Educational Media, 1995. (15 minutes) The Video Rating Guide for Libraries cites this production as containing excellent information on recycling and community sanitation.

You And Your Hospital. Rainbow Educational Media, 1995. (19 minutes) Introduces students to a community hospital and the staff and their jobs.

Down The Drain. 3-2-1 Contact, Children's Television Workshop, 1991. (30 minutes) Students are shown the water cycle, water conservation, and what happens in a water treatment plant.

Health Video Series by Harcourt *The Cleanup Kids* This video is referenced at point-of-use in this Teacher's Edition.

Your Health Webliography

The **Webliography** provides links to the Health Background and teaching resources that will support you as you teach the topics in *Your Health.* Simply choose a keyword and you will be taken to a page of links with descriptions of the content you can obtain at each site. The **Webliography** is located on the Teacher Resources page at **www.harcourtschool.com/health** Please review websites before referring your students to them.

Organizations and Agencies

The Indoor Air Quality Information Clearinghouse
P.O. Box 37133
Washington, D.C. 20013-7133
800-438-4318
Answers questions and provides information about carbon monoxide, radon, asbestos, and formaldehyde.

Kids Against Pollution (KAP)
At the Children's Museum
311 Main St., 3rd Floor
Utica, NY 13501
A network of students working for the environment through letter-writing campaigns and community action.

Environmental Protection Agency
Office of Solid Waste
1200 Pennsylvania Ave. N.W.
Washington, D.C. 20460
800-424-9346

Provides educational information on a variety of environmental issues.

For more information about health organizations and agencies, please see the *Teaching Resources* book.

Community Health

EMT Invite an emergency medical technician to talk to the class about emergencies he or she has handled on the job. Encourage each student to think of questions to ask prior to the person's scheduled arrival.

Free and Inexpensive Material

The Izaak Walton League of America, Inc.
Save Our Streams
707 Conservation Lane
Gaithersburg, MD 20878-2983
800-453-5463
Distributes a pamphlet explaining what students can do to save our water resources.

Kids For a Clean Environment
Attn: Newsletter
P.O. Box 158254
Nashville, TN 37215
800-952-3223
Written by kids for kids, this newsletter will help students learn about recycling and the environment.

Note that information, while correct at time of publication, is subject to change.

Visit **The Harcourt Learning Site** for related links, activities, resources, and the health **Webliography**.

www.harcourtschool.com

WELCOME TO THE LEARNING SITE

"If a disease is made by human beings, we should be able to prevent it."

Raising Children Toxic Free

CHAPTER SUMMARY

In this chapter students
- find out about the people involved in assuring the health of a community.
- learn about sources of air, noise, and water pollution as well as ways to reduce these types of pollution.
- discover ways to reduce, reuse, and recycle.

LIFE SKILLS Students practice *setting goals* to improve the community and the environment.

HUMAN BODY Students learn about the circulatory system and blood pressure, how asthma affects the respiratory system, and how some hearing loss is associated with noise pollution.

Literature Springboard

Use the excerpt "Running Water" to spark interest in the chapter topic. See the Read-Aloud Anthology on page RA-10 of this Teacher's Edition.

School-Home Connection

Distribute copies of the School-Home Connection (in English or Spanish), TR page 49. Have students take the page home to share with their families as you begin this chapter.

Follow Up Have volunteers share what they found out about their local hospital(s). Does the hospital offer more services than they expected?

Alternative Use the School-Home Connection page as a classroom resource for enrichment activities.

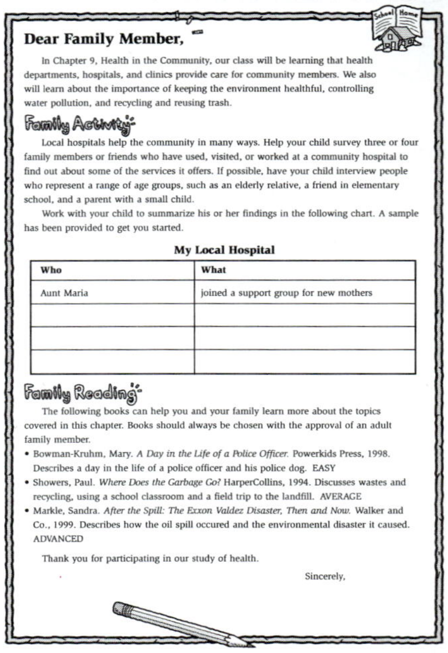

Dear Family Member,

In Chapter 9, *Health in the Community*, our class will be learning that health departments, hospitals, and clinics provide care for community members. We also will learn about the importance of keeping the environment healthful, controlling water pollution, and recycling and reusing trash.

Family Activity

Local hospitals help the community in many ways. Help your child survey three or four family members or friends who have used, visited, or worked at a community hospital to find out about some of the services it offers. If possible, have your child interview people who represent a range of age groups, such as an elderly relative, a friend in elementary school, and a parent with a small child.

Work with your child to summarize his or her findings in the following chart. A sample has been provided to get you started.

My Local Hospital

Who	What
Aunt Maria	joined a support group for new mothers

Family Reading

The following books can help you and your family learn more about the topics covered in this chapter. Books should always be chosen with the approval of an adult family member.
- Bowman-Kruhm, Mary. *A Day in the Life of a Police Officer.* Powerkids Press, 1998. Describes a day in the life of a police officer and his police dog. EASY
- Showers, Paul. *Where Does the Garbage Go?* HarperCollins, 1994. Discusses wastes and recycling, using a school classroom and a field trip to the landfill. AVERAGE
- Markle, Sandra. *After the Spill: The Exxon Valdez Disaster, Then and Now.* Walker and Co., 1999. Describes how the oil spill occured and the environmental disaster it caused. ADVANCED

Thank you for participating in our study of health.

Sincerely,

220

Health in the Community

REUSE CLASSROOM ITEMS

Develop a plan for reusing items in your classroom. Find out what kinds of things would be useful for art projects or other classroom projects. Decide where those things can be collected. Write a plan to share with other classes.

For other activities, visit the Harcourt Learning Site. www.harcourtschool.com

221

Introduce the Chapter

REUSE CLASSROOM ITEMS

Access Prior Knowledge Use this activity as a baseline assessment of students' understanding of the term *reuse*. Assign groups the following items to reuse: glass jars, metal cans (steel and aluminum), plastic milk jugs, soda bottles, and paper. Provide large cardboard boxes for collecting the items. After students have determined which items could be reused in your classroom, have them consider several ways in which they can be reused.

Performance Assessment The project can be used for performance assessment. Before students begin, explain how you will evaluate their performance. (See the Project Evaluation Sheet, Assessment Guide, p. 53.)

Prereading Strategies

Scan the Chapter Have students preview the chapter content by scanning the titles, headings, pictures, and charts. Ask volunteers to speculate on what they will learn.

Preview Vocabulary Have students copy the vocabulary words. Have them look up the terms in the glossary and write a definition next to each term. Have students keep the definitions handy for reference as you begin each lesson.

Visualize Key Concepts Display the Graphic Organizer Transparency. You may also wish to distribute photocopies to students. Have students complete the organizer as they work through the chapter. Suggested concepts for students to fill in are shown.

Follow Up Review the completed organizer with students as preparation for the Chapter Review and Chapter Tests.

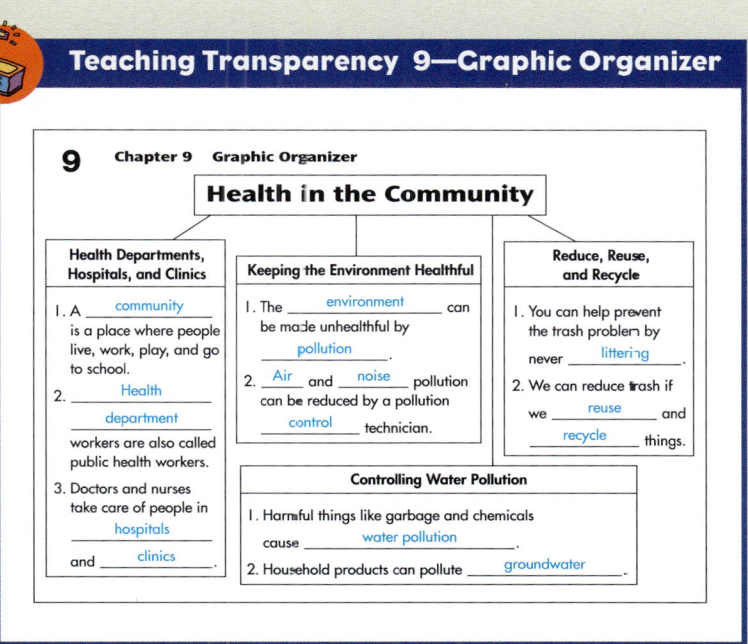

Teaching Transparency 9—Graphic Organizer

9 Chapter 9 Graphic Organizer

Health in the Community

Health Departments, Hospitals, and Clinics

1. A ___community___ is a place where people live, work, play, and go to school.
2. ___Health department___ workers are also called public health workers.
3. Doctors and nurses take care of people in ___hospitals___ and ___clinics___.

Keeping the Environment Healthful

1. The ___environment___ can be made unhealthful by ___pollution___.
2. ___Air___ and ___noise___ pollution can be reduced by a pollution ___control___ technician.

Controlling Water Pollution

1. Harmful things like garbage and chemicals cause ___water pollution___.
2. Household products can pollute ___groundwater___.

Reduce, Reuse, and Recycle

1. You can help prevent the trash problem by never ___littering___.
2. We can reduce trash if we ___reuse___ and ___recycle___ things.

OBJECTIVES

- Define *community*.
- Explain some of the responsibilities of people who work to promote public health.
- Compare and contrast hospitals and clinics.

PROGRAM RESOURCES

- Activity Book, p. 54

VOCABULARY

- community (p. 222)
- health department (p. 222)
- hospital (p. 224)
- clinic (p. 225)

Daily Safety Tip

Remind students that all medications, even over-the-counter ones, should be taken only as directed by a doctor, nurse, or pharmacist or according to the directions on the label. Also stress that prescription medications are to be taken only by the person for whom the drug was prescribed.

1 Motivate

Play a game of twenty questions based on common illnesses experienced by students. Explain that the object of the game is to guess each illness by posing questions similar to the following: How did you get ill? Did you take any medications? Did you have a rash? Did you vomit? How long were you ill? Did you have a fever? Were other family members also ill?

2 Teach

Learn from Pictures

Have two volunteers role-play the situation shown in the photograph on this page. Make sure the nurse is able to

---

LESSON 1

MAIN IDEA
Health departments, hospitals, and clinics treat people who are hurt or ill. They help people stay well, too.

WHY LEARN THIS? You can use what you learn to find places in your community to get health care.

VOCABULARY
- community
- health department
- hospital
- clinic

Health Departments, Hospitals, and Clinics

A **community** (kuh•MYOO•nuh•tee) is a place where people live, work, play, and go to school. Doctors, nurses, and other health care workers help keep the community healthy.

What does a health department do?

A **health department** is a group of health workers that serves a community. Health department workers are also called public health workers. The pictures on pages 222 and 223 show some of the jobs they do.

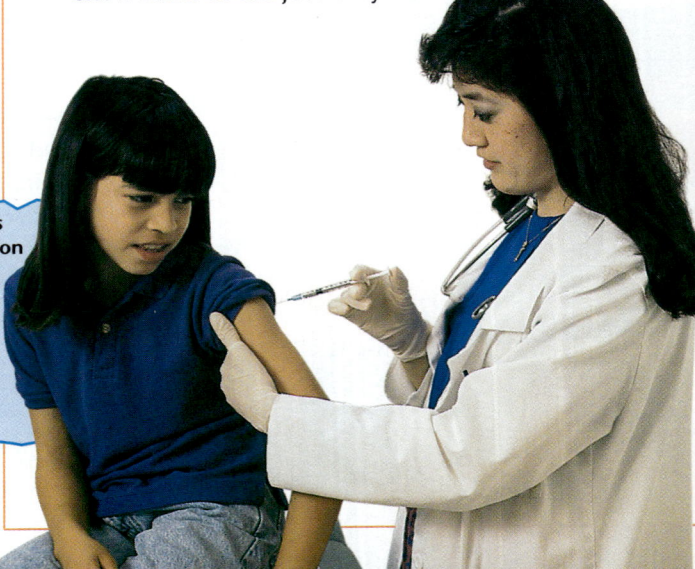

This public health nurse is giving this girl a vaccination that will protect her from a disease such as mumps or measles. The health department also gives adults shots that protect them from diseases such as flu.

222

MULTILEVEL ACTIVITIES

EASY **Research Careers** Have each student research and write a paragraph about a health-care job he or she might like to do. **INTRAPERSONAL/ LINGUISTIC**

AVERAGE **Make Rabies Posters** Direct students to find out more about rabies and how it affects people. Then have small groups of students make posters explaining the importance of having family pets vaccinated against rabies. **VISUAL/INTERPERSONAL**

ADVANCED **Tour the Health Department** Select a group of students to present the jobs in a health department to the rest of the class through role-playing. The "director" can give a tour of the department, and when introduced, each "employee" can talk about his or her job. **KINESTHETIC/INTERPERSONAL**

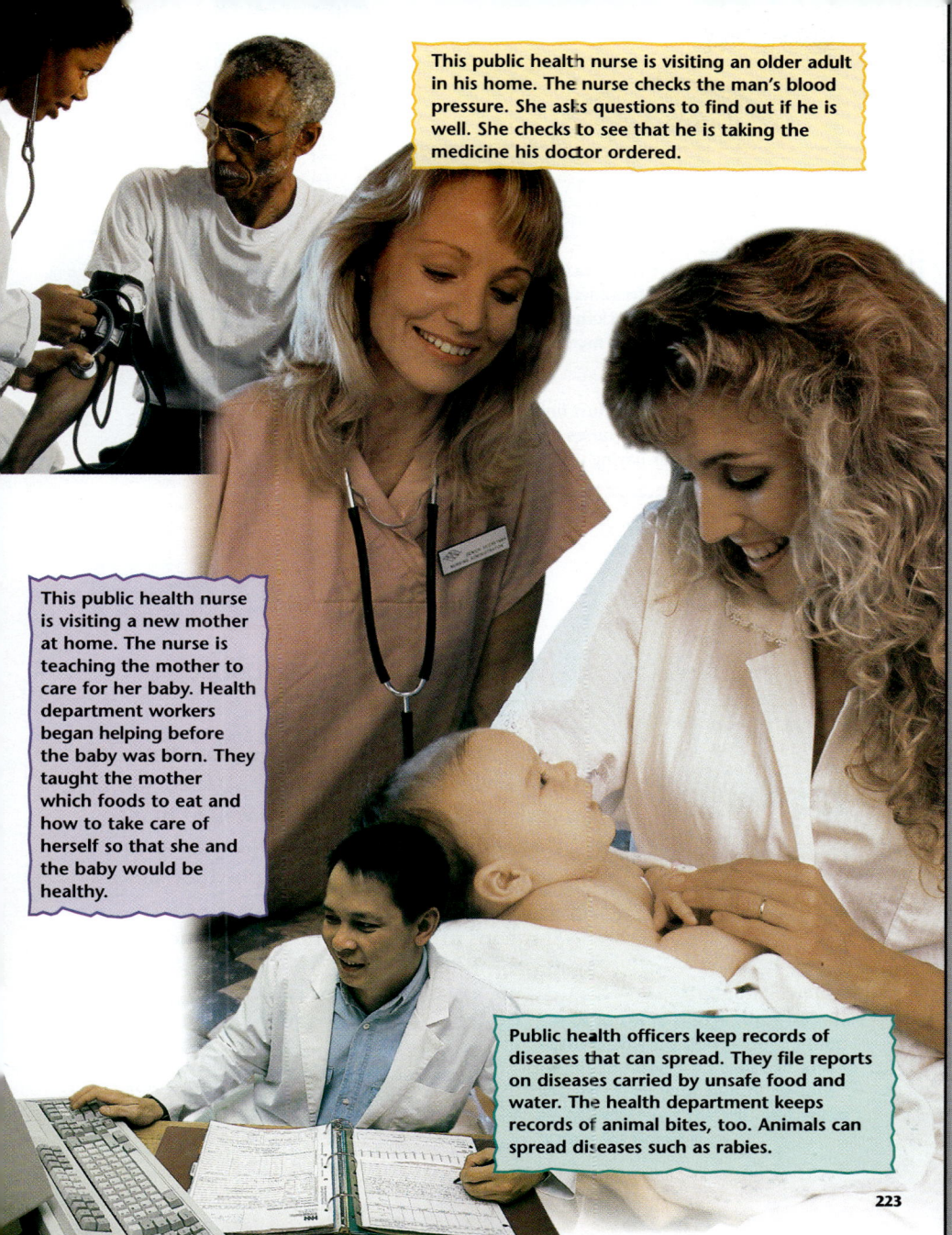

This public health nurse is visiting an older adult in his home. The nurse checks the man's blood pressure. She asks questions to find out if he is well. She checks to see that he is taking the medicine his doctor ordered.

This public health nurse is visiting a new mother at home. The nurse is teaching the mother to care for her baby. Health department workers began helping before the baby was born. They taught the mother which foods to eat and how to take care of herself so that she and the baby would be healthy.

Public health officers keep records of diseases that can spread. They file reports on diseases carried by unsafe food and water. The health department keeps records of animal bites, too. Animals can spread diseases such as rabies.

223

explain what he or she will do to the patient, whether or not it will hurt, and why it is being done. Likewise, encourage the patient to ask questions about the procedure or the disease for which he or she is being inoculated.

Critical Thinking In addition to the people shown on these two pages, who are some other health-care workers in your community? Answers will vary but could include pharmacists, doctors, optometrists, dentists, physical therapists, and dietitians.

Human Body Connection

Circulatory System Have students study the parts of the circulatory system shown on pages 10 and 11. Now explain or have the school nurse demonstrate how to take a person's blood pressure, which is a measure of the force that the blood exerts on the vessels in the body. Make sure students realize that blood pressure rises when the ventricles of the heart contract and drops when the ventricles relax.

DEVELOP READING SKILLS

Identify Cause and Effect
Explain the difference between a cause and an effect. Then help students identify some of the cause-and-effect relationships discussed in this lesson. Have students summarize the information in tables in their Health Journals. An example is given below.

Cause	Effect
Give shots.	Help protect people from diseases.
Teach pregnant women how to eat a proper diet and care for themselves.	Babies and mothers are healthier.
Keep records of diseases.	Help keep people safe from diseases that can spread.

Teach *continued*

Discuss

Broken bones are often treated at a hospital. Once a broken arm or leg bone is set, or put back in place, the doctor often applies a splint or cast to the arm or leg. A splint or cast is made from hard, inflexible material.

Critical Thinking **Why is a splint or cast applied?** The splint or cast keeps the bone in the proper position, allowing it to mend properly. A splint or cast also limits movement of the bone, preventing re-injury.

Critical Thinking **In addition to the examples on this page, what are some situations that might require hospital care?** Answers will vary but could include poisoning and treatment for diseases such as cancer.

Health Journal

Students' answers will vary. They might describe the busy, efficient atmosphere of the hospital. They might talk about the specific reason they were at the hospital. This feature is designed to provide students with an opportunity to reflect on health decisions they are making in their personal lives. The journal should *not* be used to evaluate or assess students, nor do the results need to be shared among students.

Career

Contact the following organization for more information on careers in nursing.

American Nurses Association
600 Maryland Avenue SW
Washington, D.C. 20024–2571

Or visit the **Webliography** on the Teacher Resources page at:
www.harcourtschool.com/health
Keyword health careers

Career

Registered Nurse

What They Do
- Care for people who are ill or hurt
- Help people stay healthy
- Keep records
- Help doctors during treatments and checkups
- Give medicines

Education and Training
To be a registered nurse, you must finish high school and nursing school. Nurses who also finish college get higher-paying jobs.

JOURNAL

In your Health Journal, write about a time that you went to a hospital. Perhaps you were visiting a friend or a new baby. If you've never been to a hospital, describe what you think it would be like. Remember, your journal is private and need not be shared with others.

How do hospitals help the community?

A **hospital** (HAHS•pih•tuhl) is a place where hurt or ill people get medical treatment. Hospitals care for people who are too ill to get well at home.

Doctors also take care of people who come to the emergency room. For example, they sew up deep cuts and set broken bones.

Surgeons are doctors who do operations. A surgeon might remove a person's unhealthy appendix. Surgeons also repair organs, such as a person's damaged heart.

Doctors or midwives help women give birth in hospitals. New mothers and their babies get nursing care. Nurses teach mothers how to feed their babies.

MULTICULTURAL LINK

Acupuncture Have students research and report to the class about acupuncture, a Chinese method for relieving pain, curing certain diseases, and improving general health.

DRAMA

General Hospital Have small groups of students do hospital role-plays. They might act out a surgery or an emergency room treatment of a patient who has broken a leg or arm or who needs sutures. Provide students with markers, paper, and cardboard to make simple props, such as scalpels and bandages. In the re-enactments, encourage the hospital staff to respond to the patients quickly, professionally, and with good bedside manners.

How do clinics help the community?

A **clinic** (KLIH•nik) is another place where people go for medical treatment. Sometimes the cost is low or even free. Clinics also teach things such as baby care and car-seat safety.

Doctors and nurses in clinics treat people who are ill or have small injuries. (Very ill or badly hurt people go to the hospital.) Women who are going to have babies often see doctors in clinics.

Clinics offer health screenings—tests to check for diseases. Technicians take blood from patients for tests. Nurses check blood pressure and give eye exams. Nurses also give shots to prevent diseases.

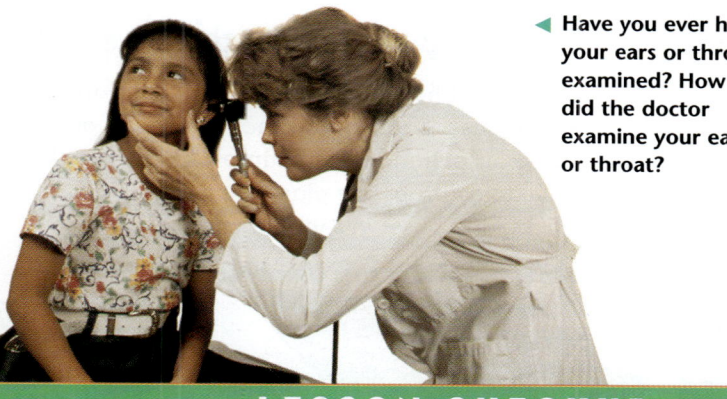

◀ Have you ever had your ears or throat examined? How did the doctor examine your ears or throat?

LESSON CHECKUP

Check Your Facts

① Describe three things a health department does.

② Name two places in the community where ill or hurt people can get care.

③ CRITICAL THINKING Why is it important for the health department to keep good records?

④ Name two services offered at clinics.

Use Life Skills

⑤ MANAGE STRESS Write about a health problem that could cause stress. How could a nurse help with this problem?

225

Discuss

How are clinics and hospitals alike? How are they different? Health care workers at both clinics and hospitals treat people who are sick or injured and provide information on how to get well. Clinics are designed for minor injuries and illnesses. Hospitals generally involve extended treatment of people who are too ill to get well at home.

Learn from Pictures

Direct students to the questions in the caption. Most students have probably had their ears and throats examined. Invite volunteers to answer the second question. They might say the doctor used a tongue depressor, asked them to say "aah," or looked into their ears with a lighted instrument.

❸ Wrap Up

Lesson Checkup

1. Possible answers: Health-care workers in a health department give shots to prevent certain diseases, keep records of contagious diseases, give home health care, and teach people how to care for themselves and their children.

2. hospitals and clinics

3. Keeping good records allows the department to track diseases, which often can help prevent the spread of these diseases. Such records also can make people aware of the diseases to which they might be exposed.

4. Possible answers: prenatal care, health screenings, health education, and treatment of minor injuries and illnesses.

5. Answers will vary. As an example, a broken leg could cause stress if a person can't do the things he or she wants to do. In this situation a nurse could suggest ways to reduce stress until the leg is healed.

OBJECTIVES

- Define *pollution*.
- List several sources of air pollution.
- Explain how noise pollution can be harmful to humans.

PROGRAM RESOURCES

- Activity Book, p. 55

 Computer Graphing Activity, Teaching Resources p. 66

 Teaching Transparency 11

VOCABULARY

- environment (p. 226)
- pollution (p. 226)
- air pollution (p. 226)
- pollution control technician (p. 227)
- noise pollution (p. 228)

Daily Safety Tip

Common "combustion" appliances, such as gas clothes dryers, ovens, furnaces, water heaters, and stoves; kerosene space heaters; and wood-burning fireplaces, are common sources of indoor air pollutants. Such appliances should be properly installed and maintained and vented to the outdoors, when necessary.

1 Motivate

Optional Materials pictures of erupting volcano, forest fire, fireplace, cigarette, car, factory, aerosol can, and gas stove burner

Show students the pictures listed above, or put the list on the board. Challenge students to identify the objects that contribute to air pollution. Some students might be surprised to find out that all of these objects are sources of air pollution.

MAIN IDEA Clean air and protection from noise are important to your health.

WHY LEARN THIS? You can use what you learn to reduce air and noise pollution and to help keep yourself healthy.

VOCABULARY
- environment
- pollution
- air pollution
- pollution control technician
- noise pollution

Keeping the Environment Healthful

Everything around you is part of the **environment** (in•VY•ruhn•muhnt). The environment includes all nonliving things, such as rocks and air. It also includes living things, such as trees. You are part of the environment, too.

The environment can be made unhealthful by pollution. **Pollution** (puh•LOO•shuhn) is dirt and harmful materials in the air, water, or land.

How do people keep the air safe?

Dirt and harmful materials in the air are **air pollution**. Some things that people use or do cause air pollution. For example, many people drive to get from one place to another. Cars, trucks, and buses give off materials that pollute the air.

▶ The exhaust from cars and trucks has harmful gases and other materials in it. In some areas laws limit the amounts of polluting gases cars and trucks can give off. Drivers in these areas must have their vehicles tested to make sure they meet pollution control laws.

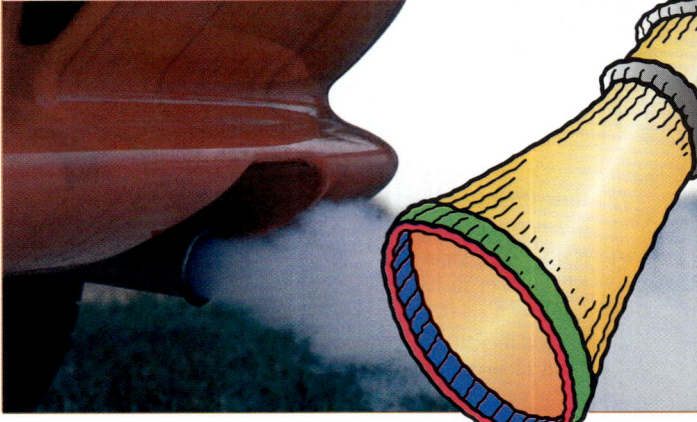

226

MULTILEVEL ACTIVITIES

EASY **Pollution Poems** Have students write short poems about air pollution and its sources. They can use the information on these pages. **LINGUISTIC**

AVERAGE **Record Noise** Have students tape record (or list) noises in their environments that are louder than they would like them to be. Have them play back the recorded noises or read their lists to the class. **AUDITORY/INTERPERSONAL**

ADVANCED **Determine Volume Changes** Show students a rectangular box, and tell them its volume (length x width x height). Inform them that incineration reduces solid waste to about one-tenth of its original volume. Then have pairs of students determine what the volume of solid wastes that filled the box would be after incineration. **MATHEMATICAL**

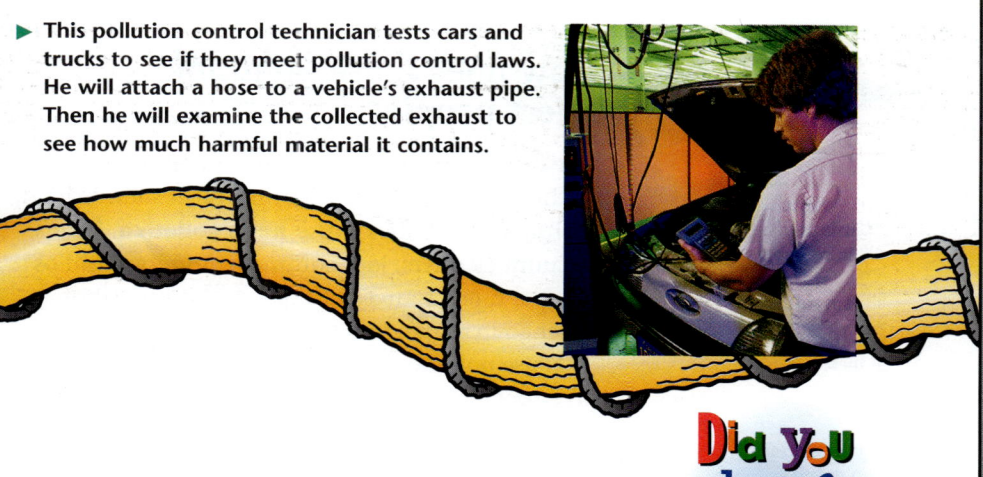

► This pollution control technician tests cars and trucks to see if they meet pollution control laws. He will attach a hose to a vehicle's exhaust pipe. Then he will examine the collected exhaust to see how much harmful material it contains.

Many communities have laws to help reduce air pollution. These laws limit the amount of smoke and harmful fumes released into the air. The laws apply to smoke and harmful fumes from factories, cars and trucks, and tobacco products.

Burning trash outside causes air pollution too. Why? Smoke from the trash causes pollution. Also, many things that people throw away give off harmful gases as they burn. Burning things such as batteries or plastic, for example, pollutes the air.

Many cities burn trash inside special buildings to help reduce air pollution. These buildings have pollution control devices. As the trash is burned, gases and solids that can pollute the air are removed.

Some people have jobs working to reduce air pollution. A **pollution control technician** (puh•LOO•shuhn kuhn•TROHL tek•NIH•shuhn) tests water, air, or soil for harmful substances.

Did you know?

There are natural sources of air pollution, too. Forest fires and volcanoes pollute the air with smoke and harmful gases. Dust storms and ocean waves also add materials to the air that are considered pollution.

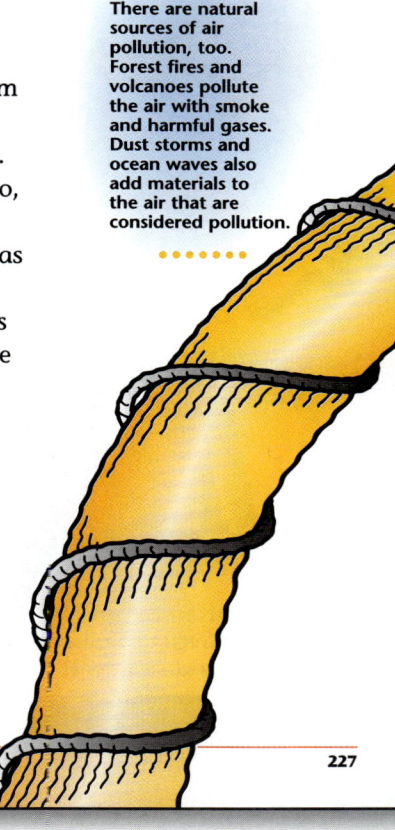

227

2 Teach

Human Body Connection

Respiratory System Have students review the respiratory system shown on pages 12 and 13. Inform students that car emissions and other air pollutants commonly trigger asthma attacks. Explain that during an attack, a person with asthma has a difficult time breathing because the smooth muscles of the tubes leading to the lungs (the bronchi) go into spasm. At the same time, tissues lining the air tubes swell and secrete excess mucus, which narrows the air passages even more.

Learn from Pictures

Once students have looked at the pictures and read the captions on pages 226–227, pose the following questions.

Critical Thinking At what time of day do you think the levels of exhaust fumes are the highest in a city? during morning and evening rush hours Which vehicle—a family car or a school bus—probably produces more exhaust? the school bus Which probably produces more pollution per passenger? the car

227

Teach *continued*

Discuss

Use the question posed in the student text as a springboard for a discussion of noise pollution.

Critical Thinking **What other sources of noise pollution can you think of?** Answers might include video games and arcades, rock concerts, leaf blowers, power saws, mixers, blenders, food processors, telephones, pagers, radios or stereos, firecrackers, and cars without mufflers.

Consumer Focus

Access Valid Health Information If students are having difficulties with finding information, suggest they try to research noise level charts in science textbooks. Students might also be interested in finding information on animals' different hearing ranges.

Human Body Connection

Senses Have students study the ear diagram shown on page 2. Explain that loud or prolonged noises can damage parts of the inner ear and can cause permanent hearing loss.

Different animals hear sounds of different frequencies, which are measured in a unit called hertz. The higher the frequency, the higher the pitch of the sound is. People, for example, hear sounds with frequencies between 20 and 20,000 hertz. Cats hear sounds between 15 and 50,000 hertz. Dogs hear sounds between 60 and 65,000 hertz.

Critical Thinking **Which animal—human, dog, or cat—hears the widest range of sound frequencies?** the dog **Why can a dog's ears be hurt by a sound that doesn't hurt our ears?** because a dog can hear sounds that humans can't

CONSUMER FOCUS

Access Valid Health Information

Noise is measured by how loud it is. Use the steps on page *xvi* to help you research the loudness level of at least five different noises. Make a poster showing ways people can control some of these noises.

How does noise pollution affect people?

Noise can pollute the environment, just as dirt in the air can. Disturbing or harmful sounds made by human activities cause **noise pollution**. Sirens, vacuum cleaners, jackhammers, and loud radios are just a few sources of noise pollution. What other sources can you think of?

Noise pollution makes people tired and angry. It gives people headaches and stomachaches. Worst of all, it hurts people's ears. Noise pollution causes most people in the United States to lose some hearing by the time they are 30 years old. If you need to raise your voice for people to hear you, then you are in a place where there is enough noise to damage your hearing.

Pollution control experts help reduce noise pollution. They check factories to make sure workers are not being harmed by unsafe noise levels. Cities make noise control laws. People can help reduce noise pollution by turning down the volume of radios, CD players, and televisions. They can also replace noisy machines, such as lawn mowers, with quieter ones.

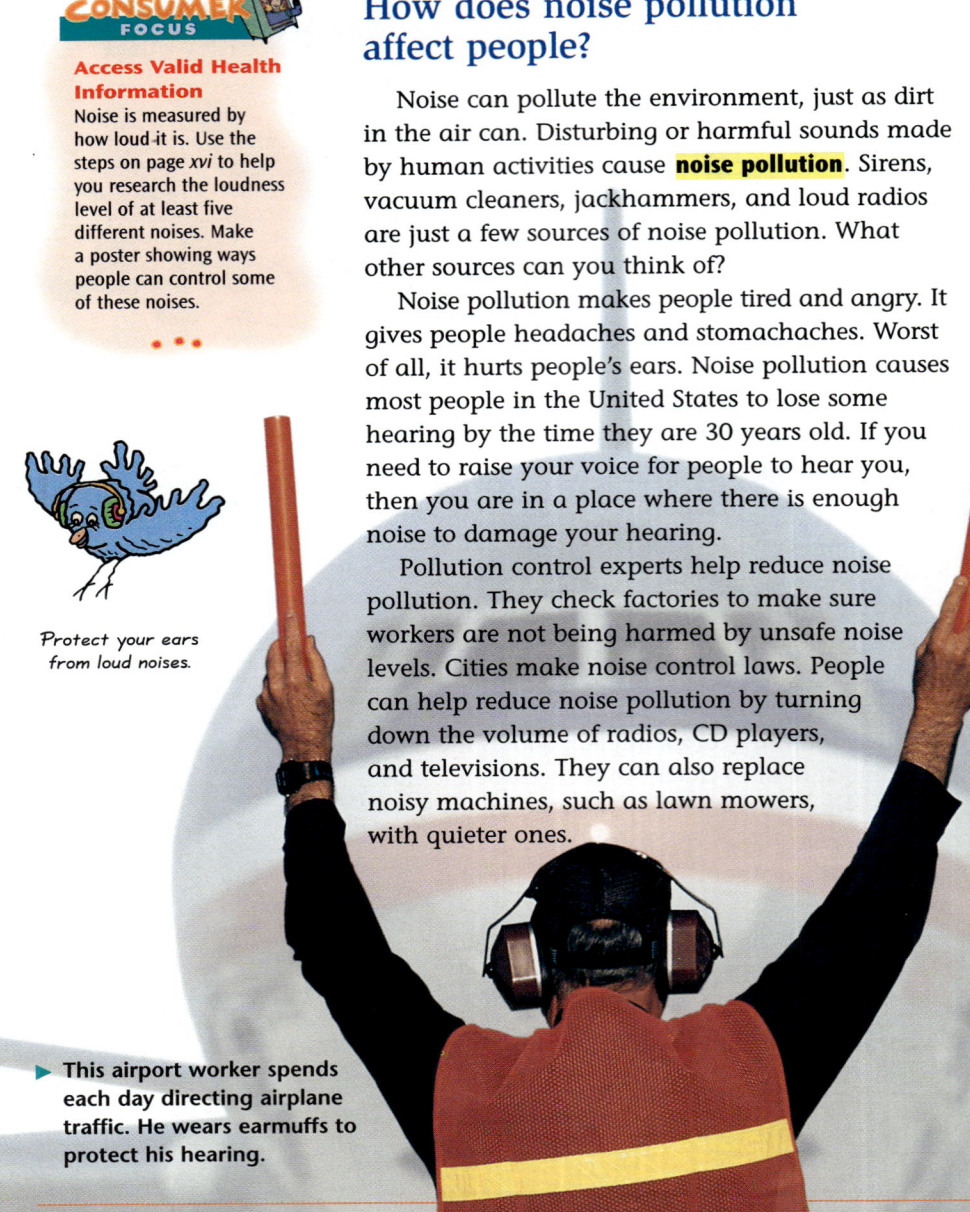

Protect your ears from loud noises.

▶ **This airport worker spends each day directing airplane traffic. He wears earmuffs to protect his hearing.**

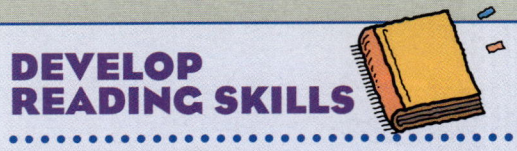

DEVELOP READING SKILLS

Identify Related Words

Compound words are single words made up of two smaller words. Ask students to find the six compound words listed on these two pages: jackhammers, headaches, stomachaches, airport, airplane, and earmuffs. Have students write definitions next to each word based on their understanding of the individual word parts. Then challenge students to add at least five other compound words and definitions to their lists.

LOUDEST →

- jet plane
- thunder
- train
- lawn mower
- jackhammer
- stereo
- traffic
- conversation

Activity

Compare Noises The intensity of a sound is measured in decibels. Normal conversation is about 30 decibels, while the sound of a jet taking off measures more than 100 decibels.

Sounds that are hard to avoid include conversation, traffic, and stereos. Continuous sounds that can damage hearing include loud stereos, jackhammers, lawn mowers, trains, and jet planes.

Activity **Compare Noises** This chart shows several sources of noise pollution. List the sounds from softest to loudest. Put a star next to the sounds that are hard to get away from. Put a check mark next to the sounds that can hurt your hearing if they go on for a long time.

3 Wrap Up

Lesson Checkup

1. air pollution and noise pollution

2. Pollution control technicians test air, water, and soil for harmful substances. They also monitor pollutants given off by motor vehicles and factories and check factory noise levels to make sure they don't harm workers' hearing.

3. People can turn down the volume on radios, televisions, stereos, and CD players and replace noisy tools and equipment with quieter substitutes.

4. Possible answers: barking dogs, loud music, traffic along a busy street, or noisy lawn equipment. You can protect yourself from these noises by avoiding the noises or wearing ear plugs to muffle the sounds.

5. Answers might include places near the student's home, such as school, the mall, the library, a friend's home, or a park. Walking or biking to nearby places reduces air pollution because these two modes of transportation don't produce pollution.

LESSON CHECKUP

Check Your Facts

❶ Name two kinds of pollution.

❷ What does a pollution control technician do?

❸ Name two things people can do to help reduce noise pollution.

❹ **CRITICAL THINKING** Name two noises that hurt your ears. How can you protect yourself from those noises?

Set Health Goals

❺ Make a list of places you have gone in a car, bus, or truck in the past two days. Make a check mark beside any places you could go safely on foot or on a bike. How does walking or biking when you usually go by car help reduce air pollution?

229

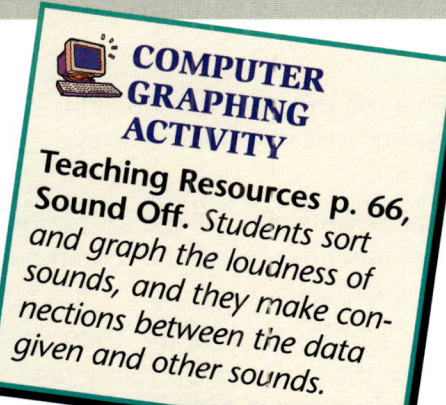

COMPUTER GRAPHING ACTIVITY

Teaching Resources p. 66, Sound Off. *Students sort and graph the loudness of sounds, and they make connections between the data given and other sounds.*

TEACHING TRANSPARENCY

Teaching Transparency 11: The Ear *shows the structure of the ear.*

OBJECTIVES

- List several sources of water pollution.
- Describe how water is treated so that it is safe for human consumption.
- Explain how groundwater becomes polluted.

PROGRAM RESOURCES

- Activity Book, p. 56

VOCABULARY

- water pollution (p. 230)
- groundwater (p. 232)

Daily Safety Tip

While most people would not drink water from a lake or river near a city, they might drink from a clear mountain stream. Explain to students that many harmful substances in water are dissolved in the water or are very small and thus invisible to the unaided eye. When camping or hiking, students should drink only bottled or treated water.

1 Motivate

Optional Materials **tap water, two empty glass jars, sand, mud, cooking oil, spoon, and coffee filter**

Have a volunteer add the sand, mud, and a teaspoon of oil to a few cups of water in one of the glass jars and stir the mixture for a few minutes. Direct another volunteer to hold the coffee filter over the other jar while you slowly pour the water through the filter. (As an alternative, describe the demonstration to students.)

Critical Thinking **What does this demonstration show?** This demonstration simulates part of the water treatment process and shows that some substances can be removed from water by filtering. Other pollutants, such as oil and dissolved chemicals, cannot be removed completely with filters.

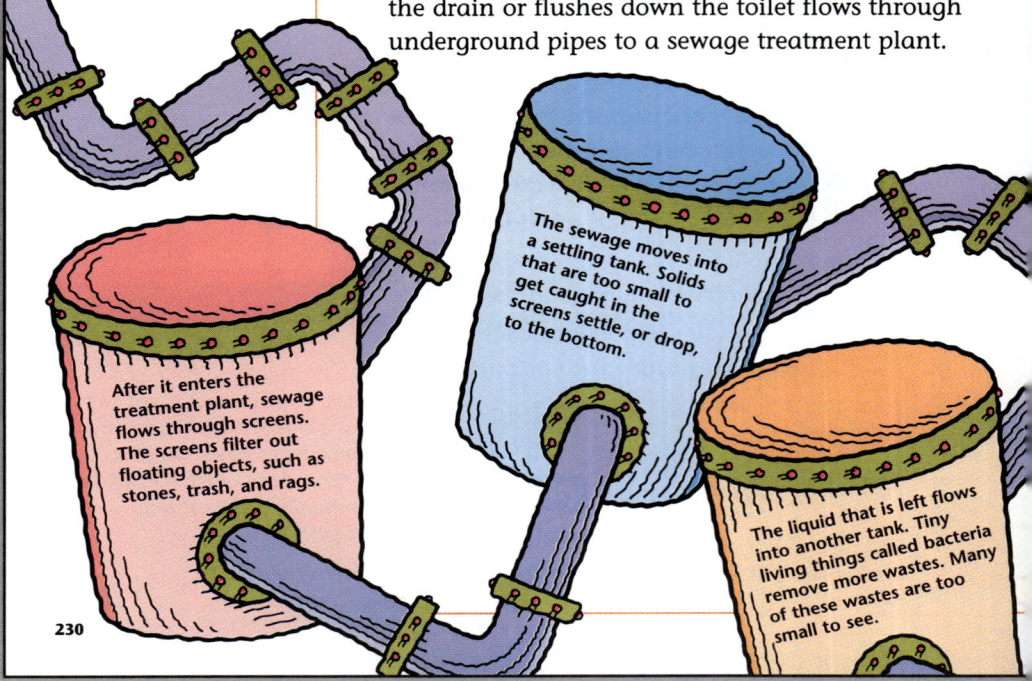

LESSON 3

MAIN IDEA
Water is polluted in many ways. Pollution technicians and other people can help control water pollution.

WHY LEARN THIS? You can use what you learn to help protect our water.

VOCABULARY
- water pollution
- groundwater

Controlling Water Pollution

Harmful material in lakes, oceans, or rivers is called **water pollution**. Harmful things poured on the ground can also pollute the water. Garbage and chemicals in a river are examples of water pollution.

How is water kept clean?

Because there is only a certain amount of water on Earth, communities use the same water again and again. The water used to do dishes today will be used for drinking later. Of course, water must be cleaned before it is used for cooking, cleaning, and drinking. That is why dirty water that washes down the drain or flushes down the toilet flows through underground pipes to a sewage treatment plant.

The sewage moves into a settling tank. Solids that are too small to get caught in the screens settle, or drop, to the bottom.

After it enters the treatment plant, sewage flows through screens. The screens filter out floating objects, such as stones, trash, and rags.

The liquid that is left flows into another tank. Tiny living things called bacteria remove more wastes. Many of these wastes are too small to see.

230

 MULTILEVEL ACTIVITIES

EASY **Diagram Water Treatment** Have students use the steps described in the illustration on these pages to create another type of graphic display explaining water treatment. **VISUAL/LOGICAL**

AVERAGE **Caves and Groundwater** Have students work in small groups to find out about the role groundwater plays in cave formation. Have them share the information with the class. **INTERPERSONAL/VERBAL**

ADVANCED **Oil Spill Facts** Write on the board a list of results of the 1989 oil spill off the coast of Alaska that occurred when the tanker *Exxon Valdez* ran aground. Have students copy the list and put the items in order from most significant to least significant, in their opinions. **SPATIAL/INTRAPERSONAL**

At the sewage treatment plant, the used water, or *sewage*, is treated to make it clean. The pictures on pages 230 and 231 show the main steps in sewage treatment.

The man in the picture is a pollution control technician. He is checking water that has been treated at a sewage treatment plant. He tests it to make sure the water is clean.

Pollution control technicians also check a community's water sources. They take samples from places where communities get their water. They check the samples for pollutants. Some pollutants include used motor oil from cars and trucks and many kinds of chemicals from factories.

If a pollution control technician finds a pollutant, such as oil, in the water, he or she reports it. Then the people or factory that spilled the oil usually pay to clean it up.

Did you know?

One quart (about 1 L) of used motor oil poured onto the ground can pollute 250,000 gallons (about 950,000 L) of groundwater. That's enough water to fill 17 backyard swimming pools.

• • • • • • •

In another tank, chemicals are added. A chemical called chlorine makes the water clear and kills pathogens.

231

2 Teach

Learn from Diagrams

Have students paraphrase the information shown in the illustration along the bottom of pages 230 and 231 and put the water treatment steps in order. Sequences should be similar to the following: Screens remove large objects. Smaller debris settles to the bottom of a second tank. Bacteria remove very small wastes. Chemicals are then added to kill pathogens and to make the water clear.

Discuss

Clean water is vital to the health of the people in a community. Ask students to name ways in which they use clean water every day. Write their answers on the board. Have volunteers put a check mark next to each situation that would harm them if the water were polluted. Have interested students research health problems caused by polluted water. Have them display their findings on a poster or chart.

Teach *continued*

Discuss

Nonpoint-source pollutants are pollutants that run off the land with rainwater. Such pollutants do not come from municipal or industrial sources, but they account for up to 80 percent of the water pollution in the United States. **Other than factories and motor oil, what are some sources of water pollution?** chemicals used on farms, salt used on icy highways, products used to grow grass and kill garden pests

Social Studies Connection

Locate Water Sources Provide pairs of students with detailed maps of your community. Have students list the lakes, rivers, streams, and reservoirs in separate columns. Make sure students realize that in many places drinking water does not come from these sources but from groundwater, which is water trapped beneath Earth's surface.

Learn from Pictures

Have a volunteer read aloud the caption. Ask the caption question. Groundwater should be kept clean because it provides some people with most of their drinking water.

▲ Groundwater fills cracks and spaces in rocks under Earth's surface. Why is it important to keep groundwater clean?

SOCIAL STUDIES
CONNECTION

Locate Water Sources

With a Partner On a map of your community, find water sources such as streams and lakes. After you have located these water sources, talk to an adult in your family about where your community's water comes from.

• • •

How is groundwater protected?

Many people think we get all our drinking water from lakes and rivers. Yet a lot of drinking water comes from groundwater. Groundwater is water that sinks into the soil and fills cracks and spaces in buried rocks. The picture on this page shows an area under Earth's surface where groundwater lies.

Chemicals, such as those used on farms, can travel into the ground and pollute groundwater. Other chemicals, such as those used in factories, can pollute groundwater, too. And salt used on icy highways pollutes groundwater. So can many products that people use to grow grass and to kill garden pests.

232

Health Background

Organic Pesticides Homeowners use up to ten times more toxic chemicals per acre than farmers do. The average homeowner uses 5 to 10 pounds per lawn. If only 10 percent of homeowners started using organic pesticides, that would remove from the environment between 2.5 and 5 million pounds of toxic chemicals that can pollute groundwater.

For more background, visit the **Webliography** on the Teacher Resources page at:
www.harcourtschool.com/health
Keyword community/environmental health

MEET INDIVIDUAL NEEDS

Visual Learners Use a sponge with large pores and a bucket of water to demonstrate how groundwater is trapped in pores in certain underground rocks.

These household products can pollute groundwater. If you use them, make sure to get rid of them safely. For example, after you paint a picture, store the paint jar with the lid on tight. Never put leftover paint into the trash or down the drain. Set it aside for a special trash pick-up of toxic, or poisonous, wastes.

Clean water is important to everyone's health. You need clean water for drinking, cooking, bathing, and washing. Talk with friends and classmates about things you can do to help protect groundwater.

LIFE SKILLS FOCUS

Communicate
You and a friend have been painting signs at his house. Your friend wants to pour the leftover paint down the drain. He says it's okay because the water will get treated. What would you say to him? Use the steps for communicating shown on page *xii*.

LESSON CHECKUP

Check Your Facts

1. What happens to sewage?
2. Where does most drinking water come from?
3. CRITICAL THINKING Would it be a good idea to eat a fish that you caught in a lake that is too polluted to swim in? Explain.

4. CRITICAL THINKING List three ways you can think of to protect rivers where people fish, boat, and swim.

Use Life Skills

5. COMMUNICATE Draw a picture to show a younger student why it is important to keep groundwater clean.

233

ACTIVITY BOOK, p. 56

Groundwater | **Critical Thinking**

Read the information below about groundwater. Then answer the questions.

Nearly three-fourths of Earth is covered with water. Very little of this water, however, is freshwater. In fact, if all Earth's water could be put into a gallon milk jug, only about one tablespoon of the water would be freshwater. Even less would be fresh, clean water that could be used for drinking, cooking, bathing, and cleaning.

Most communities get their fresh water from the ground. Groundwater is water that is trapped in the small spaces in soil and rocks beneath Earth's surface. Some of this water must be pumped from the ground. Some groundwater is taken from streams that reach Earth's surface.

Because the need for groundwater keeps growing, some communities have passed laws to help conserve it. In one state farmers use laser beams to level their fields. Making the fields level reduces the amount of water needed for irrigation. People whose sprinklers water the sidewalks instead of their lawns are fined. Wastewater is reused before being discarded. These conservation methods reduce the communities' dependence on groundwater.

1. How much of the Earth is covered with water?
   About three-fourths of Earth is covered with water.

2. What do people use water for?
   Water is used for bathing, cooking, washing, watering crops and lawns, and drinking.

3. What is groundwater?
   Groundwater is freshwater that is trapped in soil and rocks beneath Earth's surface.

4. What are some ways people have found to conserve groundwater?
   Leveling fields to prevent runoff, carefully watering only the lawn (and not the sidewalk), and reusing wastewater can help conserve groundwater.

LANGUAGE ARTS

Pollution Speech Have students write speeches to persuade others to not pollute groundwater. Their speeches could include information about the importance of groundwater, how groundwater is polluted, health problems that can be caused by polluted water, and ways to stop groundwater pollution.

Discuss

Phosphorus and nitrogen from lawn fertilizers and pesticides are common lake and stream pollutants. These pollutants eventually enter groundwater systems. Planting vegetation with adaptations to the climatic conditions of an area is one way to keep a lawn looking nice without polluting the groundwater. Such plants don't require a lot of extra chemicals to keep them healthy. Composting vegetable scraps and using the nutrient-rich soil for planting also makes a yard look nice without the use of chemicals.

Problem Solving **What is another non-polluting way to keep a lawn looking nice?** Possible answer: pulling weeds by hand rather than using herbicides.

Life Skills Focus

Communicate Most students should realize that pouring the paint down the drain could lead to pollution of nearby water systems. Encourage students to use the steps for communicating to plan what they will say. They may decide to offer suggestions to the friend, such as putting the paint in a container and taking it to a hazardous waste collection site.

3 Wrap Up

Lesson Checkup

1. Sewage is treated with filters, bacteria, and chemicals to make it clean.

2. groundwater

3. No; because the fish lives in polluted water, it absorbs many of the pollutants, which makes it unsafe to eat.

4. properly disposing of motor oil, cleaning products, pesticides, and fertilizers; limiting the use of these chemicals; not littering

5. Drawings will vary but should show that groundwater is the primary source of drinking water in many communities.

OBJECTIVES

- Identify steps in the goal-setting process.
- Use goal-setting skills to protect the environment.

PROGRAM RESOURCES

- Activity Book, p. 57
- HEALTH VIDEO: The Cleanup Kids

1 Motivate

Pass out paper, and have students draw beautiful nature scenes. Have each student write one to three sentences telling why his or her picture is beautiful. Then have them draw litter in their scenes. Ask students how they feel about their pictures now, and have them write a few sentences explaining how litter can harm our environment.

2 Teach

Discuss how Grant's family has experienced the same problem students illustrated in their pictures. Ask students to compare the first and second set of sentences they wrote about their pictures. Do members of Grant's family have similar feelings when they see the lake? yes

Learn from Pictures

Step 1

What is Grant's goal? to make the area around the lake cleaner

Critical Thinking Why is it important to set goals? A goal will keep you motivated to solve a problem. It will give you something to work toward. It will help you make a plan that will lead to accomplishing the goal.

SET GOALS to Improve Community and Environment

You can do things to improve your community and your environment. Using the steps for setting and reaching goals can help you make a difference in your surroundings.

Learn This Skill

Grant's family went to a lake for a picnic. When they arrived, they saw trash all around. Follow Grant as he uses goal-setting steps to clean up the picnic area.

1. Set a goal.

Grant wanted to make the lake a cleaner place.

2. List steps to reach that goal.

Grant mapped out an area that needed to be cleaned and asked his club friends to help.

HEALTH VIDEO
The Cleanup Kids: Working with Others
Demonstrates the value of working together for a common goal. See the Health Video Series Teacher's Guide for discussion and activity ideas.

PHYSICAL EDUCATION

Goal Posters Have students design posters showing how Grant reached his goal. Encourage them to use sports analogies, such as a football goalpost or a hockey goal, as their motifs.

3. Monitor progress toward the goal.

4. Evaluate the goal.

Grant and the other members worked together to clean the area around the lake. When each person finished, he or she put an X through his or her section on the map.

After Grant and his friends cleaned up the litter, the entire club enjoyed a picnic at the lake.

Practice This Skill

Use the steps to help you solve the problems below.

Steps for Setting Goals

1. Set a goal.

2. List steps to reach that goal.

3. Monitor progress toward the goal.

4. Evaluate the goal.

A. Ellen's family recycles aluminum cans. She was upset when she saw all the cans thrown away at school. Use what you know about goal setting to help Ellen.

B. Ray found out that some household products can pollute the groundwater. What goal setting steps could Ray take?

235

Step 2

To meet the goal, Grant asked his friends to help.

Critical Thinking Why was it a good idea to involve other people in his goal? His project was too large to be accomplished by just one person. When more people are involved, it is more fun to work. Everyone will feel good about helping reach the goal.

Step 3

How did the friends keep track of the progress they were making? As they finished each section, they put an X through the section on the map.

Critical Thinking Why is it important to monitor progress on your goal? So you can see if you are getting closer to your goal. You also can tell if your plan to reach your goal is working or if you need to make changes.

Step 4

Did Grant meet his goal? yes

Critical Thinking What were the positive results of meeting his goal? He felt good about doing something to help his community; the lake was cleaner.

3 Wrap Up

A. Students should state a goal such as finding out how to get recycling containers for the school and creating signs to remind students to recycle. Students should include a way to monitor progress and indicate how they would evaluate the goal.

B. Students should state a goal such as safely disposing of household products. Their plans might include getting more information about ways to dispose of these products and planning ways to educate others. They should include ideas for monitoring progress and evaluating the goal.

ACTIVITY BOOK, p. 57

Set Goals

Life Skills

At the beach Lorenzo and Purdy notice garbage on the sand. They want to help clean up the mess. Put an X next to the statement that would be the best goal for Lorenzo and Purdy:

____ To clean all of the beaches in the United States.

__X__ To clean an area of the beach they use.

Number the order of the steps in their plan:

3 Get trash bags and heavy gloves

1 Set aside a day to do the work, and set a time to meet on the beach.

2 Ask family and adult friends to help.

4 Find a place to dispose of the filled bags.

Write two ways they could monitor their plan. **Possible answers are shown.**

1. **Count the bags they fill.**

2. **Check their progress each hour.**

Write one way they could reward themselves for reaching their goal. **Possible answer is shown.**

3. **Have a picnic on the beach.**

What are two safety rules to remember when picking up trash? **Possible answers are shown.**

4. **Wear heavy gloves.**

5. **Tell an adult if you find anything sharp or dangerous. Do not pick it up.**

 **ART**

Before-and-After Posters Have students make posters showing the effects of polluting the environment. Have them choose a specific environmental feature, such as a lake, stream, sidewalk, beach, or forest. Suggest that they write slogans that encourage everyone to keep the environment clean. Arrange to display the posters in a public place, such as a library or local store.

235

OBJECTIVES

- Discuss how to prevent litter from becoming an unsightly part of the community.
- List ways to reduce, reuse, and recycle.

PROGRAM RESOURCES

- Computer Graphing Activity, Teaching Resources p. 67
- Activity Book, pp. 58–59

VOCABULARY

- littering (p. 236)
- reduce (p. 238)
- reuse (p. 238)
- recycle (p. 238)

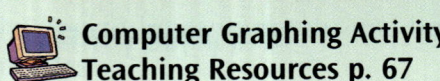

Bits of glass and metal litter the streets and sidewalks of many communities. Remind students that they should always wear shoes when outdoors to prevent injuries from these kinds of debris.

1 Motivate

Optional Materials **empty plastic 2-liter soft-drink bottle with its label removed**

Tell students an empty plastic bottle was found in the garbage. Display the bottle, or draw one on the board. **What was the object's original purpose?** It held a soft drink.

Critical Thinking **What other uses could the object have?** Possible answers: as a watering can, a scoop (when cut in half) for dog or cat food, a terrarium, a bird feeder, a bank for loose coins, a flower pot (when cut in half) The purpose of this question is to get students to think about recycling and reusing their trash. Encourage creative uses as well as practical applications.

MAIN IDEA
You can help solve the trash problem by reducing, reusing, and recycling.

WHY LEARN THIS? You can use what you learn to protect our water and land.

VOCABULARY
- littering
- reduce
- reuse
- recycle

Reduce, Reuse, and Recycle

How can you help the trash problem?

The children in the picture are helping protect the land and water. How? By picking up litter. **Littering** (LIH•ter•ing) means dropping trash on the ground or in water. Littering makes beaches, parks, and roadsides ugly. It also harms ocean animals. Many sea turtles die because they eat balloons or plastic bags in the water. They mistake them for jellyfish, their favorite food.

▼ The children cleaning up the beach are wearing heavy gloves. They do this to keep from getting cut by glass or other sharp things found on the beach.

236

MULTILEVEL ACTIVITIES

EASY **Write Jingles** Have pairs of students write radio jingles to encourage people to reduce, reuse, and recycle. **MUSICAL/VERBAL**

AVERAGE **Debate Littering** Have students engage in brief debates about whether littering is a problem. Assign opposing sides of the issue to different groups of students. **LOGICAL/VERBAL**

ADVANCED **Design Symbols** Draw on the board the recycle symbol. Have students design other appropriate symbols for reusing items and for reducing trash. Have them list items such as egg cartons and products with reduced packaging, respectively, on which these symbols could be placed. **KINESTHETIC/LOGICAL**

You can help prevent the trash problem by never littering. You might encourage your friends and family members not to litter. You might also pick up litter left by others. If you want to pick up litter in your neighborhood, take a trash bag the next time you take a walk. Spend a few minutes picking up litter at the park or at the beach, too.

Follow two safety rules when you pick up litter. Wear heavy gloves to protect your hands, and get an adult to help you.

The picture below shows many, colorful balloons. The balloons are filled with helium gas, which makes them rise. Never let go of helium balloons. The balloons can travel for many miles and litter the land or the ocean.

LIFE SKILLS FOCUS

Make Decisions

You are outdoors at a friend's house for her birthday party. Her grandfather gives everyone a helium balloon. What should you do with your balloon? Use the steps for making decisions shown on page *ix*.

• • •

◀ If you get a helium balloon, do not let go of it outside. Keep it indoors.

237

2 Teach

Discuss

A common hazard for marine mammals and birds is plastic six-pack rings that are used to package soft drinks and juices. Small mammals and birds can become entangled in these rings and strangle or starve.

Problem Solving How can this problem be prevented? Cut each of the rings before throwing out the holder; avoid buying products that are packaged with the rings; recycle the plastic rings.

Life Skills Focus

Make Decisions Answers will vary; encourage students to be gracious in accepting the balloons but to realize how to safely dispose of the balloons after use.

Discuss

According to the Consumer Product Safety Commission, thousands of children are treated at hospital emergency rooms for injuries related to balloons each year. Have interested students design and make posters depicting the dangers of young children playing with balloons.

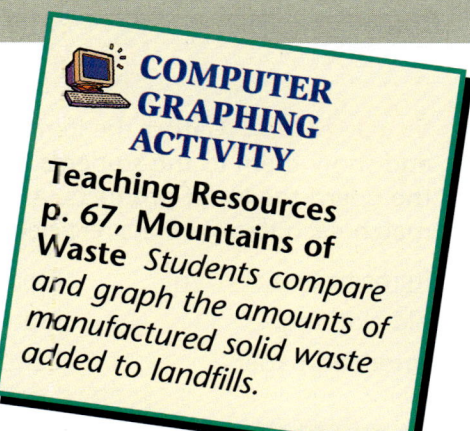

COMPUTER GRAPHING ACTIVITY

Teaching Resources p. 67, Mountains of Waste Students compare and graph the amounts of manufactured solid waste added to landfills.

Health Background

Choking Rubber balloons are a choking hazard for small children. If a child between birth and one year old is conscious but choking, five back blows between the shoulder blades alternating with five chest thrusts just below the breastbone should be administered until the object is dislodged. In older children and adults, abdominal thrusts just below the rib cage will often dislodge the object.

For more background, visit the **Webliography** on the Teacher Resources page at: **www.harcourtschool.com/health** **Keyword** first aid

Discuss

According to the Environmental Protection Agency, or EPA, the United States generates the most trash of any country—approximately 200 million tons per year! Two-thirds of this amount, which includes about 52 million tons of newsprint alone, is taken to landfills. However, the EPA estimates that by early in the twenty-first century, 80 percent of all landfills in this country will reach capacity and will have to be closed.

Problem Solving **What are some ways in which you can reduce the amount of paper you throw away?** use washable dishes and cups rather than paper, write on both sides of a sheet of paper before recycling it, share newspapers and magazines with others.

Learn from Charts

As students study the chart on this page, pose the following questions. **What can be made from recycled plastic soft-drink bottles?** surfboards, skis, carpets, and new soft-drink bottles **What happens to recycled yogurt cups?** They can be used to make food trays and car battery parts. **What are foam egg cartons made from?** recycled meat trays or foam cups **What might happen to your shampoo bottle if you recycle it?** It could become part of a floor mat, a plastic pipe, a hose, or mud flaps for a truck.

Direct students to the question in the caption. Students' answers will vary but will probably include soft-drink bottles, grocery bags, meat trays, and hangers.

Project Checkup

Reuse Classroom Items (p. 221) Have students use the information given on this page to help them plan to reuse classroom items for the chapter project.

How can you reduce, reuse, and recycle?

Clean land is important to your health. Litter left in uncovered dumps draws flies, mosquitoes, and rats, which may carry disease. We should **reduce**, or make less, trash to stay healthy. For example, you could drink from a glass instead of from a paper cup that would be thrown away.

Another way to reduce trash is to **reuse** something, or use it again. You could reuse outgrown clothes by giving them to someone smaller. You could also reuse books by borrowing them from the library.

Recycling also helps lessen the trash problem. To **recycle** (ree•sy•kuhl) means to collect used things so they can be made into new things.

Some communities recycle newspapers, glass and plastic containers, and cans.

▼ Plastics are stamped with a number code. The numbers 1 through 7 help people at the recycling center sort the plastics. Most (88 percent) of recycled plastics are marked with a 1 or a 2. What products are made from the plastics you recycle?

RECYCLING PLASTICS

Code	Original Objects		New Products
1	Soft-drink bottles, peanut butter jars, precooked frozen-food trays	become...	surfboards, skis, carpets, soft-drink bottles.
2	Detergent bottles, milk and water jugs, margarine cups	become...	flowerpots, trash cans, stadium seats, toys.
3	Shampoo bottles, clear food wrap	become...	floor mats, pipes, hoses, mud flaps on trucks.
4	Grocery bags, bread bags, frozen-food bags	become...	grocery bags, other types of bags.
5	Bottle caps, yogurt cups, other food containers	become...	food trays, car battery parts.
6	Plastic spoons, meat trays, foam cups	become...	trash cans, egg cartons, hangers.
7	Packages with many layers of materials	become...	plastic lumber.

238

MEET INDIVIDUAL NEEDS

Visual Learners Gather the items listed below, and show them to the students. Then write on the board the list of products. Ask students to match each item with its recycled product.

Items to Be Recycled	Product
old clothing	industrial rags
shredded paper	bedding for farm animals
aluminum can	nails (aluminum)
newspaper	cardboard boxes
writing paper	paper towels and tissues
plastic soda bottle	stuffing for pillows

Learn to Reuse Look at the things on this page. Tell how each thing was used. Think of at least one new way each thing could be reused. (Hints: You could think about making art. You could also think about gardening.) Tell which of the things are easy to reuse and which are hard to reuse.

LESSON CHECKUP

Check Your Facts

❶ Name four ways you can help solve the trash problem.

❷ What two safety rules should you follow when you pick up litter?

❸ CRITICAL THINKING Which helps prevent the trash problem, buying a cone or a cup of frozen yogurt? Explain.

❹ What types of plastic items are commonly recycled? Give at least three examples.

Set Health Goals

❺ Write a plan for how you can help solve the trash problem in your classroom. Include in your plan ways you can reduce, reuse, and recycle.

239

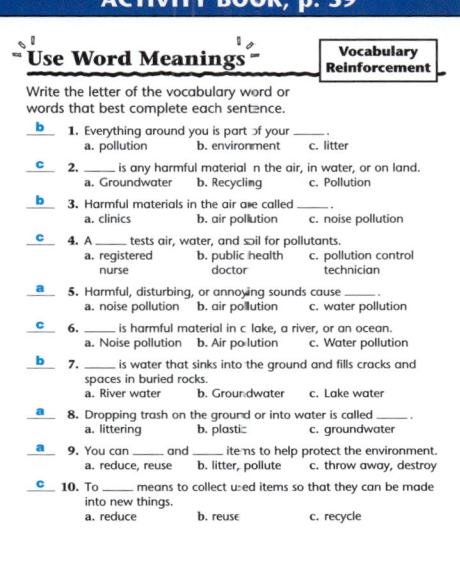

Learn to Reuse Most students should easily recognize that the plastic jug probably contained milk, juice, or some other beverage; the foam carton held eggs; the small plastic tub once contained margarine, sour cream, or cottage cheese; the box most likely held a pair of shoes; the piece of cloth might have been a shirt or some other garment.

New uses for these items will vary. Examples include using the beverage container to make a bird feeder; the foam egg carton can be used to hold small items; the plastic tub might be used as a flower pot; the shoe box can hold a variety of things. The piece of cloth could be used as a dust rag. All students should be able to come up with at least one new use for each item shown.

CAUTION: Be sure foam egg cartons are washed with soap and water before they are reused.

3 Wrap Up

Lesson Checkup

1. by not littering, by reducing the amount of trash produced, by reusing items that are still in good condition, and by recycling glass, paper, metals, and plastics

2. always wear heavy gloves and be accompanied by an adult

3. Buying the cone is better because the cone is eaten while the cup must be thrown away or recycled.

4. milk jugs, juice containers, foam cups and egg cartons, plastic peanut butter containers, detergent or bleach bottles, shampoo bottles, grocery bags

5. Plans will vary but should incorporate the goal-setting steps and the information presented in this lesson, such as throwing away only what they must, reusing items in good condition, finding new uses for trash, and recycling paper, plastics, glass, and metals.

239

CHAPTER 9 Review

Use Vocabulary 2 pts. each

1. groundwater
2. clinic
3. air pollution
4. reuse
5. community
6. hospital
7. recycle
8. environment
9. littering
10. health department
11. noise pollution
12. reduce
13. pollution
14. water pollution
15. pollution control technician

Check Your Facts 5 pts. each

16. Possible answers: Health-care workers visit new mothers and babies at home and teach mothers how to care for babies, give children and adults shots to protect them from diseases, keep records of animal bites and diseases that spread, visit older adults to give health checkups.

CHAPTER 9 Review
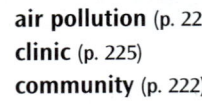

USE VOCABULARY

air pollution (p. 226)
clinic (p. 225)
community (p. 222)
environment (p. 226)
groundwater (p. 232)
health department (p. 222)
hospital (p. 224)
littering (p. 236)
noise pollution (p. 228)
pollution (p. 226)
pollution control technician (p. 227)
recycle (p. 238)
reduce (p. 238)
reuse (p. 238)
water pollution (p. 230)

Use the terms above to complete the sentences. Page numbers in ( ) tell you where to look in the chapter if you need help.

1. Many Americans get their drinking water from _____.
2. A place where people may be able to get health care at a low cost is a _____.
3. Dirt and harmful materials in the air are called _____.
4. When you give a sweater you have outgrown to a younger child, you _____.
5. A place where people live, work, and play is a _____.
6. People who are badly hurt or very sick can get health care at a _____.
7. When you collect glass jars so they can be made into new jars, you _____.
8. Everything around you is part of the _____.
9. If you throw trash on the ground, you are _____.
10. Home health care workers and public health nurses work for the _____.
11. Disturbing or harmful sounds made by human activities cause _____.
12. When you make less trash, you _____.
13. Dirt or harmful materials in the air, water, or land are called _____.
14. Materials that harm lakes, oceans, or rivers are called _____.
15. A worker who tests air, water, or soil for harmful substances is a _____.

CHECK YOUR FACTS

Page numbers in ( ) tell you where to look in the chapter if you need help.

16. Tell three things a health department does. (pp. 222–223)

17. Name three sources of noise pollution. Tell how noise pollution harms health. (p. 228)

18. Describe what happens at a sewage treatment plant. (pp. 230–231)

19. What are some things that can be made from recycled milk jugs? (p. 238)

THINK CRITICALLY

20. If someone has fallen and thinks he might have a broken leg, should he go to the hospital or a clinic? Why?

21. Suppose you buy a loaf of bread at the store. The clerk asks if you want a bag for it. Do you say yes or no? Why?

22. Why do you think it is important for clinics to offer low-cost or free health care?

APPLY LIFE SKILLS

23. **Communicate** Maria's older sister has the radio on very loud. Maria is getting a headache from the loud music. What could Maria say to her sister?

24. **Set Goals** You may have seen your classmates throw away lots of trash every day. Using the goal-setting steps, make a plan to reduce the amount of trash in your classroom.

Promote Health  Home and Community

1. Cars, trucks, and buses cause air pollution. Talk to your classmates about ways you can help reduce the air pollution problem. For example, could you walk or bike instead of going by car? Make a poster that shows your ideas.
2. With several classmates, think of some new ways your school could recycle. (For example, teachers and staff could use only recycled paper.)

PERFORMANCE ASSESSMENT

Project—Reuse Classroom Items

The chapter project (introduced on page 221) can be used for individual or team performance assessment. Allow students the opportunity to revise and complete their projects before submitting them for evaluation. Students can use the Project Summary Sheet (Assessment Guide, p. 17) to tell about their projects. You can use the rubric provided on the Project Evaluation Sheet (Assessment Guide, p. 53) to evaluate student performance.

17. Sources of noise pollution include jet engines, traffic, sirens, vacuum cleaners, jackhammers, loud radios, CD players, televisions, and noisy tools, such as leaf blowers and lawn mowers. Noise pollution harms health because it can damage hearing, give people headaches or stomachaches, and make people tired and cross.

18. Used water flows through screens that filter out solids. Then it moves into a settling tank where small solids sink to the bottom. Next it goes into a tank where bacteria remove more wastes. Finally the water flows into another tank where chlorine kills pathogens and makes the water clear.

19. Flowerpots, trash cans, stadium seats, new milk jugs, and toys can be made from recycled milk jugs.

Think Critically 10 pts. each

20. Because a broken leg can be serious, the person should go to a hospital, which is better able to care for serious injuries.

21. Most grocery bags get thrown away. Saying *no* to a bag to carry only a loaf of bread would reduce the trash you throw away.

22. Some people who are sick or hurt might not be able to get the health care they need without low-cost or free health care.

Apply Life Skills 10 pts. each

23. Possible answer: Maria could ask her sister to turn down the radio and explain why she wants her to do so. She might also point out to her sister that loud music can harm a person's hearing.

24. Answers will vary but should show an understanding of the goal-setting steps. For example, set a goal to reduce, reuse, or recycle certain items. Steps to reach the goal include informing the class and setting up collection areas. Progress could be monitored and evaluated by tracking the number of full trash cans each week.

Activities

In the News

On Your Own • Have an adult help you write a letter to your local newspaper. Give ideas for how your community can reduce noise pollution.

Checking Up

With a Partner • Call or visit the health department to find out what children's services they provide. Make a poster to show what you learned.

Save the Groundwater

At Home • Call your trash collection company to find out how your community handles household hazardous wastes such as batteries, paint, and motor oil. Then make a plan for safely getting rid of these harmful wastes in your home.

Payback Time

With a Team • Many states and communities have laws that charge deposits on soft-drink bottles and cans. Then you can return the empty bottles and cans to the grocery store for money. Find out if your state or community has such a law. If so, ask what the grocery does with the bottles and cans. Tell how this can help protect the environment.

242

Chapter Test

Multiple Choice

Choose the letter of the correct answer.

1. Many people in the United States get their drinking water from _____.
   a. oceans
   b. groundwater
   c. rivers
   d. lakes

2. A place where people live, work, play, and go to school is _____.
   a. a health department
   b. a clinic
   c. a community
   d. a hospital

3. Workers who test water, air, or soil for harmful substances are _____.
   a. pollution control technicians
   b. home health care workers
   c. public health officers
   d. registered nurses

4. A place where a person can get health care is _____.
   a. a hospital
   b. a clinic
   c. a health department
   d. all of these

5. Used water is treated at _____.
   a. a clinic
   b. a hospital
   c. the health department
   d. a sewage treatment plant

Modified True or False

Write *true* or *false*. If a sentence is false, replace the underlined term to make the sentence true.

6. People who are badly hurt can get care at a <u>health department</u>.

7. Harmful materials in the air, water, or land are called <u>pollution</u>.

8. Rocks, air, and trees are all part of the <u>environment</u>.

9. Farm chemicals and salt used on icy roads pollute the <u>air</u>.

10. Giving your clothes to a younger child is an example of <u>reusing</u>.

Short Answer

Write a complete sentence to answer each question.

11. How does burning trash outside harm the environment?

12. Why is it important to keep groundwater clean?

13. What safety rules should you follow when you pick up litter?

Writing in Health

Write paragraphs to answer each item.

14. Tell what happens at a sewage treatment plant.

15. Why do some communities have laws that require car and truck exhaust to be tested for pollutants?

Two options are provided for Chapter Tests—the in-book test and the reproducible test in the Assessment Guide. In addition to providing students with the opportunity to show what they have learned, both tests provide practice in taking standardized tests.

Multiple Choice (5 pts. each)

1. b   3. a   5. d
2. c   4. d

Modified True or False (5 pts. each)

6. false; hospital
7. true
8. true
9. false; groundwater
10. true

Short Answer (10 pts. each)

Sample answers are shown; accept other reasonable answers.

11. Burning trash can give off harmful gases and materials that pollute the air.

12. Groundwater should be kept clean because most people in the United States get their drinking water from it.

13. Wear heavy gloves, and have an adult along when picking up litter.

Writing in Health (10 pts. each)

Sample answers are shown; accept other reasonable answers.

14. Used water flows through screens that filter out solids. Then it moves into a settling tank where small solids sink to the bottom. Next it goes into a tank where bacteria remove more wastes. Finally it goes into another tank where chlorine kills pathogens and makes the water clear.

15. Cars and trucks give off gases and other substances that pollute the air. The law sets limits on the polluting gases that cars and trucks can give off. Pollution control technicians test the cars and trucks to make sure they meet pollution control laws.

These pages are available in reproducible format in the *Teaching Resources* book.

Using the Health Handbook

This section of the Pupil Edition provides information that addresses important health concerns of children, such as nutrition, physical fitness, safety, and first aid. It is intended to supplement and extend the content of the Pupil Edition. Copying masters of these pages are available in the *Teaching Resources* book.

In the Classroom

You can use these pages as stand-alone lessons. Discussion questions, activities, and additional background information are provided for you.

You may wish to make copies of these pages for students to refer to as you teach core lessons from the chapters in the Pupil Edition.

At Home

You may wish to send copies home so that students can discuss the topics with their families. These pages can also serve as a reference if students are completing health projects at home.

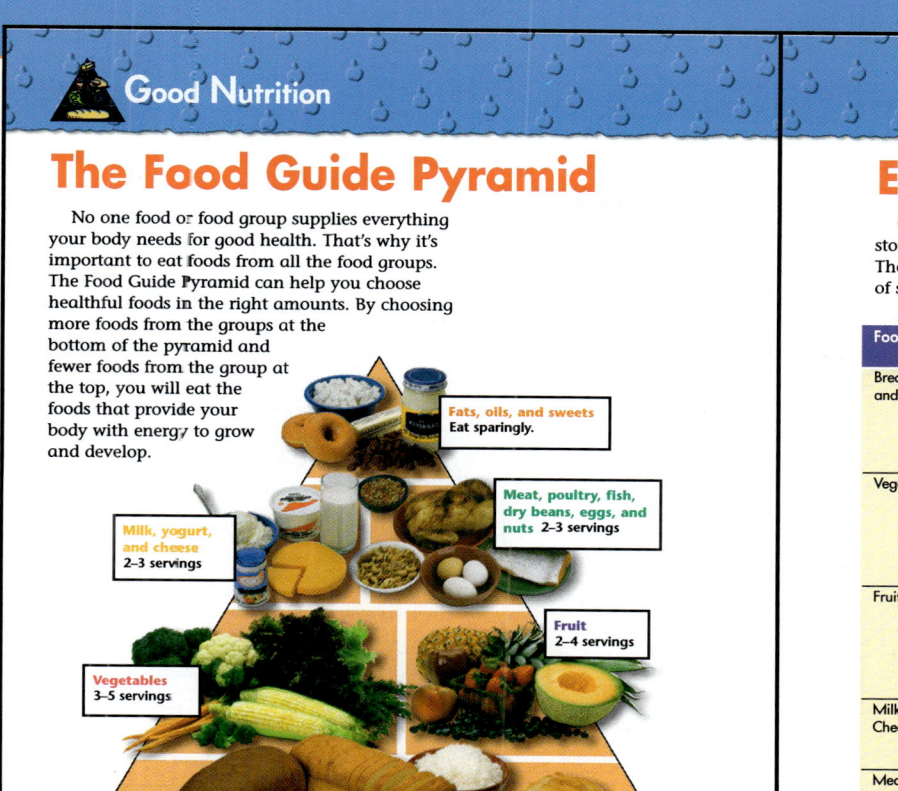
The Food Guide Pyramid

No one food or food group supplies everything your body needs for good health. That's why it's important to eat foods from all the food groups. The Food Guide Pyramid can help you choose healthful foods in the right amounts. By choosing more foods from the groups at the bottom of the pyramid and fewer foods from the group at the top, you will eat the foods that provide your body with energy to grow and develop.

Fats, oils, and sweets
Eat sparingly.

Meat, poultry, fish, dry beans, eggs, and nuts **2–3 servings**

Milk, yogurt, and cheese
2–3 servings

Fruit
2–4 servings

Vegetables
3–5 servings

Breads, cereals, rice, and pasta **6–11 servings**

246

Estimating Serving Sizes

Choosing a variety of foods is only half the story. You also need to choose the right amounts. The table below can help you estimate the number of servings you are eating of your favorite foods.

Food Group	Amount of Food in One Serving	Some Easy Ways to Estimate Serving Size
Bread, Cereal, Rice, and Pasta Group	1 ounce ready-to-eat (dry) cereal	large handful of plain cereal or a small handful of cereal with raisins and nuts
	1 slice bread, $\frac{1}{2}$ bagel	
	$\frac{1}{2}$ cup cooked pasta, rice, or cereal	ice cream scoop
Vegetable Group	1 cup of raw, leafy vegetables	about the size of a fist
	$\frac{1}{2}$ cup other vegetables, cooked or raw, chopped	
	$\frac{3}{4}$ cup vegetable juice	
	$\frac{1}{2}$ cup tomato sauce	ice cream scoop
Fruit Group	medium apple, pear, or orange	a baseball
	$\frac{1}{2}$ large banana or one medium banana	
	$\frac{1}{2}$ cup chopped or cooked fruit	
	$\frac{3}{4}$ cup of fruit juice	
Milk, Yogurt, and Cheese Group	$1\frac{1}{2}$ ounces of natural cheese	two dominoes
	2 ounces of processed cheese	$1\frac{1}{2}$ slices of packaged cheese
	1 cup of milk or yogurt	
Meat, Poultry, Fish, Dry Beans, Eggs, and Nuts Group	3 ounces of lean meat, chicken, or fish	about the size of your palm
	2 tablespoons peanut butter	
	$\frac{1}{2}$ cup of cooked dry beans	
Fats, Oils, and Sweets Group	1 teaspoon of margarine or butter	about the size of the tip of your thumb

247

These pages are available in reproducible format in the *Teaching Resources* book.

Health Background

Water Content Water content of foods varies. Fruits and vegetables generally have a higher water content than other foods. For example, lettuce, watermelon, broccoli, and grapefruit are more than 90 percent water. Milk is about 89 percent water; orange juice about 88 percent. Carrots and apples are also more than 80 percent water. In the 70 percent range are foods such as cottage cheese, yogurt, baked potato with skin, and canned, drained tuna. Rice, beans, pasta, roasted chicken, and lean beef are in the 60 percent range.

Discussion

What are the six groups of the Food Guide Pyramid? What kinds of food should you eat the most of? the least of? Discuss the foods given as examples for each group. Ask students to try to name other foods they commonly eat that might be included in each group. Then discuss the shape of the pyramid. Help them understand that the decreasing size of sections moving from the base to the top reflects the number of servings needed from each group, not the importance of the foods.

Activities

Language Arts

Describe Food Ask each student to think of three foods he or she likes and write a sentence for each food, using at least three adjectives that describe the food. Example: "I like milk because it is cool, smooth, and refreshing."

Math

How Much Is Really Juice? Have students pick a juice drink and bring the carton or can to class. Tell them to find out how much fruit juice is in the drink by studying the label. Use water and a measuring cup to show them or help them measure approximate amounts for varying percentages.

More Food Guide Pyramids

The Food Guide Pyramid from the U.S. Department of Agriculture (USDA) (page 246) shows common foods from the United States. Foods from different cultures and lifestyles also can make up a healthful diet. These other pyramids can help you add new foods to your diet. Use the serving guide on page 247 with all four pyramids.

Vegetarian

Vegetarians (vej·uh·TEHR·ee·uhns) are people who choose not to eat any meat, poultry, or fish. A balanced vegetarian diet is just as healthful as a balanced diet that includes meats.

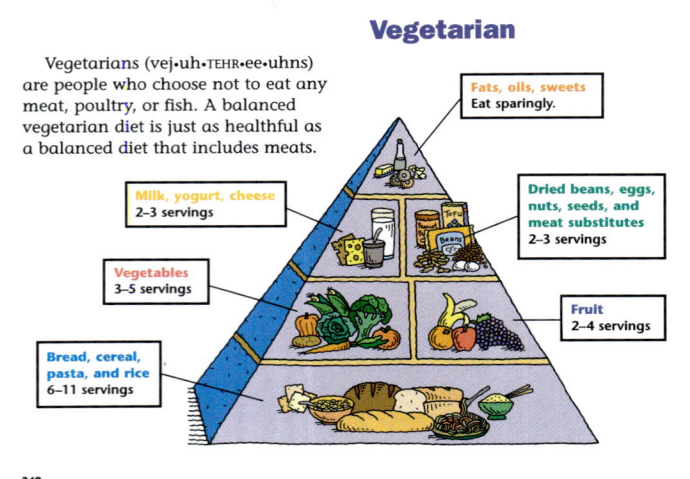

Fats, oils, sweets
Eat sparingly.

Milk, yogurt, cheese
2–3 servings

Dried beans, eggs, nuts, seeds, and meat substitutes
2–3 servings

Vegetables
3–5 servings

Fruit
2–4 servings

Bread, cereal, pasta, and rice
6–11 servings

248

The tops of these two pyramids differ from the one on page 246. They suggest eating seafood, poultry, eggs and meat each week or month rather than each day. Moderate daily use of vegetable oils is also recommended. What other differences do you notice?

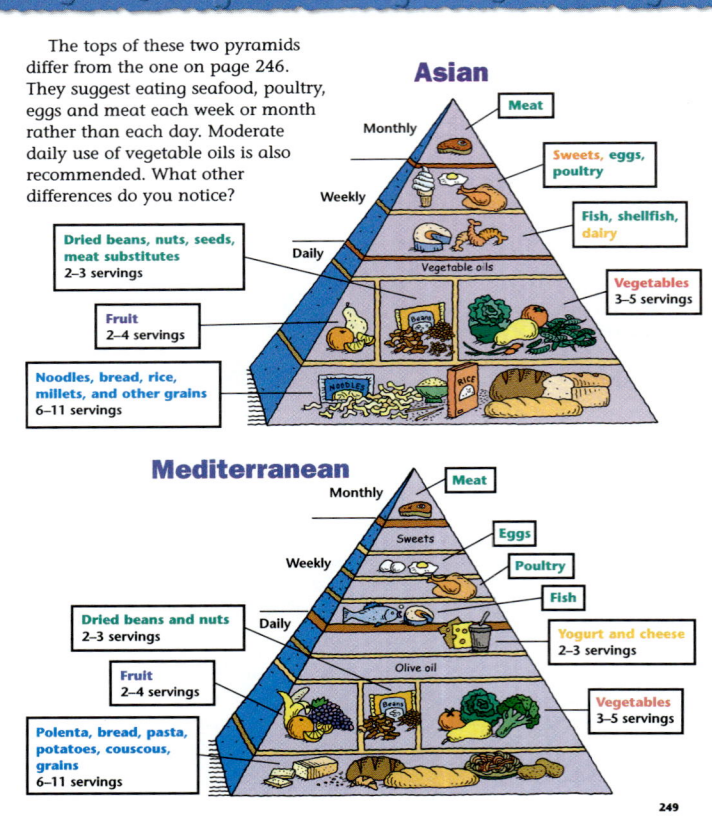

Asian

Monthly — **Meat**

Weekly — **Sweets, eggs, poultry**

Daily — **Fish, shellfish, dairy**

Dried beans, nuts, seeds, meat substitutes
2–3 servings

Vegetable oils

Vegetables
3–5 servings

Fruit
2–4 servings

Noodles, bread, rice, millets, and other grains
6–11 servings

Mediterranean

Monthly — **Meat**

Weekly — **Sweets**, **Eggs**, **Poultry**, **Fish**

Daily — **Dried beans and nuts**
2–3 servings

Olive oil

Yogurt and cheese
2–3 servings

Fruit
2–4 servings

Vegetables
3–5 servings

Polenta, bread, pasta, potatoes, couscous, grains
6–11 servings

249

These pages are available in reproducible format in the *Teaching Resources* book.

Health Background

Other Food Guide Pyramids The pyramid-shaped food guide, introduced in 1992 in the United States, has also been used by other countries, including Mexico, Chile, and Panama. Still others have used the model but have adapted it to suit their individual cultures. For example, Canada uses a rainbow, China and South Korea rely on a pagoda, and Zimbabwe uses a square. Guatemala, where pyramids have some negative cultural messages, uses a bean pot instead.

Discussion

Why is the USDA Food Guide Pyramid important? Accept reasonable answers. Possible answer: to provide information so consumers can choose foods wisely to stay healthy

Why is it important to eat foods from all the food groups? No one food or food group supplies everything your body needs to grow and develop properly.

Activities

Language Arts

 Vegetarian Food Guide Pyramid Remind students that a balanced vegetarian diet is just as healthful as a balanced diet that includes meats. Have students plan a menu for one meal, selecting foods and servings from the Vegetarian Food Guide Pyramid. Suggest students share their menus with their classmates. Students should be prepared to discuss and defend their choices.

Social Studies

The Mediterranean Diet Have students use the Internet or library resources to find more information about the Mediterranean diet. Then have them list the differences between the Mediterranean Food Guide Pyramid and the USDA Food Guide Pyramid. Suggest they present their findings to the rest of the class.

Dietary Guidelines for Americans

These guidelines come from the USDA. They promote good nutrition and healthful choices. If you follow these simple rules, you will feel better and be healthier your whole life.

Aim for Fitness

- Aim for a healthy weight. Find out your healthy weight range from a health professional. If you need to, set goals to reach a healthier weight.

- Be physically active each day. (Use the Activity Pyramid on page 254 to help you.)

Build a Healthy Base

- Use the Food Guide Pyramid to guide your food choices.

- Each day choose a variety of grains such as wheat, oats, rice, and corn. Choose whole grains when you can.

- Each day choose a variety of fruits and vegetables.

- Keep food safe to eat. (Follow the tips on pages 252–253 for safely preparing and storing food.)

Choose Sensibly

- Choose a diet that is moderate in total fat and low in saturated fat and cholesterol.

- Choose foods and drinks with less sugar. Lower the amount of sugars you eat.

- Choose foods with less salt. When you prepare foods, use less salt.

250

251

These pages are available in reproducible format in the *Teaching Resources* book.

Health Background

Dietary Guidelines The U.S. government wasn't the first to create dietary guidelines. Sweden and Canada established theirs in the 1970s. But in the 1980s, Congress required a five-year review of the guidelines and has since set high standards for the rest of the world. Guidelines vary somewhat among countries. For example, Argentina's include drinking enough water, and Zimbabwe's list the protein content of insects. However, they all share some things: eat a variety of foods; avoid too much fat, sugar, salt, and alcohol; and increase fruits, vegetables, and whole grains.

Discussion

Why is fitness important? Being physically active and maintaining a healthy weight helps people feel better and stay healthier.

Why are there no specific serving amounts for the fats, oils, and sweets food group? because these should be used sparingly

Activities

Language Arts

Make Shopping Lists Have students make food shopping lists to plan one meal by choosing foods from the Food Guide Pyramid. Remind students to select foods from all food groups to ensure getting all the needed nutrients.

Social Studies

Breads Around the World Grain products, including breads, cereals, rice, and pasta, are at the base of the Food Guide Pyramid because we need more servings (6 to 11) from this group of foods than from any other group. Have students research kinds of breads such as pita, tortillas, and cornbread that are eaten in other regions or countries. Some students may want to bring in samples of different breads. **CAUTION:** Check for food allergies before allowing students to sample any foods.

Fight Bacteria

You probably already know to throw away food that smells bad or looks moldy. But food doesn't have to look or smell bad to make you ill. To keep your food safe and yourself from becoming ill, follow the steps outlined in the picture below. And remember—when in doubt, throw it out!

FIGHT BAC!

Keep Food Safe From Bacteria

CLEAN Wash hands and surfaces often.

SEPARATE Don't cross-contaminate.

CHILL Refrigerate promptly.

COOK Cook to proper temperatures.

™

252

Food Safety Tips

Tips for Preparing Food

- Wash hands in warm, soapy water before preparing food. It's also a good idea to wash hands after preparing each dish.
- Defrost meat in the microwave or the refrigerator.
- Keep raw meat, poultry, fish, and their juices away from other food.
- Wash cutting boards, knives, and countertops immediately after cutting up meat, poultry, or fish. Never use the same cutting board for meats and vegetables without washing the board first.

Tips for Cooking Food

- Cook all food completely, especially meat. Complete cooking kills the bacteria that can make you ill.
- Red meats should be cooked to a temperature of 160°F. Poultry should be cooked to 180°F. When done, fish flakes easily with a fork.
- Never eat food that contains raw eggs or raw egg yolks, including cookie dough.

Tips for Cleaning Up the Kitchen

- Wash all dishes, utensils, and countertops with hot, soapy water. Use a soap that kills bacteria, if possible.
- Store leftovers in small containers that will cool quickly in the refrigerator. Don't leave leftovers on the counter to cool.

253

These pages are available in reproducible format in the *Teaching Resources* book.

Health Background

Food Safety Following are important food safety tips for the home: Refrigerating foods below 40° Fahrenheit significantly slows the growth of bacteria, the most common pathogen affecting foods. Freezing stops bacteria growth but does not kill bacteria. Heating food to a temperature of 160° Fahrenheit destroys bacteria. Always wash hands before handling foods, and wash dishes in hot, soapy water. Refrigerate leftover foods as quickly as possible.

Discussion

Why is it important to store foods properly? They can spoil and become unsafe.

Why shouldn't you eat spoiled food? Spoiled food is unsafe to eat because it can make you very ill.

Name four foods that must be kept in the refrigerator. Accept all reasonable answers. Possible answers include meat, poultry, eggs, milk, and some fruits.

Why might you want to store meat in the freezer instead of the refrigerator? Foods keep longer when they are frozen.

Activities

Language Arts

Food Safety Announcement Have students write public service announcements for radio or television about the proper handling of food.

Art

Food Storage Posters Suggest students use photos of food cut out of magazines to make posters showing where foods should be stored.

Science

Helpful Bacteria Ask students to find out how some bacteria are used to make food products such as yogurt, some kinds of cheese, and vinegar. Ask students to give short reports about their findings.

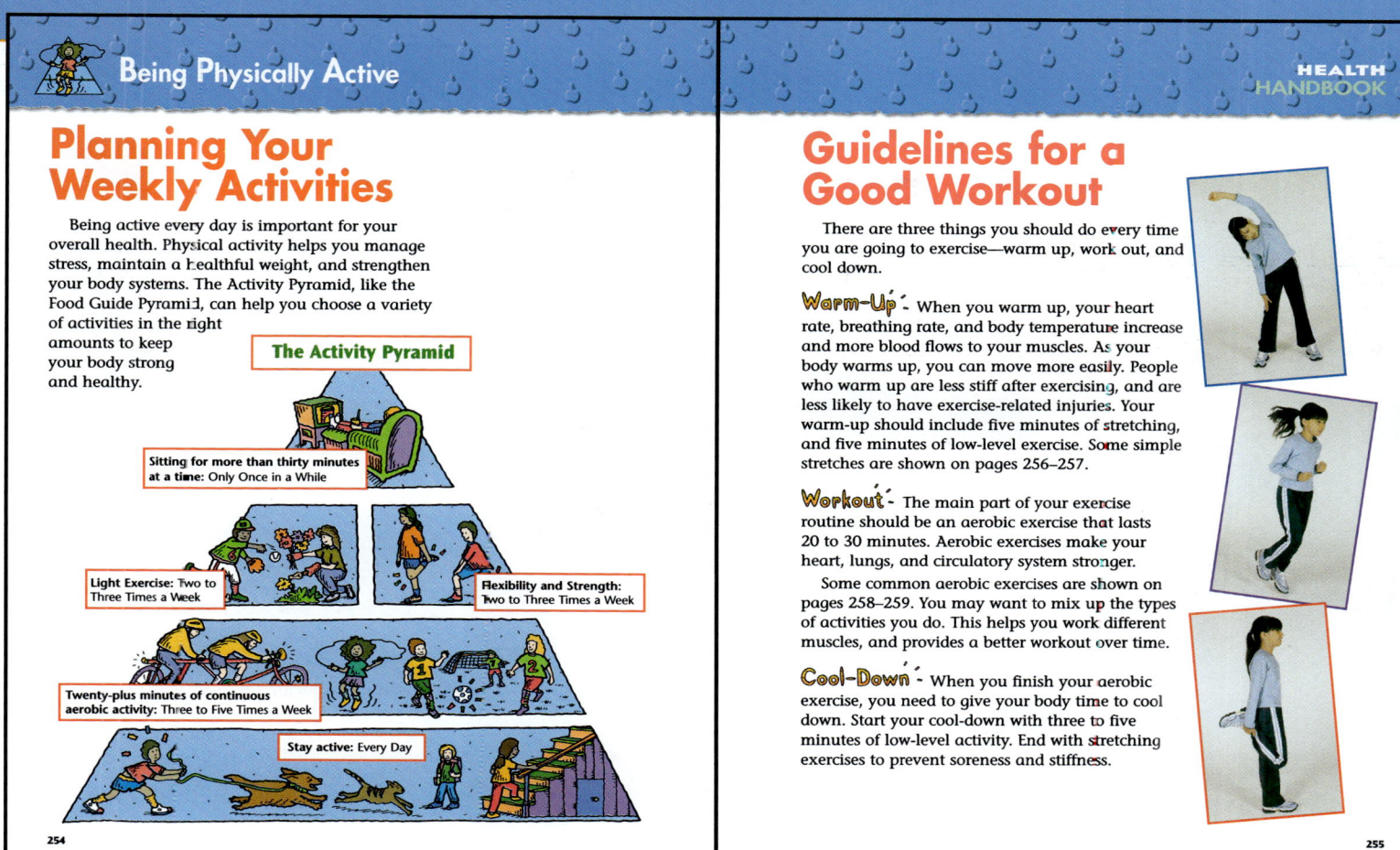

Planning Your Weekly Activities

Being active every day is important for your overall health. Physical activity helps you manage stress, maintain a healthful weight, and strengthen your body systems. The Activity Pyramid, like the Food Guide Pyramid, can help you choose a variety of activities in the right amounts to keep your body strong and healthy.

The Activity Pyramid

Sitting for more than thirty minutes at a time: Only Once in a While

Light Exercise: Two to Three Times a Week

Flexibility and Strength: Two to Three Times a Week

Twenty-plus minutes of continuous aerobic activity: Three to Five Times a Week

Stay active: Every Day

254

Guidelines for a Good Workout

There are three things you should do every time you are going to exercise—warm up, work out, and cool down.

Warm-Up When you warm up, your heart rate, breathing rate, and body temperature increase and more blood flows to your muscles. As your body warms up, you can move more easily. People who warm up are less stiff after exercising, and are less likely to have exercise-related injuries. Your warm-up should include five minutes of stretching, and five minutes of low-level exercise. Some simple stretches are shown on pages 256–257.

Workout The main part of your exercise routine should be an aerobic exercise that lasts 20 to 30 minutes. Aerobic exercises make your heart, lungs, and circulatory system stronger.

Some common aerobic exercises are shown on pages 258–259. You may want to mix up the types of activities you do. This helps you work different muscles, and provides a better workout over time.

Cool-Down When you finish your aerobic exercise, you need to give your body time to cool down. Start your cool-down with three to five minutes of low-level activity. End with stretching exercises to prevent soreness and stiffness.

255

These pages are available in reproducible format in the *Teaching Resources* book.

Health Background

Steps in Muscle Healing Once a muscle has been injured, blood vessels in the area grow larger. At the same time, white blood cells rush in to fight infection and remove dead cells. These changes cause redness, heat, and swelling. Movement becomes painful. The pain is the body's sign to let the area rest. In a day or two, the body begins manufacturing a protein called collagen, which helps make up muscle tissue. Additional small blood vessels develop and bring more oxygen and nutrients to feed the new cells. The collagen covers the injury site. As collagen forms, it needs to be gently stretched and strengthened so that it does not leave a scar that can't be stretched. It may take months for the muscle to gain normal or close-to-normal flexibility and strength.

Discussion

Swimming and biking aren't always aerobic exercises. What makes the difference? You need to do them strenuously for at least 20 minutes.

If you feel sad, what could you do that might help you feel better as well as improve your fitness? Possible answer: Do some exercise, especially aerobic exercise.

Why might it be better to exercise with others rather than alone? Accept reasonable answers. Possible answers: It's more fun, it's safer, you can play games you wouldn't be able to do alone.

Activities

Language Arts

Keep an Exercise Diary Have students make lists of the different kinds of exercise they do in a week. Suggest they include physical education classes, team sports or athletics classes, other classes, and home activities. Have them put checks next to exercises they think strengthen their heart and lungs.

Music

Exercise to Music Have students find a song that would work well for an aerobic exercise, such as jumping rope or dancing. Encourage them to design an exercise routine to go with the music and demonstrate it to the class.

Warm-Up and Cool-Down Stretches

Before you exercise, you should warm up your muscles. The warm-up exercises shown here should be held for at least fifteen to twenty seconds and repeated at least three times. At the end of your workout, spend about two minutes repeating some of these stretches.

▶ **Sit-and-Reach Stretch** HINT—Remember to bend at the waist. Keep your eyes on your toes!

◀ **Hurdler's Stretch** HINT—Keep the toes of your extended leg pointed up.

▶ **Upper Back and Shoulder Stretch** HINT—Try to stretch your hand down so that it rests flat against your back.

▼ **Thigh Stretch** HINT—Keep both hands flat on the ground. Lean as far forward as you can.

▶ **Calf Stretch** HINT—Keep both feet on the floor during this stretch. Try changing the distance between your feet. Is the stretch better for you when your legs are closer together or farther apart?

▼ **Shoulder and Chest Stretch** HINT—Pulling your hands slowly toward the floor gives a better stretch. Keep your elbows straight, but not locked!

Tips for Stretching

- Never bounce when stretching.
- Hold each stretch for fifteen to twenty seconds.
- Breathe normally. This helps your body get the oxygen it needs.
- Do NOT stretch until it hurts. Stretch only until you feel a slight pull.

256
257

These pages are available in reproducible format in the *Teaching Resources* book.

Health Background

Stretching Three major types of stretching are static, contract-relax, and ballistic. Ballistic stretching, as the name suggests, is not gentle; it involves bouncing and forcing muscles to move quickly, which can easily harm muscles and does not provide an effective stretch. Tell students to avoid ballistic stretching. Static and contract-relax stretching are helpful because they are gentle and slow. A static stretch is a gradual movement until resistance is met, a holding at that point, and a gradual return to a starting position. For contract-relax stretching, muscle groups are contracted, held, and then relaxed.

Discussion

Demonstrate the importance of stretching the muscles to warm up for exercise. Form plastic modeling compound into a ribbonlike band. Hold the band at both ends, and tug sharply until it snaps in half. Remold the compound to form another band. This time, hold both ends, and gently stretch the band so that it remains in one flexible piece.

What happens when I tug hard on the "muscle" while it is still cool? It breaks.

What happens when I gently stretch the "muscle"? It stays in one piece and can stretch out and be flexible.

Activities

Social Studies

World of Dancing Have students research and learn about dances from around the world, such as the tarantella from Italy and the hukilau hula from Hawai'i. Some of these dances are good aerobic activities. Others provide stretching or strengthening of muscles. Have students share pictures and music of the dances.

Art

Warm-Up and Cool-Down Collage Have students brainstorm good ways to warm up before and cool down after different kinds of hard exercise. A warm-up and a cool-down should use the same muscles that the hard exercise does. Suggest students make a collage using pictures of the exercises they brainstormed.

Building a Strong Heart and Lungs

Aerobic activities cause deep breathing and a fast heart rate for at least twenty minutes. These activities help both your heart and your lungs. Because your heart is a muscle, it gets stronger with exercise. A strong heart doesn't have to work as hard to pump blood to the rest of your body. Exercise also allows your lungs to hold more air. With a strong heart and lungs, your cells get oxygen faster and your body works more efficiently.

Swimming Swimming is great for your endurance and flexibility. Even if you're not a great swimmer, you can use a kickboard and have a great time and a great workout just kicking around the pool. Be sure to swim only when a lifeguard is present.

In-line Skating Remember to always wear a helmet when skating. Always wear protective pads on your elbows and knees, and guards on your wrists, too. Learning how to skate, stop, and fall correctly will make you a safer skater.

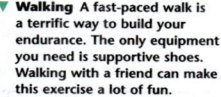

Walking A fast-paced walk is a terrific way to build your endurance. The only equipment you need is supportive shoes. Walking with a friend can make this exercise a lot of fun.

Jumping Rope Jumping rope is one of the best ways to increase your endurance. Remember to always jump on an even surface and always wear supportive shoes.

Bicycling Bicycling provides good aerobic activity and a great way to see the outdoors. Be sure to learn and follow bicycle safety rules. And always remember to wear your helmet!

258   259

These pages are available in reproducible format in the *Teaching Resources* book.

Health Background

Muscle Cramping Most children have probably experienced muscle cramps, which can occur at rest or during exercise. Tell students that when a cramp, or muscle spasm, occurs, they should stretch the muscle and gently massage the area to relax the muscles. If they get a cramp during hard exercise, they should drink more water. Water helps prevent an imbalance of certain minerals in the blood that can cause cramping.

Discussion

Explain to students that you can count the number of times your heart beats in a minute by using your pulse. Your pulse is pressure you can feel each time your heart pumps blood. Have students use a finger to find a pulse on the palm side of the wrist, below the thumb. Direct them to count the pulses as you time one minute. Ask them to take their pulses again after running outside or in place for several minutes.

How do your pulse rates before and after exercise compare? You will have a faster pulse rate after exercise.

What does your heart do when you exercise? It pumps blood more often when you exercise.

Activities

Math

Graph Exercise Favorites Have students take a survey of ten people. Have them ask what healthful sport or activity is each person's favorite. Students should make a bar graph of the results.

Physical Education

Demonstrate Safety Equipment Tell students that many sports and aerobic activities require special safety equipment. Have pairs of students choose a sport and find out what safety equipment is suggested. Ask students to prepare a demonstration or diagrams of the equipment to show how it helps prevent injury.

The President's Challenge

The President's Challenge is a physical fitness program designed for students ages 6 to 17. It's made up of five activities that promote physical fitness. Each participant receives an emblem patch and a certificate signed by the President.

The five awards:

 Presidential Physical Fitness Award—presented to students scoring in the top 15 percent in all events.

 National Physical Fitness Award—presented to students scoring in the top 50 percent in all events.

 Health Fitness Award—awarded to all other participants.

 Participant Physical Fitness Award—presented to students who complete all items but score below the top 50 percent in one or more items.

 Active Lifestyle Award—recognizes students who participate in daily physical activity of any type for five days per week, 60 minutes a day, or 11,000 pedometer steps for six weeks.

The Five Activities

1. **Curl-Ups or Sit-Ups** measure abdominal muscle strength.

- Lie on the floor with your arms across your chest and your legs bent. Have a partner hold your feet.
- Lift your upper body off the ground, then lower it until it just touches the floor.
- Repeat as many times as you can in one minute.

2. **Shuttle Run** measures leg strength and endurance.

- Run to the blocks and pick one up.
- Bring it back to the starting line.
- Repeat for the other block.

3. **One Mile Run or Walk** measures leg muscle strength and heart and lung endurance.

- Run or walk a mile as fast as you can.

4. **Pull-ups** measure the strength and endurance of arm and shoulder muscles.

- Hang by your hands from a bar.
- Pull your body up until your chin is over the bar. Lower your body again without touching the floor.
- Repeat as many times as you can.

5. **V-Sit Reach** measures the flexibility of your legs and back.

- Sit on the floor with your feet behind the line. Your feet should be shoulder-width apart.
- Reach forward as far as you can.

These pages are available in reproducible format in the *Teaching Resources* book.

Health Background

The President's Council The President's Council on Physical Fitness and Sports stresses physical activity and fitness for children and youth. The five awards recognize students for their success related to physical activity and fitness. Students who achieve high levels of fitness can earn the Presidential or National Physical Fitness Award. Other students can be rewarded for participating in the fitness test or for achieving a healthy standard of physical fitness. A new award has been added to the President's Challenge, the Active Lifestyle Award. Students of all fitness and skill levels can achieve this award by participating in physical activity for at least 60 minutes, five days per week, for six weeks. The President's Challenge also recognizes that students with disabilities or special needs have the right to an individualized fitness program and suggests guidelines for accommodating these students.

For more background, visit the **Webliography** on the Teacher Resources page at:
www.harcourtschool.com/health
Keyword physical fitness

Discussion

Who can participate in the President's Challenge? all students, including those with special needs, who are between the ages of 6 and 17

Activities

Language Arts

 Favorite Fitness Fun List on the board the five activities in the President's Challenge program. Ask each student to select his or her favorite activity and write a sentence describing why he or she likes it. Example: "I like the One Mile Run or Walk because I can do this with a friend," and "I like fresh air."

Math

Walk for Life Walk, hike, or engage in other physical activity with a friend or family member several times this week. Keep a log of the activities and the times you spent doing them.

Being Safe

Good Posture at the Computer

Good posture is important when using the computer. To help prevent eyestrain, stress, and injuries, follow the posture tips shown below. Also remember to grasp the mouse lightly and take frequent breaks for stretching.

top of screen at or just below eye level

shoulders in line with ears and hips

neck and shoulders relaxed

arms at sides, bent as shown

wrists straight

feet flat on floor

262

Safety on the Internet

You can use the Internet for fun, education, research, and more. But like anything else, you should use the Internet with caution. Some people compare the Internet to a real city—not all the people there are people you want to meet and not all the places you can go are places you want to be. Just like in a real city, you have to use common sense and follow safety rules to protect yourself. Below are some easy rules to follow to help you stay safe on-line.

Rules for On-line Safety

- Talk with an adult family member to set up rules for going on-line. Decide what time of day you can go on-line, how long you can be on-line, and appropriate places you can visit. Do not access other areas or break the rules you establish.

- Don't give out information like your address, telephone number, your picture, or the name or location of your school.

- If you find any information on-line that makes you uncomfortable, or if you receive a message that is mean or makes you feel uncomfortable, tell an adult family member right away.

- Never agree to meet anyone in person. If you want to get together with someone you meet on-line, check with an adult family member first. If a meeting is approved, arrange to meet in a public place and take an adult with you.

263

These pages are available in reproducible format in the *Teaching Resources* book.

Health Background

Repetitive Strain Injuries The carpal tunnel is the structure of bones in the wrist through which the median nerve runs. Tendons in the carpal tunnel can swell and become inflamed, pinching the median nerve, which connects to the thumb and first three fingers. Symptoms of carpal tunnel syndrome (CTS) include pain, weakness, numbness, and tingling, especially in the thumb and fingers. For mild cases, rest and varied movement lead to improvement. For more serious cases, treatment involves steroid drugs or surgery. If not treated, CTS can lead to permanent paralysis.

Discussion

How does good posture affect breathing? It's easier to take a deep breath when sitting up. **Explain that when you breathe deeply, your body gets more oxygen and you stay more relaxed.**

Even if you don't use a computer much now, why should you develop good habits working at the computer? You might use a computer more later on, and the good habits you develop now will be helpful then.

Who invented the computer? No one person invented the computer. Today's computers have evolved through the work of many different people over many years.

Activities

Language Arts

Learning the Keyboard Encourage students to devise a list of simple words or a sentence that they can type to learn the positions of letters on the computer keyboard. Tell them their words or sentences should include all the letters of the alphabet, as in this example: A quick brown fox jumps over the lazy dog.

Art

Internet Safety Suggest students design posters listing safety rules that should be observed while using the Internet. Suggest they list rules such as "Keep your passwords private, even from your best friend!" and "Always delete unknown e-mail attachments without opening them. They can contain destructive viruses." Students can display their posters for others to see.

Evaluating Health Websites

Many people find health facts on the Web. However, it's important to remember that almost anyone can put information on the Web. Here are some questions to think about when you are looking at health websites.

Does everyone agree?

Always check the information in more than one source. If several sites agree, the information is probably reliable, or trustworthy.

Who is saying it?

Information from health professionals is usually reliable. Look for the initials of a college degree, such as M.D., R.N., or Ph.D., after the writer's name.

Does the site look good?

Bad design and poor spelling or grammar are signs of a less reliable site.

Are they selling something?

Websites that sell products or services may tell you only what makes their items sound good.

What is the evidence?

Personal stories may sound convincing, but they're not the same as proof. Look for sites that show evidence from science research.

Double-check your facts!

Who controls the website?

Look for sources that you know about. Sites run by universities and the government are usually more reliable (their addresses usually end with .edu or .gov).

264

Backpack Safety

Carrying a backpack that is too heavy can injure your back. Carrying one incorrectly also can hurt you.

A Safe Weight

A full backpack should weigh between 5 and 10 percent of your body weight. To find 10 percent, divide your body weight by 10. Here are some examples:

Your Weight (lbs)	Maximum Backpack Weight (lbs)
60	6
65	$6\frac{1}{2}$
70	7

▲ This is the right way to wear a backpack.   ▲ This is the wrong way to wear a backpack.

Safe Use

- Always use both shoulder straps to carry the pack.
- Use a pack with wide shoulder straps and a padded back.
- Put heavier items in the pack so that they will be closest to your back.
- Store as many books in your locker as you can. Visit your locker often to switch books.
- Avoid carrying a heavy backpack on a bicycle. The weight makes it harder to stay balanced. Use a basket or saddlebags instead.

265

These pages are available in reproducible format in the *Teaching Resources* book.

Health Background

The World Wide Web The Internet is a publicly accessible computer network connecting many smaller networks around the world. By 1995 the Web became the most popular part of the Internet. However, because anyone can put information on the Web, it's important to recognize legitimate websites such as those from government or educational sources. Other sources may not supply reliable and up-to-date health information, may be selling something, or may be someone's personal opinion.

Backpacks Children's backs are strong and flexible and can provide a logical way to carry a heavy load. However, children must be instructed to use backpacks safely. Heavy backpacks and those carried incorrectly can alter the fluid-filled discs of the spine. That alteration can make the wearer susceptible to herniated or slipped discs and osteoarthritis later in life. According to the Consumer Products Safety Commission, there are almost 5,000 annual emergency room visits nationwide because of injuries related to backpacks.

Discussion

Why should you not rely completely on health information found on a website? The website should be considered an information supplement, not a substitute for a doctor, nurse, or pharmacist. Get an adult's permission before consulting with a health professional.

What is wrong if a person must lean forward while wearing a backpack? The backpack is probably overloaded. Ask a friend to help judge your posture while you are wearing your backpack.

Activities

Math

Use the Internet to Compare Costs Have students use the Internet to research information about backpacks. Review the rules with students on evaluating credible health websites. Students should find the costs and features of several backpacks and make charts of their choices. Have them explain how they found their information, and which backpack design offers the most features for the money.

When Home Alone

Everyone stays home alone sometimes. When you stay home alone, it's important to know how to take care of yourself. Here are some easy rules to follow that will help keep you safe when you are at home by yourself.

Do These Things

- Lock all the doors and windows. Be sure you know how to lock and unlock all the locks.
  - If someone calls who is nasty or mean, hang up. Your parents may not want you to answer the phone at all.
    - If you have an emergency, call 911 or 0 (zero) for the operator. Describe the problem, give your full name, address, and telephone number. Follow all instructions given to you.
    - If you see anyone hanging around outside, tell an adult or call the police.
  - If you see or smell smoke, go outside right away. If you live in an apartment, do not take the elevator. Go to a neighbor's home and call 911 or the fire department immediately.
- Entertain yourself. Time will pass more quickly if you are not bored. Try not to spend your time watching television. Instead, work on a hobby, read a book or magazine, do your homework, or clean your room. Before you know it, an adult will be home.

266

Do NOT Do These Things

- Do NOT use the stove, microwave, or oven unless an adult family member has given you permission, and you are sure about how to use these appliances.
- Do NOT open the door for anyone you don't know or for anyone who is not supposed to be in your home.
  - If someone rings the bell and asks to use the telephone, tell the person to go to a phone booth.
  - If someone tries to deliver a package, do NOT open the door. The delivery person will leave the package or come back later.
  - If someone is selling something, do NOT open the door. Just say, "We're not interested," and nothing more.
- Do NOT talk to strangers on the telephone. Do not tell anyone that you are home alone. If the call is for an adult family member, say that they can't come to the phone right now and take a message. Ask for the caller's name and phone number and deliver the message when an adult family member comes home.
- Do NOT have friends over unless you have gotten permission from your parents or other adult family members.

▼ A telephone with a caller ID display can help you decide whether or not to answer the telephone.

267

These pages are available in reproducible format in the *Teaching Resources* book.

Health Background

Strangers Children are aware of the need to be careful around strangers, but they may not know exactly what to do if confronted by a stranger. Inform children never to talk to a stranger, get into a car with a stranger, or accept a gift from a stranger. Tell children to yell loudly if they feel threatened or scared. Teach them to shout things like "I don't know you!" and "Help! This isn't my dad!"

Discussion

Have students name trusted adults in their lives, such as parents, guardians, grandparents, aunts, uncles, adult siblings, adult friends, religious leaders, teachers, principals, school nurses, and counselors.

What should you do if you are home alone and have an emergency? Call 911 or 0 (zero) for the operator.

What should you do if you are home alone and you see or smell smoke? Go outside right away; do not take the elevator if you live in an apartment; go to a neighbor's home and call 911 or the fire department immediately.

Why is it important that you know and follow safety rules? to avoid getting hurt

Activities

Art

Draw Your Responsible Self Have students draw pictures of themselves taking responsibility for their own safety when home alone. Display students' drawings in the classroom.

Drama

Dramatic Reenactment Encourage partners to write a scene in which a stranger tries unsuccessfully to entice a child their age to open the door when he or she is home alone. Have students rehearse their scenes and present them to the class.

Bike Safety Check

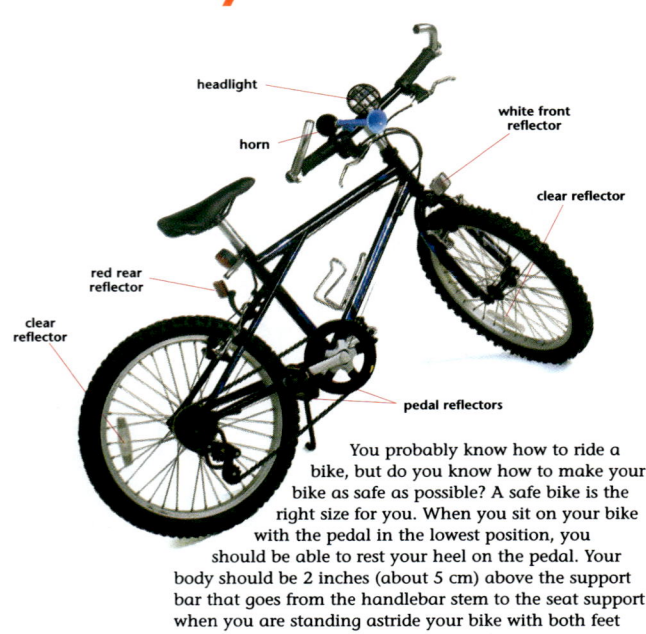

headlight

horn

white front reflector

clear reflector

red rear reflector

clear reflector

pedal reflectors

You probably know how to ride a bike, but do you know how to make your bike as safe as possible? A safe bike is the right size for you. When you sit on your bike with the pedal in the lowest position, you should be able to rest your heel on the pedal. Your body should be 2 inches (about 5 cm) above the support bar that goes from the handlebar stem to the seat support when you are standing astride your bike with both feet flat on the ground. After checking for the right size, check your bike for the safety equipment shown above. How safe is *your* bike?

268

Your Bike Helmet

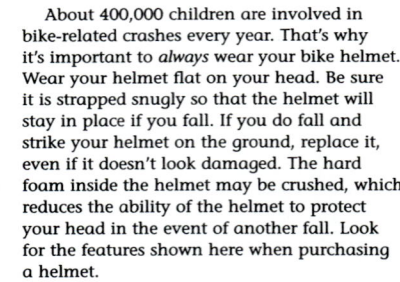

quick-release strap

approval sticker

air vents

hard shell

padding

About 400,000 children are involved in bike-related crashes every year. That's why it's important to *always* wear your bike helmet. Wear your helmet flat on your head. Be sure it is strapped snugly so that the helmet will stay in place if you fall. If you do fall and strike your helmet on the ground, replace it, even if it doesn't look damaged. The hard foam inside the helmet may be crushed, which reduces the ability of the helmet to protect your head in the event of another fall. Look for the features shown here when purchasing a helmet.

Safety While Riding

Here are some tips for safe bicycle riding.

- Check your bike every time you ride it. Is it in safe working condition?
- Ride in single file in the same direction as traffic. Never weave in and out of parked cars.
- Before you enter a street, **STOP**. **Look** left, then right, then left again. **Listen** for any traffic. **Think** before you go.
- Walk your bike across an intersection. **Look** left, then right, then left again. Wait for traffic to pass.
- Obey all traffic signs and signals.
- Do not ride your bike at night without an adult. Be sure to wear light-colored clothing and use reflectors and front and rear lights for night riding.

269

These pages are available in reproducible format in the *Teaching Resources* book.

Health Background

Bicycle Helmets Bicycle helmets do not provide adequate protection for skating and other sports. However, skating helmets will adequately protect bicyclists. When purchasing a bicycle helmet, students should look for helmets that have the ANSI (American National Standards Institute) or The Snell Memorial Foundation label. These stickers ensure that the helmet has been stringently tested to protect against head injuries.

Discussion

Why is it important to obey traffic signs when bicycling? to avoid collisions with other vehicles on the road

Why should you ride your bicycle only in bright daylight? to avoid accidents with car, whose drivers might not see you in the dark

How can bicycle riders make themselves more visible to car drivers? wear light-colored clothing; make sure bicycles have front and rear reflectors

Why do you suppose it is important to fit a bicycle helmet properly before wearing it? so that it stays in place and does not slip off the head during riding; so that it is comfortable to wear

Activities

Math

Compare Helmet Costs Suggest students visit area sporting goods stores with older family members to find the costs of several bicycle helmets. Have them make charts that compare the costs and features of the different models. Then have them determine which model offers the most safety features for the least amount of money.

Language Arts

Safety Announcements Have students write brief public service announcements to remind young people of the importance of wearing helmets while bicycling. Suggest students incorporate rhyme, humor, or any other creative device to make their announcements interesting and informative.

Safety Near Water

Water can be very dangerous. A person can drown in five minutes or less. The best way to be safer near water is to learn how to swim. You should also follow these rules:

- Never swim without a lifeguard or a responsible adult.
- If you cannot swim, do not use a blow-up raft to go into deep water. Stay in shallow water.
- Know the rules for the beach or pool and obey them. Do not run or shove others while you are near the water.
- Never dive in head-first the first time. Go feet-first instead to learn how deep the water is.

Pool Rules
1. Public use of pool is permitted only when a lifeguard is on duty.
2. All patrons must shower before entering the pool.
3. No food, drink, gum, glass, or smoking in the pool or on the deck.
4. No animals in pool or on pool deck.
5. Children under 5 years of age must be accompanied by an adult guardian (16 yrs. or older) Children under 6 years of age must be accompanied by an adult in the water THIS INCLUDES THE PLAY POOL.
6. In appropriate behavior such as horseplay, fighting, or use of abusive language is not permitted.
7. Running is not allowed anywhere in the pool area
8. Diving from the side of the pool in the shallow area is not allowed.
9. Flips or back dives from the side of the pool are not allowed.
10. Only one person at a time is allowed on the diving board. Only one bounce is allowed on the diving board.
11. Only Coast Guard approved flotation devices may be used in the pool.
12. Use of mask, fins, or snorkel is prohibited
13. Loitering or playing in or around the locker rooms, showers, or restrooms is not allowed
14. Only regular, clean bathing suits may be worn Street clothes are not allowed in the pool
15. Bathing load and pool operating hours are posted at the office

▶ Protect your skin with sunblock and your eyes with sunglasses.

▲ Wear a Coast Guard approved life jacket anytime you are in a boat. Wear one when you ride a personal watercraft, too. Know what to do in an emergency.

◀ Watch the weather. Get out of the water at once if you see lightning or hear thunder.

270

271

These pages are available in reproducible format in the *Teaching Resources* book.

Health Background

Water Safety In the United States, drowning is the second leading cause of death from unintentional injuries for people ages 5 to 24. Drowning claims the lives of over 4,000 people every year. Although all age groups are represented, children from birth to age 4 have the highest rates of death due to drowning. Most drownings and near drownings happen when a child falls into a pool or is left unattended in a bathtub. It is surprising to many parents that young children tend not to splash or make noise when they get into trouble in the water and thus usually drown silently.

Discussion

Why should you not chew gum or eat while swimming, diving, or playing in the water?
to prevent choking

Why should buckets or other open containers of liquid never be left around small children? a toddler can drown in as little as one inch of water

Activities

Drama

Act It Out Suggest partners act out a scene in which one member plays the role of a "swimmer" and the other plays an "adult" engaged in some distracting activity, such as talking on the phone, mowing the lawn, or reading a book. Have students present their scenes to the rest of the class. Encourage discussion about the potential dangers for a child who is swimming when an adult does not pay close enough attention.

Language Arts

Sunglasses Have students use the Internet, library resources, or product advertisements to find information about sunglasses and write a report they can present to the class. Suggest they look specifically for information about the UV protection in sunglasses.

Fire Safety

Fires cause more deaths than any other type of disaster. But a fire doesn't have to be deadly if you prepare your home and follow some basic safety rules.

- Install smoke detectors outside sleeping areas and on every other floor of your home. Test the detectors once a month and change the batteries twice a year.
- Keep a fire extinguisher on each floor of your home. Check them monthly to make sure they are properly charged.
- Make a family emergency plan. Ideally, there should be two routes out of each room. Sleeping areas are most important, as most fires happen at night. Plan to use stairs only, as elevators can be dangerous in a fire. See pages 274–275 for more about emergency plans.
- Pick a place outside for everyone to meet. Choose one person to go to a neighbor's home to call 911 or the fire department.
- Practice crawling low to avoid smoke.
- If your clothes catch fire, follow the three steps shown here.

1. STOP

2. DROP

3. ROLL

Storm Safety

- **In a Tornado** Take cover in a sheltered area away from doors and windows. An interior hallway or basement is best. Stay in the shelter until the danger has passed.
- **In a Hurricane** Prepare for high winds by securing objects outside or bringing them indoors. Cover windows and glass with plywood. Listen to weather bulletins for instructions. If asked to evacuate, proceed to emergency shelters.
- **In a Winter Storm or Blizzard** Stock up on food that does not have to be cooked. Dress in thin layers that help trap the body's heat. Pay special attention to the head and neck. If you are caught in a vehicle, turn on the dome light to make the vehicle visible to search crews.

Earthquake Safety

An earthquake is a strong shaking or sliding of the ground. The tips below can help you and your family stay safe in an earthquake.

Before an Earthquake	During an Earthquake	After an Earthquake
• Attach tall, heavy furniture, such as bookcases, to the wall. Store the heaviest items on the lowest shelves. • Check for fire risks. Bolt down gas appliances, and use flexible hosing and connections for both gas and water lines. • Strengthen and anchor overhead light fixtures to help keep them from falling.	• If you are outdoors, stay there and move away from buildings and utility wires. • If you are indoors, take cover under a heavy desk or table, or in a doorway. Stay away from glass doors and windows and from heavy objects that might fall. • If you are in a car, drive to an open area away from buildings and overpasses.	• Keep watching for falling objects as aftershocks shake the area. • Check for hidden structural problems. • Check for broken gas, electric, and water lines. If you smell gas, shut off the gas main. Leave the area. Report the leak.

272

273

These pages are available in reproducible format in the *Teaching Resources* book.

Health Background

Smoke Detectors Smoke detectors reduce the chances that a person will die in a fire by 50 percent. Smoke detectors should be installed on every level of a home and in or near all the bedrooms. Families should be sure that every member can hear and recognize the sound of a smoke detector. Also, parents should test detectors frequently, preferably once a month, to be sure they are working. Batteries should be replaced at least once a year.

Discussion

Have students divide a sheet of paper in half. On one half of the paper, they should draw a picture that shows how fire can be helpful. On the other half, they should draw a picture that shows how fire can be dangerous. Invite students to display and explain their pictures.

When is fire helpful? Possible answers: when it is used to cook food or to warm rooms.

When is fire dangerous? Possible answers such as, when it is burning out of control, as in a house fire; when it could burn skin.

What did you do to stay safe during the emergency? Accept all reasonable answers.

Have children share experiences they have had with earthquakes or powerful storms.

Activities

Language Arts

Fire Escape Plans Ask students to make escape plans for their homes, with at least two exits from each room. Students should practice their escape plans with their families. Then have students write out the rules for escaping a fire and post them in their kitchens for everyone to review.

Art

Earthquake and Safety Rules Have students work in pairs to illustrate and label a Do poster and a Don't poster about earthquakes. Suggest they get ideas for their posters from the information in the chart on page 273.

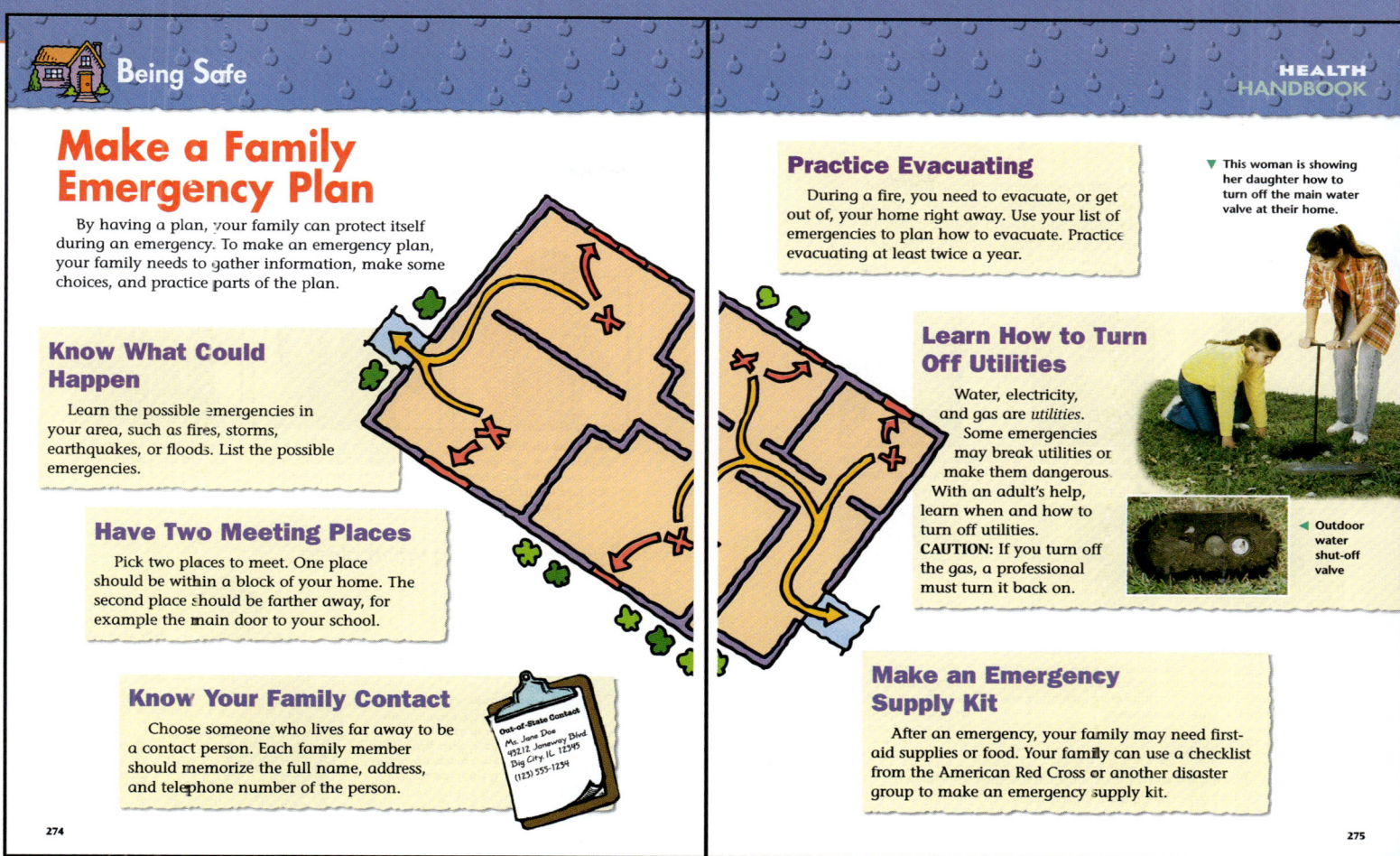

Make a Family Emergency Plan

By having a plan, your family can protect itself during an emergency. To make an emergency plan, your family needs to gather information, make some choices, and practice parts of the plan.

Know What Could Happen

Learn the possible emergencies in your area, such as fires, storms, earthquakes, or floods. List the possible emergencies.

Have Two Meeting Places

Pick two places to meet. One place should be within a block of your home. The second place should be farther away, for example the main door to your school.

Know Your Family Contact

Choose someone who lives far away to be a contact person. Each family member should memorize the full name, address, and telephone number of the person.

Out-of-State Contact
Ms. Jane Doe
45212 January Blvd
Big City, IL 12345
(123) 555-1234

Practice Evacuating

During a fire, you need to evacuate, or get out of, your home right away. Use your list of emergencies to plan how to evacuate. Practice evacuating at least twice a year.

▼ This woman is showing her daughter how to turn off the main water valve at their home.

Learn How to Turn Off Utilities

Water, electricity, and gas are *utilities*. Some emergencies may break utilities or make them dangerous. With an adult's help, learn when and how to turn off utilities. **CAUTION:** If you turn off the gas, a professional must turn it back on.

◄ Outdoor water shut-off valve

Make an Emergency Supply Kit

After an emergency, your family may need first-aid supplies or food. Your family can use a checklist from the American Red Cross or another disaster group to make an emergency supply kit.

274

275

These pages are available in reproducible format in the *Teaching Resources* book.

Health Background

Be Prepared Disaster can strike quickly and without warning. It can force people to evacuate their neighborhoods or can confine them to their homes. Local officials and relief workers respond after a disaster, but they cannot reach everyone right away. It is important to know what types of disasters are most likely to happen and to be prepared to deal with them while waiting for help to arrive. Disaster relief groups such as the American Red Cross also provide assistance, expertise, and inventive solutions.

Discussion

Why is it important to have an out-of-state family member or friend be your family contact in an emergency? If family members are separated, there is one person unaffected by the disaster that they can contact. Also, it is sometimes easier to call long distance after a disaster.

Activities

Language Arts

Home Hazard Hunt Suggest students conduct a hunt with a responsible adult for hazards at home. Suggest they look for things such as defective electrical wiring, unsecured shelving, and flammable liquids stored near a heat source. Students can list the hazards they found.

Social Studies

Make a Map Remind students of the importance of knowing the kinds of emergencies that might occur in their area. For example, Tornado Alley is a region in the middle of the United States where more tornadoes occur than anywhere else in the world. Have students research areas where earthquakes, floods, and other disasters are common. They can use maps to show their findings.

Universal Precautions

You can get some diseases from another person's blood. Universal precautions are steps to protect you from that. Because there is no easy way to tell if someone's blood will make you ill, you should avoid touching anyone's blood. To treat a wound, follow the steps below.

If someone else is bleeding . . .

Wash your hands with soap, if possible.

Put on protective gloves, if available.

Wash small wounds with soap and water. Do *not* wash serious wounds.

Place a clean gauze pad or cloth over the wound. Press firmly for ten minutes. Don't lift the gauze during this time.

If you don't have gloves, have the injured person hold the cloth in place with his or her own hand.

If after ten minutes the bleeding has stopped, bandage the wound. If the bleeding has not stopped, continue pressing on the wound and get help.

If you are bleeding . . .

Follow the steps shown above. You don't need gloves to touch your own blood. Tell an adult about your injury.

276

For Choking

If someone else is choking . . .

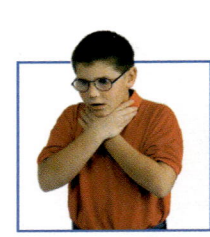

1. Recognize the Universal Choking Sign—grasping the throat with both hands. This sign means a person is choking and needs help.

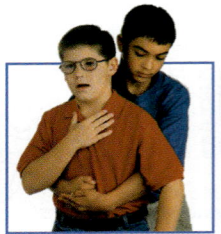

2. Put your arms around his or her waist. Make a fist and put it above the person's navel. Grab your fist with your other hand.

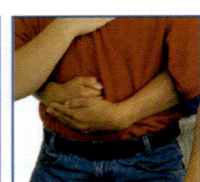

3. Pull your hands toward yourself and give five quick, hard, upward thrusts on the choker's belly.

If you are choking when alone . . .

1. Make a fist and place it above your navel. Grab your fist with your other hand. Pull your hands up with a quick, hard thrust.

2. Or, keep your hands on your belly, lean your body over the back of a chair or over a counter, and shove your fist in and up.

277

These pages are available in reproducible format in the *Teaching Resources* book.

Health Background

Assessing a Wound Not all wounds that bleed heavily are life threatening. Nosebleeds, cuts to the lip or mouth, and scalp wounds often ooze or gush but may actually be minor injuries. Other wounds with little external bleeding may be more serious, such as a puncture wound, which could lead to infection. Wounds that produce internal bleeding can lead to shock and death.

Discussion

What are the first two steps to control bleeding? Wash your hands with soap. Protect your hands.

Why is it important to protect yourself from another person's blood? to avoid spreading diseases, such as HIV and hepatitis B

What is the universal choking sign? grasping the throat with both hands

What should you do if someone is badly injured? Tell an adult, and call 911 or an emergency number for your area.

Activities

Art

First-Aid Steps Give each student two sheets of drawing paper. Have students draw and number several pictures showing the basic first-aid steps for treating choking or bleeding. Students should label their illustrations with a sentence or two describing each procedure.

Drama

Help! I'm Hurt Have students work in pairs to role-play what to do when a friend is choking or bleeding. Then have students role-play what to do when they are alone and start choking or bleeding. They should choose who will be the victim, what the emergency is, and who will administer first aid. Have them perform their plays for the class.

For Burns

Minor burns are called first-degree burns and involve only the top layer of skin. The skin is red and dry and the burn is painful. More serious burns are called second- or third-degree burns. These burns involve the top layer and lower layer of skin. Second-degree burns cause blisters, redness, swelling, and pain. Third-degree burns are the most serious. The skin is gray or white and looks burned. All burns need immediate first aid.

Minor Burns

- Run cool water over the burn or soak it in cool water for at least five minutes.
- Cover the burn with a clean, dry bandage.
- Do *not* put lotion or ointment on the burn.

More Serious Burns

- Cover the burn with a cool, wet bandage or cloth.
- Do *not* break any blisters.
- Do *not* put lotion or ointment on the burn.
- Get help from an adult right away.

For Nosebleeds

- Sit down, and tilt your head forward. Pinch your nostrils together for at least ten minutes.
- You can also put an ice pack on the bridge of your nose.
- If your nose continues to bleed, get help from an adult.

278

For Insect Bites and Stings

- Always tell an adult about bites and stings.
- Scrape out the stinger with your fingernail.
- Wash the area with soap and water.
- Ice cubes will usually take away the pain from insect bites. A paste made from baking soda and water also helps.
- If the bite or sting is more serious and is on the arm or leg, keep the leg or arm dangling down. Apply a cold, wet cloth. Get help immediately!

- If you find a tick on your skin, remove it. Crush it between two rocks. Wash your hands right away.
- If a tick has already bitten you, do not pull it off. Cover it with oil and wait for it to let go, then remove it with tweezers. Wash the area and your hands.

▲ Deer ticks can carry diseases.

For Skin Rashes from Plants

Many poisonous plants have three leaves. Remember, "Leaves of three, let them be." If you touch a poisonous plant, wash the area. Put on clean clothes and throw the dirty ones in the washer. If a rash develops, follow these tips.

- Apply calamine lotion or a baking soda and water paste. Try not to scratch. Tell an adult.
- If you get blisters, do *not* pop them. If they burst, keep the area clean and dry. Cover with a bandage.
- If your rash does not go away in two weeks or if the rash is on your face or in your eyes, see your doctor.

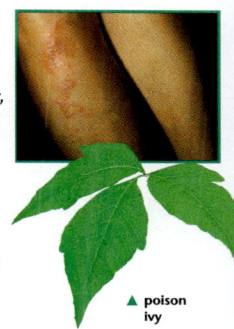

▲ poison ivy

279

These pages are available in reproducible format in the *Teaching Resources* book.

Health Background

Allergic Reactions Determine if any students in your class are allergic to insect bites or stings (or foods). You should know what to do in case one of these students suffers an allergic reaction from a bite or sting. You can also invite students to explain in as much detail as they wish what happens to them when they get bit or stung and what emergency first-aid treatment is necessary to prevent them from becoming ill or even dying.

Discussion

How can you help prevent burns in the home?
Accept all reasonable answers. Possible answers: by keeping chemicals that could cause burns out of the reach of children; by being safe around the stove, for example: keeping pot handles turned in, using potholders, and keeping shirt sleeves turned back so they won't catch on pots.

Name three ways you can deal with a nosebleed.
Sit down, tilt your head forward, and pinch your nostrils together; put an ice pack on the bridge of your nose; get help from an adult

Activities

First-Aid Kit Ask children to visit the school nurse or office to find out which first-aid supplies the school has. They can list the supplies that a classroom first-aid kit might need. Suggest that they work together to plan a kit for their classroom.

Language Arts

A Hiking Story Have students write short stories about a group of friends who are on a hiking adventure in which two of the friends have a first-aid emergency. Invite students to share their stories with the class.

Art

Poison Bearers Have students research poisonous plants or venomous animals. They should make a poster to show what they learn. Suggest that they draw a picture of each plant or animal, describe the effects and signs of each kind of poison, and tell about first-aid treatment.

What to Do When Others Use Drugs

You should make a personal commitment to not use alcohol, tobacco, or other drugs. But you may be around other students or adults who make unhealthful choices about drugs. Here is what you can do.

Know the Signs

Someone who has a problem with drugs may be sad or angry all the time, skip school or work, or forget events often.

Talk to a Trusted Adult

Do not keep someone's drug use a secret. Ask a trusted adult for help. You can also get support from adults to help you resist pressure to use drugs.

Be Supportive

If a person decides to stop using drugs, help them quit. Suggest healthful activities you can do together. Tell them you are happy that they have quit.

Stay Healthy

Do not stay anywhere that drugs are being used. If you cannot leave, politely ask others not to use drugs while you are there.

Where to Get Help
- Hospitals
- Alateen
- Alcoholics Anonymous
- Narcotics Anonymous
- Al-Anon
- Drug treatment centers

A Drug-Free School

Many schools make rules and sponsor activities to encourage people to say *no* to drugs. This makes the schools a more healthful environment for everyone.

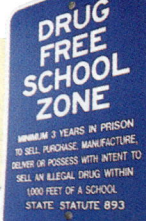

School Rules

Many schools decide to be drug free. They often have strict penalties for anyone found with drugs. For example, a person found with drugs may be expelled or suspended from school.

Positive Peer Pressure

Peer pressure can be bad or good. *Positive peer pressure* is when people the same age encourage each other to make healthful choices. For example, students may make posters or hold rallies to encourage others to choose not to use drugs.

These pages are available in reproducible format in the *Teaching Resources* book.

Health Background

Medicines and Drugs Explain to students how the development of medicines has helped people live longer, more comfortable lives. For example, before the discovery of vaccinations, many people lost their lives to infectious diseases like smallpox, polio, diphtheria, cholera, tetanus, and yellow fever. Penicillin and other antibiotics can cure some of these diseases and many others. Other medicines have been developed to treat chronic diseases such as diabetes, asthma, and heart disease. However, using drugs for purposes for which they were not intended, or using illegal drugs, such as marijuana, cocaine, or heroin, can be dangerous or can lead to dangerous behavior. People who abuse drugs can become addicted to them. Addiction can lead to serious illness or death.

Discussion

Why is tobacco smoke harmful? It contains nicotine, a highly addictive poison found in tobacco leaves; carbon monoxide, a poisonous gas; tar; and at least 60 other harmful substances.

Why is alcohol considered a drug? Where is it found? It is a substance, other than food, that causes changes in the way the body or mind works; it is found in beer, wine, and liquor.

Activities

Art

Antidrug Campaign Have students design and create an antidrug campaign. Suggest they use various media such as magazine ads, billboards, and bumper stickers. Students can display their media campaign during a drug-awareness program at school.

Science

Cigarette Tar Remind students that cigarette smoke contains tar, a sticky substance left by the smoke of certain burning substances. Suggest that with an adult's help they search for tar on barbeque grills, or in chimneys, and take samples to observe and record its properties.

Glossary

Numbers in parentheses indicate the pages
on which the words are defined in context.

PRONUNCIATION RESPELLING KEY

Sound	As in	Phonetic Respelling	Sound	As in	Phonetic Respelling
a	bat	(BAT)	oh	over	(OH•ver)
ah	lock	(LAHK)	oo	pool	(POOL)
air	rare	(RAIR)	ow	out	(OWT)
ar	argue	(AR•gyoo)	oy	foil	(FOYL)
aw	law	(LAW)	s	cell	(SEL)
ay	face	(FAYS)		sit	(SIT)
ch	chapel	(CHAP•uhl)	sh	sheep	(SHEEP)
e	test	(TEST)	th	that	(THAT)
	metric	(MEH•trik)	th	thin	(THIN)
ee	eat	(EET)	u	pull	(PUL)
	feet	(FEET)	uh	medal	(MED•uhl)
	ski	(SKEE)		talent	(TAL•uhnt)
er	paper	(PAY•per)		pencil	(PEN•suhl)
	fern	(FERN)		onion	(UHN•yuhn)
eye	idea	(eye•DEE•uh)		playful	(PLAY•fuhl)
i	bit	(BIT)		dull	(DUHL)
ing	going	(GOH•ing)	y	yes	(YES)
k	card	(KARD)		ripe	(RYP)
	kite	(KYT)	z	bags	(BAGZ)
ngk	bark	(BANGK)	zh	treasure	(TREZH•er)

abdominal muscles (ab•DAH•muh•nuhl MUH•suhlz): body muscles located in the area of the stomach (6)

abstinence (AB•stuh•nuhnts): avoiding a behavior that harms health (139)

addiction (uh•DIK•shuhn): is a constant need that makes people keep using drugs even when they want to stop (174)

aerobic exercises (air•OH•bik EK•ser•sy•zuhz): exercises that strengthen the heart and lungs by making them work harder (82)

air pollution (AIR puh•LOO•shuhn): dirt and harmful materials in the air (226)

alcohol (AL•kuh•hawl): a drug found in beer, wine, and liquor (173)

alcoholism (AL•kuh•haw•lih•zuhm): a disease in which a person can't stop using alcohol (181)

allergy (A•ler•jee): the body's reaction to a substance (132)

anger (ANG•ger): a feeling of being very mad (26)

apologize (uh•PAH•luh•jyz): to say a person is sorry (35)

arteries (AR•tuh•reez): blood vessels that carry blood away from the heart throughout the body (11)

asthma (AZ•muh): a disease that causes people to have difficulty breathing (134)

bacteria (bak•TIR•ee•uh): living things that are so tiny they cannot be seen without a microscope (70, 124)

balanced diet (BA•luhnst DY•uht): a diet in which foods from each food group are eaten each day (105)

biceps (BY•seps): front upper arm muscles (6)

bloodstream (BLUHD•streem): the blood flowing through the body (178)

blood vessels (BLUHD VEH•suhlz): arteries, capillaries, and veins that carry blood throughout the body (11)

body language (BAH•dee LANG•gwij): how the body shows feelings (21)

brain (BRAYN): main organ of the body's nervous systems; control center of body's activities (15)

bully (BU•lee): someone who hurts or frightens others, especially those who are smaller or weaker (200)

caffeine (ka•FEEN): a drug that speeds up the heart (156)

cancer (KAN•ser): a disease that makes cells grow wildly (175)

cavity (KA•vuh•tee): a hole in a tooth (74)

cell (SEL): the smallest working part of the body (58)

chewing tobacco (CHOO•ing tuh•BA•koh): moist tobacco used for chewing (174)

clavicle (KLA•vih•kuhl): collarbone (4)

clinic (KLIH•nik): a place where people get health care (225)

cocaine (koh•KAYN): an illegal drug made from the leaves of the coca plant (161)

communicate (kuh•MYOO•nuh•kayt): to share information (34)

community (kuh•MYOO•nuh•tee): a place where people live, work, play, and go to school (222)

compassion (kuhm•PA•shuhn): the ability to feel what others feel (34)

cool-down (KOOL-down): slow exercise and stretching done for five minutes after hard exercise to help prevent muscle soreness later (89)

deltoid (DEL•toyd): shoulder muscle (6)

dental floss (DEN•tuhl FLAHS): a special thread to remove plaque from between teeth (75)

diabetes (dy•uh•BEE•teez): a noninfectious disease that prevents the body from using sugar properly (135)

diaphragm (dy•uh•FRAM): partition that separates the chest and abdomen (12)

diet (DY•uht): the foods a person usually eats and drinks (99)

disease (dih•ZEEZ): something that causes the body not to work normally (122)

divorce (duh•VORS): when a couple is no longer married to each other (49)

drug (DRUHG): something other than food that changes the way the body works (148)

ear canal (IR kuh•NAL): part of the outer ear where sound enters (2, 78)

eardrum (IR•druhm): located at the end of the ear canal; is moved back and forth by sound waves (2, 79)

emergency (ih•MER•juhnt•see): a situation in which help is needed right away (204)

emotions (ih•MOH•shuhnz): strong feelings (22)

environment (in•VY•ruhn•muhnt): everything, living and nonliving, around you (226)

environmental tobacco smoke (in•vy•ruhn•MEN•tuhl tuh•BA•koh SMOHK): smoke that fills an area when someone is smoking (176)

esophagus (ih•SAH•fuh•guhs): tube made of muscle that squeezes food into stomach (9)

exercise (EK•ser•syz): any activity that makes the body work hard (82)

family (FAM•lee): the group of people with whom a person lives (44)

fear (FIR): the feeling of being scared (24)

feelings (FEE•lingz): the way a person reacts to people and events (18)

femur (FEE•mer): upper leg bone (4)

fever (FEE•ver): a body temperature that is higher than normal (126)

fiber (FY•ber): the woody part of plants; important part of a healthful diet (99)

fibula (FIH•byuh•luh): the outer and smaller of the two bones between the knee and the ankle (4)

first aid (FERST AYD): caring for small injuries (214)

flexors (FLEK•serz): muscles that help bend body parts such as limbs (6)

fluoride (FLAWR•yd): a nutrient the body needs in small amounts that helps keep teeth strong and hard (76, 104)

Food Guide Pyramid (FOOD GYD PIR•uh•mid): a tool to help choose foods for a healthful diet (102)

food label (FOOD LAY•buhl): found on packaged food; gives information about how nutritious a food is (111)

grief (GREEF): a deep sadness (27)

groundwater (GROWND•waw•ter): water that sinks into the soil and fills cracks and spaces buried in rocks (232)

growth rate (GROHTH RAYT): how quickly or slowly a person grows (60)

hazard (HA•zerd): a danger that could lead to an injury (195)

health department (HELTH dih•PART•muhnt): a group of health workers that works for the government and serves the community (222)

heart (HART): organ that pumps blood and keeps it moving through the body at all times (10)

honest (AH•nuhst): truthful (19)

hospital (HAHS•pih•tuhl): a place where hurt or ill people get medical treatment (224)

humerus (HYOO•muh•ruhs): upper arm bone (4)

immune (ih•MYOON): to be protected against a pathogen that causes a disease (129)

infectious disease (in•FEK•shuhs dih•ZEEZ): a disease that can spread from one person to another (124)

ingredients (in•GREE•dee•uhnts): the things that go into a food (110)

inhalants (in•HAY•luhnts): substances that give off fumes (158)

injury (INJ•ree): harm done to a person's body (195)

iris (EYE•ruhs): colored part of the eye that changes size to adjust the amount of light coming into the pupil (2)

large intestine (LARJ in•TES•tuhn): hollow tube in the lower part of the digestive system in which wastes are stored until they leave the body (8)

life cycle (LYF SY•kuhl): four stages of growth people go through (54)

limit (LIH•muht): a point at which a person must stop doing something (195)

littering (LIH•ter•ing): dropping trash on the ground or in water (236)

lungs (LUHNGZ): large, spongy organs used for breathing, located in the chest (12)

marijuana (mair•uh•WAH•nuh): an illegal drug that comes from the hemp plant (160)

medicine (MEH•duh•suhn): a liquid, powder, cream, spray, or pill used to treat illness (130)

mouth (MOWTH): opening through which food passes into the body (8, 12)

mouth guard (MOWTH GARD): a protective plastic shield worn in the mouth (208)

nasal cavity (NAY•zuhl KA•vuh•tee): main opening inside the nose (3)

nerves (NERVZ): bundles of cells that carry messages to and from the brain (14)

nicotine (NIH•kuh•teen): a drug in tobacco (173)

noise pollution (NOYZ puh•LOO•shuhn): disturbing or harmful sounds made by human activities (228)

noninfectious diseases (nahn•in•FEK•shuhs dih•ZEE•zuhz): diseases that are not spread by pathogens and cannot be caught from or spread to other persons (132)

nose (NOHZ): the part of the face between the mouth and eyes that has two openings for breathing and smelling (3)

nostril (NAHS•truhl): opening to the nose (3)

nutrients (NOO•tree•uhnts): the parts of food that help the body grow and get energy (98)

nutrition (nu•TRIH•shuhn): the study of food and how it affects the body (98)

olfactory bulb (ahl•FAK•tuh•ree BUHLB): contains nerves that carry information about odors (3)

olfactory tract (ahl•FAK•tuh•ree TRAKT): part of the nose that carries information from the olfactory bulb to the brain (3)

optic nerve (AHP•tik NERV): part of the eye that transmits nerve signals to the brain (2)

organs (AWR•guhnz): groups of tissues joined together, such as the heart (59)

organ system (AWR•guhn SIS•tuhm): organs that work together (59)

over-the-counter medicine (OH•ver-THUH-KOWN•ter MEH•duh•suhn): a medicine an adult can buy without a doctor's order (150)

passenger (PA•suhn•jer): someone riding in a car or bus with a driver (196)

pathogens (PA•thuh•juhnz): germs that cause disease (115, 124)

peer (PIR): a friend within the same age group (33)

peer pressure (PIR PREH•sher): when friends want someone to do something just because "everyone is doing it" (33)

pelvis (PEL•vuhs): hipbone (4)

plaque (PLAK): a sticky coating that is always forming on teeth (74)

poison (POY•zuhn): a substance that causes illness or death when it gets in the body (206)

pollution (puh•LOO•shuhn): harmful material in the air, water, or land (226)

pollution control technician (puh•LOO•shuhn kuhn•TROHL tek•NIH•shuhn): a person who tests water, air, or soil for harmful substances (227)

pores (POHRZ): tiny holes in the skin (70)

prescription medicine (prih•SKRIP•shuhn MEH•duh•suhn): a medicine that must be ordered by a doctor (151)

private (PRY•vuht): belonging only to a specific person (63)

pupil (PYOO•puhl): hole in center of eye through which light enters the eye (2)

quadriceps (KWAH•druh•seps): front thigh muscles (6)

radius (RAY•dee•uhs): the bone on the thumb side of the forearm (4)

recycle (ree•SY•kuhl): to collect used things so they can be made into new things (238)

reduce (rih•DOOS): to make less of something (238)

refuse (rih•FYOOZ): to say *no* (162)

relationship (rih•LAY•shuhn•ship): the way one person gets along with another person (30)

respect (rih•SPEKT): belief in someone (19)

responsible (rih•SPAHNT•suh•buhl): when a person acts so other people can count on him or her (19)

retina (REH•tuh•nuh): tissue at the back of the eyeball which contains cells that turn images into nerve signals (2)

reuse (ree•YOOZ): to use something again (238)

rib cage (RIB KAYJ): the bones that protect the chest, including the ribs and the bones that connect them (5)

safety gear (SAYF•tee GIR): clothing or equipment worn to protect players from injury (208)

safety rules (SAYF•tee ROOLZ): rules that help protect people from injury (195)

self-control (SELF-kuhn•TROHL): power over emotions (22)

serving (SER•ving): the measured amount of a food probably eaten during a meal or as a snack (102)

sibling (SIH•bling): a brother or sister (49)

side effects (SYD ih•FEKTS): unwanted changes in the body caused by a medicine (155)

skull (SKUHL): the connected bones that protect the brain (4)

small intestine (SMAWL in•TES•tuhn): hollow tube between the stomach and the large intestine through which the body absorbs digested nutrients (8)

smokeless tobacco (SMOHK•les tuh•BA•koh): powdered or shredded tobacco people put between their cheeks and gums (174)

snacks (SNAKS): food between meals (106)

spinal cord (SPY•nuhl KAWRD): bundle of nerves that relays messages between the brain and the rest of the nerves in the body (14)

spine (SPYN): backbone (4)

spoiled (SPOYUHLD): unsafe to eat (114)

stomach (STUH•muhk): organ between the esophagus and the small intestine that squeezes and mashes food (8, 9)

stranger (STRAYN•jer): someone not known well (198)

stress (STRES): a feeling of pressure (25)

sunscreen (SUHN•skreen): a lotion or cream that can protect a person from the sun's harmful rays (73)

symptom (SIMP•tuhm): a sign that something is wrong with the body (122)

tar (TAR): a dark, sticky substance that coats the lungs and air passages of people who breathe in tobacco smoke (175)

taste buds (TAYST BUHDZ): tiny nerve cells on the tongue that pick out tastes and send signals to the brain (3)

tibia (TIH•bee•uh): the inner and larger of the two bones between the knee and the ankle (4)

tissues (TIH•shooz): cells that work together to get a job done (59)

trachea (TRAY•kee•uh): tube that lets air go from the nose and mouth into the chest; also called the windpipe (12)

triceps (TRY•seps): back upper arm muscles (6)

trusted adult (TRUHS•tid uh•DUHLT): a grown-up known well or an adult in a responsible position (198)

ulna (UHL•nuh): the bone on the little-finger side of the forearm (4)

vaccine (vak•SEEN): a substance given to keep someone from getting a certain kind of disease (129)

values (VAL•yooz): strong beliefs, such as honesty and caring about others (44)

veins (VAYNZ): blood vessels that carry blood to the heart (10)

virus (VY•ruhs): a tiny pathogen that causes disease (125)

warm-up (WAWRM-uhp): stretching and slow exercises done for about five minutes that get muscles ready for hard exercise and help prevent pulled muscles (89)

water pollution (waw•ter puh•loo•shuhn): harmful materials in lakes, oceans, or rivers (230)

Index

Boldfaced numbers refer to illustrations.

CREDITS

Read-Aloud
Anthology

Read-Aloud Anthology

CONTENTS

My Puppy

by Aileen Fisher

Using the Selection

This selection can be used to begin a discussion about different feelings and different ways people show their feelings. Invite students who have or know pets to tell how animals communicate. Then have students look at the picture on page 16 and name feelings they think the children in the picture are expressing. Some students may want to include a copy the poem in the feelings booklet they will be making for the project on page 17.

AILEEN FISHER was born in 1906 and grew up in a logging and mining community. When she was a high-school senior, she decided she wanted to be a writer. During World War II, Fisher wrote children's dramas for the United States government, but she always loved writing poetry best. In 1978, the National Council of Teachers of English chose Fisher to receive the Excellence in Poetry for Children Award.

Wouldn't it be nice to have a friend who always understands just how you feel? If you have a pet, maybe you already do.

My Puppy

by Aileen Fisher

It's funny
my puppy
knows just how I feel.

When I'm happy
he's yappy
and squirms like an eel.

When I'm grumpy
he's slumpy
and stays at my heel.

It's funny
my puppy
knows such a great deal.

Mark's Fingers

by Mary O'Neill

Using the Selection

Read aloud "Mark's Fingers" as students listen. Reread the poem slowly and encourage students to pantomime actions to go with the words. Then ask which actions that they can do now are things they could not have done when they were in kindergarten. (Students may mention whistling, shooting rubber bands, snapping their fingers, buttoning buttons, and tying shoelaces.) Explain that developing coordination is part of the growth process. In this chapter students will learn about families and about growth and development.

MARY O'NEILL wrote and directed plays for her younger brothers and sisters as she was growing up in Berea, Ohio. She always knew she wanted to be a writer, so she became an advertising copywriter and wrote stories in her spare time. Soon her stories began to be published, too. Now Mary O'Neill lives with her family in New York City and is a partner in her own advertising agency. She still finds time to write stories and poems.

Fingers are pretty "handy" things to have. Listen to find out all the things Mark's fingers can do. What would you add to the list?

Mark's Fingers
by Mary O'Neill

I like my fingers.
They grip a ball,
Turn a page,
Break a fall,
Help whistle
A call.
Shake hands
And shoot
Rubber bands.
When candy is offered
They take enough.
They fill my pockets
With wonderful stuff,
And they always tell me
Smooth from rough.
They follow rivers
On a map,
They double over
When I rap,
They smack together
When I clap.
They button buttons,
Tie shoelaces,
Open doors to
Brand-new places.
They shape and float
My paper ships,
Fasten papers to
Paper clips,
And carry ice cream
To my lips. . . .

A Pig Is Never Blamed

by Babette Deutsch

Using the Selection

Ask students to explain what they already know about why keeping clean is important. Ask them to name times when it is especially important to wash their hands and whether they have ever felt annoyed when they have to stop doing something they are enjoying to take a bath. Then invite students to listen to a poem about a creature who never has to worry about keeping clean.

BABETTE DEUTSCH was born in New York City in 1895 and died in New York in 1982. She graduated from Barnard College and became a college lecturer. Besides writing books and poetry for children, Deutsch also wrote, edited, and translated many scholarly publications, sometimes working in partnership with her husband.

Wouldn't it be nice to be a pig? No one cares if a pig is dirty. No one nags a pig to wash its face and hands or take a bath. Of course, there may be some drawbacks as well. . . .

A Pig Is Never Blamed
by Babette Deutsch

A pig is never blamed in case
he forgets to wash his face.
No dirty suds are on his soap,
because with soap he does not cope.
He never has to clean the tub
after he has had a scrub,
for whatever mess he makes,
a bath is what he never takes.
But then, what is a pool to him?
Poor pig, he never learns to swim.
And all the goodies he can cram
down his gullet turn to ham.
It's mean:
keeping clean.
You hardly want to, till you're very big.
But it's worse to be a pig.

Greedy Mable

by Georgie Adams

Using the Selection

Read aloud "Greedy Mable." Reread the poem as students listen to name the things Mable ate. Have volunteers write the names of the foods on the board. Then help children preview Chapter 4 by looking at the picture of the Food Guide Pyramid on page 103. Invite them to study the pyramid and draw conclusions about the kinds of foods that would help Mable solve her problem.

GEORGIE ADAMS lives in England with her husband, two daughters, and many, many pets. She has been interested in children's books for a long time. For thirty years, she was an editor. Now she is a full-time writer.

Is there one kind of food you really love? Do you wish you could eat and eat and eat it until it was all gone? If so, listen carefully to the story of Greedy Mable. It may make you change your mind.

Greedy Mable

by Georgie Adams

Greedy Mable
at the table
ate as much as
she was able.

Pies and pastries
cold or hot.
Greedy Mable
ate the lot.

Chili, chicken
fish in batter. . .
Wider Mable grew
and fatter.

Till at last
her mother said,
"Mable, it is
time for bed."

But when upon
the bed she sat,
Greedy Mable's
bed fell flat.

It really couldn't
stand the weight
from all that
Greedy Mable ate.

Said Greedy Mable
on her heels,
"I'll eat a little
LESS at meals!"

excerpt from   **No Measles, No Mumps for Me**
by Paul Showers
Thomas Y. Crowell, 1980

Using the Selection

Ask students to describe childhood diseases they have
heard older relatives or friends mention that children
today do not worry about catching. (Students may
mention diseases such as polio, measles, and mumps.)
Read aloud "No Measles, No Mumps for Me." After
students listen to the selection, encourage them to
predict how advances in medicine may change life for
children of the future and then retell the story as if
one of their grandchildren were telling it about them.

No Measles, No Mumps for Me by Paul Showers

Shots are no fun. But isn't it better to get a shot than to get a disease?
Listen to hear what life was like for a typical child in the days before
doctors learned to prevent or cure some common childhood diseases.

I like to hear my grandmother tell stories. I like the
stories about when she was a little girl. My grandmother
was sick a lot when she was little.

First she got whooping cough. She coughed all day
and all night. Sometimes she had trouble catching her
breath. She had to go to bed and stay there.

Grandmother got over whooping cough. Later she
got the mumps. Her face swelled up on both sides. It
hurt her to chew and swallow. Pickles hurt her the most.
She couldn't eat them at all.

Grandmother got over the mumps. Later she got the
measles. She had a fever and a runny nose. There were
red spots all over her body. She had to go to bed with
the measles, too.

I'm glad I didn't live in those days. Children got
whooping cough, measles, and mumps. They got rubella,
polio, tetanus, and diphtheria. Some children got very
sick. Some even died.

I've never had whooping cough or mumps or
measles or polio or any of the rest. And I never will,
either. Because I've had shots, and sometimes special
drops.

When you get the shots, or the drops, you are
helping your body to keep well.

PAUL SHOWERS was a newspaperman for over thirty years.
When his children were learning to read with typical 1950's
reading books, he became interested in writing children's books
himself. His goal was to write children's books that were "lively
and worthwhile." Now retired from the newspaper business,
Showers has written over twenty children's books.

selection from   **The Circle of Thanks**
Native American Poems and Songs of Thanksgiving
told by Joseph Bruchac
BridgeWater Books, 1996

Using the Selection

Ask students to tell about the kinds of medicines their families give them when they are ill. Discuss different forms medicines can take, such as pills or capsules, liquid, inhalers, sprays, and rub-on creams. Explain that some medicines are made from natural substances, such as plants, and some are made in a laboratory. But long before medical technology was developed, people knew how to use medicines to cure illnesses.

Native American people have known how to use medicines for thousands of years. The Cherokee people of the North American Southeast have handed down this legend that explains how people began using plants as medicines.

JOSEPH BRUCHAC is proud of both the Abenaki Indian and the European parts of his heritage. He shows his pride in his books and also through storytelling. Bruchac and his wife live in New York state, where they have founded their own publishing house.

HOW MEDICINE CAME

Cherokee, Southeast

Long ago,
the animals and the birds,
the fish and insects and plants
could all talk.
They lived with the people
in peace and friendship.

Then the people invented
bows and blowguns and spears.
They began to kill
the animals and birds and fish
for their flesh and their skins.
The animals then joined together.
They invented diseases
to weaken the people.

The plants remained friendly
to the people.
Each tree and shrub and herb agreed
to offer a cure for each new disease.
Each said, "When I am called upon,
I shall help the humans in their need."

So it is that the plants gave us medicine.
So it is that we must be thankful to them.

excerpt from   **Where There's SMOKE**
by Janet Munsil,
Annick Press, 1993

Using the Selection

Write *New Year's Resolution* on the board and help students define *resolution*. Invite volunteers to tell about resolutions they have made or would like to make. Help children recognize that keeping a resolution to stop doing something they do all the time, or to break a habit, is much more difficult.

Where There's SMOKE by Janet Munsil

Have you ever tried to break a bad habit? Sometimes its easier if two people help each other . . .

On the very last night of the year, Daisy's parents always get dressed up really fancy and go cha-cha dancing at the Topaz Ballroom. When they get home very late at night, Daisy's mom wakes her up with a lipsticky kiss.

"Happy New Year, Daisy. We've made New Year's resolutions! That's a promise you make to yourself that you want to keep all year. I resolve to learn to play a musical instrument this year!"

"Now, what do you resolve to do?"

Daisy and her dad looked at each other for a long time.

Daisy nibbled her nails. Her dad smoked a cigarette.

They pretended they didn't hear the question.

Daisy thought about it. And she chomped. And she thought. And she chomped.

Think, chomp, think, chomp, think, chompchompchomp.

And then she said, "I resolve to pick up my toys."

"That's a good one, but is there anything else?" asked her mum.

"I resolve to turn off the lights when I leave the room."

"Maybe a bad habit you'd like to break?" asked her dad.

"I resolve not to punch my friends in the nose."

"That's a good one," said her mom, "but isn't there one other thing that you'd like to stop doing?"

"I don't think so," chomped Daisy. Chompchompchomp.

"Well, maybe just one. I'll stop biting my nails. I will not bite my nails ever again. Now, what's your resolution, Dad?"

"Not to eat a whole lemon meringue pie before dinner?" suggested Dad.

"I can think of one for you," said Daisy. "It's something that makes the house smoky and your clothes smelly and our eyes sting-y and it makes you cough all night and all morning long."

"But I've tried to stop smoking lots of times and I can't," whined Dad. "I'll help you," said Daisy, "and you'll help me. Starting tomorrow." "It's a deal," said Dad.

Daisy chomped all night, since it was her last chance. Her dad puffed so much he set off the smoke detector.

Daisy woke up the next morning to the sound of her mum playing the trumpet. SQEEeekeeSQREEkeeSQREEKEES QEEeeEEeEEe! Her dad was wearing a deep-sea diver's helmet to keep the noise down.

"Good morning, Daisy," he said. "Ready to stop biting your nails?" "Yes. Ready to stop puffing?" "Yes. But all the noise from mum's resolution is making me nervous. I'm going to go for a walk. Bye." "All this noise makes me nervous," said Daisy. "I'm going to play outside. Bye."

Daisy didn't REALLY want to play outside. There was something else she wanted to do. Something she hadn't done for a long time. She wanted to bite her nails, really-really badly. But she also didn't want to bite them, because she'd made a deal with her dad. She decided to go to her treehouse. That way, if she started to chomp by accident, nobody would see.

She went outside.
She looked all around.
She made sure nobody was

following her.
She climbed up to her treehouse.
She peeked over the ledge. . .

"DAD!" said Daisy.
"Daisy!" said Dad.
"WHAT ARE YOU DOING HERE?"

"I'm having trouble with my resolution," said Dad.

"Me too," said Daisy. "I want to stop biting my nails like crazy, but I don't know how."
"I want to stop smoking, but I don't know how."
"We need to think of some ways to help each other out," said Daisy.

So they went up to Daisy's room and thought and listened to Mom practicing the tuba. And they made a plan.

Daisy gave her dad some chewing gum and a bubble pipe so he could chew and blow bubbles instead of puff. Daisy's dad helped put bandages on all her fingers so she wouldn't chomp. And he shared his gum.

Everything worked for a little while, but sooner or later, Daisy and her dad would catch each other in the treehouse. And they'd sit there, and sigh, and listen to mom play the drums.

So Daisy and her dad did things together to keep their minds off chomping and puffing.
They baked cookies.
They did jigsaws.
They made spice racks.
They did fingerpainting.
They built things out of frozen treat sticks.
They built things out of spaghetti.
They built things out of macaroni and cheese.
They built things out of the cookies that burned.

Daisy and her dad learned how to knit.
They knit teacosies, 100 pairs of socks, 60 hats, 59 mittens, 30 pairs of long underwear, two scarves that were a thousand meters long, and a muffler for the car. They knit mom a cover for her tuba, even though it was now on its way to the attic.

"Well, we've done it, Daisy," said her dad. "We've been so busy with our hobbies that we forgot all about our bad habits! Now I think I'll go for a little walk. Bye." "Wait!" said Daisy, who had heard that one before.
"I'll go too." And they went to the corner store together.

"We have certainly been good at keeping our resolutions!" said Mom.
"I'll call Grandma right now and ask her to take us to the symphony! Oh, and thank you very much for the tuba cover, but I have decided to play the electric guitar instead."

Grandma came right over.
"WOW!" she said. "I can't believe it! NO smoking? No chomping? Quick, everybody in the taxi!" she yelled. "We're going to the symphony orchestra!"

Not once in the whole concert did Daisy bite her nails.
Not once did her dad cough or look in his pocket for his cigarettes.

I Need My Knees, but No More, Please
by Stan Lee Werlin

Using the Selection
Read aloud "I Need My Knees, but No More, Please" and invite students to tell about times when they have had similar problems. Ask students to describe the circumstances that caused their injury and to suggest ways they can prevent the same kind of injury in the future.

Look at your knees. Do they have cuts, scrapes, or scars? If they do, you'll probably understand poet Stan Lee Werlin's mixed feelings about knees. . . .

I Need My Knees, but No More, Please
by Stan Lee Werlin

I am very displeased
to discover that knees
can be banged up and bruised
with incredible ease.

They're so bony and bumpy,
lamentably lumpy,
and sorer than sore
when I crash on the floor
or dance without looking
right into the door—
I'm just glad that I haven't got four!

● ●

excerpt from   **Keeping Clean**
by Vicki Cobb
Lippincott-Raven Publishers, 1989

Using the Selection

Ask students to tell where they think the water we use in our homes comes from and how it gets into our homes. Then read aloud "Running Water." Connect the selection to Lesson 3 by asking students to use what they learned to explain why a clean, unpolluted water supply is important to every member of the community.

Imagine what life was like before people could turn on a faucet to bring water right into the house. Then listen to find out how water gets into our homes.

Running Water

● ●

Want to wash your hands? Go turn on the faucet. Out comes clean water. Dirty water disappears down the drain. Today about half the people in the world have hot and cold running water in their homes.

The pipes that bring clean water to your house and carry away waste water are called <u>plumbing</u>.

There are many places in the world where there is no plumbing. People have to carry in pails of water from a well or river or stream to take a bath. They have to heat the water on a fire.

They may pour the water into a tub. A family may take turns using the same bathwater.

If you live in a city or town, your water may come from a river or lake. It goes through huge pipes to a special plant that makes it clean before it is piped to homes.

If you live in the country, your water probably comes from a well. A well is a deep hole in the ground that reaches pure, clean underground water.

Here's how modern plumbing works. A pipe carrying clean water comes into your house from your water supply.

Some of the clean water goes into a heating tank called a <u>hot-water heater</u>. Both hot and cold water travel through pipes to sinks, showers, tubs, toilets, and washing machines.

Machines called <u>pumps</u> push water through pipes. Clean water pushes against closed faucets. The push of the water is called water pressure. When you turn on a faucet, pumps make the water rush out.

Waste water goes down into a different set of pipes, called <u>drainpipes</u>. All the drainpipes empty into one large drainpipe, which leaves your house and carries waste water into a sewer or septic tank.

VICKI COBB has degrees in zoology and in elementary science education. She has put her knowledge to work by writing many children's books about science. She has also appeared on television as the host of a show called "The Science Game," which she invented herself.

Teacher Reference Section

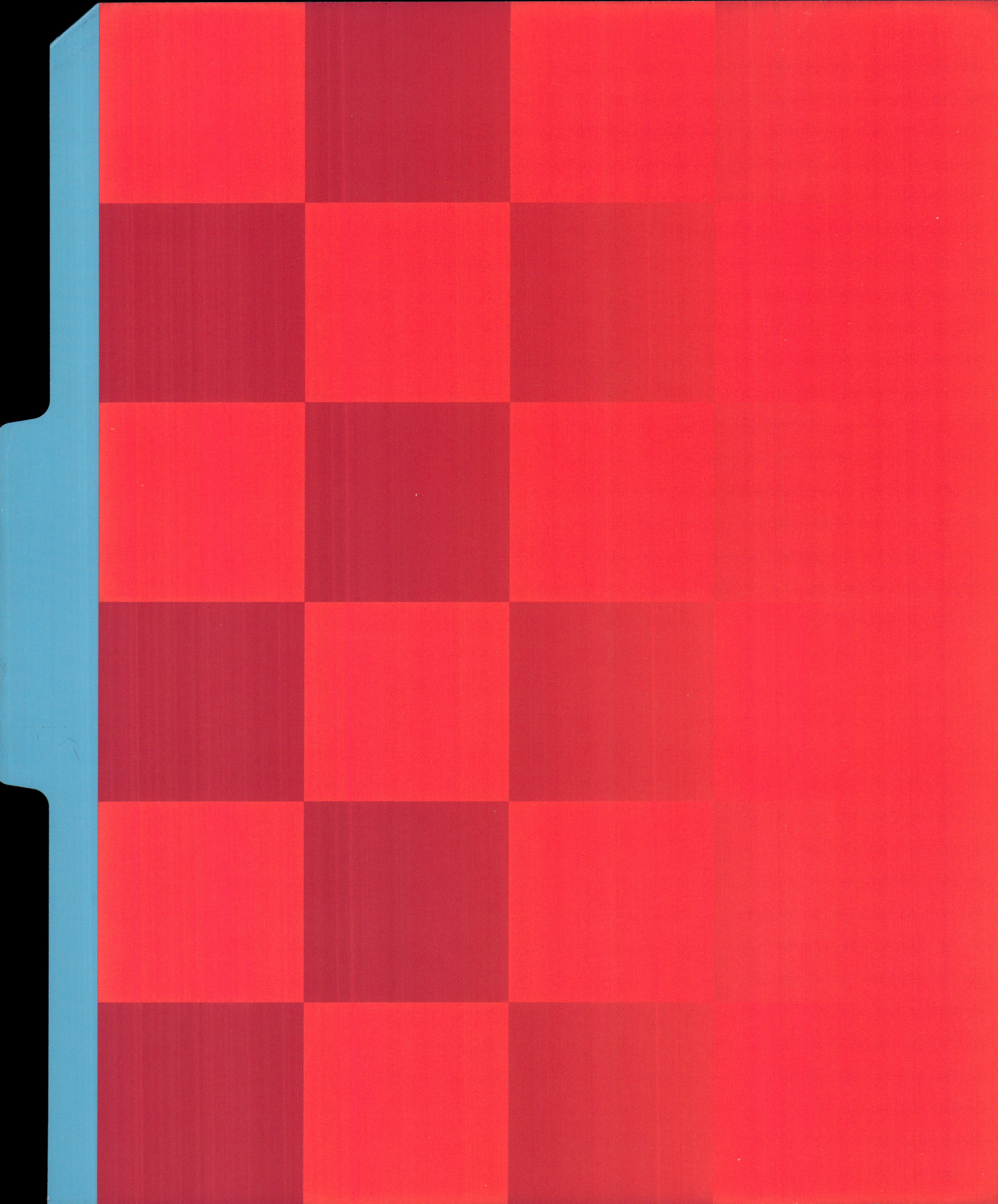

Teacher Reference

Author Articles

Scope and Sequence, Grades 3–6

Injury Prevention Is a Partnership

Jan Marie Ozias, Ph.D., R.N.

Why are injury prevention and control of concern to schools?

- Injuries are the leading killer of children and youth in the United States and a major cause of hospital care and long-term disability. Of the 22 million injuries to children that occur yearly in the United States, it is estimated that 10 to 25 percent occur in and around schools and school events.

- Schools are not only where students learn about safety practices but also where students spend many hours daily. The community expects schools to teach students knowledge and skills for safe, responsible lifestyles. Parents want to trust that school buildings, the ways to and from schools, and school activities are safe—all the time.

- Schools are work sites for many adults in every community. The people who staff schools need protection from unnecessary risks and need to take responsibility for injury prevention practices.

Why don't we use the term accidents anymore?

The U.S. Centers for Disease Control and Prevention analyzed "accidents" using the concept of epidemiology (the study of diseases that affect people) and determined that most accidents are not random occurrences. They are predictable and preventable.

Let us examine a fatal car collision caused by a teenage driver who was drinking, showing off, and driving on a rain-slick road without using a seat belt. None of these factors is a random occurrence, that is, a true accident. The event and the injuries that resulted follow a predictable pattern. Epidemiology examines the relationship among three elements:

- **Host**—a person who could become ill or injured due to his or her own resistance, skills, or state of mind
- **Agent**—a direct cause of illness, such as a virus, or of harm, such as a car
- **Environment**—such as rules, weather conditions, and cleanliness

If we can alter any one of the three epidemiological elements, we can break the chain of events that lead to a high risk of illness or harm. For example, immunizing a child breaks the chain of events leading to disease if the child is later exposed to a virus. Here is a home safety example:

> *Host:* Curious 5-year-old child
> *Agent:* Cigarette lighter
> *Environment:* unsupervised garage with flammable materials

Changing any of the three elements breaks the link between the host and the agent. If you teach young students the skill of self-discipline and the risks of fire, add adult supervision to the environment, or keep lighters out of reach, no fire!

In order to help students and staff identify what can and cannot be controlled, we use *unintended injury* to refer to burns, crashes, and falls. (These were previously called *accidents*.) We distinguish unintended injuries from deliberate or *intended injuries*, injuries caused by violence, assault, and self-harm.

Do children think injuries are preventable?

Children can tell us about injury prevention—they know it's not just about "accidents" or "kids being kids." In a study of 12 elementary schools, students were asked about their playground injuries. Almost a third of the injured students thought they could have prevented their injuries. When they were asked how, the most common replies were *not going so fast, watching, being more careful, not fighting,* and *avoiding the situation.* About half the same injured students thought someone else or something in the environment had influenced the injury. The most frequent reasons were *actions of another student* or *an object,* such as a rock or playground equipment. Developmentally, students can learn to use their senses to recognize hazards like these, connect them to unsafe situations, and then act to prevent injuries.

What do we know about students' injuries?

Detailed reports about student injuries come from the National Pediatric Trauma Registry study of school-age children (5- to 18-year-olds) seen in 74 emergency rooms between 1988 and 1995. Here are some results from that study:

- More injuries (49 percent) occurred in recreational areas than in any other school area.

- Falls were the most common cause of injury (46 percent), followed by sports activities (30 percent).

- Assaults or intended injury caused 10 percent of the injuries.

- Students with disabilities were more likely to be hurt; 17 percent of the injured students already had a disability or chronic illness.

- Forty-six percent of the injuries occurred among 10- to 14-year-olds.

- Almost 40 percent of the cases involved head injuries.

Do schools handle injuries properly?

The same hospital emergency room study also found that 16 percent of the children received no or inadequate first aid; they were sent home rather than sent to receive care. How prepared is your school to handle injuries? Does it have a registered nurse and staff trained in first aid? Who fills in for the nurse if he or she is unavailable?

Where do violence and abuse fit in injury prevention?

Assault injuries to students seen in emergency rooms included beatings (more than 50 percent of the assaults), stabbings (14 percent), gunshot wounds (10 percent), or being deliberately hit by an object. Although violence receives much more media attention and causes staff to worry, most of the students injured at school—in a ratio of 9 to 1—are injured *un*intentionally. Regardless, conflict resolution as a life skill can reduce aggression and intended injuries, especially when it is taught in elementary school and applied in the home, community, and workplace. The Children's Safety Network identified over 40 curricula that include violence prevention, but few were well evaluated for effectiveness. One reference for developing age-appropriate violence prevention curriculum is *Promoting Social and Emotional Learning: Guidelines for Educators*. Alexandria, VA: Association for Supervision and Curriculum Development (1997).

"Stranger" danger addresses community concerns for children when they are unsupervised. Many children also may be at risk in the presence of a neighbor, a family acquaintance, or even a relative. Teachers should work with approved school resources to include opportunities for students to learn how to handle uncomfortable situations involving touch, secrets, or pressure by an older person to do something that children feel is wrong or unsafe.

Are school buses safe?

While much attention is being given to installing seat belts (safety belts) in school buses—primarily to reinforce the habit of using them in cars and to prevent disruptive behavior—school buses are quite safe. Considering the number of passenger miles they travel, school buses are 37 times safer than cars. Even so, an average of 11 children die annually in school bus crashes. Another 30 pedestrians die getting on or off a bus, or are hit by a bus or a passing vehicle. Half of these pedestrians are children between the ages of five and seven!

What needs to happen in schools?

In addition to quality student instruction, the Centers for Disease Control and Prevention (2001) recommends that schools

- establish a safety council that includes parents and students as part of a school health program advisory committee. The safety council would identify and correct safety hazards and establish safety policies.

- develop reporting methods so that school staff can analyze unintended and intended injuries and target the most common or most serious situations and develop better prevention strategies.

- develop and implement emergency plans to properly assess, manage and refer injured students.

What are safety education priorities for elementary grades?

Among elementary-school children, common unintended injuries are related to the following:

- traffic
- bicycles
- water
- playgrounds
- fire
- personal trauma (falls, cuts)

Appropriate education goals for elementary grades are to develop in students **habits** of safety that will guide **behaviors** and prepare students for the risk-taking years of middle school. We must convey more than just knowledge of safety risks and rules, we must focus on habits and behaviors (*what to do*) and skills (*how to perform the behaviors*). Positive role models at school and at home, guided practice, and social reinforcement of emerging skills are appropriate strategies to build these habits and behaviors. 🌀

Preventing Drug Use

Kathleen Middleton

Education to prevent drug use is most effective when it is included as part of a comprehensive health education program that begins in elementary school and continues through high school. Such an education starts in kindergarten with basic messages about safe behavior around unknown substances and about appropriate use of medicines, and continues with developmentally appropriate instruction throughout the school years.

Effective education to prevent drug use must include more than facts about the effects of drugs. Knowledge alone about the effects of drugs is not enough to prevent drug use; children must develop the skills they need to be able to remain drug-free. To effectively resist the pressures toward drug use that permeate our society, children must learn they have the ability to *refuse* to use drugs. Research over the past several years has indicated success in programs in which children practice life skills, including refusals, decision making, goal setting, conflict resolution, communication, and stress management.

Before they reach adolescence, most children report that they are strongly opposed to drug use. But with the onset of adolescence comes the desire to experiment, coupled with the need to assert one's independence. This stage of growth and development makes children much more susceptible to pressures to experiment with drug use.

In primary grades, children can be taught facts about dangerous substances and can begin to practice the skills they need to say *no* to pressures and to protect themselves in dangerous situations. By the time they are in sixth grade, many children will have been approached to try tobacco, alcohol, or other drugs, as well as to participate in other unsafe behaviors. By this time children must already have had the reinforcement of repeated practice in saying *no*. They also need the confidence to withstand peer pressure, make safe decisions, communicate effectively, manage stress, and set goals for the future.

Drug Use Statistics

In the 1980s, the U.S. Centers for Disease Control and Prevention began conducting national school-based surveys to measure the prevalence of health-risk behaviors among students in grades 9 through 12. In 1999, the Youth Risk Behavior Survey (YRBS) reported the following drug use behaviors:

- More than 47 percent of the students surveyed had used marijuana during their lifetimes.
- Over 8 percent had used a form of cocaine at some point, and at least 4 percent had used it within the last month.
- More than 3 percent had used steroids without a doctor's prescription.

- Nearly 2 percent had injected illegal drugs.
- Over 14 percent reported inhalant use; or sniffing intoxicating substances and just over 4 percent had used inhalants within the last month.

Perhaps not surprisingly, the drugs most commonly used were the drugs that are legal for adult use—tobacco and alcohol. The YRBS survey reported the following statistics:

- More than 80 percent of the students surveyed had had at least one drink of alcohol during their lifetimes, and more than 50 percent had had a drink in the last 30 days.
- More than 70 percent had tried cigarette smoking, and 34 percent had smoked during the last month.
- Almost 8 percent of the students surveyed had used smokeless tobacco during the last 30 days.

Although these statistics reflect high-school drug use, the behaviors are an outgrowth of what has been learned in earlier grades. Many researchers feel that by the time students are in high school, it's almost too late to prevent drug use. The foundation for drug-use prevention must be laid during childhood.

Healthy People 2010

Healthy People 2010: Understanding and Improving Health includes objectives for youths 12 to 17 years old to reduce the prevalence of personal health risks. The goal of Objectives 27-4a, 26-9a, and 26-9b is to "increase the average age of first use" of tobacco products, alcohol and marijuana by adolescents and young adults aged 12 through 17 by 2, 3, and 4 years respectively. Baseline data from 1997–1998 indicated an average age of first use for cigarettes to be 12 years; for alcohol, 13.1 years; and for marijuana, 13.7 years. A 1999 review of trends indicated that little progress had been made in the attempt to reduce the initiation of cigarette smoking by children and youth. Downward trends in alcohol and marijuana use among students 12 to 17 years old were reversed in 1995.

Young adults are unlikely to develop problems of alcohol and drug use if the age of first use can be delayed beyond childhood and adolescence. The U.S. Department of Health and Human Services review indicated a consensus that children are never too young to be reached with consistent messages about the health effects of alcohol and other drugs.

Effective Education

Evaluation of drug-use prevention programs has identified some key elements of success. Programs that work include not only information but activities to help build students' personal social skills. Essential skills include the following:

- communication
- stress management
- decision making and goal setting
- refusing

The first three skills provide the basis for the skills of refusing. Communication skills help students clearly communicate their feelings and thoughts. Stress-management skills help students handle their stress without turning to drug use. Decision-making and goal-setting skills help students consider consequences and look to the future. Effective refusals incorporate all these skills.

Finally, students need to feel confident in order to remain drug-free. Research has shown that students who practice skills in an education setting not only develop the skills but also develop a feeling of empowerment and the belief that they can use the skills. This feeling of confidence is considered a key aspect of adolescent success in remaining drug-free. When we provide children opportunities to practice these skills throughout the elementary grades, we offer them the foundation they need to protect themselves in adolescence.

Nutrition Behaviors for Children

Carl A. Stockton, Ph.D.

As I think about promoting positive dietary behaviors in children, I have to look at my three-year-old's current eating habits. Her eating practices are being molded at this early stage in her life. Children learn at a young age what kinds of food adults around them eat. In trying to teach her about positive nutritional choices, I find myself selecting healthful foods for her, such as green beans, apples, oranges, and other fruits and vegetables, that are part of my own diet. Nutritional eating practices are learned behaviors, and it is important that we start molding these behaviors early in a child's life.

Poor Health Habits

Our society has been extremely negligent in promoting positive eating behaviors in our children. Many studies have shown that poor diets and lack of physical activity together account for more than 300,000 premature deaths among adults each year. These poor health habits begin in our children. According to the U.S. Centers for Disease Control and Prevention, the percentage of children who are overweight has more than doubled in the past 30 years, and more than 5.3 million children (13 percent) are seriously overweight. Studies have shown that obese children are more likely to become obese adults. As adults, they are at increased risk for many premature diseases.

Eating habits of children and young people in the United States are poor. Children make poor nutritional choices that put them at risk for health problems. Contrary to common misconceptions, children do not instinctively select the nutrients that they need for proper growth and development. If I allowed my three-year-old daughter to select food instinctively, she would have a diet of candy, soda, and cookies—hardly a healthful diet.

Another common misconception is that children can handle a poor diet when they are young because they will burn off the Calories; this is a dangerous misconception. Although it is true that children are able to metabolize the extra Calories because of increased activity, the poor eating habits they develop in childhood will continue into adulthood and can be detrimental. Establishing good nutritional habits during childhood is critical because changing poor eating behaviors in adulthood is difficult. Think about your own nutritional habits. I challenge you to choose one nutritional habit that you would like to change and to spend one week trying to change that habit. You can probably guess that trying to change the habit would be difficult. Now consider that if you had developed a more positive eating pattern as a child, you would most likely not need to make this behavior change as an adult.

Poor Diets

Children would get the proper amount of nutrients if they could only learn proper eating habits. Contrary to common beliefs, children do not need vitamin and mineral supplements. Unless there is a medical reason for vitamin and mineral supplements, children receive all the nutrients they need through a balanced diet. Taking vitamin pills only seems to be an easy solution for making up the nutrients missed in a child's dietary intake.

On another note, did you know that pound per pound children need to consume more water than do adults? Children lose a greater percent of water through evaporation than adults. Therefore, children need to consume more water per pound of body weight than adults need to consume.

Even though adults have shown some improvement in their dietary patterns, our children's eating habits remain poor. According to the U.S. Department of Health and Human Services, more than 84 percent of children eat too much fat. Children on average consume about 40 percent of their calories from fat. Children are not consuming enough fruits and vegetables in their diet. The National Cancer Institute recommends that children consume five servings of fruits and vegetables per day. Only 20 percent of our children actually meet this recommendation. Did you know that 51 percent of our children eat less than one serving of fruit a day? Furthermore, fried potatoes account for a large proportion of the vegetables eaten by children.

Did you know that one in five students skips breakfast on a regular basis? Several research studies have found that not eating breakfast can affect children's intellectual performance in school. Even moderate malnutrition can have a long-term effect on how well a child performs in school. Several studies have reported that undernourished children become sick, miss school, and score lower on tests than do children who receive the proper amount of nourishment. Therefore, it is important for children to eat properly and not skip meals.

Promoting Good Nutrition

What can we do as teachers to encourage our students to become better eaters? The opportunity to promote better eating habits is in front of us. We have a captive audience to whom to promote good nutrition and also positive health behaviors. We as teachers need to develop a comprehensive scope and sequence for nutrition education. It is important to keep reinforcing positive eating behaviors at every grade level. Nutrition education involves more than just educating students about healthful eating. We need to help children learn skills, not just facts about nutrition. The USDA's *Nutrition and Your Health: Dietary Guidelines For Americans, 2000* is a good source for learning diet and lifestyle skills. In this document, you can find healthful activities and practices that students can actually put into practice.

Give children repeated opportunities to practice healthful eating. Practicing a positive health behavior enough times will usually make that behavior the norm for children, not the exception. Teaching children about nutrition is no different from teaching children math skills. If we want our children to excel in mathematics, we give them multiple opportunities to practice math problems. The same holds true for developing positive eating practices. Practice, practice, practice!

Practicing Good Nutrition

What types of activities can teachers do to promote positive nutritional practices in children? First of all, request healthful snacks for class parties. This will create a positive atmosphere for eating these kinds of foods. Give students many chances to taste foods low in fat, sodium, and added sugar and foods high in vitamins, minerals, and fiber. Also teach children how to make healthful choices in the school cafeteria or when packing their lunches. This promotes positive behaviors and keeps children involved in learning about nutrition. Emphasize the positive aspects of healthful eating rather than the harmful effects of unhealthful eating.

Finally, make nutrition education activities fun. Be creative with your activities, and try to show your students that learning can be fun. Nutrition education curricula resources exist and are readily available, often for free. Many nutrition-based materials can be obtained from volunteer agencies and governmental offices. Use them!

I would be remiss if I failed to mention the use of computers and technology in the classroom. If you are fortunate enough to have computers in your classroom, integrate the use of these learning tools with nutrition education. Surf the nutrition information highway, search CD-ROMs, and experience nutrition multimedia along with your students. Who knows, even your own nutritional habits may improve!

Becoming Physically Active

Charlie Gibbons, Ed.D.

Children have always enjoyed the opportunity to play outdoors and rarely refuse to take advantage of an opportunity to run and have fun. However, in recent years not as many children are outdoors playing. Some studies have shown that children are less active and that childhood obesity is on the rise. How true is this? Are children in the United States becoming less active and more overweight? If they are, what are the influencing factors?

Physical activity and fitness have become such a national health concern that several national documents from the U.S. Department of Health and Human Services have emphasized the importance of physical activity and fitness. *Healthy People 2010,* the national initiative that established health objectives for the first decade of this century, includes objectives to increase levels of moderate and vigorous physical activity among adolescents, to increase the proportion of trips made by walking and bicycling, and to decrease the amount of time young people spend watching television. *Physical Activity and Health: A Report of the Surgeon General* emphasizes that regular participation in moderate physical activity is an essential component of a healthy lifestyle.

How physically active are children and adolescents?

Numerous national studies (First and Second National Children and Youth Fitness Study, The President's Council on Physical Fitness and Sports School Population Fitness Study, Youth Fitness Behavior Surveillance System, and *Healthy People 2010*) have been conducted to determine the physical activity levels of children and adolescents in the United States. The general finding is that children and youth in the United States are less active and physically fit than is recommended for optimal protection against future chronic diseases.

In addition to studies conducted on fitness levels of children and adolescents, a number of studies have been conducted to determine the prevalence of childhood obesity in the United States. The general finding is that children and youth are getting more overweight.

Why are children and adolescents less physically active and fit?

If children and adolescents are less active and are becoming more overweight, there must be some influencing factors. Researchers have emphasized the influencing role of television watching on sedentary (inactive) behavior and obesity. Television watching is a popular childhood leisure activity. The majority of children spend more time watching television than they spend in school. During television watching, physical activity ceases and metabolism slows down. As television watching increases among children and adolescents, physical activity decreases. As physical activity decreases among children and adolescents, obesity increases. According to the U.S. Centers for Disease Control and Prevention (CDC), the percentage of young people who are overweight has more than doubled in the past 30 years, and the number of deaths due to inactivity and poor diet is at least 300,000 a year for all ages.

In recent years there also has been an explosion in the use of computers, computer games, and video games by children and adolescents. These advances in technology also may help to promote sedentary behavior among children and adolescents and to increase the likelihood of obesity and the development of chronic diseases.

Television is a very powerful medium that has a pervasive influence on the health knowledge, attitudes, and behavior of children, adolescents, and adults. Researchers have suggested another avenue in which television watching influences obesity. Television watching may influence obesity among children and adolescents by increasing the number of nutritional messages to which they are exposed. Much too often foods in commercials and the foods shown in television programs are high in Calories and low in nutritional value.

What health problems are associated with inactivity?

Researchers have found obesity in childhood and adolescence to be associated with developmental risk factors for cardiovascular diseases, hypertension, high blood cholesterol, and diabetes. These problems become more pronounced in adulthood. Obese children are at an increased risk of obesity as adults. Recent studies have shown that the problems of obesity and physical inactivity among young adults are increasing at alarming rates. As the prevalence of adult obesity increases, morbidity and mortality increase.

At the same time, children and adolescents today are being bombarded with societal messages that emphasize thinness. These social pressures for thinness increase the health risk for overweight youth suffering from eating disorders.

What are the benefits of regular physical activity?

According to the *Report of the Surgeon General,* regular physical activity that is performed on an almost daily basis reduces the risk of developing or dying from some of the leading causes of illness and death in the United States.

Regular physical activity improves health in the following ways:

- It reduces the risk of dying prematurely from heart disease.
- It reduces the risk of developing high blood pressure.
- It reduces feelings of depression and anxiety.
- It helps control weight.
- It reduces the risk of developing diabetes.
- It helps build and maintain healthy bones, muscles, and joints.
- It promotes psychological well-being.
- It helps alleviate stress.

What is physical activity and fitness?

Have you ever gone for a walk? Have you ever done any gardening? If your answer is *yes* for these activities, or for any activities of this energy level or higher, you have been involved in physical activity. And if you have engaged in these types of activities for at least 30 minutes per day, you have been improving your fitness. You have been engaging in physical activity that will help ensure Calories are expended and health benefits will be conferred. Children and adolescents should engage in

- aerobic activities that will help improve and maintain the cardio–respiratory system,
- physically challenging activities that will improve and maintain the muscular system, and
- stretching activities that will improve and maintain flexibility and help prevent injuries.

Children should learn the importance of warm-up activities, which prepare the body for physical activity and prevent injuries, and of cool-down activities, which allow for continual blood return from the lower extremities of the body to prevent blood from pooling in the legs.

How can teachers help?

It is important to remember that children and adolescents are less likely to engage in physical activity and will choose inactivity if they are not enjoying the physical activity. A healthy level of physical activity requires regular participation in activities that increase energy expenditure above resting levels. An active child participates in physical education classes, plays sports, performs regular household chores, spends recreational time outdoors, and regularly travels by foot, bicycle, or roller blades. Opportunities for physical activity should be fun, increase confidence in participation in physical activity, and involve friends and peers. Positive role models for physical activity include parents and teachers.

If children and adolescents are supposed to be able to carry out only everyday tasks with vigor and alertness and without undue fatigue, then for too many of them there is no need for physical activity because their everyday tasks do not require much energy. With the increase in television watching, computer use, and playing computer and video games, more and more children and adolescents are engaging in more sedentary practices. The lack of participation in physical activity by the youth of the United States is a national concern. It is imperative that this concern be addressed by the families, schools, and communities in the United States.

As a teacher, you can help alleviate this problem with your students by modeling a physically active lifestyle, helping them understand the importance of being physically active, and encouraging them to participate every day in physical activity that they enjoy.

Program Organization

Content Areas	Kindergarten	Grade 1	Grade 2
Emotional, Intellectual, and Social Health	1 All About Me	1 Me and My Feelings	1 My Feelings
Family Life, Growth, and Development	2 Growing and Learning	2 My Senses Help Me Grow	2 My Family
Personal Health and Physical Fitness	3 Caring For My Teeth 4 Staying Fit and Healthy	3 My Teeth 4 Taking Care of My Body	3 Caring for My Teeth 4 Keeping Fit and Healthy
Nutrition	5 Food for Health	5 Wonderful Food	5 Food for Fitness
Disease Prevention and Control	6 Staying Well	6 Staying Well	6 Staying Well
Drug Use Prevention	7 Medicines Help–Drugs Hurt	7 About Medicines and Drugs	7 Medicines and Drugs
Injury Prevention	8 Keeping Safe	8 Being Safe	8 Staying Safe
Community and Environmental Health	9 A Healthy Community	9 Keeping My Neighborhood Healthy	9 Caring for My Neighborhood

Integrated content areas: human body systems, consumer health

Grade 3	Grade 4	Grade 5	Grade 6
1 About Myself and Others	1 Your Needs and Feelings	1 Dealing with Feelings	1 Setting Goals
2 Me and My Family	2 Living and Growing	2 Growth and Development	2 Patterns of Growth
3 Keeping My Body Fit	3 Your Health and Fitness	3 Keeping Fit and Healthy	3 Health and Fitness
4 Food for a Healthy Body	4 Food and Your Health	4 Foods for Good Nutrition	4 Preparing Healthful Foods
5 Preventing Disease	5 Guarding Against Disease	5 Learning About Disease	5 Controlling Disease
6 Medicines and Other Drugs	6 Medicines, Drugs, and Your Health	6 Legal and Illegal Drugs	6 Drugs and Health
7 Avoiding Alcohol and Tobacco	7 Harmful Effects of Alcohol and Tobacco	7 About Tobacco and Alcohol	7 Tobacco and Alcohol
8 Keeping Safe	8 Staying Safe	8 Planning for Safety	8 Safety and First Aid
9 Health in the Community	9 Living in a Healthful Community	9 Working for a Healthful Community	9 Community Health

Scope and Sequence

Emotional, Intellectual, and Social Health

Grade 3	Grade 4	Grade 5	Grade 6
• Recognize the importance of respecting and taking care of oneself.	• Identify the four types of traits that contribute to personality.	• Recognize that each person shapes his or her self-concept.	• Identify elements that contribute to a person's self-concept.
• Describe ways to exhibit responsible behavior.	• Differentiate between traits that can and cannot be changed.	• Realize that a positive self-concept helps a person make healthful choices.	• Explain the importance of being aware of personal strengths and weaknesses.
• Recognize that feelings are expressed by words, actions, and body language.	• Apply decision-making skills.	• Identify basic physical and emotional needs.	• Explain the differences between long-term and short-term goals.
• Identify effective ways to change or cope with unpleasant feelings.	• Identify four basic physical needs.	• Learn practical strategies and identify sources for help in setting and achieving long-term goals.	• Identify steps for setting goals.
• List situations involving fear that require immediate help from a trusted adult.	• Identify examples of basic emotional, mental, and social needs.	• Identify strategies for making and keeping friends.	• Explain how having goals can help you make choices.
• Identify effective strategies for dealing with fear, stress, anger, and grief.	• Recognize how setting goals helps people meet their needs.	• Explain how to deal with peer pressure.	• Explain the meaning and importance of self-control.
• Identify ways to manage stress.	• Recognize the importance of expressing feelings in safe ways.	• Practice communication skills.	• Describe strategies for coping with anger, stress, and grief.
• Apply stress-management skills to situations at school.	• Identify symptoms of stress.	• Identify three ways in which people communicate feelings.	• Recognize the need for help in dealing with unpleasant feelings.
• Describe practical methods for establishing and building healthful relationships.	• List and apply effective steps for anger management.	• Identify and practice effective strategies for stress management.	• Identify ways to manage stress.
• Recognize the importance of standing up for personal values when faced with negative peer pressure.	• Identify steps to cope with or to manage stress.	• Identify steps to cope with and manage stress.	• Apply stress management skills to situations at school.
• Recognize that effective communication skills include both speaking and listening skills.	• Use stress management skills to deal with stress in a healthful way.	• Use stress-management skills to deal with stress.	• Recognize that lasting friendships depend on shared interests and values.
• Realize the importance of compassion, kindness, apology, and forgiveness.	• Recognize shared interests, goals, and values as factors in friendship.	• Define and identify common sources of boredom, anger, loneliness, shyness, and grief.	• Recognize the positive and negative aspects of peer pressure.
• Identify strategies for resolving conflicts.	• Identify and practice effective strategies for resolving conflicts using negotiation and compromise.	• Learn effective strategies for coping with uncomfortable feelings.	• Explain the role of brainstorming in mediation and conflict resolution.
• Use negotiation to resolve conflicts with friends and peers.	• Identify skills to resolve conflicts.	• Learn effective strategies for resolving conflicts.	• Summarize the components of an equitable resolution to a conflict.
	• Apply conflict resolution skills to conflicts at school.	• Identify the five steps in the peer mediation process.	• Identify ways to resolve conflicts.

Emotional, Intellectual, and Social Health

Grade 3	Grade 4	Grade 5	Grade 6
	• Explain the importance of respecting differences in people. • Describe how people can work together to help others.	• Identify skills to resolve conflicts. • Use conflict resolution skills to work through conflicts between friends.	• Use negotiation to resolve conflicts with friends and peers. • Describe skills that people can use to work collaboratively. • Analyze ways students can make a difference in their communities.

Family Life, Growth, and Development

Grade 3	Grade 4	Grade 5	Grade 6
• Describe different kinds of families and the basic needs that families of all kinds attempt to meet.	• Identify different types of families and how they meet the needs of their members.	• Identify the kinds of changes that families experience.	• Identify the skills of a responsible family member.
• Describe ways family members can work and play together.	• Discuss the roles that people have in families.	• Describe how children's responsibilities change as they mature.	• Describe how each skill contributes to the functioning of the family.
• Describe some of the big changes that can affect the members of a family.	• Describe the roles that extended family members may play in families.	• Describe ways to communicate effectively with family members.	• Identify strategies to resolve conflicts.
• Identify ways that family members can help each other when big changes happen.	• Describe three things that children learn from their families.	• Identify causes of conflicts in the family and ways to resolve them.	• Practice strategies to resolve conflicts with family members.
• Identify communication skills.	• Identify ways that values are taught.	• Identify effective communication skills.	• Identify changes that affect families.
• Use communication skills to get along with family members.	• Identify ways to show cooperation and respect to other family members.	• Practice communication skills to express feelings to family members.	• Describe ways that children in a family may respond to changes.
• Describe each stage of the human life cycle.	• Identify communication skills.	• Identify the stages of growth and development.	• Identify when help outside the family may be needed.
• Compare the four stages of the human life cycle.	• Use communication skills to get along with family members.	• Describe some of the changes a person experiences at each stage.	• Outline the major events that occur during the prenatal period of life.
• Describe how growth occurs.	• Explain how inherited traits and acquired traits both contribute to making an individual unique.	• Identify the significance of reaching puberty.	• Describe the stages of mitosis.
• Compare kinds of cells and how they are designed to do special jobs.	• Describe the parts of a cell and how cells are organized.	• Identify and describe factors that affect growth.	• Describe the role of genes in heredity.
• Describe one kind of growth in addition to physical growth and the changes that occur as a result.	• Compare growth during early and late stages of childhood.	• Describe the functions of the major glands of the endocrine system.	• Describe how puberty relates to adolescence and identify several glands and the function of each.
• Identify ways to care for your body.	• Explain how the brain controls the body.	• Describe the role of the endocrine system in the growth process.	• Identify some of the physical changes that occur during puberty.
	• Describe how the brain and the central nervous system respond to the body's needs.	• Describe how the growth spurt experienced during puberty affects your interests and your ability to solve problems.	• Describe the varying emotions that adolescents experience and ways to deal with them.
		• Describe the feelings and problems that are common during adolescence and ways to handle these new feelings.	• Explain how relationships change during adolescence.
		• Explain how exercise and a proper diet help growing bodies.	• Describe the three forms of exercise that contribute to total fitness.
		• Describe other choices that can affect growth.	• Explain the role of diet in maintaining health.

Personal Health and Physical Fitness

Grade 3	Grade 4	Grade 5	Grade 6
• Identify the parts and functions of the body's sense organs, skeletal, muscular, digestive, circulatory, respiratory, and nervous systems.	• Identify the parts and functions of the body's sense organs, skeletal, muscular, digestive, circulatory, respiratory, and nervous systems.	• Identify the parts and functions of the body's sense organs, skeletal, muscular, digestive, circulatory, respiratory, nervous, immune, and endocrine systems.	• Identify, differentiate, and explain various parts of each of the sense organs, skeletal, muscular, digestive, circulatory, respiratory, nervous, immune, and endocrine systems.
• Explain how and why to keep skin clean.	• Describe the structure and function of skin.	• Explain the importance of choosing a good sunscreen.	• Describe the structure of the skin.
• Explain how and why to protect skin and eyes from the sun.	• Explain how to take care of skin.	• Describe the function and care of skin, hair, and nails.	• Explain how and why to take good care of skin, hair, and nails.
• Explain how plaque can lead to cavities and loss of teeth.	• Explain why using sunscreen is important.	• Identify and compare teeth types.	• Describe the importance of protection from the sun.
• Describe and demonstrate how to brush and floss correctly.	• Describe tooth and gum problems and explain how to prevent them.	• Explain how to care for teeth and gums.	• Explain the importance of making wise choices of hair and skin products.
• Explain how to protect teeth from injury.	• Describe and demonstrate how to brush and floss correctly.	• Define orthodontia and explain its importance.	• Describe and demonstrate how to use labels to make wise product choices.
• Explain how the parts of the ear function.	• Identify and explain the causes of common vision and hearing problems.	• Identify parts of the eye and the ear and explain how the parts of each function together as a unit.	• Identify the importance of caring for teeth and gums.
• Describe how to take good care of the ears and the nose.	• Describe and demonstrate how to take good care of eyes and ears.	• Describe how to take good care of eyes and ears.	• Describe and demonstrate ways to prevent tooth decay and gum disease.
• Describe different ways exercise helps the body.	• Describe the importance of and demonstrate good posture.	• Explain the importance choosing health care products wisely.	• Describe the structure and function of the eyes and the ears.
• Explain how and why to get aerobic exercise.	• Define muscle strength, flexibility, and endurance.	• Identify and evaluate sources of health information.	• Explain how and why to take good care of the eyes and ears.
• Explain why sleep is helpful.	• Explain how aerobic exercise affects the cardiovascular system.	• Demonstrate how to use labels to make wise product choices.	• Describe the importance of correct body position and lighting for computer use.
• Identify goal-setting steps.	• Develop a personal exercise plan.	• Describe how exercise benefits the respiratory and circulatory systems.	• Analyze how to work at a computer.
• Practice goal-setting steps to get enough rest.	• Describe how sleep and rest affect health.	• Explain how to use the Activity Pyramid to improve physical fitness.	• Explain the importance of exercise to maintaining physical fitness.
• Explain how to use safety gear, warm-ups, cool-downs, and water to stay safe during exercise.	• Identify goal-setting steps.	• Identify ways to set goals.	• Describe how to use the Activity Pyramid to improve physical fitness.
• Describe what to do in case of injury.	• Practice goal-setting steps to get enough rest.	• Use goal-setting steps to create a fitness plan.	• Identify goal-setting steps.

Personal Health and Physical Fitness

Grade 3	Grade 4	Grade 5	Grade 6
		• Describe the right way to warm up, exercise, and cool down. • Describe exercise for strength, flexibility, and endurance.	• Practice goal setting for fitness • Describe the importance of different types of exercise. • Develop a personal exercise and fitness program.

Nutrition

Grade 3	Grade 4	Grade 5	Grade 6
• Identify healthful food choices.	• Identify the six major nutrients, their sources, and their functions in the body.	• Describe how the digestive system works.	• Identify six types of nutrients important to health.
• Explain why eating healthful foods is important to good health.	• Describe how the body digests and uses food.	• Explain how each nutrient helps the body.	• Explain the role of each type of nutrient in the body.
• Describe where food comes from.	• Explain how fiber is important to health.	• Identify the role of proteins in the body.	• Identify the food groups on the Food Guide Pyramid.
• Explain how to use the Food Guide Pyramid to plan a healthful diet.	• Identify the food groups and explain why they are important.	• Describe how the body gets and uses vitamins and minerals.	• Use the Food Guide Pyramid to plan a balanced diet.
• Describe how people get the water they need to stay healthy.	• Explain what a balanced diet is and why it is important.	• Define dietary supplements and explain why they are used by some people.	• Describe a healthful vegetarian diet.
• Explain why food is needed at regular intervals.	• Use the Food Guide Pyramid and the steps for making decisions to identify and choose healthful snack foods.	• Identify decision-making steps.	• Compare healthful foods from Mexico, China, and Italy.
• Describe how to choose healthful snacks.	• Identify the steps for decision making.	• Use decision-making steps to make healthful food choices.	• Recognize that different kinds of foods can provide a healthful diet.
• Identify steps for making decisions.	• Use the decision-making steps to make healthful food choices.	• Identify the food groups.	• Recognize that good health depends on food choices that satisfy nutritional needs.
• Use the decision-making steps to make healthful snacks choices.	• Identify the types of information found on food labels.	• Explain how to use the Food Guide Pyramid to plan and achieve a balance diet.	• Describe some consequences of unhealthful eating practices.
• Define ingredients and tell how to use labels to choose foods with the most nutritious ingredients.	• Explain how food labels can be used to compare the nutritional value of foods.	• Explain how family, friends, and culture affect food choices.	• Identify steps for making decisions.
• Explain why a food's price varies.	• Describe or demonstrate ways to handle and prepare foods safely.	• Explain how food choices may be affected by health, the seasons, emotions, and knowledge about foods.	• Use the decision-making steps to make healthy choices about nutrition.
• Explain why it is important to store foods properly.	• Explain how a person can tell if a food is spoiled.	• Explain how to use food labels to evaluate nutritional values of foods.	• Explain the importance of food choices to good health.
• Describe ways to handle foods safely.		• Describe the influences advertising has on food choices.	• Explain how to select healthful foods in supermarkets and restaurants.
		• Explain how pathogens get into food. Describe the effects of pathogen contamination.	• Describe how to store and prepare foods safely.
		• Describe how to store and prepare food safely.	• Identify spices used to enhance food flavors.

Disease Prevention and Control

Grade 3	Grade 4	Grade 5	Grade 6
• Define symptom and disease, and list some common symptoms of disease.	• Compare and contrast infectious and noninfectious diseases.	• Compare and contrast infectious and noninfectious diseases.	• Distinguish among hereditary, environmental, and behavioral risk factors.
• Explain what a disability is, and discuss how to treat a person with a disability.	• Differentiate between chronic and acute diseases and give two examples of each.	• List some ways to respond to people with disabilities.	• Define pathogen.
• Define infectious disease.	• Explain what a disability is.	• Distinguish among diseases caused by different pathogens.	• Name some environmental risk factors.
• Compare and contrast bacteria and viruses.	• Distinguish between diseases caused by viruses and bacteria.	• Explain how pathogens are transmitted and how they enter the body.	• Explain the advantages of preventive health care.
• List some infectious diseases and their symptoms.	• Explain how diseases can spread.	• Explain how HIV is transmitted and how it affects the body.	• Analyze five infectious diseases.
• Explain two ways a person can become immune to a disease.	• Explain how food and water spread pathogens.	• Name the body's defenses against pathogens.	• Distinguish among bacteria, viruses, fungi, and protozoa.
• Define medicine, and explain the importance of taking all medicines only as directed.	• List some of the body's defenses against disease.	• Explain the relationship between a pathogen and an antibody.	• Explain how to prevent STDs.
• Define noninfectious diseases, and list three examples.	• Explain the function of antibodies.	• Explain how the body develops immunity to a disease.	• Explain how AIDS is transmitted.
• Compare and contrast allergies and asthma.	• Discuss how vaccines help the body fight certain diseases.	• Name some tests used to determine the treatment of illnesses.	• Name the body's defenses.
• Explain what happens to sugar in a person with diabetes.	• Distinguish between noninfectious and infectious diseases.	• Define immunization and list some diseases that can be prevented by immunization.	• Explain the function of antibodies.
• Explain how a healthful lifestyle reduces a person's chances of getting certain diseases.	• Discuss heart diseases and cancer and explain how skin cancer can be prevented.	• Distinguish between chronic and acute diseases.	• Explain how a person develops immunity to a disease.
• Identify ways to manage stress.	• Differentiate among allergies, arthritis, diabetes, and asthma.	• Recognize the relationship between lifestyle choices and the risk of developing some chronic diseases.	• Discuss vaccines, immunizations, and antibiotics.
• Apply stress-management skills to help control disease.	• Explain how a healthful lifestyle reduces one's chances of getting certain diseases and illnesses.	• Discuss the roles of diet, exercise, and managing stress in determining a person's overall health.	• Define noninfectious diseases.
	• List ways to deal with stress.	• Identify steps to manage stress.	• Analyze two cardiovascular diseases.
	• Explain the effects of tobacco use.	• Practice steps to manage stress to keep your body healthy.	• List the warning signs of cancer.
	• Identify skills to manage stress.		• Describe diabetes and asthma.
	• Practice skills to manage stress at the doctor's office.		• Cite ways to lower one's risk of contracting infectious diseases.
			• Explain the importance of exercise, diet, and sleep to health.
			• Analyze dangers of tobacco use.
			• Identify steps for managing stress.
			• Practice managing stress to prevent disease.

Drug Use Prevention

Grade 3	Grade 4	Grade 5	Grade 6
• Explain what drugs are.	• Recognize that medicines are drugs that help the body.	• Explain that medicines are drugs that cause helpful changes in the body when used correctly.	• Explain that medicines are drugs that can help you stay healthy when used safely.
• Distinguish between drugs that help the body and drugs that harm the body.	• Distinguish between prescription and over-the-counter medicines.	• Differentiate between OTC and prescription medicines.	• Distinguish between prescription and over-the-counter medicines.
• Differentiate between OTC medicines and prescription medicines.	• Recognize that some common substances, such as caffeine and OTC medicines, can be addictive.	• Interpret information on how to use a medicine.	• Describe the dangerous consequences of drug abuse.
• Describe ways medicines can help people and how medicines are taken or applied.	• Describe the harmful effects of marijuana and cocaine.	• Discuss how to use medicines safely.	• Explain why the reasons people give for using drugs are really based on myths.
• Understand that medicines can be helpful only if they are used correctly.	• Recognize the dangerous effects of marijuana and cocaine.	• Interpret a medicine label.	• Describe the harmful effects of powerful stimulants, such as amphetamines, cocaine, and crack.
• List the rules for using medicines safely.	• Recognize that cocaine use can lead to instant addiction.	• Distinguish between medicine misuse and medicine abuse.	• Analyze how depressants affect the body and brain, and what happens when these drugs are abused.
• Explain what caffeine is and what it does to the body.	• Explain why saying no to drugs is a healthful decision.	• Explain how the use of illegal drugs can harm the body.	• Describe the dangers of using cannabis, narcotics, inhalants, hallucinogens, and steroids.
• Suggest ways to avoid foods and drinks with caffeine.	• Demonstrate how to say no to illegal drugs.	• Describe crack and cocaine and their effects on the body.	• Describe the immediate and long-term effects of using drugs.
• List the dangerous physical effects of using inhalants, marijuana, or cocaine, and tell why these drugs should be avoided.	• Identify steps for refusing.	• Describe marijuana, inhalants, and steroids and effects they have on the body.	• Explain who can help people avoid drugs.
• Describe how to avoid breathing inhalants.	• Practice refusing over-the-counter medicines.	• Describe the negative consequences of drug abuse.	• Identify steps for refusing.
• Emphasize the importance of saying no to drugs.	• Recognize the warning signs of drug abuse.	• Explain how drug abuse can interfere with activities and goals.	• Use refusal steps to say no to drug use.
• Suggest ways to avoid dangerous drugs.	• Identify people and organizations that can help with drug recovery.	• Suggest ways to say no to drug abuse.	• Name three harmful substances in tobacco smoke.
• Identify refusal skills.	• Describe tobacco products and the harm they cause to the body.	• Identify refusal skills.	• Identify parts of the body that are affected by tobacco use.
• Use refusal skills to say no to drug use.	• Explain why some young people begin smoking and why stopping is difficult.	• Use refusal skills to stay drug free.	• Describe the effects of tobacco use on parts of the body.
• Describe the harmful effects of nicotine and alcohol on the body.	• Describe alcohol and the harm causes to body systems and behavior.	• Recognize when someone needs help refusing or getting off drugs.	• Define environmental tobacco smoke (ETS).
• Identify products that contain tobacco or alcohol.	• Identify some effects of problem drinking.	• Explain where to get help for drug abuse.	• List three dangers of using smokeless tobacco.
• Identify the effects of tobacco on specific human body parts.	• Describe laws regarding alcohol and tobacco purchase and use by minors.	• Name three harmful substances in tobacco smoke.	

Drug Use Prevention

Grade 3	Grade 4	Grade 5	Grade 6
• Describe the hazards of environmental tobacco smoke.	• Demonstrate strategies for refusing the use of alcohol and tobacco.	• Describe the effects of tobacco use on parts of the body.	• Explain why it is difficult for an addicted person to stop using tobacco.
• Describe some effects of alcohol on specific body organs and on behavior.	• Recognize truths behind misleading tobacco and alcohol advertising.	• Identify reasons people use tobacco.	• Describe the effects of alcohol on a person who drinks it.
• Identify safety risks associated with alcohol use.	• Identify ways to say no.	• Explain what blood alcohol level is and what it measures.	• Explain blood alcohol level (BAL) and its relation to the amount of alcohol a person drinks.
• Describe some laws regarding the sale, use, and packaging of alcohol and tobacco products.	• Practice ways to refuse alcohol and tobacco.	• Describe the ways in which alcohol affects a person's health, abilities, and functioning.	• List four ways that drinking alcohol can affect a person's safety.
• Explain reasons for refusing and demonstrate ways to refuse tobacco and alcohol.	• List warning signs of alcohol and tobacco use.	• Explain what an alcoholic is and who might become one.	• Define peer pressure and describe its effects.
• Identify skills for refusals.	• Name sources of help for alcohol or tobacco users.	• List reasons for choosing not to use alcohol.	• Analyze the motives behind advertisements for tobacco and alcohol products.
• Use refusal skills to say no to alcohol and tobacco.		• Develop strategies for dealing with peer pressure.	• Practice strategies for refusing offers of alcohol or tobacco products.
		• Analyze advertisements for alcohol and tobacco products.	• Identify ways of refusing.
		• Identify ways of refusing.	• Apply various refusal strategies to situations in which alcohol or tobacco are offered.
		• Use refusal skills to say no to alcohol and tobacco.	• List four places where a person with alcoholism can get help.
		• List warning signs of a problem with alcohol.	• Identify types of people who might be able to help a young person with an alcohol problem.
		• Explain why people who are addicted to alcohol or tobacco need help to stop using these drugs.	• Describe three kinds of recovery programs.
		• Identify sources of support available to people who want to stop using alcohol or tobacco.	

Injury Prevention

Grade 3	Grade 4	Grade 5	Grade 6
• Recognize that there are people who are responsible for keeping children safe.	• Recognize an emergency situation and know how to respond.	• Recognize and reduce hazards that lead to unexpected injuries.	• Describe potential hazards in and around the home and how to prevent injury from them.
• Practice safety rules on the way to and from school and at school.	• Practice first aid for minor injuries.	• Explain how to respond to emergency situations.	• Explain safe baby-sitting practices.
• Describe how to stay safe around strangers.	• Describe how to prevent home injuries from electricity, falls, fire, and poison.	• Practice first aid for injuries.	• Explain swimming and boating safety rules.
• Explain how to avoid conflicts and get along with bullies.	• Explain camping safety measures.	• Practice safety at play and in motor vehicles.	• Describe how to respond to a water emergency.
• Identify steps to resolve conflicts.	• Describe appropriate safety gear for sports and outdoor activities.	• Analyze safety equipment.	• Explain how to prepare for emergency situations.
• Use negotiation to handle conflicts with friends.	• Recognize safety hazards present in cold weather and thunderstorms.	• Explain first-aid treatment for common injuries.	• Describe how to respond to emergency situations in order to reduce risks.
• Make a home fire escape plan.	• Identify steps in the decision-making process.	• Compare road rules for safe bicycling and safe driving.	• Identify steps for effective communication.
• Describe how to safely escape a home fire.	• Apply decision-making steps to staying safe.	• Practice safe bicycling.	• Practice communication skills for handling emergencies.
• List safety rules for using electricity and household products.	• Explain how to prevent injuries and practice safety when bicycling, skating, skateboarding, and riding in a motor vehicle.	• Identify traffic signs and signals.	• Recognize common injuries.
• Identify safety gear.	• Recognize and follow swimming and boating safety rules.	• Identify steps used to make decisions.	• Describe first-aid treatment for common injuries.
• Explain safety rules for bicycling.	• Describe how to respond to a water emergency.	• Apply decision-making steps to protecting health and safety.	• Recognize life-threatening injuries.
• Know what features to look for when purchasing a helmet.	• Recognize how to avoid conflicts in sports and play situations.	• Explain how to prevent home fires.	• Describe first aid for medical emergencies.
• Identify steps to make decisions.	• Explain how to prevent injuries from firearms.	• Recognize fire hazards in the home.	• Describe the danger of gangs and how to avoid conflicts with them.
• Use decision-making steps to stay safe.	• Identify steps to resolve conflicts.	• Describe how to survive a home fire.	• Explain how the media affects violent behavior.
• Learn how to get emergency assistance when someone has been injured or accidentally poisoned.	• Apply conflict resolution skills to handle conflicts with friends.	• Recognize situations that can lead to violence.	• Identify steps for conflict resolution.
• Describe first aid for cuts, scrapes, insect bites, and stings.		• Describe how to respond to threatening situations.	• Use conflict resolution steps to resolve conflicts that could lead to violence.
		• Practice ways to avoid violence.	
		• Identify skills used to resolve conflicts.	
		• Apply skills to resolve conflicts before conflicts become violent.	

Community and Environmental Health

Grade 3	Grade 4	Grade 5	Grade 6
• Define community. • Explain some of the responsibilities of people who work to promote public health. • Compare and contrast hospitals and clinics. • Define pollution. • List several sources of air pollution. • Explain how noise pollution can be harmful to humans. • List several sources of water pollution. • Describe how water is treated so that it is safe for human consumption. • Explain how groundwater becomes polluted. • Identify steps in the goal-setting process. • Use goal-setting skills to protect the environment. • Discuss how to prevent litter from becoming an unsightly part of the community. • List ways to reduce, reuse, and recycle.	• Recognize that the environment includes living and nonliving things. • Analyze why people need clean air, water, and land. • Describe some recreational activities. • Explain how groundskeepers, janitors, police officers, and firefighters keep the community clean and safe. • Describe the jobs of emergency medical technicians and dispatchers. • Define natural resources, list seven kinds, and describe some of the ways that people use them. • Explain how fossil fuels are used. • List sources of air pollution and explain how polluted air affects a person's health. • Name some sources of water pollution and explain how these pollutants affect human health. • List several ways to prevent land pollution. • Define conservation. • Describe ways to conserve water, air, land, and other resources. • Identify strategies to set goals. • Practice setting goals to conserve resources.	• Define public health and list public health agencies and their responsibilities. • List three volunteer groups that work to improve public health. • Explain how the spread of disease can be controlled or prevented. • Sequence the steps involved in water treatment. • List organizations that help communities prepare for and respond to emergencies. • List some causes of forest fires, and explain why some forest fires are allowed to burn. • Describe the role of consumer advocate groups. • Compare and contrast the FDA and CPSC. • Describe some of the effects of noise pollution on a person's health. • List at least four ways to reduce noise pollution. • List examples of the three Rs of improving the environment. • Explain ways in which fresh water can be conserved. • Explain how air pollution affects people's health. • Identify strategies to set goals. • Practice setting goals to help protect land resources.	• Describe damage caused by tornadoes, hurricanes, and earthquakes. • Explain how local governments and volunteer groups help people before, during, and after natural disasters. • Describe how to prepare for earthquakes and severe weather. • Distinguish between a storm watch and a storm warning. • List items that should be contained in a natural disaster emergency kit. • Define sanitarian. • List the steps involved in water treatment. • Explain how waste is disposed of in a sanitary landfill and by incineration. • Define resources, and explain why it is necessary to conserve them. • Describe ways to conserve water, paper, metals, and glass. • Identify sources of air and water pollution and health problems they cause. • Describe harm done by acid rain. • List examples of the three Rs that help improve the environment. • Name several sources of noise pollution and explain how loud noises can damage hearing. • Identify the steps in the goal-setting process. • Apply goal-setting skills to protecting the environment.